WritersMarket.com
WHERE & HOW TO SELL WHAT YOU WRITE

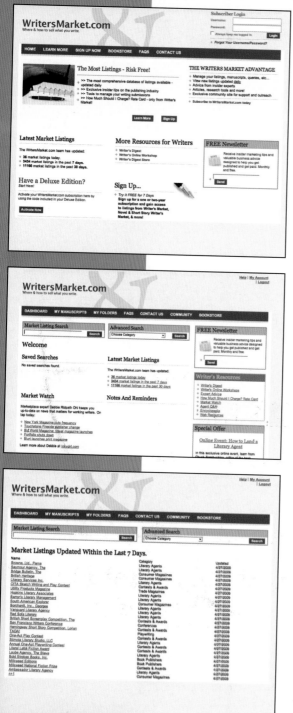

Activate your WritersMarket.com subscription to get instant access to:

- **Updated listings in your writing genre** — Find additional listings that didn't make it into the book, updated contact information and more. WritersMarket.com provides the most comprehensive database of verified markets available anywhere.

- **Easy-to-use searchable database** — Looking for a specific magazine or book publisher? Just type in its name. Or widen your prospects with the Advanced Search. You can also search for listings that have been recently updated!

- **Personalized tools** — Store your best-bet markets, and use our popular record-keeping tools to track your submissions. Plus, get new and updated market listings, query reminders, and more – every time you log in!

- **Professional tips & advice** — From pay rate charts to sample query letters, and from how-to articles to Q&A's with literary agents, we have the resources freelance writers need.

- **Industry Updates** — Debbie Ridpath Ohi's Market Watch column keeps you up-to-date on the latest publishing industry news, so you'll always be in-the-know.

YOU'LL GET ALL OF THIS
WITH YOUR INCLUDED SUBSCRIPTION TO
WritersMarket.com

To put the full power of WritersMarket.com to work for you, upgrade your subscription and get access to listings from all of our best-selling Market books. Find out more at www.WritersMarket.com

2010

22ND ANNUAL EDITION

CHILDREN'S WRITER'S & ILLUSTRATOR'S MARKET®

Alice Pope, Editor

WRITER'S DIGEST BOOKS
CINCINNATI, OH

Publisher & Editorial Director, Writing Communities: Jane Friedman
Managing Editor, Writer's Digest Market Books: Alice Pope

Writer's Market Web site: www.writersmarket.com
Writer's Digest Web site: www.writersdigest.com

Distributed in Canada by Fraser Direct
100 Armstrong Avenue
Georgetown, ON, Canada L7G 5S4
Tel: (905) 877-4411

Distributed in the U.K. and Europe by David & Charles
Brunel House, Newton Abbot, Devon, TQ12 4PU, England
Tel: (+44) 1626 323200, Fax: (+44) 1626 323319
E-mail: postmaster@davidandcharles.co.uk

Distributed in Australia by Capricorn Link
P.O. Box 704, Windsor, NSW 2756 Australia
Tel: (02) 4577-3555

ISSN: 0897-9790
ISBN-13: 978-1-58297-587-0
ISBN-10: 1-58297-587-6

Cover design by Claudean Wheeler
Production coordinated by Greg Nock

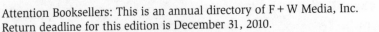

Contents

© Gilbert Ford

Reprinted with permssion of Delacorte Press.

INTERVIEWS

Reprinted with permssion of Simon & Schuster Children's Publishing.

MARKETS

RESOURCES

INDEXES

From the Editor

As I planned the (terrific) article lineup for this edition of *Children's Writer's & Illustrator's Market*, I was e-mailing author Sara Zarr discussing deadlines and topics she might like to tackle:

Sara: I have just embarked on a somewhat hellish revision of book #3, which is why I'm slow on everything else these days...

Me: Maybe you could write about hellish revisions.

Sara: Seriously. (And is there any other kind?)

Writing really *is* revision. And revision is seldom easy. Even as editor Cheryl Klein offers practical, hands-on revision strategies for writers (page 58), she shares this quote from author Carolyn See: "Revision is when you first get to recognize the distance between what you wanted to write, what you thought you were writing, and what you actually did write. That recognition often makes you want to throw up."

For debut novelist Erin Dionne (page 143) revision isn't nauseating but she admits she's a bit obsessed with it. "I've always wanted to be one of those one-revision writers," she says. "You know, the ones who draft a full story, get some feedback, polish it up, and voila—shiny, stunning book! Yeah, that's not me." Erin completed seven full revisions of her manuscript for *Models Don't Eat Chocolate Cookies* before she began looking for an agent, then she got interest from two who both asked for (very different) revisions. When she settled on the right agent and got her contract, she went through revisions again with her editor at Scholastic.

"I think writers need to learn to love revision and constructive criticism ... a good reader plus a willingness to rewrite can make a ton of difference. Nothing is good enough the first time it goes down on paper. Or the second."

When picture book author Hope Vestergaard (page 35) decided to finally pursue her desire to write novels, she had to revise her whole work strategy as she adapted to the new form. Hope identified the obstacles as she travelled down career revision road, and came up with solutions that helped her through the transition.

Authors like Sara, Erin and Hope have come to realize that for writers, revision is not just part of the job—it's a way of life. "What I've learned about the reality of writing is that, for me, it's mostly about overcoming self-doubts, exercising humility, and practicing failure. It's about revision," says Sara Zarr (page 52). "Not just revision of my creative work, but revision of self-image, revision of ideas of success and failure, and revision of my expectations for the writing life."

Writers aren't the only ones revising and rethinking these days, however. The publishing industry as a whole is in a period of adaptation and change as it comes to grips with both the economic downturn and the effect of new technology on the industry. Kelly Milner Halls tackles this topic, offering five suggestions for the evolution of children's publishing (page 20). And here at *Children's Writer's & Illustrator's Market* we've done our best to keep up with staff and policy changes and pass them onto you.

As for Sara Zarr's "hellish revision of book #3," it was well worth the effort. I devoured my advance copy of *Once Was Lost* in one sitting. (A detail from the cover is above.)

Alice Pope
alice.pope@fwpubs.com
http://cwim.blogspot.com
www.twitter.com/alicepope

How to Use This Book

As a writer, illustrator, or photographer first picking up Children's Writer's & Illustrator's Market, you may not know quite how to start using the book. Your impulse may be to flip through the book and quickly make a mailing list, then submit to everyone in hopes that someone will take interest in your work. Well, there's more to it. Finding the right market takes time and research. The more you know about a company that interests you, the better chance you have of getting work accepted.

We've made your job a little easier by putting a wealth of information at your fingertips. Besides providing listings, this directory includes a number of tools to help you determine which markets are the best ones for your work. By using these tools, as well as researching on your own, you raise your odds of being published.

USING THE INDEXES

This book lists hundreds of potential buyers of freelance material. To learn which companies want the type of material you're interested in submitting, start with the indexes.

Names Index

This index lists book and magazine editors and art directors as well as agents and art reps, indicating the companies they work for. Use this index to find company and contact information for individual publishing professionals.

Age-Level Index

Age groups are broken down into these categories in the Age-Level Index:
- **Picture books or picture-oriented material** are written and illustrated for preschoolers to 8-year-olds.
- **Young readers** are for 5- to 8-year-olds.
- **Middle readers** are for 9- to 11-year-olds.
- **Young adults** is for ages 12 and up.

Age breakdowns may vary slightly from publisher to publisher, but using them as general guidelines will help you target appropriate markets. For example, if you've written an article about trends in teen fashion, check the Magazines Age-Level Index under the Young Adult subheading. Using this list, you'll quickly find the listings for young adult magazines.

Subject Index

But let's narrow the search further. Take your list of young adult magazines, turn to the Subject Index, and find the Fashion subheading. Then highlight the names that appear on both lists (Young Adult and Fashion). Now you have a smaller list of all the magazines that would be interested in your teen fashion article. Read through those listings and decide which ones sound best for your work.

Illustrators and photographers can use the Subject Index as well. If you specialize in painting animals, for instance, consider sending samples to book and magazine publishers listed under Animals and, perhaps, Nature/Environment. Since illustrators can simply send general examples of their style to art directors to keep on file, the indexes may be more helpful to artists sending manuscripts/illustration packages who need to search for a specific subject. Always read the listings for the potential markets to see the type of work art directors prefer and what type of samples they'll keep on file, and obtain art or photo guidelines if they're available through the mail or online.

Photography Index

In this index you'll find lists of book and magazine publishers that buy photos from freelancers. Refer to the list and read the listings for companies' specific photography needs. Obtain photo guidelines if they're offered through the mail or online.

USING THE LISTINGS

Many listings begin with one or more symbols. Refer to the inside covers of the book for quick reference and find a handy pull-out bookmark (shown at left) right inside the front cover.

Many listings indicate whether submission guidelines are available. If a publisher you're interested in offers guidelines, get them and read them. The same is true with catalogs. Sending for and reading catalogs or browsing them online gives you a better idea of whether your work would fit in with the books a publisher produces. (You should also look at a few of the books in the catalog at a library or bookstore to get a feel for the publisher's material.)

Especially for artists & photographers

Along with information for writers, listings provide information for illustrators and photographers. Illustrators will find numerous markets that maintain files of samples for possible future assignments. If you're both a writer and an illustrator, look for markets that accept manuscript/illustration packages and read the information offered under the **Illustration** subhead within the listings.

If you're a photographer, after consulting the

Getting Started

2010 CHILDREN'S WRITER'S & ILLUSTRATOR'S MARKET KEY TO SYMBOLS

N market new to this edition

Canadian agents

listing outside U.S. and Canada

publisher producing educational material

electronic publisher or producer

book package/producer

A publisher accepts agented submissions only

award-winning publisher

ms, mss manuscript(s)

SCBWI Society of Children's Book Writers and Illustrators

SASE self-addressed, stamped envelope

SAE self-addressed envelope

IRC International Reply Coupon, for use in countries other than your own

b&w black & white (photo)

(For definitions of unfamiliar words and expressions relating to writing, illustration and publishing, see the Glossary.)

Photography Index, read the information under the **Photography** subhead within listings to see what format buyers prefer. For example, some want 35mm color transparencies, others want black and white prints. Note the type of photos a buyer wants to purchase and the procedures for submitting. It's not uncommon for a market to want a resume and promotional literature, as well as tearsheets from previous work. Listings also note whether model releases and/or captions are required.

SPECIFIC
CONTACT
NAMES

INFO ON
WHAT A
PUBLISHER
HANDLES

TIPS
DIRECTLY
FROM
EDITORS

E-MAIL
ADRESSES
AND WEB
SITES

DETAILED
SUBMISSION
GUIDELINES

FLUX

Llewellyn Worldwide, Ltd., 2143 Wooddale Drive, Woodbury MN 55125. (651)312-8613. Fax: (651)291-1908. E-mail: submissions@fluxnow.com. Web site: www.fluxnow.com. **Acquisitions Editor:** Brian Farrey. Imprint estab. 2005; Lllewellyn estab. 1901. Publishes 21 young abult titles/year. 50% of books by first-time authors. "Flux seeks to publish authors who see YA as a point of view, not a reading level. We look for books that try to capture a slice of teenage experience. We are particularly interested in books that tell the stories of young adults in unexpected or surprising situations around the globe."

• See First Books for an interview with Carrie Jones, author of Flux title *Tips on Having a Gay (ex) Boyfriend.*

Fiction Young Adults: adventure, contemporary, fantasy, history, humor, problem novels, religion, science fiction, sports, suspense. Average word length: 50,000. Recently published *Blue Is for Nightmares,* by Laurie Faria Stolarz; *Dream Spinner,* by Bonnie Dobkin; *How It's Done,* by Christine Kole MacLean.

How to Contact/Writers Query. Responds to queries in 1-2 weeks; mss in 1-3 months. Will consider simultaneous submissions and previously published work.

Terms Pays royalties of 10-15% based on wholesale price. Offers advance. Authors see galleys for review. Book catalog available on Web site. Writer's guidelines available for SASE or available online.

Tips "Read contemporary teen books. Be aware of what else is out there. If you don't read teen books, you probably shouldn't write them. Know your audience. Write incredibly well. Do not condescend."

Quick Tips for Writers & Illustrators

I f you're new to the world of children's publishing, buying *Children's Writer's & Illustrator's Market* may have been one of the first steps in your journey to publication. What follows is a list of suggestions and resources that can help make that journey a smooth and swift one:

1. Make the most of *Children's Writer's & Illustrator's Market.* Be sure to read How to Use This Book on page 2 for tips on reading the listings and using the indexes. Also be sure to take advantage of the articles and interviews in the book. The insights of the authors, illustrators, editors, and agents we've interviewed will inform and inspire you.

2. Join the Society of Children's Books Writers and Illustrators. SCBWI, more than 19,000 members strong, is an organization for both beginners and professionals interested in writing and illustrating for children. They offer members a slew of information and support through publications, a Web site, and a host of Regional Advisors overseeing chapters in almost every state in the U.S. and in a growing number of locations around the globe (including France, Canada, Japan, and Australia). SCBWI puts on a number of conferences, workshops, and events on the regional and national levels (many listed in the Conferences & Workshops section of this book). For more information, contact SCBWI, 8271 Beverly Blvd., Los Angeles CA 90048, (323)782-1010, or visit their Web site: www.scbwi.org.

3. Read newsletters. Newsletters, such as *Children's Book Insider, Children's Writer*, and the *SCBWI Bulletin*, offer updates and new information about publishers on a timely basis and are relatively inexpensive. Many local chapters of SCBWI offer regional newsletters as well. (See Helpful Books & Publications on page 367 for contact information on the newsletters listed above and others. For information on regional SCBWI newsletters, visit www.scbwi.org and click on "Publications."

4. Read trade and review publications. Magazines like *Publishers Weekly* (which offers two special issues each year devoted to children's publishing and is available on newsstands), *The Horn Book*, and *Booklinks* offer news, articles, reviews of newly-published titles, and ads featuring upcoming and current releases. Referring to them will help you get a feel for what's happening in children's publishing.

5. Read guidelines. Most publishers and magazines offer writer's and artist's guidelines that provide detailed information on needs and submission requirements, and some magazines offer theme lists for upcoming issues. Many publishers and magazines state the availability of guidelines within their listings. Send a self-addressed, stamped envelope (SASE) to publishers who offer guidelines. You'll often find submission information on publishers' and magazines' Web sites.

6. Look at publishers' catalogs. Perusing publishers' catalogs can give you a feel for their line of books and help you decide where your work might fit in. If catalogs are available (often stated within listings), send for them with a SASE. Visit publishers' Web sites, which often contain their full catalogs. You can also ask librarians to look at catalogs they have on hand. You can even search Amazon.com by publisher and year. (Click on "book search" then "publisher, date" and plug in, for example, "Lee & Low" under "publisher" and "2006" under year. You'll get a list of Lee & Low titles published in 2006, which you can peruse.)

7. Visit bookstores. It's not only informative to spend time in bookstores—it's fun, too! Frequently visit the children's section of your local bookstore (whether a chain or an independent) to see the latest from a variety of publishers and the most current issues of children's magazines. Look for books in the genre you're writing or with illustrations similar in style to yours, and spend some time studying them. It's also wise to get to know your local booksellers; they can tell you what's new in the store and provide insight into what kids and adults are buying.

8. Read, read, read! While you're at that bookstore, pick up a few things, or keep a list of the books that interest you and check them out of your library. Read and study the latest releases, the award winners, and the classics. You'll learn from other writers, get ideas, and get a feel for what's being published. Think about what works and doesn't work in a story. Pay attention to how plots are constructed and how characters are developed or the rhythm and pacing of picture book text. It's certainly enjoyable research!

9. Take advantage of Internet resources. There are innumerable sources of information available on the Internet about writing for children (and anything else you could possibly think of). It's also a great resource for getting (and staying) in touch with other writers and illustrators through listservs, blogs, social networking sites and e-mail, and it can serve as a vehicle for self-promotion. (Visit some authors' and illustrators' sites for ideas. See Useful Online Resources on page 370 for a list of Web sites.)

10. Consider attending a conference. If time and finances allow, attending a conference is a great way to meet peers and network with professionals in the field of children's publishing. As mentioned above, SCBWI offers conferences in various locations year round. (See www.scbwi.org and click on "Events" for a full conference calendar.) General writers' conferences often offer specialized sessions just for those interested in children's writing. Many conferences offer optional manuscript and portfolio critiques as well, giving you a chance for feedback from seasoned professionals. See the Conferences & Awards section for information on SCBWI and other conferences. The section features a Conferences & Workshops Calendar to help you plan your travel.

11. Network, network, network! Don't work in a vacuum. You can meet other writers and illustrators through a number of the things listed above—SCBWI, conferences, online. Attend local meetings for writers and illustrators whenever you can. Befriend other writers in your area (SCBWI offers members a roster broken down by state)—share guidelines, share subscriptions, be conference buddies and roommates, join a critique group or writing group, exchange information, and offer support. Get online—sign on to listservs, post on message boards and blogs, visit social networking sites and chatrooms. (The Institute of Children's Literature offers regularly scheduled live chats and open forums. Visit www.institutechildrenslit.com and click on Scheduled Events. Also, visit author Verla Kay's Web site, www.verlakay.com, for information on workshops. See Useful Online Resources on page 370 for more information.) Exchange addresses, phone numbers, and e-mail addresses with writers or illustrators you meet at events. And at conferences, don't be afraid to talk to people, ask strangers to join you for lunch, approach speakers and introduce yourself, or chat in elevators and hallways.

12. Perfect your craft and don't submit until your work is its best. It's often been said that a writer should try to write every day. Great manuscripts don't happen overnight; there's time, research, and revision involved. As you visit bookstores and study what others have written and illustrated, really step back and look at your own work and ask yourself—honestly—*How does my work measure up? Is it ready for editors or art directors to see?* If it's not, keep working. Join a critique group or get a professional manuscript or portfolio critique.

13. Be patient, learn from rejection, and don't give up! Thousands of manuscripts land on editors' desks; thousands of illustration samples line art directors' file drawers. There are so many factors that come into play when evaluating submissions. Keep in mind that you might not hear back from publishers promptly. Persistence and patience are important qualities in writers and illustrators working toward publication. Keep at it—it will come. It can take a while, but when you get that first book contract or first assignment, you'll know it was worth the wait. (For proof, read First Books on page 142.)

Before Your First Sale

If you're just beginning to pursue your career as a children's book writer or illustrator, it's important to learn the proper procedures, formats, and protocol for the publishing industry. This article outlines the basics you need to know before you head to the post office with your submissions.

FINDING THE BEST MARKETS FOR YOUR WORK

Researching publishers thoroughly is a basic element of submitting your work successfully. Editors and art directors hate to receive inappropriate submissions; handling them wastes a lot of their time, not to mention your time and money, and they are the main reason some publishers have chosen not to accept material over the transom. By randomly sending out material without knowing a company's needs, you're sure to meet with rejection.

If you're interested in submitting to a particular magazine, write to request a sample copy or see if it's available in your local library or bookstore. For a book publisher, obtain a book catalog and check a library or bookstore for titles produced by that publisher. Most publishers and magazines have Web sites that include catalogs or sample articles (Web sites are given within the listings). Studying such materials carefully will better acquaint you with a publisher's or magazine's writing, illustration, and photography styles and formats.

Most of the book publishers and magazines listed in this book offer some sort of writer's, artist's, or photographer's guidelines for a self-addressed, stamped envelope (SASE). Guidelines are also often found on publishers' Web sites. It's important to read and study guidelines before submitting work. You'll get a better understanding of what a particular publisher wants. You may even decide, after reading the submission guidelines, that your work isn't right for a company you considered.

SUBMITTING YOUR WORK

Throughout the listings, you'll read requests for particular elements to include when contacting markets. Here are explanations of some of these important submission components.

Queries, cover letters, & proposals

A query letter is a no-more-than-one-page, well-written piece meant to arouse an editor's interest in your work. Many query letters start with leads similar to those of actual manuscripts. In the rest of the letter, briefly outline the work you're proposing and include facts, anecdotes, interviews, or other pertinent information that give the editor a feel for the manuscript's premise—entice her to want to know more. End your letter with a straightforward request to write or submit the work, and include information on its approximate length, date it could be completed, and whether accompanying photos or artwork are available.

In a query letter, think about presenting   book as a publisher's catalog would present it. Read through a good catalog and examine how the publishers give enticing summaries of their books in a spare amount of words. It's also important that query letters give editors a taste of your writing style. For good advice and samples of queries, cover letters, and other correspondence, consult *Formatting & Submitting Your Manuscript*, Second Edition, by Cynthia Laufenberg and the editors of *Writer's Market* and *How to Write Attention-Grabbing Query & Cover Letters*, by John Wood (both Writer's Digest Books).

• **Query letters for nonfiction.** Queries are usually required when submitting nonfiction material to a publisher. The goal of a nonfiction query is to convince the editor your idea is perfect for her readership and that you're qualified to do the job. Note any previous writing experience and include published samples to prove your credentials, especially samples related to the subject matter you're querying about.

• **Query letters for fiction.** More and more, queries are being requested for fiction manuscripts. For a fiction query, explain the story's plot, main characters, conflict, and resolution. Just as in nonfiction queries, make the editor eager to see more.

• **Cover letters for writers.** Some editors prefer to review complete manuscripts, especially for picture books or fiction. In such cases, the cover letter (which should be no longer than one page) serves as your introduction, establishes your credentials as a writer, and gives the editor an overview of the manuscript. If the editor asked for the manuscript because of a query, note this in your cover letter.

• **Cover letters for illustrators and photographers.** For an illustrator or photographer, the cover letter serves as an introduction to the art director and establishes professional credentials when submitting samples. Explain what services you can provide as well as what type of follow-up contact you plan to make, if any. Be sure to include the URL of your online portfolio if you have one.

• **Résumés.** Often writers, illustrators, and photographers are asked to submit resumes with cover letters and samples. They can be created in a variety of formats, from a single page listing information to color brochures featuring your work. Keep your resume brief, and focus on your achievements, including your clients and the work you've done for them, as well as your educational background and any awards you've received. Do not use the same resume you'd use for a typical job application.

• **Book proposals.** Throughout the listings in the Book Publishers section, publishers refer to submitting a synopsis, outline, and sample chapters. Depending on an editor's preference, some or all of these components, along with a cover letter, make up a book proposal.

A *synopsis* summarizes the book, covering the basic plot (including the ending). It should be easy to read and flow well.

An *outline* covers your book chapter by chapter and provides highlights of each. If you're developing an outline for fiction, include major characters, plots and subplots, and book length.

Sample chapters give a more comprehensive idea of your writing skill. Some editors may request the first two or three chapters to determine if she's interested in seeing the whole book.

Manuscript formats

When submitting a complete manuscript, follow some basic guidelines. In the upper-left corner of your title page, type your legal name (not pseudonym), address, and phone number. In the upper-right corner, type the approximate word count. All material in the upper corners should be single-spaced. Then type the title (centered) almost halfway down that page, the word "by" two spaces under that, and your name or pseudonym two spaces under "by."

The first page should also include the title (centered) one-third of the way down. Two spaces under that type "by" and your name or pseudonym. To begin the body of your manuscript, drop down two double spaces and indent five spaces for each new paragraph. There should be one-inch margins around all sides of a full typewritten page. (Manuscripts with wide margins are more readable and easier to edit.)

Set your computer to double-space for the manuscript body. From page two to the end of the manuscript, include your last name followed by a comma and the title (or key words of the title) in the upper-left corner. The page number should go in the top right corner. Drop down two double spaces to begin the body of each page. If you're submitting a novel, type each chapter title one-third of the way down the page. For more information on manuscript formats, read *Formatting & Submitting Your Manuscript*, by Cynthia Laufenberg and the editors of *Writer's Market* (Writer's Digest Books). SCBWI members and nonmembers can refer to their publication *From Keyboard to Printed Page: Facts You Need to Know*. Visit their Web site www.scbwi.org and click on "Publications."

For More Info

Picture book formats

The majority of editors prefer to see complete manuscripts for picture books. When typing the text of a picture book, don't indicate page breaks and don't type each page of text on a new sheet of paper. And unless you are an illustrator, don't worry about supplying art. Editors will find their own illustrators for picture books. Most of the time, a writer and an illustrator who work on the same book never meet or interact. The editor acts as a go-between and works with the writer and illustrator throughout the publishing process. *How to Write and Sell Children's Picture Books*, by Jean E. Karl (Writer's Digest Books), offers advice on preparing text and marketing your work.

If you're an illustrator who has written your own book, consider creating a dummy or storyboard containing both art and text, and then submit it along with your complete manuscript and sample pieces of final art (color photocopies or computer printouts—never originals). Publishers interested in picture books specify in their listings what should be submitted. For tips on creating a dummy, refer to *How to Write and Illustrate Children's Books and Get Them Published*, edited by Treld Pelkey Bicknell and Felicity Trotman (North Light Books), or Frieda Gates' book, *How to Write, Illustrate, and Design Children's Books* (Lloyd-Simone Publishing Company).

For More Info

Writers may also want to learn the art of dummy making to help them through their writing process with things like pacing, rhythm, and length. For a great explanation and helpful hints, see *You Can Write Children's Books*, by Tracey E. Dils (Writer's Digest Books).

Mailing submissions

Your main concern when packaging material is to be sure it arrives undamaged. If your manuscript is less than six pages, simply fold it in thirds and send it in a #10 (business-size) envelope. For a SASE, either fold another #10 envelope in thirds or insert a #9 (reply) envelope which fits in a #10 neatly without folding.

Another option is folding your manuscript in half in a 6 × 9 envelope, with a #9 or #10 SASE enclosed. For larger manuscripts, use a 9 × 12 envelope both for mailing the submission and as a SASE (which can be folded in half). Book manuscripts require sturdy packaging for mailing. Include a self-addressed mailing label and return postage.

If asked to send artwork and photographs, remember they require a bit more care in packaging to guarantee they arrive in good condition. Sandwich illustrations and photos between heavy cardboard that is slightly larger than the work. The cardboard can be secured by rubber bands or with tape. If you tape the cardboard together, check that the artwork doesn't stick to the tape. Be sure your name and address appear on the back of each piece of art or each photo in case the material becomes separated. For the packaging, use either a manila envelope, a foam-padded envelope, brown paper, or a mailer lined with plastic air bubbles. Bind nonjoined edges with reinforced mailing tape and affix a typed mailing label or clearly write your address.

Mailing material first class ensures quick delivery. Also, first-class mail is forwarded for one year if the addressee has moved, and it can be returned if undeliverable. If you're concerned about your original material safely reaching its destination, consider other mailing options, such as UPS or certified mail. If material needs to reach your editor or art director quickly, use overnight delivery services.

Remember, companies outside your own country can't use your country's postage when returning a manuscript to you. When mailing a submission to another country, include a self-addressed envelope and International Reply Coupons, or IRCs. (You'll see this term in many listings in the Canadian & International Book Publishers section.) Your postmaster can tell you, based on a package's weight, the correct number of IRCs to include to ensure its return.

If it's not necessary for an editor to return your work (such as with photocopies), don't include return postage. You may want to track the status of your submission by enclosing a postage-paid reply postcard with options for the editor to check, such as "Yes, I am interested," "I'll keep the material on file," or "No, the material is not appropriate for my needs at this time."

Some writers elect to include a deadline date. If you don't hear from the editor by the specified date, your manuscript is automatically withdrawn from consideration. Because many publishing houses and companies are overstocked with material, a minimum deadline should be at least three months.

Unless requested, it's never a good idea to use a company's fax number or e-mail address to send manuscript submissions. This can disrupt a company's internal business. Some publishers and magazines, however, may be open to e-mail submissions. Study the listings for specifics and visit publishers' and publications' Web sites for more information.

Keeping submission records

It's important to keep track of the material you submit. When recording each submission, include the date it was sent, the business and contact name, and any enclosures (such as samples of writing, artwork, or photography). You can create a record-keeping system of your own or look for record-keeping software in your area computer store.

Keep copies of articles or manuscripts you send together with related correspondence to make follow-up easier. When you sell rights to a manuscript, artwork, or photos, you can "close" your file on a particular submission by noting the date the material was accepted, what rights were purchased, the publication date, and payment.

Often writers, illustrators, and photographers fail to follow up on overdue responses. If you don't hear from a publisher within their stated response time, wait another month or so and follow up with a note asking about the status of your submission. Include the title or description, date sent, and a SASE for response. Ask the contact person when she anticipates making a decision. You may refresh the memory of a buyer who temporarily forgot about your submission. At the very least, you'll receive a definite "no" and free yourself to send the material to another publisher.

Simultaneous submissions

If you opt for simultaneous (also called "multiple") submissions—sending the same material to several publishers at the same time—be sure to inform each editor to whom you submit that your work is being considered elsewhere. Many editors are reluctant to receive simultaneous submissions but understand that for hopeful writers and illustrators, waiting several months for a response can be frustrating. In some cases, an editor may actually be more inclined to read your manuscript sooner if she knows it's being considered by another publisher. The

Society of Children's Book Writers and Illustrators cautions writers against simultaneous submissions. They recommend simultaneously submitting to publishers who state in their submission guidelines that they accept multiple submissions. In such cases, always specify in your cover letter that you've submitted to more than one editor.

It's especially important to keep track of simultaneous submissions, so if you get an offer on a manuscript sent to more than one publisher, you can instruct other publishers to withdraw your work from consideration.

AGENTS & ART REPS

Most children's writers, illustrators, and photographers, especially those just beginning, are confused about whether to enlist the services of an agent or representative. The decision is strictly one that each writer, illustrator, or photographer must make for herself. Some are confident with their own negotiation skills and believe acquiring an agent or rep is not in their best interest. Others feel uncomfortable in the business arena or are not willing to sacrifice valuable creative time for marketing.

About half of children's publishers accept unagented work, so it's possible to break into children's publishing without an agent. Some agents avoid working with children's books because traditionally low advances and trickling royalty payments over long periods of time make children's books less lucrative. Writers targeting magazine markets don't need the services of an agent. In fact, it's practically impossible to find an agent interested in marketing articles and short stories—there simply isn't enough financial incentive.

One benefit of having an agent, though, is it may speed up the process of getting your work reviewed, especially by publishers who don't accept unagented submissions. If an agent has a good reputation and submits your manuscript to an editor, that manuscript will likely bypass the first-read stage (which is generally done by editorial assistants and junior editors) and end up on the editor's desk sooner.

When agreeing to have a reputable agent represent you, remember that she should be familiar with the needs of the current market and evaluate your manuscript/artwork/photos accordingly. She should also determine the quality of your piece and whether it is saleable. When your manuscript sells, your agent should negotiate a favorable contract and clear up any questions you have about payments.

Keep in mind that however reputable the agent or rep is, she has limitations. Representation does not guarantee sale of your work. It just means an agent or rep sees potential in your writing, art, or photos. Though an agent or rep may offer criticism or advice on how to improve your work, she cannot make you a better writer, artist, or photographer.

Literary agents typically charge a 15 percent commission from the sale of writing; art and photo representatives usually charge a 25 to 30 percent commission. Such fees are taken from advances and royalty earnings. If your agent sells foreign rights to your work, she will deduct a higher percentage because she will most likely be dealing with an overseas agent with whom she must split the fee.

Be advised that not every agent is open to representing a writer, artist, or photographer who lacks an established track record. Just as when approaching a publisher, the manuscript, artwork, or photos and query or cover letter you submit to a potential agent must be attractive and professional looking. Your first impression must be as an organized, articulate person. For listings of agents and reps, turn to the Agents & Art Reps section.

For additional listings of art reps, consult *Artist's & Graphic Designer's Market*; for photo reps, see *Photographer's Market*; for more information and additional listings of agents see *Guide to Literary Agents* (all Writer's Digest Books).

Running Your Business

The Basics for Writers & Illustrators

A career in children's publishing involves more than just writing skills or artistic talent. Successful authors and illustrators must be able to hold their own in negotiations, keep records, understand contract language, grasp copyright law, pay taxes, and take care of a number of other business concerns. Although agents and reps, accountants and lawyers, and writers' organizations offer help in sorting out such business issues, it's wise to have a basic understanding of them going in. This article offers just that—basic information. For a more in-depth look at the subjects covered here, check your library or bookstore for books and magazines to help you. We also tell you how to get information on issues like taxes and copyright from the federal government.

CONTRACTS & NEGOTIATION

Before you see your work in print or begin working with an editor or art director on a project, there is negotiation. And whether negotiating a book contract, a magazine article assignment, or an illustration or photo assignment, there are a few things to keep in mind. First, if you find any clauses vague or confusing in a contract, get legal advice. The time and money invested in counseling up front could protect you from problems later. If you have an agent or rep, she will review any contract.

A contract is an agreement between two or more parties that specifies the fees to be paid, services rendered, deadlines, rights purchased, and for artists and photographers, whether original work is returned. Most companies have standard contracts for writers, illustrators,

Sources for Contract Help

Writers organizations offer a wealth of information to members, including contract advice:

Society of Children's Book Writers and Illustrators members can find information in the SCBWI publication Answers to Some Questions About Contracts. Contact SCBWI at 8271 Beverly Blvd., Los Angeles CA 90048, (323)782-1010, or visit their Web site: www.scbwi.org.

The Authors Guild also offers contract tips. Visit their Web site, www.authorsguild.org. (Members of the guild can receive a 75-point contract review from the guild's legal staff.) See the Web site for membership information and application form, or contact The Authors Guild at 31 E. 28th St., 10th Floor, New York NY 10016, (212)563-5904. Fax: (212)564-5363. E-mail: staff@authorsguild.org. Web site: www.authorsguild.org.

and photographers. The specifics (such as royalty rates, advances, delivery dates, etc.) are typed in after negotiations.

Though it's okay to conduct negotiations over the phone, get a written contract once both parties have agreed on terms. Never depend on oral stipulations; written contracts protect both parties from misunderstandings. Watch for clauses that may not be in your best interest, such as "work-for-hire." When you do work-for-hire, you give up all rights to your creations.

When negotiating a book deal, find out whether your contract contains an option clause. This clause requires the author to give the publisher a first look at her next work before offering it to other publishers. Though it's editorial etiquette to give the publisher the first chance at publishing your next work, be wary of statements in the contract that could trap you. Don't allow the publisher to consider the next project for more than 30 days and be specific about what type of work should actually be considered "next work." (For example, if the book under contract is a young adult novel, specify that the publisher will receive an exclusive look at only your next young adult novel.)

For More Info

(For more information about SCBWI, The Authors Guild, and other organizations, turn to the Clubs & Organizations section and read the listings for the organizations that interest you.)

Book publishers' payment methods

Book publishers pay authors and artists in royalties, a percentage of either the wholesale or retail price of each book sold. From large publishing houses, the author usually receives an advance issued against future royalties before the book is published. Half of the advance amount is issued upon signing the book contract; the other half is issued when the book is finished. For illustrations, one-third of the advance should be collected upon signing the contract; one-third upon delivery of sketches; and one-third upon delivery of finished art.

After your book has sold enough copies to earn back your advance, you'll start to get royalty checks. Some publishers hold a reserve against returns, which means a percentage of royalties is held back in case books are returned from bookstores. If you have a reserve clause in your contract, find out the exact percentage of total sales that will be withheld and the time period the publisher will hold this money. You should be reimbursed this amount after a reasonable time period, such as a year. Royalty percentages vary with each publisher, but there are standard ranges.

Book publishers' rates

According to figures from the Society of Children's Book Writers and Illustrators, first-time picture book authors can expect advances of $2,000-3,000; first-time picture book illustrators' advances range from $5,000-7,000; text and illustration packages for first-timers can score $6,000-8,000. Rates go up for subsequent books: $3,500-5,000 for picture book text; $7,000-10,000 for picture book illustration; $8,000-10,000 for text and illustration. Experienced authors can expect higher advances. Royalties for picture books are generally about five percent (split between the author and illustrator) but can go as high as ten percent. Those who both write and illustrate a book, of course, receive the full royalty.

Advances for hardcover novels and nonfiction can fetch author's advances of $4,000-6,000 and 10 percent royalties; paperbacks bring in slightly lower advances of $3,000-5,000 and royalties of 6-8 percent.

As you might expect, advance and royalty figures vary from house to house and are affected by the time of year, the state of the economy, and other factors. Some smaller houses may not even pay royalties, just flat fees. Educational houses may not offer advances or offer smaller amounts. Religious publishers tend to offer smaller advances than trade publishers. First-time writers and illustrators generally start on the low end of the scale, while established and high-profile writers are paid more. For more information SCBWI members can request or download SCBWI publication "Answer to Some Questions About Contracts." (Visit www. scbwi.org.)

Pay rates for magazines

For writers, fee structures for magazines are based on a per-word rate or range for a specific article length. Artists and photographers have a few more variables to contend with before contracting their services.

Payment for illustrations and photos can be set by such factors as whether the piece(s) will be black and white or four-color, how many are to be purchased, where the work appears (cover or inside), circulation, and the artist's or photographer's prior experience.

Remaindering

When a book goes out of print, a publisher will sell any existing copies to a wholesaler who, in turn, sells the copies to stores at a discount. When the books are "remaindered" to a wholesaler, they are usually sold at a price just above the cost of printing. When negotiating a contract with a publisher, you may want to discuss the possibility of purchasing the remaindered copies before they are sold to a wholesaler, then you can market the copies you purchased and still make a profit.

KNOW YOUR RIGHTS

A copyright is a form of protection provided to creators of original works, published or unpublished. In general, copyright protection ensures the writer, illustrator, or photographer the power to decide how her work is used and allows her to receive payment for each use.

Essentially, copyright also encourages the creation of new works by guaranteeing the creator power to sell rights to the work in the marketplace. The copyright holder can print, reprint, or copy her work; sell or distribute copies of her work; or prepare derivative works such as plays, collages, or recordings. The Copyright Law is designed to protect work (created on or after January 1, 1978) for her lifetime plus 70 years.

If you collaborate with someone else on a written or artistic project, the copyright will last for the lifetime of the last survivor plus 70 years. The creators' heirs may hold a copyright for an additional 70 years. After that, the work becomes public domain. Works created anonymously or under a pseudonym are protected for 120 years, or 95 years after publication. Under work-for-hire agreements, you relinquish your copyright to your "employer."

Copyright notice & registration

Some feel a copyright notice should be included on all work, registered or not. Others feel it is not necessary and a copyright notice will only confuse publishers about whether the material is registered (acquiring rights to previously registered material is a more complicated process).

Although it's not necessary to include a copyright notice on unregistered work, if you don't feel your work is safe without the notice, it is your right to include one. Including a copyright notice—(c) (year of work, your name)—should help safeguard against plagiarism.

Registration is a legal formality intended to make copyright public record, and it can help you win more money in a court case. By registering work within three months of publication or before an infringement occurs, you are eligible to collect statutory damages and attorney's fees. If you register later than three months after publication, you will qualify only for actual damages and profits.

Ideas and concepts are not copyrightable, only expressions of those ideas and concepts. A character type or basic plot outline, for example, is not subject to a copyright infringement lawsuit. Also, titles, names, short phrases or slogans, and lists of contents are not subject to copyright protection, though titles and names may be protected thZrough the Trademark Office.

You can register a group of articles, illustrations, or photos if it meets these criteria:

- the group is assembled in order, such as in a notebook
- the works bear a single title, such as "Works by (your name)"
- it is the work of one writer, artist, or photographer
- the material is the subject of a single claim to copyright

It's a publisher's responsibility to register your book for copyright. If you've previously registered the same material, you must inform your editor and supply the previous copyright information, otherwise, the publisher can't register the book in its published form.

For more information about the proper way to register works and to order the correct forms, contact the U.S. Copyright Office, (202)707-3000. The forms available are TX for writing (books, articles, etc.); VA for pictures (photographs, illustrations); and PA for plays and music. For information about how to use the copyright forms, request a copy of Circular I on Copyright Basics. All of the forms and circulars are free. Send the completed registration form along with the stated fee and a copy of the work to the Copyright Office.

For specific answers to questions about copyright (but not legal advice), call the Copyright Public Information Office at (202)707-3000 weekdays between 8:30 a.m. and 5 p.m. EST. Forms can also be downloaded from the Library of Congress Web site: www.copyright.gov. The site also includes a list of frequently asked questions, tips on filling out forms, general copyright information, and links to other sites related to copyright issues. For members of SCBWI, information about copyrights and the law is available in their publication: Copyright Facts for Writers.

The rights publishers buy

The copyright law specifies that a writer, illustrator, or photographer generally sells one-time rights to her work unless she and the buyer agree otherwise in writing. Many publications will want more exclusive rights to your work than just one-time usage; some will even require you to sell all rights. Be sure you are monetarily compensated for the additional rights you relinquish. If you must give up all rights to a work, carefully consider the price you're being offered to determine whether you'll be compensated for the loss of other potential sales.

Writers who only give up limited rights to their work can then sell reprint rights to other publications, foreign rights to international publications, or even movie rights, should the opportunity arise. Artists and photographers can sell their work to other markets such as paper product companies who may use an image on a calendar, greeting card, or mug. Illustrators and photographers may even sell original work after it has been published. And there are a number of galleries throughout the U.S. that display and sell the original work of children's illustrators.

Rights acquired through the sale of a book manuscript are explained in each publisher's contract. Take time to read relevant clauses to be sure you understand what rights each contract is specifying before signing. Be sure your contract contains a clause allowing all rights to revert back to you in the event the publisher goes out of business. (You may even want to have the contract reviewed by an agent or an attorney specializing in publishing law.)

The following are the rights you'll most often sell to publishers, periodicals, and producers in the marketplace:

First rights. The buyer purchases the rights to use the work for the first time in any medium. All other rights remain with the creator. When material is excerpted from a soon-to-be-published book for use in a newspaper or periodical, first serial rights are also purchased.

One-time rights. The buyer has no guarantee that she is the first to use a piece. One-time permission to run written work, illustrations, or photos is acquired, then the rights revert back to the creator.

First North American serial rights. This is similar to first rights, except that companies who distribute both in the U.S. and Canada will stipulate these rights to ensure that another North American company won't come out with simultaneous usage of the same work.

Second serial (reprint) rights. In this case, newspapers and magazines are granted the right to reproduce a work that has already appeared in another publication. These rights are also purchased by a newspaper or magazine editor who wants to publish part of a book after the book has been published. The proceeds from reprint rights for a book are often split evenly between the author and his publishing company.

Simultaneous rights. More than one publication buys one-time rights to the same work at the same time. Use of such rights occurs among magazines with circulations that don't overlap, such as many religious publications.

All rights. Just as it sounds, the writer, illustrator, or photographer relinquishes all rights to a piece—she no longer has any say in who acquires rights to use it. All rights are purchased by publishers who pay premium usage fees, have an exclusive format, or have other book or magazine interests from which the purchased work can generate more mileage. If a company insists on acquiring all rights to your work, see if you can negotiate for the rights to revert back to you after a reasonable period of time. If they agree to such a proposal, get it in writing. Note: Writers, illustrators, and photographers should be wary of "work-for-hire" arrangements. If you sign an agreement stipulating that your work will be done as work-for-hire, you will not control the copyrights of the completed work—the company that hired you will be the copyright owner.

For More Info

Foreign serial rights. Be sure before you market to foreign publications that you have sold only North American—not worldwide—serial rights to previous markets. If so, you are free to market to publications that may be interested in material that's appeared in a North American-based periodical.

Syndication rights. This is a division of serial rights. For example, if a syndicate prints portions of a book in installments in its newspapers, it would be syndicating second serial rights. The syndicate would receive a commission and leave the remainder to be split between the author and publisher.

Subsidiary rights. These include serial rights, dramatic rights, book club rights, or translation rights. The contract should specify what percentage of profits from sales of these rights go to the author and publisher.

Dramatic, television, and motion picture rights. During a specified time, the interested party tries to sell a story to a producer or director. Many times options are renewed because the selling process can be lengthy.

Display rights or electronic publishing rights. They're also known as "Data, Storage, and Retrieval." Usually listed under subsidiary rights, the marketing of electronic rights in this era of rapidly expanding capabilities and markets for electronic material can be tricky. Display rights can cover text or images to be used in a CD-ROM or online, or they may cover use of material in formats not even fully developed yet. If a display rights clause is listed in your contract, try to negotiate its elimination. Otherwise, be sure to pin down which electronic rights are being purchased. Demand the clause be restricted to things designed to be read only. By doing this, you maintain your rights to use your work for things such as games and interactive software.

STRICTLY BUSINESS

An essential part of being a freelance writer, illustrator, or photographer is running your freelance business. It's imperative to maintain accurate business records to determine if you're making a profit as a freelancer. Keeping correct, organized records will also make your life easier as you approach tax time.

When setting up your system, begin by keeping a bank account and ledger for your business finances apart from your personal finances. Also, if writing, illustration, or photography is secondary to another freelance career, keep separate business records for each.

You will likely accumulate some business expenses before showing any profit when you start out as a freelancer. To substantiate your income and expenses to the IRS, keep all invoices, cash receipts, sales slips, bank statements, canceled checks, and receipts related to travel expenses and entertaining clients. For entertainment expenditures, record the date, place, and purpose of the business meeting, as well as gas mileage. Keep records for all purchases, big and small. Don't take the small purchases for granted; they can add up to a substantial amount. File all receipts in chronological order. Maintaining a separate file for each month simplifies retrieving records at the end of the year.

Record keeping

When setting up a single-entry bookkeeping system, record income and expenses separately. Use some of the subheads that appear on Schedule C (the form used for recording income from a business) of the 1040 tax form so you can easily transfer information onto the tax form when filing your return. In your ledger include a description of each transaction—the date, source of income (or debts from business purchases), description of what was purchased or sold, the amount of the transaction, and whether payment was by cash, check, or credit card.

Don't wait until January 1 to start keeping records. The moment you first make a business-related purchase or sell an article, book manuscript, illustration, or photo, begin tracking your profits and losses. If you keep records from January 1 to December 31, you're using a calendar-year accounting period. Any other accounting period is called a fiscal year.

There are two types of accounting methods you can choose from—the cash method and the accrual method. The cash method is used more often: You record income when it is received and expenses when they're disbursed.

Using the accrual method, you report income at the time you earn it rather than when it's actually received. Similarly, expenses are recorded at the time they're incurred rather than when you actually pay them. If you choose this method, keep separate records for "accounts receivable" and "accounts payable."

Satisfying the IRS

To successfully—and legally—work as a freelancer, you must know what income you should report and what deductions you can claim. But before you can do that, you must prove to the IRS you're in business to make a profit, that your writing, illustration, or photography is not merely a hobby.

The Tax Reform Act of 1986 says you should show a profit for three years out of a five-year period to attain professional status. The IRS considers these factors as proof of your professionalism:

- accurate financial records
- a business bank account separate from your personal account
- proven time devoted to your profession
- whether it's your main or secondary source of income
- your history of profits and losses
- the amount of training you have invested in your field
- your expertise

If your business is unincorporated, you'll fill out tax information on Schedule C of Form 1040. If you're unsure of what deductions you can take, request the IRS publication containing this information. Under the Tax Reform Act, only 30 percent of business meals, entertainment and related tips, and parking charges are deductible. Other deductible expenses allowed on Schedule C include: car expenses for business-related trips; professional courses and seminars; depreciation of office equipment, such as a computer; dues and publication subscriptions; and miscellaneous expenses, such as postage used for business needs.

If you're working out of a home office, a portion of your mortgage interest (or rent), related utilities, property taxes, repair costs, and depreciation may be deducted as business expenses—under special circumstances. To learn more about the possibility of home office deductions, consult IRS Publication 587, Business Use of Your Home.

The method of paying taxes on income not subject to withholding is called "estimated tax" for individuals. If you expect to owe more than $500 at year's end and if the total amount of income tax that will be withheld during the year will be less than 90 percent of the tax shown on the current year's return, you'll generally make estimated tax payments. Estimated tax payments are made in four equal installments due on April 15, June 15, September 15, and January 15 (assuming you're a calendar-year taxpayer). For more information, request Publication 533, Self-Employment Tax.

The Internal Revenue Service's Web site (www.irs.gov) offers tips and instant access to IRS forms and publications.

Social Security tax

Depending on your net income as a freelancer, you may be liable for a Social Security tax. This is a tax designed for those who don't have Social Security withheld from their paychecks. You're liable if your net income is $400 or more per year. Net income is the difference between your income and allowable business deductions. Request Schedule SE, Computation of Social Security Self-Employment Tax, if you qualify.

If completing your income tax return proves to be too complex, consider hiring an accountant (the fee is a deductible business expense) or contact the IRS for assistance. (Look in the White Pages under U.S. Government—Internal Revenue Service or check their Web site, www.irs.gov.) In addition to offering numerous publications to instruct you in various facets of preparing a tax return, the IRS also has walk-in centers in some cities.

Insurance

As a self-employed professional, be aware of what health and business insurance coverage is available to you. Unless you're a Canadian who is covered by national health insurance or a full-time freelancer covered by your spouse's policy, health insurance will no doubt be one of your biggest expenses. Under the terms of a 1985 government act (COBRA), if you leave a job with health benefits, you're entitled to continue that coverage for up to 18 months—you pay 100 percent of the premium and sometimes a small administration fee. Eventually, you must search for your own health plan. You may also choose to purchase disability and life insurance. Disability insurance is offered through many private insurance companies and state governments. This insurance pays a monthly fee that covers living and business expenses during periods of long-term recuperation from a health problem. The amount of money paid is based on the recipient's annual earnings.

Before contacting any insurance representative, talk to other writers, illustrators, or photographers to learn which insurance companies they recommend. If you belong to a writers' or artists' organization, ask the organization if it offers insurance coverage for professionals. (SCBWI has a plan available to members in certain states. Look through the Clubs & Organizations section for other groups that may offer coverage.) Group coverage may be more affordable and provide more comprehensive coverage than an individual policy.

Evolving Children's Book Publishing

by Kelly Milner Halls

Like most post-2008 industries, children's literature has struggled to survive a bottomed-out national economy. Bailout billions tossed at banks and brokers never trickled down to publishers, writers or illustrators.

Even as I interviewed *Publishers Weekly* Editor-in-Chief Sara Nelson about the long term outlook for children's publishing, another axe fell and her job was eliminated. Clearly, the cuts are deep and painful. But as Nelson herself insisted, hope does yet endure.

"We should be shaken up by economic realities," she admitted in a PW column. But Nelson also saw the turmoil as opportunity. "There is no question that some of our old-fashioned ways—and, sorry to say, the people who perform them—need to change. As the old adage goes, change or die."

If evolution is the path to survival, what shifts might be necessary along the road? Many experts agree, these five steps are a great place to start.

1. Publish the best, not the most

According to Nelson, more than 300,000 titles are published each year, "a ridiculous number," she insists. (Recent Bowker stats put that number at more than 560,000 in 2008 if you include POD books.) If the children's book industry and other branches of the publishing family exchange excess for exception, hope may be within sight.

When Vice President and Publisher of Greenwillow Books, Virginia Duncan agreed to publish my 2009 nonfiction picture book, *Saving the Baghdad Zoo: A True Story of Hope and Heroes*, it was an exception to the her general rule. "We do so little nonfiction," she said. "It needs to be of broader interest," to even be considered.

Duncan and many other editors feel nonfiction books that tell a very specific and dramatic tale—like animals endangered by war—might fare better in today's economy than less pointed proposals. And librarians seem to agree.

"For nonfiction books," says Southlake Public Library media specialist Jesse Ephraim, "I look for subjects that aren't covered well by other available titles."

Marin County Day School librarian Anie Schafer agrees. "Make it good—well researched with great art and/or photographs; not like anything out there to make it into my collection," she says.

KELLY MILNER HALLS is a freelance writer and lover of all things weird, including her latest books, *Dinosaur Parade* (Lark, 2008) and *Saving the Baghdad Zoo* (Greenwillow/HarperCollins 2009), and other classics including *Mysteries of the Mummy Kids* (2007) and *Tales of the Cryptids* (2006), both from Darby Creek. She lives in Spokane, Washington with two daughters, two dogs, too many cats and a 4-foot rock iguana named Gigantor.

Dig deep when you prepare your nonfiction book proposals and find a slant that gives readers and book buyers something new to think about. When it comes to writing fiction, the considerations are very nearly the same.

Laurena Schultz, Teen Services Librarian at the Mount Lebanon Public Library says, "I'd rather read a book that's true to itself and the author's ability than just another copycat vampire thriller or chick-lit fluff."

"Authors that write books in genres that are underrepresented in the publishing world stand a good chance of getting in my collection," Ephraim continues. "For example, action-oriented contemporary war fiction that isn't 'issues' based is grossly underrepresented in YA publishing these days. It's hard to find YA books geared for boys in general, to be honest."

2. Serve neglected readerships

Ephraim leads seamlessly to the next survival tip. Write for neglected audiences. Even if you find it easy to imitate various success stories, selling the work will be hard as acquisition dollars shrink. If you already publish Stephenie Meyer, why pay for a clone?

Avoid reinventing the wheel and blaze a trail of your own. Write for readers underserved, including boys and reluctant readers.

"I think the biggest and most hopeful trend is the rise in graphic novels for children," says *Publishers Weekly* children's book editor Diane Roback, "created both for entertainment and educational purposes. This area of the market continues to grow and should help give reluctant readers more choices in reading material they can enjoy."

Breakthrough novelist Andrew Smith, *Ghost Medicine* (Feiwel & Friends, 2008) and *In the Path of Falling Objects* (Feiwel & Friends, 2009), thinks more men should step up to write books expressly for boys—or even to publish them.

"What do boys' brains need in books?" he wrote in one blogs. "They need male characters; they need spatial-kinesthetic action, technical and mechanical content, and graphics and visual stimulation. This is exactly how I focused the content of *Ghost Medicine* because I wanted boys to read again, like we used to when I was a boy."

"I'm on a mission, as a member of a fairly quiet minority—male authors," he continued, "to give boys back the literary connections they once had."

Nelson agrees. "I think anything that can be done to increase interest in reading by young boys is great—but I think it's false and insulting to assume that because women are 'in charge' in publishing, they're all too prissy to publish for boys. Have you ever met Carrie Kania over at Harper Perennial?" Kania, according to the *New Yorker*, has a passion for "losers" or writers who have lived life close to the edge.

And the truth is, it's not just about gender. Some young readers—male and female—are not finding the subjects they long to read about in their libraries—kids outside the norm in terms of childhood interests. They're dying inside—isolated and alone because everyone else seems to love typical books, but they can't find their titles. They are the reason I write quirky fiction about dinosaurs and lake monsters. They are the kids I once was. Want to rise above economic disaster? Serve a reading population—with authenticity—that normally falls through the cracks. It's irresistible.

3. Rethink traditional covers, titles and advertising

Never judge a book by its cover. It's often said. And yet, from a book buyer's perspective, it's an impossible aim. "I automatically overlook an ugly cover or one with juvenile looking art," says teen services librarian Schultz. And many others agree. In fact, many authors lament the weakness of their book cover designs, knowing the power of visuals in relation to kids.

Awkward titles can be just as dangerous. *Tales of the Cryptids* (Darby Creek, 2006) seemed like a fun play on words when I wrote my book of mysterious animals. And it's sold very,

very well. But literacy expert Katherine Baxter made an excellent point when I talked with her by email.

"Kids don't know what a 'cryptid' is," she observed. "Why make them guess?" Baxter felt the book itself was compelling, but said the title should have been more direct, and the cover more compelling.

Traditional advertising dollars are shrinking along with publishing budgets, so marketing efforts must also evolve. Case-in-point, Jay Asher's *13 Reasons Why* (Razorbill/Penguin, 2007). Word-of-mouth briefly launched the author's debut novel onto the New York Times Children's Books Best-Seller list shortly after its release. But creative marketing gave it a return engagement more than a year later.

Digital strategist Regan Meador at Grey New York, a PR firm (hired by Razorbill) helped create *YouTube* video shorts drawn from key scenes in the book to revive interest and sales. Once the book hit #3 on its second bestseller list run, the campaign's success was undeniable.

"I think my best advice for publishers [and authors] is, 'go where the readers are,'" says Nelson. "If that's Facebook, MySpace, etc, then that's where the publishers [and authors] should be."

4. Embrace Innovation—Electronic

Just the thought of digital book publishing sends panic into the hearts of many authors and illustrators. But with innovation comes opportunity. Thanks to Amazon's Kindle—a wireless reading device as thin as a magazine launched in November of 2007—the e-book craze might be here to stay.

As many as 280,000 Kindle readers reportedly sold in its first year of availability. In fact, Amazon's initial inventory sold out in just over five hours, the day it debuted. Founder Jeff Bezos insists that number will skyrocket as the "new product" fear-factor subsides. Each Kindle can hold up to 200 non-illustrated book downloads. Amazon offered 88,000 options its first year out of the box—along with newspapers and magazines. With an optional memory card, an e-library of illustrated options becomes more feasible.

Downloads are more affordable than traditional books, so there is less cash to divvy up per unit. But production costs are lower (no paper or bindings), and storage costs are all but nonexistent—no warehousing digital downloads. Even distribution is simpler. Though limited to key online outlets for now, in-store kiosks could easily bring chains and independent bookstores into the game.

It's only natural in a digital age, according to Nelson. "The first word my son learned to spell was 'install,'" she says. "So yes, I do think digital availability will help further the sales and consumption of children's books. I also think children can and will still learn the value of holding an actual book in their hands." Nelson sees no real conflict in coexistence.

What she does see is resistance from the older generation. "The biggest hurdle to the future of digital books will be the parents, who may still tend to think that digital books aren't 'real.' But between the publishers and kids themselves, this impression is bound to dissipate."

4b. Embrace Innovation—Design

Traditionalists, take heart. Electronics is not the only road to innovation. Book design also represents a brave new horizon. Consider the appeal of books like *Lincoln Shot: A President's Life Remembered* (2008, Feiwel & Friends). Written by Barry Denenberg and illustrated by Christopher Bing, the oversized (12 × 18 trim size) hardcover picture book uses the look of Lincoln era newspaper reports—and modern facsimiles—to transport readers back in time.

In an interview on the publisher Web site, Denenberg explained how the unique format eventually evolved after meetings with the author, illustrator and publisher, Jean Feiwel—and later, the entire production team.

"The discussion immediately focused on our obsession with historical accuracy," he said, "and the challenge of presenting history to young readers in a new, edgy way. This flowed naturally to creating a newspaper or magazine that was written back then," he explained.

Feiwel charged them with meeting that challenge as they parted. Denenberg said, "Christopher constructed three mock-ups representing three possible approaches. We both were in favor of the one that had a folded newspaper inside a custom made box, possibly with a CD."

Newspaper folds and the potential damage they represent took the box and "insert" idea off the production table, but inspired the final design. *Lincoln Shot* became a large book to mirror exactly the 1866 newspaper format, literally bringing history home. Why go to so much trouble?

As a writer-in-residence, Denenberg had observed that elementary school age kids didn't read much nonfiction. He, Bing and Feiwel wanted to make *Lincoln Shot* a book that was impossible to ignore. It was daring. The oversized design would also be hard to shelve in bookstores and libraries. But it was a risk they were willing to take.

"[We were] creating an object, not just a book," Denenberg said, "an object that was physically and visually inviting. As much as I might believe the writing in *Lincoln Shot* is the most important aspect, it doesn't matter if no one is going to look at the book. We wanted to create something that a 10- or 12-year-old would pick up and open, and then enter a world we had constructed; an historical tour of sorts. A conventionally formatted book just couldn't do that."

Almost immediately, dozens of publications validated their decision. *Booklist* named it an Editors' Choice. *School Library Journal* named it a Best book of the Year. Glowing response appeared in *Horn Book, Kirkus,* the *New York Times, the San Francisco Chronicle, USA Today* and the *Washington Post.* The gamble—and bold innovation—paid off.

5. Outreach, outreach, outreach

Once you've found your new angle and your new audience, once you've welcomed digital and other futuristic inclusions, once you've designed a book that stands out in value and appearance, the human connection remains a crucial element. So reach out and make them.

Bookstores, especially independent bookstores, still welcome author interaction in their children's departments. But step outside of the reading box. Make yours an in-store event—literally. Bake book related cookies and have a tea party. Prepare a craft even a kindergartener can master. Teach little readers how to draw. Create masks and have a dinosaur parade. Do something that makes your bookstore event impossible to ignore or deny.

Happy kids make happy parents. Happy parents buy books. Happy booksellers make enthusiastic recommendations even after you've gone home. Innovative bookstore events are the gifts that keep on giving, even if you're not around to watch most of it unfold.

School visits can also improve with innovation. When I talk about *Dinosaur Parade* (Lark, 2008), I don't just read from my book. I share fossils drawn directly from the pages. And in one school, I sold more than three dozen copies.

When Nancy Roe Pimm shares her book *Indy 500* (Darby Creek, 2006) she brings her Indy 500 husband's helmet and driving suit, along with checkered flags and pieces of thrown off tread.

Bring your book pages to life with fun and facts, and you'll see your speaking calendar fatten. Visit more and more schools, and you'll sell a lot more books. Why wait for your publisher? Take the success or failure of your book into your own hands.

Simply put, evolve, and you'll live to write another day. Resist and you may face extinction.

Articles

What's in a Name?

Probably More than You Think

by Carmela Martino

What do Gloria, Holling, Octavian, Olivia, Opal, and Salamanca have in common? Give up? They're all names of characters in award-winning books for children and young adults. Read the list again. Have you "met" all of these characters? If not, what's your first impression of them, based solely on their names? Are you surprised you already have an impression? (To check out your responses, see the list of corresponding titles at the end of this article.)

I spend a great deal of time thinking about character names. Before I can begin to imagine how my characters will move, act, or speak, I need to know at least their first names. I try to choose those names based on a character's personality and ethnicity, as well as the time period and location of the story. At the same time, I avoid names that are too common. I want my characters to be like those listed above—unique!

The young authors I teach in my children's writing workshops (typically in grades 3-8) seem to have the opposite approach. Most of their stories are populated by people with names like "Mike" and "Sarah." There's nothing "wrong" with these names. However, it seemed that my students weren't putting much thought into the naming process. In particular, they weren't thinking about how a name contributes to a reader's perception.

To help students think along these lines, I now begin my discussion of characterization with an exercise on names. I start out by asking students to share the names of memorable fictional characters. Interestingly, most of the names they remember aren't ones you typically hear on school playgrounds. They usually include Harry Potter, Hermione Granger, Lyra Belacqua, Hugo Cabret, Opal Buloni, Stanley Yelnats, Ramona Quimby, Percy Jackson, and even Clifford (the big red dog).

For the next step, I prepare the class by explaining that I will write a name on the board. (I make sure no one in the class has the same name.) Before I begin writing, I tell the students to try to picture this person based solely on the name. I list three specific questions to consider:

What does this person look like?

How does this person dress?

How would you describe his or her personality?

CARMELA MARTINO is a freelance writer who also teaches writing workshops for children and adults. Her first book, *Rosa, Sola* (Candlewick Press), was named to *Booklist* magazine's "Top Ten First Novels for Youth: 2006." Carmela's humorous short story, "Big Z, Cammi, and Me," will be published in the middle-grade anthology *I Fooled You* (Candlewick Press, 2010). She recently launched www.TeachingAuthors.com, a blog of writing and teaching tips from six children's authors who are also writing teachers. To learn more, visit www.carmelamartino.com.

You can try the exercise right now. Think about your first impression of someone with the following name. Jot down your answers to the three questions before you read on.

The name is: **"Hubert"**

In class, I explain that, since this is a fictional character, there are no right or wrong answers. Therefore, it's okay to disagree with how another student sees the person. I've tried this exercise several times with students in grades 3-5 and have come up with surprisingly consistent results. "Hubert" usually wears glasses and dresses in stripes or plaids. Instead of gym shoes, he wears brown or black leather shoes, either loafers or with laces. Most students think he's brown-haired, though occasionally someone will say he's blonde. (No one's ever said he's a redhead.) Most students also see him as having an average build, though some say he's stocky. And most say he's smart and good at solving problems. I find the last trait particularly interesting. According to the baby-naming book I use, "Hubert" is old German for "brilliant mind." (How did your answers compare?)

When we're done talking about "Hubert," I repeat the exercise with a more common name, usually **"Kyle."**

What's your impression of someone named "Kyle"? Even though girls can be named Kyle, my students assume he's a boy. They almost always say he's athletic, with a slender or muscular build. He usually doesn't wear glasses. He dresses in the latest styles and wears the "best" gym shoes. He can have blonde or brown hair, be blue-eyed or brown-eyed, or sometimes green-eyed. But he's always good-looking. The origin of the name "Kyle"? It's from the Irish Gaelic for "handsome."

For girls' names, I've used Eleanor and Erika, with similar results. Of course, I deliberately chose stereotypical names for this exercise. But even *I* was surprised by how consistent the responses were.

The exercise reinforced two things I instinctively knew:

1) Character names can create instant images in our readers' minds.

2) As authors, we need to be aware of those images so that we can use them to our advantage.

How, then, do we find a name that creates the intended image? I'll share some techniques I've used, along with tips from other children's authors.

One of the first references I consult when choosing a character's name is a baby-naming book. (See Resources sidebar.) These books typically provide lists of names with their meanings and origins. They may also include articles on naming customs and trends. I use the books in two ways: to help me find a character name when I can't think of one, and to verify that the meaning of a name I've already chosen doesn't conflict with my image of that character. A name's meaning doesn't always match common perceptions as overtly as "Hubert" and "Kyle." But even when it doesn't, I believe a name's origin may still have an unconscious effect on readers.

I recently discovered a naming book especially for writers—*The Writer's Digest Character Naming Sourcebook* by Sherrilyn Kenyon. (See Resources sidebar.) In the book's second edition, Kenyon includes a list of ten guidelines for naming characters. Her first guideline: "Capture the Persona." To do that, she says, we must take time to become familiar with our characters, even the secondary ones. We need to know a character's personality before we can figure out how to project that image to our readers.

One way to know our characters is to base them on real people. I'm working on a picture book inspired by my niece, Natalie Grace. My made-up character has Natalie's spunk and imagination. So I gave her a name derived from my niece's: Gracie Lee.

Even when characters aren't based on family members or friends, authors sometimes still name them for real people. Regarding the characters in her picture book, *New Year at the Pier: A Rosh Hashanah Story* (Dial), April Halprin Wayland says, "I chose the name of a favorite uncle who is now deceased for my young male protagonist, Izzy. His sister is named Miriam—Moses' sister, from a small book about Moses I treasured as a child."

Wayland didn't choose the name "Izzy" simply to honor her uncle. The name also fits the ethnicity of her character. This is key to creating authentic characters. Yet authenticity can be tricky for authors writing about characters outside their own ethnic group.

Naming books and Web sites can help to some extent. (See Resources sidebar.) However, Elsa Marston, author of *Santa Claus in Baghdad—And Other Stories about Teens in the Arab World* (Indiana University Press) uses her own sources to ensure authenticity. She says, "For contemporary Arabic names, I have many personal contacts and publications with lists of names, such as the American University of Beirut alumni magazine. . . . I try to choose a name that has an appropriate meaning, that is easy for the reader to pronounce, and that doesn't sound too much like another name in the same story. And that isn't used so often in stories as to be another form of stereotype. There *are* other names besides Ali and Muhammad!"

Choosing easily pronounced names is critical when writing for children and young adults because these stories are often read aloud. Peni Griffin learned this the hard way after publishing her middle-grade time-travel novel, *11,000 Years Lost* (Amulet). She says, "I got carried away and decided to name a character 'Plum,' and that the word for 'Plum' was the sound a perfectly ripe one makes when it collapses in a perfect rush of liquid sweetness in your mouth. Unfortunately, this sound is spelled *Shusskt*. This trips up those who read aloud and I shouldn't have done it."

Picture book authors, in particular, need to pay attention to sound and rhythm. Regarding the names in her rhyming picture book, *The Recess Queen* (Scholastic), Alexis O'Neill says, "'Jean,' the bully, rhymed with 'mean,' thus the first line, 'Mean Jean was recess queen, and nobody said any different.' I like how you have to sneer and hiss to say 'mean,' 'Jean,' 'queen' and 'recessssssss.' . . . The bouncy new kid who disarms Mean Jean is 'Katie Sue'–a perky 'Southern howdy' type of name."

Of course, sound and rhythm are also important in prose, and especially when names are used in a title. While working on a humorous short story called "Big Z, Amy, and Me," I began to have second thoughts about the name "Amy" for my main character's younger sister. The name didn't seem to fit a contemporary second-grader. At the time, I had a job in an elementary school (K-5) library, and I realized we didn't have one "Amy" in the whole school. However, we did have a precocious girl named "Cammi" who often visited the library. When I changed "Amy" to "Cammi" it felt perfect. The sound and rhythm of "Cammi" worked better in the title. Plus, the new name was more distinctive. I eventually sold "Big Z, Cammi, and Me" to Candlewick Press for inclusion in *I Fooled You*, a forthcoming middle-grade anthology.

Just as contemporary stories need modern names, stories set in the distant past (or future) require names that fit their times and places. For stories set in the United States, a great resource for both contemporary and historical names is the Social Security Administration Web site. (See Resources sidebar.) The Web site lists the top 1000 names given babies every year dating back to 1880. The Web site's search features also allow writers to find the popularity of a particular name in a given time period, popularity by state, and even the most frequently used names for twins.

Unfortunately, the Web site doesn't help for characters born before 1880, or outside of the United States. In that case, finding appropriate names becomes part of the research process. Regarding the names in her upcoming middle-grade Civil War novel, *Finding My Place* (White Mane Kids), Margo Dill says, "I used first names and last names that I saw during researching, but I mixed them up and put different first names with different last names."

Finding appropriate names for characters in the two-volume novel, *The Astonishing Life of Octavian Nothing,* was a special challenge for M.T. Anderson. The title character,

Carmela Martino's main character in *Rosa, Sola* (Candlewick, 2005), Rosa Bernardi, is part of an Italian American family in Chicago in the 1960s.

Articles

Naming Resourses for Writers

BOOKS

- *Beyond Jennifer & Jason, Madison & Montana: What to Name Your Baby Now,* by **Linda Rosenkrantz and Pamela Redmond Satran**. This is one of countless baby-naming books for parents. It discusses the psychological and sociological impact of names. This book also provides lists of first names organized into interesting categories such as popular names, old-fashioned names, "comfy" names, unpopular names, and creative names.
- *The Writer's Digest Character Naming Sourcebook,* by **Sherrilyn Kenyon**. Second edition includes tips for how to research names online and ten guidelines for naming characters. The name lists are organized by ethnic group and include information about corresponding surnames. The name meaning lists themselves are briefer than those in typical baby-naming book.
- *Names and Naming in Young Adult Literature,* by **Alleen Pace Nilsen and Don L. F. Nilsen**. Explores specific examples of how names are used by authors of novels for twelve- to eighteen-year-olds. Discusses not only character names but also "names for events, inventions, animals, attitudes, social developments, and imagined concepts."
- *The Language of Names: What We Call Ourselves and Why it Matters,* by **Justin Kaplan and Anne Bernays**. A biographer and a novelist discuss American naming practices and their implications. Includes a chapter on literary names.

WEB SITES

- **www.ssa.gov/OACT/babynames** Social Security Web site listing most popular names given babies in the United States from 1880 to the present. You can search by gender, time period, state, etc. However, note that different spellings of similar names are not combined.
- **www.behindthename.com** Provides the history and etymology of first names from around the world. Includes a "popularity" feature—a listing of the most popular first names in various countries, by year. Contains some interesting background information on naming practices within an ethnic group. For example, if you follow the "about Italian names" link at the top of the list of Italian first names, you'll learn about a naming custom practiced in my family and many others. There's a companion site for last name information, **surnames.behindthename.com**, which lists the meaning, ethnicity, and popularity of surnames around the world. Both sites include links to other helpful name-related Web sites.
- **www.writing-world.com/links/names.shtml** links to a wide range of Web sites, from basic baby-naming sites to name-generating sites and archives of medieval names. A number of the linked-to sites are for names within specific ethnic groups, such as Chinese, Indian, and Sikh.
- **www.parents.com/baby-names** baby-naming Web site from the publishers of *Parents* magazine. Among its search features: the ability to find names with specific meanings.
- **switchboard.com** and other online telephone directories.
  Phone directories are a great source for lists of both first and last names.

Octavian Nothing, is an African slave being educated as an experiment by a group of natural philosophers (what we now call scientists) in 1770s Boston. Anderson says, "Octavian's name was important to me from the beginning of the project—especially because the whole use of names played out so tragically in this period. For the African transported to America, the loss of names meant the loss of history, of culture, and specifically, the loss of sacred ties to community. The erasure of enslaved Africans' names was an unbearably cruel psychological measure—and white slave-traders undertook it knowingly as a method of control and disorientation. So I always knew that rather than take his master's name, Octavian would opt for 'Nothing.' As for 'Octavian,' I wanted an imperial name to go with his imperial lineage—but something Classical, of course, to suggest his learning."

Prolific author Jane Yolen has faced a different sort of naming challenge while working on historical novels. Yolen occasionally auctions off the placement of a name in a book to raise money for charity. This can cause problems, though, as she explains: "I sold off such a placement several years ago for a new baby named Julia Nathanson. However, the books I was working on at the time were Scottish historical novels. Ooops. It has taken enough time so that when the book Julia is finally featured in comes out, she will likely be old enough to read it." That book, a contemporary novel tentatively called *B. U. G.*, is scheduled for publication by Dutton in 2010.

My middle-grade novel, *Rosa, Sola* (Candlewick), is set in Chicago in the 1960s. The main character, a ten-year-old girl, is the daughter of Italian immigrants. I wanted her to have an obviously Italian name that was easy to pronounce. I originally named her Rosa Bruno. "Bruno," is a very common last name in Italy, just as the corresponding "Brown" is in English. However, Rosa's father is obsessed with having a son to "carry on the family name." That obsession doesn't make much sense with a common last name. So I changed the name to "Bernardi." Not only is "Bernardi" more unusual, but it connotes bravery, which Rosa shows in facing a family tragedy.

Last names, like first, can help reinforce a story's themes. M. T. Anderson's "Octavian Nothing" is an example of this. Anderson says he chose "Nothing" in part because it "tied in to a lot of the themes of emptiness and erasure I was discussing."

Holling Hoodhood, the main character in Gary Schmidt's *The Wednesday Wars* (Clarion), has one of the most distinctive character names of recent years. (He is the "Holling" in the list that opens this article.) Schmidt talks about how he came up with the unusual name in a PublishersWeekly.com interview: ". . . my middle son actually has a friend whose last name is Hoodhood. It's such an inherently funny name. And I gave him Holling, in part to honor Holling Clancy Holling, who wrote children's books in the 1950s, and because I liked the alliteration."

Schmidt's editor initially objected to "Holling Hoodhood" as *too* unusual. In response, Schmidt, who is a literature professor at Calvin College in Michigan, showed her some of his class lists, which, he says, contained "incredibly funny and odd names." That convinced her of the name's plausibility.

But some adult readers I know still dislike the name. For them, "Holling Hoodhood" is too strange, making it hard to "suspend disbelief." While I don't have a problem with the name, I was curious about how young readers have reacted to it. I asked Schmidt about his feedback from children. He says, "I have never had any comments on the name being unusual; I have had lots of comments on how the name is funny—which is, of course, what I was hoping for!"

A character's name, especially an unusual one, can be a way to provide background information. After all, someone, usually a character's parents, had to bestow that name. What was their motivation? Also, if the character doesn't like the name, it can create conflict. Lisa Yee is the author of several novels featuring distinctive character names, including *Millicent Min, Girl Genius*. She says of her latest young adult novel *Absolutely Maybe* (Arthur A. Levine), "The main character's name is Maybelline Mary Katherine Mary Ann Chestnut— however the teen refers to herself as 'Maybe.' Because her mother is an ex-beauty queen, I wanted to acknowledge this and saddle Maybe, a goth-ish girl, with a name that would be a burden to her. I also liked the idea of her being named after a cosmetics company, and Maybelline fit perfectly."

I could say much more about names—whole books have been written on the subject. One of special interest to children's writers is *Names and Naming in Young Adult Literature* by Professors Alleen Pace Nilsen and Don L. F. Nilsen. (See Resources sidebar.) The Nilsens' book is filled with examples of how authors ranging from Sherman Alexie to J. K. Rowling manipulate names for multiple purposes. However, their overriding purpose is to create characters readers will remember.

As promised, the book titles associated with the character names in the opening sentence are listed below. The authors of these books have succeeded in creating memorable characters, in part, by giving them distinctive names. A distinctive name alone won't make a character memorable—but it's a good starting point.

Gloria: Officer Buckle and Gloria written and illustrated by Peggy Rathmann (Caldecott winner)

Holling Hoodhood: *The Wednesday Wars* by Gary D. Schmidt (Newbery honor winner)

Octavian Nothing: *The Astonishing Life of Octavian Nothing, Traitor to the Nation* by M.T. Anderson, (National Book Award Winner, Young People's Literature)

Olivia: Olivia written and illustrated by Ian Falconer (Caldecott honor winner)

Opal Buloni: Because of Winn-Dixie by Kate DiCamillo (Newbery honor winner)

Salamanca Tree Hiddle: Walk Two Moons by Sharon Creech (Newbery winner)

Storyboarding

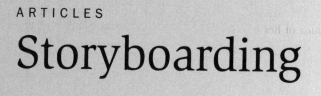

by Sue Bradford Edwards

I f you've studied picture book writing for any length of time, you know how tricky it is to pace your story for rising tension, develop your characters and give the illustrator just enough to work with. Whenever I tried to use a picture book dummy to do all of this, I had to flip back and forth through the pages so that I could move blocks of text and try, with no success, to see the big picture. Frustrated, I would give up with little accomplished in the way of improving my picture book manuscript.

Then, at a writing event, I saw just the thing I needed. A storyboard worksheet. This illustrators' tool let's you see your whole book at a glance. Even if you can't draw, you can learn to use it and take your own picture book writing to the next level.

A STORYBOARD IS WHAT?

If you're not sure what a storyboard is, you're not alone. Many writers are unfamiliar with this tool that let's illustrators and cartoonists plot out their work. Think back to *The Wonderful World of Disney.*

"I learned about storyboards when I was watching 'Uncle Walt' as a child," says author Anastasia Suen. "Walt Disney came on the TV every Sunday night at 7 to introduce his show. He showed the storyboards the artists made for his movies."

A storyboard is a worksheet or chart that shows all 32 pages of a picture book manuscript at once. A single box represents a single-page spreads, and a double box represents a two-page spread. Your storyboard will consist of 1 one-page spread (page 1), 15 two-page spreads (pages 2-31) and 1 final one-page spread (page 32).

"They can be done many ways but I usually draw them on one piece of paper," says author/illustrator Scott E. Franson. "This allows me to see at a glance the visual narrative." Author/illustrator Karen Lee uses a slightly different technique. "Ultimately mine are done on two sheets of letter size paper with eight very small double page spreads indicated on each. Storyboards can be sketched images, text only, or both," says Lee. "I like to write the essential action or dialog on index cards or sticky notes and then organize them into scenes. This allows me to move them around, combine them, divide them, or change their order."

Is all this work worth it?

SUE BRADFORD EDWARDS writes and edits from her office in St. Louis, Missouri. Her work has recently appeared in *Children's Writer* newsletter and *WOW Women on Writing* Newsletter. She is the managing editor of 21st Century Family, a new virtual magazine. Visit her site (www.suebradfordedwards.com) or blogs (suebe.wordpress.com, suebe2.wordpress.com) to find out more about her and her work.

Consider what you can see on your storyboard. "It is an extremely useful way of looking at the pacing of the story. I can really 'see' if things bog down in an area or move too quickly. I use it to establish a rhythm or build suspense," says Lee. "Page turns are an important tool in manipulating pace. They are literally a pause, so scene changes or surprises may best happen after a page turn. A climactic event in a story will probably deserve a spread. All these things can be manipulated in a storyboard and revisions to the story made if needed."

My storyboard is an approximately 2½ × 3 foot piece of cardboard on which I've rubber-cemented 17 paper rectangles. I use post it notes with a sentence or two for each scene. Shuffling them around on my piece of cardboard, I plot out new picture book ideas. As a non-illustrating writer, it forces me to keep the illustrator in mind and to recall that each spread is a unique scene.

SCENE BY SCENE

As writers, we write. Usually this means opening a word processing document and typing away until double-spaced text fills numerous pages and the story is told. We do this with novels and with picture books too. With picture books, *sometimes* we cut the text apart and try to fit it into a dummy to see how it works in picture book form. Do this without storyboarding first and you miss an opportunity to work out potential problems before you even turn on your computer.

Storyboarding helps not only by presenting the big picture, but also because it forces us to think more like an illustrator, not just visually, but also by forcing us to think of what a spread is—a clear, distinct scene. A single unit of story telling.

For some writers, this is easier than it is for others. "I'm a visual thinker," says Suen, "so I use a storyboard to plan my books. I draw a small box for each page of the book, and then I write what I want to *see* on each page." This isn't the place that she carefully crafts her text. Instead, she focuses on the visual aspects of the story. The scene.

Other writers force themselves to think visually with basic sketches. "Even if you don't have any artistic talent, you can still draw stick figures that show the characters, setting and action in each 'shot,' or beat, of your storybook," says editor Eve Heidi Bine-Stock. "Remember, the storyboard is a tool for you to use—you do not have to show it to anyone, so it doesn't matter if you don't have any artistic talent."

Don't use not being able to draw as an excuse not to storyboard. If you find yourself panicking at the sight of inept stick figures, do what you do best. Write. "I write a short phrase describing the main action on that page," says Suen. "I don't draw the art, I use words to describe it."

Whether you draw or write your storyboard, think about your story scene by scene. How does it open? What is going on? Who is there? Work through your action and plot one scene at a time. Think about what is going on, who is doing it and where they are. Fill out your storyboard.

You might be surprised at what you discover. "One of the main function of the storyboard is to help the author or illustrator evaluate their use of resources. An example of a resource is the number of pages," says Franson.

PICK UP THE PACE

Lay out your idea on a storyboard and you'll quickly be able to tell how it uses the space allotted. Remember that most often a picture book is 32 pages long, but that up to four pages will be taken up by the title page and other necessities. Your story must fill the space that is left and no more.

"With the storyboard you can quickly figure out if your story will fit into a 32 page book," says Suen. "One action per square is all you need. If you have too many actions to fit in the page squares, you need to cut. If you have empty squares, you need to add more actions to your story."

What might you need to add? First, ask yourself the following. "What happens in the allotted space? How long is the beginning? How long is the middle? How does it end? Plan each scene and put them together in a logical narrative sequence," says Franson. "Plan transition from place to place or time to time. It soon becomes apparent if you have too much content or too little." If you didn't introduce your character or it took only one attempt to solve the story problem, flesh your story out now.

Storyboards can also reveal when there is too much. "By laying out the text and anticipating where page turns might be, I find it helpful to see what might need cutting," says author Lisa Wheeler. "Sometimes, there is a whole mess of stuff in the middle that does not move a story forward." How do you tell if a scene is 100% essential? Take it out. If the story makes perfect sense without that particular scene, it isn't really part of the plot.

Scott Franson echoes this in his experience storyboarding *Un-Brella*. "I had originally planed to show the little girl using the 'un-brella' to create the opposites of all kinds of weather. Changing summer green leaves to colorful fall leaves, wind on a still day so that she could fly a kite, splashing in rain puddles on a sunny day. It seemed great until I started to storyboard. I soon discovered that these different weather events were 'events' that didn't help the story move forward. Telling the story became more important than showing all of the capabilities of the un-brella. It is surprising how short 32 pages is," says Franson. "I was forced to edit and tighten the narrative and I think that it made the story much better."

COUNTING CHARACTERS

Just as each scene must serve a purpose in your story, each character also has a job to do. Author/illustrator Joan Holub uses her storyboard to spy out when they aren't doing all they should.

"Using a storyboard let's me see if I've forgotten a character for too many pages," says Holub. Fortunately, there are a variety of ways for an author who illustrates his or her own work to solve this problem. "I try to weave the character back into the story or into the art background in some small way," she says. "Or I look at the other characters to determine if one of them could serve the same function as that 'lost' character in the story. Is so, I do away with the superfluous character altogether."

This type of problem is easiest to spot when you sketch out your storyboard. If you use written descriptions, take the time to *see* who is present in each scene. You may catch a character slacking off.

PICTURE THIS

Last but not least, the storyboard can also help you determine if there is enough for the illustrator to do. "Seeing the story as a 'whole' helps me catch places where the story may have become stagnant and doesn't move forward. Picture books are all about forward movement," says Wheeler. "I want there to be enough illustrative possibilities and a storyboard can help me see if I have done my job in that respect."

The same characters on every spread, a static location, talking heads. All of these represent problems for the illustrator and may indicate that a story would be more appropriate for a magazine than a picture book.

"So many times when I hear a manuscript that isn't going to work its because there isn't enough to it," says author Jan Peck. "A lot of people will write a short story and think they can make it into a picture book, but it's all set in one place and usually that won't work. You want 15 different scenes for a picture book."

Author Verla Kay agrees. "Storyboarding keeps me from having 'blank spots' where there's nothing visual going on and lets me see if I have enough visual possibilities for a strong story. It also helps me determine if there are enough different scenes in the story to make it worth illustrating."

Another way the illustrator can change things from spread to spread is by giving the reader a variety of points of view within each scene. "Changing the point of view adds interest. It helps to transport your reader into the world of your story," says Franson. "Move them up into the sky looking down, take them underground, or look through a keyhole. A word of caution: Radical changes in point of view can jar a reader out of the story. Make sure that it is enhancing the readers experience." Visual variety is key to a successful picture book manuscript. A storyboard let's you survey the possibilities from start to finish.

Storyboards aren't a quick fix but they are a worthwhile tool. "I've seen it when another writer and I came in for a book project," says Peck. "I ended up selling and their's didn't, because I'd done both a storyboard and a dummy." Why not add this tool to your collection and give yourself an edge? Its worked for Peck and many others. Let it work for you too.

Dummy Too

If a storyboard can do all of these things, do you still need to dummy? You bet! Dummies and storyboards work well together because they let you look at different things. Where a storyboard pulls back to view the big picture, a dummy zooms in on the details.

"For me the storyboard is a planning tool, while the book dummy is an editing tool. With a storyboard you can see the entire story at once. With a book dummy, you can test the text," says author Anastasia Suen.

This means that you begin with the storyboard. "I always storyboard before I make a dummy simply because it's easier to work out problems in both text and art on a small scale, before moving to a big scale. If I start out working 'big' as in a real-size dummy, I tend to focus on rendering details in the illustration," says author/illustrator Joan Holub. "If I haven't looked at the overall book as a whole and decided what needs to be depicted first, I may find out later that I've wasted a lot of time."

Once you have your story down on paper, a dummy will help you polish it. If you've never used one before, a dummy is a mock-up of the actual picture book. Says author/illustrator Scott E. Franson, "The dummy simulates the reader's experience. Turning pages adds to the experience. Looking at a book one spread at a time is different than looking at it all at once."

Start with a blank dummy. "To make a book dummy, you fold 16 sheets of paper in half, and it's a 32-page book," says Suen.

Next, work in your text. "I print out my text in chunks that I think are what I want for each page, cut them out and use a glue stick to put them in the blank dummy book," says author/illustrator Karen Lee. "It is a very flexible way of working out content for each page."

The dummy can also help you judge whether a scene is too text heavy. "This is *very* helpful when you are trying to see how much text is on each page," says Suen. "I find this to be a useful editing tool, especially for my students who write longer books. It helps them see how much room they have left for the artist."

For an author/illustrator, dummies are a way to submit text and illustration together. If you're not an illustrator a dummy can still help you think visually. "When you make a dummy, you have to choose the one 'shot' or image that best conveys the information on one particular page," says editor Eve Heidi Bine-Stock. "The dummy also forces you to decide where each page break will be, and helps you to create books that are 'page-turners.'"

If you're a writer who doesn't illustrate, you won't be showing the dummy to your editor or publisher, but if you're smart, you'll use it to polish your work until it shines. That will be the time to take your treasure to an editor.

From Picture Book Writer to Novelist

by Hope Vestergaard

> Writing a novel is like driving a car at night. You can see only as far as your headlights, but you can make the whole trip that way.
>
> —*E.L. Doctorow*

Because I read so many picture books aloud as a preschool teacher, I have an instinctive understanding of the **form**. I rarely need to ponder plot, length, setting, or other structural elements of picture books when I get a new idea for a picture book—I generally know where I'm headed. I've long aspired to writing novels, but every time I sat down to work, I felt totally lost. So many words! So few road signs! I had no internal compass or bossy GPS to get me to my destination.

I collected at least half a dozen abandoned novels before I decided to ask for help. Unfortunately, the yellow pages and personal ads had no listings for "Novel writer's hand-holder/cheerleader/taskmaster/guide." Then a writer friend invited me to do a page swap to keep us both on task. It wasn't easy. There were weeks when producing my promised pages was *worse* than pulling teeth. But we made a plan and we stuck to it. Much to my surprise, some 78,000 + words later, I had a novel manuscript.

Everyone approaches writing differently. I'm not saying my route is the most efficient way to complete a novel, but it got me where I needed to go. Whether you decide to follow the tracks I've laid or blaze your own trail, being methodical will significantly improve your chances of reaching The End. I present herewith a sort of Trip-Tik for finishing a draft of a novel, including detours, roadside attractions, and breakdown assistance. Fasten your seatbelts!

OBSTACLE: A LONG, LONG ROAD STRETCHING OUT IN FRONT OF YOU

Contemplating a project that will eventually have 30,000 or more words can be utterly overwhelming, especially for picture book writers who are used to manuscripts of 800-300 words or fewer.

Solution: Set an arbitrary word count.

Most picture books are 32 pages long. This format dictates scope, complexity, and pacing. I wanted some basic parameters before I began my novel, so I started with an estimated word count: 60,000 words. I based this on existing books that I thought shared an audience with the book I wanted to write. Renaissance Learning has a database that's helpful for this step: http://www.renlearn.com/store/quiz home.asp. You search for books by title or author and they'll tell you the word count. Remember, your projected word count is merely a guesstimate. Once you decide your book will be approximately "X" words long, you can map out some very general milestones: inciting incident, escalating incidents, climax, resolution. Whenever your writing slows down, having these checkpoints can help you get back on track.

Solution: Make a plan.

Don't say, "I want to finish a first draft within six months." That's too nebulous. Figure out a reasonable schedule and stick to it. You can commit to writing two pages or up to 1,000 words per day. You might want more flexibility, as I did: make a commitment to 10 pages per week. This way, you can find your own writing rhythm. After a few weeks with a 10-page commitment, I realized I wrote better (less painfully and more effectively) when I did my 10 pages in one or two long sittings. Other writers do better with a daily goal. Once you set this goal, give it a chance. Try a daily goal for two weeks and a weekly one for at least a month and see how much progress you make. If the goal you start with isn't productive, try something new.

Solution: Give yourself mini-goals along the way.

Whenever you feel yourself lagging, don't think about the big finish line. Just get over the next big hurdle: finishing a chapter, a scene, a page, even a paragraph. If you're having trouble meeting your goals, lower the bar temporarily. You can write an entire novel in little chunks.

OBSTACLE: RUNNING ON EMPTY

Completing a novel requires a full tank of gas. The following tips can keep your energy up so you don't stall at crossroads.

Solution: Lower your standards

It took me a long time to truly embrace the crappy draft. I had a habit of revising each thing I wrote before moving forward. But that perfectionism was a real obstacle for progress, because the rewriting took energy I needed to continue writing. And I didn't really know how to revise the manuscript well until I had completed the big picture. Instead of looking back, insert revision notes to yourself within brackets. For example: [TIGHTEN GROCERY SCENE]. Use this technique for research, too—anything that will divert you from the task at hand: finishing that crappy draft. I also employ placeholders [INSERT BRILLIANT TRANSITION HERE] whenever I start to dither. Sometimes when I go back to revise a placeholder, the solution is so obvious it's laughable, which affirms my decision not to waste time with it whenever I inserted the placeholder. While I'm writing, I keep a running list of "things to revisit" on my desk. Having this list helps me maintain momentum during the first draft *and* during revisions.

Solution: Bribe yourself.

Give yourself concrete rewards for meeting milestones. Whatever works for you: a trip to the movies, coffee with a friend, videogames, chocolate. Make the goal something you'll have to work to obtain, but not so challenging that you're more likely to fail than succeed.

Solution: Work on something else.

At some point, your manuscript will begin to feel like a family member who's overstayed her welcome. You know, the relative you can't wait to see but are happy to send on her way at the end of the visit. When the novel writing has you so crabby you begin to hate the

Tool of the Trade: Recommended Reading

- *20 Master Plots (And How to Build Them),* by Ronald B. Tobias (Writer's Digest Books)

- *Novel Metamorphosis: Uncommon Ways to Revise Novels with Creative Writing Tips, Tools and Strategies,* by Darcy Pattison (Mims House)

- *Novelist's Essential Guide to Crafting Scenes,* by Raymond Obstfield (Writer's Digest Books)

- *Revising Fiction: A Handbook for Writers,* by David Madden (Barnes and Noble Books)

Articles

project, work on something else for a while. I like to hop between picture books and novels. Sometimes I write poems about the process—wretched, melodramatic poems that make me laugh and remind me that the opportunity to write a book isn't so bad, after all.

OBSTACLE: DISTRACTIONS

Writing a novel is a long trip. Is it really so awful to pause along the way, to give in to the roadside attractions and life's demands? Yes and no. It is great idea to pause *between drafts,* to let your words gel (or not) and to process your feelings about the characters and their escapades. But pausing too long during the *process* of writing may make you lose enthusiasm for the project. If you believe that writing is mostly re-writing, you have to be committed to finishing that first draft. Some ways to stick to your itinerary:

Solution: Find a writing buddy

When I committed to swap pages with a writer friend, I learned that I hated the thought of disappointing my pal more than I enjoyed wallowing in my own ineptitude. (Okay, so I didn't *enjoy* wallowing, but I was comfortable there.) I knew how to *not* finish a novel. I needed a tough task master to teach me how to *finish* one. Pick a writing buddy with similar goals to your own. E-mail each other your pages each week for two reasons: accountability and safekeeping. The buddy system also jumpstarted my competitive nature: I didn't want to be left behind. Having a writing buddy and sticking to a page commitment were the two most important elements in finishing my novel.

Solution: Find useful detours.

When you feel yourself succumbing to distractions, maybe it's because you really *do* need a little break. Make it productive! Why not take a little sightseeing trip related to your W-I-P? Go somewhere that you can engage your senses in things relating to your story: smell the smells, hear the sounds, enjoy the views. Read travel books or watch movies. Give yourself a day off or even a week, but get back in the driver's seat quickly so you can let all the sensations you soaked up spill over into your story.

Solution: Switch lanes.

Ever drive home and forget the trip entirely? Autopilot can both help and hurt the first-draft writer. Establishing a routine—writing first thing in the morning, for example– is a good way to get going, but when you start losing focus, it may be time to take the road less traveled. If you usually write from home, go to the library or a coffee shop. If you write on a desktop computer, try a laptop or a pad of paper. Even small changes can do the trick: shift the time of day you write, change the clothes you wear when you write, or take your laptop to a different room.

OBSTACLE: ROAD RAGE

Writing a novel—even a crappy first draft that will revised beyond recognition—can be a gut-wrenching experience. We all have emotional roadblocks: jealousy, insecurity, whatever. Identifying your hot buttons will help you navigate this journey safely and successfully.

Solution: Watch out for emotional bombshells along the road.

If reading about other peoples' book deals or bestsellers makes your blood boil or lose faith in your own ability, stop. Do not read book blogs or Web sites. Sign off any networking lists or online bulletin boards. Issue yourself an industry news moratorium until you're done with the first draft. Reading about other people's "overnight" successes is self-defeating. First, more often than not, you are not hearing the whole story. There are really very few true ingénues. Second, it's true—some people *do* get lucky. But far more people are successful writers because they work at it. You may never get lucky, but you can control the amount of effort you put into your craft. If you have a hard time identifying your own emotional roadblocks, ask a trusted friend or family member to let you know when you're wallowing. Sometimes anxiety is just a socially acceptable form of procrastination. Your first draft of a book is not the sum total of your skill or potential as a writer. It's just a draft. Deal with it as such.

Solution: Slow down, enjoy the ride.

What is the part of writing that you love? When writing is no longer fun, it's up to you to rediscover that spark, that joy. You are the driver. What thrilled you about the story or characters to begin with? If you love certain elements of your manuscript, spend more time on those scenes. Figure out what part of the process is most satisfying to you: character development, reality building, plotting—and concentrate your efforts there. You can use placeholders for entire scenes or chapters if you need to. By concentrating on the part of the writing you're good at, you can build the skeleton of a novel that you can flesh out later.

Here's the bottom line for why you should do whatever it takes to get through that intimidating first draft: **You can always go back and fix a crappy draft, but you can't revise something that isn't written.**

YOU ARE HERE: Revision tips

So you have a complete first draft! What now?

First, savor this accomplishment. I put a post-it on my computer screen that said simply, "You did it." This reminded me, when revising got tough, that I'd already done the hardest part. Next, put the manuscript away for a while. A week, maybe a month, however long it takes for you to stop feeling dread/anxiety/unreasonable elation when you think about the book. This cooling off period is critical to give you fresh perspective. Resist the temptation to tinker with the manuscript again until it feels new to you. When you're ready to revise, concentrate on one aspect of your manuscript each time you sit down to tackle it. Pick your poison from the list below:

• **Pacing:** Does the story start soon enough? Does something important (internal or external) happen in every chapter? Have you varied the emotional tone from chapter to chapter? Do you want to keep turning pages?

• **Characters:** Are your characters fully developed? Do they have flaws? Do they change over the course of the story? Are they distinct from one another? Do they earn their space in the story?

• **Setting:** Does the reader know where they story takes place? Does the setting affect the storyline in any way? Do you include setting elements in every scene? Do you use sensory details such as smells, sounds, and textures to give the story dimension?

• **Dialogue:** Do the characters sound like real people? Are the character's voices unique? Does dialogue further the action and/or reveal the characters, or does it merely restate what's in the surrounding text? Have you balanced dialogue with descriptive passages and active scenes? Do you punctuate dialogue with actions that underscore the emotional tilt of what the character's saying?

• **Plot:** What is the problem or quest of the story? How is it resolved? Do all the scenes/chapters propel the plot forward? How do your subplots complement the main story?

The plodding, mechanical approach to finishing a crappy first draft that I outlined above may not be very sexy. It bears little resemblance to the romantic, magical mystery tour of self-discovery and literary genius that many wannabe writers imagine when they think about writing a novel. However, it gets the job done. It's novel writing for beginners. Remember the first time you drove a car? You probably lurched down the road at 10 or 15 miles per hour, braking clumsily and feeling like you were totally out of control. After enough driving, you don't have to think about braking or shifting, your body just remembers how to do it. Novel writing will get easier, too, as you internalize things like plot and structure and begin to recognize and correct your own writing foibles.

What are you waiting for?

Outlining: Your Mileage May Vary

Do novelists need to outline? A brief survey of published novelists tells me the answer is decidedly *maybe*. Most seasoned writers I polled said they outlined as beginning novelists, but don't any longer. Several newer novelists said they write synopses or sketchy outlines. Some use index cards to brainstorm and organize plot points. Other writers outline after the fact: they write a draft, then synopsize before they revise. And some novelists, seasoned and new, reported they write detailed outlines and/or character sketches before beginning a project. I find that writing a synopsis before I start a book is a good exercise – it helps me work through some of the plot kinks and see if I really care about the characters before I invest too much time in them. Just remember that your outline, synopsis, and character sketches are not prescriptions, but suggestions.

Writing Humor

12¾ Ways to Tickle Young Readers' Funny Bones

by Donna Gephart

Humor in children's books satisfies ravenous readers and reaches reluctant ones. It generates excitement from agents, editors, books sellers and librarians.

Powerful stuff!

Below, you'll find tips and techniques to get kids giggling.

Different levels of humor are appropriate for different stages of development.

The very young understand opposites, incongruity and slapstick, such as a dog that's very large and not a standard color—*Clifford the Big Red Dog* by Norman Bridwell. Or a duck who types notes to a farmer—*Click Clack Moo: Cows That Type* by Doreen Cronin. Or a child being turned into a pizza—*Pete's a Pizza* by William Steig.

Children in early elementary school giggle at potty humor. What young child can resist a book titled: *Captain Underpants and the Perilous Plot of Professor Poopypants* by Dav Pilky? Or Andy Griffith's book, *The Day My Butt Went Psycho*?

Children at this age also understand and enjoy books with wordplay, like *Amelia Bedelia* by Peggy Parish, in which Amelia, when asked to draw the curtains, pulls out a marker and creates a picture of curtains. In *Deputy Dan and the Bank Robbers* by Joseph Bloom, when the sheriff tells Deputy Dan to hop over to the bank, he stands on one foot and literally hops to the bank. And Avi's *A Beginning, A Muddle, and an End: The Right Way to Write Writing* brims with fun wordplay.

Middle grade readers appreciate more complex humor.

Humor evolves naturally from the characters' quirks and situations in which they find themselves, like *Ella Enchanted* by Gail Carson Levine, about a spirited girl who is forced to be utterly obedient. When Ella is told to do something she doesn't want to, she uses funny tactics to stall, such as doing what the person asks, but not in the way she intended.

Young adult readers delight in sarcasm, irony and subtle complexities. *Ella Minnow Pea* by Mark Dunn fits the bill. It's an epistolary novel about a tiny town that pays homage to the man who invented the sentence: "The quick brown fox jumps over the lazy dog,"

DONNA GEPHART's first novel, *As If Being 12¾ Isn't Bad Enough, My Mother Is Running for President!* won the prestigious Sid Fleischman Humor Award. Her new novel, *ive Middle School (without getting your head flushed), Deal With an Ex-best Friend, Um, Girls and a Heart-breaking Hamster*, will be available April 2010 from Delacorte Press/Random House. When Donna's not writing or creating ridiculously long titles, she enjoys speaking at schools, conferences and book festivals. To learn more, visit www.donnagephart.com.

which uses every letter of the alphabet. A statue is erected with those words on it. As age and wear cause letters to fall off, citizens aren't allowed to use those letters in correspondence. It's hilarious to observe Ella creatively use fewer and fewer letters in her correspondence.

Whether you write picture books, early readers, middle grade or young adult novels, there are 12¾ things to keep in mind when creating humor:

THE BIG ISSUES . . .

1. Take risks.

A book that does this beautifully is *The True Meaning of Smekday* by Adam Rex. In this novel, the world is invaded by aliens, um, twice. The main character, Gratuity ("Tip") Tucci befriends a renegade alien, J. Lo, and ventures to Happy Mouse Kingdom to find Gratuity's mother, figure out what's going on and, um, save the planet.

2. Tell the truth.

Those things we recognize as true are often the funniest. *The Absolutely True Diary of a Part-Time Indian* by Sherman Alexie is heartbreaking in its truth-telling, yet hilarious. Mark Twain once said, "Humor is tragedy plus time."

How to Survive Middle School (without getting your head flushed), Deal with an Ex-Best Friend, um, Girls, and a Heart-Breaking Hamster, is Donna Gephart's upcoming comic novel (Delacorte, 2010).

In the picture book, *Diary of a Worm*, Doreen Cronin tells the truth of young children—it's hard to be small and unnoticed.

Erma Bombeck once said, "There is a thin line that separates laughter and pain, comedy and tragedy, humor and hurt."

3. Mine your embarrassment.

What an odd lot we writers are. When something embarrassing happens, we brush ourselves off and think, this will make a great story.

David LaRochelle writes brilliantly about an embarrassing situation in his novel *Absolutely Positively Not*. While Steven DeNarski is purchasing a *Playboy* magazine, his former first grade teacher strolls into the store. Under the watchful eyes of a clerk, Steven ends up buying breath mints, a box of plastic forks, a can of WD-40, *New Baby, The Magazine for Young Mothers* and extra absorbent diapers.

Embarrassment, when not happening to you, is downright hilarious.

4. Surprise your reader.

Surprise is a delightful tool, especially in picture books. Especially at the end of picture books. Endings should always satisfy and provide a promised resolution, but in an unexpected way.

Think of The Monster at the End of This Book by Jon Stone. (Spoiler alert here.) The monster that Grover worries about meeting is actually himself. Surprise!

Tips from the Pros . . .

The Sid Fleischman Humor Award is an award for authors whose work exemplifies the excellence of writing in the genre of humor. The SCBWI established the award to honor humorous work, so often overlooked in children's literature by other award committees.

Here are tips for writing humor from Sid Fleischman Humor Award winners:

Sid Fleischman (*The Whipping Boy, McBroom's Wonderful One-Acre Farm: Three Tall Tales*, etc.) says that when writing humor for young people, "Make sure they have the references or the humor will completely misfire. Today's kids, for example, know bubble gum, but not Wrigley's. So a pun such as this would fail and confound: A snake got stuck in a wad of spearmint and went all Wrigley."

One book he finds hilarious is Ramona the Pest by Beverly Cleary.

Lisa Yee (*Millicent Min, Girl Genius*) says one thing to keep in mind is the humor has to resonate immediately. She also finds Ramona the Pest by Beverly Cleary very funny.

David LaRochelle (*Absolutely Postively Not*) offered the following advice: "Putting your characters in embarrassing situations can be very funny, but humiliating your characters is not. The difference is subtle, but I think it comes when the author genuinely cares about his or her characters and is not just using them as pawns to create funny situations."

When asked to name one children's book he finds hilarious, he replied: "Only one? That's not fair! *The Wednesday Wars*, by Gary Schmidt—it made me laugh out loud and cry. *Don't Let the Pigeon Drive the Bus*, by Mo Willems—those pigeon's emotions are all too true. *How to Make an Apple Pie and See the World*, by Marjorie Priceman—deliciously subtle humor, and a last line that always cracks me up. But if I have to choose only one, I'll pick *Millicent Min, Girl Genius*, by Lisa Yee—fresh characters, genuine emotional depth, and a laugh-out-loud opening."

Sara Pennypacker (*Clementine*) advises: "Let children be part of making the joke. An example: on the first page of *Clementine* I felt the phrase "Margaret's hair was not my fault and besides she looks okay without it" would be funnier than "I cut off Margaret's hair" because with the former, the readers have to be part of figuring out the punchline." When it comes to favorite funny book, she says, "I've been studying Jeff Brown's Flat Stanley books lately - that guy was a genius at delightfully ridiculous adult characters!"

5. Character quirks create empathy, affection and humor.

In *Walter the Farting Dog* by William Kotzwinkle, Glenn Murray and Audrey Colman, what seems like a detriment—Walter's unbelievably bad-smelling farts—ends up saving the day.

Lisa Yee's Millicent (*Millicent Min: Girl Genius*) has such a high I.Q., she's unable to understand social cues. The first sentence of Yee's novel clues the reader into the quirks of her character: "I have been accused of being anal retentive, an overachiever, and a compulsive perfectionist, like those are bad things."

6. Create funny situations.

Put your character in an uncomfortable situation or one that's the opposite of what's expected, such as a brash tomboy being forced to go to charm school.

Freaky Friday, the classic switcheroo novel by Mary Rodgers, puts a child in an adult's world when the main character wakes one morning to discover she's inhabiting her mother's body. With this perspective, a parent-teacher conference has never been so amusing.

A pigeon should obviously be poking around a city sidewalk or flying, not contemplating driving a bus. But when one does, the unexpected situation makes Mo Willem's *Don't Let the Pigeon Drive the Bus* a rip-roaring success.

Quotations on Humor

"I realize that humor isn't for everyone. It's only for people who want to have fun, enjoy life and feel alive."—Anne Wilson Schaef

"Good humor isn't a trait of character; it is an art which requires practice."—David Seabury

"We're young only once, but with humor, we can be immature forever."—Art Gliner

"Humor is just another defense against the universe."—Mel Brooks

"Humor is a rubber sword—it allows you to make a point without drawing blood."—Mary Hirsch

TECHNIQUES & DETAILS TO HONE YOUR HUMOR . . .

7. Use creative formats.

You need to think not only about the story you want to tell, but how you want to tell it. Consider the variety of formats available: diary, cartoons, poems, songs, symbols, charts, footnotes, e-mails, etc.

In Jennifer L. Holm's *Middle School Is Worse than Meatloaf: A Year Told Through Stuff*, every manner of "stuff" is used to create a meaningful novel. Between the covers of this inventive book, you'll find a drug store receipt, notes from the fridge, English assignments, comic strips, etc.

Louise Rennison uses the "list" format within her young adult novel, *Angus, Thongs and Full-Frontal Snogging: Confessions of Georgia Nicolson* to great effect:

11:35 a.m.
There are six things very wrong with my life:
1. I have one of those under-the-skin spots that will never come to a head but lurk in a red way for the next two years.
2. It is on my nose.
3. I have a three-year-old sister who may have peed somewhere in my room.
4. In fourteen days the summer hols will be over and then it will be back to Stalag 14 and Oberführer Frau Simpson and her bunch of sadistic "teachers."
5. I am very ugly and need to go into an ugly house.
6. I went to a party dressed as a stuffed olive.

8. Pay attention to the sound of language, especially in books that will be repeatedly read aloud.

The "K" sound is funny (even when it's made by a "C" or "CK") as in the following: Chicken is funny. Roast beef is not. Pickle is funny. Cucumber is not. Twinkie is funny. Pie is not.

An example of a title that employs the "K" sound is *The Chicken Doesn't Skate* by Gordon Korman.

Alliteration can produce fun sounds, too, such as Margaret Atwood's picture book, *Princess Prunella and the Purple Peanut*, which is full of more "P" words than you could shake a pickle at.

9. Use specific details in your writing.

Don't say, "He ate his lunch." Opt instead for: "He nibbled on his peanut butter and hot dog sandwich with a side of Granny's prize-winning Cheez Whiz cookies."

In my favorite picture book, *Cloudy with a Chance of Meatballs* (It's sequel is *Pickles to Pittsburgh*) by Judi and Ron Barrett, food doesn't simply fall out of the sky, but "After a brief shower of orange juice, low clouds of sunny-side up eggs moved in followed by pieces of toast. Butter and jelly sprinkled down for the toast. And most of the time it rained milk afterwards."

The more specific your details, the more clearly your reader can envision the scene and the funnier it will be.

10. Exaggeration and understatement are excellent tools in your humor writing toolbox.

The tall tale is exaggeration at its finest. For an excellent example of exaggeration, take a peek at Sid Fleishman's *McBroom's Wonderful One-Acre Farm: Three Tall Tales*. On McBroom's farm, the soil is so rich that even nickels grow into quarters.

To employ understatement, when something big happens, downplay it, like referring to a hurricane as a tropical breeze or rock music as a gentle lullaby.

An example of understatement can be found in *The Dumb Bunnies' Easter*, by Dav Pilkey:

> "Oh, yeah?" said Poppa Bunny. "Well, I hope the Easter Bunny brings me a THOUSAND dollars."
> "I hope the Easter Bunny brings me a balloon," said Baby Bunny.
> "Now don't be greedy," said Momma and Poppa Bunny.
> "I'm sorry," said Baby Bunny.

11. Nonsense/Silliness.

When all else fails, employ complete and utter nonsense and silliness.

In *Purple, Green and Yellow* by Robert Munsch, when Brigid says she needs new colouring markers, her mother goes out and gets "500 super-indelible-never-come-off-till-you're-dead-and-maybe-even-later colouring markers."

In Jon Scieszka's *Math Curse*, readers are delighted by unique ways of looking at math in everyday life, including this silly math equation: "Does tunafish + tunafish = fournafish?"

For an absurd situation, look no further than the classic, *Mr. Popper's Penguins* by Richard and Florence Atwater. At 432 Proudfoot Avenue, Mr. Popper ends up caring for twelve penguins!

12. Give humorous characters funny names.

For inspiration, consider some of these names from children's literature:

Ron Weasly, Cindy Lou Who, Ramona Quimby, Mrs. Biddlebox, Mrs. Piggle-Wiggle, The Remarkable Farkle McBride, Joey Pigza, Fudge, Henry and Mudge, Pippi Longstocking, Anastasia Krupnik, etc.

You can find names in playbills, obituary listings, the phone book, the masthead of magazines, etc. I've even glanced at lists of pet names, such as in this site: http://www.babynames.com/Names/Pets/

12¾. Don't try to be funny.

Forced humor is no fun for anyone.

Sometimes it's best to get the story out, then find opportunities to add humor as you work through revisions.

At a conference, Dave Barry said his first drafts really weren't that funny. He added humor during revisions.

Ultimately, aim to please an audience of one—yourself! If what you write cracks you up, chances are young readers will enjoy it, too.

A Funny Reading List

There are many humorous books in which to find examples and inspiration, not to mention a lot of laughs.

PICTURE BOOKS

- *Miss Nelson is Missing,* by Harry Allard
- *Martha Speaks,* by Susan Meddaugh
- *Alexander and the Terrible, Horrible, No Good, Very Bad Day,* by Judith Viorst
- *Parts,* by Tedd Arnold
- *Don't Make Me Laugh,* by James Stevenson
- *Frankenstein Makes a Sandwich,* by Adam Rex
- *The True Story of the Three Little Pigs,* by Jon Scieszka
- *The Wump World,* by Bill Peet
- *Green Eggs and Ham,* by Dr. Seuss
- *Chester,* by Melanie Watt

CHAPTER BOOKS

- *The Golly Sisters Go West*, by Betsy Byars
- *Freckle Juice,* by Judy Blume
- *Agapanthus Hum and the Eyeglasses,* by Joy Cowley
- *Frog and Toad are Friends*, by Arnold Lobel
- Marvin Redpost series by Louis Sachar
- Time Warp Trio series by Jon Scieszka
- Chet Gecko Mystery series Bruce Hale
- Junie B. Jones series by Barbara Park

MIDDLE GRADE NOVELS

- *Lawn Boy,* by Gary Paulsen
- *My Big Sister Is So Bossy She Says You Can't Read This Book*, by Mary Hershey
- *The Cat Ate My Gymsuit,* by Paula Danziger
- *Squashed,* by Joan Bauer
- *The Prince of the Pond: Otherwise Known as De Fawg Pin,* by Donna Jo Napoli
- *Joey Pigza Swallowed the Key,* by Jack Gantos
- *Invasion of the Road Weenies,* by David Lubar
- *A Crooked Kind of Perfect,* by Linda Urban
- *Bunnicula,* by James Howe
- *Ben and Me: An Astonishing Life of Benjamin Franklin by His Good Mouse Amos,* by Robert Lawson
- *Anastasia Krupnik,* by Lois Lowry
- *101 Ways to Bug Your Parents,* by Lee Wardlaw

YOUNG ADULT NOVELS

- *The Earth, My Butt and Other Big Round Things*, by Carolyn Mackler
- *The Princess Diaries,* by Meg Cabot
- *Storky: How I Lost My Nickname and Won the Girl,* by D. L. Garfinkle
- *Son of the Mob,* by Gordon Korman
- *Dairy Queen,* by Catherine Murdock
- *Audrey, Wait!,* by Robin Benway
- *The Year My Life Went Down the Loo,* by Katie Maxwell

Articles

Don't Be Afraid to Write GLBTQ Characters

by Ellen Wittlinger

What the heck do all those letters in the title mean? You may not immediately recognize the initials GLBTQ which stand for *gay, lesbian, bisexual, transgender or questioning*. I hope to persuade you that even if you (like me) don't personally fall into any of the above categories, you might still want to write characters who do.

Maybe you're thinking: *I'm not part of the gay community. What if I get it wrong?* On the one hand, I understand that writing about someone unlike you is not as simple as writing about someone you see as more similar. On the other hand, you *are* part of the human community; there are more ways in which we're all alike than ways in which we're different. And that's where you start.

I should probably say up front that I don't think you have to be African American, Latino or Asian to write characters of those ethnicities into your books either, nor do you need to be a member of a particular religion to write about people who are. I know these are all sensitive areas and that there are people who will argue vociferously that I am wrong on all counts. My feeling is that if you know what you're talking about and you stay as far away from stereotypes as possible, you'll be okay.

My feeling is that we ought not to limit what people are *allowed* to write about. Writers use their imagination in every other aspect of their craft—why shouldn't they be able to enter the soul of a character who is different from themselves? Should I be restricted to writing about straight, white, middle-class, middle-aged women? *That* would be boring. We take it for granted that women will write male characters and men will write female characters; otherwise every book's characters would be of a single gender. Of course some people leap these divides more agilely than other, but that doesn't mean none of us should attempt it.

About ninety percent of the population identify themselves as straight. So, it follows that most writers are also straight. But if they write only about straight children, teens and adults, we get too many of the kinds of books we've always gotten for kids which don't represent the full spectrum of possibilities. GLBTQ teens will continue to have relatively few books which speak to them personally, and, perhaps even more importantly, straight kids won't be challenged to open their minds about their GLBTQ peers.

ELLEN WITTLINGER is the author of 14 novels for young adults, including such titles as *Sandpiper, Blind Faith, Parrotfish, Hard Love* (winner of a Michael L. Printz Honor Award and a Lambda Literary Award), and her newest book, *Love & Lies*. Her middle-grade novel *This Means War!* will be released in 2010. Many of her novels have been listed on the yearly best books lists of the New York Public Library and the American Library Association; she has also won state book awards in Massachusetts, Michigan and Pennsylvania. She has a bachelor's from Millikin University and an M.F.A. from the University of Iowa Writer's Workshop. A former children's librarian, she lives with her husband in western Massachusetts.

So, I'm hoping to convince you that with thoughtfulness—and maybe some research—you will feel comfortable including lesbian, gay, bisexual, transgender, and questioning characters in your fiction, if not as the protagonists, at least as secondary characters, as a natural part of the world your characters inhabit.

Perhaps you're asking yourself if we really need more books with GLBTQ characters—aren't there a lot of them already? Well, there are some, to be sure, and many of them are excellent, but no, there aren't enough. Because there are as many stories to tell about GLBTQ youth as there are about any other kids. Not just the coming-out stories, but the living-a-regular-life stories. And all kids need to read these stories, not just GLBTQ kids.

The first book of mine to deal with homosexuality was Hard Love in which John, formerly "immune to emotion," falls hard for Marisol, an out and proud lesbian. At the time I was writing this book my own children were in high school, and I was happy to

Reprinted with permission of Simon & Schuster Children's Publishing.

Love & Lies: Marisol's Story, by Ellen Wittlinger (Simon & Schuster Children's Publishing, 2008) is a companion title to her book *Hard Love* (written in 1999).

see how much certain things had changed over the years. There was a Gay-Straight Alliance in their school and some kids felt safe enough to announce their sexual identity to the community. Marisol, I hoped, would be not only a role model for the gay kids, but also a character straight kids could relate to.

My goal in writing books with gay, lesbian, bisexual, transgender or questioning characters has always been to normalize all types of gender and sexuality, to help kids to see that a person's gender and sexuality are only two of the many ways in which we're all different from one another, and not such a big deal. I wanted the books to appeal not only to readers who saw themselves in the GLBTQ characters, but also to straight kids who didn't know, or thought they didn't know, any GLBTQ people.

The proof that this can indeed happen, that books can make a difference, came to me in a letter from a girl I call Anne. Her letter and my answer are reproduced in the book, Dear Author: Letters of Hope, edited by Joan Kaywell. After reading Hard Love, which is about a boy falling in love with a lesbian girl, Anne wrote this to me, "I learned a lot about gay people. I don't think I was ever really prejudiced, but I didn't understand them. I guess I was even scared of them. But now, after knowing Marisol, I know that gay people are just regular, normal people."

The phrase that continues to give me chills each time I read it is, "after knowing Marisol." Anne embraced the character so completely that she felt she knew her, and, as usually happens, once you know someone, your prejudices fall away.

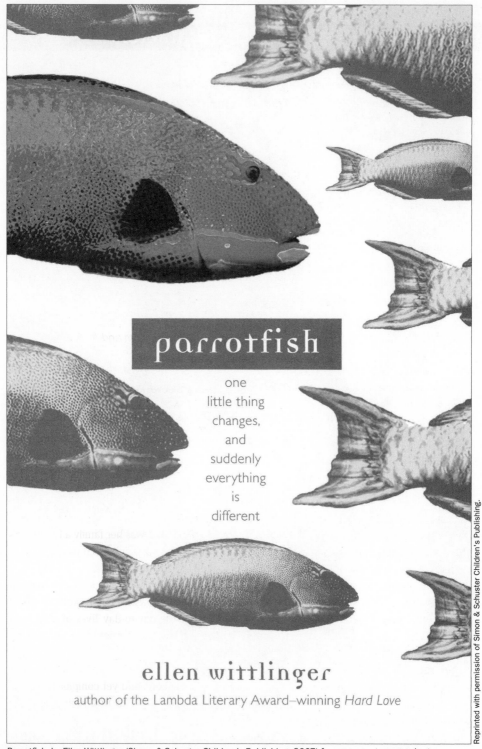

parrotfish

one
little thing
changes,
and
suddenly
everything
is
different

ellen wittlinger
author of the Lambda Literary Award–winning *Hard Love*

Parrotfish, by Ellen Wittlinger (Simon & Schuster Children's Publishing, 2007) focuses on a transgender teen.

Authors Writing GLBTQ Characters

- **Steve Berman:** *Vintage: A Ghost Story*
- **Paul Cameron**: *Someday This Pain Will Be Useful To You*
- **Nancy Garden:** *Hear Us Out!: Lesbian and Gay Stories of Struggle, Progress and Hope, 1950 to the Present.*
- **Brent Hartinger:** *Geography Club, The Order of the Poison Oak, Split Screen*
- **James Howe:** *The Misfits, Totally Joe*
- **James St. James:** *Freak Show*
- **Maureen Johnson:** *The Bermudez Triangle*
- **Carrie Jones:** *Tips on Having a Gay Ex-Boyfriend*
- **Ron Koertge:** *Boy Girl Boy*
- **David Larochelle,** *Absolutely, Positively Not*
- **David Levithan:** *Boy Meets Boy, Wide Awake*
- **E. Lockhart:** *Dramarama*
- **Perry Moore:** *Hero*
- **Lauren Myracle:** *Kissing Kate*
- **Julie Ann Peters:** *Luna, Keeping You A Secret, Between Mom and Jo, Far From Zanadu, Grl2grl*
- **Alex Sanchez:** *Rainbow Boys trilogy, So Hard To Say, Getting It, The God Box*
- **Ellen Wittlinger:** *Hard Love, Razzle, Heart on my Sleeve, Parrotfish, Love & Lies: Marisol's Story*
- **Jacqueline Woodson:** *From the Notebooks of Melanin Sun, The House You Pass on the Way*

So, how *do* you write about someone who seems to be very unlike you? The way I do it is to start at the core of the character, their insides, their soul, the place in which all people are the same. Then I layer on their personality. What else makes this person unique besides being gay? What are her secrets and fears? What was his childhood like? Was her family a loving one? These are the kinds of things you ought to know about any of your characters if you don't want them to be one-dimensional. Your GLBTQ character is no different.

Maybe you don't know any GLBTQ people and you're afraid you'll write a very stereotypical character. If you've been to Provincetown or the Castro, or watched The L-Word or Queer as Folk, you have a cursory and overly-dramatic idea of the day-to-day lives of most gays and lesbians. GLBTQ people come in as many shapes and styles as straight people. The only difference is in their sexual or their gender orientation.

The thing to remember is that a GLBTQ character is no more unknown to you than any character you might create. Every person is the same at the core, and yet completely unique in his or her presentation to the world. Your job as the writer is to understand both the humanity and the individuality of each character.

Having said this, I will admit that before I began to write my novel Parrotfish, which is about a transgender teenager, I did quite a bit of research. And, in fact, I probably would not have had the nerve to delve into this subject at all if I hadn't met my daughter's female-to-male transgendered friend, Toby. (Let me remind you again: once you know someone, your prejudices drop away.)

As luck would have it, Toby was a fan of mine, having read Hard Love as a teenager. He was 23 when I met him and a little shy, so I asked my initial question through my daughter, Kate. Might Toby be interested in talking to me about the emotions of growing up feeling like a boy and looking like a girl? He was thrilled to be asked!

So I began my research, but not, at first, with Toby. I didn't want my questions to him to be either ignorant or invasive. I wanted to know the basics before I went to him. So I read books: memoirs about transitioning from one sex to the other, research books from therapists, books on gender theory. I visited numerous online sites and even became a member of a bulletin board called The Transgender Planet.

Then I e-mailed Toby a long list of questions, primarily about growing up, and he typed back long stories, a few of which I adapted for the book (for example, not knowing which line to stand in when the swimming teacher said to make two: boys and girls.) Even though Toby was painfully honest in his e-mails back to me, I felt that I needed to talk to him in person, to make sure he really trusted me with this information.

So we met in a coffee shop, sat in a corner with cups of tea, and talked all afternoon. He told me things I wouldn't have thought to ask. For instance, that there is still a lot about masculinity that makes him uncomfortable (for instance, the fact that men don't touch each other as much as women do—it's seen as sexual—and that male bonding is often done by putting down women or making fun of them.) Because his socialization was as a girl, he still feels he's more aware of injustice towards women than most born-male men.

Toby also told me about the problems of using public bathrooms and the fact that he never feels completely safe or comfortable in either the men or the women's rooms. "Women," he told me, "look at each other a lot and make comments which make transpeople feel ashamed." Men, on the other hand, seldom meet each other's eyes in restrooms for fear they'll be taken as gay. So he was less likely to be challenged in a men's room, but if he was challenged, the outcome could be much worse. (Toby reminded me that bathrooms were also a racial battleground during the civil rights movement, which gave me a glimmer of hope for the future.)

What I wanted from Toby was not the story of his life, but the emotional truth that would make my character real. I needed to know what it felt like to be called a girl when he knew he wasn't. Toby asked me, that afternoon, if I would please not make the book too dark—no physical abuse, no suicidal tendencies. I agreed readily. Not because such things don't happen to transgendered people—of course they do. Julie Ann Peters has looked at this phenomenon in her groundbreaking book, *Luna*. But that isn't the only story there is to tell. I wanted to tell a happier one, a story Toby would have loved reading when he was s16. And with his help—he vetted every word—I think I've done that.

There are no hard and fast numbers yet available for how many people struggle with their gender identity, but it seems likely that at least 1-2% of the population fall into the category of questioning themselves about it. Of course, at this point, only the bravest of them defy societal expectations and actually live outside the gender into which they were born. But that closet door is creaking open too. As is happening with homosexuality, we'll begin to understand gender dysphoria, we'll meet someone who is transgendered, and we'll see that it's not such a big deal. My hope is that *Parrotfish* will encourage that understanding in teenagers.

Of course, not all my GLBTQ characters are the book's protagonists. In *Razzle*, the main character hangs out with Frank, a muscley plumber who's fixing up all the old bathrooms in his parents' cottage colony. He's shocked to learn, weeks into their friendship, that the older man is gay. In *Heart on my Sleeve*, it's the sister of the protagonist whose coming-out is a secondary plot line in the book. And in *What's in a Name*, one of the 12 interlocking stories is told by a gay boy.

Even though these secondary gay characters may not lead the main action in the book, I feel it's important that the protagonist's world is peopled by them. They are a part of the fabric of the story; even when they're in the background they serve the purpose of normalizing GLBTQ people for teens.

Perhaps you don't see why this is necessary. I think we sometimes lull ourselves into believing that homophobia is a problem that's just about solved, that GLBTQ kids today are free of the problems of their predecessors. And certainly some teenagers do find it easier to come out to their families and peers now, but by no means is this true for everyone.

A new study done by Boston Children's Hospital researchers found that GLBTQ youth are three to four times more likely to be bullied than those who identified as heterosexual. GLBTQ teens are five times more likely than the general population to skip school, often because of the harassment they face there, and they tend to do worse academically. And it's estimated that gay, lesbian and bisexual youth attempt suicide two to three times more often than their heterosexual peers. *For transgendered youth, some studies say the rate of attempted suicide is as high as 50%.*

If you wrote the book that stopped one straight kid from harassing a gay peer, or helped one gay or lesbian teen deal with the bullies at their school, or helped one transgender child see that he or she was not alone in the world, wouldn't that be amazing?

There's no harm in trying.

Articles

For Research & Insight

BOOKS

- *Transparent: Love, Family, and Living the T with Transgender Teenagers,* by Chris Beam
- *Gender Outlaw: On Men, Women and the Rest of Us.* by Kate Bornstein
- *Out of the Ordinary: Essays on Growing Up with Gay Lesbian and Transgender Parents,* by Kate Bornstein
- *GLBTQ: The Survival Guide for Queer and Questioning Teens,* by Kelly Huegel
- *Full Spectrum: A New Generation of Writing about Gay, Lesbian, Bisexual, Transgender, Questioning and Other Identities,* David Levithan and Billy Merrell, editorsl

WEB SITES

- **I'm Here, I'm Queer, What the Hell Do I Read? www.leewind.org**
Writer Lee Wind's comprehensive site on books with GLBTQ themes for children and teens.

- **Worth the Trip, http://worththetrip.wordpress.com**
Librarian and children's and YA literature specialist, K.T. Horning's blog about GLBTQ books.

Life in Revision

When the Honeymoon is Over

by Sara Zarr

During the 10 years between when I started writing seriously and when I sold my first book, I spent a lot of time fantasizing about my life as a published author. A lot. Here were some of my favorite fantasies:

Me reclining in bed with my laptop. Late morning sun lights my workspace and a gentle breeze stirs the curtains as I refill my coffee. I sip, then write another four or five pages of good, solid prose.

Me at my desk in the hush of night, a glass of wine sitting near the pile of manuscript pages I'm revising. With laser-like focus, I'm killing my darlings and showing, not telling. Tightening plot, deepening characters. I go to bed exhausted, but happy.

Me on the phone with my future editor, feet up, having a great conversation about how wonderful my book is now but hey, we're going to make it even better, why not. In total agreement with all her suggestions, I hang up, sharpen my pencils, and get to work.

After writing seven novels (three of them published) and living the dream of writing full-time for four years, none of my fantasies have quite come true. What I've learned about the reality of writing is that, for me, it's mostly about overcoming self-doubts, exercising humility, and practicing failure. It's about revision. Not just revision of my creative work, but revision of self-image, revision of ideas of success and failure, and revision of my expectations for the writing life.

I want to talk about revising books. Not the craft of that, the technique, but the emotional complications of engaging deeply with your work and accepting, even embracing, failure and humility as part of the process.

THE HONEYMOON

The honeymoon could be the excitement you feel with the (often secret) knowledge that you're writing a book and you know you'll finish. Among all the people in the world who say they want to write a book, you're doing it.

Or, it could be the period of time when you're discovering your place in the world of published and would-be authors, making online and real-time friends who share your interests and goals, who encourage you and offer critiques.

SARA ZARR is the critically acclaimed author of three novels for young adults: Story of a Girl (a 2007 National Book Award finalist), Sweethearts, and Once Was Lost. She's also been published in the quarterly journal IMAGE, and has had short pieces in several anthologies. She lives in Salt Lake City, UT, and online at www.sarazarr.com.

It could also be when you get an agent, get a contract, first go to New York and meet all the people who love your book enough to pay you for it, or get a good blurb from an author you admire.

For me, the most blissful honeymoon is when I have a new idea and I'm writing those first chapters. I haven't gotten bogged down yet, I haven't run into any walls, I haven't painted myself into a corner. I haven't yet failed.

All of these honeymoon phases are great. I've learned (and am still learning) that it's important to enjoy and celebrate them and not let my inner Eeyore ruin it for me with dire predictions of rejection or a displeased editor or bad reviews and disappointed fans.

But, no honeymoon can last forever. Nearly all positive life events (marriage, babies, houses, jobs, even vacations) bring new challenges and frustrations. If we were under zero pressure in life, we'd never change or grow. It's the same with writing.

WRITING IS REVISING & REVISING IS WORK

Most people—readers as well as other writers—are surprised and maybe a little appalled to find out how hard I have to work to make my writing good. The published version of my first novel, *Story of a Girl*, is pretty much all revision. I'd been working on it for years before it sold, and a lot of that work happened while I was in a great writing group. I'm sure I rewrote that book ten times. Then, when I signed with my agent, he asked me to rewrite it yet again. By the time it sold and got to my editor, I was fairly certain it was as good as it could possibly be. Then, she asked for more—more emotional depth and complexity, more details, more description, a clearer look at the relationship dynamics.

I remember the physical sensation of getting that first editorial letter. Criticism makes my adrenaline pump, my face get hot. The hackles of my ego are on alert. Some part of me thought, "More depth? It's pretty darn deep, if you ask me." I wasn't sure where the blood from that particular turnip was going to come from.

This was not like my fantasies. This required a revision of my expectations for what being a contracted, paid author looked like in reality. Somehow I'd led myself to believe it would all be easy, that a contract was like a magic wand that would transform me into someone who was never insecure, never lazy, never filled with doubts. It's not just writers who fall into this thought trap. It's a human thing. We have dreams and goals (making more money, losing weight, falling in love, getting a better job) and think when we meet them, it will be the end of all our problems.

So, I was faced with this first editorial revision and yet not granted special powers by my contract. Fortunately, deadlines are a powerful thing, and so is the desire to please people. Somehow, I was able to sit down to work that I'd thought was already at the very limits of my abilities and make it better. It was a triumph to get the phone call from my editor, Jennifer, telling me I was done. I'd done it—written, sold, and successfully edited my first book. Subsequent books would be so much easier, I thought, now that I'd cleared that first hurdle.

At the time, I didn't realize how very wrong I was, and how very minor those editorial revisions were compared to the work I'd wind up doing on my second novel, *Sweethearts*. When I turned it in, I thought I had a really solid book. Never mind I did it in one fourth of the time I took to write *Story of a Girl*. Never mind I hadn't had the peer support of a writers group. I managed to conveniently forget all of the drafts Story took. After all, I was a Real Writer now, so surely I was an expert.

Oh, the crushing reality! The editorial letter was long and brutal. I'd love to share some of the highlights, but it was so traumatizing that I eventually deleted it from my email archives, forever. I do remember the emotions, though. In addition to the aforementioned physical reaction, a variety of thoughts ran through my head such as:

Why does Jennifer hate me so much?

Once Was Lost (Little, Brown; 2009) is acclaimed author Sara Zarr's latest novel.

I should return my advance and cancel this book.

I'll never be able to make it good enough.

God is punishing me for ever being dumb and selfish enough to think I could do this for a living.

What will I tell my family when they realize my writing "career" was never meant to be?

Maybe there is a slight chance that this book will actually come out some day, and when it does, I will disappoint all my friends, fans, and family.

Et cetera.

It's not an exaggeration to say I had a little bit of a dark night of the soul. Was a writing career really for me? Maybe I couldn't handle the stress and pressure of publication. I felt like a fool for thinking it would be easy this time, and felt doubly foolish about my naive fantasies of the writing life. Curled into a ball on the kitchen floor, crying, I was forced to revise my expectations.

My wonderful agent helped me pick myself up and get to work.

Something happens when you sit down to your work with an open mind and open heart, and manage to build some kind of mental fence to keep fear and doubt away. You soften to your editor's notes, and soften to yourself, as you're back in the story and get your fingers moving on the keyboard. It's a mystery to me how, exactly, this all works, where the resolve or patience or strength or clarity or whatever it is that you need comes from. It takes humility, which isn't my favorite thing, and it takes being willing to leave open the possibility that you may fail again, that this draft may not be the last.

Sweethearts took five rounds with my editor, a number about which I could easily feel humiliated, but I don't, as humility was exactly what I needed to learn with that book.

Did I really learn it? Do we ever really, finally learn it and get an A? Not me. While drafting this very article, the second round of revision notes for my third novel arrived in my e-mail inbox. And I couldn't open it. Just seeing Jennifer's unopened e-mail made me want to go out for a few martinis then buy a one-way ticket to Jamaica. I tried to figure out how to forward to my agent without opening it, so that he could read it and then relay an easier version of the truth to me. But there is no "easier version" of the truth, and this particular truth is that very few of us (I'll go on record by saying none) ever write a book that has no room for improvement. We can never write the Perfect Draft.

THE PROBLEM OF PERFECTIONISM, THE GIFT OF PERFECTIONISM

Perfectionism is perhaps the single biggest obstacle to getting published, and, after that, being happy in your writing career. Perfectionism makes you clench, seize up, and can eventually stop you altogether if you don't recognize it, and tame it. On the other hand, perfectionism can drive you to finish what you start, stir up your competitive nature, and make you a hard worker.

Intuition might tell you that the difference between a published author and an unpublished author is that the published authors are "better." Maybe. But why are they better?

My theory is that published writers are perfectionists who have learned how to control their perfectionism and make it work for them, and not against them. I've learned to put it on hold during drafting and revising, and then let it out when working on that very last draft or two. Perfectionism is a bloodhound you've got to train to sniff out and alert you to potential problems in your manuscript when it's time to do that, but the last thing you need while you're drafting is the howling and panting beast running loose.

THERAPY HELPS

You probably came to this article hoping to know the secret to making revision a little easier,

Writers & Editors on Revisions

If you have a problem with something your editor suggests, keep the lines of communication open. Sometimes you might have to get your agent involved. But no matter what, don't keep your uncertainties to yourself.

—Wendy Toliver, author, *Miss Match*

In my experience, the key to a good editorial working relationship is honesty and communication. Ultimately, it's my job to be flexible and accommodating so my writers can do their best work. That's what everybody wants. But this can only work when writers tell me how I can best help them. The worst thing an author can do is hide. As long as we're talking regularly, a book isn't really in trouble.

—Andrew Karre, Editorial Director, Carorhoda Books

I'm a much better rewriter than writer. Once I get something down on the page, I can always make it better. If I couldn't revise, I couldn't write, pretty much.

—Janni Lee Simner, author, *Bones of a Faerie*

If you're starting a new author/editor relationship, have a talk with your editor before your start the revision process. Do you know that you're especially sensitive to line edits? Do you prefer to receive comments mainly in an editorial letter, or do you prefer to get them mostly marked directly on the manuscript? Do you like getting suggestions as to how to "solve" issues, or would you prefer the editor just point out that there is a problem and leave it up to you? You may not yet know the answers to these questions, but anything you can tell the editor will help the revision process run more smoothly.

—Alvina Ling, Editor, Little, Brown Books for Young Readers

That first editorial letter can make you want to go to bed and pull the covers up over your head. Remind yourself that your editor really, really likes your book. He wouldn't have bought it if he didn't.

—Ann Cannon, Author, *The Loser's Guide to Life and Love*

I don't revise the first draft. It's just an exercise to offer me an opportunity to get to know my world, my hero, and what he or she wants. When I finish, I print it, read it, toss the draft, delete the file, and start over again. That way I can get to the "real" first draft, the one that's a strong enough foundation to build a novel on."

–Cynthia Leitich Smith, Author, *Eternal*

The edits are not a personal judgment on you or your authorial worth. In case it bears saying: Your editor does not hate you. Your editor does not think you're stupid because your work needs revision.

—Cheryl Klein, Editor, Scholastic Books, Inc.

I actually really like revision because when I am drafting I am so aware of how the words I'm writing aren't as good as my idea of what they could be. But revision is satisfying in the same way cleaning a toilet is satisfying; whatever you do, there's no way you're going to make things worse.

—Holly Black, Author, *Ironside*

not looking for a psychological diagnosis, but don't underestimate the power of good mental health in enjoying the writing life. When I was in the middle of revising *Sweethearts*, I ran into Chris Crutcher at a conference and shared my tale of revision woe. He said to just get it done, that he could list off names of people he knew who never finished their second books because of pressure, and not being able to overcome the psychological aspects of being a published author. Talk therapy with a trained professional can help. Bouncing your feelings off someone who has no investment in your career, your contract, your success or failure, how much money you make, or any of those other things that can cloud our view is super helpful. Just as important is having writer friends who are at about the same stage of their careers as you. Stay away from people who tend toward uncontrolled envy or "sky is falling" thinking.

I hope this all doesn't sound too dire. Revision will be easier if you can realize and accept that it's part of the process, every single time, whether it's your first book or your tenth, and that life as a published author won't always be you and your editor running hand in hand through a sun-drenched field of buttercups. Sometimes it will be like that, yes, but the potential for the buttercup field has a direct correlation to the time you spend in the dark, dank, bat-poop-encrusted cave—by yourself, or with your editor holding the flashlight.

There are so many wonderful things about being a writer that sometimes I think to myself, "I can't believe I get paid to do this!" Other times, I totally believe it. Revision is where you earn your money—and if you haven't made any money yet, revision is where you pay your dues. Every act of revision you do now, in writing and in life, everything you learn about staying balanced while practicing humility and failure, will help prepare you for the day you land the contract.

Articles

Putting the Vision Back in Revision

by Cheryl Klein

When I talk to writers about how they revise, I sometimes think the key syllable they hear there is "vise"—as in a large set of pincers that will slowly crush their spirits, their souls, and the life out of their work. But the word "revise" actually comes from the Latin *revisare* or *revidare*; literally, "to visit again" or "to see again." And I believe the revision process should indeed start with *seeing again*: the writer taking a step back to look at the project whole, not just to see what's been accomplished and what remains to be done, but to reconnect with his or her artistic vision after the practical problems of the first draft. Here I hope to suggest some techniques by which writers can consider their work with fresh eyes, and then revise, if not in comfort, then at least with less of a sense of impending death by simple machine.

Before I begin, I want to note that all of these ideas come with two giant asterisks. **First, proceed only if these techniques fit into your own process.** Some writers thrive on momentum, and taking a week off to get distance from a project would succeed only in killing their interest in it. An author I work with hated outlining so much that she asked if she could rewrite her entire 300-page novel rather than writing out a 10-page book map of it. The exercises below are worth doing at least once (I hope), but they're by no means the last word in revision; the only way to know what works for you is to try what you like and trust what feels right.

Second, give yourself time, space, and kindness as you revise. Many people who call themselves writers never even manage to complete first drafts of their books. You've done that, which in itself is an accomplishment to be proud of. You shouldn't beat yourself up if you reread the manuscript and it isn't as fantastic as you thought it was when you were writing; getting it to that fantasticness is the point of the revision process. Every great author from Jane Austen to J.K. Rowling has gone through multiple drafts in crafting their masterpieces, and I hope these techniques might help you make a masterpiece of your own.

First of all, try to get away from the manuscript for at least a week, or better yet, two. Read something fun; go on vacation; see all the friends or movies you missed while you were writing; start another project in a totally different genre or style. The goal is to move

CHERYL KLEIN is the senior editor at Arthur A. Levine Books/Scholastic. Among the titles she has edited are *A Curse Dark as Gold*, by Elizabeth C. Bunce, winner of the inaugural William C. Morris Award for a YA debut novel; *Moribito: Guardian of the Spirit*, by Nahoko Uehashi, translated by Cathy Hirano, winner of the Mildred L. Batchelder Award for a book in translation; *The Light of the World: The Life of Jesus for Children*, by Katherine Paterson, illustrated by Francois Roca; and *Marcelo in the Real World*, by Francisco X. Stork. She also served as the continuity editor for the last three books of the Harry Potter series. Please visit her editorial Web site at www.cherylklein.com.

your brain away from your book long enough to defamiliarize it, so you can look at it again without being blinded by the fever or pain or joy of composition—so you can see what's actually *on the page* and not just the emotion you felt in writing it or the ideas crowded behind it.

Once you come back to the manuscript, but before you reread it, write a letter to a friend about your book. This friend could be your spouse, your mother, your writing partner—anyone who'd be interested in and sympathetic to your writing. In the letter, quickly summarize the story, including the ending, and then share your answers to some or all of these questions:

- What was your initial idea for the book? What made you excited about that idea?
- What artistic goals did you have in mind as you wrote?
- What ideas (themes, characters, settings, plot concepts) did you want to explore?
- Who did you envision as the book's ideal reader? What do you want him or her to feel as they read and when they finish the book?
- What aspects of the book do you love madly (characters, scenes, lines)?
- What aspects do you already suspect might need revision?
- In the larger philosophical sense: What is this book about?

Don't stress out over length here or making your summary or answers perfect; you're just casually writing to a friend, after all, and you don't even have to send this letter if you don't want to. Because in the end, this letter is really an exercise for *you* to reconnect with what excites you about the project and define the ideal book you want to create. (It will also make a great first draft of a query letter when you reach the submissions stage.) I often ask my authors to write me a letter like this at the start of the editorial process, and it's enormously useful in helping me see what they had in mind in writing the novel and where it might need revision to meet their goals.

In his letter for *Marcelo in the Real World*, Francisco X. Stork told me that he wanted to explore the question of suffering—why it happens in the world and what response thoughtful people should make to it. I loved this question and ambition passionately, but I also felt that the plot developments at the end of the first draft greatly distracted the reader from the novel's answer, as the romantic relationship between the characters overshadowed the plot strand involving suffering. Francisco agreed and revised the conclusion to allow that plot strand pride of place at the climax, in keeping with its role as the central theme of the book. I referred to his letter at every stage of the editing, reminding myself again and again what this book we were making was all about; and our focus on his authorial vision paid off in a novel that has thus far received four starred reviews. Ideally your letter can work the same way, helping you articulate the questions your book in the end will answer.

If the letter explores the themes of your book, this next exercise examines its plot. Digressing here briefly with a bit of literary theory: The story inside every work of literary fiction has two intertwined strands like DNA: the Action Plot and the Emotional Plot. The Action Plot is simply the external action that the characters experience in the course of the story, and its central spine will usually fall into one of three categories:

- A Conflict—where one character's desires conflict with another character's, or even her own
- A Mystery—where the characters are searching for something: an object, a person, a piece of information
- A Lack—where a character needs something to be complete and live a full life: love, friends, family.

Novels often incorporate more than one of these plots; *Harry Potter and the Sorcerer's Stone*, for instance, has all three (Conflict: Harry vs. Lord Voldemort; Mystery: What is the Sorcerer's Stone and where is it located?; and Lack, in that Harry goes from being essentially friendless and homeless to finding his place in the Wizarding world). The

Emotional Plot of a book, meanwhile, is the internal action—the moral and emotional development of your characters as a result of the Action Plot. Both kinds of plot revolve around change: a conflict being settled; a mystery being solved; an emotional need getting fulfilled, and the way that the protagonist grows and develops because of those events. And while the proportions of Action Plot and Emotional Plot will vary from book to book, they are both absolutely essential in crafting a meaningful work of fiction.

So if you do one thing in a revision, you should be sure that those changes, how they happen, and what they mean are all clearly shown to and felt by the reader. And at this stage in the revision process, it can be useful for writers to delineate those changes for themselves as well. A few years ago, I created a Plot Checklist to help writers (and myself as an editor) identify and work through their changes. The most important part of this checklist reads:

> The overall change my protagonist experiences is:
>
> At the beginning, what does the protagonist want?
>
> My central Action Plot is (*circle all that apply*):
>
> Conflict Mystery Lack
>
> And that Conflict/Mystery/Lack is:
>
> The stakes are:
>
> My subplots are:
>
> My central Emotional Plot is:

(The complete checklist is available at www.cherylklein.com/id19.html.) "Stakes" are the consequences for the protagonist if s/he fails to win the conflict, solve the mystery, or fulfill the lack. **Run this checklist on your book** and see what it reveals. Does your protagonist change over the course of the book? What events make that change happen in him? What does he have to lose or to win? Is that big enough in the world of the story to justify the action he'll undertake here? If you have more than one type of plot, are all of them satisfactorily concluded? Just as the letter exercise hopefully helped you define the theme of the book, this checklist is meant to help you clarify the story you're telling here and how it and all its related subplots elucidate that theme.

Once you know the ends you want to achieve, it's time to read the manuscript and start the process of reworking it to meet those goals. (I strongly advise you to print out the manuscript for this reading, as words on paper truly have a different feel than words onscreen.) You might make notes and mark up the page as you go; you might wish to concentrate on overarching revision work first; or you might want to just take in the whole thing before you touch the text at all. In any case, please **read the *entire* manuscript** before you start making revisions on the computer: Your goal at this point is to get a holistic view of the book and what it needs, not to revise piecemeal and possibly throw it off balance.

To get a sense of that balance, on either your first reading or a second, **make a book map.** A book map is a chapter-by-chapter outline that generally includes the chapter number; the first page number of that chapter; the date and time of the scene within the action of the novel; and a brief summary of the scene/chapter's events: what happens in both the action and the characters' feelings, crucial new information the reader learns, any lines that especially reveal character or set up the theme. A book map is a fantastic tool for practical revision because it shows you the events of the book without distracting you with their actual wording. That is, you can't worry about the phrasing of a sentence or the tone of the dialogue; you can see only the information each contains and judge how it's serving the overall story. Moreover, when I'm mapping out a novel editorially, I often make notes and record my emotional reactions in bullet points below each chapter summary; it's a clear and easy way to keep track of my observations and start to develop a "to do" list for the revision.

Once you've completed the book map, use it for these exercises and questions:

• With a Conflict Action Plot: What sets off the conflict and sets up the antagonists here? Each new event in this plot (aka the "Escalating or Complicating Events") should increase the stakes or the intensity of the conflict. Does it? The climax will most likely be a confrontation between the antagonists: Are the means by which one triumphs established earlier in the story?

• With a Mystery Action Plot: The Escalating Events here are the discovery of clues or revelation of backstory; a good mystery usually has at least three of these. Again, is the solution to the mystery set up earlier in the story?

• With a Lack Action Plot: The Escalating Events here show the step-by-step fulfillment of a lack. Be sure that these events are dramatized for the reader, not just mentioned in passing. How does the climax prove this lack no longer exists?

• With all three of these, how can you see in the denouement that the characters and their lives have changed?

• Does your protagonist drive the action and make a difference in the plot, or does he mostly observe or talk? If the manuscript primarily chronicles his reactions to events instigated by others, then think about giving him more to do in the Action Plot, or (at the least) adding a subplot in which he can be the prime actor.

• What events in the manuscript lead your protagonist toward the change of the Emotional Plot? Are those events dramatized in the manuscript, not just narrated? Have you allowed quieter moments in the story for the protagonist to reflect upon what she's going through?

• Highlight the events of each plotline/subplot/relationship in a different color on the book map, then read just that color. Do the events of each plotline follow each other naturally, or are there jumps in logic or feeling that need to be better coordinated? Do some colors disappear for a long time? If so, consider writing new scenes or moving them around to make their development more regular.

Anita Nolan's article "The End Is Only the Beginning," available online at http://www.anitanolan.com/theend. html, offers some excellent further tips on using a book map to master a revision.

Of course, a plot only matters if the reader connects with the character who's living it, and at this stage it's wise to take a second look at how that connection is made. To accomplish this, **list the first ten things your main character and any important supporting characters say or do in the novel.** Viewed objectively, out of the context of the action, who do these people seem to be? You the writer have a long-term view of your characters' development and behavior, but when we readers first meet them in a novel, we know only what we see on the page. So if the first thing your hero does is flop down on his bed and say "I hate Smallville. There's nothing to do in this town!", it doesn't matter if he will later save Smallville from rampaging aliens: He seems like a whiner to me-the-reader, and he (and the book) will have to overcome that negative first impression. On the other hand, if he's first seen building a raft to get the heck out of Smallville, then he's creative and resourceful and someone I want to follow. Your protagonist doesn't have to be a morally good or likeable person, but he has to be interesting enough upfront to justify the time the reader will spend with him; so if these first ten actions or lines of dialogue don't reveal something of what's interesting about him, then think about bringing out more of those qualities upfront.

Once you've completed your letter, plot checklist, and book map, considered your characters, and compiled your notes on the manuscript, **make a list of the larger revisions you have in mind and why you want to make them.** This will provide a list of principles to refer to as you embark on the complicated, often minutiae-filled process of revision, and help keep you on track as you work.

With that done, you can start revising the manuscript itself. It's natural to feel a fair amount of psychological stress at this stage, particularly if you're a perfectionist (as I am). Try to **remember that nothing is irreversible, and you still don't have to get it right** in your second draft; you can (and very likely will) have a third draft, and a fourth, and a fifth as you work toward that ideal book. Some writers incorporate all the big overarching changes first—any new plot developments or thematic reworkings based upon the analytic techniques above, saving the smaller corrections for a line-by-line review later. Others work straight through and juggle both macro and micro changes at the same time. Whatever your process is, continue to give yourself time and kindness as you work.

If cutting things worries you, **keep an outtakes file** to preserve any material you're excising. When I write an editorial letter or essay, the very first time I find myself cutting any material, I scroll to the bottom of my document and type OUTTAKES, then paste the cut lines beneath it. Likewise, in a terrific essay on her writing process at notforrobots.blogspot.com, novelist Laini Taylor says that she keeps two files open onscreen at all times—one the actual draft of her book, and the other what she calls a "working document," where she warms up in the morning, makes notes as she's writing, and files her own outtakes. As she feels her way through writing a manuscript, testing different plot directions and character interactions, Laini also tries to **save each "exploratory draft" as a new file**, labeled 1, 1a, 2, 2a, 2b, etc. You could also maintain just one file, but then all **e-mail a copy of each day's draft to a free e-mail account** you set up especially for that purpose; this will give you an ongoing archive of your revisions, and instant backup in case your computer crashes.

However many drafts it takes, when you've feel you've gotten to a place where your characters are thoroughly developed, your plot is solidly in hand, and your themes there for the perceptive reader to see, **read the book aloud**—or better yet, have a friend read it aloud to you. This time, pay attention solely to *language*. Hearing your words aloud can help you fix any awkward rhythms or infelicitous phrasing; it's also an easy way to identify places where where you may need a different word or punctuation. When you've made your corrections based on that reading, you should have a manuscript that's ready to share with the world.

The writer Carolyn See says, "Revision is when you first get to recognize the distance between what you wanted to write, what you thought you were writing, and what you actually did write. That recognition often makes you want to throw up." It's never an easy process, even if you can avoid the vomiting and vises. But at every stage you're digging deeper toward the truth and the story you most want to tell, creating something you alone can offer to the rest of the world. As a reader, I thank you for your efforts; as an editor, I hope they succeed; and in the end, I wish you all the best with your work.

An Agent's Career Outline for Illustrators

by Steven Malk

Breaking into the publishing industry is never easy, but getting your foot in the door as a new illustrator can be particularly challenging. Whereas writers choose a specific project to submit and get a definite yes or no on their manuscript, illustrators who aren't also writers have a less clear path to follow—which can leave them wondering exactly how to go about getting illustration jobs from publishers.

The aim of this article is to give illustrators concrete steps to follow in order to get published. For the purposes of this piece, I'm going to address illustrators who aren't writing their own work, and who are looking to illustrate manuscripts already under contract with a publisher.

Educating yourself

The first thing I tell anyone who's looking to get their foot in the door is to educate yourself about the market. This may sound obvious, but it's always surprising to me how many new artists aren't familiar with a lot of the work out there beyond the most popular titles. It's essential that you have a good understanding of both the history of children's illustration and what's currently going on in the market. This may seem daunting, and rest assured that I'm not suggesting that you need to have a PhD in children's literature in order to get published. However, by immersing yourself in the field, spending time in a good independent children's bookstore, reading periodicals such as *The Horn Book,* and looking at recent award lists, as well as the bestseller lists, you'll come away with a solid understanding of what else is out there, and, hopefully, where your work fits in. And it should be fun as well.

Spend time understanding and appreciating how masters like Marc Simont, Maurice Sendak, William Steig, Barbara Cooney and others used their art to complement the text in their stories and how carefully and thoughtfully they made each decision. You'll also be surprised how often you'll draw on this knowledge throughout your career, and how much other books are referenced by editors, art directors and designers. I'll never forget the first time I visited my client Marla Frazee's studio in Pasadena and saw that she had every single issue of *The Horn Book*—dating back to 1978—right next to her desk. Similarly, another one of my clients, Lane Smith, keeps a library of his favorite books right next to him as he works. It may be surprising

---

STEVEN MALK is an agent with Writers House where he represents a wide range of projects for children and young adults. He opened a West Coast office for Writers House in 1998, and some of his clients include Jon Scieszka, Lane Smith, Kadir Nelson, Cynthia Rylant, Marla Frazee, Sara Pennypacker, Adam Rex, Elise Primavera, Karma Wilson, Sonya Sones, and Jennifer Donnelly.

that two illustrators who have each achieved such success in the field continue to look at what's new and stay current on what different houses are publishing, but I would argue such awareness is central to their achievements.

As you're doing research and looking through new books, pay attention to which publishers are putting out books that you really like, and whether there are certain houses that seem like a good fit for your style. You should also browse publishers' Web sites and see what they're currently publishing. Try to come away with a general sense of which houses seem to work with illustrators most often, and which publishers primarily publish non-illustrated books, and therefore won't be a good fit for you.

Once you've taken the time to build a strong foundation in terms of your knowledge about the market and the history of picture books, you'll be ready to move on to the next step: your portfolio.

Building your portfolio

Putting together a portfolio might seem simple—just a matter of choosing your favorite pieces—but it's something you need to think very carefully about. Think of it this way: This is your opportunity to tell an agent, editor, art director, or designer exactly who you are through your work, and they will be paying almost as much attention to the time and thought you put into constructing your portfolio (i.e. the pieces you selected, the order you put them in, etc.) as they will to the work itself. You never get another chance to make that first impression, so it's worth spending a good deal of time to put together the right portfolio.

First of all, think about exactly what you'd like that impression to be. Do you want an editor to think of you for young picture books? Slightly older, historical picture books? Black and white art in novels? All of the above? Try to decide on the feeling you want your portfolio to create for an editor (beyond "We want to do a book with this person," obviously). Then, construct your portfolio in such a way that's most likely to leave that impression.

In terms of practical advice for putting together your portfolio, try to decide on at least 12 pieces, but no more than 20. Be sure to have some variety, i.e. show that you can illustrate both characters and landscapes. Include both children and animals. Throw in a little black and white as well as color. Also—and I can't stress this enough—you need to demonstrate to a publisher that beyond being a talented illustrator, you understand the art of visual storytelling; that you can create a visual narrative that works with the text, making use of page turns and other conventions of an illustrated book.

Being a talented illustrator is only half the battle. Publishers are just as eager to see that you understand the art of the picture book, and this will be evident when they look at your portfolio. To that end, think about including a couple of sequential spreads that show that you understand how to move a story along with your art. This takes us back to the research you did; don't hesitate to refer back to some of your favorite illustrators and picture books, both for inspiration and to see the command they have over their craft.

The most common mistake that I see illustrators make with their portfolios is that in their eagerness to get their work out there, they haven't taken the time to really fully develop a portfolio that's specific to children's books illustration. A lot of illustrators come to this from other fields, such as commercial or editorial art, animation, fine art, etc. Often, their portfolios are strong, but the work doesn't look like it belongs in children's books. The illustrators will sometimes explain that they expected the person evaluating their work to be able to make a mental leap in imagining the work for a picture book. If I've learned one thing, it's that while editors, art directors, and designers are obviously capable of making this leap, they're unlikely to do it until they see real evidence that the illustrator can do work that's suited for children's books. It's a big decision for them to hand over a picture book to an illustrator, and editors want to see the work and not have to go on faith, at least not

Image © Gilbert Ford. Reprinted with permission of Writers House.

Image © Gilbert Ford. Reprinted with permission of Writers House.

image © Nikki McClure. Reprinted with permission of Writers House.

Agent Steven Malk advises illustrators to send out promotional postcards two or three times a year just as he does for his clients. Here are sample cards for his illustrators Gilbert Ford, Carson Ellis and Nikki McClure, each featuring one striking image.

entirely. If you're having trouble coming up with new images to illustrate, think about taking a classic scene (or scenes) from one of your favorite fairy tales or folk tales.

I've personally encouraged several people who had been successful in other areas of illustration to try children's books. These clients include Carson Ellis, who was very well-known for her artwork for the band The Decemberists, and has since illustrated two New York Times Best-Sellers, *The Mysterious Benedict Society* and *The Composer Is Dead*; Nikki McClure, who had successfully self-published a calendar in her distinctive paper-cut style for many years, and whose first picture book, *All In a Day*, has also been a New York Times Best-Seller; and Yoko Tanaka an accomplished fine artist, who just finished illustrating Kate DiCamillo's next book, *The Magician's Elephant*. However, in each case, they'd done extra work to make sure their portfolios reflected the fact that they could do illustration that was specific to children's books, and they all shared a love for children's books and a strong desire to work in this field.

Designing your Web site

The first thing that you can do with your portfolio is to post it on your Web site. You really do need a Web site, but if you're saying to yourself, "I'm an illustrator, not a web designer," don't worry. It doesn't have to be anything fancy; it should be something that you can design yourself or have built for a modest fee. You just want something clean, professional, and easy to navigate, with sections for news/blog, portfolio, bio, contact info, and anything else that you'd like to include. I will say that while the site doesn't need to have all sorts of bells and whistles, you do want to take the time to make sure that it reflects who you are. In the same way that you took so much time to carefully construct your portfolio, take a little extra time to make sure that your entire site (beyond just the images) is sending the right message about you. It's another chance to make that good first impression.

You should post the images that you selected in a portfolio or gallery section, and, ideally have them displayed as thumbnails that can be enlarged for easy and detailed viewing. Of course, you'll want your contact information on the Web site so agents and publishers can get in touch if they're interested or if they'd like to see more art. In addition, you can post new images on the news or blog section on a regular basis.

Getting your work out there

Now that you've really taken the time to put together a strong portfolio that you feel confident about, it's time to get your work out into the world and hopefully find the agent or publisher who will help you get your first book. I'm going to outline some concrete steps that you can take, beyond following the guidelines of various agents, publishers, and magazines (which you'll find in this book).

A great first step is to attend as many conferences—especially those affiliated with the Society of Children's Book Writers and Illustrators (SCBWI)—as possible. Many of the SCBWI conferences feature portfolio displays and they also award prizes for best portfolio. In addition, you often have the opportunity to sit down with an agent, art director, editor, or a published illustrator and have your portfolio critiqued. This one-on-one time can be an invaluable experience, but, beyond that, the conferences are essential for your continuing education about the industry and about your craft.

Earlier I discussed the importance of understanding your field and having a firm grasp on what else is out there. Remember that this sort of learning doesn't stop once you get beyond that initial phase. You always want to be aware of what's coming out, and, while I always encourage illustrators not to follow specific trends, it's not a bad idea to keep the corner of your eye on the market. You'll also be surprised about the little tips you'll pick up in speeches or even in conversation that might help you tweak your portfolio. Or you might hear of a certain type of piece or style that a specific art director likes, and you can tailor your portfolio specifically for that person if you have the opportunity to submit your work to him or her. You can also make good contacts at conferences, and the speakers will likely give extra consideration to your portfolio if you've chatted with them or heard them speak.

Promotional postcards

Another great way to get your work out there is to send out promotional postcards featuring your art. This is something that I do frequently with my clients, and it's produced great results over time. Before you can get to the stage of producing the cards, you should come up with a list of editors, art directors, designers, agents, magazines and others to whom you'd like to send your work. There are many sources for these lists, and the book that you're holding is the best one. SCBWI is also an excellent source. Once you have your list, print enough cards for everyone on it, plus at least 50 or so to have with you at conferences.

The postcard itself should feature one image on each side (some people try to put multiple images on the card, but I don't find this as effective, unless there's an organic reason for it, e.g. the art is in panels) and you can just choose two of your favorite images or a couple of recent images. Be sure to include your name, your email address, and your Web site on the postcard. You can send these mailings out two or three times a year. I wouldn't recommend more frequent mailings than that, but if you do one in the early fall, one in the spring, and one in the summer, you should be in good shape, and it's a great way to remind agents and publishers about your work and encourage them to take another look at your site.

It's also not a bad idea to update your site before each mailing so it looks fresh when people come back to it and they're more encouraged to take a closer look. Don't be discouraged if you don't get an immediate response to the postcards. People in the industry really do pin them on their bulletin boards or keep them in a file that they'll refer to when they need an illustrator for a project. So, just because you haven't heard from someone, it doesn't mean they don't enjoy receiving your cards and they very well might be trying to find the right project for you.

There are many ways to get your work out to a wide audience online. You can post your images to sites like www.illustrationmundo.com, www.childrensillustrators.com, or www.theispot.com. Agents, art directors, and designers browse those sites regularly. There are also many great sites for illustration enthusiasts that aren't necessarily specific to children's books and also aren't sites where you post your work, but I still recommend them in terms of a way to be part of the illustration community and to see who else is out there. These include www.drawn.ca, www.tinyshowcase.com, and www.illustrationfriday.com.

Be patient and don't get discouraged!

My final few points aren't as concrete as some of the steps above, but I think they're as—if not more—important than anything else that I've discussed. The first one is to be patient. I know that's not something people always want to be hear, or they think it's just a way of being put off. But, truly, you need to have a lot of patience to succeed and thrive as an illustrator in this field. There are not definite yeses or nos when you're sending your work out into the world. In many cases, people are bookmarking your site, filing your samples away, and waiting until they have the absolute perfect project for you.

It's easy to be at home in your studio thinking that what's actually happening is no one is seeing your work at all and your break is never going to come, but that's not true—I have many, many examples to the contrary. I've helped to break many new illustrators into this field, and, while I've also been guilty of getting a bit impatient at times, I've also seen—time and time again—that if you have faith and do everything that's in your power (sending out promo cards, reminding people of the work, etc.), your break will come. Although it may sound like a cliché, staying positive and working hard are the best things that you can do.

Essential Picture Books

Three top illustrators (who are clients of Steven Malk's) share their top 10 lists of picture books every illustrator should have in their collection. (Number one is unanimous.)

Marla Frazee's list:

1. *Where the Wild Things Are*, illustrated by Maurice Sendak
2. *The Carrot Seed*, illustrated by Crockett Johnson
3. *The Tub People*, illustrated by Richard Egielski
4. *The Stray Dog*, illustrated by Marc Simont
5. *Snow*, illustrated by Uri Shulevitz
6. *Roxaboxen*, illustrated by Barbara Cooney
7. *Peek-a-Boo*, illustrated by Janet Ahlberg
8. The entire Mr. Putter and Tabby series, illustrated by Arthur Howard (I realize that they aren't quote/unquote picture books)
9. The four Will books—*Will Gets a Haircut, Will's New Cap, Will Goes to the Post Office, Will Goes to the Beach*, illustrated by Olof and Lena Landstrom
10. And everything that's been illustrated illustrated by Lisbeth Zwerger

Kadir Nelson's list:

1. *Where the Wild Things Are*, illustrated by Maurice Sendak
2. *Green Eggs and Ham*, illustrated by Dr. Seuss
3. *The Polar Express*, illustrated by Chris Van Allsburg
4. *Goodnight Moon*, illustrated by Clement Hurd
5. *John Henry*, illustrated by Jerry Pinkney
6. *Swamp Angel*, illustrated by Paul O. Zelinsky
7. *The Giving Tree*, illustrated by Shel Silverstein
8. *The Very Hungry Caterpillar* illustrated, by Eric Carl
9. *The Snowy Day*, illustrated by Ezra Jack Keats
10. *John, Paul, George, & Ben*, illustrated by Lane Smith

Lane Smith's list:

1. *Where the Wild Things Are*, illustrated by Maurice Sendak
2. *The Snowman*, illustrated illustrated by Raymond Briggs
3. *The Carrot Seed*, illustrated by Crockett Johnson
4. *The Gashlycrumb Tinies*, illustrated by Edward Gorey
5. *The Happy Day* illustrated by Marc Simont
6. *David's Little Indian*, illustrated by Remy Charlip
7. The "This is..." series, illustrated by M. Sasek
8. Anything illustrated by William Steig
9. *My Father's Dragon*, illustrated by Ruth Chrisman Gannett
10. *Mr. Rabbit and the Lovely Present*, illustrated by Maurice Sendak

What about after you get your first job? My advice there is quite simple: Be easy to work with and always strive to exceed expectations. I've seen some illustrators so eager to get more work that when they get a job, they knock it out quickly and don't end up doing their best work. This is the worst thing that you can do. Don't simply *finish* the assignment (whether it's a piece for a magazine or illustrations for a 32-page picture book)—*wow* the person who hired you. You want them to look at your work and realize that they never could have imagined someone doing quite what you did. You want them to know you did your work carefully, thoughtfully, and enthusiastically. The work will ultimately speak for itself, but I can guarantee that publishers will be much more eager to work with you again if they like your attitude, find you easy to work with, and know that you'll put everything you have into each job.

Breaking into the publishing business as an illustrator isn't easy. However, I'm confident that if you follow the steps that I've outlined—educating yourself about the history of children's illustration and the current market, spending a lot of time to build your portfolio carefully, and then patiently putting your work out there in a number of different ways— you'll be far ahead of the game and your chances for landing your first book will increase exponentially.

Articles

Under One Roof

An Author & An Illustrator, Married

by Laini Taylor & Jim Di Bartolo

In general, publishers keep authors and illustrators apart. One reason for this is to insulate the artist from the author's criticism. After all, it's very difficult for writers to relinquish their private mind's-eye vision of their characters to the hands of another. No matter how wonderful the art is, there's no way it can fit precisely with the author's own ideas.

On the other hand, an illustrator needs to have the freedom to bring their own vision to a project and breathe fresh creative life into it—that's why they're hired. The close oversight of an author could be stifling.

So for many authors, the moment their publisher e-mails the jpeg of their book's cover is one of excitement and terror—as they click to open the file, they have no idea what they are about to see. They might love it or hate it; the tension can be excruciating. It's quite different, however, when the author and illustrator are married to each other.

That's my situation. All three of my (Laini Taylor's) novels feature cover art and interior illustrations by my husband Jim Di Bartolo.

Jim and I met on the first day of art school (at the California College of the Arts in San Francisco) when we were assigned to draw each other. In the 10 years since, we've seen each other's artistic skills and careers develop and diversify. Whereas once I dreamed of writing and illustrating picture books, I now write middle grade and young adult novels and my art has gone in a different direction: gift licensing, and the creation of my product line "Laini's Ladies."

Jim was initially most interested in graphic novels and comic books, but is now working largely in the children's and teen book illustration market. As luck would have it, his drawing style perfectly suits my books.

Our first collaboration was the graphic novel *The Drowned*, published by Image Comics, written by me and illustrated by Jim. Since then, Jim has been hired by both Putnam and Scholastic to illustrate my novels *Dreamdark: Blackbringer; Dreamdark: Silksinger;* and *Lips Touch: Three Times*, as well as doing a variety of projects with other companies.

LAINI TAYLOR's middle-grade novels, *Dreamdark: Blackbringer and Dreamdark: Silksinger* are published by G.P. Putnam's Sons; her illustrated YA novel, *Lips Touch,* is from Arthur A. Levine Books. She also creates a line of stationery and gift products called Laini's Ladies, which are available in over 5,000 stores. Visit www.lainitaylor.com and www.growwings.blogspot.com.

JIM DI BARTOLO has worked with Arthur A. Levine Books, Simon & Schuster, Scholastic Press, G.P. Putnam's Sons, Dark Horse Comics, and Image Comics, among others. He has contributed cover artwork and interiors to all of his wife's novels, as well as their 2004 collaborative graphic novel. Visit www.jimdibartolo.com and www.jimdibartolo.blogspot.com

LAINI & JIM live in Portland, Oregon, and at the time of writing are expecting their first child (the ultimate collaboration).

So what's it like for an author and an illustrator to live under one roof and collaborate on books? Below Jim and I have a conversation about collaboration and share both sides of the story.

How did the collaborations come about?

Laini: When I sold *Blackbringer* to Putnam, there was no guarantee they would hire Jim to do the art. We hoped so, but he had to earn the job by submitting concept drawings, and he finally nailed it down by creating the piece that would become the cover (which I love so much). I think everyone who saw it was immediately sold that he was the right artist for the job.

That's not the ordinary process by which an artist is chosen, and it was a risk for Jim to commit the time "on spec" when he might not get the job, but in this case it paid off, and we were grateful my editor at Putnam, Timothy Travaglini, gave him that opportunity.

With *Lips Touch* we had a vision of the book as a collaboration from the start, and we pitched it together as a joint effort, so that was quite different. We were thrilled that Arthur Levine liked our idea and signed up the book.

I want to stress that authors are not expected or encouraged to come along with an artist in tow. This is a question I hear a lot from writers trying to break into the field, especially in picture books. They think they must submit an illustrated manuscript and need to hire an artist themselves. Nothing could be further from the truth. Editors want to see your manuscript alone, unless the collaboration is an integral part of the project for you, as was the case for us with *Lips Touch*.

What does the actual process of collaboration look like?

Laini: Though Jim has read my manuscripts many times by the art stage, it helps him if I pull out the passages that describe the characters or scenes he's illustrating. He takes it from there and does his sketches.

Here's where I'm so very lucky. I get to see things at an early stage and give feedback. Before he even sends his sketches to the art director and editor, usually he's addressed my comments and made sure everything meshes with my vision. Of course, being an artist, he brings so much more to the design than just breathing life into *my* vision—he brings his own to it too.

I think it would be terrible, as an author, to see final art that misses the mark and doesn't convey one's characters or book. I've been very lucky not to experience that.

Jim: What always comes first for me—after reading the source material of course—is doing "thumbnail sketches." I work very small on thumbnails to keep from getting carried away by details of expression, hairstyle, etc. Working small, I'm forced to think purely in terms of composition.

I then do slightly larger versions of my favorite thumbnail (or selection of a few) and run them by Laini (if it's one of her books), then tighten up or alter based on her input and present it to the art director. With the art director's feedback, I create the final drawing, knowing that requests for changes may still be made before it can truly be considered "finished."

There are a lot of people to satisfy in this scenario, not least of all myself. And if the piece is a cover, the marketing team has final approval. It has happened that a finished cover has satisfied myself, Laini, the art director, the editor, and the publisher, only to be sent back to the drawing board by the marketing team.

It's important to be flexible and accommodating and not invest too much ego when trying to please so many different people.

Articles

Jim, what are the upsides and downsides of having the author close at hand?

Jim: The good news is that the "downsides" are never insurmountable or relationship-damaging. I feel extremely lucky to be working with Laini's richly imagined stories. They give me so many ideas sometimes that it's hard to rein them all in, and this can lead me down a number of unforeseen creative paths.

As an artist herself, Laini has a particular creative vision that can give me valuable insight; however, she would admit that she doesn't always articulate her vision with perfect clarity, so we do have to come back and forth a little before we've got something we both like. Also, her vision might differ from that of the editor or art director, leaving me a little caught in the middle. Thankfully however, she's not a control-freak, so, if I capture the essence of what she has imagined, she's fine with me running with it and exercising my own creativity.

Also, her insight is helpful on my separate projects. Sometimes when you're working on a piece of art, you lose sight of what's good and bad, and having another artist with strong opinions giving feedback can lead to a better final product.

Laini: Likewise, having Jim as an in-house reader is helpful for me. He reads my books at various stages and gives me great suggestions. I call him my "action scene consultant" because with his comic book background he's got a really good feel for pacing in dramatic scenes—especially fights!

And when it comes to projects with a strong visual component, like *Lips Touch*, it's great to be able to develop them together from the beginning, so we have a strong sense of the interplay of text and art that is crucial to the finished project.

Jim: Overall, I think we both value each other's taste and opinions enough to know that any criticism or suggestions are coming from a positive place. That mutual respect (and never critiquing while angry) are healthy for both of our careers as well as for our marriage.

Do problems ever arise?

Laini: For me the only issue is that I'm put in a position to critique Jim's work more than is always comfortable. When he's illustrating somebody else's work, I'm not nearly as invested, and can be more purely positive. But when it's my own characters in question, I can be quite nitpicky (as Jim can tell you). I do like it when he's doing other projects and I can just cheerlead, instead of saying things like, "I imagined her eyes would be a little bigger," or "Can you make his nose less pointy?"

Jim: Well, in general, Laini is my muse so even on projects that she's not involved in, I'm always wanting to knock her socks off a bit. While there can be some tension in working together—and Laini did mention a "nitpicky" quality she has sometimes—it's always (always!) worth it in the end. There's just something special about that feeling of visually breathing life into something that I've seen created from early on, or—as in the case of our graphic novel *The Drowned*—had a hand in developing. Truly, as much as I love every job I've worked on, strong personal investment in a project brings added enjoyment to the whole process.

Laini, how does working with Jim give you, as an author, insight into the design process?

Laini: I imagine that for most authors there's much more mystery. Because Jim is communicating with a whole different set of people than me (me with my editor; he with the art department, as well as hearing feedback from marketing meetings), I can follow along in the decision-making process regarding cover design. This has been really interesting. Covers are, of course, hugely important, and a lot of people can be involved in making those decisions. As an author I think generally you're shielded from that, but I hear Jim's end of things, and if he does three or four final versions for a cover, I see them all, rather than just the final choice. The risk is: I might fall in love with one that ultimately is not chosen. I can watch, but I don't have any power over the decisions that are made. At least I see the cover creation process too, and I know there will be no cover choices that I *don't* like!

Jim, how have the projects you've worked on with Laini differed from other jobs you've done?

Jim: Hmm. There is definitely more freedom to create something that is purely my own vision, and pleasing the art director is sometimes easier than pleasing the author—and certainly easier than pleasing them both at the same time!

I still like to get Laini's feedback, and because she isn't personally invested and usually hasn't read the source material (be it a comic book script, a novel, or art notes from a client), her opinion in these cases is based on a gut reaction to the art, rather than any preconceptions stemming from the text.

Again, another set of trained eyes is never a bad thing. While Laini's detached from the project, she'll still tell me if something is bad or not, and that's one of the jobs of the muse, right?

Are there more collaborations in your future?

Laini: There surely are. We have lots of ideas.

Jim: What she said. Times four.

Lips Touch: Three Times (Arthur A. Levine Books, 2009) is one of several collaborative projects written by Laini Taylor and illustrationed by Jim Di Bartolo.

An Interior illustration by Jim Di Bartolo from *Lips Touch* written by his wife Laini Taylor.

Articles

How We Got Our 'Breaks'

Laini: The sale of my first book is inextricably intertwined with the SCBWI annual conference in Los Angeles. It was at that conference that I got my first nibble of interest—an editor had seen the faerie characters in my art portfolio and wondered if I'd considered writing a book around them. I had, in fact. I had written several chapters, and getting interest and feedback from an editor was magical and really spurred me to keep writing. On top of that, there were terrific workshops that helped me shape the simple early story into a complex novel. I kept working. At the same conference a year later, I attended talks given by editors, including Timothy Travaglini from Putnam. From what he said that day, I thought he might like my manuscript, and he did! I met my agent at the conference as well, so I can really say that from start to finish, it was the inspiration, teaching workshops, and networking opportunities from those days in Los Angeles (over several years) that led to the completion and publication of *Dreamdark: Blackbringer*. I somehow avoided ever writing a single query letter, by being lucky enough to meet the right people at the right time.

Jim: My earliest consistent work came from the role-playing-game company White Wolf, who first hired me based on a packet of artwork I mailed them. Seven years on, I've worked on over 20 of their gaming manuals as well as trading cards.

In the beginning I was pursuing comic books and graphic novels as a career, and my first work in that industry came from attending the San Diego Comic Con for a few years. We pitched our graphic novel *The Drowned* and got some good feedback, but didn't find a publisher on

An Interior illustration by Jim Di Bartolo from *Lips Touch* written by his wife Laini Taylor.

our first trip, so I returned the following year with new art samples to accompany Laini's now-completed script. I spent all of my time meeting other artists, editors, art directors, and publishers at the Con as well as at evening parties (never underestimate the value of meeting people in a more casual setting!). I was introduced to the Managing Editor at Image Comics and met with him the following morning; after reviewing our pitch, he wanted to publish it!

After doing some work in comics, I began to look to expand into book publishing. I attended some SCBWI conferences at about the same time Laini's first novel, *Dreamdark: Blackbringer,* sold. Since winning the job of artist on that, I have continued sending postcard mailings and have tried to do a big Web site update about once a year. This past year has been a rewarding one in terms of finding work in the children's publishing market. Some jobs have come from meeting people at conferences, and others from having a presence online. A recent project that I was hired for came from an art director surfing the Internet and clicking from Web site to Web site until she happened upon mine.

Reaching Reluctant Readers

by Sue Bradford Edwards

Reluctant Reader.

If you read at all, you are familiar with the term. Reluctant readers are in the headlines. They're in our schools. They are also the audience that certain publishers and writers target. To write for this audience, you have to understand who reluctant readers are.

"A reluctant reader is a child who tends to be intimidated by books," says ABDO Group editor-in-chief Paul Abdo. Some of them have problems reading, perhaps because of dyslexia or simple inexperience.

Other reluctant readers are reluctant only when they don't chose the book. "When I was an elementary and middle school student, I loved to read—comic books, science fiction, fantasy, mythology, astronomy. I even read the Robert Lawson *Pilgrim's Progress*, because it was a rip-roaring quest story," Stone Arch Books editorial director Michael Dahl says. "But I was a reluctant reader at school, because the topics didn't interest me. I didn't want to read about American history; I wanted to read about pyramids and pharaohs. I didn't want to learn about rocks and minerals; I wanted to find out more about volcanoes and earthquakes. Reluctant readers haven't met the book that grabs them by the collar and demands to be read."

Give a child a book on a topic they aren't interested in and its no surprise when they choose to play a computer game instead. Fortunately, there is a solution. "As a publisher to the reluctant reader we need to make books fun and less intimidating," Abdo says. "We need to let them see that reading is not a chore but more of a fun activity." One way to do this, especially for those who are reading below grade level, is by publishing hi-lo material.

HI-LO THERE!

"Hi-lo books are high interest and low readability. We try to create books with subjects such as cars, pirates, sports. In our research from our Advisory Board, this audience typically tends to be boys," says Abdo. "So we focus our publishing plan with subjects generally that appeal to boys. For instance cars, sports, dinosaurs, animals, high profile biographies. Some of our newer titles are: *Mighty Machines*, *Fantasy and Folklore*, *World of Science Fiction*, and Buddy Biographies which are high profile biographies on people such as Miley Cyrus, Michael Phelps, and the Jonas Brothers to name a few."

SUE BRADFORD EDWARDS writes and edits from her office in St. Louis, Missouri. Her work has recently appeared in *Children's Writer* newsletter and *WOW Women on Writing* Newsletter. She is the managing editor of 21st Century Family, a new virtual magazine. Visit her site (www.suebradfordedwards.com) or blogs (suebe.wordpress.com, suebe2.wordpress.com) to find out more about her and her work.

Reluctant May Not Mean Remedial

When a publisher's guidelines tell you that they target reluctant readers, this may not mean that they publish hi-lo material or that all of their high-interest titles are low reading level. Stone Arch Books publishes both hi-lo titles, at only 40 pages, and other high-interest books, some of which are over 100 pages in length. Why the variety?

"Keep in mind that reluctant readers are not necessarily low-achieving students. They are as varied as any group of students found in any classroom," says Dahl. "I spent some time with a group of six-graders last month who were considered reluctant. But, wow, were they smart and articulate! One girl sat down at her desk and announced, 'I'm a tough critic, and I hate reading!' She liked books with action and 'big endings.' And she could tell you exactly what she didn't like about books that she had to read for class."

In addition to getting to know reluctant readers, Dahl recommends looking at what *you* read. "Think about the various types of books your adult friends read. Kids are reluctant to pick up certain books for the same reasons adults are. When was the last time you picked up George Eliot's *The Mill on the Floss* or read Edmund Spenser's *Faerie Queene*? Or James Joyce's *Ulysses*? They're good for you, and have a great moral – shouldn't you be reading them instead of Robert Parker or Jan Karon or Lorna Landvik or Alexander McCall Smith? We read what makes us happy, or gets our blood boiling, or makes us laugh, or sweat, or cry, or jump out of our seat. Whether young or old, it's the same thing. Our job as writers, and my job as an editor, is to get kids to equate reading with pleasure. Then to stand back and watch them grab a book." You don't want to be bored even if its good for you. Neither do reluctant readers. Give them what they're looking for and you can hook any kid.

High interest is a term many writers have troubles defining, but young readers don't. "A high-interest topic is one that interests a child without the direct supervision of a teacher or parent. For example, classic high-interest topics have been sports, horror, humor, sci fi, mystery, and adventure," says Dahl. "Some of our hi-lo books are the Library of Doom adventure/fantasy series, the Rex Jones high-action series, Keystone books, which have wide variety of genres, and our newest set Dragonblood, a contemporary adventure-light horror combo that is a mix of *Heroes* with modern-day monsters. It is only 40 pages long and roughly 400 words. The design resembles a shadowy fantasy video game."

To write hi-lo, start with a topic a child will read voluntarily, even greedily. Think about what your son or daughter reads instead of going to bed, feeding the dog or taking out the trash. Once you have a topic in mind, consider how to write hi-lo, starting with the need to hook the reader. Fast.

QUICK & QUIRKY

Reluctant readers won't read a whole chapter to get into the topic. "The biggest thing a writer should remember is that the books need to be fun to hold the reader's interest," says Abdo. "Many of these readers are reading a book for the first time so it can't be intimidating and it can't be difficult."

This is especially difficult when dealing with an academic topic the reluctant reader may not be familiar with. Because of their reading problems, learning is often intimidating. "Find a hook that will engage struggling readers and encourage them to keep reading," says author Buffy Silverman. "One of the topics that I was assigned to write was about the brain and nervous system. I used a basketball metaphor throughout the book—the brain was

Graphic Expectations

Not interested in hi-lo, but still want to write for reluctant readers? Try the graphic novel. "Our new Graphic Novels are really doing wonders for the reluctant readers. These books take the fun and action from comic books that this audience is looking for," says Abdo.

Graphic novels encompass but aren't limited to standard comic book topics. "Some of the titles we have are: the Marvel Age books from Spider-Man to Iron Man our Graphic Planet imprint which is nonfiction titles in Graphic Novel form," says Abdo. "And we just produced the classic Box-Car Children in graphic novel form – this was done in cooperation with the original publisher, Albert Whitman and Co. What we believe with the Box-Car Children graphic novels is that we will capture the reluctant reader who then in turn may move on to the Box-Car chapter books. Our hope is that books will lead to more books."

Straightforward text and high-powered graphics combine to hook readers of all reading levels, including those who'd rather have fun than read for school.

compared to a coach, telling the body what to do. Signals between players were compared to electrical signals that travel through the nervous system. Through these analogies, and by following a player on a basketball court, the book introduced concepts like neurons, nerves, spinal cord, different parts of the brain, sense organs, and reflexes. Photographs of the action on a basketball court complemented diagrams of different parts of the nervous system." Silverman connected with readers through something they already knew—sports.

Hi-lo also takes the familiar and makes it both academic and fun. "We do fun variations on subjects for the curriculum. Next month for instance we are releasing a science series but instead of the usual look at science we are doing it in a 'gross' way," says Abdo. "The series is titled That's Gross and it looks at the backyard, the body, and home to see what is gross in the world of science in these areas. The writing is very fun and engaging and the design and images draws in the reader even more."

Author Ana Maria Rodriguez combines both the gross and the unusual in her series, Animal Secrets Revealed! "Tell the story, so to speak, behind the facts," she reminds writers. "For example, my series is about how animals do amazing things, such as how the limbless hagfish uses a gooey trap he produces in his mouth to repel predators. Another chapter presents the story of how scientists discovered what the lion's mane is for using life-size toy lions." Children may think they know all about fish or lions, but Rodriguez surprises them with the latest unusual facts about some of their favorite animals.

No matter how fun you make your writing, hi-lo writing is serious business. "Each of my books combines high interest topics with carefully written and researched text and photos to create a book even reluctant readers will find of interest and accessible. The goal is to help them gain confidence through quirky but legitimate nonfiction," says author Kelly Milner Hall. "Find a fresh twist on old, popular ideas, then do the most careful and thoughtful research of your life. Go right to the experts sources and be bold enough to ask the questions you *know* kids would ask. Cater to the educators, yes, but don't forget the kids. Find a balance that respects them both." Part of this balance is in how you introduce new material.

EASE INTO WHAT'S NEW

In addition to connecting unfamiliar topics to what is fun and familiar, hi-lo writers must introduce new concepts in a way that doesn't overwhelm readers who are less enthusiastic or may be struggling. This is done through how they write, special features included in the manuscript and design elements from the publisher.

With each sentence you write, remember the audience is reluctant to read. Don't give them a reason to stop. "You have to keep the struggling reader in mind and make sure your sentences are simple and straight-forward, but not babyish," says author Joanne Mattern, "and you have to keep the tone and the subject matter exciting so it grabs the reader and makes him or her want to keep reading."

Do this by remembering the story behind the facts. "Do it almost like if you were talking to them in person," says Rodriguez. "Imitate a story-line style used in fiction to grab their interest." This means bringing out the story elements of your topic—strong characters, a gripping plot and suspense. Think of the ways that you can do this without distorting the facts and you'll have a gripping real-life tale.

Successful hi-lo writers find ways to keep their writing straightforward but still include enough detail to make things interesting. "Be streamlined, not simplistic. Details are good, but only telling details. Stay away from too much description," says Dahl.

Which details are telling? "Focus on the essence of the story and the person or fact you are describing," says Rodriguez. Once you have narrowed down your topic, focusing on a single narrative line, eliminate all facts that don't inform the reader about this narrow focus. Some of the rest may make its way into a sidebar, or it may have to be eliminated altogether.

Authors use a variety of special features to introduce new ideas in ways that reinforce them in the minds of young readers. "Concepts are age-appropriate," Silverman reminds authors, "while new vocabulary and concepts are reinforced multiple times. Unfamiliar words are defined in context and as glossary words."

Author Joanne Mattern also reinforces new material by introducing it in several different ways. "My books contain features to help children learn new words and concepts, such as glossaries, sidebars, and a further reading list." Such features work together to help readers take in new material without feeling overwhelmed.

The publisher also uses various design elements to reinforce this learning process.

"Books are highly illustrated with appealing photographs and captions," says Silverman. "A limited number of words per spread increases appeal and encourages success."

Book design is vital in hooking reluctant readers. "One thing it does *not* look like is a remedial or lower-level book," says Dahl of a hi-lo book. "Kids know if they have difficulty reading. It's embarrassing and frustrating." Why make it worse by handing them a book that looks like less than what their peers are reading?

Give them something fascinating in an accessible way and you'll have a win-win situation. "Respect your reader, and give him or her a reason to conquer your book," says Silverman. Do this and you'll also give the editor a reason to sign you on.

MAKING THE SALE

How to approach an editor varies from house to house. Some publishers pull hi-lo titles from the slush. "I developed the idea for all of my books except *Wild Dogs*, which was assigned by my editor," says Kelly Milner Hall.

Many titles are developed in-house, within on-going series. Publishers like Abdo, Stonecrest, Raintree, and Mitchell Lane assign the titles they want to a stable of writers who have applied to write for them. "We ask for resumes and writing samples and then we assign the actual book/series," says Abdo. "We do that for all of our nonfiction books."

Some writers think series writing won't let them be creative. These writers need to follow Mattern's advice. "Read the books out there and get an idea of the language and the format. Then see how you can put your own style into play," she says. "Publishers are always looking for new and exciting voices and presentations. Hi-lo books can be a great field because they are usually assigned in series which means more work and more pay. Once you are connected with a publisher, you tend to get fairly steady work."

This means repeated opportunities to connect with young readers. "The kids never disappoint me in their enthusiasm for the books I love to write," Hall says. "I feel so lucky to have the chance to reach out to those kids. Especially considering I was once one of them myself."

Consider bringing these reluctant readers into the fold. If you possess the necessary skills, you'll find yourself with steady work and a demanding audience. What more could a writer want?

The Hi-Lo Shelf

Start your hi-lo reading with titles by the authors interviewed.

Kelly Milner Halls:

- *Albino Animals*
- *Dinosaur Mummies*
- *Dinosaur Parade*
- *Mysteries of the Mummy Kids*
- *Saving the Baghdad Zoo*
- *Tales of the Cryptids*
- *Wild Dog Wild Horses*

Joanne Mattern:

- *Animal Geography* series
- *First Facts: Snakes*
- *First Ladies* series
- *Great Artists*
- *The Jonas Brothers*
- *Learn about Cats*
- *Outrageous Animals*
- *Peyton Manning*
- *Safety First*
- *World Cities*

Buffy Silverman:

- *Blame Your Parents: Inheritance and Reproduction*
- *Follow that Food!: Distribution of Resources*
- *Going Underground!: City Infrastructure*
- *States of Confusion: Solids, Liquids, and Gases*
- *Who's in Control: Brain and Nervous System*
- *You Scratch My Back: Interdependence and Symbiosis*

Articles

Writing a Series for a Packager

by Tracy Barrett

I had recently tangled with a computer virus, so I hesitated to open the e-mail from an unknown sender. But in the end, the subject line proved irresistible: "I loved your book." The writer went on to say, "Let me introduce myself. I'm Jane Stine, president of Parachute Publishing, an independent book producer in New York. Parachute has been in the business of creating books for children and young adults for 20 years.

"I am writing to you to see if you would be at all interested in doing some writing for us. We are looking for writers both to do writing on some of our existing series—and most importantly, we are looking for writers to work with us to develop new ideas.

"If you are interested, curious, or just want to chat with someone who admires your ear for dialogue, give me a call."

Naturally I was interested, and she was right—I was indeed curious. What is an independent book producer? The term was new to me, and when I asked around and was told that it was another term for "book packager," I wasn't greatly enlightened, so I did some research.

WHAT DOES A BOOK PACKAGER DO?

A packager, I found, is an independent company (or sometimes an individual) that provides many of the functions that a publisher does. Editors at a packager read queries and manuscripts sent to them, or more they often solicit book projects (more on that later); they edit the manuscripts; they often provide illustrations, including sometimes the jacket art.

Packagers usually deal with series, both fiction and nonfiction, for adults or young readers, sometimes both. A series can mean books with the same characters who do the same kind of thing—solve a mystery, for example, or travel in time—but it can also mean books with a similar theme and feel to them but different characters from book to book, as in the Goosebumps series.

Packagers of books for young readers tend to focus on the middle-grade market although there are some who work with YA, early readers, and picture books. Many produce books based on licensed characters from Disney, Sesame Street, etc. These books are almost always

TRACY BARRETT's series The Sherlock Files includes *The 100-Year-Old Secret* (2008), *The Beast of Blackslope* (2009), *The Case That Time Forgot* (2010), and a fourth title to be published in 2011, all by Henry Holt Books for Young Readers. She is also the author of the novels *Anna of Byzantium, Cold in Summer, On Etruscan Time,* and *King of Ithaka* (fall, 2010) as well as ten works of nonfiction for young readers. She served for ten years as the Midsouth Regional Advisor with the Society of Children's Book Writers and Illustrators and is on the faculty of Vanderbilt University.

work for hire. Some packagers work with the educational market, in which case they're called "developers," or the trade market, but they tend to focus on mass-market fiction.

In the case of very long series, multiple authors frequently write under one name. This could be the name of the author of the original book or books, as in the case of Francine Pascal, who wrote the first Sweet Valley High books, which are now mostly written by other people. Sometimes the "author" named on the jacket is a fictional person, as in the case of Carolyn Keene, whose name appears on the Nancy Drew series of mysteries.

In shorter series, one author tends to write all the books, as with my "Sherlock Files," packaged by Parachute Publications and published by Henry Holt Books for Young Readers.

In some cases the books are set up with traditional advances and royalty, with the author holding the copyright as with a traditional publisher. With books based on a licensed character, neither the packager nor the author but the holder of the license (Disney, etc.) usually retains copyright.

So what does a packager *not* do? They don't publish the book. They submit either a proposal or a finished product to an editor at a publishing company, who accepts it or rejects it. This means that a book written for and edited by a packager will be published by Random House or Henry Holt or Dutton or any other publisher.

In work-for-hire, the packager pays the author a flat fee and any earnings beyond that flat fee are kept by the packager. If the book doesn't do well, the author keeps the fee and the loss is borne by the packager (and the publisher), but if the book is a bestseller, the author receives no more payment. In an advance-and-royalty situation, the packager splits both the advance and the royalty with the author, either 50-50 or in some other agreed-upon configuration.

So now I knew what a packager did. I still didn't know how they operated, and more importantly, I didn't know what this meant for me. So after having published 13 books on my own, I took the plunge and acquired an agent. This turned out to be a very wise step. My new agent was very good at making an advantageous contract and explaining it to me. Even so, the learning curve has been steep. I found it helpful to look at some books produced by a packager, but I found that they're not always easy to identify. Sometimes you have to look at the copyright page where you'll see a line like this: Copyright © by Parachute Publishing, LLC

The cover is sometimes helpful—for example *Francine Pascal's Sweet Valley High*. The use of the possessive (Francine Pascal's) tells you that this particular book was written by someone other than the originator of the series, and thus was probably produced by a packager. Pascal's name on the cover indicates that the series is hers, but not this book.

In my research I found that many well-known authors (for example, Bruce Coville, R.L. Stine, and Ann Brashares) write or have written for packagers. Jane Stine explains, "Sometimes an author will call me up and say, 'My kid needs braces' or 'I have to put on a new roof—give me a book to write.'" It's quick money, and someone who has experience in writing for a particular packager and knows what they're looking for can find it fun to do. Packagers' books are usually what is described as "high concept." The series that I'm writing with Parachute, The Sherlock Files, can be described as: Two American kids in London discover that they're descended from Sherlock Holmes and are given his cold-case notebook and set about solving these cases using modern technology.

Chris Tebbetts describes his series this way: "The Viking, Sagas 1-4: a comedic middle grade fantasy adventure series, about Zack, a high school freshman, who finds himself back and forth in time, between modern Minneapolis and 9th Century Scandinavia, where he falls into the middle of a mythical Viking quest, populated by doppelgangers of the people back home."

The concept, then, is crucial for most series done by packagers. I got involved with The Sherlock Files after another writer had submitted an idea and a sample first chapter. Parachute

Useful Organizations

- **American Book Packagers Association**
  611 Broadway, Suite 611
  212-563-5904
  800-209-4575
  www.abpaonline.org

- **Society of Children's Book Writers and Illustrators**
  8271 Beverly Blvd. Los Angeles, CA 90048
  323-782-1010
  www.scbwi.org

  SCBWI members have access to the "Book Producers List" of book producers in the U.S. and U.K. who have expressed interest in working with freelancers.

loved the concept but not the writing, so they paid the author for his idea and looked for an author to do the actual writing. R.L. Stine, whose wife, Jane Stine, is Parachute's publisher, recommended me to Jane, and she asked me to write a sample first chapter. They pitched it to Reka Simonsen at Henry Holt, who's published two of my other books, and she picked it up.

I asked Susan Lurie, Senior Vice President and Publisher at Parachute Publications, whether it was typical for one person to come up with a series concept and for another to actually write the series. She told me that it was, and said that they work in two ways: They have a project that interests them—one they've come up with in-house or one that was sent to them—and then they "look for a writer we think would be really terrific for the series," or they receive a query through the mail and work on it with the person who generated the idea. They ask the same as a standard publisher: The entire manuscript of a picture book, an outline and sample chapter of a longer work. She said they especially like at least an idea of the plot of the other books in the series as well as some character sketches.

HOW DO PACKAGERS FIND AUTHORS?

Some authors connect with a packager through their agent or other authors. Author Chris Tebbetts says, "I met a guy at Barbara Seuling's summer manuscript workshop, who had done some work on the Sweet Valley High books, for Alloy (then 17th Street Productions). I'd never heard of packagers before, and he explained that they were often looking for writers, and that I should email his editor there to inquire. They just happened to be looking for someone to write a boy-centered MG fantasy adventure series called The Viking, and the editor asked me to write a sample chapter, which I did. Once they sold the project to Puffin, I was hired to write it."

Australian author Chris Cheng was also contacted by the packager. He said, "The packager . . . actually the fiction coordinator was approached by an overall packager to get together a bunch of prominent Aussie kid's writers who could also write for the education market." His book in the Whole Child series is called *William's Backyard*.

Author Debby Garfinkle ("The Band" trilogy, Berkley, 2007) says, "I had written a book in a paperback series and told my agent I'd like to do more of that type of work. Shortly thereafter, a packager contacted my agent, asking her if she could refer a writer for a trilogy they were pitching to publishers. She gave the packager my name. The publisher bought the proposal from the packager about six months later, and then the packager asked me to write the trilogy."

Packager Mini-Glossary

Packager. A company (or sometimes an individual) that performs much of the work of a traditional publisher but does not publish the work. The packager may generate series, solicit manuscripts (or receive them through an agent or the slush pile), edit them, copy edit and/or proofread them, typeset them, provide cover art and/or interior art, or any combination. The packager submits the proposal or the finished product (or the work at any stage along that continuum) to a publisher. The author or illustrator almost always deals with the editor at the packager, not the editor at the publishing company, at least initially.

Work for hire. Any work, whether artistic (writing, drawing, etc.) or technical (an invention, etc.), created by an employee or contractor. The copyright (or trademark, etc.) is held by the employer. The employee may or may not be compensated for this work beyond the salary drawn when the work was created; a contractor (such as an author writing for a packager) is paid.

High concept. A book, television series, movie, etc., that can be described in a sentence or two.

Chris Snowden of Working Partners, a packager based in the UK that also works with many authors in the United States, says, "We proactively look for new talent. We approach agents but also have an open invitation on our Web site. Our editors work with groups like the Society of Children's Book Writers and Illustrators to identify new writers. We also host writer's workshops to educate writers about our process and projects that are under development." He adds, "We work with both established writers who like to have a second writing home and new writers who want to build their profile and experience."

PACKAGER PROS & CONS

Susan Lurie agreed with me that the most difficult aspect for writers is the fact that you're the servant of two masters—you have to satisfy the editor at the packager, who is doing her best to make the book or books acceptable to the editor at the traditional publishing company while maintaining the author's distinctive voice and style. Sometimes—fortunately, this is rare—due to miscommunication or misunderstanding or a change in direction, the author winds up having to undo work that looked to be done. I had two big changes to my work after I was already several drafts into *The 100-Year-Old Secret*, Book 1of The Sherlock Files. They're both good changes but they did add to my workload. They wanted the books to be longer—24,000 words instead of 20,000, which is a big percentage change—and the books are coming out in hardcover and are released on a slower schedule, one a year instead of all four in two years.

Chris Tebbetts echoes the sentiments of many authors when he says, "I felt as though my editor at the packager was very much interested in creating as good a series of books as we could, in the time allowed. (The 'time allowed' is a big caveat—the schedule was insane!)"

One author says that when she writes her own books, that is, books not for a packager, "I find that the money is much better, even if I'm just doing ghostwriting or licensed character books, because the packager isn't taking a cut. I also find the editorial process generally easier, because there aren't so many different editors to deal with. But sometimes I just need some quick money, and writing and selling my own books can take a long time. The big advantage that packagers offer is that they're a good source of freelance work when you're broke and their projects are usually pre-sold, so at least you know that what you're working on will be published and you'll get paid. My own books are more idiosyncratic and mean more to me, and I feel as if I have more control over the whole publishing process with them. Plus I can earn royalties from them." (Remember that in some cases, series books through a packager *are* royalty-based and not work for hire.)

Chris Tebbetts agrees, saying, "The pros were all about getting into the game. I'd been trying unsuccessfully to get published, and here was a chance. Also, I liked the idea of getting paid up front, rather than writing on spec. The biggest con was that it would not be my copyright. But really, at that point, it was a small consideration. Once I was offered the project, I didn't think much about not taking it."

Jo Kittinger says of the pros and cons of working with a packager were the "time constraints (very, very tight deadline), the fee that was being offered, the prestige of the DK Inc and Smithsonian names (which would look good on my resume), and whether or not I would get my name on the book." Her field guides in the Birds of America series were published through the packager Crane Hill.

Debby Garfinkle adds, "I didn't know if I was capable of doing the work, as the packager wanted the entire young adult trilogy completed in a year. Also, I would be writing about a topic I didn't know much about, and it was the first non-humorous work I'd get published. Also, it would tie up my writing for a year so that I couldn't work on my own projects. Finally, I worried I'd get burned out writing three books about the same characters. I'd always written stand-alones before."

On the other hand, I was being offered a three-book deal and I didn't even have to submit a proposal. Also, they were putting a lot of promotion and marketing into the trilogy. And I was eager to spread my wings by trying to write something different. My other publisher wanted me to write only humorous young adult fiction."

What kinds of series are popular now? Mysteries are big, as are "adventure" books. "Junior chick-lit," about friendships and problems between girls, are popular. But all the editors I spoke to confirmed that the genre doesn't really matter. Almost any theme can work as long as it can be sustained through several books. Susan Lurie said, "I'm looking for really fresh voices." When I asked her to elaborate, she said, "If I could describe it, then it wouldn't be fresh.

Something that touches middle-grade and YA readers that's genuine but has a new feeling to it. A lot of personality."Some subsidy presses bill themselves as packagers and while they may be legitimate businesses, they do not perform the same function as a packager. If you want to check out a press, find out if they belong to the ABPA. This organization has high standards—members have to deal honorably with their clients (they have specific regulations defining this) and have to be actively publishing books. Membership in this organization does not, of course, mean that this is the right packager for you, but it's an indication that they're on the level.

Am I glad I opened that email from Jane Stine? You bet. I've had a lot to learn—not an outliner by nature, I've gone through as many as seven drafts of an outline before my packager editor and I agree on it, I've faced deadlines that seemed impossible, and I've had to learn a different style of writing. But I have four books that I'm very proud of and that have received good reviews and have been picked up by the Junior Library Guild, and I kept my name visible while I worked on longer-term projects. Signing with a packager was a good decision for me, and it might be for you too. Just be sure to do your homework to make sure it's a good fit for you!

Intensive Publisher Research

by Deanna Caswell

After collecting enough form rejections to wallpaper our bathrooms, my critique partner and I were weary. We wondered if we would ever understand this business. It felt like we had better odds of being simultaneously struck by lightning than either of us getting a career in children's literature off the ground. I just knew that if an editor would talk to me, interact with me about my writing, I could become A Really Decent Writer...eventually. But, as we all know, that doesn't happen without good writing AND good targeting. So, after a great deal of teeth-gnashing and e-mail whining, we buckled down and revisited the basics:

- Don't send your picture book to a company that publishes cookbooks. *Check.*
- Buy a *Children's Writer's & Illustrator's Market* and learn to use it. *No kidding, it's falling apart from overuse.*
- Read each company's catalog and see what they publish. *Seriously?*

I knew which companies had published my favorite picture books. Wasn't that enough? My crit partner already was deep in the monumental task of "getting to know the list" of each of the 35 publishers we'd been hounding with our unwanted submissions, but I was resistant. It seemed like more work than should be expected. I wasn't an agent and I had no desire to be one. I not-so-secretly hoped that it really was all "a numbers game," that my statistically inevitable moment was fast approaching, and that my crit partner was wearing off her fingerprints in futility. Yes, I was lazy. But, after a few more stacks of letters from "The Editors" arrived, set askew on the page, and pockmarked with what I imagined was the photocopied evidence of some poor intern's blueberry crumble muffin, I gave in. Sigh. It was time to put in the effort. A lot of effort.

The immediate response was *ink* from publishers. A pen in an editor's hand actually came in contact with a sheet of paper addressed to me! (Well, "addressed" might be an exaggeration. It was a redacted form rejection, but still!) Mark McVeigh, bless his heart, gave me my Very First Ink. He crossed out "Dear Author" and wrote "Deanna." He wrote the name of my manuscript at the top and crossed out "The Editors" at the bottom. He signed it with his initials "MM." I was ecstatic. From that point on, I rarely got a form rejection. I got rejected all the time, of course, but with comments! I was finally getting the feedback I desperately needed to improve. And I did improve, quickly. In under two years, I went from

DEANNA CASWELL secretly dreams of being a ballerina someday. But, being a graceless, 5'10" thirty-three year old with an excessive affinity for all things salty and a deep, abiding hatred for high-waisted tights... it's probably never going to happen. So, she has poured her aspirations into her debut picture book. In *First Ballet* (Hyperion, October 2009), Caswell uses poetic imagery and sparse language to capture a young child's excitement and wonder as she watches her first ballet.

crumb-Xeroxed form rejections, to personal comments and letters, to an accomplished agent and two picture book contracts.

Before we buckled down, we were already doing some things correctly. We weren't sending picture books to cookbook publishers. We owned a *Children's Writer's & Illustrator's Market* and learned to use it, especially the subject index. In fact, when I use it, that's the first place I go. (I may love the press and success of a certain company, but if they don't publish what I write, then my odds of getting in there are negligible.) If I write humor, I need to know what companies buy humor. If I write multicultural, I need to know which companies characterize their books as multicultural. If I write both, I need to generate a list for each. Once we had the list of people who said they printed what we write, we read their full entries. A children's writer never really finishes with the *Children's Writer's & Illustrator's Market*, but there comes a stopping point when it is marked up sufficiently and/or stuffed with enough post-it notes and loose-leaf notebook paper to say that we have a pretty good list of companies we want publishing our books.

And we did. We already had our dream list (affectionately named The Snob List). We'd had it for months and had been snubbed three times over by everyone on it! Now we needed to Get To Know The List. My crit partner was too impatient to wait for catalogs and I was too lazy to search every publisher's Web site. Our tool of choice was Amazon.com. Through Amazon Advanced Search, we could generate lists of books according to a single publisher/imprint, for a single year. We suspected that houses like Farrar, Straus & Giroux who bought *Shrek* 20 years ago might not be buying those kinds of manuscripts today. We wanted to know what a given publisher had put out this year and last year before we spent energy learning about anything else they'd done. That would tell us what they'd been buying from authors for the last four years.

Amazon.com offers searches restricted to its book section. If this option is chosen, an Advanced Search tab appears at the top of the page. Clicking on it produces a form with a dozen blanks. If I am interested in researching trade, hardcover picture books and am interested in Abrams, I would type "Abrams" in the publisher blank, change the format to "Hardcover," choose a reader age of "4-8 years," and set the publication date for "During 2007." Leaving everything else alone or empty and clicking Search generates a list of every hardcover picture book Abrams published in the last year.

The book reviews on Amazon quickly told us what each book was about, if it was in rhyme, if it was funny, multicultural, taught a lesson, if it was a fairytale, fractured or traditional, a song rewrite, etc. We picked about ten buzz words to describe different aspects of books like: funny, light lesson, heavy lessons, rhyme, song, rewrite, serious, fluff, or educational. We wanted to know about the manuscripts they were buying from unknowns, so we read the reviews for each of the books on the list, skipping any book that was licensed, a sequel, a reprint, a novelty book, or written by a celebrity, an author/illustrator, or a perennial author. We listed out the titles that remained and read each with our buzz words in mind, recording our findings. You can't tell a book by it's cover, but you can certainly tell if it's something in your ballpark by the review!

By the time we reached the end of the list, we had a much better idea of the "character" of each house and what kind of manuscripts they would buy from an unknown and put the time in to hunt down an illustrator. But the realizations didn't set in until we started counting. At the time, we were both writing mostly fun, anthropomorphic. For each house, we counted how much rhyme they published. We asked how many anthropomorphic books were light lessons or pure fun or heavy, like ducks with cerebral palsy. We found ourselves saying things like, "This house only bought two funny manuscripts and both were author/illustrator! Everything else is nonfiction. No wonder they wouldn't talk to us!"

We had been so wrong about the companies we'd been subbing. There were whole lists that we said, "I have nothing that would interest these people!" There were others that we felt we could have written any number of books on the list, but we had never submitted a manuscript to that company. After getting a good overview of each house's tendencies, we went back to the *Children's Writer's & Illustrator's Market* to see how the publishers categorized themselves and compared that to the books they published this year. We were shocked!

Charlesbridge and Abrams were both listed under humor. And they both belonged there, but Charlesbridge would probably never publish a book about tinkling monkeys and Abrams did! If we'd written a knee-slapper about learning fractions, we'd be more on track for Charlesbridge. And some companies that we'd be submitting to as "funny" companies hadn't bought any humor in ages. But they had funny licensed material that landed them in the category!

Armed with this new perspective on publishers and a dog-eared, post-it filled *Children's Writer's & Illustrator's Market*, we went to the library and read all of the books that we felt favored our style. The ability to mention exactly what about X book reminded us of our own work manuscript seemed to go a long way toward receiving a personal response. I'm quite sure, given my free-association style of thinking that some submission readers would have never made the connections I did between my work and the books I mentioned, but I wasn't as interested in being their opinion-twin as much as showing that I had put effort and thought into my submission. I tried to speak to them as a group of people that had produced material I identified with.

Each house has a personality, just like people. What is funny to one, is rude to another. What is educational to one, is heavy-handed to another, but they may have characterized themselves using the same words. By conducting your publisher research this way, you will no longer be submitting into a black hole. You will have well-earned confidence and be able to write effective query letters.

EXTRA CREDIT

Now, at this point in the process, I'd say that the critical work is done. Sending well-targeted material to the submissions editor will get attention (and got my crit partner her first contract), however, if you want, you can get fancy and try targeting individual editors. There is a big debate among writers whether it's more effective to send material to General Submissions or to Mr. Editor, specifically. First of all, submission editors do a good job. They know better than we do where to funnel the material. But, you may think sending it to a specific editor will get you farther. We did both and both worked well.

To research editors, we felt we first needed to find out if they were still working where we last saw them. Some years it seems all the editors are changing positions, so it was important to know where each one was currently working to avoid sending submissions to the trash can beside an empty desk. There was no sense in building an editor list from scratch and I was way too chicken to call the front desk at each house and verify my list. We found that the best option was to make alterations to the entries in our poor, long-suffering *Children's Writer's & Illustrator's Market* volumes.

The first stop was www.underdown.org/chchange.htm. Harold Underdown lists most of the children's publishing moves for the past eighteen months. We started at the beginning just to make sure we caught everyone. The second stop was www.vistacomp.com/pub moves/pub moves.html. This site chronicles the moves for the whole publishing industry, so we scanned the entries for anything mentioning the children's department for the companies on our list. Any mentions of promotions or hiring in other areas of the company were skipped. We focused exclusively on people exiting or entering the editorial department of a given company. Between these two Web sites, we kept an editorial move list that stayed months ahead of any of our other resources.

Next we wanted to collect information about individual editor's tastes and preferences. We felt that the best information about an editor was the list of books they'd edited. Just like an individual publisher, an editor could say, "I like humor," but their definition of that word may be quite different from ours. We used five basic resources to research editors. The first stop was www.robinfriedman.com. Robin has put together a large collection of interviews with editors discussing their past and present works. Gold mine!

Second, as members of SCBWI, we had access to a great publication, "Edited By: A House By House Listing of Editorial Credits." Even if an individual editor was no longer at the same house, the list of books they'd helped create told us a great deal about how that person might react to our work.

The third resource was Amazon. We plugged individual editors into the general search box. Out popped all mentions they'd received in acknowledgments (i.e., "Thanks to my dear editor, Jane Doe") and, surprisingly, several editors had written their own books.

The fourth source, and possibly the most important, was our friends. Our writer pals were spread out all over the United States and we each were active in different areas of the writing community. Some were active on Verla's Boards. Some attended lectures. Others liked weekend workshops. So, together, we amassed a great deal of information. The last resource was good old Google. Some editors were so new that there was no track record. Some books weren't listed in our other resources and we just *knew* that whoever edited that book would love something we'd written, so we Googled the titles with additions like "edited by" or "editor."

I cut and pasted all of this information into a spreadsheet by house. We read the reviews on Amazon, noting which ones leaned toward anything we'd written. Then, we headed back to the library and got familiar with those books.

In the end we'd compiled a huge list of editors, their submission preferences, their past work, and what they said about their preferences in interviews. Those details, combined with the current character of the publishing house gave us a *person* to contact, not just a name on a list. We had finally gone beyond "Ooo, her name sounds like a nice person who likes puppy stories," to "Mr. Editor said in an interview two years ago that he wants adventure and historical fiction, but his house hasn't ever published anything like that. They clearly support his history interest, but through their nonfiction offerings. And oddly, he seems to have edited a lot of song rewrites."

The most important thing to remember in all of this, is to not get hung up on the One Perfect Submission. Searching for the golden bullet is a wild goose chase that ends with a frustrated writer. There are factors and unknowns that we as writers can't possibly nail down, but the submission process (read: rejection process) is where we learn the business. At least, it's where I learned the business. I truly believe that if I hadn't gone through this process, if I hadn't written and submitted dozens of manuscripts, if I hadn't pored over a hundred responses, I don't believe I would have produced the manuscripts that have finally made it. Additionally, I have a confidence in talking about the field that I wouldn't have had otherwise and an affection for editors I've never met whose comments and encouragement helped me get my career off the ground. You've already got the *Children's Writer's & Illustrator's Market* in your hands. So you're off to a great start. So roll up your sleeves and dig into the internet for the rest. Good luck in your researching—May you learn helpful things from your rejections!

Summary of Our Research System

1. Read everything in *Children's Writer's & Illustrator's Market* about companies who publish what you like to write.

2. Choose a tentative list of houses based on your preferences, gut reactions, and beliefs.

3. Profile this year's book list for each house, skipping material that doesn't fit your situation. (Author/illustrator, celebrity, licensed, etc.)

4. Make a note of all books that you feel are similar to your work and go read them. Write brilliant letters to the submissions editor and immediately proceed to step six—or—do the Extra Credit below.

5. Pore over the responses, dissecting every word and gabbing about it to your writer friends.

6. Send out more work.

Step 4—Extra Credit

- Make a current editor list for each house using *Children's Writer's & Illustrator's Market*, www.underdown.org/chchange.htm, and www.vistacomp.com/pub moves/pub moves.html.

- Check out the "Edited By" publication at SCBWI.org, www.robinfriedman.com, Amazon, and your writing community to find specific editorial credits and preferences.

- Google if you have to.

- Make a note of all books (edited by people working at houses on your list) that you feel are similar to your work and go read them.

- Write brilliant letters to Ms. Editor

The Acquisitions Process

by Harold Underdown

If you're a typical aspiring children's book writer, a contract is the reward you are hoping for at the end of the labor of writing, learning, rewriting, submitting, rewriting again, and submitting again. But to be offered a contract, an author must inspire an editor to want to offer her a contract for her manuscript and develop it into a book. The steps that lead to a contract, known as "the acquisition process," can be mysterious and prolonged. Why is that? How does the process work?

And does it really matter? As an editor I contacted for this article pointed out, there's a certain irony in writing about the acquisition process in 2009, at a time when most houses have slowed acquisitions to a crawl, and will most likely keep them at that pace for most of the coming year. And yet, the worst recession in the U.S. in at least 30 years has not stopped the process cold at any children's book publisher.

It can't. Publishers must acquire manuscripts and develop them into books, just as farmers must plant in the spring if they are to harvest in the fall, or as a manufacturer must do research and development to create new products. Acquisition is the way publishers choose the books that they will publish in the future, and if a publisher stops acquiring, it won't be long before they will stop publishing.

That basic principle is simple, and yet the process often is not. To start with, there's no one process—different publishers go about acquiring manuscripts in different ways—and different manuscripts at the *same* publisher don't necessarily follow the same path. Broadly speaking, though, there are three paths that can lead to the acquisition of a manuscript.

WE TRUST YOUR JUDGMENT: THE OLD-FASHIONED WAY

Legend has it that in the early decades of children's publishing, the heads of children's imprints, who were generally former librarians publishing books for libraries, signed up the books they wanted to publish. Their staff too needed only their boss's approval of the books they wanted to sign up. Today, so continues the legend, corporate processes require editors to get approval by committee after "doing the numbers" and justifying an acquisition financially.

Legend has part of the story right. That was the process, one that was simply the practice in publishing generally, whether of adult or children's books. One person approved acquisitions, making the final decision of what to publish. The title of "publisher" goes with that power, and is still used to this day.

HAROLD UNDERDOWN is a children's book editor and the author of *The Complete Idiot's Guide to Publishing Children's Books*. He works with publishers and writers, teaches the "Kid's Book Revision" online class with Eileen Robinson, and runs The Purple Crayon Web site at http://www.underdown.org.

Legend is wrong, though, in saying that as multinational media corporations have come to dominate publishing, that practice has died out. It's still in use, and not just at small, independent houses, the ones that one might assume would carry on such a tradition. Yes, the traditional process is still used at independents such as Holiday House and Candlewick, but it is also used at the children's trade imprints at one of New York's large corporate publishers, Penguin. The practice there is not a simple one of taking a manuscript straight to the publisher, as Kate Harrison, an editor at Dial, explained it to me: "Dial does (as do several other imprints) have a manuscript meeting about once a month to which editors can bring picture books or partial novels on which they'd like editorial feedback before taking something to Lauri [Lauri Hornik, the Dial publisher]. This meeting is only attended by the editors and assistants—not by the publisher or any sales or marketing." Still, with the addition of the editorial meeting, their process is little different from the traditional one.

It's heartening that the traditional process is still in use, but that method of acquiring isn't the one that causes anxiety in writers, so I'll move on to investigate the dreaded acquisitions committee.

THE ACQUISITIONS COMMITTEE: THE CORPORATE WAY

In the "corporate" acquisition process, an editor must prepare an acquisition proposal, circulate it, present the title at an acquisition or publishing meeting, attended by heads of marketing, subsidiary rights, and other departments as well as a publisher, and get the committee's approval.

This is a relatively new process, though long established at Macmillan Children's Books when I joined the company in the late 1980s in my first publishing job. In a conversation with Leonard Marcus, author of the children's book industry history, *The Minders of Make-Believe*, I learned that acquisition meetings developed as publishers looked beyond the library market and the marketing department grew in importance, and as children's publishing became more corporate. They didn't appear at the same time at every company, however. They are now widespread, standard these days at publishers such as HarperCollins, Simon & Schuster, Little, Brown, and others.

Why is this process necessary? Children's publishing is big business now, and for many companies that means not leaving acquiring decisions up to one person. The books still matter, but so do the finances. Emma D. Dryden, vice president and publisher of Atheneum Books for Young Readers and Margaret K. McElderry Books, imprints of Simon & Schuster Children's, looks at today's realities this way: "Authors need to recognize that when they submit a manuscript for publication, they are proposing to enter into a business contract with a publisher—and so it is with a business head and a creative heart that authors should acknowledge that the acquisitions meeting is a necessary part of the process whereby a publisher can feel 100% certain that they can do a project justice by publishing it —and thereby making money for the author and the publisher alike."

How the process plays out varies widely. Typically, it begins with a discussion within an imprint, either informally or at a regular meeting of editors. If the editor takes the project forward from there, she must prepare an acquisitions proposal, to justify the acquisition and set up a proposed budget. She circulates this to the acquisitions committee (the group that must approve the acquisition), and schedules time to present her project at an acquisitions meeting. These meetings are held regularly, even weekly, or only as needed, and may get postponed if a crucial person is at a conference or on vacation. Once a proposal gets to the meeting, that isn't always the end of the process. Some acquisition committees routinely approve almost all of the proposals that come to them. More typically, some approved, some are turned down, and some are returned to the editor for more information or a rethink.

Here's one specific example, as described to me by Yolanda LeRoy, editorial director at Charlesbridge:

An editor finds a manuscript they like and brings it my attention. I may make some suggestions or I may have them bring it to Team Meeting (all the editors and designers) for a group discussion/brainstorming session. From there it would go to our Acq Board. Or sometimes a book might skip the Team Meeting step and go straight to Acq Board, which consists of me, the art director, the head of publicity and promotions, the associate publisher, and the publisher. We all read the text and leave written comments on a standardized form. Sometimes no further discussion is needed, and a project will get a yea or nay based on the feedback. More often than not, though, we have a meeting to discuss it, with the sponsoring editor present to answer questions and articulate their vision. There are three voting members of Acq Board: me, the associate publisher, and the publisher. Two out of three of us need to approve any acquisition. It's a fairly simple, streamlined procedure, and so far it's been working for us.

Other companies, particularly larger companies, may require more people to approve an acquisition, or require that all manuscripts be discussed in an acquisitions meeting. It is any wonder that this takes time?

PUBLISHER-INITIATED ACQUISITION

The third type of acquisition process is little known but common, widely used in library-oriented nonfiction and mass market publishing, but not unheard of elsewhere. In this process, the process of acquisition is kicked off by the publisher, who plans a title or series of titles internally, and then goes in search of a writer.

Eileen Robinson, formerly of Scholastic Library, led me through the steps involved from inception: "The process begins from the moment the editor has an idea or concept he or she wants to pursue; a book or series that will expand upon or add value to the publishing plan and continue to build upon the publisher's guiding principles while increasing revenue." The editor develops the idea, researches the competition and needs in the market, and discusses it in an editorial meeting. If others like the idea, work on a P&L follows, leading to a formal presentation: "the editor can now work with Creative (Design) to create a visual, a prototype of the possible covers and interior layouts for the book or series. The editor presents the full package (concept, supporting materials, i.e., curriculum information, articles or other material found during research, and competition) to the management team." Then the project is approved, and only then is an author or authors hired to write what the editor has planned.

The impetus for the acquisition comes from inside the publisher, in other words, but the manuscript is still brought in from outside. To work with a publisher using this process, a writer must have contacts and the ability to write to specifications and often to a very tight deadline, so it has its frustrations. They are not the same frustrations, of course, as a writer waiting to hear what an acquisition committee thinks of an already-completed manuscript.

WHY IS IT SO FRAUGHT?

Over and over again, on discussion boards, at conferences, and in e-mails, I hear from writers frustrated by the acquisitions process, writers usually experiencing the acquisition committee process. This frustration is not only felt by beginners, as this comment by Jane Yolen demonstrates:

The most frustrating thing from this writer's pov (and this has happened more times recently than I can count) is the editor who tells me how much she loves a manuscript, already has ideas for how to illustrate it, can't wait to get started with it, and one, two—even six months later—turns it down because she "can't get enough enthusiasm" from the rest of the troops. Give me back the Ursula days when she bought what she loved; she would tell them to find a way to sell the book. That was their job, after all.

Part of the reason why the process can be difficult and time-consuming is simply that it couldn't possibly be more important to publishers. As noted above, this is how publishers build their future, and they want to get it right. So publishers think, and debate, and then think some more.

As Alvina Ling notes, the committee tends to err on the side of caution: "My main frustration is that I think acquisition by committee results in more "safe" projects, and prevents the more risky or experimental books from getting signed up." That's not the whole story, though, because as Alvina goes on to say, the committee sometimes does take risks, and the publisher at Little, Brown, who has the final say, will from time to time agree to go ahead with a project that did not have unanimous support.

Caution isn't the only reason why acquisitions can take time. As Yolanda LeRoy points out, there are competing interests in play:

> Why can the acquisition process get contentious? Well, because for the most part people don't go into publishing unless they really, really care about books. And that means we are all rather opinionated. . . . I also think that there are necessary, inherent tensions in any publishing house. For example, editorial is not in charge of how a book is sold or promoted, yet we are judged on its financial success and want it to succeed because of our personal creative investment in the book. But achieving that success is largely out of our hands. On the flip side, marketing is stuck selling and promoting a product that they had very little to do with creating. So when a book does poorly, is it that "marketing didn't push it enough," as we in editorial would say, or is it that "editorial didn't deliver a saleable product"? Hence the tension. I think there are similar competing goals between design and production and even to some extent between design and editorial. But these conflicting interests and tensions are healthy and natural. It's what makes us question our choices or stand firm in our convictions.

And, I would add, when the process goes right, that's what leads to better books.

WHY EDITORS (SOMETIMES) LIKE THE PROCESS

In spite of the inherent difficulties and delays, the acquisition process gives an editor the opportunity to get the rest of the company, particularly sales and marketing, excited about and supportive of a book. Kate Harrison had this to say about her experiences before she came to Dial: "Acquisitions meetings are very good for some things, like getting sales excited about a promising project from the get-go, getting extra insight into the sales possibilities for a particular topic, or hearing a great illustrator idea for a picture-book manuscript." Alvina Ling of Little, Brown said something similar: "As I think we all know, in-house support and enthusiasm can be important to a project's success in the market. Decisions made by committee can mean that key people are already invested in the book's success." And so did Cheryl Klein, editor at Arthur A. Levine Books, Scholastic: "When I have a project I'm tremendously excited about, I actually really like the Acquisitions process, because it's my first chance to share the ms. with our sales and marketing staff and get them as excited as I am. Everyone brings their expertise to the table to figure out the best way to publish the book."

Regardless of whether or not one likes the way acquisitions are done at most children's publishers, the unavoidable reality is that they *are* done that way, and will continue to be for the foreseeable future. What to do, in these tough times? Listen to the words of wisdom of Judy O'Malley, independent editor: "In the current economic climate, when publishers are understandably cautious about acquiring books for which they can't expect strong initial sales, authors and their editors need to be particularly conscientious in developing the manuscript and building a strong case for a book before beginning the acquisitions process." Forewarned is forearmed, in other words. Know what to expect, and do what you can to make the process go as smoothly as possible.

RESOURCES

I've found surprisingly little information online or in print about the acquisitions process at children's publishers. Books by editors, including my *Complete Idiot's Guide to Publishing Children's Books*, or Olga Litowinsky's *It's a Bunny-Eat-Bunny* World, have some general information. Online, other than Alvina Ling's acquisitions stories, mentioned earlier, I know only of an article I wrote, which covers some of the same ground but with different details, at http://www.underdown.org/acquisition-process.htm. I'll add any others that I discover to that page.

What's in an Acquisition Proposal?

Some of the information included or attached:

- description of the book and rationale for publishing
- it planned specifications for the book, such as page count and trim size
- biography of the author
- same for the intended illustrator, if the book will be illustrated
- author's sales history, reviews of previous books
- a profit and loss (P&L) or budget statement for the book proposed
- contract terms the manuscript itself

For more details, see http://www.underdown.org/acquisition-proposal.htm

Read Some Case Studies

Alvina Ling of Little, Brown has posted some detailed accounts of particular acquisitions on her blogs.

- Her first acquisition: http://bloomabilities.blogspot.com/2006/06/do-you-remember-your-first.html
- A later one: http://bloomabilities.blogspot.com/2006/07/another-star.html
- A particularly complicated story: http://bluerosegirls.blogspot.com/2008/09/publication-story-of-wabi-sabi-part-one.html

For more, go to bloomabilities.blogspot.com, and on the right side towards the bottom, you will find links to posts about various books she's edited.

Social Networking

The Path to Cyber-Success

by Kelly Milner Halls

Even at its inception, the Internet held vast potential when it came to promoting good books. Jeff Bezos proved it in 1994 when he launched Amazon.com, the groundbreaking online bookstore, complete with a community of reader reviews. Carol Fitzgerald and Jesse Kornbluth unveiled The Bookreporter Network two years later in 1996. Like Amazon, it survived and is thriving still, today.

Can smaller, more specialized groups follow in their successful footsteps? Considering millions of bloggers compete for recognition everyday, the odds may be against it. But innovators learn to ignore the odds—and heat always, always rises.

Three smokin' hot examples are ReaderGirlz, Classof2k7 and ReadKiddoRead. Thanks to their unique points of view and sheer determination, these social networking experiments beat the odds and found a way to shine. But how did they do it?

We asked a representative from each site to share their secrets. Fantasy author, Dia Calhone stepped up for ReaderGirlz. Humor author Greg Fishbone spoke up for Classof2k7. And Ned Rust, a long-time associate of author James Patterson represents ReadKiddoRead. Study their strategies and you may be better prepared to blaze a social networking trail of your own.

Who came up with the idea and how did it come about?

Dia/ReaderGirlz: When Justina Chen Headley went on her book tour for *Nothing But the Truth (and a few white lies)* in 2006, she made a huge effort to include schools who couldn't afford author visits. The students were thrilled to see and speak with an author. They were eager, attentive, and asked the best questions. Justina went away thinking that there had to be a way to bring authors to teens regardless of the teens' location or socio-economic status. Very quickly she brainstormed the concept of readergirlz—the foremost innovative online book community where teen girls can discuss books directly with authors. The first task was to build a team of award-winning young adult authors, or divas, to begin the work.

Greg/Classof2K7: I woke up with the idea one morning in early 2006. I had my middle-grade children's novel, *The Penguins of Doom*, coming out in 2007 and I was becoming overwhelmed by how much publishers are relying on authors to help with marketing and

KELLY MILNER HALLS is a full-time freelance writer specializing in quirky nonfiction for young readers. Her books include *Saving the Baghdad Zoo* (Harpercollins/Greenwillow, 2009), *Dinosaur Parade* (Lark, 2008), *Tales of the Cryptids* (Darby Creek Publishing 2006) and *Albino Animals* (Darby Creek Publishing, 2004). Her new book, *In Search of Sasquatch* will be published in 2011 by Houghton Mifflin/Harcourt. She lives in Spokane, Washington with two dogs, too many cats and a four-foot iguana named Gigantor.

publicity, how much there is to learn, and how quickly it all has to come together. I figured there had to be other debut authors in a similar situation, and wouldn't' it be great if we could come together as a group and help each other? So I put out the word and within 48 hours we had enough interest to form a core group, the Class of 2k7.

Ned/ReadKiddoRead: James Patterson came up with the idea last year. At least partly, he relates, it was inspired by the experience of finding good summer books for his young son, Jack, to read.

What were your initial goals in forming the community?

Dia/ReaderGirlz: We had—and still have—three goals. We want teen girls to read, reflect, and reach out based on what they have read. So, we feature the best YA books in all different genres. To get girls to reflect, we've established the rgz Web site www.readergirlz.com which carries the monthly issue, including author information, a playlist, and book-party ideas. Then, the rgz MySpace Group Forum http://groups.myspace.com/readergirlz enables girls to chat with the featured author, other teens, and the rgz divas about the featured book. To encourage girls to reach out, we include a monthly related community service project at the rgz Web site and blog. http://readergirlz.blogspot.com

Greg/Classof2K7: We were looking to do things as a group that would be difficult or impossible for any of us to do on our own. It wouldn't be a replacement for our individual book efforts but an enhancement for us all. The focus of the Class of 2k7 was on the BLTs who help to put books into the hands of readers: Booksellers, Librarians, and Teachers. Our goal was to get their attention in an environment where we were all still new and unknown.

Ned/ReadKiddoRead: It seemed like a natural extension of the whole idea. When we set out to create the program, it was with the notion that here's James Patterson, this guy who knows a thing or two about books that people like, and it's almost as if we're talking to him over the back-yard fence about his insights into books that work. So starting the community seemed like a logical way to make that fence lower—and a way to accommodate even more people in the yard.

How did you decide which blog/community format would work best for your goals?

Dia/ReaderGirlz: Studies show that the majority of teen girls have online profiles. Currently, we have our major presence at Myspace and Facebook. MySpace offers the group forum for discussion threads and our live online chat, rgz LIVE! Our blog can be read at both MySpace www.myspace.com/readergirlz and BlogSpot http://readergirlz.blogspot.com This allows us to reach a wide audience which includes: teens, college students, librarians, teachers, booksellers, and mothers. We have added an exciting new YouTube presence called rgz TV to showcase interviews with authors as well as fun YA events.

Greg/Classof2K7: A group blog was something we thought would work well, because itwould have so much points of view, so much information, and could be updated frequently with just a little effort from any one individual. We also did a group Web site, group ezine, group brochure, group media releases, group social networking campaign, and group tour.

Ned/ReadKiddoRead: We'd been keeping our eye on Ning for some time and in fact we'd already created an online (separate) space for James's online fans with the service. We liked Ning because they offer all the important features—at least to us—of a Facebook or a MySpace, but it allows for more design flexibility and personalization. So, when people come to visit, it's more of a truly interest-centered community.

How long did it take from conception to launch?

Dia/ReaderGirlz: The four rgz co-founders: I, Dia Calhoun (*Avielle of Rhia*), Janet Lee Carey (*Dragon's Keep*), Lorie Ann Grover (*On Pointe*), and Justina Chen Headley (*North of Beautiful*) had our first meeting in November, 2006. We eagerly launched four months later, March, 2007, in honor of Women's History Month.

Greg/Classof2K7: The Class of 2k7 started forming in March of 2006 and closed membership in August. We had a soft launch in the fall followed by a hard launch in January 2007, and we ran our campaign through the 2007 calendar year. The Classes of 2k8 and 2k9 followed similar schedules.

Ned/ReadKiddoRead: About eight months. It would have been faster but we all have day jobs, unfortunately!

Who designed your logo? Did each of you have a responsibility of some kind?

Dia/ReaderGirlz: I designed our logo that we used during our first year at rgz. The cat tail art often seen with the original logo was drawn by Lorie Ann Grover. Her brother, Dale Leary (Prodigy, Strategic Marketing Advertising) created our first Web site homepage and nav bar. He then went on to design our current logo and Web site.

We now have five active divas. Justina Chen Headley is our visionary. Lorie Ann Grover operates as the program manager, Chief of Operations. Holly Cupala (A *Light that Never Goes Out*) is our graphic designer and manages our YouTube site. Melissa Walker is our primary blogger, and I act as the author liaison and logo designer.

The divas have essential help from Mitali Perkins (*Secret Keeper*), our rgz talent scout; Martha Brockenbrough, (*Things-That Make Us [Sic]*) our media specialist; and Sara Easterly (*Artlab: Fashion Studio*) our PR advisor. Karen Wennerstrom offers office work for the team, and Little Willow http://slayground.livejournal.com acts as our webdiva. Led by Little Willow, the postergirlz comprise our advisory board of five of the best kidlit bloggers: Jackie Parker http://interactivereader.blogspot.com, Miss Erin http://misserinmarie.blogspot. com, HipWriterMama http://hipwritermama.blogspot.com, and Shelf Elf http://shelfelf. wordpress.com. These women offer up recommended reads to accompany the featured novel of the month, and they keep the divas abreast of the season's must reads.

Greg/Classof2K7: The Class of 2k7 logo was designed by one of our members, Ruth McNally Barshaw, who also illustrates her own books and is a brilliant graphic artist. We were lucky that so many members of our group had talents and knowledge that could help us with our goals.

Ned/ReadKiddoRead: A longtime New York friend of James's, Frank Nicolo, designed the logo. There are several people involved in the project that James knows, and he brought in Judy Freeman who you may know is something of a resource unto herself! She's been fabulous in helping us find books as well as other people who believe in the mission of getting kids addicted to reading.

As to us each having a responsibility, there's no organization chart or anything like that. It's a new and pretty collaborative thing, so we're all just pulling together to make things work

When did you know, at what point did you realize, your experiment was in fact a success?

Dia/ReaderGirlz: Well, there are several measures of success. One is the response of girls whose lives we touch. "You girls make my heart SING. I love reading even more now since you girls have inspired me!!!" Our special literacy projects are solid measures. During 31 Flavorite Authors for Teens in October 2007, we hosted 31 authors, including Stephanie Meyer (*Twilight Series*). We had hundreds of girls around the world attend her chat, from

Saudi Arabia, to the Netherlands, to Argentina, to Korea. Afterward, one teen girl said: "Do you have any idea at all of how much I love you people? Monuments shall be erected in your honor!" Partnering with YALSA (Young Adult Library Services Association) and having vast publisher support is another wonderful encouragement to us. Winning a James Patterson PageTurner Grant was very validating along with being named a Great Web Site by ALSC (Association for Library Services to Children).

Greg/Classof2K7: I thought it was already a success early on when potential memberswould ask their editors whether they should join our group, and the editors already knew who we were. They were buzzing about us within the industry before we even had our Web site up!

Ned/ReadKiddoRead: Well we all immediately clicked with James's inspiring notion of creating a place where the very best books for this mission were highlighted from among the often daunting array of titles out there. As a parent or teacher (in a former life I taught high school English, so I can attest!), or librarian, you can walk into a store, or a library and are confronted with a dizzying array. I mean just looking at the online listings, there appear to be almost a million different books for kids for sale in today's world. It's just too much.

And of course what often is getting the most attention out there is just what's new and what the industry is putting resources into, so it's not always easy to uncover last year's—or last decade's—true try-em-and-love-em books. So this is a way to take a step back and give adults an easy, hassle-free way to find the absolutely right books for their kids.

How have you drawn more authors and readers into the program?

Dia/ReaderGirlz: First, I believe we've attracted membership and attention by remaining true to our mission to challenge girls to read, reflect, and reach out. We truly are a community service organization. That fact garners trust and respect from girls and librarians. Secondly, our special literacy projects bring new readers to rgz. When we celebrated YALSA's Teen Read Week in October 08, we presented Night Bites and hosted three different authors an evening. Genres were crossed, and the energetic experience brought in excited new members.

Greg/Classof2K7: We never had a problem attracting authors to the group. Our biggestproblem was having to turn them away after we were full. I hated writing those emails! I wanted to be all-inclusive, even if it meant having 50 authors or more, but the consensus of the group was that we should stay smaller, work harder, and be more effective that way. I've come to accept that the consensus of the group was right.

Ned/ReadKiddoRead: Well interest by folks like you certainly helps! Really, it's been a lot of word-of-mouth so far. We of course had a nice publicity boost from a piece that ran in *People* magazine as well as shout-outs from bloggers, school librarians, and others online.

How much traffic do you get on a good week, and on a bad week? A range is fine.

Dia/ReaderGirlz: To our Web site, a slower week brings in roughly 500 visits. During a strong week, we might have 1,600. We currently have over 8,500 members at our MySpace site.

Greg/Classof2K7: We never used Web site or blog traffic as a measure of effectiveness because we had a narrow target audience: the BLTs. If they were talking to us, or blogging about us, or subscribing to our ezine, or friending our MySpace page, our campaign was succeeding.

Ned/ReadKiddoRead: Our traffic has been about doubling every month so far. In terms of actual people at the community and Web site, we're up to 20,000 people for December according what I believe is a pretty conservative estimate. Our best week by this measure saw 6,500 people (unique visitors) in a given week. Last week—which was a little slow due to the holiday and people being away from the computer—had about half that, but it looks like it's picking back up now that people are back in their routine. Little secret of web usage we've discovered is that people do a lot of their surfing at work!

What has been the most fruitful "event" to date?

Dia/ReadersGirlz: I think we are most proud of Operation Teen Book Drop (TBD 08) in which we partnered with YALSA to celebrate their Support Teen Literature Day. We solicited new YA books from 21 publishers which were distributed to over 10,000 teen patients in pediatric hospitals across the country. We hope to repeat the effort in '09 and 2010.

Greg/Classof2K7: We put together some great bookstore events and panels for SCBWI conferences, but our strength was being able to present ourselves online as a big united group. Our members were spread all over the country, so it was harder to get more than a few in one place at the same time.

Ned/ReadKiddoRead: We've had a number of them. That *People* article was a great send-off for the site, but we've also had great success with posting interviews with Julie Andrews, Jeff Kinney, Rick Riordan, and other authors, as well as just getting the word out through some print and online ads we've run.

Were there any surprises, good or bad, in this endeavor?

Dia/ReaderGirlz: I think each diva, founding and current, has been surprised by both the time commitment that readergirlz requires and by the huge amount of satisfaction that comes from doing such major philanthropic work.

Greg/Classof2K7: The first surprise was that nobody had done something quite like thisbefore. The second surprise was that the Class of 2k8 could build so successfully on what we accomplished and have such a great year of their own. And the third surprise is how many other authors and illustrators have been inspired to start similar groups based ondifferent genres or themes, or targeting readers as well as the BLTs. It's like we threw the first snowball off the mountain, and now it's become an avalanche.

Ned/ReadKiddoRead: So far I'd say they've all been on the positive side and, for me, the biggest surprise has just been the enthusiasm people have shown in the project. I mean from Carl Hiaasen to Lemony Snicket to publishers and booksellers, it's been a true wellspring of interest. I realize I'm in danger of earning myself brown-nose points here, but it seems to me that James, the guy who came up with the "I'm a Toys R Us Kid" slogan has once again put his finger on something that resonates out there: people have a great desire to get their kids reading. And offering them a fun—and *easy*—way to do it, is something that just makes sense.

What's next for your group?

Dia/ReaderGirlz: Our newest exciting component is the rgz Salon, where prominent experts of the YA lit community, including Nancy Pearl, Judy Nelson, Rene Kirkpatrick, and Sharon Levin, will be sharing their reviews of YA Lit at our blog.

Greg/Classof2K7: As I'm writing this in December 2008, the Class of 2k9 just launchedtheir Web site and have some very ambitious plans underway. It looks like another great year for debut middle-grade and YA fiction.

Ned/ReadKiddoRead: Hopefully more of the same! Retailers, schools, libraries, volunteer groups and others have been showing a lot of interest in the program and I think it would be great if we one day took James's notion out of the strictly electronic space and planted a foot or two in the "dirt" world. Just what that foot will look like... well, you'd better read the e-newsletters. We'll be sure to let you know as soon as anything happens!

Articles

Can we expect any spin off groups?

ia/ReaderGirlz: In December, 2008, Lorie Ann Grover and Joan Holub (*Knuckleheads*) started readertotz (http://readertotz.blogspot.com), a blog devoted to raising the profile of infant-toddler books. We count GuysLitWire (http://guyslitwire.blogspot.com) our brother site and direct male readers there. We have a charge out to the kidlit world for other authors to begin readerkidz!

Greg/Classof2K7: We've been talking for a while about forming a 2k Classes umbrella group to conduct "alumni outreach" from the previous three classes and serve as an incubator for future groups starting with the Class of 2k10. At this point we're known in the industry, we have connections with the BLTs, and we've refined the year-long campaign format, so it makes sense to not have to reinvent the wheel with every new class.

Ned/ReadKiddoRead: Well, for that, I'd just keep an eye on the community. It's a people-driven thing so I think you'll see groups getting together (as they've already begun to) and pursuing the interests that spin-off best for them.

What advice would you offer other writers hoping to launch a reader outreach online?

Dia/ReaderGirlz: Be prepared to give a great deal of your time! Be as organized and professional as possible from the beginning. Consider constructing a team. And then be prepared to make enduring friendships with the people you choose to work with. That has certainly been one of the most rewarding parts of readergirlz for me.

Greg/Classof2K7: Go for it. The online tools are available, most are free or low-cost, and they get better and more effective every year.

Ned/ReadKiddoRead: Just to drop us a line! We'd love to collaborate with anybody looking to spread the joy and excitement of books.

Book Promotion

From Blog Tours to Book Trailer

by Tina Nichols Coury

Back in the fall of 2006, I used my computer for e-mail and word processing. That was about it. I had heard of blogs, but I was Internet challenged. The thought of learning more technology was about as appealing as a root canal. It also wasn't my intention to add even more work to my very busy life. But during a lunch with my then editor from Dutton, Mark McVeigh, after much discussion about rewrites, my next book and the writing life, his last words to me were, "Start a blog."

Being the dutiful author, I immediately investigated my options. Lucky for me, I was already a longtime member of the SCBWI (Society of Children's Book Writers and Illustrators), and in January 2007 my local chapter offered a weekend retreat centering on promotion. One of the workshops was on blogs. Little did I know then that becoming a blogger would enrich my life through new friendships, make me part of a newfound community, and provide a professional stage to promote my work.

WHAT IS A BLOG?

The word blog comes from the longer term, "web log." To put it simply, a blog is an interactive Web site, and more user-friendly and accessible than a traditional Web site. Blogs have morphed over the years from chatty teenage Web pages to serious venues for news and information. You can discuss important social issues or find the best recipe for cheesecake by surfing the blogs. Many blogs allow readers to leave comments. If you are a children's book author or illustrator, a blog is an important tool in your promotional cyber arsenal. Many authors are daunted by the thought of yet another Web site to maintain, possibly on a daily basis. But not all blogs are alike. It is important to recognize that you can create a blog to fit your style, professional needs and time constraints.

WHAT KIND OF BLOGS ARE THERE?

My blog is a full-time job that finds me a writing tri-weekly column with interviews, writing tips and news regarding the SCBWI. Some authors post to their blog every day, with comments from readers creating the topic of discussion for the next day. Some well known authors offer a once a month commentary on their blogs. Other blogs are hosted by editors, who discuss

---

TINA NICHOLS COURY is blogger, children's book author, artist, illustrator, muralist and all around renaissance woman, as well as a longtime member of the SCBWI and a contributor to the regional newsletter. Her first picture book, *Hanging Off Jefferson's Nose: Growing up on Mount Rushmore,* is scheduled for release by Dutton in the spring of 2011, in time for the 70th anniversary of Mount Rushmore. You can surf Tina's popular children's lit blog, Tales from the Rushmore Kid at www. tinanicholscouryblog.com.

everything from slush piles to their favorite books.

Many free sites are available to start your blog, such as Blogspot, Livejournal and Blogger. I opted to use Typepad, which is a fee-based blog site. As an artist, I was drawn to the greater number of options in type color, style and pages of posts. Also, I can write my articles in advance to be posted on a specific date. While a fee-based option is not necessary for everyone, I find it useful, and the cost is minimal, around $10 a month.

WHAT CAN I WRITE ABOUT?

Content is king. No longer will musing about your day and jotting general thoughts about children's books suffice. Step outside the box to create a niche for your blog. If your new book takes place at a county fair with apple pies you can start a kid's lit and apple pie blog.

When I first started my blog I wanted to promote my new book on the building of Mount Rushmore. The focus of my blog is Mount Rushmore, art, and children's books. My critique group partner, Barbara Bietz, wrote a middle grade novel set during Hanukah. She chose to focus her blog (http://barbarabbookblog.blogspot.com) on Jewish books for children. My friend Greg Pincus blogs about Fibonacci poetry on his blog, Gottabook, (http://gottabook. blogspot.com), and through his blog he landed a book deal with Arthur A. Levine books.

Another option is to participate in a group blog like I.N.K. (http://inkrethink. blogspot.com) Interesting Non-Fiction for Kids, or Shrinking Violets Promotion (http:// shrinkingvioletpromotions.blogspot.com) specializing in children's book marketing for introverts.

If you are on the fence about taking the blogger plunge, you can still be active in the blog community by reading blogs and sharing your comments. Familiarize yourself with children's literature blogs and kidlit networks like Jacketflap and Kidslitosphere.Choose several that resonate with you, and join the community.

The reality of publishing in children's literature is that unless you are well established or a Newbery winner, money for marketing and promotion is limited. A publishing house will typically provide support for one year: six months before a book comes out and six months after. Promoting your book is mostly your own responsibility, especially beyond that one-year window. Proactive authors will have their promotional ducks in a row long before their book comes out. One possibility is a blog tour.

BLOG TOURS

There are several variations of blog tours. Group blog tours include a number of authors and can be fun and synergistic. But at the release of your book, try to do a solo tour. This can be as simple as posting four interviews in one month on different blogs. A more extensive tour might include twice as many interviews over twice as many months.

Some publishing houses favor a one-week blog tour, promoting your book on five different blogs every day during the week your book comes out. This creates a splash and is usually set up by the publicity department of your publishing house. But with some careful planning, an author can set up his or her own blog tour.

HOW DO I FIND BLOGS FOR MY TOUR?

The publicity department of your house might have blogs to suggest for your tour. Through your own research and networking you can add your own venues. Send an e-mail to the blog host requesting him or her to be part of the tour for a specific week. Include all the information regarding the book, including the publisher, publicity department contact, reviews and a link to your Web site. Arrange your blog tour two to three months before the book is released. Ask your author friends about their favorite blogs or network at SCBWI events to find some. I have been asked to host many blog tours. My only criterion is that I don't host blog tours or interviews for self-published books. Most serious KidLit blogs have a similar policy.

HOW DO I PREPARE FOR A BLOG TOUR?

Have your e-mail press packet ready to send, including JPEG head shots, one in black and white and one in color; a short biography; links to your Web site and your publisher's contact person; a JPEG of the cover of the book, and a short interview, around 500 words. Some bloggers may choose to send you their own interview questions. Where it is applicable, you can add the contact at the publicity department of your house who can send the book to blog reviewers. Be sure to send a follow-up thank you to all your blog hosts.

THE SUPER BLOG TOUR

When I arrange blog tours, I prefer to stretch them over a two-month period of time, with seven to eight postings. The key is to make each post different so you are not sending out the same interview over and over. The order is not essential, but here is an example of how I might break down the Super Blog Tour:

- Week one: Book trailer
- Week two: Interview
- Week three: Podcast interview
- Week four: Interview with book editor
- Week five: Interview with book illustrator or cover artist
- Week six: Reviews of the book
- Week seven: Interview with the art director
- Week eight: Book launch coverage

Week one: Book trailer

You might opt to spend some of your own money to invest in a professional book trailer created by a company that specializes in creating video trailers. Your publishing house can recommend one, but if you have a knack and the proper equipment, you can produce one yourself. If you are already published, create a different trailer for each of your books. Multiple books in one trailer tend to muck up the look and the message.

A book trailer should be from 30-90 seconds long. Longer trailers risk losing the attention of the viewer. A book trailer should be a tease, not the whole text of the book. The trailer should begin and end with a photo of the book cover. It should include a credit page with the ISBN number, publishing house and Web site links. If you use music, it has to be royalty free. You cannot legally use established songs unless you pay a fee. There are Web sites that specialize in royalty free music, such as Music Bakery, Royalty Free Music.com, and Beatsuite, to name a few.

Week two: Interview

In advance, you have sent out your e-mail press packet. Ask your interviewers if they want you to supply the interview questions or if they want to send out their own questions. When I host an author or illustrator on my blog, I like to use my own questions since I use the same format for every interview—including my famous last question, "What is your favorite dessert?" If a blogger has specific questions, give him or her a deadline for supplying them to you so you have time to answer them thoughtfully. Let them know the approximate date you would like the interview to be posted and send them a reminder a week before the posting.

Week three: Podcasting

Podcasting blogs are easy to find and can be done over the phone. You can ask your house's publicity department or you can just Google Kid's Lit podcasting. Some podcasters send you their questions in advance so your answers are clear and precise. Others want a spur of the moment, spontaneous interview. You can prepare for that by having water handy for a quick sip and remembering to slow down and articulate your responses. Be sure to have a list of talking points in front of you. Again, before the podcast is posted, send out your e-mail press kit. Give your host the approximate date you'd like to have the interview posted and send them a reminder a week before the posting.

Week four: Interview with the editor

Many bloggers are eager to do editor interviews. Editors and art directors now have to go through the publicity department for any blog interviews. Be sure you go through proper channels and make sure your editor is willing to be interviewed before you commit to a blogger. Let the interviewer know you want the discussion to be about your book.

Week five: Interview with the illustrator or cover artist

An illustrator blog might be good for this interview. For picture books and middle grade novels, the blogger can talk about the art. For YA books, the cover artist can discuss what inspired them to create the powerful cover. In advance, send out your e-mail press kit. Give the blog host a deadline for the questions and the approximate date you'd like the interview to be posted. Send a reminder a week before the posting.

Week six: Book review

If a review is available online, you can announce it on your blog and direct your readers to the site. You also can send the book out in advance and ask librarians to review it for your blog. If you have done your research you will see which blogs do book reviews. Your publicity department will have some reviewers they use. Also, kid lit bloggers review on Amazon. Make sure you request your publicity department to send out the book for reviews.

Week seven: Art director interview

Art Directors are also an interest to many readers of blogs. You can conduct your interview with the art director, highlighting your book. Then offer it up to one of the blog sites that you haven't used for the blog tour. Since you are doing the interview you can ask about the art in your book, then you can expand to general art director questions, like "How did you get into children's publishing?" "What do you look for in a portfolio?" "Do you use first time illustrators?" In advance, send out your e-mail press packet with information about the art director and the approximate date you'd like the interview to be posted. Send a reminder a week before the posting.

Week eight: Book launch

A book launch is like a birthday party for your book. Call in friends and family to help make this a memorable event, with food and games for the kids. Notify local newspapers. Have your event at a local bookstore or library. A weekend afternoon party works the best, but no longer than two to three hours. Do a reading or make your picture book into a play and have audience members act it out. Puppets are great for a young picture book crowd. Designate a photographer and set up in advance with a local kid lit blogger to cover the event. Every time a photo is taken of you, hold up the book in the picture. But most of all, enjoy this day. You've worked hard for it.

WORKING THE BLOG TOUR

It is important that every week of the tour you send out announcement e-mails to authors, schools, librarians and your editor, art director and house publicity. Because the tour is spread out and varied, people won't mind looking at it every week. Spend a small amount of money to announce the blog tour through a public relations web company, like www.prweb. com. These companies will send your press release to newspapers nationwide. On your own blog, announce the tour's progress every week and provide links. Also, have a category on your blog that is just for the tour. You can also put your book trailer in the side column of your blog where readers can easily access it. These tips will help you gain a good following so your promotional efforts will pay off.

Tina's Top Promo Tips

- **Join SCBWI.** If you are already a member, get more active. This organization provides a wealth of information and is filled with generous souls. Attend every SCBWI event that you can, including the national conference in Los Angeles every August. It is the major event for our industry. The networking and workshops are invaluable.

- **Continue to learn the craft of writing:** Take more classes. We can all benefit from the growth a class offers. The stronger your work, the more books you will sell.

- **Adopt a school in need.** Set up e-mail chats with students. Hold a book drive for their school library. You will become known in your community and feel good about giving back.

- **Continue to expand your web presence.** Comment on blogs. Join MySpace, Facebook and Kidlit blogger sites. Cruise YouTube book trailer sites. Every month watch 10 book trailers and vote for The New Covey Book Trailer Awards, http:// thenewcoveytrailerawards.blogspot.com. Six months after your blog tour, make another book trailer and promote it. You can have more than one trailer.

- **Read, read, and read.** Read the Newbery and Caldecott winners and honor books every year. Read the Golden Kite winners, the National Book Award winner and nominees, and the Printz winner and honor books. Not only will it keep you in the loop about your competition, you'll be able to see how an award-winning book is promoted. Vote for the Cybils, http://dadtalk.typepad.com/cybils (the children's and young adult blogger literary awards.)

- **Know what is going on in children's publishing.** Subscribe online to *Publishers Weekly*. Sign up for the PW Daily newsletter for daily update on the industry, and PW Children's Bookshelf which is send out every Thursday and is devoted to children's publishing. The opportunities for promotion and marketing are ever changing and it's important to keep informed of new options.

- **Do as many school visits as possible.** Through networking with the SCBWI you will find many authors who will recommend you to different schools.

- **Become a local celebrity.** Have professional photographs taken of you in black and white and in color. The photos should be headshots with plain backgrounds. Don't wear any flashy jewelry that tends to stand out in a photo. Have a hard copy press packet ready to send out. Get in touch with your local papers and TV stations. Do book signings at local charity events.

- **Expand your e-mail list for promotions.** At book fair, raffle away your books and request e-mail information from individuals who enter the raffle.

- **Enjoy your journey.** A happy person is a magnet for success.

Rachel Cohn

Queen of Teen Lit

Photo: Taylor Hooper Photography

by Aaron Hartzler

Seven years ago Rachel Cohn was profiled in the pages of the *Children's Writer's & Illustrator's Market* as a brand new author who was hanging onto her day job while her first book *Gingerbread* made its debut. Since that time Cohn has established herself as one of the most prominent, prolific, and respected voices in literature for young adults.

"Rachel's writing is like that one song you want to put on every mix CD to every person you know," said David Levithan, Executive Editorial Director at Scholastic Press. "It means something really special to you, but you also know that other people will love it and get it, too."

And Levithan would know. Two of Rachel's nine books have been co-written with him, and last fall, their first team effort, *Nick & Norah's Infinite Playlist* became a major motion picture, and a box-office success.

When we caught up with her, Cohn informed us that she has, indeed, officially quit her day job.

Did you have any idea when *Gingerbread* was published that this is where'd you be seven years later?

No, no. I wish I had a big master plan for how it's all going to go, but I'm still making it up as I go along. Everything that happens is a big surprise, success or otherwise.

Had you planned a series about Cyd Charisse when you sold *Gingerbread*?

No, I did not plan a series at all, and you know the publisher had very low expectations for that book. They only printed like 6,000 copies in the first printing—even they didn't expect anything. I think how well the book did was as big a surprise to them as to me. Sometimes I was surprised that it did so well, because, it seemed to me it was just littered with in-jokes to my friends. So when other people got it I was like, "What?!"

Is there one piece of advice that might have made your path easier if you'd heard it seven years ago?

There's *so* much. First of all, have a really good agent, and have very realistic expectations. Be prepared to do a lot on your own separate from the publisher in terms of online marketing and stuff like that.

AARON HARTZLER is a writer, and the Director of Communications at the Society of Children's Book Writers & Illustrators in Los Angeles.

So, keep your expectations low?

No, don't have *low* expectations—have *realistic* expectations; that's an important distinction. People have this image that in order to be a success you have to have a huge marketing and publicity campaign, and that you have to get a huge advance, and that you have to go get sent on a tour, and be mentioned in every newspaper or magazine, and not all of those things are realistic, especially in teen publishing.

You can get a big launch, but in the end, the books that are going to do the best sales-wise are really going to be developed by word of mouth. So, you really want to have the most grass-roots approach you can. A publisher can put out a ton of money and they can put out no money, and you'll see two books come from opposite ends of that spectrum and do equally well. The bottom line is that when a book does well it is really because of word of mouth, not necessarily the big marketing campaign.

People just have such a romanticized vision of how it's going to work. When it actually happens it can feel a little bit anti-climactic, which is so hard on everything you went through to get there. You want to be able to cherish that journey, but have realistic expectations for how it's all going to work out.

What's your best recommendation to writers on staying realistic as they pursue publication?

Have a really open and honest dialogue with your agent. How can you know what to expect if you've never been through it before? Don't put off hard conversations because you think you might get an answer you don't like.

Ask your agent what you need to do for yourself in order to make that next leap. What can I do on my own and what can I expect? Also ask "What are good numbers?" Most books just don't sell a lot of copies, and it's hard to understand what "good" is. Quite honestly, in Young Adult hardcover, if you sell 20,000 copies that's considered really good.

Your first and last tip to writers at your Web site is "Read!" What do you recommend?

A lot of books inspire me. I love *A Confederacy* of Dunces by John Kennedy Toole. I love anything by Dawn Powell. Ellen Gilchrist was a big influence. When I first started writing kids books I didn't really know what I was doing, I was kind of going from what I thought I remembered, and if there's any model for that, it's Judy Blume. It all begins and ends with her.

You wrote adult fiction first. Did you shop that around and not have success with it?

Yes, I had written two adult books that made it all the way to the editorial board and then were rejected. Then, I'd written a third book called The Steps, which eventually did get published, but initially was rejected. I kept getting told how I wrote "whiny narrators," which really pissed the f--- out of me. Finally, I was really depressed, and I thought, "Well, it's never going to work out for me to be a writer, so I'm just not going to worry about it anymore because nobody wants my books. I'm going to write the whiniest protagonist I can imagine because 'Who cares?'" So I started writing a book that I really considered to be unpublishable, just for my own pleasure. That was Gingerbread, and if it wasn't for a Nick & Norah movie, that would probably still be the book of mine that sold the most copies.

You've achieved a certain amount of success, obviously, and you've also written for quite a long time—over a decade.

(Laughing) Yes! And I'm only 19! I started really young.

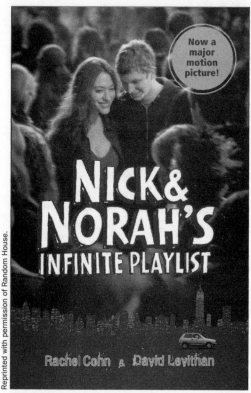

Reprinted with permission of Random House.

Nick & Norah's Infinite Playlist, by Rachel Cohn and David Levithan (Knopf, 2008) was made into a major motion picture in 2008.

Do you think that success or experience has had more of an effect on your writing?

Both. Success in the sense that what is considered to be success hinders me at times. I feel intimidated by success and it's very hard to work against that. I think "Nobody else will like anything that I do." So, there's a lot of fear that comes along with success for me. You think that it will get easier, but for me, it actually gets harder with each book, because you're working against an accumulated expectation. That's hard on your psyche.

Experience is helpful because it will sort of off-set the fear. You begin to have enough experience to know that you've been through this before, and you'll get through it this time. You get better each time. The more you work it, the more you develop that muscle.

What's the one question that you get from aspiring writers the most?

"How do I get published?" which I think sort of misses the point, because the answer is, "Develop your craft and take your time."

Be the best writer that you can be. Don't think that just because you have a good idea you're ready to have a book published. It takes a lot more than that. You need to polish your words and your story and your characters, and treat it like a craft, not like a money-making or fame-getting endeavor.

I am very grateful now for those unpublished books because they were a really good learning curve. If I had known that they were a learning curve at the time I was struggling through writing them, I would have been apoplectic, but in retrospect I'm really glad to have had that really private learning time. Quite honestly, they're not very good. They're good concepts—I have always been big on ideas—but I was bad on execution back then.

Do you ever go back to those manuscripts and think about retooling them?

The book I'm writing now was initially a re-do of the very first book I ever wrote, but what I found out was that I couldn't recreate the voice I had so long ago. My voice has changed so much I couldn't replicate it.

When I started revisiting it, a part of me thought, "When I reach a certain point, I'll just take out the old book and insert it." But now the new characters have all taken on lives of their own, so there's no copy and paste; none whatsoever. I'm writing a whole book from scratch, and that's wonderful. And while the idea that I could somehow take this book out of a box and re-do it failed, the premise of it was so good that it would have been a shame not to use it in some way. I'm glad to be doing that.

Speaking of voice, do you ever feel stuck, voice-wise?

No, voice is the one thing that comes to me very naturally. If I feel stuck it usually has to do more with plot points and stuff like that. For better or for worse, voice is the one part that comes really easily for me. (Laughing) Of course, sometimes it can be for the worse. I can just go off on a stream of consciousness tangent forever, and it's just this person talking, but you're really going nowhere. Voice is the one thing that I get the most positive feedback about, but it's also the thing that can twist me into circles.

Do you think voice is something that can be taught?

No, and that's the other "number one question" that I get. When it's not about the business it's "How do you write a voice?" Voice is just something that you can't quantify or qualify in any way. It is a totally ephemeral thing. You know it when you see it, but can you explain it? Not really.

For me, especially when you're talking about writing voices for teens, it's really

Very LeFreak is celebrated author Rachel Cohn's latest novel (releasing from Knopf in 2010).

about making the narrator sound like a very recognizable personality. It's about assembling the words so that when you read them you see that character.

I think the best thing you can do is study voice. Get recommendations for books that have "really powerful voice" and read them. Try to really dissect when voice was at play. When was it really strong? When did you really connect to something? Try to analyze it that way. It's really the only way to learn or absorb voice that's ever worked successfully when I've taught.

How do you describe the work that you've put out over the past seven years?

Fun and funny…(laughs) with one notable exception. It's always my goal to deal with teen voices and lives with respect and humor. Any book that I write is a book that I would have wanted to read as a teen.

Do you have specific advice to adult writers who might be starting their first book for a young adult audience?

Whatever your first 50 pages are, toss them. Just start on page 51. That's probably where you're supposed to start for teens. Cut. It. Down. I think that YA books are the very same books as adult books. They deal with the same themes; everything's the same, except for two things: The characters tend to be teenagers, and they say everything they have to say in half the time.

Above all, write from your heart and don't worry about anything else. Write the story you want to tell. Don't try to write for the market or what you think is a trend. It never works. The best, best, best books always come from the story you really want to tell.

Sara Varon

Telling Stories Picture by Picture

by Erzsi Deàk

Comic and picture book creator Sara Varon chooses her words carefully. For the author of *Chicken and Cat*, *Robot Dreams*, *Chicken and Cat Clean Up* and the earlier *Sweaterweather*, it's the images that light her imagination, get the story flowing. Words are details included within the illustrations, whether comics or picture books. As Varon notes: "I think I do the wordless stories best. I am working on a story now that has words, and I think the wordless sections are better. But as stories become more complicated, at some point, you need words."

Her reading public might agree. Recently, there's been much discussion about wordless books—are they easier to read than books with words, are they for younger or older audiences? These questions amuse Varon. "Here's something I hear *all* the time and I think it's *so* weird: People say, 'Oh, your books are great because kids can look at the pictures and make up their own stories!' But I totally don't get it, because the story is already there! Maybe they mean that kids can articulate the stories? I haven't quite figured this out. Or maybe they are getting something out of my books that I didn't anticipate? But I do think a lot of people are kind of freaked out by picture-stories. Or they look at them and immediately think they are for children. Maybe a cultural bias, I guess, because Americans associate comics with kids."

But whether a comic book or a picture book, these seemingly simple stories are quite complicated when examined closely. Robot and Dog in *Robot Dreams* are friends, but in addition to an entertaining premise (in the vein of mail order brides, Dog orders a robot kit to build a robot friend), there's a great deal of angst and sorrow. As one reader, Eva Volin (http://www.schoollibraryjournal.com/blog/540000654.html) writes, "*Robot Dreams* is a beautiful book and can be read on many different levels. I do think a 6-year-old can read *Robot Dreams* and come away satisfied. I think a 16-year-old will be more satisfied. I think a 36-year-old will be even more satisfied. This makes it a true all-ages title."

So who was Varon creating for when she made Robot Dreams?

"I *love* that quote! I really wanted my book to be for everyone, and in a way, it makes me sad to see it limited to the kids' shelf. I'm pleased that a 6-year-old can enjoy it, but I also think some things are lost. So I am grateful for her recognition that people of different ages

ERZSI DEÀK, a journalist for more than 30 years, has covered fashion and children's features from Alaska to San Francisco to Paris. She has tramped the Alaska Pipeline looking for environmental problems, worked as a camp counselor managing the craft hut, and always as a writer. Her writing has appeared in a number of anthologies and her book, *Period Pieces: Stories for Girls*, edited with Kristin Litchman (HarperCollins, 2003), was named to the 2004 Bank Street Best Books List (starred) and the NYPL Women in Books for the Teenage. Erzsi lives in Paris, France, with her husband, 2-3 of her 3 daughters (depending on the season), and their dog, Bingley. Visit her at: www.ErzsiDeak.com.

will bring different life experiences to the story. Also, I like the idea that it can be a bridge between parents and teens. Honestly, though, I didn't much think about my audience when I was making it—I just made something I liked, so in a way, I was my intended audience . . . I do always like things that are all-ages, and I think it's something to aspire to. I like that about *The Simpsons*, and about shows like *Rocky and Bullwinkle.* In fact, I was recently watching *Tennessee Tuxedo*, which I was pleased to purchase. I loved it as a kid, but watching it now, I realize I must have missed so much! Like in one episode, a tiger comes to stay at the zoo, and he is a punch-drunk former boxer. The character is hilarious. I'm sure he must have been a reference to a popular boxer from the time it was made, but a 5-year-old would never get that. However, as a 5-year-old, I just liked watching the funny talking animals."

FINDING INSPIRATION

Varon often cites that she's from Brooklyn-via-Chicago and loves dogs and chickens. (Her Web site is www.chickenopolis.com, as just one outlet for this fowl obsession).

"In a way, I am not very creative, so I just include the things I see everyday. And now that I live in Brooklyn, Brooklyn really figures into my books. Like, if I can't think of a background, I just go to the corner of my block and draw what's there. Or I go to a favorite place and draw that...I think it's fun for readers to look at a picture and think, 'Hey, I know that place!' Like Central Park, in *Chicken and Cat*. It might help people to identify with the story, and also, I just think it's funny to put fictional characters in a non-fictional setting."

And who and/or what (else) has influenced her in her work and style? "Certainly the cartoons of my youth," says Varon. "I loved all Jay Ward cartoons (OK, maybe not Dudley Do-Right; he was a little tedious, but certainly Rocky and Bullwinkle, Underdog and Tooter Turtle, etc). Also, I was really influenced by *Sesame Street*. I liked the puppets but I also loved the short animated segment they'd show in-between longer scenes of the puppets. And I love stories. Anything that tells a good story. I read more novels than picture books/graphic novels these days, but it's exciting when I find a graphic novel that tells a story in a new way. When I first started doing comics around 2000, I was really impressed by Craig Thompson's comics. Books that have impressed me more recently are the graphic novels *Aya* (Drawn and Quarterly) and *Skim* (Groundwood Books)."

Both *Aya* and *Skim* are night and day different from Varon's own work. Her straightforward, yet whimsical, drawing style is a combination of sophisticated *New Yorker* magazine spot art and expressive quiet charm. Her simple brush and ink work combined with flat colors, as she says, "automatically makes something look young and comic-booky."

When Varon starts a project, she thinks of scene or a character she wants to draw and then of other things she likes to draw and connects them. In *Sweaterweather* she managed to connect a pie-eating contest to a pawn shop and of her upcoming title from First Second, *Bakesale*, she says, "I tried to fit in a bunch of things that I like. I love baking (and drawing baked goods) and traveling, so the book is about a cupcake who works in a bakery and dreams of traveling abroad to meet a foreign pastry."

Unlike Joann Sfar, the prolific French comics creator whose Little Vampire and Rabbi's Cat collections (both published by First Second) are making a splash in the U.S., Varon says she doesn't have a ton of ideas. But book-by-book, her work is building a strong following of readers of all ages—and with the recent publication of *Robot Dreams* in France, across oceans. "I don't do more than a book a year, so if I only have one idea a year, it's fine. It's not a fast process for me. I have to spend a lot of time thinking about these characters and let them stew in my head."

PICTURE BOOKS VS. COMICS

Whether an idea for a picture book or a comic comes to her while she's out jogging where "there are no other distractions," Varon sees the difference between comics and picture books as basically a matter of panels. "They are similar," she says, "except that picture books have one picture per page, and comics have many. In the beginning, my stories were simple, and I could tell a story in, say, 40 individual pictures. But after working on long projects, I find it very difficult to come up with a story and distill it into 40 single and simple drawings. I had a tough time with *Chicken and Cat Clean Up*. (Mostly out of laziness) I wanted it to be 32 pages, but I couldn't get it down past 48. I hope to be able to get back there though, to be able to tell a simple story."

No matter the page length, so far, Sara Varon is doing something right. Both *Robot Dreams* and *Chicken and Cat* are multi-award-winners and future projects on the horizon include *Bakesale* and a book called *Odd Duck*, which is her first collaboration. Written by Cecil Castelluci, *Odd Duck* a funny story about an uptight duck and her friend. For *Odd Duck*, says Varon, "the format is different, too, and it has lots of copy, so that will be a fun experiment for me." (Both books, First Second.)

When not working on her picture books and comics, Varon works in the print shop at the School of Visual Arts in New York and for an amateur boxing tournament sponsored by a New York City newspaper. "You asked what I find inspiring, and I think my jobs are inspirational. I really like being around all different kinds of people, just living their lives. There are so many stories, and I think they give me fuel for my work."

Interior illustration from Sara Varon's *Chicken and Cat Clean Up* (Scholastic Press, 2009), the sequel to *Chicken and Cat* (Scholastic Press, 2006).

Interviews

Interior illustration from *Chicken and Cat Clean Up* (Scholastic Press, 2009), Sara Varon's wordless picture book in which Chicken hires Cat to help out with his housekeeping business causing a strain on their friendship.

Q&A with Editor Jennifer Rees

Jennifer Rees got her start in children's books as a children's bookseller at Joseph-Beth Booksellers in Cincinnati. Since then, she's found great joy in working as an editor at Scholastic Press, where she acquires and edits fiction and nonfiction picture books, middle grade and YA novels. A sampling of the projects she's edited include *Looking for Miza*, by Craig Hatkoff; *Jibberwillies at Night*, by Rachel Vail and Yumi Heo; *Chicken and Cat Clean Up*, by Sara Varon; *Sunny Holiday*, by Coleen Murtagh Paratore; *11 Birthdays*, by Wendy Mass; *Purge*, by Sarah Darer Littman; and *The Hunger Games*, by Suzanne Collins.

What was it that hooked you when you saw Sara Varon's bound art school version of *Chicken and Cat*?

I simply fell in love—head over heels!—with the characters. They were distinctive, fresh, charming, and felt sweet without being sentimental or cutesy. I noticed right away (without really knowing her comics background at that point) that Sara had a wonderful knack for storytelling. The details in the illustrations were irresistible—you couldn't help but want to find out what happened next—and it all helped to tell a compelling, satisfying story.

We know that *Chicken and Cat* started out with a good amount of text and ended up nearly wordless. Yet you seem to be a word person. Once it was set that the book would be nearly wordless, was it a challenge to edit?

Sara and I struggled quite a bit with the text because, even from the very beginning, the text seemed redundant. No matter how we changed the manuscript, the words repeated what the illustrations were already telling us. We tried a million different ways to edit the text, and Sara and I were both extremely frustrated. It took us a long time, but finally a light bulb went off and we removed the text completely. The book read beautifully on its own, and from that point on *Chicken and Cat* was a dream to edit because I was working with what Sara does best: telling a story through her illustration. It was clear this book was asking to be wordless from the very beginning, only we hadn't quite realized that until the end of the process!

Is editing a wordless book different than editing a "wordful" book?

In some ways it is a different experience, but in the end you are still trying to tell the best, most genuine story possible, so whether a book is wordless or not you are taking a lot of things into consideration like age-level, accessibility, plot, resolution, etc. Of course, there are some different considerations. If one part of a wordless story needs to be changed or edited, it means that the illustrator has to re-draw or touch-up the art, and that change can affect other parts of the book so you have to be careful. Overall though, from experience, I tend to feel that every project I've worked on—wordless or not—has been a different experience to edit, because every project is unique and presents different challenges.

Did you find a blurring of the lines between editor and art director working on *Chicken and Cat*?

As a picture book editor, I've always relied on trusting my artists and respecting their vision for their work (I never want to mess with that!). So my intention is never to be directing per se, but rather to be asking questions and saying, "Wow, this is great." Of course, with *Chicken and Cat* especially and with Sara's follow-up book out this spring, *Chicken and Cat Clean Up*, I had the brilliant guidance of creative director David Saylor who was deeply involved. He was a big fan of Sara's from the very beginning and I always had the sense that his involvement was definitely one of, "I love this!" rather than out of ordinary obligation. Sara and were both fortunate to have had David on board.

Were you aware that there is a reading public which thinks it's more difficult to read a wordless book and did this concern you at all?

Yes! When we first decided to make *Chicken and Cat* wordless there was definitely discussion in-house as to whether this would be a viable product. Would readers buy a wordless picture book? Fortunately, everyone was in love with Sara's work and we knew that if people simply opened up *Chicken and Cat,* they would keep reading.

Do you think *Chicken and Cat* helps educate the public in terms of learning to read pictures and understand the story?

As a parent of two young boys, I do understand where the hesitation to wordless picture books comes from. If a child is not reading on his or her own yet, it can be a scary, uncertain experience for an adult to "make up" a story on the spot to go along with a book's illustrations. I always coax parents I know to give it a try. And I give them this tip: Instead of "reading to" your child, ask them questions instead like, "What is Chicken doing here?" or "Why do you think Cat feels sad?" Because the emotional connection a reader makes to a story is part of what makes reading so important and satisfying.

With *Chicken and Cat,* and other wordless picture books, the child also gets to be an active participant in the story, rather than a spectator; I think that's very important for the developing emotional and intellectual health of a child (as well as creating future readers!). It's interesting to me that all of the parents to whom I've given *Chicken and Cat* have come back to me and said their family loved the book. Many of them also said that after they took the book home, what surprised them initially was how their children (who weren't of reading age yet) "read" the story aloud. They could have cared less if the book had words or not! They were compelled by the illustrations and followed the story just fine. It's encouraging to see that. I challenge anyone—with or without kids—to pick up *Chicken and Cat* and not be charmed. By the end, I bet they won't even notice that the book doesn't have words!! A story, after all, is more than just its words—it's an experience. It's all about connecting with the characters and being drawn in by their tale.

Sara's stories are seemingly simple and numerous reviewers have mentioned that they are even mistakenly simple and are really quite complicated in the friendship realm. How would you say that *Chicken and Cat Clean Up* develops the relationship between these two characters since the first book, *Chicken and Cat*?

In *Chicken and Cat Clean Up*, Sara really takes Chicken and Cat's friendship to a whole new level. Chicken and Cat will always be friends, but there are definitely some stumbling blocks and things that the pair needs to accept, forgive, and discover about the other one before their friendship can move on. The story is very gentle and sweet, but I think everyone, kids and adults, can relate. One of the many things I love about Sara's work is how nothing is what it seems at first glance. There's no black and white, good or bad. It's an interesting mix of real life and real emotions, and yes, real friendships. And in the end, cooperation and honesty and being true to one's self triumphs.

In addition to picture books, which categories do you acquire? Do you have a favorite genre?

I also acquire distinctive middle grade and young adult fiction. I tend to like variety so I don't have a favorite genre. I do like stories with authentic, fresh voices and exceptionally drawn characters, which have a great hook, are addictive, and have writing that sings. I love stories that make me cry, laugh out loud, make me think, take me on a journey, are provocative and take risks, have plenty of kid/teen appeal, resonate deeply with readers of all ages, and stay with me long after I've put the book down. I'm open to everything: gripping and well-researched historical fiction, intriguing/intense or humorous/silly mysteries, sweet love stories, steamy romance, edgy teen fiction, urban fantasies with a new spin, and funny, laugh-out-loud fiction on any subject. And, of course, as always, no matter the genre or age level, I'm looking for that perfect, incredible, "You have to read this" book. What stands out to me is the writing. If I'm sucked in by page 5, I'm in for as long as I'm interested. If an author's writing is clunky or can't hold my attention, then I'm not that excited to continue. What really stands out to me is great voice. If an author has a great voice, I'm in. You can change plot, you can work on structure, but a fabulous voice is very hard to come by.

As Sara's other publishing life is in comic books, have you worked on any graphic novels with her or others? Do you want to? If yes, how can a writer who doesn't draw submit to you?

I haven't worked on any graphic novels with Sara or others, which isn't to say that I wouldn't be open to doing that. The submission process, no matter the project or scope, is always the same: please submit a query letter to me with SASE at Scholastic Press via regular post.

Do you accept unagented submissions? Queries? And if so, how do you like to receive these submissions/queries—regular post? E-mail?

I do not accept unagented submissions unless the writer is a member of SCBWI or has been previously published by relevant children's publications. I will accept unsolicited queries and those can be sent via regular post to me at my Scholastic address (Jennifer Rees, Editor, Scholastic Press, 557 Broadway, New York, NY 10012).

For illustrators, do you look at portfolios? Accept samples?

Unless, an illustrator has a manuscript or an idea for a story he or she wishes to tell, I don't really look at portfolios or accept samples.

For author/illustrators, do you like to see a completed dummy or . . .?

Yes, completed dummy is preferable, even if some of the dummy is in sketch form and other pieces are finished art.

When an author submits to Scholastic Press and you pass on the manuscript is it a problem, not worth it, or definitely worth it, for the writer to submit to another Scholastic imprint that might be a better fit? Do you ever run down the hall to a colleague suggesting a manuscript for him/her, the other imprints?

If something is excellent but isn't right for Scholastic Press, I will definitely show it to one of my colleagues (if it seems right for them). Otherwise, a writer is probably spinning their wheels. That said, I do realize that every editor's taste is different and that I can't pretend to know everyone's tastes within the company in great detail, so I would hate to advise that an author give up completely if I pass on a manuscript.

Authors and illustrators want to get it right when submitting to you and other publishers. Anything you'd like to add to help them get it right?

I would advise authors and illustrators to please do their homework. I am always surprised by the number of queries and manuscripts I receive that start out, "Dear Editor." So, not only do they not know what Scholastic Press is looking for, but they also don't know what I'm looking for. I do understand that once an author has completed and polished a project, he or she is eager to get it "out there," but I would encourage everyone to take the extra time to find out where it makes sense to submit her or his work. It will pay off in the end, hopefully!

Writing Series

Three Author Tell All

by Fiona Bayrock

Multiple-book contracts, a stream of advance checks, work sold before it's written, readers chomping at the bit for your next book—for many writers, this is the stuff of dreams and goals. For series writers, it's a common reality. But does this silver lining come with a cloud? What about deadlines, boredom, or review fatigue? What is writing a series *really* like? We invited three successful series writers to share the nitty gritty of their experiences and dish their best advice.

Pam Withers (http://www.takeittotheextreme.com) is the author of the 10-book young adult series, Take It to the Extreme (Whitecap Books, 2003-07), in which each book finds best friends Jake and Peter involved in a new extreme sport and a heap of trouble. Withers has also published three stand-alone teen novels with Orca Books, and an adult biography: *Going Vertical: The Life of an Extreme Kayaker* (Menasha Ridge Press, 2008).

Award-winning author **Deborah Hodge** (http://www.deborahhodge.com) is a nonfiction series veteran. Her long-running Kids Can Press Wildlife Series began in 1996, and her latest, the six-book Who Lives Here? series (Kids Can Press), debuted in 2008. In between, she contributed to several multi-author series (KCP), and published two stand-alone picture books with Tundra Books: *Emma's Story* (2003), and *Lily and the Mixed-Up Letters* (2007).

The Queen of Disguises (Orca, 2009) is the sixth book in **Melanie Jackson's** (http://dinahgalloway.blogspot.com) humorous middle grade *Dinah Galloway Mystery* series about a wisecracking, bespectacled and freckled, tween detective with a big singing voice and an even bigger sense of curiosity. Jackson also has two stand-alone novels out this year: *The Midnight-Blue Marble* (Gumboot Books), and *The Big Dip* (Orca Currents).

Did you set out to write and sell a series?

Pam Withers: I pitched it as a series, and the publisher called my bluff. It was pretty intimidating when they said, "Yes, we're interested in accepting your first novel, but only if you submit outlines of the next five in the series and we like those." I took a deep breath and outlined the next five novels. They accepted that first book (*Raging River*), and then I spent five years putting out a new novel every six months—a coup for an unpublished writer, but

FIONA BAYROCK is the author of *Bubble Homes and Fish Farts* (Charlesbridge, 2009; a Junior Library Guild selection), 14 other quirky science books for the school and education market, and 60+ articles, stories, and poems in children's magazines such as *Highlights for Children, KNOW,* and *Odyssey.* Over the years, Fiona has delighted in chasing questions through most of the "ologies," talking to scientists around the world about all kinds of neat stuff, from palindromes to solar wind. She currently lives with her zany family on the side of a mountain in rural British Columbia, Canada, where she is constantly in search of the "Aha!" clever puns, and her coffee. She enjoys visiting schools and speaking at conferences. Visit her at www.fionabayrock.com.

also hard work and scary. Sometimes you have to be careful what you ask for.

Deborah Hodge: Each series was different. The *Wildlife* series began with a one-off book, (*Bears*, 1996) followed by a second, (*Wild Cats,* 1996) and later evolved into a series. The *Who Lives Here*? series was conceived and proposed as a series. My editor and I spent a lot of time working out the format, and collaborating with the designers to get the right look and feel. I also wrote several books as part of existing multi-author series. Although I had good experiences with those books, I missed the creative aspect of working on the design.

Melanie Jackson: I wrote *The Spy in the Alley* as a stand-alone novel. Dinah was a lively, irrepressible, spunky character who'd evolved in my imagination. I saw *Spy* as a home for her, not a springboard. I thought it'd be great to get one book published in my lifetime, just one! I was thrilled when my publisher suggested the series.

How and when did you establish the parameters of your series? Is this easier to do if you know ahead of time it will be a series?

Withers: I naively hoped the first book would become a series. I had the characters work for a company called Sam's Adventure Tours, which I thought would allow for a variety of future adventures. I could then choose any source of tension, character development, location, and additional characters. The major parameter was the new sport in which the characters were engaged in each book—a stretch by the tenth book. I just said they were natural athletes able to pick up and excel at almost any sport.

Hodge: When I knew in advance I was writing a series, I established the parameters at the proposal and outline stage. I don't know if it's any easier knowing ahead of time that it'll be a series. In a way, there's more pressure to make the right decisions about the format because you know it'll have to be viable for multiple books.

Do series parameters help or hinder?

Withers: I think established parameters help. The writing goes faster because you know the characters so well; you know what they'd do and how they'd react and it becomes more fun, faster, easier to write, like you're on a roll. You may feel slightly straitjacketed by their set personalities after many books, but all it takes is a little imagination to get around that.

Hodge: Each style of book has its own challenges. Whether initially a one-off or part of a series, I really agonize over format decisions in the first book. For subsequent books in a series, I know I'm not going to make any major format changes, and this is helpful in steering my writing.

Jackson: Parameters make it easier. The characters you reintroduce are like old friends. You know them well, and it's easy to figure out how they'll behave and react to developments.

Have series parameters ever become a problem later?

Withers: My main characters are best friends who'd grown up together, with one having just moved away. Fine. That worked for one book, but it's not realistic for "best friends" to stay best friends when one moves away. It was highly annoying and ended up being a challenge to deal with, both in settings and in their relationship, all the way through the series.

Hodge: Establishing parameters early in the series really hasn't cause me problems (knock on wood!). However, I'm lucky to have had great editors who allowed each series to evolve in a natural way, and didn't require me to be too rigid too early.

Jackson: My problem was Dinah's age—how to keep her as an adolescent suitable for intermediate readers over the years it would take the series to be released. My solution was to schedule Dinah's adventures close together in time. I may write the books one or two years apart, but in the time of the novels, only a few weeks have elapsed.

What challenges did you face in sustaining the series?

Withers: I occasionally hankered to write differently: in first person, or with a girl as a main character, or with more humor or edgier material. I couldn't do so within the established framework. I got around that by writing some stand-alone novels between the series books.

Hodge: As I moved toward the end of a series, sustaining a fresh, energetic sound and keeping the content original became a bigger challenge.

Jackson: The plots weren't a problem. The challenge was having Dinah grow, change and learn in her relationships. The old series books I grew up with didn't bother about characters evolving. Nowadays, authors know characters have to change or else...yawn. Dinah changes as real-life kids do. For example, she is more aware of boys in her later adventures.

Rain Forest Animals, by Deborah Hodge (Kids Can Press, 2008) is in the Who Lives Here? series.

Reprinted with permission of Kids Can Press.

How did you keep things fresh?

Withers: By coming up with innovative and sometimes outrageous actions or settings. For instance, in BMX Tunnel Run (2007), the boys acquire night vision goggles and oxygen meters, and bike through old mining tunnels. The research that doesn't involve the sport itself also helps keep things fresh and interesting.

Hodge: I approached each new book—whether stand-alone or part of a series—with excitement, and I worked very hard to find engaging content that I could present in a child-friendly way.

Jackson: Dinah's singing career allows her to travel to new places. Her sister acquires a boyfriend, who becomes part of Dinah's close-knit circle, and in The Mask on the Cruise Ship (2004), Dinah finds another good friend, Talbot.

Did you encounter any surprises—good or bad—mid-series?

Withers: I sprained my back badly and had to write several books using voice recognition software. I almost gave up the series at that point. It was phenomenally difficult to get into the right frame of mind to write a book on extreme climbing when I could neither sit nor walk, but I had a deadline, so I did it.

Hodge: Sometimes the market can change unexpectedly mid-series. For example, nonfiction books for young children shifted toward a more narrative stand-alone style as I was working on the Who Lives Here? series, catching me (and my publisher) by surprise. When you're committed to a series, it's hard to change direction in mid-stream.

Jackson: Dinah was so vivid to me. For a long time it was difficult to create a new protagonist who was equally compelling.

How did writing within a series affect your marketing and promotion?

Withers: Fantastically. I developed a niche and reputation, and undoubtedly ended up far more prolific than if I'd been marketing stand-alones.

Hodge: Each time a new book in the series came out, earlier books got mentioned and

Interviews

BMX Tunnel Runner, by Pam Withers (Walrus Books, 2007) is in the Take It to the Extreme series.

promoted. This had the positive effect of keeping all of my books in the front of people's minds. New books help sell the older ones.

Jackson: Dinah became a brand with the second book. When promoting later books, we were able to refer to the praise and honors previous books had garnered. The challenge is to assure readers that each adventure stands alone; they don't have to read previous books in the series to enjoy the latest one.

How did/will you know it's time to end the series?

Withers: I started feeling tired of the characters and restraints in book eight, and I worried that if I was tired of them, it would show. But ten seemed like a nice, even number, so I rallied and challenged myself to make the last two the best of the set. That carried me through. But when the series was finished, it was like a ball and chain had been removed.

Hodge: When I start running out of steam and the thought of another book in the series feels like a chore instead of a joy, I know it's time to quit. Six books seems to be the magic number for me.

Jackson: There seems to be a fading out point for series of around five or so. Dinah has wriggled past that mark, so she's already outlasted expectations. She's drawing close to her dream of singing at Carnegie Hall. If there's a seventh Dinah book, I'll get her there somehow, and that'll probably be the end of the series.

Have you experienced any stigma due to series writing?

Withers: I reflected more than once that I was developing a reputation as "that woman who writes about extreme sports." How lucky that I love this niche, because otherwise I might feel like an actor who had been typecast. Another possible disadvantage: I've heard that series books are less likely to garner awards than stand-alones. I don't know if that's true or not.

Hodge: A certain series fatigue exists. I'm not sure I'd call it a stigma, though. Reviewers tend to review the first one or two books in a series, then pass on the subsequent books. This also seems to be true for award committees. Conversely, I think booksellers and kids love series.

Jackson: I haven't felt any stigma, but I wouldn't be surprised. The detective genre, for adults or children, has traditionally not been accorded the respect that other fiction receives.

How has writing a series affected your career?

Withers: Tremendously positively. It put rocket launchers behind my career and gave me confidence and a base of fans. I went from unknown and unpublished to established in the blink of an eye.

Interviews

Hodge: It's allowed me to make a (modest) living, which is a wonderful thing for a children's author! It also contributed to recognition from teachers, librarians, and children.

Jackson: Giving school presentations about the series got rid of my shyness. I discovered my inner ham.

What was the best part of writing and marketing a series?

Withers: Getting to know the characters so intimately, and meeting young fans who knew and loved the series so much they felt free to suggest what I should do for the next in the series! The discipline of deadlines.

Hodge: It gave me peace of mind that I'd be receiving regular advances and wouldn't have to worry about how and where to sell my work once it was completed. That was very reassuring. I also care deeply about making books accessible to beginning readers. Since they find comfort in the consistency and familiarity of series books, series writing allowed me to feel that I was contributing to a less daunting reading experience for young children.

Jackson: Dinah has opened up new circles of friends for me. A teacher-librarian is now one of my very best friends, and I still correspond with one of my early young fans who's now attending high school on the other side of the continent.

Queen of Disguises, by Melanie Jackson (Orca, 2009) is in the Dinah Galloway Mysteries series.

Reprinted with permission of Orca Book Publishers.

What's the most frustrating about writing and marketing a series?

Withers: There's not much space between deadlines.

Hodge: Sometimes when I'm writing a series, people think that's the only kind of writing I'm able to do. I begin to feel a little boxed in, and it becomes necessary to demonstrate my writing versatility beyond those limited expectations.

Jackson: I'm not sure there is a "most frustrating"...

If you could go back and do it all over again, would you choose to write a series?

Withers: Definitely.

Hodge: Yes, absolutely!

Jackson: Definitely!

Would you write another series?

Withers: Yes, but with a break first.

Hodge: Yes, but I would alternate writing stand-alone books with series books in order to try new challenges, stay fresh, and grow as a writer.

Jackson: Sure! After writing my first novel for reluctant readers (The Big Dip), I'm interested in exploring more of that genre.

Interviews

What do you know now about series writing that you wish you'd known going in?

Withers: That the main challenge is finding a new source of tension between the same old characters, and that you have to guard against repetition of phrases and plot twists from book to book.

Hodge: It's a big commitment of time and energy. My most recent 6-book series took me 2½ years of solid work, without breaks. It was worth it to have the guaranteed work, but it was exhausting as well. It didn't leave room in my schedule to create stand-alone books (or cook dinner!).

Jackson: Nothing. I have no regrets.

Any last words of advice for someone considering writing a series?

Withers: Each book needs to be able to stand alone and refer less to the others in the series than did series books of a generation or two ago. In the days of Nancy Drew and Hardy Boys, I think a much higher percentage of people started at the first book and read the series all the way through. Nowadays, readers are more likely to read fewer of a series, and read them out of sequence. And...a publisher can end a series at any time.

Hodge: If you have a great idea, go for it! If you like creative control, make sure there's room in the process for you to have a say in the series format. Also, alternate series writing with stand-alone books, if possible. The variation keeps your imagination flowing and allows the public (and your publisher) to see that you're multi-talented.

Jackson: If you have a passion—writing mysteries, knitting, collecting doorknobs—you should fulfill it, no matter what. Don't let your dream get away. Chase after it.

Holly Black

Author of Other Worlds

Photo: D. Williford

by Deborah Bouziden

Holly Black was groomed from childhood to write stories about other worlds. Born in New Jersey in 1971, she grew up in a decrepit Victorian house listening to her mother's other-world stories.

"My mother very much believed in ghosts and so she would talk about her experiences," Black said. "When she was a kid, she apparently had a ghost she would play with that she said still played in our house. As a sensitive child, I was pretty freaked out all of the time."

Freaked out or not, those stories paved the way for Black to create her other worlds, enter in to them with her characters, and become a bestselling author.

Her work takes readers from modern living to fantasy where adventures await. Her first book, *Tithe: A Modern Fairy Tale* was published in 2002 by Simon & Schuster. The book received starred reviews from *Publishers Weekly* and *Kirkus Reviews*. It was also included in the American Library Association's Best Books for Young Adults. Two more books, *Valiant* and *Ironside*, from this same world were published next. *Valiant* was a finalist for the Mythopoeic Award for Young Readers and the recipient of the Andre Norton Award for Excellence in Young Adult Literature.

In 2003, the first two books of the bestselling Spiderwick Chronicles series, *The Field Guide* and *The Seeing Stone*, were released by Simon & Schuster. In this series, Black collaborated with her long-time friend and Caldecott award winning artist, Tony DiTerlizzi. Three more books, *Lucinda's Secret*, *The Ironwood Tree*, and *The Wrath of Mulgarath*, quickly followed with *The Wrath of Mulgarath* climbing to number one on the New York Times Bestseller List. In February 2008, the *Spiderwick Chronicles* was released in film version by Paramount Pictures in conjunction with Nickelodeon Films.

The three companion books and lavishly illustrated *Authur Spiderwick's Field Guide to the Fantastical World Around You, The Notebook for Fantastical Observations,* and *Care and Feeding of Sprites* have been translated in to 32 languages. The popularity of Black's books keep expanding with each one published.

Black continues to stretch her worldly borders. Her first graphic novel, *Kin*, in The Good Neighbors series, with author and illustrator, Ted Naifeh, was released in September 2008. *Kith* and *Kind* are the next two titles scheduled for publication.

In the meantime, Black keeps contributing to anthologies and working on her latest project. "My newest book is *The White Cat*," Black said, "which features a charming con

DEBORAH BOUZIDEN has been writing and publishing articles and books since 1985. She has had hundreds of articles published in such magazines as *Woman's Day, Writer's Digest,* and *Oklahoma Today,* eight books published, and contributed to nine more. To learn more about Bouziden, visit her Web site at www.deborahbouziden.com.

artist named Cassel, curse magic, and a cat in a dress. Despite the cat, it's a pretty dark book and the first in a trilogy of caper novels."

What drew you to writing? How did you start? Why did you decide to start writing and publishing? Why did you choose the children and teen genre?

Like most professional writers, I've been making up stories since I was a kid. The part that was hardest for me was finishing my first book, Tithe. It took me about five years and changed so much over the writing and rewriting that it barely looked like the same book. When I was first writing it, I didn't think of Tithe as being specifically a teen book. I chose a teenage protagonist because I knew Kaye was going to discover she was a changeling and I thought if that happened to her when she was too much older, it would seem silly, but I thought I was writing an adult fantasy in the tradition of Terri Windling or Charles de Lint. I had a friend who was a children's librarian and she was the one who pushed me to consider thinking of Tithe as a novel for teens. She also pushed me to start reading in that genre again, causing me to discover a lot of books I absolutely love.

When you wrote Tithe did you write it for publication or were you writing it for yourself? How and where did you meet your first editor?

I was writing Tithe in the hopes it would someday be published, but after many years of working on it, publication was a pretty distant dream. What I mostly dreamed of was finishing a book with a plot that made sense, rather than writing endless vignettes about elves drinking coffee and killing one another.

I met my first editor, Kevin, because he was (and is) Tony DiTerlizzi's editor. With Tony's blessing, Kevin agreed to take a look at my book and tell me if he thought Tithe was a book for teens, since I still wasn't sure. Happily for me, he both decided it was a teen book and he wanted to acquire it.

What are some challenges and obstacles you faced on the road to publication?

I was very lucky to sell Tithe quickly. The hardest thing for me was to keep going when the actual writing the book itself was so daunting. With a first novel, one has to teach oneself a lot about characterization, plotting, dialogue and all the other elements that go into a novelist's bag of tricks. It can often feel overwhelming, especially with a drafting process like mine which meant I would reach a certain point, rip the whole thing apart and go back to the beginning. I was really afraid I would never finish that book.

How in depth do you go into the background of your characters, in particularly your faerie characters?

I often change my ideas of who characters are over the course of writing a novel. I don't start out with extensive biographies—I start out with a name (which sometimes takes me a while, because I find having the right name oddly important) and a lot of vague notions. I need to put the character in situations and try out reactions before I really feel like I know who they are. By the time I finish a book, the character feels really solid and at that point I will often have extensive notes about him or her. One of the joys of writing sequels and series is being able to take a character I know really well and putting him or her in a new situation.

How do you plot? Outline? Storyboard? Fly by the seat of your pants? What are your most common plot problems? How do you solve them?

I have a kind of crazy process in that I start with ideas that don't always seem like they'll go together. Like for my new novel, The White Cat, I wanted to retell that fairy tale, but I

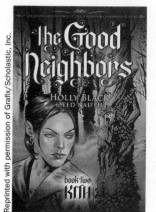

Kith is the second book in Holly Black's The Good Neighbors graphic novel series illustrated by Ted Naifeh (Graphix, 2009).

wanted to combine that somehow with grifters, curse magic and I wanted one of the settings to be a garbage house. I try to outline, but mostly that's to make me feel like I know what I'm doing. I always change things as I go. After each chapter, I will go back to the beginning and change around edit all the preceding chapters, so it's often slow movement forward, but by the end, the early and middle chapters are in very good shape.

What advice can you give new writers about rough drafts?

Find your own process and trust it. I love sitting at a coffee shop and writing across from other writers, but it has made me even more aware of how all of us create books very differently. I have a friend who starts with themes and scenes that come to her out of order, who then patchwork quilts them together. I know someone who writes a first draft, then destroys it and writes the whole thing over. I've met a few people who do my strange slow half-backwards crawl through a book and I know others who write a first draft from beginning to end without looking back. There's no right way; there's only the way that works for you.

What do you enjoy about the writing process? Not enjoy?

I love editing. I love the part where the scenes are in place, blocked and I get to go into them and really make them better. Where I get to push the characters and ask myself about their reactions. That's when the book really comes to life for me and where I feel like I can play around with what I have done.

When you finish a project, how do you reward yourself?

This is a terrible answer, but it is so hard to know when a project is done. I just bundled off a manuscript to my critique group, but I am very aware of the many things I have to fix before it goes to my editor. Then my editor will find new things to fix. Then the copyeditor will point out that I have misspelled my own name and so on. Sometimes, when I turn in a final draft to my editor, I will take a few days off to indulge in reading books for pure pleasure, but more often I will just start a new project.

In the Spiderwick Chronicles, you worked with Tony DiTerlizzi, your friend. How did a working relationship begin and why did you decide to add illustrations to your stories?

I met Tony when I interviewed him for his illustration work on Dungeons & Dragons and other role playing games. I was amazed to see his beautiful work up close and we bonded over our love of turn of the century illustrators like Arthur Rackham and also books of our childhood, like Brian Froud and Alan Lee's Faeries. We started hanging out and I saw several of his projects in their early stages. He had been working on a field guide to faeries, with paintings in an Audubon style that I really loved. I really wanted him to make that his next project and offered to write the descriptions of the faeries—they were about a paragraph—having no idea what I was getting myself into. Once we started talking about it, we got more and more excited, and our Spiderwick partnership was born.

Tell readers about The Spiderwick Chronicles being adapted into a film. Where were you when you heard the news? What was your family's reaction? Were

you a consultant on the film? In your opinion, how true did they stay to your book characters?

Tony and I were very lucky in that we were involved from the beginning. Mark Waters, the director, was very generous in terms of letting us read all the versions of the script and give our thoughts, but it was a long process. When the film was finally greenlit, I think Tony and I were both a little stunned and, of course, really excited. We got to go to the set and Tony worked with the visual effects people.

Of course, in the process of being made into a film, things change, but I really think the movie captures the essence of the characters. The faeries remain organic and evocative of folkloric faeries. And, most of all, I think the film is really satisfying to watch, which is what we hoped for most when we began the process.

How and why did the SC *Field Guide* come about? What are readers saying about it?

Arthur Spiderwick's Field Guide to the Fantastical World Around You was the book Tony and I wanted to do

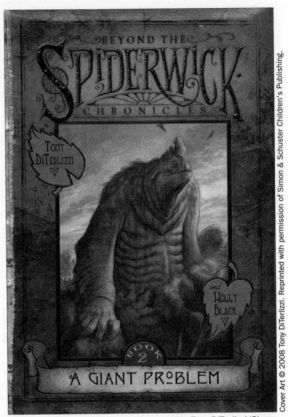

A Giant Problem, by Holly Black, illustrated by Tony DiTerlizzi (Simon & Schuster, 2008) is part of the pair's Beyond the Spiderwick Chronicles series.

first. The chapter books wound up coming out before the field guide, but we were extremely excited to finally get to do the book we considered the centerpiece of The Spiderwick Chronicles. Tony spent a year laboring on the gorgeous artwork and we tried to be really thoughtful in terms of including traditional folklore and expanding on it based on natural history. Our hope is that readers take it out into their backyards, nearby parks and woods and try to find evidence of faeries on their own.

Your first graphic novel is *Kin*. How did this series come about? Explain this book's birth process? How did you and Ted work on the project? Did he do his illustrations first or did you write words first? Was it done in sections? Scenes?

I've been really interested in the story of Bridget Cleary, a young woman who was killed in front of her family by her husband, Michael Cleary, in Ireland only about a hundred years ago. He thought (and her family agreed) that she was a faerie changeling and that if he killed the changeling the real Bridget would ride home on a white horse in the morning. When she didn't, the reality of what they had done started to become clear to the family members present. There was a much publicized trial and even a children's rhyme came out of it: "Are you a witch, are you a fairy, or are you the wife of Michael Cleary?"

From there, I decided I wanted to write a modern mystery trilogy, The Good Neighbors (the three individual books are Kin, Kith, and Kind), where a girl, Rue, is investigating the disappearance of her mother. It is loosely based on the story of Bridget Cleary, but also heads off in a very different direction.

It was a lot of fun to try out a totally new medium. Working with Ted Naifeh, who is so knowledgeable and such a wonderful illustrator (I was a fan of his work from his book How Loathsome), made the process easier and more fun. I did write the manuscript first, but he had a lot of great suggestions for improvement.

Why do you present faeries as you do?

All of my books draw on traditional faerie folklore, primarily Celtic and Scandinavian (although there's faerie folklore all over the world). Folklorically, faeries are capricious and dangerous; behaving according to a moral system can seem wholly alien. They cry at weddings and laugh at funerals, so they can be difficult to write, but I find them really fascinating. Unlike many other supernatural creatures, such as the werewolf or vampire, faeries are not and have never been human. They are utterly other. And, although some people think of them as little, sparkly creatures with wings, according to folklore people were at one time so afraid of getting the attention of faeries—for fear of having their crops blighted, their family members stolen and replaced with changelings, and their cows' milk soured—that they wouldn't even say the word "faeries." Instead people had euphemistic names for faeries, like the People of Peace, The Little People, and The Good Neighbors.

What do you do to feed your muse, recharge your creative batteries, keep your writing fresh?

I read a lot and I read a lot of nonfiction, which is really helpful in terms of being. I believe that writers are often people that get obsessed with a topic and read tons about it, then move on to something else. I try to indulge those impulses. It might take a while for my interest to find its way into a story, but I think when it gets there, it gets there organically.

interviews

Ellen Hopkins

Reaching YA Readers Through Verse

by Travis Adkins

I f you opened one of Ellen Hopkins' novels in a bookstore, your first glance could lead you to think that it had been placed in the wrong section. "This is written all in verse," you might say, "so it must belong in children's books, not young adults." But after reading a few of the raw, honest lines about drug and methamphetamine addiction (*Crank* and *Glass*), abused teenaged runaways (*Burned*), or young people struggling with suicidal thoughts (*Impulse*), you'd realize that Hopkins' verse is about as far from Dr. Seuss as can be.

Hopkins says that writing in verse allows her "to get into my character's heads and take a good look around." That unflinching perspective has won her a following of readers who respond to the painful honesty and intensity of her writing. Perhaps the ultimate compliment comes from fans who have faced similar ordeals as those that Hopkins describes and tell her how much her writing means to them. One wrote to her to tell her "this book has helped me more than you will ever know." Here, Hopkins talks about her writing style, how she researches her difficult material, and why writers should "buck trends and the marketplace and write the story you have to write."

How does writing in verse allow you to access your characters' thoughts in a way that prose can't?

Verse is an internal form of writing. A poem is a poet's private view of the world. Writing in verse, as a character, feels very internal, too. I basically become the character, as poet. Prose often feels more like you're telling a story. Too much detail interferes with the internal thought processes of my characters.

How did you discover that writing in verse was the right style for you? Did you try writing in prose first and find that it just wasn't working for you?

I did start *Crank*, my first novel, as a prose novel. But the voice felt too angry. It was *my* voice, not Kristina's. The voice of Kristina, as poet, simply felt right. And then I discovered a certain talent for storytelling through verse.

Your novels so far have been about young adults coping with traumatic circumstance, whether it's methamphetamine addiction or suicidal impulses. Aside from your writing style, what else do you do to try to get into the minds of such characters? Do you do a lot of research?

TRAVIS ADKINS is a freelance writer and a frequent contributor to Writer's Digest Market Books. He lives in Brooklyn.

I research heavily. Thank goodness for my nonfiction and journalism background! In addition to "expert" input, I rely on input from friends or family members who have experienced some of these things, as well as readers, many of whom have shared their own stories with me.

Which of your novels so far has been the toughest for you to write, in terms of getting a handle on the issues you're tackling? Why?

Probably *Identical*, which deals with father/daughter incest. Tough topic to research. Tough topic to identify with. Tough topic to write about. I wanted to write with sensitivity to readers who might have experienced this issue, and yet it's of prime importance to write honestly about it. Many readers have thanked me for not "hinting" at the issue, but hitting it straight on. They want to know they're not alone, that someone understands.

You've published a sequel to your first novel, *Crank,* and have said that you're considering writing a third. Had you planned all along to write a series, or did that just happen unexpectedly?

Nope. Never planned sequels originally. But reader demand for "more of Kristina's story" was overwhelming. Even after *Glass*, they wanted to know the rest of it. I am, in fact, currently writing *Fallout*, the third and final Kristina book. Only, because I didn't want to write the same book, nor leave the ultimate hope of the story with Kristina, I'm writing from the POVs of three of her children, now teens and dealing with the fallout of their [absent] mother's choices.

What's your greatest challenge as a writer?

Time! Never seems to be enough of it. That, and my determination to always make the next book as good, or better, than the last. If I can't keep doing that, I'll quit.

With 20 nonfiction books and five novels published in the past nine years, you're amazingly productive. What's your secret?

Easy. I love to write. Love everything about it. Love the process. The journey. The growth. Fiction. Nonfiction. Articles. Poetry. Words. I love words, and I love that I can put them down on paper so others want to read them. The great thing about realizing the success that I have is I used to have to apologize for the time I spent writing. Now my family and friends stand back and say, "You go, girl."

What projects are you working on now?

We're in the final production phases of *Tricks,* about five teens who fall into prostitution, for five very different reasons. It's due out in August. As I mentioned, I'm writing Fallout. And I'm guest editing Flirtin' With the Monster, which will publish in May. This is a collection of essays about Crank and Glass. It's several YA authors, talking about themes, etc.; a criminal court judge and a drug counselor giving their take on the books; plus four essays by members of my family. So readers will get personal glimpses of that time by "Kristina," her sister, my husband ("Scott" in the books), and Orion, aka "Hunter," now 12.

On your Web site, you share some of the responses from readers who say that they've gone through similar struggles as your characters and that your novels have touched them. What does that mean to you to get that kind of response?

Every day brings messages like that, and each and every one touches me in the most amazing way. I want them to know they're not alone. Not weird. Not stupid. Not emo. Not any of the labels others insist on giving them. Whose life is perfect? Who doesn't experience pain? Who doesn't ask for that pain sometimes? What I always try to give them as a takeaway (and I always respond!) is that the future is theirs. They can allow the past to take them down, or choose a more positive tomorrow. I am honored, and humbled, to know my words may have helped them toward that tomorrow.

Crank (McElderry, 2004) is Ellen Hopkins' first novel-in-verse.

Reprinted with permission of Margaret K. McElderry Books/Simon & Schuster Children's Publishing Division.

You sold *Crank* without an agent by approaching an editor (Julia Richardson, then with Simon & Schuster and now at Houghton Mifflin) at a book festival. How did you get her to take a look at your novel without an agent? Did you prepare a quick pitch to give her a good idea of the book? Had you researched her before you spoke to her so that you knew a little about her editorial preferences?

Not at all. Julia was critiquing manuscripts, and I showed her a picture book (a quiet one, in verse!) I had written. She said, "This is the best writing I've seen in a long time, but I don't do picture books. Do you have anything else?" I had five pages of Crank written at the time, and showed her that. She loved it and said to send it when it was finished. Two months later, I had 75 pages written. I emailed and asked if she'd like an exclusive first look. She said yes, and the next thing I knew, I had a contract.

You're now with the Andrea Brown Literary Agency. Why did you decide to go with a literary agency even though you'd managed to launch your career without one?

Knowing what I know now, I suggest anyone who is trying to sell a novel length manuscript look for an agent first. It's not just about bigger advances, but about contractual issues a new writer cannot negotiate for themselves. Sub rights, especially. You need someone learned on your side. And now, I don't want to have to worry about contracts, rights, etc. I don't want to have to go to my editor, with whom I have an exceptional working relationship (and truthfully, a wonderful friendship), griping about money or movie rights. When I have a problem, I want a champion. My agent is that, and should be.

You maintain a very active schedule of appearances at writer's conferences and book festivals. What are some of the lessons you've learned about successfully promoting your books?

It's really important to be "out there" and accessible not only to readers, but also to other writers, editors and agents. I feel I've developed an excellent reputation within the industry by being open and giving back where I can. Maintaining a positive buzz among peers and

Tricks (McElderry, 2009) is Ellen Hopkins' latest novel-in-verse.

industry professionals keeps your name circulating—never a bad thing. I suppose "bad press" can serve that purpose, too. But respect within the publishing world is important to me.

You also speak frequently at schools. Have you learned anything from talking to students—who are, after all, your primary audience—that's helped you with your writing?

Some authors do school visits to boost their income. Others hate them and refuse to do them. Personally, I love the outreach. My readers want to know I'm a real person, and I want them to see for themselves that I truly care about them. I also think anyone writing for children or young adults should spend lots of time around them. It helps you get in touch with your inner child, as sappy as that might sound. But when I observe today's teens, it not only puts me in touch with the teen I used to be, it helps me gain perspective on the issues that touch them today. Every visit brings at least one (and sometimes several) young person to me privately, to share a personal story. Sometimes that generates a character thread or story idea, so yes, every visit is valuable.

What's the best writing advice you've ever been given?
To buck trends and the marketplace and write the story you have to write, the one that hides in a deep, dark corner of your heart. The one that whispers to you at night and refuses to shut up until you sit down and write it.

Books by Ellen Hopkins

- ***Crank,*** Hopkins' first novel, is the story of 17-year-old Kristina Snow's terrifying descent into methamphetamine addiction and her attempt at recovery.
- ***Glass,*** a sequel to *Crank*, follows Kristina Snow as she deals with the fallout of her addiction and tries to put her life back together.
- ***Identical*** is told through the point-of-view of two identical twins, one of whom is being sexually abused by her father.
- ***Impulse*** takes readers into the lives and minds of a group of teenagers struggling with suicidal urges.
- In ***Burned,*** a young woman raised in the Mormon church struggles with her faith, her family and her first love.

Interviews

Lisa Yee

*On Quirky Characters, Series
& Crossover Readers*

Photo: Mieke Kramer

by Travis Adkins

Lisa Yee sold her first book thanks to the kind of big break that many writers dream of. Arthur Levine, the American editor of the *Harry Potter* series and the head of his eponymous imprint at Scholastic Books, found another of Yee's books on the slush pile and was interested enough to ask her if she had anything else for him to see. That turned out to be *Millicent Min, Girl Genius*. Since then Yee has published three more books with Arthur Levine, including two featuring characters from her debut.

It's fitting that Yee's publishing success should be a bit of a Cinderella story, since the main characters in her novels are often misfits and outsiders with hidden talents that shine through in the end. Here Yee talks about her fascination with quirky characters, her thoughts on writing a series, and why her books have a surprising appeal for adults.

You seem to have a strong affinity for quirky characters who are trying to fit in with the crowd at the same time that they're trying to find their own identity. What interests you in characters like that?

I find quirky fascinating. I think we all have our little peccadilloes; it's what sets us apart from the person sitting to our right. As for fitting in, and standing out, that's something that kids (and adults) seem to struggle with. When we're young, we're tethered to our parents. But as we work our way through school we have to find our own footing. That can be pretty scary. I think it's a universal fear and therefore something that I love exploring because even though each person experiences this, how they go about it is different and unique.

You say on your Web site that *Millicent Min, Girl Genius* started out as a much different book, and that you rewrote it several times. What was the first draft of *Millicent Min* about, and what made you decide to rewrite it?

The first draft of *Millicent Min* was about an 11-year old genius who had a job as a psychologist, solving problems for adults. When I sent it in to Arthur Levine, my editor, he said that he wanted to know what Millicent was like with younger people. So I threw the entire novel away, but kept Millicent.

The book went through several other major revisions, however the one constant was Millicent's character and voice—that never wavered.

TRAVIS ADKINS is a freelance writer and a frequent contributor to Writer's Digest Market Books. He lives in Brooklyn.

You've written two more books featuring characters from *Millicent Min*. Did you intend all along to return to those characters, or did they just take on a life of their own after you finished *Millicent Min*?

I'm not clever enough to have planned that trilogy! After I was done with Millicent Min, I was wondering what to write next. At that time, my daughter was eleven years old and hated boys. (That has since changed. Oooh yeah.) So I thought I'd write about a boy to prove to her that they were human.

Stanford Wong, Millicent's enemy, instantly came to mind. I wasn't interested in writing a sequel, so instead I wrote about the same summer as Millicent's story, only from Stanford's point of view.

Later, lots of kids asked me about Emily Ebers, a character in both Millicent and Stanford's book. So it made sense to complete the trilogy by giving Emily a novel of her own.

Do you think writing a series of books featuring the same characters has helped build you an audience, since readers who like one of the books might be more apt to read the rest of them? When you hear from fans, do they say that they follow you from book to book?

I hear from readers all the time who have read one book and tell me that now they're going to read the other two. Or I hear from kids who have read them all and they have very definite opinions about each character, and sometimes even tell me what should happen to them next. What I like hearing most though is when a reader says something like, "I didn't like Stanford when I read about him in Millicent's book. Then I read his book and have totally changed my opinion."

Although your books are written for a pre-teen and young adult audience, it seems that you have many fans among adult readers, as well. Why do you think adults like your books? Do you think it's for the same reasons that pre-teens and young adults like them?

Having so many adult readers has taken me by surprise. I'm thrilled though, because when I was working on Millicent Min, I kept asking Arthur Levine, "Who's my target audience?" And he'd say, "Don't worry about that. Just write the book." So I decided that I was the target audience and I wrote a book I'd want to read.

I think the adults read my books and reflect back upon their days as a tween/teen. And the pre-teens and young adults read the books in real time, and are experiencing some of the same emotions and dilemmas as my characters. What I love the best is when parents and their kids read the books together and talk about them.

Your first three books are all pretty lighthearted in tone and subject, but your newest book, *Absolutely Maybe,* is considerably darker. The main character is a teenaged runaway who's been abused by her mother's boyfriend. What made you decide to tackle such a difficult subject? Did you have a hard time adjusting your writing style to match the change in theme?

I honestly don't know what came over me. Too much chocolate, maybe? What I do know is that I enjoyed every moment of writing Absolutely Maybe. It was a writing high that I had not experienced before. Perhaps it was because for the longest time I thought I was a fluke. But when I started Absolutely Maybe, I realized, "Yes, I can do this." And I stopped being scared and just started writing.

As far as the subject matter goes, even though I outlined the book, a lot of what happened in the novel took me by surprise. The subject matter is dark at times, but it was liberating to write without any constraints.

Are you concerned at all that some of the fans of your other books might be a little put off by *Absolutely Maybe*?

I didn't shy away from any issues with Absolutely Maybe. There's alcoholism, homelessness, and an attempted rape in the book. But these are things that do happen. The book is also warm and funny, and heartbreaking.

I am aware that of my younger readers might find the novel disturbing in places. Whenever I speak at schools I always stress that Absolutely Maybe is for ages 12 and up. I would hate for a fourth grader to read it. That's one of the reasons the cover looks so different from my other books, so as not to confuse them.

However, I like to think that my readers are growing up with my books. So that someone who read the Millicent/Stanford/Emily novels when they were younger, will pick up Absolutely Maybe when they are ready for it. To me, writing this YA novel was an extension of who I am as an author.

Absolutely Maybe (Arthur A. Levine Books, 2009) is Lisa Yee's latest novel.

Reprinted with permission Arthur A. Levine Books/Scholastic Inc.

It's pretty rare for editors to pluck a writer out of the slush pile, as Arthur Levine did with you. What do you think he saw in your work that made him want to take it on? What has it been like working with him?

Actually, what drew Arthur to me was not the quality of my manuscript, but my query letter. He said he liked my voice.

The first thing of mine he pulled from the slush pile wasn't Millicent Min, but something else. He said it wasn't right, but to send him more. I told him I had this idea about a girl genius and that I'd send him the synopsis and the first three chapters.

After he read those he was very enthusiastic and asked to see the rest of the book. Only there was no rest of the book. It took me six years to write Millicent Min and Arthur never lost patience. He is a dream editor.

For Millicent Min, I also worked with a talented newcomer named Cheryl Klein. I believe Millicent Min was the first book she edited. I didn't know it was rare to have two editors work on your book. It's totally to my benefit to get input from both Arthur and Cheryl. They don't always agree and that makes for interesting author letters!

Who is your agent now, and how does working with her compare with working without one?

I am represented by Jodi Reamer at Writers House. For my first two books I was unagented. I was working on a novel for adults and thought that would be easier to sell via an agent. I wanted someone who represented both children's and adult books. Jodi happened to be keynoting at the SCBWI national conference in Los Angeles. So we connected there and hit it off.

I love working with Jodi. She does more than just agent my work, she gets on my case and says things like, "Um, Lisa should you really be goofing off? Shouldn't you be devoting more time to writing?"

(By the way, I still haven't gotten around to finishing my adult novel.)

Interviews

Millicent Min, Girl Genius (Arthur A. Levine Books, 2004) is Lisa Yee's first novel.

In addition to maintaining a web site (www. lisayee.com), you're a very active blogger. Is blogging something you enjoy doing, or is it more of a promotional tool for you? Is it especially important for authors of YA novels, since so many pre-teens and young adults spend so much time online now?

I love blogging. It's a journal of sorts for me. I blog about the writing process and my author adventures. I don't know how many books are sold because of my blog, but I do know that I've met some great people because of it. It's always nice when I go into a new city to meet fellow bloggers. I feel I already know them because we correspond via the blog all the time.

I believe it's very important for an author to have an Internet presence. This generation of kids is internet savvy. When I was a kid we sent letters via snail mail. Not any more! Today's kids are really plugged in and we need to react to that.

I don't think everyone needs a blog. That's a personal preference. However, I think a Web site is a must, especially if you write MG or YA. Students will often do book reports or author studies and the Internet of today is what al those volumes of the World Book Encyclopedia used to be to me when I was a kid. Oops. Now you know how old I am!

What are some of your upcoming projects?

I have the first of a chapter book series coming out in September 2009. It's called Bobby Vs. Girls (Accidentally) and will be published by Arthur A. Levine Books/Scholastic. The second one comes out in 2010.

Also in 2010 will be a sequel to the Millicent Min trilogy. This book will feature a boy named Marley. He was a minor character in Stanford Wong Flunks Big-Time. It also has a lot of Digger, Stanford's nemesis, in it. Millicent, Emily, and Stanford will all appear, but really the book is about Marley. It takes place the following school year.

What advice do you have for aspiring writers?

Read. Read, and then read some more. Also, don't fall in love with your writing. As soon as you finish a manuscript, don't love it to death and keep reworking it forever. Send it out, or set it aside, and begin a new one.

Also, to make things easier on yourself, don't say, "I want to get published." Say, "I want to write well." Do that and the getting published part will follow.

Interviews

A Q&A with Peepy

If you visit Lisa Yee's blog you can't miss her plush Peeps bunny friend Peepy. Peepy accompanies Yee to all her author events like conference and parties, and she's been photographed with pretty much any children's publishing luminary you can name. We've asked Peepy for the inside scoop on life with Lisa Yee.

Photo: Lisa Yee

Peepy poses with the lovely Julie Andrews in New York City.

You've been the Lisa Yee Entourage for some time now. How did you hook up with your famous author friend?

Actually, Lisa Yee is part of my entourage. We first met after I discovered that she was blowing up marshmallow Peeps in her microwave and posting photos of the destruction on her blog. I felt that she ought to know that there was more than one kind of Peep in the world—we aren't all just marshmallow, you know. For the record, I am a soft plush Peep...and I'm fabulous.

What role have you assumed in the development of Ms. Yee's career? Muse? Adviser? Proofreader? Social director?

If it weren't for me, Ms. Yee would not have a career. I feed her all of her ideas and I write her stories for her. Of course, I let her think that she's in control of her creativity. Also, when we are in public, it's me who people tend to gravitate to. Ms. Yee serves as my bodyguard, stylist and chauffeur.

Not long ago you went missing in New York City. It's time to tell the truth: what were you really doing in those hours you were "missing"?

Shhhh...just between us, I did get lost in the New York Public Library—at first. Then, while I was wandering around, I realized they had a gift shop! Later, a kind lady brought me to the security guards. I was brutally manhandled when one used me as a hand exerciser. I still have nightmares about that.

You've had your picture taken in many locations and with many celebrities of the children's publishing world. Do you have a favorite event or favorite photo shoot you could tell us about?

It's true that famous authors, editors and agents have all had their photos taken with me. Posing with me for a picture has become sort of a status symbol. My favorite photo op was in New York at a book festival. Julie Andrews and I were backstage at the same time. Ms. Yee got all weirded out, she does that a lot, but not me. I just went right up to Ms. Andrews and we had a lovely chat and then she asked for a photo with me!

You probably know Ms. Yee better than anyone. Can you reveal a secret about her? (The juicier the better.)

Well, no matter how much time Ms. Yee has to write a book, she always ends up pushing it to the limit. I can't tell you how many times I've had to stay up until the wee morning hours rewriting her work after she has crashed.

Finally, what's your advice to writers who are trying to get published? Anything you've learned from Ms. Yee you could pass along?

From my own experience, I'd caution writers not to stalk agents. I once followed Curtis Brown agent Ginger Knowlton into the ladies room and slipped a manuscript under the stall. Some paparazzi caught this and incriminating photos appeared in Ms. Yee's blog. Now I'm banned from that agency.

As for what I've learned from Ms. Yee, always have a good stash of chocolate within reach at all times.

Lisa Yee's Favorite Books

- **_Honestly, Katie John!,_ by Mary Calhoun**

   I identified with Calhoun's spunky tomboy so much that I named my daughter Katie, after her. Recently, I wrote a HORN BOOK essay mentioned the book. Mary Calhoun contacted me and now we are friends. Imagine that! She's one of my childhood idols.

- **The All of a Kind Family Books, by Sydney Taylor**

   Oh, how I longed to be Jewish and live with all my sisters in New York at the turn-of-the-century! (Um, that would be the 1900s.) Taylor's descriptions of the street scenes put me squarely in the action.

- **_Look Homeward Angel,_ by Thomas Wolfe**

   This was a massive book, but I drank it up and wanted more. Wolfe is a master storyteller.

- **_Walk Two Moons,_ by Sharon Creech**

   I read and reread this as a study of what a great children's novel should be like.

- **Winnie the Pooh, by A. A. Milne**

   These stories are delightful, plus slightly subversive. Because of these books I started collecting Winnie-the-Poohs and now have the second largest collection in America.

- **_To Kill a Mockingbird,_ by Harper Lee**

   I cried at the last page of this book, I never wanted it to end. Scout, Dill and Jem were my friends. Harper Lee only wrote one novel, but it was perfect.

Mitali Perkins

'Story Became My Fire Escape'

Photo: Bethany MacLeod

by Rebecca Ward

Few adults remember their adolescent selves with much clarity, because most don't want to revisit the throws of the unavoidable and all-too-common teenage identity crisis. Mitali Perkins is not like most adults. She not only vividly remembers her younger self, but embraces her old friend without inhibition: "Part of my soul got stuck at 13," she says.

There are some writers whose work represents a break from their own reality, taking the reader into a world very unlike one they have ever known. Others draw from their personal histories to create familiar characters and conflicts. Although Perkins leans toward the latter, she takes her work one step further. She sees writing as an opportunity to connect to an audience that is often forgotten, one that she herself can relate to, that of immigrant teenagers who try to create an identity despite being "squeezed between cultures." When diving into a Mitali Perkins' novel, readers will notice that her unique characters from all over the globe share a common thread—they are all displaced adolescents struggling to navigate multiple worlds and traditions while also doing the tough business of growing up.

Before settling in California at the age of 11, Perkins was well traveled. Born in Calcutta, her father's career as a civil engineer developing ports took the family all over the world, including Mexico, Ghana, Cameroon, London, and New York City. She credits stories as her "rock and stability" while growing up and recalls being particularly drawn to books about children steering through life's difficulties without parental support.

"When I was growing up, reading fiction helped me understand myself and gain insight into North American mainstream culture," she says. "I've experienced firsthand the heightened power of a story to transform a childhood, so that's why I write for a younger audience."

Perkins believes YA literature is the most powerful genre. "Our protagonists suffer and rejoice intensely, as do our readers. I write for young teens in middle-school because that's when I experienced the heat of rejection as an outsider and stories became my fire escape," she explains.

Although she has always been drawn to stories, Perkins did not start out her career dreaming up characters. After earning a degree in political science from Stanford University and a Masters in public policy from the University of California Berkley, Perkins became a visiting political science professor at Pepperdine University. Even while attending these top California universities, she continued to take solace in children's literature, often stealing away to the children's section of the local public library to unwind.

REBECCA WARD is a middle school language arts teacher and curriculum designer in Chicago, IL. During her summer, she runs young adult book clubs for her students. She has written for several Writer's Digest Market Books, including *Novel & Short Story Writers, Artist's & Graphic Designer's Market, Poet's Market,* and *Writer's Market*.

Perkins later uprooted herself from American culture and moved overseas with her husband to find herself wedged between cultures once again, although this time as an adult. Together they lived in Thailand, India, and Bangladesh, where Perkins worked as a grant writer for World Vision, a humanitarian organization dedicated to fighting poverty for children and families. Perkins also taught English at an international school, where she gained deeper insight into the world of adolescents. In fact, she wrote her first novel, *The Sunita Experiment,* during her afternoons after teaching.

"I liked tuning into their conversations and culture to find out how they see things," Perkins says of her students. She has found listening to young adults often allows for more authentic language and even some surprises. In some instances, these revelations have taken her characters in a different direction than she originally planned.

"I also tune into the artifacts of their culture—the music, television, movies, video games, and hobbies they enjoy." Although it might seem unusual to play the latest video game or change the channel on your radio under the guise of "research," recognizing and investigating the cultural artifacts of current adolescents is all part of the job when you're a YA writer. How else do adults imagine they can really understand their adolescent characters?

Perkins' exposure to middle and high school culture has enriched her writing, however she is careful to make sure it does not define or limit it. "I never imagine my audience," Perkins insists. "I only imagine my characters."

Her investment in her characters is what has kept Perkins in the game. After the publication of her first book, Perkins' life changed course when she and her husband returned to the states, settled in Massachusetts, and decided to adopt twin boys from India. Motherhood occupied her much of her energy during the years between her first book, published in 1993, and her second book in 2006, but Perkins also used this time to rethink her career path. In the end, she left academia and pursued writing, but it was not an easy decision. After taking a two-day silent retreat filled with prayer, journaling, and reflection, Perkins resolved that writing was her life's vocation. "It became clear that my calling was to connect children to stories," she explains. "I enjoyed teaching my students strategies to battle against poverty and human rights violations, but I wanted to inspire an early passion in their hearts for the task. That's why I turned to story."

Her turn to the story was not without its share of difficulties. Unlike many writers whose biggest hurdle is getting a publisher to take that first manuscript seriously, Perkins struggled much more with her second novel, Monsoon Summer, which faced repeated rejection. "Those years of rejection were crucial in shaping my vision as a children's author. My desire to be a writer grew, as did my determination to improve my craft," Perkins says.

Despite more than a decade lapse in publication, Perkins refused to give up on Monsoon Summer because of her love for its main character, Jazz. "Jazz was alive in my imagination," she insists. "I couldn't terminate her by stashing her in a desk drawer or archiving her on my husband's hard drive. I had to keep slogging on so that readers could meet her. And now they can!"

Early on Perkins recognized the ugly truth of publishing—rejection is part of the process that most writers become very familiar with. Her experience with Monsoon Summer and unwillingness to abandon her vocation was important preparation when later manuscripts were turned down. Both Rickshaw Girl and Bamboo People were rejected by numerous publishers before eventually finding a home with Charlesbridge.

"Any worthwhile vocation requires sweat and tears," says Perkins, who credits her years of rejection and revision with Monsoon Summer for honing her craft. "When discouragement and disappointment inevitably arrive, I echo Winston Churchill's famous words: 'Nevah, nevah, nevah give in!'"

But persistence isn't the only key ingredient to finding success in publishing. Equal

Interviews

The Secret Keeper (Delacorte, 2009) is Mitali Perkins' latest novel.

parts discipline is vital if a writer wants to ever quit her day job. Perkins divides the year into academic quarters and set individual goals for fall, winter, spring, and summer—a habit no doubt picked up during her years in academia, and a smart one! She sets aside the fall and spring for author visits and promotions, and uses the winter and summer as her time to research and write.

"When I'm under deadline, I go to a café with my laptop, order a latte, set a word count goal of 2,000 words and write until I meet that goal," says Perkins. "It doesn't matter that 1,850 of them are total balderdash, because at the end of the day I've got 150 keepers and some momentum in the story for tomorrow." This kind of self-control and her self-professed "love of revision" are saving graces, especially when you are the kind of writer who fears a blank page.

"It's a first draft that scares me silly," admits Perkins. She begins the brainstorming process in a journal and often during long showers, allowing the characters and narrative arc to slowly develop in her mind. "Once I have a narrative arc and a strong protagonist, I start writing and usually get stuck after three or four chapters," confesses Perkins. "That's when it gets excruciating. I have to take Jane Yolen's advice then and keep my 'butt in chair.' That chair for me is usually in a local coffee shop."

However, the first draft is only the preliminary layer of a story. Like many of her novels, Perkins most recent project coming out this year, Bamboo People, a tale of two 15-year-old boys living amidst war along the Thai-Burma border, required a considerable amount of research. Long after she tackled the initial draft of her story, there was considerable work to be done adding layers to enrich the setting and characters. In addition to her experience living in Chiang Mai, Thailand for three years where she visited refugee camps, Perkins also investigated the Burmese government's record of child soldier recruitment and slaughter of the Karenni people. "I stay in touch with friends who translate for the Karenni people and work to get food and medicine to the internally displaced refugees hiding in the jungle. I'm still in the process of fine-tuning cultural details and will send the manuscript to some of my Burmese friend as well as to a Karenni expert," says Perkins. She is committed to getting the details of her backdrop correct.

If the first draft, research, and revisions are layers one, two and three of a successful manuscript, then self promotion is the necessary and equally important fourth step that cannot be overlooked. In such a congested young adult market, Perkins feels self promotion is absolutely crucial. She advises writers to create an online presence to showcase their voices via blogs and social networks. "Strive for excellence in writing in those venues as well as in snail mail and e-mail. Your writing is your best ad for your writing," says Perkins who focuses on promoting locally, regionally, and virtually.

She also credits her involvement in writing organizations PEN and the Boston's Author Club as helping her to maintain stamina and feel a sense of community. "I wouldn't be published without SCBWI, and I would probably sell half as many books without the Kidlitosphere, readergirlz, Facebook, Twitter, and my other online connections. I delight in the community that we have formed around books for children and teens; it's unlike any other part of the publishing industry." Perkins asserts that relationships both online and face to face are the key to getting published. She adamantly believes young writers should take advantage of conferences and retreats, as well as try to find themselves an agent. Even with multiple publications under her belt, Perkins still devotes considerable energy to fostering and developing new connections with local bookstores, libraries, and schools. In fact, meeting young people, teachers, parents, librarians, and local businesses invested in the arts are an aspect of the profession that she finds not only essential, but rewarding.

Finally, Perkins advises novice writers to treat their craft as a serious profession rather than a hobby and regrets having not thought of her own work as a vocation earlier in life. She urges writers to feel a sense of urgency and commit to their art. Waiting with your ideas scribbled down in a journal means those characters might stay stuck in your desk drawer. Successful authors have many things in common, one being a willingness to take chances.

"Good books take time to write, edit, get published, and reach the hands and hearts of readers. Writing is also a risky, potentially heartbreaking venture. I wish I had treated myself as a professional years ago so I could have started setting aside the time and taking the risks earlier. But I was scared to fail," admits Perkins. "So I dawdled and dabbled instead of diving in the deep end. Learn from my mistakes, people!"

Mitali Perkins Reading List

Writing for young adults for more than 15 years, Mitali Perkins continues to expand the bookshelf for adolescents balancing two different cultures. For reviews and synopsis of her novels, visit her Web site at www.mitaliperkins.com.

- *The Sunita Experiment* (YA novel, 1993)
- *Ambassador Families: Equipping Your Kids To Engage Popular Culture* (Nonfiction, 2005)
- *Monsoon Summer* (YA novel, 2006)
- *Rickshaw Girl* (YA novel, 2007)
- *First Daughter: Extreme American Makeover* (YA novel, 2008)
- *First Daughter: White House Rules* (YA novel, 2008)
- *Secret Keeper* (YA Novel, 2009)
- *Bamboo People* (YA novel, 2010)

Interviews

First Books

Characters Struggling with Confidence

by Kelly Milner Halls

Two of the writers in this group of First Book interviewees had defining writing-life moments when they were in sixth grade. Megan Frazer rewrote a story for a class assignment and knew her efforts were better than the original; Jenny Meyerhoff wrote a story that was so well written, the teacher thought she was plagiarizing. Each of them came away with one of those glorious, crystal-clear realizations we all hope for as writers: my writing is good.

As aspiring writers, there are far too few such moments in our lives. Instead, we're faced with the more mundane and unwelcome daily struggles of confidence: Are our stories compelling? Is our writing as sharp as it can be? Will anyone want to read our words?

But as writers, we need to remember that struggling with confidence isn't a new challenge. It's actually part of the process of writing—and of life. And that there's a payoff.

As each of the books by this group of writers demonstrates, our childhood and teenage years are rife with challenges to our self-esteem, whether we're struggling with our weight, worried about losing our baby teeth, or hating our seemingly too-big noses or too-big breasts. But as each of the protagonists learn, the issue is never really about what we physically look like, but how we actually think about ourselves.

The same can be said for our writing. All of the writers in this group have experienced crises of confidence. It took Jenny Meyerhoff several other careers before she realized she wanted to pursue writing for kids. Erin Dionne received 37 straight rejections before she found an agent and publisher. Megan Frazer cut 20,000 hard-earned words from her manuscript before it was ready for publication. Sydney Salter lists the number of rejections she's received that year in her annual Christmas letter. And our First Books Follow-up author Marlene Perez, an interviewee from our 2005 First Books, has four other published books coming out, but describes the years between the sale of her first and latter books as nerve-wracking.

Despite these things, all of these women have kept writing. They've pushed beyond those scary moments or patiently endured them, because of how they think of themselves: they're writers. And their writing is good.

If we keep pushing, keep trying, keep writing, we're all bound to discover, sooner or later, for however fleeting, that same crystal-clear realization of knowing our writing is good.

We're writers, after all. And those moments make it all worth it.

MEG LEDER is the co-author of *The Happy Book* (Sourcebooks 2009) and a nonfiction book editor. She lives in Brooklyn.

Erin Dionne
Models Don't Eat Chocolate Cookies
(Dial)
www.erindionne.com

Erin Dionne always wanted to be a writer. Except, that is, for the brief period she thought about going down a slightly different career path. "For a while," she says, "around age 10 or 11—I decided that I wanted be a detective (I was reading lots of Nancy Drew and The Hardy Boys at the time), but since my parents wouldn't let me build a crime lab over the garage, I went back to being an author again."

The crime-solving world's loss is the middle-grade readers' gain, as Dionne's first book, *Models Don't Eat Chocolate Cookies,* published by Dial in February 2009, is sure to resonate with any young girl who's ever felt uncomfortable in her body (in other words, *all* young girls). The voice of her protagonist, Celeste, an unwilling contestant in a Miss HuskyPeach pageant for plus-sized girls, is achingly on spot when it comes to the humor, embarrassment, sarcasm, and hope in being in an adolescent.

"I don't think I can write in another voice," says Dionne. "Those middle school/early teen years were tough for me (as they are for most kids, I think), and it was a time when I learned a lot about myself. My theory is that writers have a time/experience that stays with them—resonates with them—and that contributes to the development of their voice. For some writers, different 'adult' milestones resonate and that's what they write about or explore. For others, it's childhood. Twenty-odd years out of junior high, I feel as though I have a handle on the emotions and experiences that constitute that time in my life, and can explore them through my fiction."

Dionne's fiction writing process includes drafting, and then revision, revision, revision. In fact, along with Boston College football, the Red Sox, and making her infant daughter laugh, she counts that part of the process as one of her obsessions. "I've always wanted to be one of those one-revision writers," she says. "You know, the ones who draft a full story, get some feedback, polish it up, and voila—shiny, stunning book! Yeah, that's not me."

Instead, she's found that she gets her best work done well after the first draft. When she began looking for an agent for *Models Don't Eat Chocolate Cookies*, the manuscript had already been through seven full revisions. And, she points out, "that doesn't count the step where I bought colored note cards and jotted each scene on a card—yellow for family, green for friends, pink for the HuskyPeach pageant, blue for school—and spread them out so I could see how the subplots were distributed and if there were any missing scenes/information!"

Not only did Dionne's diligence pay off in terms of creating her manuscript, it also paid off when she was searching for an agent. "I sent out 42 queries, and received 37 requests for more pages/full manuscripts, etc. And 37 ultimate rejections. I queried from August of 2006 to March 2007." After receiving the rejections, Dionne discovered that Sally Harding, an agent who had favorably reviewed her work in the past, had expanded her client list to include children's authors. "On a whim, I e-mailed and asked if she'd like to look at this project, and she was interested. Three weeks later, we had a contract."

While Harding decided that the manuscript was ready to go out to publishing houses in its current state, the revision work was far from over. "Sally told me that one of the editors liked the story, but wanted me to rework the opening chapters a little. I was fine with that, and took her notes and started working. Then another editor asked for revisions to the first three chapters. I was okay with that, too. They were asking for different types of revisions, so the two editors guided the book in two different directions. I was definitely partial to one set of instructions over the other, but I happily did what they asked—and it was interesting to see the shape those opening chapters were taking with their input. We resubmitted when I was done."

Models Don't Eat Chocolate Cookies (Dial, 2009) is Erin Dionne's debut novel.

Soon after, an offer came in. When her agent called to let her know, Dionne's knees buckled. "The phone call was a blur. I giggled through the whole thing, especially when she told me that there were two other houses interested. When I hung up and called my husband, I started shaking and lost my voice. He could barely hear me when I croaked out that there was an offer. After I hung up from him, I actually got sick from the shock! I couldn't believe that everything I'd worked for had actually come to fruition. It was surreal."

Since two other houses came in with offers shortly thereafter, Dionne had a decision to make. "It wasn't an auction situation, but it made for a *very* interesting weekend!" says Dionne. "What really helped me make the decision were the editorial notes from my now-editor, Alisha. She was so excited about the book, and I really felt as though she connected with the character of Celeste and that she shared my vision for what the book *could* be. I went with her—and Penguin/Dial Books—and I couldn't be happier."

Her working relationship with her editor has continued to be nothing but positive throughout the process. "Alisha 'gets' me, she 'gets' my books. I call her my 'Awesome Editor'—and she is. She's a fantastic reader, who is able to pinpoint the missing elements that give my stories depth. She is always encouraging, but doesn't shy away from telling me when I can do better and ways I can improve."

And of course, that process has included more revision. "I revised the first three chapters according to her notes before she bought it," says Dionne. "After she bought it, we did two revisions together. The first one was a bit broader, looking at themes and characterization. The second was to catch any loose ends and focused on specific scenes."

She sees this rewriting process as critical to her success, as well as to any other writer's. "I think writers need to learn to love revision and constructive criticism—that's the problem that I see the most with any type of writing…. We writers are not objective about our work, and a good reader plus a willingness to rewrite can make a ton of difference. Nothing is good enough the first time it goes down on paper. Or the second."

In Dionne's case, it took seven pre-agent revisions, two editor revisions, and multiple smaller edits along the way, but it's obvious her publisher and readers definitely think her finished book and her writing are not only good enough—they're great. Models was chosen as a featured titled for Scholastic's Spring 2009 Book Fairs, meaning "it'll be at just about every Scholastic book fair across the country this year—and at a bunch in Canada!" says Dionne. And her deal with Dial/Penguin was for two books, with an option for a third. Currently, she's working with the "Awesome Editor" on book two, making her way through, of course, a revision.

Megan Frazer
Secrets of Truth and Beauty
(Disney Hyperion)
www.meganfrazer.com

A self-professed fan of *Lost, Freaks and Geeks,* and *Buffy the Vampire Slayer,* Megan Frazer has always found inspiration in pop culture. In fact, it was through a movie that she discovered the sparks that would turn into her first YA novel, *Secrets of*

Truth and Beauty. "I was watching *Little Miss Sunshine,* and, during the pageant scene at the end, I thought, 'What would happen if one of those girls got fat?' What would that do to her self-perception? How would her parents and friends react? Once I had that idea, Dara's voice just jumped into my head," says Frazer.

Dara is *Secrets of Truth and Beauty's* protagonist, an overweight 17-year-old former Little Miss Maine who spends a summer coming to terms with her body image, meeting a sister she never knew she had, falling in love for the first time, and finding a smart and powerful role model in Mama Cass. Her voice came naturally to Frazer. "I lived with that voice for a while—I tend to let my characters live in my head for at least a few weeks before I start writing—and once I started writing, it flowed really quickly."

While she doesn't rely on pop culture references to drive her stories ("Publishing takes a long time, and by the time your book comes out, that reference could be passe. Also, pop culture isn't static, so your reference could

Secrets of Truth & Beauty (Hyperion, 2009) is Megan Frazer's debut novel.

have a totally different meaning now than it did five years ago."), she does use movies, books, and TV shows as idea generators and jumping-off points for creating momentum. "When I see something really impressive in the way it's done, or in the creator's vision, I want to get to work on my own stuff. I like to think about how they did what they did, and wonder if I can use any of those techniques myself," Frazer says. "Also, the emotions brought up can spur memories and ideas for me."

While the love for pop culture came later in life, Frazer developed her love for writing early on, a fact she attributes to her education. "I was lucky to go through a school system that placed a lot of emphasis on writing," she says. "The idea was that kids are natural storytellers, so get them writing, and from there you can also hook them into reading. So, as early as kindergarten, we were writing stories, and 'publishing' them."

In sixth grade, one such story led her to a realization. "We had one of those assignments where the teacher reads the first part of a story, and then you write your own ending. It was about something scary in a basement," she says. "I remember I thought my ending was better than the real ending. I think that's when I first started thinking about being a writer as a career."

Frazer recalls wishing for "more smart literature for smart teens" when she was in high school, but the desire to write YA literature wasn't fully realized until later, after composing what she refers to as "a whole bunch of forgotten novels in my past."

"There's the super-angsty one I wrote in high school. There's a big mess of chick-lit coming of age fiasco that I wrote after college. There's the mostly-finished mystery-esque novel based on a story that happened near my hometown," she says. "Then I wrote a novel about a woman coaching her daughter's little league baseball team—when unbeknownst to everyone but the mom, the girl's father was a former pitcher for the Red Sox. That one was where I started to get how to write a novel. I got a lot of positive feedback on it."

After receiving positive rejections for her earlier writing, a week came when two people—one a friend and one in the industry—both suggested she try YA. Frazer says, "I figured why not." She started Dara's story in January, and wrote it on the way to work. "At the time, I lived in Boston and commuted by train. I would write longhand on the train, and then type it up at night, adding details and expanding the scenes," she says. "I probably had a rough draft done in maybe six months. Then I put it aside while I let other people read it."

From there, she did revisions and began sending out agent queries, "at a really leisurely pace," she adds, because she was busy planning her wedding. "Instead of checking my e-mail frantically, I was desperately trying to get place cards finished. For once, getting published was in the back of my mind." In the midst of wedding prep, she received an e-mail from Sara Crowe at Harvey Klinger asking to call her about the manuscript. They talked, and Frazer signed with Crowe the next day. "The wedding was a great distraction," she says. "Once I stopped focusing on getting an agent, I got one." After a few rounds of back and forth editing, Crowe began to send out Frazer's manuscript in the fall. They received a few initial offers, and then Disney-Hyperion editors Donna Bray (before she left Hyperion) and Emily Schultz offered a preempt, and Frazer accepted. It was a surreal moment. "I had expected to be jumping up and down and screaming when I found out it sold, but I was calm. I think it was shock. It didn't feel real to me—this thing I had wanted for so long was happening over the course of days. I really couldn't believe it was true," Frazer says. "Part of me thought it was some elaborate hoax by someone I had wronged long ago. I even mentioned that to Emily, just to get reassurance that it was really real."

Not only did Frazer's editor provide her with initial emotional support and enthusiasm, she also "saw a lot of potential that I hadn't tapped yet," says Frazer. "We completely revamped the beginning section…. Her thought, which I agreed with, was that the beginning needed to be stronger in order to make the end resonate more. I'd say we did three major revisions, with a bunch of little minor ones."

Those revisions entailed growing the manuscript by almost 20,000 words, and cutting it by nearly as much. For Frazer, the process was "arduous, but worth it."

"My self-confidence took a beating—not because of how I was treated, but because my self-confidence is always looking for a chance to get down on itself," she says. However, Frazer thinks such a reaction is natural in the writing process: "As writers we are in love with our words, and our biggest fear is that people won't understand them, or will try to take them away from us somehow."

That wasn't the case with Schultz. Frazer says, "Her suggestions were always made with a gentle hand. She sent me at least three manuscripts that were covered with her tiny scrawl. She sent me lengthy, thoughtful e-mails, asking me questions, making suggestions, and forcing me to think more deeply about my work." It is this ability to take criticism and revision suggestions and work with them that has helped Frazer get to where she is today—seeing her first novel published in July 2009, and working on the draft for the next. "For me, it's a matter of perseverance. Normally I am not someone who takes rejection well, but when it comes to writing, I am able to shake it off and keep going," she says. "It's like that story of Stephen King—he had a nail above his desk where he kept all of his rejections, and when the nail was full, he used a stake. I actually had my own nail for a while, but it was too messy, so I put them all in a file folder. But I wasn't ashamed of them: they showed that I was doing the work and putting in the time."

Jenny Meyerhoff
Third Grade Baby
(Farrar, Straus & Giroux)
www.jennymeyerhoff.com

In sixth grade, Jenny Meyerhoff's teacher accused her of plagiarism. "I wrote a poem all by myself, and my teacher thought I'd plagiarized," she says. "I figured that meant it was good." Strangely enough, the incident ended up being just the encouragement she needed, and at that moment, she says, it all just clicked. "I knew writing was something I'd be doing for the rest of my life."

Photo: Mindy Garfinkle

The sixth grader found herself drawn to the world of children's publishing. "I began to carry a poetry journal with me wherever I went and soon noticed that some of my poetry sounded like picture books. I actually illustrated a couple of them." This interest in the world of children's literature would stay with her through her school years and beyond.

When Meyerhoff began teaching after college, it was, as she calls it, "the dawn of desktop publishing." She decided to put out a zine for kids, and ended up with 60 subscribers. However, while she was connected to the world of kids' books at the time, she wasn't seeking to get her own work published. "At that period in my career I knew nothing about how the business of children's publishing worked. I never submitted anything I wrote to book publishers or other children's magazines. It didn't even occur to me."

She did, however, want to know more about publishing. She got an internship at a local parenting magazine, began to freelance for the publication as well as local newspapers, and went back to school to get her master's degree in education. "Suddenly I was writing more about children than for them," she says.

Third Grade Baby (FSG, 2008) is Jenny Meyerhoff's debut novel.

Reprinted with permission of Farrar, Straus & Girous

But children's literature kept calling. "Even though I had stopped writing for children, my love of children's books was evident in my choice of reading material throughout these years," she says. "I might have told myself that I spent all that time in the children's section of the library for my students, but really I was there for myself."

In 2004, Meyerhoff made a discovery that would again kick-start her desire to write children's books, even more so than her sixth-grade teacher. "I learned about an organization called The Society for Children's Book Writers and Illustrators (SCBWI)," she says. "I recognized my true calling the moment I read their Web site and I joined instantly. Through SCBWI, I've learned so much about both business and craft sides of writing. And they connected me with my wonderful critique group."

It was both SCBWI and her critique group that helped Meyerhoff get her first book published: Third Grade Baby, the tale of sweet and spunky Polly, a late bloomer who fears she's the only third grader in the world with her baby teeth intact.

"I'm going to have to sing the praises of SCBWI again. (I promise, they haven't paid me!)" she says. "Shortly after I joined my critique group one of my critique partners, Brenda Ferber, sold her first book, Julia's Kitchen. Brenda mentioned that in one of her early conversations with her editor, her editor mentioned that chapter books were one of her favorite things to edit. I filed that bit of information away, since I had only just begun working on my book, but a year and a half later, when I was ready to submit, I knew I wanted to send it to that editor."

Before she did that, however, she revised, continuing to get feedback from her critique group. She also sought out a different set of reviewers: her daughter's third-grade class! "The teacher read the book out loud to the class, and then a hard copy remained for the students to read on their own. It was a great confidence boost to know that kids were choosing to read it over and over."

Meyerhoff eventually sent the manuscript to Ferber's editor Beverly Reingold, received feedback, revised, and sent the manuscript again. She also signed with an agent and then waited to hear from Reingold.

"After she received my revision, the editor told me she planned to take my book to

Interviews

acquisitions. The days spent waiting to hear the results of that meeting were some of the most nerve-wracking days of my life," she says. "I spent a lot of time on the Internet Googling the phrase acquisitions meeting. I think some part of me believed that if I searched hard enough and long enough I might somehow find the future results of that meeting already posted on the Internet in some weird time-folding-back-on-itself way."

When the call finally did come, Meyerhoff's cell phone was lost in her purse. "I could hear it ringing, but no amount of digging through my cluttered purse could produce it," she says. When she found it and checked her voice-mail, she had a message from her agent saying there was an offer for the book from Farrar, Straus & Giroux. And with the voice-mail, Meyerhoff could to relive the moment—repeatedly! "I was able to play the message for friends and family and listen to it as many times as I liked."

Her relationship with her editor at FSG was extremely positive, and the editing process a smooth one. "Every suggestion she made, question she posed, made so much sense to me. I couldn't believe I hadn't already thought of them," she says. "Working with her was a joy."

It also helped to have an editor who was familiar and appreciative of standalone chapter books. "I always hear that librarians and booksellers want them," says Meyerhoff, "but most books for this age groups are series books. I definitely submitted to some editors who didn't know what to do with this kind of book." Because her editor had worked on similar books before, it was a good match. "Since she was so familiar with the genre, I knew she was the perfect editor to make my book the best it could be."

And now that the manuscript has become the best book it could be, Meyerhoff has fun promotional opportunities planned to welcome it to the world. "Promoting the book turns out to be a lot more fun than I imagined, and I think that's because my book is best marketed to libraries and schools, two places where I truly feel at home," she says. "I'm really focusing on doing as many school visits as possible. I even do virtual school visits, videoconferencing with classrooms who've read my book." And for live visits? "I am accompanied by a character from my book, Martha Molar, a woman in a tooth costume who loves to talk about dental hygiene. I actually made the costume myself!"

It's somewhat fitting that Meyerhoff finds herself at home with students, as she still considers herself one. "Early on in my attempts to write children's book I read an out-of-print book by Jane Fitz-Randolph called How to Write for Children and Young Adults. She wrote that those starting out should think of themselves as apprentice writers, should focus on learning everything they can in the first year or two before sending submissions out into the world," she says. "I amend this advice to say never stop thinking of yourself as a student. I still attend as many workshops, classes and conferences as I can. I read as many craft books as I can."

And for Meyerhoff, it's the student's determination and willingness to learn and improve that can lead to success and happiness as a writer. "There is so much about this business that, as writers, is out of our control. We cannot influence which publishers take unagented submissions, how long editors take to read our manuscripts or whether a particular editor will connect with a story about believing in the tooth fairy," she says. "The only thing we absolutely can control is our craft. It is perfectly within our power to keep writing and learning and improving."

Sydney Salter
My Big Nose and Other Natural Disasters
(Graphia/Harcourt)
www.sydneysalter.com

Sydney Salter got the inspiration for her first published novel from one of the worst days of her teenage life. "The summer before my senior year in high school I worked delivering flowers, pies, and cakes for The Cake & Flower Shoppe in Reno, Nevada," she says. "One morning, I managed to tear a metal post through the van's sliding door, only hours before a big wedding."

But the disaster didn't stop there. "We had to load the huge tiered wedding cake through the van's front doors. Feeling terrible, I tried to be extra helpful at the wedding by setting the little columns in the cake and placing the layers on top. Within minutes the top layers of cake fell from the columns into a ball of frosting and grass."

Jory, the heroine of Salter's first book, My Big Nose and Other Natural Disasters, goes through the same set of mishaps, and like the teenage Salter, Jory's fired. However that wasn't the only part of Salter's life that inspired the book.

Like Jory, who spends most of the summer before her senior year saving for a nose job, Salter too struggled with confidence about her appearance. "The big nose part comes from my insecurity about my looks in high school, and my realization after high school that confidence is a far more attractive trait than traditional

My Big Nose and Other Natural Disasters (Graphia, 2009) is Sydney Salter's debut novel.

Reprinted with permission of Graphia/Houghton Mifflin Harcourt.

beauty," she says. "I wanted to write about a girl who thinks that her looks are her problem, when it's really her thinking that's the problem."

Salter wrote Jory's story during National Novel Writing Month (NaNoWriMo, www. nanowrimo.org). Being challenged to write 50,000 words in the month of November helped spur her writing on—some much-needed motivation at the time. "At this point, I'd written three other manuscripts, but had not found publishing success," she says. "My other three novels had each won local writing contests, and while I'd received some lovely rejection letters, I was feeling kind of discouraged."

Writing so much so quickly gave Salter a creative momentum that led to the creation of what she calls a "surprisingly cohesive" 60,000 word first draft. "I loved the rush of writing so many words so fast—I didn't have time to second-guess myself and I smashed my writing rituals to pieces. I learned that I could write with my kids fighting, while baking Thanksgiving pies, early in the morning, late at night, and in a variety of locations—all skills essential to a writing mom."

Manuscript in hand, Salter decided to go the agent route rather than submitting to publishing houses on her own, and sent off a series of queries. She received a response from Ted Malawer, then an assistant with Nadia Cornier, and soon signed with him. He helped Salter prepare the manuscript for submission at the same time he began taking on his own clients. The match has been a good one for Salter. "I really appreciate having someone to help me make career decisions. As I've often told Ted, I can't imagine doing this alone."

Salter was at the airport, waiting for her flight to the SCBWI conference in Los Angeles when Malawer called her to let her know that Julie Tibbott at Harcourt had made a two-book offer for Salter's work. Salter's response was ecstatic. "I could hardly believe it—and I didn't really sleep for about four days. I kept waking in the night, amazed that I would be paid for doing what I loved," she says. "My books would be in bookstores and libraries! People would read my words! Everyone would know that I had a big nose. Yikes!" Salter was thrilled to share the news with her friends and colleagues at SCBWI, "people who really understand the long struggle toward publication."

It was the realization of a lifelong dream for Salter, one that started in her teens. "When I was 15, I started writing in a daily diary that I've kept ever since. I'd always secretly wanted to become a writer, but the fear of failing prevented me from taking a single writing class while getting my B.A. in English at Whitman College," she says. After college, she began taking classes at the University of Washington, and while there, wrote "serious—and seriously awful—short stories about professional footballs players and other subjects that I knew nothing about." The stories she did receive positive feedback on were about children. "My classmates would encourage me to pursue those stories further, but I wanted to be a real writer so I ignored their advice."

It took a few more years, another college major (in history this time), two children, several more notebooks of "awful writing," and a trip to Mexico to convince Salter that she had what it took to be a real writer, especially when writing for children. On a family vacation to Mexico, Salter decided to write and research a short story that would teach her daughters about Mayan culture. What resulted was the first draft of a novel and a newfound confidence. "I was hooked on writing. If I could write one, I could write two, or maybe even 200."

She began to work daily on her writing, doing writing exercises, starting on new novels and revising old ones, writing magazine stories, and reading children's novels. During that time, she also became a Regional Advisor for SCBWI, a role that helped her learn a lot about the business of writing. After five years of solid writing, she sold My Big Nose and Other Natural Disasters—it was her fourth manuscript.

Now, Salter's definitely on her way to achieving her writing dream of "maybe even 200" books. Along with *My Big Nose*, Harcourt will be publishing *Jungle Crossing* (the novel that arose from her trip to Mexico) in 2009 and *Swoon at Your Own Risk* in 2010. She's polishing a tween manuscript, planning on revising some manuscripts she's already written, and has notebooks full of ideas. Plus, she has some source material living in her own home. "I have two daughters on the verge of their teen years," she says. "I keep threatening to chaperone one of my daughter's junior high dances—I just know it would give me the plots for at least two novels!"

Salter's main advice for writers is evident in her own habits: "Keep writing. Don't just write the first book and wait for an editor to fall in love with it. Write the second book, the third one. Then take what you've learned and go back and revise the first one."

She's also an advocate for making rejection "fun." "I keep all my rejection letters in a big fat Notebook of Rejection. I also list the number of rejections I receive in my annual Christmas letter," she says. "Don't fear rejection; learn from it. I started collecting small turtle statues to remind me to have a strong shell—and to remind myself that the tortoise *did* win that race!"

First Books Follow-Up: Marlene Perez

When we last left talked with Marlene Perez (www.marleneperez.com), she was awaiting publication of her first book *Unexpected Development,* nervous about her book's imprint Roaring Press Books being sold to Macmillan, but excited to see the book published and eager to continue her writing journey. The day a copy of the book arrived in her hands, was, as she puts it, glorious. "I felt like life couldn't get any better," she says. The good news? It did get better. "Having a second book in your hand feels just as good, maybe even better. Because now I feel like I've proven to myself that I'm in it for the long haul."

So what's been going on in Perez's life since her first book? Well, there's one new agent, two new editors, two new publishing homes, and five new books. What hasn't changed? The intense fear and excitement that comes with waiting for a book offer.

"There were a couple of years between sales, and that was a little scary. *Unexpected Development* came out in September 2004, and I didn't sell another book until October 2006," she says.

But when she did, she not only sold one book, she sold three. At auction, the day before her birthday, Perez's agent Stephen Barbara sold to Harcourt her YA supernatural trilogy: *Dead Is the New Black; Dead Is a State of Mind; Dead Is So Last Year.*

A month later, a few days before her husband's birthday, Perez's agent sold the young adult novel *Love in the Corner Pocket* to Scholastic/Point. "He ended up selling four books of mine in five weeks," she says. "We really like birthdays around here."

Even though she had a published book under her belt, getting the next books published wasn't a complete breeze. "It was nerve-wracking, especially during the auction," she says. However, she did learn a few things along the way that helped ease some of the nerves. For one thing, she had the experience of the first book under her belt. "I think, like many writers, that I was so focused on getting that first book published, that I hadn't even given a thought to what happens after a book is purchased. So that's where my expectations just kind of stopped. I hadn't thought about what happened next," she says. "I didn't really know enough about the review process or that anything could go wrong after a sale. In my case, it was that my imprint was going to be sold. So my first book was an education."

Between her first book and her later sales, Perez also immersed herself in a self-education crash course in publishing. "During that time, I did my homework and learned as much about literary agents and the publishing industry as I could. I truly believe writing is a calling, a craft, but it's also a business. I needed to learn more about the business side of things and I did," she says. The knowledge—from how much sales matter, what sell-through means, and how independent bookstores hand-sell books—paid off. "It made my life easier. And maybe my expectations were more realistic this time, although my agent managed to surpass those expectations."

Working with Barbara has been invigorating, mainly because they're on the same page. "We have the same long-term views and ideas about the trajectory of my career, he's incredibly enthused about my writing... and most importantly, I'm comfortable and confident in way in which he represents me."

While she's discovered more about the business, she's also working on her own writing process, in particular, how to work with her inner critic. "I'm learning when to shut her up and when to let her in. I think you have to turn that internal editor off when you're writing a first draft or you'll get bogged down in editing. But definitely invite that critic back during revision!"

Other parts of her writing process have remained the same. "As with anything, I think you get better with practice. So I don't really approach the process differently, except that

I may show my agent and editor a couple of chapters of something, rather than a completed manuscript. But every writer is different."

Perez's new books feature female protagonists, but their quests this time around are a bit different than the heroine of *Unexpected Development*, Megan, a teen dealing with the challenges of being in high school and being large-breasted.

Her *Dead* series is a YA humorous paranormal mystery trilogy featuring a family of psychic sisters who solve mysteries in Nightshade, California. The topics intrigued Perez from the get-go. "I have seven sisters (and four brothers) so I really loved writing about those familial relationships," she says. "And the supernatural really intrigues me, so I had a blast writing about vampires, werewolves, ghosts, and other things that go bump in the night," says the fan of *Dark Shadows* and the Vampire Lestat books.

Love in the Corner Pocket, a YA novel about a love and billiards triangle set in Laguna Beach, California, is a change too. "I loved writing about the main character, Chloe because she was so different from me," says Perez. "And I played pool (badly) in high school, so it was fun to learn about competitive pool."

Marlene Perez has had four novels published since her 2004 debut Unexpected Development, including *Dead is the New Black* (Harcourt, 2008).

Throughout it all, the only regret Perez has is not writing earlier. "Honestly, I wish I would have started sooner. I was always one of those people who were going to write a book 'some day.'" Now, Perez works on writing down her goals and dreams, so that she doesn't postpone them until "some day."

"We have this dry erase board hanging on our fridge that my family calls the 'magic white board' because I wrote down a dream—'a three book contract with a major publisher' and it came true!" she says. "You have to put in a lot of work to make that dream a reality, but it can happen."

Book Publishers

There's no magic formula for getting published. It's a matter of getting the right manuscript on the right editor's desk at the right time. Before you submit it's important to learn publishers' needs, see what kind of books they're producing and decide which publishers your work is best suited for. *Children's Writer's & Illustrator's Market* is but one tool in this process. (Those just starting out, turn to Quick Tips for Writers & Illustrators on page 5.)

To help you narrow down the list of possible publishers for your work, we've included several indexes at the back of this book. The **Subject Index** lists book and magazine publishers according to their fiction and nonfiction needs or interests. The **Age-Level Index** indicates which age groups publishers cater to. The **Photography Index** indicates which markets buy photography for children's publications. The **Poetry Index** lists publishers accepting poetry.

If you write contemporary fiction for young adults, for example, and you're trying to place a book manuscript, go first to the Subject Index. Locate the fiction categories under Book Publishers and copy the list under Contemporary. Then go to the Age-Level Index and highlight the publishers on the Contemporary list that are included under the Young Adults heading. Read the listings for the highlighted publishers to see if your work matches their needs.

Remember, *Children's Writer's & Illustrator's Market* should not be your only source for researching publishers. Here are a few other sources of information:

- The Society of Children's Book Writers and Illustrators (SCBWI) offers members an annual market survey of children's book publishers for the cost of postage or free online at www.scbwi.org (SCBWI membership information can also be found at www.scbwi.org)
- The Children's Book Council Web site (www.cbcbooks.org) gives information on member publishers.
- If a publisher interests you, send a SASE for submission guidelines or check publishers' Web sites for guidelines *before* submitting. To quickly find guidelines online, visit The Colossal Directory of Children's Publishers at www.signaleader.com.
- Check publishers' Web sites. Many include their complete catalogs that you can browse. Web addresses are included in many publishers' listings.
- Spend time at your local bookstore to see who's publishing what. While you're there, browse through *Publishers Weekly* and *The Horn Book*.

SUBSIDY & SELF-PUBLISHING

Some determined writers who receive rejections from royalty publishers may look to subsidy and co-op publishers as an option for getting their work into print. These publishers ask writers to pay all or part of the costs of producing a book. We strongly advise writers and illustrators to work only with publishers who pay them. For this reason, we've adopted a policy not to include any subsidy or co-op publishers in *Children's Writer's & Illustrator's Market* (or any other Writer's Digest Books market books).

If you're interested in publishing your book just to share it with friends and relatives, self-publishing is a viable option, but it involves time, energy, and money. You oversee all book production details. Check with a local printer for advice and information on cost or check online for print-on-demand publishing options (which are often more affordable).

Whatever path you choose, keep in mind that the market is flooded with submissions, so it's important for you to hone your craft and submit the best work possible. Competition from thousands of other writers and illustrators makes it more important than ever to research publishers before submitting—read their guidelines, look at their catalogs, check out a few of their titles and visit their websites.

N ABBEVILLE FAMILY

Abbeville Press. 137 Varick St.New York NY 10013.Estab. 1977. (212)366-5585. Fax: (212)366-6966. E-mail: cvance@abbeville.com. Website: www.abbeville.com. Specializes in trade books. **Manuscript/ Art Acquisitions:** Cynthia Vance, Director of Abbeville Family. Publishes 8 picture books/year. 10% of books by first-time authors and 20% for subsidy published.

Fiction Picture Books: Animal, anthology, concept, contemporary, fantasy, folktales, health, hi-lo, history, humor, multicultural, nature/environment, poetry, science fiction, special needs, sports, suspense. Average word length 300-1000 words. Recently published *Everett, the Incredibly Helpful Helper,* by Sue Anne Morrow with illustrations by CG Williams (ages 1-4, picture/nonfiction book); *Red, Yellow, Blue, and You,* by Cynthia Vance with illustrations by Candace Whitman (ages 2-5 picture/board book) with padded cover and rhyming text; *The Journey: Plateosarus (Dinosaurs illustrated comics series),* by Matteo Bacchin and Marco Signore, with foreword by Mark Norell (ages 9 and up). Educational comic series, 64 pages with hardcover.

How to Contact Fiction: Please refer to web site for submission policy. Initial submission by mail only.

HARRY N. ABRAMS BOOKS FOR YOUNG READERS

115 W. 18th St.New York NY 10011. (212)519-1200. Website: www.abramsyoungreaders.com **Publisher, Children's Books:** Howard W. Reeves.
  • Abrams title *365 Penguins,* by Jean-Luc Fromental, illustrated by Joelle Jolivel, won a Boston Globe-Horn Book Picture Book Honor Award in 2007. See first books on page 133 for an interview with Boni Ashbum, Author of Abram's title *Hush, Little Dragon.; Abrams no longer accepts unsolicited works of fiction.*

Fiction Picture books ages 0-12, fiction and non-fiction.

How to Contact Does not accept unsolicited manuscripts or queries.

ABSEY & CO.

23011 Northcrest Dr.Spring TX 77389. (281)257-2340. Fax: (281)251-4676. E-mail: abseyandco@aol.com. Website: www.absey.com. New York address: 45 W. 21st Street, Suite 5, New York NY 10010. (212)277-8028. (Send mss to Spring TX address only.) **Publisher:** Edward Wilson. "We are looking for education books, especially those with teaching strategies based upon research, for children's picture books and Young Adult fiction. We haven't done much with nonfiction." Publishes hardcover, trade paperback and mass market paperback originals. Publishes 5-10 titles/year. 50% of books from first-time authors; 50% from unagented writers.

Fiction "Since we are a small, new press, we are looking for good manuscripts with a firm intended audience." Recently published *Stealing a Million Kisses* (board book); *Adrift* (YA fiction).

How to Contact Fiction: Query with SASE. Does not consider simultaneous submissions. Responds to queries in 3 months. No e-mail submissions. "We do not download from unknown sources."

Terms Pays 8-15% royalty on wholesale price. Publishes book 1 year after acceptance of ms. Manuscript guidelines for #10 SASE.

Tips "Absey publishes a few titles every year. We like the author and the illustrator working together to create something magical. Authors and illustrators have input into every phase of production."

ALADDIN/PULSE

1230 Avenue of the Americas, 4th Floor, New York NY 10020. (212)698-2707. Fax: (212)698-7337. Website: www.simonsays.com. **Vice President/Publsher, Aladdin/Pulse:** Bethany Buck; **Vice President/Associate Publisher, Aladdin:** Ellen Krieger; Liesa Abrams, executive editor (Aladdin); Emily Lawrence, associate editor (Aladdin); Kate Angelella, assistant editor (Aladdin) Jennifer Klonsky, Editorial Director (Pulse); Anica Rissi, editor (Pulse); Michael del Rosario, associate editor (Pulse), Manuscript Acquisitions: Attn: Submissions Editor. **Art Acquisitions:** Karin Paprocki, Aladdin; Russell Gordon, Simon Pulse. Hardcover/paperback imprints of Simon & Schuster Children's Publishing Children's Division. Publishes c. 175 titles/year.

Fiction Aladdin publishes picture books, beginning readers, chapter books, middle grade and tween fiction and nonfiction, and graphic novels and nonfiction in hardcover and paperback, with an emphasis on commercial, kid-friendly titles. Simon Pulse publishes original teen series, single title fiction, and select nonfiction, in hardcover and paperback. Recently published Nancy Drew and the Clue Crew chapter book series (Emily Lawrence, editor); Pendragon middle grade series (Liesa Abrams, editor); Edgar & Ellen middle grade series (Ellen Krieger, editor); Uglies series (Bethany Buck, editor); *Wake, bloom, Uninvited, Disenchanted Princess, The Straight Road to Kylie* (Jennifer Klonsky, editor); *Chill*; *Model* (Anica Rissi, editor); *I Heart You, You Haunt Me*; *Unleashed*; *My Summer on Earth*; Drama series (Michael del Rosario, editor).

How to Contact Fiction: Accepts query letters with proposals (Aladdin); accepts query letters (Simon Pulse).

ALASKA NORTHWEST BOOKS

Imprint of Graphic Arts Center Publishing Co.P.O. Box 10306, Portland OR 97296-0306. (503)226-2402. Fax: (503)223-1410. E-mail: editorial@gacpc.com. Website: www.gacpc.com. **Executive Editor:** Tim Frew. Imprints: Alaska Northwest Books. Publishes 3 picture books/year; 1 young reader/year. 20% of books by first-time authors. "We publish books that teach and entertain as well as inform the reader about Alaska or the western U.S. We're interested in wildlife, adventure, unusual sports, inspirational nature stories, traditions, but we also like plain old silly stories that make kids giggle. We are particular about protecting Native American story-telling traditions, and ask that writers ensure that it's clear whether they are writing from within the culture or about the culture. We encourage Native American writers to share their stories."

Fiction Picture books, young readers: adventure, animal, contemporary, fantasy, history, humor, multicultural, nature/environment, poetry. Middle readers, young adult/teens: adventure, animal, anthology, contemporary, history, humor, multicultural, nature/environment, suspense/mystery. Average word length: picture books—500-1,000; young readers—500-1,500; middle readers—1,500-2,000; young adults—35,000. Recently published *Seldovia Sam and the Wildfire Rescue*, by Susan Woodward Springer, illustrated by Amy Meissner (ages 6-10, early chapter book); *Ten Rowdy Ravens*, by Susan Ewing, illustrated by Evon Zerbetz (age 5 and up, humor); *Berry Magic*, by Teri Sloat and Betty Huffmon, illustrated by Teri Sloat (age 6 and up, legend).

Nonfiction Picture books: animal. Young readers: animal, multicultural, sports. Middle readers, young adults/teens: animal, history, multicultural, nature/environment, sports, Alaska- or Western-themed adventure. Average word length: picture books—500-1,000; young readers—500-1,500; middle readers—1,500-2,000; young adults—35,000. Recently published *Big-Enough Anna: The Little Sled Dog Who Braved the Arctic*, by Pam Flowers and Ann Dixon, illustrated by Bill Farnsworth (5 and up); *Recess at 20 Below*, by Cindy Lou Aillaud (ages 6-10).

How to Contact Fiction: Submit complete ms for picture books or submit outline/synopsis and 2 sample chapters for YA novels. Nonfiction: Submit complete ms for picture books or submit 2 sample chapters for YA nonfiction chapter books. Responds to queries/mss in 3-5 months. Publishes book 2 years after acceptance. Will consider simultaneous submissions.

Terms Pays authors royalty of 5-7% based on net revenues. Offers advances (average amount: $2,000). Pays illustrators royalty of 5-7% based on net revenues. Pays photographers royalty of 5-7% based on net revenues. Sends galleys to authors; dummies to illustrators. Originals returned to artist at job's completion. Book catalog available for 9 × 12 SASE and $3.85 postage; ms, art, and photo guidelines available for SASE. All imprints included in a single catalog. Catalog available on Web site.

Tips "As a regional publisher, we seek books about Alaska and the West. We rarely publish YA novels, but are more interested in the pre-school to early reader segment. A proposal that shows that the author has researched the market, in addition to submitting a unique story, will get our attention."

☐ ALL ABOUT KIDS PUBLISHING

9333 Benbow Drive, Gilroy CA 95020. (408)846-1833. Fax: (408)846-1835. E-mail: lguevara@aakp. com. Website: www.aakp.com. **Acquisitions:** Linda Guevara. Publishes 3-5 picture books/year; 3-5 chapter books/year. 80% of books by first-time authors.

Fiction Picture books, young readers: adventure, animal, concept, fantasy, folktales, history, humor, nature, poetry, suspense/mystery. Average word length: picture books—450 words. Recently published *Dillan McMillan, Please Eat Your Peas*, by David Schneider (picture book); *The Titanic Game*, by Mike Warner (chapter book).

Nonfiction Picture books, young readers: activity books, animal, biography, concept, history, nature. Average word length: picture books—450 words. Recently published *Shadowbox Hunt: A Search & Find Odyssey*, by Laura L. Seeley (picture book).

How to Contact Fiction: Submit complete ms. Nonfiction: Submit complete ms for picture books; outline synopsis and complete ms for young readers. Responds to mss in 3 months. Publishes a book 2-3 years after acceptance. Manuscript returned with SASE only.

Terms Pays author royalty. Offers advances (average amount: $1,000). Pays illustrators by the project (range: $3,000 minimum) and/or royalty of 3-5% based on discounted. Pays photographers by the project (range: $500 minimum) or royalty of 5% based on discounted price. Sends galleys to authors; dummies to illustrators. All imprints included in a single catalog. Writer's, artist's and photographer's guidelines available for SASE and on Web site.

Tips "Not accepting submissions until July 2009. Please check our Web site in June and December for updates and submission guidelines."

AMERICAN GIRL PUBLISHING

8400 Fairway Place, Middleton WI 53562-2554. (608)836-4848. Fax: (608)836-1999. Website: www. americangirl.com. **Manuscript Acquisitions:** Submissions Editor. Publishes 30 middle readers/ year. 10% of books by first-time authors. Publishes fiction and nonfiction for girls 8-12.

Fiction American Girls publishes 2-3 titles per year for its Girl of the year character and 3 mystery titles per year for its historical characters. American Girl does not accept ideas or manuscripts.

Nonfiction Middle readers: activity books, arts/crafts, cooking, history, hobbies, how-to self help, sports. Recently published *A Smart Girl's Guide to Friendship Troubles*, by Patti Kelley Crisswell, (ages 8 and up; self-help); *Paper Punch Art*, by Laura Torres (ages 8 and up; craft); *Quiz Book 2*, by Sarah Jane Brian, illustrated by Debbie Tilley (ages 8 and up; activity). Also publishes *American Girl* magazine. See the listing for *American Girl* in the Magazines section.

How to Contact Nonfiction: Submit well-focused concepts for activity, craft or advice books. "Proposals should include a detailed descripton of your concept, sample chapters or spreads and lists of previous publications. Complete manuscripts also accepted." Responds in 3 months. Will consider simultaneous submissions.

Terms Pays authors royalty or work purchased outright. Pays illustrators by the project. Pays photographers by the project. Sends galleys to authors; dummies to illustrators. Originals returned to artist at job's completion. Book catalog available for 8½ × 11 SAE and 4 first-class stamps. All imprints included in a single catalog.

AMULET BOOKS

Amulet Books/ Harry N. Abrams, Inc, 115 W. 18th St.New York NY 10001. (212)229-8000. Website: www.amuletbooks.com. Estab. 2004. Specializes in trade books, fiction. **Manuscript Acquisitions:** Susan Van Metre, editorial director. **Art Acquisitions:** Chad Beckerman, art director. Produces 10 middle readers/year, 10 young adult titles/year. 10% of books by first-time authors.

Fiction Middle readers: adventure, contemporary, fantasy, history, science fiction, sports. Young adults/teens: adventure, contemporary, fantasy, history, science fiction, sports, suspense. Recently published *Diary of a Wimpy Kid*, by Jeff Kinney; *The Sisters Grimm*, by Michael Buckley (midgrade series); *Ttyl*, by Lauren Miracle (YA novel).

How to Contact Fiction: Does not accept unsolicited manuscripts or queries.

Terms Offers advance against royalties. Illustrators paid by the project. Author sees galleys for review. Illustrators see dummies for review. Originals returned to artist at job's completion. Catalog available for 9 × 12 SASE and 4 first-class stamps.

ATHENEUM BOOKS FOR YOUNG READERS

Imprint of Simon & Schuster Children's Publishing Division, 1230 Avenue of the Americas, New York NY 10020. (212)698-2715. Website: www.simonsayskids.com. Estab. 1960. **Publisher:** Vice President, Publisher Emma D. Dryden. Editorial Director, Caitlyn Dlouhy. Executive Editor, Namrata Tripathi. Atheneum publishes original hardcover and paperback trade books for children from pre-school age through young adult. Our list includes picture books, chapter books, mysteries, biography, science fiction, fantasy, graphic novels, middle grade and young adult fiction and nonfiction. The style and subject matter of the books we publish is almost unlimited. We do not, however, publish textbooks, coloring or activity books, greeting cards, magazines or pamphlets or religious publications."

- Atheneum title *The Underneath*, by Kathi Appelt; illustrated by David Small won a 2009 Newbery Honor. Recently published: *Someday*, by Alison McGhee, illustrated by Peter Reynolds (picture book); *That Book Woman*, by Heather Henson; illustrated by David Small (picture book); *Olivia Helps With Christmas*, by Ian Falconer (picture book); *Dark Dude*, by Oscar Hijuelos (teen novel); *Shift*, by Jennifer Bradbury (debut novel); *Tweak*, by Nic Sheff (teen memoir); *The Higher Power Of Lucky*, by Susan Patron (Newbery Medal).

Terms Pays royalty on hardcover and paperback retail price: 10% fiction; 5% illustrator (picture book). Publishes MSS up to 3 years after acceptance. Pays illustrators advance and royalty or by the project. Pays photographers by the project. Original artwork returned at job's completion.

Tips "Atheneum has a 40+ year tradition of publishing distinguished books for children. Study our titles

AVALON BOOKS

160 Madison Ave.5th Floor New York NY 10016. Phone: (212)598-0222 Fax: (212)979-1862. E-Mail: editorial@avalonbooks.com; Website: www.avalonbooks.com. **Acquisitions:** Faith Black, editor. Chelsea Gilmore, assistant editor. Established: 1950. Publishes hardcover originals. **Publishes 60 titles/year.** Publishes manuscript 10-12 months after acceptance. Responds in 6 No Answer to manuscripts. **Pays 15% royalty Offers True advance.**

Fiction "We publish wholesome contemporary romances, mysteries, historical romances and westerns. Our books are read by adults as well as teenagers, and the characters are all adults. All mysteries are contemporary. We publish contemporary romances (4 every 2 months), historical romances (2 every 2 months), mysteries (2 every 2 months) and traditional westerns (2 every 2 months). Submit first 3 sample chapters, a 2-3 page synopsis and SASE. The manuscripts should be 40,000-70,000 words. Manuscripts that are too long will not be considered. The books shall be wholesome fiction, without graphic sex, violence or strong language. We are actively looking for romantic comedy, chick lit."

Needs Mystery, Romance, Western. Submission method: Query with SASE. Recent Titles: *Miss Delacourt Speaks Her Mind*, by Heidi Ashworth (historical romance); *Everything But A Wedding*, by Holly Jacobs (contemporary romance); *Murder Express*, by Robert Scott (mystery); *Judgment at Gold Butte*, by Terrell L. Bowers (western).

ⓐ AVON BOOKS/BOOKS FOR YOUNG READERS

1350 Avenue of the Americas, New York NY 10019. (212)261-6500. Fax: (212)261-6668. Website: www.harperchildrens.com.

• Avon is not accepting unagented submissions. See listing for HarperCollins Children's Books.

AZRO PRESS

PMB 342, 1704 Llano St. B, Santa Fe NM 87505. (505)989-3272. Fax: (505)989-3832. E-mail: books@azropress.com. Website: www.azropress.com. Estab. 1997. Specializes in illustrated children's books. **Writers contact:** Gae Eisenhardt. Produces 3-4 picture books/year; 1 young reader/year. 75% of books by first-time authors. "We like to publish illustrated children's books by Southwestern authors and illustrators. We are always looking for books with a Southwestern look or theme."

Fiction Picture books: animal, history, humor, nature/environment. Young readers: adventure, animal, hi-lo, history, humor. Average word length: picture books—1,200; young readers—2,000-2,500. Recently published *The Magical Mrs. Iptweet & Me*, by Barbara Mayfield; *Tis for Tortilla*, by Jody Alpers, ill by Celeste Johnson; *Cactus Critter Bash*, by Sid Hausman; *Loco Dog and the Dustdevil in the Railyard*, by Marcy Heller, ill by Nancy Poes; *Pancho Finds a Home*, by Karen Gogan, ill by Blanche Davidson.

Nonfiction Picture books: animal, geography, history. Young readers: geography, history.

How to Contact Accepts international submissions. Fiction/nonfiction: Query or submit complete ms. Responds to queries/mss in 3-4 months. Publishes book 1-2 years after acceptance. Considers simultaneous submissions.

Terms Pays authors royalty of 5% to 10% based on wholesale price. Pays illustrators by the project ($2,000) or royalty of 5%. Author sees galleys for review. Illustrators see dummies for review. Originals returned to artist at job's completion. Catalog available for #10 SASE and 3 first-class stamps. Catalog on line. See website for artist's, photographer's guidelines.

Tips "We are not currently accepting new manuscripts. Please see our Web site for acceptance date."

Ⓝ BALZER & BRAY

HarperCollins Children's Books. 1350 Avenue of the America's, New York NY 10019.Estab. 2008. (212)307-3628. Fax: (212)261-6538. Specializes in fiction. Imprints: Balzer & Bray Alessandra Balzer, Co-Publisher; Donna Bray, Co-Publisher; Jill Santopolo, Senior Editor; Kristin Daly, Editor; Ruta Rimas, Editorial Assistant; Corey Mallonee, Editorial Assistant. Publishes 10 picture books/year; 8 middle reader/year; 7 young adult/year.

Fiction Picture Books, Young Readers: adventure, animal, anthology, concept, contemporary, fantasy, history, humor, multicultural, nature/environment, poetry, science fiction, special needs, sports, suspense. Middle Readers, Young Adults/Teens: adventure, animal, anthology, contemporary, fantasy, history, humor, multicultural, nature/environment, poetry, science fiction, special needs, sports, suspense.

Nonfiction All levels: animal, biography, concept, cooking, history, multicultural, music/dance, nature/environment, other, science, self help, social issues, special needs, sports. We will publish very few non-fiction titles, maybe 1-2 per year.

How to Contact Interested in agented material. Publishes a book 18 months after acceptance.

Terms Offers advances. Pays illustrators by the project. Sends galleries to authors. Originals returned to artist at job's completion. Catalog is available on our web site.

BANTAM DELACORTE DELL BOOKS FOR YOUNG READERS

Random House Children's Books, 1745 Broadway, Mail Drop 9-2, New York NY 10019. (212) 782-9000.Web sites: www.randomhouse.com/kids, www.randomhouse.com/teens.

- Publishes middle-grade and young adult fiction in hard cover, trade paperback, mass market and digest formats.

How to Contact Unsolicited manuscripts are only accepted as submissions to either the *Delacorte Dell Yearling Contest for a First Middle-Grade Novel* or *Delacorte Press Contest for a First Young Adult Novel*. See www.randomhouse.com/kids/about/faq for rules and guidelines or send a written request addressed to *Delacorte Press Contest*, Random House, Inc.1745 Broadway, New York, NY 10019 and include a SASE. All other query letters or manuscript submissions must be submitted through an agent or at the request of an editor. No e-mail queries.

BAREFOOT BOOKS

2067 Massachusetts Ave, 5th Floor, Cambridge MA 02140. Website: wwwbarefootbookscom.

Fiction Picture books, young readers: animal, anthology, concept, folktales, multicultural, nature/environment, poetry, spirituality. Middle readers, young adults: anthology, folktales. Average word length: picture books—500-1,000; young readers—2,000-3,000; anthologies—10,000-20,000. Recently published *The Prince's Bedtime*, by Joanne Oppenheim; *The Hare and the Tortoise*, by Ranjit Bolt; *Elusive Moose*, by Clare Beaton.

How to Contact Fiction: Submit complete ms for picture books; outline/synopsis and 1 sample story for collections. Responds in 4 months if SASE is included. Will consider simultaneous submissions and previously published work.

Terms Pays authors royalty of 5% based on retail price. Offers advances. Sends galleys to authors. Originals returned to artist at job's completion. Book catalog available for SAE and 5 first-class stamps; ms guidelines available for SASE.

Tips "We are looking for books that inspire and are filled with a sense of magic and wonder. We also look for strong stories from all different cultures, reflecting the ways of the individual culture while also touching deeper human truths that suggest we are all one. We welcome playful submissions for the very youngest children and also anthologies of stories for older readers, all focused around a universal theme. We encourage writers and artists to visit our Web site and read some of our books to get a sense of our editorial philosophy and what we publish before they submit to us. Always, we encourage them to stay true to their inner voice and artistic vision that reaches out for timeless stories, beyond the momentary trends that may exist in the market today."

☐ BARRONS EDUCATIONAL SERIES

250 Wireless Blvd.Hauppauge NY 11788. Fax: (631)434-3723. E-mail: waynebarr@barronseduc.com. Website: www.barronseduc.com. **Manuscript Acquisitions:** Wayne R. Barr, acquisitions manager. **Art Acquisitions:** Bill Kuchler. Publishes 20 picture books/year; 20 young readers/year; 20 middle readers/year; 10 young adult titles/year. Most are from packagers.

Fiction Picture books: animal, concept, multicultural, nature/environment. Young readers: adventure, multicultural, nature/environment, fantasy, suspense/mystery. Middle readers: adventure, fantasy, multicultural, nature/environment, problem novels, suspense/mystery. Young adults: problem novels. Examples — *Night at the Smithsonian*, by Leslie Goldman; *Renoir and the Boy in the Long Hair*, by Wendy Wax. Stories with an educational element are appealing.

Nonfiction Picture books: concept, reference. Young readers: biography, how-to, reference, self help, social issues. Middle readers: hi-lo, how-to, reference, self help, social issues. Young adults: reference, self help, social issues, sports.

How to Contact Fiction: Query via e-mail with no attached files. No snail mail. Nonfiction: Submit outline/synopsis and sample chapters. "Nonfiction Submissions must be accompanied by SASE for response." Responds to queries in 2 months; mss in 4 months. Publishes a book 1 year after acceptance. Will consider simultaneous submissions.

Terms Pays authors royalty of 10-13% based on net price or buys ms outright for $2,000 minimum. Pays illustrators by the project based on retail price. Sends galleys to authors; dummies to illustrators. Book catalog, ms/artist's guidelines for 9 × 12 SAE.

Tips Writers: "We publish preschool storybooks, concept books and middle grade and YA chapter books. No romance novels. Those with an educational element" Illustrators: "We are happy to receive a sample illustration to keep on file for future consideration. Periodic notes reminding us of your work are acceptable." Children's book themes "are becoming much more contemporary and relevant to a child's day-to-day activities, fewer talking animals. We are interested in fiction (ages 7-11 and ages 12-16) dealing with modern problems."d

☐ BENCHMARK BOOKS

Imprint of Marshall Cavendish, 99 White Plains Rd.Tarrytown NY 10591. (914)332-8888. Fax: (914)332-1888. E-mail: mbisson@marshallcavendish.com. Website: www.marshallcavendish.us **Manuscript Acquisitions:** Michelle Bisson. Publishes about 300 young reader, middle reader and young adult books/year. "We look for interesting treatments of only nonfiction subjects related to elementary, middle school and high school curriculum."

Nonfiction Most nonfiction topics should be curriculum related. Average word length: 4,000-20,000. All books published as part of a series. Recently published First Americans (series), Family Trees (series), Bookworms (series).

How to Contact Nonfiction: "Please read our catalog or view our Web site before submitting proposals. We only publish series. We do not publish individual titles." Submit outline/synopsis and 1 or more sample chapters. Responds to queries/mss in 3 months. Publishes a book 2 years after acceptance. Will consider simultaneous submissions.

Terms Buys work outright. Sends galleys to authors. Book catalog available online. All imprints included in a single catalog.

☐ BICK PUBLISHING HOUSE

307 Neck Rd.Madison CT 06443. (203)245-0073. Fax: (203)245-5990. E-mail: bickpubhse@aol.com. Website: www.bickpubhouse.com. **Aquisitions Editor:** Dale Carlson. "We publish psychological, philosophical, scientific information on health and recovery, wildlife rehabiliation, living with disabilities, teen psychology and science for adults and young adults."

Nonfiction Young adults: nature/environment, religion, science, self help, social issues, special needs. Average word length: young adults—60,000. Recently published *In and Out of Your Mind* (teen science); *Who Said What?* (philosophy quotes for teens); *What are You Doing with Your Life?*, by J. Krishnamurti (philosophy for teens); *The Teen Brain Book*, by Dale Carlson.

How to Contact Fiction: Submit outline/synopsis and 3 sample chapters. Nonfiction: Submit outline/synopsis or outline/synopsis and 3 sample chapters. Responds to queries/mss in 2 weeks. Publishes book 1 year after acceptance. Will consider simultaneous submissions and previously published work.

Terms Pays authors royalty of 5-10%. Pays illustrators by the project (range: up to $1,000). Sends galleys to authors; dummies to illustrators. Book catalog available for SASE with 1 first-class stamp; writer's guidelines available for SAE. Catalog available on Web site.

Tips "Read our books!"

☐ BIRDSONG BOOKS

1322 Bayview Rd.Middletown DE 19709. (302)378-7274. E-mail: Birdsong@BirdsongBooks. com. Website: www.BirdsongBooks.com. **Manuscript & Art Acquisitions:** Nancy Carol Willis, president. Publishes 1 picture book/year. "Birdsong Books seeks to spark the delight of discovering our wild neighbors and natural habitats. We believe knowledge and understanding of nature fosters caring and a desire to protect the Earth and all living things. Our emphasis is on North American animals and habitats, rather than people."

Nonfiction Picture books, young readers: activity books, animal, nature/environment. Average word length: picture books—800-1,000 plus content for 2-4 pages of back matter. Recently published The Animals' Winter Sleep, by Lynda-Graham Barber (age 3-6, nonfiction picture book); *Red Knot: A Shorebird's Incredible Journey*, by Nancy Carol Willis (age 6-9, nonfiction picture book); *Raccoon Moon*, by Nancy Carol Willis (ages 5-8, natural science picture book); *The Robins In Your Backyard*, by Nancy Carol Willis (ages 4-7, nonfiction picture book).

How to Contact Nonfiction: Submit complete manuscript package with SASE. Responds to mss in 3 months. Publishes book 2-3 years after acceptance. Will consider simultaneous submissions (if stated).

Tips "We are a small independent press actively seeking manuscripts that fit our narrowly defined niche. We are only interested in nonfiction, natural science picture books or educational activity books about North American animals and habitats. We are not interested in fiction stories based on actual events. Our books include several pages of back matter suitable for early elementary classrooms. Mailed submissions with SASE only. No e-mail submissions or phone calls, please. Cover letters should sell author/illustrator and book idea."

BLOOMING TREE PRESS

P.O. Box 140934, Austin TX 78714. Estab. 2000. (512)921-8846. Fax: (512)873-7710. E-mail: email@ bloomingtreepress.com. Website: www.bloomingtreepress.com. **Imprints:** Blooming Tree Press (Children's), CBAY Books (Edgier Fiction), Tire Swing Books (Paperback), Ready Blade (Graphic Novels). **Publisher:** Miriam Hees; Madeline Smoot, editorial director, CBAY Books; Anna Herrington, editorial director, blooming tree children's and tire swing books, Bradford Hees, editorial director, ready blade graphic novels/comics. **Art Acquisitions:** Attention Art Department. "Blooming Tree Press is dedicated to producing high quality book for the young and the young at heart. It is our hope that you will find your dreams between the pages of our books."

Fiction Picture books: adventure, animal, contemporary, fantasy, folktales, history, humor, multicultural, religion, science fiction, special needs, sports. Young readers: adventure, animal, contemporary, fantasy, folktales, history, humor, multicultural, religion, science fiction, special needs, sports, suspense. Middle readers: adventure, animal, anthology, contemporary, fantasy, folktales, history, humor, multicultural, poetry, religion, science fiction, suspense. Young adults/teens: adventure, animal, anthology, contemporary, fantasy, folktales, history, humor, religion, science fiction, suspense. Average word length: picture books: 300-1,000; young readers: 800-9,000; middle readers: 25,000-40,000; young adult/teens: 40,000-70,000. Recently published *Patrick the Somnambulist*, written and illustrated by Sarah Ackerley (picture book about a sleepwalking penguin); *Dragon Wishes*, by Stacy Nyikos (mid-grade about the mythical world of Chinese dragons); *The Girls*, by multiple authors (five mid-grade short stories about girlfriends); *The Emerald Tablet*, by P.J. Hoover (middle grade fantasy about two friends and a mysterious emerald tablet).

Nonfiction We are not accepting nonfiction at this time.

How to Contact Fiction: "Accepting agented, conference attendee and personally requested submissions only. For unsolicited submissions check Web site for dates of unsolicited submission times throughout the year. Do not send unsolicited submissions unless it is during a specified submission time. Mailings received during non-submission dates will be recycled".

Terms Pays authors royalty of 10% depending on the project. Pays illustrators by the project or royalty depending on project. Authors see galleys for review; illustrators see dummies. Writer's guidelines on Web site.

Tips "During submission times follow the guidelines listed on our Web site. Send a crisp and clean one-page query letter stating your project, why it is right for the market, and a little about yourself. Write what you know, not what's 'in.' Remember, every great writer/illustrator started somewhere. Keep submitting... don't ever give up."

BLOOMSBURY CHILDREN'S BOOKS

Imprint of Bloomsbury PLC, 175 Fifth Avenue, 8th Floor, New York NY 10010. Website: www. bloomsburyusa.com Specializes in fiction, picture books. Publishes 15 picture books/year; 10 young readers/year; 20 middle readers/year; 25 young adult titles/year. 25% of books by first-time authors.

Fiction Picture books: adventure, animal, contemporary, fantasy, folktales, history, humor, multicultural, poetry, suspense/mystery. Young readers: adventure, animal, anthology, concept, contemporary, fantasy, folktales, history, humor, multicultural, suspense/mystery. Middle readers: adventure, animal, contemporary, fantasy, folktales, history, humor, multicultural, poetry, problem novels. Young adults: adventure, animal, anthology, contemporary, fantasy, folktales, history, humor, multicultural, problem novels, science fiction, sports, suspense/mystery. Recently published Natalie & Naughtily by Vincent X. Kirsch (picture books); Dragon Princess by E.. Baker (middle reader); The Musician's Daughter, by Susanne Dunlap (young adult).

Terms Pays authors royalty or work purchased outright for jackets. Offers advances. Pays illustrators by the project or royalty. Pays photographers by the project or per photo. Sends galleys to authors; dummies to illustrators. Originals returned to artist at job's completion. Writer's and art guidelines available on http://www.bloomsburyusa.com/FAQ.

Tips All Bloomsbury Children's Books submissions are considered on an individual basis. Bloomsbury Children's Books will no longer responding to unsolicited manuscripts or art submissions. Please include a telephone AND e-mail address where we may contact you if we are interested in you work. Do NOT send a self-addressed stamped envelope. We regret the inconvenience, but unfortunately, we are too understaffed to maintain a correspondence with authors. We will continue to accept unsolicited manuscripts but we can contact you ONLY if we are interested in acquiring your work. There is no need to send art with a picture book manuscript. Artists should submit art with a picture book manuscript. Artist should submit art samples separately to the attention of the Art Department. We do not return art samples. Please do not send us original art! Please note that we do accept simultaneous submissions but please be courteous and inform us if another house has made an offer on your work. Do not send originals or your only copy of anything. We are not liable for artwork or manuscript submissions. Do not send a SASE, as we are no longer responding to submissions. Please address all submissions to the attention of Manuscript Submissions. Please make sure that everything is stapled.paper-clipped, or rubber-banded together. We do not accept e-mail or CD/DVD submissions. Be sure your work is appropriate for us. Familiarize yourself with our list by going to bookstores or libraries

BOYDS MILLS PRESS

815 Church St.Honesdale PA 18431. Website: www.boydsmillspress.com. Estab. 1990. Imprints: Calkins Creek Books, Front Street, Wordsong. 5% of books from agented writers. "We publish a wide range of quality children's books of literary merit, from preschool to young adult."

Fiction Ages 0-10: adventure, contemporary, humor, multicultural, rhyming. Picture books: all kinds. Multicultural themes include any story showing a child as an integral part of a culture and which provides children with insight into a culture they otherwise might be unfamiliar with.

Nonfiction All levels: nature/environment, history, science. Picture books, young readers, middle readers: animal, multicultural. Does not want to see reference/curricular text.

How to Contact Fiction/nonfiction: Submit complete ms or submit through agent. Label package "Manucript Submission" and include SASE. Responds in 3 months.

Terms Authors paid royalty or work purchased outright. Offers advances. Illustrators paid by the project or royalties; varies. Photographers paid by the project, per photo, or royalties; varies. Manuscripts/artist's guidelines available on Web site.

Tips "Picture books with fresh approaches, not worn themes, are our strongest need at this time. Check to see what's already on the market and on our Web site before submitting your story. Prose fiction for middle-grade through young adult should be submitted to Boyds Mills imprint Front

Street—see Front Street listing for submission information. Poetry for all ages should be submitted to Boyds Mills Wordsong imprint—see Wordsong listing for submission information. Historical fiction and nonfiction about the United States for all ages should be submitted to Calkins Creek Books—see Calkins Creek listing for submission information."

☐ BRIGHT RING PUBLISHING, INC.

P.O. Box 31338, Bellingham WA 98228. (360)592-9201. Fax: (360)592-4503. E-mail: maryann@brightring.com. Website: www.brightring.com. **Editor:** MaryAnn Kohl.

• Bright Ring is no longer accepting manuscript submissions.

CALKINS CREEK

815 Church St.Honesdale PA 18431. Website: www.calkinscreekbook.com. Estab. 2004. "We aim to publish books that are a well-written blend of creative writing and extensive research which emphasize important events, people, and places in U.S. history."

Fiction All levels: history. Recently published *Healing Water*, by Joyce Moyer Hostetter (ages 10 and up, historical fiction); *The Shakeress*, by Kimberly Heuston (ages 12 and up, historical fiction).

Nonfiction All levels: history. Recently published *Farmer George Plants a Nation*, by Peggy Thomas (ages 8 and up, nonfiction picture book); *Robert H. Jackson*, by Gail Jarrow (ages 10 and up, historical fiction);

How to Contact Accepts international submissions. Fiction: Submit outline/synopsis and 3 sample chapters. Nonfiction: Submit outline/synopsis and 3 sample chapters. Considers simultaneous submissions. Label package "Manuscript Submissions" and inlcude SASE.

Terms Authors paid royalty or work purchased outright. Offers advances. Illustrators paid by the project or royalties; varies. Photographers paid by the project, per photo, or royalties; varies. Manuscripts/artist's guidelines available on Web site.

Tips "Read through our recently-published titles and review our catalog. When selecting titles to publish, our emphasis will be on important events, people, and places in U.S. history. Writers are encouraged to submit a detailed bibliography, including secondary and primary sources, and expert reviews with their submissions."

CANDLEWICK PRESS

99 Dover Street, Somerville, MA 02144. (617)661-3330. Fax: (617)661-0565. E-mail: bigbear@candlewick.com. Website: www.candlewick.com. **Manuscript Acquisitions:** Karen Lotz, publisher; Liz Bicknell, editorial director and associate publisher; Joan Powers, editorial director; Mary Lee Donovan, executive editor; Sarah Ketchersid, senior editor; Deborah Wayshak, executive editor; Andrea Tompa; associate editor; Katie Cunningham, associate editor; Kaylan Adair, associate editor; Kate Fletcher, associate editor; Jennifer Yoon, associate editor. **Art Acquisitions:** Anne Moore. Publishes 160 picture books/year; 15 middle readers/year; 15 young adult titles/year. 5% of books by first-time authors. "Our books are truly for children, and we strive for the very highest standards in the writing, illustrating, designing and production of all of our books. And we are not averse to risk."

• Candlewick Press is not accepting queries and unsolicited mss at this time. Candlewick title *Good Masters! Sweet Ladies! Voices from a Medieval Village*, by Amy Schlitz won the John Newbery Medal in 2008. Their title *Twelve Rounds to Glory: The Strong of Muhammad Ali*, by Charles R. Smith Jr.illustrated by Bryan Collier, won a Coretta Scott King Author Honor Award in 2008. Their title *The Astonishing Life of Octavian Nothing*, by M.T. Anderson won the Boston Globe-Hornbook Award for Fiction and Poetry in 2007.

Fiction Picture books: animal, concept, contemporary, fantasy, history, humor, multicultural, nature/environment, poetry. Middle readers, young adults: contemporary, fantasy, history, humor, multicultural, poetry, science fiction, sports, suspense/mystery. Recently published *The Astonishing LIfe of Octavian Nothing, Traitor to the Nation: Volume One: The Pox Party by M.T. Anderson* (young adult fiction); *Surrender*, by Sonya Hartnett (young adult fiction); *Good Masters! Sweet Ladies! by* Laura Amy Schlitz, illustrated by Robert Byrd (middle grade poetry collection), *Drangonolgy,* by Ernest Drake; Encyclopedia Prehistorica: *Dinosaurs,* by Robert Sabuda and Matthew Reinhart.

Nonfiction Picture books: concept, biography, geography, nature/environment. Young readers: biography, geography, nature/environment. Recently published *Twelve Rounds to Glory : The Story of Muhammad Ali* by Charles R. Smith Jr.illustrated by Bryan Collier.

Terms Pays authors royalty of 2½-10% based on retail price. Offers advances. Pays illustrators 2½-10% royalty based on retail price. Sends galleys to authors; dummies to illustrators. Pays photographers 2½-10% royalty. Original artwork returned at job's completion.

CAROLRHODA BOOKS, INC.

A division of Lerner Publishing Group, 241 First Ave. N.Minneapolis MN 55401. Website: www.lernerbooks.com. Estab. 1969. Publishes hardcover originals. Averages 8-10 picture books each year for ages 3-8, 6 fiction titles for ages 7-18, and 2-3 nonfiction titles for various ages.

- Starting in 2007, Lerner Publishing Group no longer accepts submissions to any of their imprints except for Kar-Ben Publishing.

How to Contact "We will continue to seek targeted solicitations at specific reading levels and in specific subject areas. The company will list these targeted solicitations on our Web site and in national newsletters, such as the SCBWI Bulletin."

CARTWHEEL BOOKS, for the Very Young

Imprint of Scholastic Inc.557 Broadway, New York NY 10012. Website: www.scholastic.com. Estab. 1991. Book publisher. Editorial Director: Cecily Kaiser. **Manuscript Acquisitions:** Rotem Moscovich, editor; Jeffrey Salane, editor. **Art Acquisitions:** Daniel Moreton, Creative Director. Publishes 15-25 picture books/year; 10-15 easy readers/year; 40-50 novelty/concept/board books/year.

Fiction Picture books, young readers: humor, seasonal/holiday, humor, family/love. Average word length: picture books—100-500; easy readers—100-1,500.

Nonfiction Picture books, young readers: seasonal/curricular topics involving animals (polar animals, ocean animals, hibernation), nature (fall leaves, life cycles, weather, solar system), history (first Thanksgiving, MLK Jr.George Washington, Columbus). "Most of our nonfiction is either written on assignment or is within a series. We do not want to see any arts/crafts or cooking." Average word length: picture books—100-1,500; young readers—100-2,000.

How to Contact Cartwheel Books is no longer accepting unsolicited mss. All unsolicited materials will be returned unread. Fiction/nonfiction: For previously published or agented authors, submit complete ms. Responds to mss in 6 months. Publishes a book within 2 years after acceptance. SASE required with all submissions.

Terms Pays advance against royalty or flat fee. Sends galley to authors; dummy to illustrators. Originals returned to artist at job's completion.

Tips "With each Cartwheel list, we seek a pleasing balance of board books and novelty books, hardcover picture books and gift books, nonfiction, paperback storybooks and easy readers. Cartwheel seeks to acquire projects that speak to young children and their world: new and exciting novelty formats, fresh seasonal and holiday stories, curriculum/concept-based titles, and books for beginning readers. Our books are inviting and appealing, clearly marketable, and have inherent educational and social value. We strive to provide the earliest readers with relevant and exciting books that will ultimately lead to a lifetime of reading, learning, and wondering. Know what types of books we do. Check out bookstores or catalogs first to see where your work would fit best, and why."

MARSHALL CAVENDISH CHILDREN'S BOOKS

Imprint of Marshall Cavendish, 99 White Plains Rd.Tarrytown NY 10591-9001. (914)332-8888. **Publisher:** Margery Cuyler. **Art Acquisitions:** Anahid Hamparian, art director. Publishes 60-70 books/year.

Fiction Publishes fiction for all ages/picture books.

How to Contact Query nonfiction. Submit 3 chapters (or more) for fiction or for synopsis. For picture books, submit the complete manuscript. Only replies if interested. Authors may submit to other publishers simultaneously.

Terms Pays authors/illustrators advance and royalties.

CHARLESBRIDGE

85 Main St.Watertown MA 02472. (617)926-0329. Fax: (617)926-5720. E-mail: tradeeditorial@ charlesbridge.com. Website: www.charlesbridge.com. Estab. 1980. Book publisher. **Contact:** Trade Editorial Department. Publishes 60% nonfiction, 40% fiction picture books and early chapter books. Publishes nature, science, multicultural, social studies, and fiction picture books and transitional "bridge books" (books ranging from early readers to middle-grade chapter books).

Fiction Picture books and chapter books: "Strong, realistic stories with enduring themes." Considers the following categories: adventure, concept, contemporary, health, history, humor, multicultural, nature/environment, special needs, sports, suspense/mystery. Recently published *The Searcher and Old Tree*, by David McPhail; *Good Dog, Aggie* by Lori Ries; *The Perfect Sword*, by Scott Goto; *Not So Tall for Six*, by Dianna Hutts Aston; *Wiggle and Waggle*, by Caroline Arnold; *Rickshaw Girl*, by Mitali Perkins.

Nonfiction Picture books and chapter books: animal, biography, careers, concept, geography, health, history, multicultural, music/dance, nature/environment, religion, science, social issues, special needs, hobbies, sports. Average word length: picture books-1,000. Recently published *After Gandhi*, by Anne Sibley O'Brien and Perry Edmond O'Brien; *The Mysteries of Beethoven's Hair*, by Russell Martin and Lydia Nibley; *Sea Queens*, by Jane Yolen; *Trout are Made of Trees*, by April Pulley Sayre; *Life on Earth-and Beyond: An Astrobiologist's Quest,* by Pamela S. Turner. Charlesbridge title *Hello, Bumblebee Bat*, written by Darrin Lunde, illustrated by Patricia J. Wynne, won a Theodor Seuss Geisel Award in 2008.

How to Contact Send mss as exclusive submission for three months. Responds only to mss of interest. Full mss only; no queries. Please do not include a self-addressed stamped envelope.

Tips Charlesbridge publishes picture books and transitional "bridge books."We look for fresh and engaging voices and directions in both fiction and nonfiction.

CHELSEA HOUSE, AN IMPRINT OF INFOBASE PUBLISHING

Facts on File, 132 West 31st Street, 17th Floor, New York, New York 10001. (800)322-8755. Fax: (917)339-0326. E-mail: jciovacco@factsonfile.com. Website: www.chelseahouse.com. Specializes in nonfiction chapter books. **Manuscript Acquisitions:** Laurie Likoff, editorial director; Justine Ciovacco, managing editor. Imprints: Chelsea Clubhouse; Chelsea House. Produces 150 middle readers/year, 150 young adult books/year. No 10% of books by first-time authors.

How to Contact "All books are parts of series. Most series topics are developed by in-house editors, but suggestions are welcome. Authors my query with résumé and list of publications."

CHRISTIAN ED. PUBLISHERS

P.O. Box 26639, San Diego CA 92196. (858)578-4700. Website: www.ChristianEdWarehouse.com. Book publisher. **Acquisitions:** Janet Ackelson, assistant editor; Carol Rogers, managing editor; Michelle Anson, production coordinator. Publishes 80 Bible curriculum titles/year. "We publish curriculum for children and youth, including program and student books and take-home papers— all handled by our assigned freelance writers only. Do not send unsolicited manuscripts. Ask for a writer's application."

Fiction Young readers: contemporary. Middle readers: adventure, contemporary, suspense/mystery. "We publish fiction for Bible club take-home papers. All fiction is on assignment only. Do not send unsolicited manuscripts. Ask for a writer's application"

Nonfiction Publishes Bible curriculum and take-home papers for all ages. Recently published *All-Stars for Jesus*, by Lucinda Rollings and Laura Gray, illustrated by Aline Heiser (Bible club curriculum for grades 4-6); *Honeybees Classroom Activity Sheets*, by Janet Miller and Wanda Pelfrey, illustrated by Ron Widman (Bible club curriculum for ages 2-3).

How to Contact Fiction/nonfiction: Query. Responds to queries in 5 weeks. Publishes assignments 1 year after acceptance. Send SASE for guidelines or contact Christian Ed. at crogers@cehouse.com. Ask for a writer's application. Do not send manuscripts.

Terms Work purchased outright from authors for 3¢/word. Pays illustrators $15-18/page. Book catalog available for 9 × 12 SAE and 4 first-class stamps; ms and art guidelines available for SASE or via e-mail.

Tips "Read our guidelines carefully before sending us a manuscript or illustrations. Do not send unsolicited manuscripts. All writing and illustrating is done on assignment only and must be age-appropriate (preschool-6th grade). Ask for a writer's application. Do not send manuscripts."

CHRONICLE BOOKS

680 Second St. San Francisco CA 94107. (415)537-4400. Fax: (415)537-4415. Website: www.chroniclekids.com. Book publisher. **Acquisitions:** Victoria Rock, founding publisher & editor-at-large; Andrea Menotti, senior editor; Julie Romeis, editor; Melissa Manlove, associate editor, Naomi Kirsten, assistant editor, Mary Colgan, editorial assistant. Publishes 90 (both fiction and nonfiction) books/year; 5-10% middle readers/year; young adult nonfiction titles/year. 10-25% of books by first-time authors; 20-40% of books from agented writers.

Fiction Picture books, young readers, middle readers, young adults: "We are open to a very wide range of topics." Recently published *Wave* by Suzy Lee (all ages, picture book); *Ivy and Bean* (series), by Annie Barrows, illustrated by Sophie Blackall (ages 6-10, chapter book**).**

Nonfiction Picture books, young readers, middle readers, young adults: "We are open to a very wide range of topics." Recently published *Delicious: The Life & Art of Wayne Thiebaud*, by Susan Rubin (Ages 9-14, middle grade)**.**

How to Contact/Writers Fiction/nonfiction: Submit complete ms (picture books); submit outline/synopsis and 3 sample chapters (for older readers). Responds to queries in 1 month; will not respond to submissions unless interested**.** Publishes a book 1-3 years after acceptance. Will consider simultaneous submissions, as long as they are marked "multiple submissions." Will not consider submissions by fax, e-mail or disk. Do not include SASE; do not send original materials. No submissions will be returned; to confirm receipt, include a SASP.

Illustration Works with 40-50 illustrators/year. Wants "unusual art, graphically strong, something that will stand out on the shelves. Fine art, not mass market." Reviews ms/illustration packages from artists. "Indicate if project *must* be considered jointly, or if editor may consider text and art separately." Illustrations only: Submit samples of artist's work (not necessarily from book, but in the envisioned style). Slides, tearsheets and color photocopies OK. (No original art.) Dummies helpful. Résumé helpful. Samples suited to our needs are filed for future reference. Samples not suited to our needs will be recycled. Queries and project proposals responded to in same time frame as author query/proposals."

Terms Generally pays authors in royalties based on retail price, "though we do occasionally work on a flat fee basis." Advance varies. Illustrators paid royalty based on retail price or flat fee. Sends proofs to authors and illustrators. Book catalog for 9 x 12 SAE and 8 first-class stamps; ms guidelines for #10 SASE.

Tips "Chronicle Books publishes an eclectic mixture of traditional and innovative children's books. We are interested in taking on projects that have a unique bent to them-be it subject matter, writing style, or illustrative technique. As a small list, we are looking for books that will lend us a distinctive flavor. We are also interested in growing our fiction program for older readers, including chapter books, middle grade, and young adult projects."

CLARION BOOKS

215 Park Ave. S.New York NY 10003. (212)420-5889. Website: www.clarionbooks.com. **Manuscript Acquisitions:** Dinah Stevenson, publisher; Virginia Buckley, contributing editor; Jennifer Wingertzahn, editor; Marcia Leonard, editor. **Art Acquisitions:** Christine Kettner, art director.

- Clarion title *The Wednesday Wars*, by Gary D. Schmidt won a Newbery Honor Medal in 2008. Picture book recently published: The Wonderful Thing about Hiccups, by Cece Meng, illustrated by Janet Pedersen (ages 4-7, picture book)

Fiction Recently published *The Wonderful Thing About Hiccups*, by Cece Meng, illustrated by Janet Pedersen (ages 4-7, picture book); *The Wednesday Wars*, by Gary D. Schmidt (ages 10-148, historical fiction).

Nonfiction Recently published *Who Was First? Discovering the Americas*, by Russell Freedman (ages 9-12, history).

How to Contact Picture books: Send complete mss. Fiction: Please send first three chapters and a synopsis. Nonfiction: Send query with up to 3 sample chapters. Will only respond to those manuscripts they are interested in. Will accept simultaneous submissions if informed.

Terms Pays illustrators royalty; flat fee for jacket illustration. Pays royalties and advance to writers; both vary. Guidelines available on Web site.

CLEAR LIGHT PUBLISHERS

823 Don Diego, Santa Fe NM 87505. (505)989-9590. Fax: (505)989-9519. Website: www.clearlightbooks.com. **Acquisitions:** Harmon Houghton, publisher. Publishes 4 middle readers/year; 4 young adult titles/year.

Nonfiction Middle readers and young adults: multicultural, American Indian and Hispanic only.

How to Contact Fiction/nonfiction: Submit complete ms with SASE. "No e-mail submissions. Authors supply art. Manuscripts not considered without art or artist's renderings." Will consider simultaneous submissions. Responds in 3 months. Only send *copies*.

Terms Pays authors royalty of 10% based on wholesale price. Offers advances (average amount: up to 50% of expected net sales within the first year). Sends galleys to authors.

Tips "We're looking for authentic American Indian art and folklore."

◫ CLIMBING ROSES

The Wild Rose Press. P.O. Box 708, Adams NY 14410-0708.Estab. 2007. (717)497-0632. E-mail: queryus@thewildrosepress.com. Website: www.thewildrosepress.com/young-adult-c158.html. Specializes in Christian material, fiction, multicultural material. **Manuscript Acquisitions:** queryus@thewildrose.com. **Art Acquisitions:** queryus@thewildrose.com. Imprints: Climbing Roses, Kat O'Shea, senior editor. Publishes 12 young adult titles/year. 50% of books by first-time authors. "The Wild Rose Press calls itself a kinder, gentler publishing house. We try to offer constructive editorial suggestions to each author, including those we reject. This is why we ask for exclusive submissions. Our personal attention to authors is one of the many reasons we received the 2008 Best Publisher award from Predictors & Editors. Climbing Roses uses a teen focus group to review all manuscripts. Although the reviewing editor makes the final decision, the opinions of this panel of young women are crucial to the success of this line. The compilation of their opinions will guide the acceptance of the manuscripts and may be given as feedback to the authors"

Fiction Young adults: romance. Average word length: young adult/teens—7,000-65,000. Recently published *I Was a Teenage Alien*, by Jane Greenhill, (YA, humorous, light paranormal); *Enter the parrot*, by Kiki Lon, (YA, mystery with romantic elements); *Freaksville* (Book 1 in the Freaksville series), (YA, paranormal romance laced with humor).

How to Contact Fiction: query or submit outline/1-2 pg.synopsis. Responds to queries in 1 month; mss in 3 months. Publishes book 1 year after acceptance. Will consider electronic submissions only or previously published work if author has all rights.

Terms Pays authors royalty based on wholesale price. Sends galleys to authors.

Tips "Climbing Roses books encompass a variety of genres from mystery to inspirational, paranormal to historical, but all must contain at least some romantic tension. Stories may have a romantic plot or one that is only vaguely implied. Please check out the Climbing Roses guidelines on the Web site www.thewildrosepress.com/young-adult-c158.html and our author's blog at http://twrpclimbingrose.blogspot.com/ to see what we publish. Before you send anything to us please have someone knowledgeable in grammar and punctuation look it over. I highly recommend a critique group to help polish your submissions. A well-written query and short synopsis (1 page preferred) that show you know what we publish will assure you of the opportunity to submit a partial.The best way to get published with us, or with anyone, is to write a well-plotted novel with strong characterization. We're looking for novels with heart and voice. If a character jumps off the page and the plot arrests our attention from the beginning, your story will most likely be a keeper. Once you manuscript has been accepted, prepare to work hard. We are looking for authors who will work with us to make their story outstanding. Editing for quality takes a lot of time and effort on both the author's and editor's parts, so if you submit to us, know that you'll have a great deal of hard work ahead. The acceptance is only the beginning of a long process. Our goal is to put out a book that we'll all be proud to have produced, one that will appeal to teen readers and make them beg for more. Also, we are a small company, so authors need to be prepared to aggressively market their books. We do as much as we can help, but we also count on you to spend time selling your book. If you're willing to commit to working hard at revising and marketing and you've followed our guidelines, we'd love to see your story."

CONCORDIA PUBLISHING HOUSE

3558 S. Jefferson Ave.St. Louis MO 63118. (314)268-1187. Fax: (314)268-1329. Website: www.cph.org. **Contact:** Peggy Kuethe. **Art Director:**Norm Simon. "Concordia Publishing House produces quality resources that communicate and nurture the Christian faith and ministry of people of all ages, lay and professional. These resources include curriculum, worship aids, books, and religious supplies. We publish approximately 30 quality children's books each year. We boldly provide Gospel resources that are Christ-centered, Bible-based and faithful to our Lutheran heritage."

Nonfiction Picture books, young readers, young adults: Bible stories, activity books, arts/crafts, concept, contemporary, religion. "All books must contain explicit Christian content." Recently published *Three Wise Women of Christmas*, by Dandi Daley Mackall (picture book for ages 6-10); *The Town That Forgot About Christmas*, by Susan K. Leigh (ages over 5-9, picture book); *Little Ones Talk With God* (prayer book compilation, aged 5 and up).

How to Contact Submit complete ms (picture books); submit outline/synopsis and samples for longer mss. May also query. Responds to queries in 1 month; mss in 3 months. Publishes a book 2 years after acceptance. Will consider simultaneous submissions. "Absolutely no phone queries."

Terms Pays authors royalties based on retail price or work purchased outright ($750-2,000). Manuscript guidelines for 1 first-class stamp and a #10 envelope. Pays illustrators by the project.

Tips "Do not send finished artwork with the manuscript. If sketches will help in the presentation of the manuscript, they may be sent. If stories are taken from the Bible, they should follow the Biblical account closely. Liberties should not be taken in fantasizing Biblical stories."

☐ COTTONWOOD PRESS, INC.

109-B Cameron Drive, Fort Collins CO 80525. Estab. 1986. (907)204-0715. Fax: (907)204-0761. E-mail: cottonwood@cottonwoodpress.com. Website: www.cottonwoodpress.com. Specializes in educational material for the English/language arts classroom. **President:** Cheryl Thurston. Cottonwood Press strives "to publish materials that are effective in the classroom and help kids learn without putting them to sleep, specializing in materials for grades 5-12." Publishes 4 middle reader and young adult books/year. 60% of books by first-time authors.

Nonfiction Middle readers: textbooks. Young Adults/Teens: textbooks. Recently published: *UnJournaling: daily writing exercises that are NOT personal, NOT introspective, NOT boring*, by

Dawn DiPrince, illustrated by Cheryl Miller Thurston; *Singuini: noodling around with silly songs,* by Heather Stenner and Cheryl Miller Thurston; *Phunny Stuph: Proofreading exercises with a sense of humor,* by M.S. Samston.

How to Contact Nonfiction: Submit complete manuscript. Responds to queries in 2 weeks; mss in 2 months. Publishes a book 6 months-1 year after acceptance. Will consider simultaneous submissions if notified.

Terms Pay royalty of 10-15% based on net sales.

Tips "It is essential that writers familiarize themselves with our Web site to see what we do. The most successful of our authors have used our books in the classroom and know how different they are from ordinary textbooks."

CREATIVE EDUCATION

Imprint of The Creative Company, P.O. Box 227, Mankato MN 56001. (800)445-6209. Fax: (507)388-2746. **Manuscript Acquisitions:** Aaron Frisch. Publishes 5 picture books/year; 40 young readers/year; 20 middle readers/year; 40 young adult titles/year. 5% of books by first-time authors. The company name is The Creative Company. It has two imprints: Creative Editions (picture books), and Creative Education (nonfiction series). Either The Creative Company should appear as the header for this entry, or else all picture book references should be removed if Creative Education is given as the header. Currently, we are not accepting submissions for picture books, so it is only of importance to us that the nonfiction series are described here.

Nonfiction Picture books, young readers, middle readers, young adults: animal, arts/crafts, biography, careers, geography, health, history, hobbies, multicultural, music/dance, nature/environment, religion, science, social issues, special needs, sports. Average word length: young readers—500; middle readers—3,000; young adults-6,000. Recently published *Built to Last series*, by Valerie Bodden (age 7, young reader); *Colorado*, by Sheryl Peterson (age 11, middle reader); *The Story of McDonalds*, by Sara Gilbert (age 14, young adult/teen).

How to Contact We are not accepting fiction submissions. Nonfiction: Submit outline/synopsis and 2 sample chapters, along with division of titles within the series. Responds to queries in 3 months; mss in 3 months. Publishes book 2 years after acceptance. Do not accept illustration packages.

Tips "We are accepting nonfiction, series submissions only. Fiction submissions will not be reviewed or returned. Nonfiction submissions should be presented in series (4,6, or 8) rather than single."

CRICKET BOOKS

Carus Publishing Company, 70 East Lake St.Suite 300, Chicago IL 60601. Website: www.cricketmag.com. Art Acquisitions: John Sandford.;
  • Cricket Books has a moratorium on manuscripts. Queries from agents and authors who have worked with Cricket Books are still welcome. Direct queries to Jenny Gillespie. Watch Web site for updates.

Tips "You may consider submitting your manuscript to one of our magazines, as we sometimes serialize longer selections and always welcome age-appropriate stories, poems, and nonfiction articles."

CROSSWAY BOOKS

Division of Good News Publishers, 1300 Crescent St.Wheaton IL 60187-5800. (630)682-4300. Fax: (630)682-4785. Website: www.crossway.com. **Contact:** Jill Carter. Estab. 1938. "'Making a difference in people's lives for Christ' as its maxim, Crossway Books lists titles written from an evangelical Christian perspective." Midsize evangelical Christian publisher. Publishes hardcover and trade paperback originals. Averages 85 total titles, 1 fiction titles/year. Member ECPA. Distributes titles through Christian bookstores and catalogs. Promotes titles through magazine ads, catalogs.

How to Contact Does not accept unsolicited mss. Agented fiction 5%.

Terms Pays negotiable royalty. Average advance: negotiable. Publishes ms 18 months after acceptance. Ms guidelines online.

DARBY CREEK PUBLISHING

7858 Industrial Pkwy.Plain City OH 43064. (614)873-7955. Fax: (614)873-7135. E-mail: info@ darbycreekpublishing.com. **Manuscript/Art Acquisitions:** Tanya Dean, editorial director. Publishes 10-15 children's books/year.

• Darby Creek does not publish picture books.

Fiction Middle readers, young adult. Recently published *The Warriors*, by Joseph Bruchac (ages 10 and up); *Dog Days*, by David Lubar (ages 10 and up); *Four Things My Geeky-Jock-of-a-Best-Friend Must Do in Europe*, by Jane Harrington.

Nonfiction Middle readers: biography, history, science, sports. Recently published *Albinio Animals*, by Kelly Milner Halls, illustrated by Rick Spears; *Miracle: The True Story of the Wreck of the Sea Venture*, by Gail Karwoski.

How to Contact Accepts international material only with U.S. postage on SASE for return; no IRCs. Fiction/nonfiction: Submit publishing history and/or résumé and complete ms for short works or outline/synopsis and 2-3 sample chapters for longer works, such as novels. Responds in 6 weeks. Does not consider previously published work.

Terms Offers advance-against-royalty contracts.

Tips "We are currently not accepting any submissions. If that changes, we will provide all children's writing publications with our new info.."

⊞ MAY DAVENPORT, PUBLISHERS

26313 Purissima Rd.Los Altos Hills CA 94022-4539. (650)947-1275. Fax: (650)947-1373. E-mail: mdbooks@earthlink.net. Website: www.maydavenportpublishers.com. **Acquisitions:** May Davenport, editor/publisher. Publishes 1-2 picture books/year; 2-3 young adult titles/year. 99% of books by first-time authors. Seeks books with literary merit. "We like to think that we are selecting talented writers who have something humorous to write about today's unglued generation in 30,000-50,000 words for teens and young adults in junior/senior high school before they become tomorrow's 'functional illiterates.' We are interested in publishing literature that teachers in middle and high schools can use in their Language Arts, English and Creative Writing courses. There's more to literary fare than the chit-chat Internet dialog and fantasy trips on television with cartoons or humanoids." This publisher is overstocked with juvenile books.

Fiction Young readers, young adults: contemporary, humorous fictional literature for use in English courses in junior-senior high schools in U.S. Average word length: 40,000-60,000. Recently published *Charlie and Champ*, by Alysson Wagoner (a fun way to learn phonics coloring book, ages 5-7); *Suriving Sarah, the Sequel: Brown Bug & China Doll*, by Dinah Leigh (novel set in post-WWII Manhattan, ages 15-18);*The Lesson Plan*, by Irvin Gay (about an illiterate black boy who grows up to become a teacher, ages 15-18); *A Life on the Line*, by Michael Horton (about a juvenile delinquent boy who recovers from his past abusive life heroically, ages 15-18); *Making My Escape*, by David Lee Finkle (about a young boy who daydreams movie-making in outer space to escape unhappy family life, ages 12-18); *Summer of Suspense*, by Frances D. Waines*; A Young Girl visits Grandparents Who Rented Rooms to Students with Meals Included; Girl Learns about Freezing Food, Canning, Sleuthing, Too. Modern Equipment fo the Grandparents and Sheriff were Gems (ages 14-18)*.

Nonfiction Teens: shocking pathway choices. Recently published *The Runaway Game*, by Kevin Casey (a literary board game of street life in Hollywood, ages 15-18).

How to Contact Fiction: Query. Responds to queries/mss in 3 weeks. Mss returned with SASE. Publishes a book 6-12 months after acceptance.

Terms Pays authors royalty of 15% based on retail price; negotiable. Pays "by mutual agreement, no advances." Pays illustrators by the project (range: $75-350). Guidelines free on request with SASE.

Tips "Write stories with teen narrators and sharing digital camera/computer activities which today's teenages can relate to. Entertain teenagers who don't, won't, or can't read English, won't read printed pages so your book will be useful to teachers in social studies in high schools nationwide."

DAWN PUBLICATIONS

12402 Bitney Springs Rd.Nevada City CA 95959. (530)274-7775. Website: www.awnpub.com. Book publisher. Co-Publishers: Muffy Weaver and Glenn J. Hovemann. **Acquisitions:** Glenn J. Hovemann. Publishes works with holistic themes dealing with nature. "Dawn Publications is dedicated to inspiring in children a deeper appreciation and understanding of nature."
Fiction Picture books exploring relationships with nature. No fantasy or legend.
Nonfiction Picture books: animal, nature/environment. Prefers "creative nonfiction."
How to Contact Query or submit complete ms by mail (enclose self-addressed stamped envelope for reply) or by e-mail to submission@dawnpub.com (with title and your name in the subject line, ms inserted into the body of the email or attached as a Word document only). Responds to queries/mss in 3 months.
Terms Pays authors royalty based on net sales. Offers advance. Book catalog and ms guidelines available online.
Tips Looking for "picture books expressing nature awareness with inspirational quality leading to enhanced self-awareness. Does not publish anthropomorphic works; no animal dialogue."

DIAL BOOKS FOR YOUNG READERS

Penguin Young Readers Group, 345 Hudson St.New York NY 10014. Website: www.penguin.com. Vice President and Publisher: Lauri Hornik. **Acquisitions:** Kathy Dawson, Associate Publisher; Kate Harrison, senior editor; Liz Waniewski, editor; Alisha Niehaus, editor; Jessica Garrison, editor. **Art Director:** Lily Malcom. Publishes 30 picture books/year; 2 young readers/year; 8 middle readers/year; 12 young adult titles/year.
Fiction Picture books, young readers: adventure, animal, fantasy, folktales, history, humor, multicultural, poetry, sports. Middle readers, young adults: adventure, fantasy, folktales, history, humor, multicultural, poetry, problem novels, science fiction, sports, mystery/adventure. Recently published Savvy, by Ingrid Law (agent 10-14); On the Wings of Heroes, by Richard Peck (ages 10 and up); Impossible, by Nancy Werlin (ages 14 and up); Ladybug Girl, by Jacky Davis and David Soman(ages 3-7); I'm the Best Artist in the Ocean, by Kevin Sherry (ages 3-6).
Nonfiction Will consider query letters for submissions of outstanding literary merit. Picture books, young readers, middle readers: biography, history, sports. Young adults: biography, history, sports. Recently published *A Strong Right Arm*, by Michelle Y. Green (ages 10 and up); *We the Kids*, by David Catrow (ages 5 and up).
How to Contact/Writers "Due to the overwhelming number of unsolicited manuscripts we receive, we at Dial Books for Young Readers have had to change our submissions policy: As of August 1, 2005, Dial will no longer respond to your unsolicited submission unless interested in publishing it. Please do not include SASE with your submission. You will not hear from dial regarding the status of your submission unless we are interested, in which case you can expect a reply from us within four months. We accept entire picture book manuscripts and a maximum of 10 pages for longer works (novels, easy-to-reads). When submitting a portion of a longer work, please provide an accompanying cover letter that briefly describes your manuscript's plot, genre (i.e. easy-to-read, middle grade or YA novel), the intended age group, and your publishing credits, if any."
Terms Pays authors and illustrators in royalties based on retail price. Average advance payment varies. Catalogue available for 9 × 12 envelope with four 37¢ stamps. "This is one way to become informed as to the style, subject matter, and format of our books."
Tips "Because confirmation postcards are easily separated from or hidden within the manuscript, we do not encourage you to include them with your submission. Please send only one manuscript

at a time. Never send cassettes, original artwork, marketing plans, or faxes and do not send submissions by e-mail. Please know that we only keep track of requested manuscripts; we cannot track unsolicited submissions due to the volume we receive each day, so kindly refrain from calling, faxing or e-mailing to inquire after the status of an unsolicited submission as we will be unable to assist you. If you have not received a reply from us after four months, you can safely assume that we are not presently interested in publishing your work."

Ⓐ DISNEY HYPERION BOOKS FOR CHILDREN

114 Fifth Ave.New York NY 10011-5690. 914-288-4100. Fax: (212)633-4833. Website: www. hyperionbooksforchildren.com. **Manuscript Acquisitions:** Editorial Director. 10% of books by first-time authors. Publishes various categories. **All submissions must come via an agent.**

- Hyperion title *Are You Ready to Play Outside*, by Mo Willems, won the Theodor Seuss Geisel Award in 2009. Their title *We Are the Ship*, by Kadir Nelson won a Coretta Scott King Author Award. Their title *The Disreputable History of Frankie Landou-Banks*, by E. Lockhart was a National Book Award Finalist and won a Michael L. Printz Honor.

Fiction Picture books, early readers, middle readers, young adults: adventure, animal, anthology (short stories), contemporary, fantasy, history, humor, multicultural, poetry, science fiction, sports, suspense/mystery. Middle readers, young adults: commercial fiction.

Nonfiction Narrative nonfiction for elementary schooler's.

How to Contact/Writers Only interested in agented material.

Illustration Works with 100 illustrators/year. "Picture books are fully illustrated throughout. All others depend on individual project." Illustrations only: Submit résumé, business card, promotional literature or tearsheets to be kept on file. Responds only if interested. Original artwork returned at job's completion.

Photography Works on assignment only. Provide résumé, business card, promotional literature or tearsheets to be kept on file.

Terms Pays authors royalty based on retail price. Offers advances. Pays illustrators and photographers royalty based on retail price or a flat fee. Sends galleys to authors; dummies to illustrators.

Ⓐ DK PUBLISHING

375 Hudson St.New York NY 10014. Website: www.k.com. **Acquisitions:** submissions editor. "DK publishes photographically illustrated nonfiction for children of all ages."

- DK Publishing does not accept unagented manuscripts or proposals.

Ⓐ DOG-EARED PUBLICATIONS

P.O. Box 620863, Middletown WI 53562-0863. (608)831-1410. Fax: (608)831-1410. E-mail: field@ dog-eared.com. Website: www.og-eared.com. **Art Acquisitions:** Nancy Field, publisher. Publishes 2-3 middle readers/year. 1% of books by first-time authors. "Dog-Eared Publications creates action-packed nature books for children. We aim to turn young readers into environmentally aware citizens and to foster a love for science and nature in the new generation.

Nonfiction Middle readers: activity books, animal, nature/environment, science. Average word length: varies. Recently published *Discovering Black Bear*, by Margaret Anderson, Nancy Field and Karen Stephenson, illustrated by Michael Maydak (middle readers, activity book); *Leapfrogging Through Wetlands*, by Margaret Anderson, Nancy Field and Karen Stephenson, illustrated by Michael Maydak (middle readers, activity book); *Ancient Forests*, by Margaret Anderson, Nancy Field and Karen Stephenson, illustrated by Sharon Torvik (middle readers, activity book).

How to Contact Nonfiction: **Currently not accepting unsolicited mss.**

Terms Pays authors royalty based on wholesale price. Offers advances (amount varies). Pays illustrators royalty based on wholesale price. Sends galleys to authors. Originals returned to artist at job's completion. Brochure available for SASE and 1 first-class stamp or on Web site.

⚂ DUTTON CHILDREN'S BOOKS

Imprint of Penguin Group (USA), inc. 345 Hudson St.New York NY 10014. (212)4143700. Fax: (212)414-3397. Website: www.penquin.com/youngreaders. **Contact**: Lauri Hornik, president and publisher; Julie Strauss-Gabel, associate publisher (literary contemporary young adult fiction); Lucia Monfried, senior editor (picture books and middle grade fiction); Maureen Sullivan, executive editor (books for all ages with distinct narrative style). Estab.1852. Dutton Children's Books publishes fiction and nonfiction for readers ranging from preschoolers to young adults on a variety of subjects. Publishes hardcover originals as well as novelty formats Averages 50 titles/year. 10% of books form first-time authors.

How to Contact Query letter only; include SASE

Terms Pays royalty on retail price. Offers advance.

⚃ EDCON PUBLISHING GROUP

30 Montauk Blvd.Oakdale NY 11769. (631)567-7227. Fax: (631)567-8745. Website: www. edconpublishing.com. **Manuscript Acquisitions:** Editor. Publishes 6 young readers/year, 6 middle readers/year, 6 young adult titles/year. 30% of books by first-time Looking for educational games and nonfiction work in the areas of math, science, reading and social studies.

Fiction Recently adapted/published A Christmas Carol; Frankenstein; Around the World in 80 Days; The Picture of Dorian Grey.

Nonfiction Grades K-12 though primarily 6-12 remedial.

How to Contact Submit outline/synopsis and 1 sample chapter. Publishes book 6 months after acceptance. Will consider simultaneous submissions. Submission kept on file unless return is requested. Include SASE for return.

Terms Work purchased outright from authors for up to $1,000. Pays illustrators by the project (range: $100-$500). Catalog available at Web site www.edconpublishing.com.

⚃ EDUPRESS, INC.

401 S. Wright Rd.Janesville WI 53546. (800)558-9332. Fax: (800)835-7978. E-mail: edupress@ highsmith.com. Website: www.edupressinc.com. **Manuscript Acquisitions:** Elizabeth Bowie, product development manager. "Our mission is to create products that make kids want to go to school!"

How to Contact Nonfiction: Submit complete ms. Responds to queries/mss in 3 months. Publishes book 1-2 years after acceptance.

Terms Work purchased outright from authors. Pays illustrators by the project. Book catalog available at no cost. Catalog available on Web site.

Tips "We are looking for unique, research-based, quality supplemental materials for Pre-K through eighth grade. We publish all subject areas in many different formats, including games. Our materials are intended for classroom and home schooling use."

EERDMANS BOOKS FOR YOUNG READERS

An imprint of Wm. B. Eerdmans Publishing Co.2140 Oak Industrial Dr. NE, Grand Rapids, MI 49505 (616) 459-4591. Fax: (616) 776-7683. E-mail: youngreaders@eerdmans.com. Website: www. eerdmans.com/youngreaders. **Writers contact:** Acquisitions Editor. **Illustrators contact:** Gayle Brown, Art director. Produces 10-12 picture books/year; 2 middle readers/year; 2 young adult books/year. 10% of books by first-time authors. "We seek to engage young minds with words and pictures that inform and delight inspire and entertain. From board books for babies to picture books, nonfiction, and novels for children and young adults, our goal is to produce quality literature for a new generation of readers. We believe in books!"

Fiction Picture books: animal, concept, contemporary, folktales, history, humor, multicultural, nature/environment, poetry, religion, special needs, social issues, sports, suspense. Young readers: animal, concept, contemporary, folktales, history, humor, multicultural, poetry, religion, special needs, social issues, sports, suspense. Middle readers: adventure, contemporary, history, humor, multicultural, nature/environment, problem novels, religion, social issues, sports, suspense. Young adults/teens: adventure, contemporary, folktales, history, humor, multicultural, nature/environment, problem novels, religion, sports, suspense. Average word length: picture books-1,000; middle readers-15,000; young adult-45,000. Recently published *My Name is Sangoel*, by Karen Lynn Williams and Khadra Mohammed, illustrated by Catharine Stock (picture book, ages 7-10); *A River of Words,* written by Jen Bryant, illustrated by Melissa (picture book, ages 7 & up); *Garmann's Summer*, written and illustrated by Stian Hole (picture book, ages 5-8). Ethan, Suspended by Pamela Ehrenberg (middle reader fiction, ages 11-14)

Nonfiction Middle readers: biography, history, multicultural, nature/environment, religion, social issues. Young adults/teens: biography, history, multicultural, nature/environment, religion, social issues. Average word length: middle readers-35,000; young adult books-35,000. Recently published *C.S. Lewis: The Man Behind Narnia,* by Beatrice Gormley.

How to Contact We only consider submissions sent EXCLUSIVELY to Eerdmans. YA and Middle Reader fiction: Please send query, synopsis, and 3 sample chapters. Responds to exclusive queries/mss in 3-5 months. "We no longer acknowledge or respond to unsolicited manuscripts. Exceptions will be made only for exclusive submissions marked as such on outside envelope."

Terms Offers advance against royalties. Author sees galleys for review. Illustrators see proofs for review. Originals returned to artist at job's completion. Catalog available for 8 × 10 SASE and 4 first-class stamps. Offers writer's guidelines for SASE. See Web site for writer's guidelines. (www. eerdmans.com/youngreaders/submit.htm)

Tips "Find out who Eerdmans is before submitting a manuscript. Look at our website, request a catalog, and check out our books."

Ⓝ EGMONT USA

443 Park Ave South, New York NY 10016.Estab. 2008. The Egmont Group was founded in 1878. (212)685-0102. Website: egmont-us.com. Specializes in trade books. Imprints Egmont USA. **Acquisitions:** Elizabeth Law (VP & Publisher), Regina Griffin (Executive Editor). Publishes 5 picture books/year; 5 young readers/year; 20 middle readers/year; 20 young adult/year. 25% of books by first-time authors. "Egmont USA publishes quality commercial fiction. We are committed to editorial excellence and to providing first rate care for our authors. Our motto is that we turn writers in authors and children into passionate readers."

Fiction Picture Books: animal, concept, contemporary, humor, multicultural. Young Readers: adventure, animal, contemporary, humor, multicultural. Middle Readers: adventure, animal, contemporary, fantasy, humor, multicultural, problem novels, science fiction, special needs. Young Adults/Teens: adventure, animal, contemporary, humor, multicultural, problem novels, science fiction, special needs. *Leaving the Belleweathers,* by Kristen Venuti (Fall 09); *Back,* by Julia Keller (Fall 09); *The Cinderella Society,* (Spring 2010).

How to Contact Only interested in agented material. Fiction: Submit complete query. Responds to queries in 4 weeks; mss in 6 weeks. Publishes a book 18 months after acceptance. Will consider e-mail submissions.

Terms Pays authors royalties based on retail price. Pays illustrators royalties.

ENSLOW PUBLISHERS INC.

Box 398, 40 Industrial Rd.Berkeley Heights NJ 07922-0398. Fax: (908)771-0925. E-mail: info@ enslow.com. Website: www.enslow.com or www.myreportlinks.com. **Acquisitions:** Brian D. Enslow, vice president. Imprint: MyReportLinks.com Books. Publishes 30 young readers/year; 70 middle readers/year; 100 young adult titles/year. 30% of books by first-time authors.

- Enslow Imprint MyReportLinks.com Books produces books on animals, states, presidents, continents, countries, and a variety of other topics for middle readers and young adults, and offers links to online sources of information on topics covered in books.

Nonfiction Young readers, middle readers, young adults: animal, arts/crafts, biography, careers, geography, health, history, multicultural, nature/environment, science, social issues, sports. Middle readers, young adults: hi-lo. "Enslow is moving into the elementary (grades 3-4) level and is looking for authors who can write biography and suggest other nonfiction themes at this level." Average word length: young readers—2,000; middle readers—5,000; young adult—18,000. Published *It's About Time! Science Projects*, by Robert Gardner (grades 3-6, science); *Georgia O'Keeffe: Legendary American Painter*, by Jodie A. Shull (grades 6-12, biography); *California: A MyReportLinks.com Book*, by Jeff Savaga (grades 5-8, social studies/history).

How to Contact Nonfiction: Send for guidelines. Query. Responds to queries/mss in 2 weeks. Publishes a book 18 months after acceptance. Will not consider simultaneous submissions.

Terms Pays authors royalties or work purchased outright. Pays illustrators by the project. Pays photographers by the project or per photo. Sends galleys to authors. Book catalog/ms guidelines available for $3, along with an 8½ × 11 SASE and $2 postage or via Web site.

FACTS ON FILE

132 W. 31st St.New York NY 10001. (212)967-8800. Fax: (212)967-9196. E-mail: editorial@factsonfile.com. Website: www.factsonfile.com. Estab. 1941. Book publisher. Editorial Director: Laurie Likoff.

Acquisitions: Frank Darmstadt, science and technology/nature; Andrew Gyory, American history and cultural studies; Jeff Soloway, language and literature; Owen Lancer, world studies; Jim Chambers, arts, health and entertainment. "We produce high-quality reference materials for the school library market and the general nonfiction trade." Publishes 25-30 young adult titles/year. 5% of books by first-time authors; 25% of books from agented writers; additional titles through book packagers, co-publishers and unagented writers.

Nonfiction Middle readers, young adults: animal, biography, careers, geography, health, history, multicultural, nature/environment, reference, religion, science, social issues and sports.

How to Contact Nonfiction: Submit outline/synopsis and sample chapters. Responds to queries in 10 weeks. Publishes a book 10-12 months after acceptance. Will consider simultaneous submissions. Sends galleys to authors. Book catalog free on request. Send SASE for submission guidelines.

Terms Submission guidelines available via web site or with SASE.

Tips "Most projects have high reference value and fit into a series format."

FARRAR, STRAUS & GIROUX INC.

18 West 18th St.New York NY 10011. (212)741-6900. Website: www.fsgkidsbooks.com. Estab. 1946. Book publisher. Imprints: Frances Foster Books. Children's Books Editorial Director: Margaret Ferguson. **Manuscript Acquisitions:** Margaret Ferguson, editorial director; Frances Foster, Frances Foster Books; Wesley Adams, executive editor; Janine O'Malley, Senior editor. **Art Director:** Robbin Gourley, art director, Books for Young Readers. Publishes 40 picture books/year; 30 middle grade books/year; 10 young adult titles/year. 5% of books by first-time authors; 20% of books from agented writers.

- Farrar title *How I Learned Geography*, by Uri Shulevitz, won a Caldcott Honor in 2009**.** Farrar/Frances Foster title *The Wall: Growing Up Behind the Iron Curtain*, by Peter Siís, won a Caldcott Honor Medal in 2008. Farrar/Melanie Kroupa title *Rex Zero and the End of the World,* by Tim Wynne-Jones, won a Boston Globe-Horn Book Fiction and Poetry Honor Award in 2007. Farrar/Frances Foster title *Dreamquake: Book Two of the Dreamhunter Duet*, by Elizabeth Knox, won a Michael L. Printz Honor Award in 2008. See First Books on page 133 for interviews with Deborah Diesen and Dan Hanna, author and illustrator of Farrar, Straus & Giroux title *The Pout-Pout Fisho*.

Fiction All levels: all categories. "Original and well-written material for all ages." Recently published *The Cabinet of Wonders*, by Marie Rutkoski; *Last Night*, by Hyewon Yum.

Nonfiction All levels: all categories. "We publish only literary nonfiction."

How to Contact Fiction/nonfiction: for novels, query with outline/synopsis and 3 sample chapters;

for picture books send complete ms. Do not fax or e-mail submissions or queries. Responds to queries/mss in 3 months. Publishes a book 18 months after acceptance. Will consider simultaneous submissions.

Terms "We offer an advance against royalties for both authors and illustrators." Sends galleys to authors; dummies to illustrators. Original artwork returned at job's completion. Book catalog available for 9 × 12 SASE with $1.95 postage; ms guidelines for SASE1 first-class stamp, or can be viewed at www.fsgkidsbooks.com.

Tips "Study our catalog before submitting. We will see illustrator's portfolios by appointment. Don't ask for criticism and/or advice—due to the volume of submissions we receive, it's just not possible. Never send originals. Always enclose SASE."

FIRST SECOND BOOKS

Imprint of Roaring Brook Press, 175 5th Ave.New York NY 10010.Estab. 2005. (646)307-5095. Fax: (646)307-5285. E-mail: mail@firstsecondbooks.com. Website: www.firstsecondbooks.com. **Editorial Director:** Mark Siegel. Publishes 3 young graphic novels/season; 3 middle teen graphic novels/season; 3 adult graphic novels/season. "First Second aims for high-quality, literate graphic novels for a wide range of readers from middle grade to young adult to adult readers."

Fiction Graphic novels. All books 96 + pages. Recently published *Sardine in Outer Space*, by Joann Sfar and Emmanuel Guibert (graphic novel, age 6 and up); *A.L.I.E.E.E.N.*, by Lewis Trondheim (graphic novel, ages 12 and up); *American Born Chinese*, by Gene Yang (graphic novel, teen).

Nonfiction Graphic novels. Recently published *Journey into Mohawk Country*, by George O'Connor (graphic novel, YA); *Kampung Boy*, by Lat (graphic novel, YA); *Missouri Boy*, by Leland Myrick (graphic novel, YA).

How to Contact No unsolicited submissions accepted.

Terms Authors and illustrators see proofs. Original artwork returned at job's completion. Book catalog available on Web site. Writer's and artist's guidelines available with SASE and on Web site.

▧ FITZHENRY & WHITESIDE LTD.

195 Allstate Pkwy.Markham ON L3R 4T8 Canada. (905)477-9700. Fax: (905)477-9179. E-mail: gailwinskill@fitzhenry.ca. Website: www.fitzhenry.ca. Book publisher. **President:** Sharon Fitzhenry; Children's Publisher: Gail Winskill. Publishes 3 picture books/year; 4 middle novels/year; 3 young adult titles/year; 3 juvenile nonfiction titles/year. 10% of books by first-time authors. Publishes fiction and nonfiction—social studies, visual arts, biography, environment. Emphasis on Canadian authors and illustrators, subject or perspective.

How to Contact Fiction/nonfiction. Publishes a book 12-24 months after acceptance. See full submission guidelines on Web site www.fitzhenry.com.

Terms Pays authors 8-10% royalty with escalations. Offers "respectable" advances for picture books, 50/50 splite between author and illustrator. Pays illustrators by the project and royalty. Pays photographers per photo. Sends galleys to authors; dummies to illustrators.

Tips "We respond to quality."

▢ ▣ FIVE STAR PUBLICATIONS, INC.

P.O. Box 6698, Chandler AZ 85246-6698. (480)940-8182. Fax: (480)940-8787. E-mail: info@ fivestarpublications.com. Web sites: www.FiveStarPublications.com, www.LittleFivestar. com, www.FiveStarLegends,com, www.FiveStarSleuths.com, www.SixPointsPress.com. **Art Acquisitions:** Sue DeFabis. Publishes 7 middle readers/year.

Nonfiction Recently published *Tic Talk Book: Living with Tourette Syndrome*, by Dylan Peters, illustrated by Zachary Wendland (www.TicTalkBook.com); Alfie's Bark Mitzvah, by Shari Cohen, songs by Cantor Marcello Gindlin, illustrated by Nadia Komorova (www.AlfiesBarkMitvah.com).

How to Contact Nonfiction: Query.

Terms Pays illustrators by the project. Pays photographers by the project. Sends galleys to authors; dummies to illustrators.

FLASHLIGHT PRESS

527 Empire Blvd.Brooklyn NY 11225. (718)288-8300. Fax: (718)972-6307. E-mail: editor@ flashlightpress.com. Website: www.flashlightpress.com. Estab. 2004. **Editor:** Shari Dash Greenspan. Publishes 2-3 picture books/year. 25% of books by first-time authors.

Fiction Picture books: contemporary, humor, multicultural. Average word length: 1,000. Recently published: *I Need my Monster*, by Amanda Noll, illustrated by Howard Mcwilliam; *I'm Really Not Tired*, by Lori Sunshine, illustrated by Jeffrey Ebbler (ages4-8); *Grandfather's Wrinkles*, by Kathryn England, illustrated by Richard McFarland (ages 4-8, picture book); *Grandpa for Sale*, by Dotti Enderle and Vicki Sansum, illustrated by T. Kyle Gentry (ages 4-8, picture book); *Getting to Know Ruben Plotnick*, by Roz Rosenbluth, illustrated by Maurie J. Manning (ages 5-9, picture book); *Alley Oops*, by Janice Levy, illustrated by Cynthia B. Decker (ages 5-9, picture book); *Carla's Sandwich*, by Debbie Herman, illustrated by Sheila Bailey (ages 4-8, picture book).

How to Contact Query by e-mail only, after carefully reading our Submission Guidelines: http://flashlightpress.com/submissionguidelines.html. No e-mail attachments. "Do not send anything by snail mail. Responds to queries in 10 days; usually responds to mss in 3-4 months. Publishes a book 2 years after acceptance.

Terms Pays authors and illustrators royalty of 10% based on wholesale price. Offers advance of $500-1,000. Catalog available through IPG (Independent Publishers Group). E-mail to request catalog or view on Web site.

FLUX

Llewellyn Worldwide, Ltd.2143 Wooddale Drive, Woodbury MN 55125. (651)312-8613. Fax: (651)291-1908. E-mail: submissions@fluxnow.com. Website: www.fluxnow.com. Blog: http://fluxnow.blogspot.com. **Acquisitions Editor:** Brian Farrey. Imprint estab. 2005; Lllewellyn estab. 1901. Publishes 21 young abult titles/year. 50% of books by first-time authors. "Flux seeks to publish authors who see YA as a point of view, not a reading level. We look for books that try to capture a slice of teenage experience, whether in real or imagined worlds."

Fiction Young Adults: adventure, contemporary, fantasy, history, humor, problem novels, religion, science fiction, sports, suspense. Average word length: 50,000. Recently published *Blue Is for Nightmares*, by Laurie Faria Stolarz; *How to Ruin a Summer Vacation*, by Simone Elkeles; *The Shape of Water*, by Anne Spollen; *The Tree Shepherd's Daughter*, by Gillian Summers.

How to Contact Query. Responds to queries in 1-2 weeks; mss in 1-3 months. Will consider simultaneous submissions and previously published work.

Terms Pays royalties of 10-15% based on wholesale price. Offers advance. Authors see galleys for review. Book catalog available on Web site. Writer's guidelines available for SASE or in Web site at www.fluxnow.com/submission_guidelines.php.

Tips "Read contemporary teen books. Be aware of what else is out there. If you don't read teen books, you probably shouldn't write them. Know your audience. Write incredibly well. Do not condescend."

FREE SPIRIT PUBLISHING

217 Fifth Ave. N.Suite 200, Minneapolis MN 55401-1299. (612)338-2068. Fax: (612)337-5050. E-mail: acquisitions@freespirit.com. Website: www.freespirit.com. Publishes 25-30 titles/year for pre-K through 12, educators and parents. "Free Spirit is the leading publisher of learning tools that support young people's social and emotional health, helping children and teens to think for themselves, succeed in life, and make a difference in the world."

• Free Spirit does not accept fiction, poetry or storybook submissions.

How to Contact Accepts nonfiction submissions from prospective authors or through agents.

"Please review catalog and author guidelines (both available online) before submitting proposal." Reponds to queries in 4-6 months. "If you'd like material returned, enclose an SASE with sufficient postage." Accepts queries only—not submissions—by e-mail.

Terms Pays authors royalty based on net receipts. Offers advance. Pays illustrators by the project.

Tips "We do not publish fiction, poetry or picture storybooks, books with animals or mythical characters, books with religious content, or single biographies, autobiographies or memiors. Free Spirit prefers books written in a practical, pshycologically sound, and positive style."

FREESTONE/PEACHTREE, JR.

Peachtree Publishers, 1700 Chattahoochee Ave. Atlanta GA 30318-2112. (404)876-8761. Fax: (404)875-2578. E-mail: hello@peachtree-online.com. Website: www.peachtree-online.com. **Acquisitions:** Helen Harriss. Publishes 4-8 young adult titles/year.

- Freestone and Peachtree, Jr. are imprints of Peachtree Publishers. See the listing for Peachtree for submission information. No e-mail or fax queries or submissions, please.

Fiction Picture books: animals, folktales, health, history, humor, multicultural, nature/environment, special needs, sports. Young readers: history, humor, health, multicultural, sports. Middle readers: adventure, contemporary, history, humor, multicultural, problem novels, sports, suspense/mystery. Young adults/teens: adventure, contemporary, history, humor, multicultural, problem novels, sports, suspense/mystery. Recently published *Martina the Beautiful Cockroach,* by Carmen Agra Deedy, illustrated by Michael Austin (ages 4-8, picture book); *Young Charles Darwin and the Voyage of the Beagle*, written by Ruth Ashby (ages 7-10; early reader); *The Sorta Sisters,* by Adrian Fogelin (ages 8-12, middle reader); *Giving Up the Ghost,* By Sheri Sinykin (ages 12-16, young adult).

Nonfiction Picture books, young readers, middle readers, young adults: history, sports. Picture books: animal, health, multicultural, nature/environment, science, social issues, special needs.

How to Contact Responds to queries/mss in 6 months.

Terms Pays authors royalty. Pays illustrators by the project or royalty. Pays photographers by the project or per photo.

FRONT STREET

Imprint of Boyds Mills Press, 815 Church Street, Honesdale, PA 18431 Website: www.frontstreetbooks. com. Publishes 20-25 titles/year. "We look for fresh voices for children and young adults. Titles on our list entertain, challenge, or enlighten, always employing novel characters whose considered voices resonate." High-end picture books.

- Front Street title *Keturah and Lord Death*, by Martine Leavitt, was a 2007 National Book Award Finalist. Front Street title *One Whole and Perfect Day,* by Judith Clarke won a Michael L. Printz Honor Book Award in 2008.

Fiction Recently published *I'm Being Stalked by a Moonshadow*, by Doug MacLeod; *Runaround*, by Helen Hemphill; *Baby*, by Joseph Monninger.

How to Contact Fiction: Submit cover letter and complete ms if under 30 pages; submit cover letter, 1 or 2 sample chapters and plot summary if over 30 pages. Label package "Manuscript Submission." Include SASE with submissions if you want them returned. "We try to respond within three months. "

Terms Pays royalties.

☐ FULCRUM PUBLISHING

4690 Table Mountain Drive, Suite 100 Golden CO 80403. (303)277-1623. Fax: (303)279-7111. Website: www.fulcrum-books.com. **Manuscript Acquisitions:** T. Baker, acquisitions editor.

Nonfiction Middle and early readers: Western history, Nature/ Environment, Native American.

How to Contact Submit complete ms or submit outline/synopsis and 2 sample chapters. Publisher does not send response letters unless we are interested in publishing. Do not send SASE.

Terms Pays authors royalty based on wholesale price. Offers advances. Book catalog available for

9 × 12 SAE and 77¢ postage; Ms submission guidelines available on website under "Authors" tab.
Tips "Research our line first. We look for books that appeal to the school market and trade. "

🅐 DAVID R. GODINE, PUBLISHER

9 Hamilton Place, Boston MA 02108. (617)451-9600. Fax: (617)350-0250. Website: www.godine. com. Estab. 1970. Book publisher. Publishes 1 picture book/year; 1 young reader/year; 1 middle reader/year. 10% of books by first-time authors; 90% of books from agented writers. "We publish books that matter for people who care."
• This publisher is no longer considering unsolicited manuscripts of any type.
Fiction Picture books: adventure, animal, contemporary, folktales, nature/environment. Young readers: adventure, animal, contemporary, folk or fairy tales, history, nature/environment, poetry. Middle readers: adventure, animal, contemporary, folk or fairy tales, history, mystery, nature/ environment, poetry. Young adults/teens: adventure, animal, contemporary, history, mystery, nature/environment, poetry. Recently published *Little Red Riding Hood*, by Andrea Wisnewski (picture book); *The Merchant of Noises*, by Anna Rozen, illustrated by François Avril.
Nonfiction Picture books: alphabet, animal, nature/environment. Young readers: activity books, animal, history, music/dance, nature/environment. Middle readers: activity books, animal, biography, history, music/dance, nature/environment. Young adults: biography, history, music/ dance, nature/environment.
How to Contact Only interested in agented material.Query. Include SASE for return of material.
Tips "E-mail submissions are not accepted. Always enclose a SASE. Keep in mind that we do not accept unsolicited manuscripts and that we rarely use freelance illustrators."

🅐 GOLDEN BOOKS

1745 Broadway, New York NY 10019. (212)782-9000. **Editorial Directors:** Courtney Silk, color and activity; Chris Angelilli, storybooks; Dennis Shealy, novelty. **Art Acquisitions:** Tracey Tyler, executive art director.
• See listing for Random House-Golden Books for Young Readers Group.
Fiction Publishes board books, novelty books, picture books, workbooks, series (mass market and trade).
How to Contact Does not accept unsolicited submissions.

GRAPHIA

Houghton Mifflin Harcourt, 222 Berkeley St.Boston MA 02116. (617)351-5000. Website: www. graphiabooks.com. **Manuscript Acquisitions:** Julia Richardson. "Graphia publishes quality paperbacks for today's teen readers, ages 14 and up. From fiction to nonfiction, poetry to graphic novels, Graphia runs the gamut, all unified by the quality of writing that is the hallmark of this imprint."
Fiction Young adults: adventure, contemporary, fantasy, history, humor, multicultural, poetry. Recently published: *The Off Season*, by Catherine Murdock; *Come in from the Cold*, by Marsha Qualey; *Breaking Up is Hard to Do*, with stories by Niki Burnham, Terri Clark, Ellen Hopkins, and Lynda Sandoval; *Zahrah the Windseeker*, by Nnedi Okorafot-Mbachu.
Nonfiction Young adults: biography, history, multicultural, nature/environment, science, social issues.
How to Contact Query. Responds to queries/mss in 3 months. Will consider simultaneous submissions and previously published work.
Terms Pays author royalties. Offers advances. Sends galleys to authors. Catalog available on Web site (www.houghtonmifflin.com).

◪ GREENE BARK PRESS

P.O. Box 1108, Bridgeport CT 06601-1108. (610)434-2802. Fax: (610)434-2809. E-mail: greenebark@ aol.com. Website: www.greenebarkpress.com. **Acquisitions:** Thomas J. Greene, publisher. Publishes 1-6 picture books/year; majority of books by first-time or repeat authors. "We publish only quality fictional hardcover picture books for children. Our stories are selected for originality, imagery and color. Our intention is to fire-up a child's imagination, encourage a desire to read in order to explore the world through books."

Fiction Picture books, young readers: adventure, fantasy, humor. Average word length: picture books—650; young readers—1,400. Recently published *Edith Ellen Eddy*, by Julee Ann Granger; *Hey, There's a Gobblin Under My Throne*, by Rhett Ranson Pennell.

How to Contact Responds to queries in 3 months; mss in 6 months; must include SASE. No response without SASE. Publishes a book 18 months after acceptance. Will consider simultaneous submissions. Prefer to review complete mss with illustrations.

Terms Pays authors royalty of 10-12% based on wholesale price. Pays illustrators by the project (range: $1,500-3,000) or 5-7% royalty based on wholesale price. No advances. Sends galleys to authors; dummies to illustrators. Manuscript guidelines available for SASE or per e-mail request.

Tips "As a guide for future publications look to our latest publications, do not look to our older backlist. Please, no telephone, e-mail or fax queries."

GREENHAVEN PRESS

Imprint of the Cengage Gale, 27500 Drake Road, Farmington Hills MI 48331. E-mail: Kristine. burns@cengage.com. Website: www.gale.com/greenhaven. **Acquisitions:** Kristine Burns. Publishes 220 young adult academic reference titles/year. 50% of books by first-time authors. Greenhaven continues to print quality nonfiction anthologies for libraries and classrooms. Our well known Opposing Viewpoints series is highly respected by students and librarians in need of material on controversial social issues. **Greenhaven accepts no unsolicited manuscripts.** All writing is done on a work-for-hire basis. Also see listing for Lucent Book.

Nonfiction Young adults (high school): controversial issues, social issues, history, literature, science, environment, health. Recently published (series): Issues That Concern You; Writing the Critical Essay: An Opening Viewpoint Guide; Introducing Issue with Opposing Viewpoints; Social Issues in Literature; and Perspectives on Diseases and Disorders.

How to Contact/Writers Send query, resume, and list of published works by e-mail.

Terms Work purchased outright from authors; write-for-hire, flat fee.

◪ ◪ GREENWILLOW BOOKS

1350 Avenue of the Americas, New York NY 10019. (212)261-6500. Website: www. harpercollinschildrens.com. Book publisher. Imprint of HarperCollins. Vice President/Publisher: Virginia Duncan. **Art Acquisitions:** Paul Zakris, Art Director. Publishes 30 picture books/year; 5 middle readers/year; 5 young adult books/year. "Greenwillow Books publishes picture books, fiction for young readers of all ages, and nonfiction primarily for children under seven years of age."

- Greenwillow Books is currently accepting neither unsolicited manuscripts nor queries. Unsolicited mail will not be opened and will not be returned. Call (212)261-6627 for an update. Greenwillow title *Escape*!: The Story of the Great Houdini, by Sid Fleischman, won a Boston Globe-Horne Book Nonfiction Honor Award in 2007.

Terms Pays authors royalty. Offers advances. Pays illustrators royalty or by the project. Sends galleys to authors.

◪ GROSSET & DUNLAP PUBLISHERS

Penguin Group (USA), Inc 345 Hudson St.New York NY 10014. Website: http://us.penguingroup. com/youngreaders. Estab. 1898. **Acquisitions:** Francesco Sedita, Vice-President/Publisher.

Publishes approximately 140 titles/year. "Grosset & Dunlap publishes high interest, affordable books for children ages 0-10 years. We focus on original series, licensed properties, readers and novelty books."

Fiction *Recently published series*: Camp Confidential; Hank Zipzer; Katie Kazoo; Magic Kitten; Magic Puppy; The Hardy Boys; Nancy Drew; The Little Engine That Could. *Upcoming series*: Mysterious Mr. Spines; monster Squad; George Brown, Class Clown; Bedeviled. *Licensed series*: Angelina Ballerina; Disney Club Penguin; Strawberry Shortcake; Charlie & Lola; Dick & Jane (brand).

Nonfiction *Young readers:* nature/environment, science. *Recently published series*: All Aboard Reading; Who Was...? series.

How to Contact "We do not accept e-mail submissions. Unsolicited manuscripts usually receive a response in 6-8 weeks."

☐ GRYPHON HOUSE

P.O. Box 207, Beltsville MD 20704-0207. (301)595-9500. Fax: (301)595-0051. E-mail: kathyc@ghbooks.com. Website: www.gryphonhouse.com. **Acquisitions:** Kathy Charner, editor-in-chief.

Nonfiction Parent and teacher resource books, textbooks. Recently published *Reading Games*, by Jackie Silberg; *Primary Art*, by MaryAnn F. Kohl; *Teaching Young Children's with Autism Spectrum Disorder*, by Clarissa Willis; *The Complete Resource Book for Infants*, by Pam Schiller. "At Gryphon House, our goal is to publish books that help teachers and parents enrich the lives of children from birth through age eight. We strive to make our books useful for teachers at all levels of experience, as well as for parents, caregivers, and anyone interested in working with children."

How to Contact Query. Submit outline/synopsis and 2 sample chapters. Responds to queries/mss in 6 months. Publishes a book 18 months after acceptance. Will consider simultaneous submissions, e-mail submissions.

Terms Pays authors royalty based on wholesale price. Offers advances. Pays illustrators by the project. Pays photographers by the project or per photo. Sends edited ms copy to authors. Original artwork returned at job's completion. Book catalog and ms guidelines available via website or with SASE.

Tips "Send a SASE for our catalog and manuscript guidelines. Look at our books, then submit proposals that complement the books we already publish or supplement our existing books. We are looking for books of creative, participatory learning experiences that have a common conceptual theme to tie them together. The books should be on subjects that parents or teachers want to do on a daily basis."

⊠ H & W PUBLISHING INC

P.O. Box 53515, Cincinnati OH 45253.Estab. 2007. (513)687-3968. Fax: (513)761-4221. E-mail: info@handwpublishing.com. Website: www.handwpublishing.com. Specializes in African American children's literature. Publishes 2 books/year. 90% of books by first-time authors. "Our company empowers, inspires, and uplifts".

Fiction Picture Books: concept, contemporary, humor, poetry, religion. Young Readers: adventure, contemporary, nature/environment, poetry. Middle Readers: contemporary, problem novels. Average word length: picture books—1,200; young readers—850; middle readers—2,500. Recently published *Coralee's Best Run Yet*, by Karen N. Harkness, Alpha Frierson, (ages 6-8 picture book); *Obama Our Hero*, by Karen N. Harkness, Elbert Lewis Jr. (ages 5-12, biography).

Nonfiction Young Readers: biography, social issues. Average word length: picture books—700; young readers—1,200.

How to Contact Submit complete manuscript or submit outline/synopsis. Responds to queries in 1 month. Responds to mss in 2 months. Publishes a book 18 months after acceptance.

Terms Pays authors royalty 5% and Work purchased outright for $2,500-4,000. Pays illustrators by the project—range ($1,800-3,500) and royalty of 3-5% based on retail price. Originals returned to artist at jobs completion. Writers and artists guidelines available at www.handwpublishing.com.

Tips "We specialize in literature for African American children. Illustrations should be detailed and reflect positive images. Story lines should either be humorist, contemporary, or teach without being preachy. No books on slavery please."

HACHAI PUBLISHING

527 Empire Blvd.Brooklyn NY 11225. (718)633-0100. Fax: (718)633-0103. E-mail: info@hachai. com. Website: www.hachai.com. **Manuscript Acquisitions:** Devorah Leah Rosenfeld, submissions editor. Publishes 4 picture books/year; 1 young reader/year; 1 middle reader/year. 75% of books published by first-time authors. "All books have spiritual/religious themes, specifically traditional Jewish content. We're seeking books about morals and values; the Jewish experience in current and Biblical times; and Jewish observance, Sabbath and holidays."

Fiction Picture books and young readers: contemporary, historical fiction, religion. Middle readers: adventure, contemporary, problem novels, religion. Does not want to see fantasy, animal stories, romance, problem novels depicting drug use or violence. Recently published *Let's Go Visiting*, written and illustrated by Rikki Benenfeld (ages 2-5, picture book); *What Else Do I Say*, by Malky Goldberg, illustrated by Patti Argoff (ages 1-2, lift-the-flap book); *Way Too Much Challah Dough*, by Goldie Shulman, illustrated by Vitaliy Romanenko (ages 3-6, picture book); *Faigy Finds the Way*, by Batsheva Brandeis (ages 7-10, short chapter book).

Nonfiction Recently published *The Invisible Book*, by Bracha Goetz, illustrated by Patti Agroff; *My Jewish ABC's*, by Draizy Zelcer, illustrated by Patti Nemeroff (ages 3-6, picture book); *Shadow Play*, by Leah Pearl Shollar, illustrated by Pesach Gerber (ages 3-6, picture book); *Much Much Better*, by Chaim Kosofsky, illustrated by Jessica Schiffman (ages 5-8).

How to Contact Fiction/nonfiction: Submit complete ms. Responds to queries/mss in 6 weeks.

Terms Work purchased outright from authors for $800-1,000. Pays illustrators by the project (range: $2,000-4,000). Book catalog, ms/artist's guidelines available for SASE.

Tips "Write a story that incorporates a moral, not a preachy morality tale. Originality is the key. We feel Hachai publications will appeal to a wider readership as parents become more interested in positive values for their children."

HARCOURT CHILDREN'S BOOKS

Imprint of Houghton Mifflin Harcourt Children's Book Group, 215 Park Ave South, New York, NY 10003. Website: www.harcourtbooks.com. **Senior Vice President and Publisher:** Betsy Groban. **Associate Publisher:** Jennifer Haller. 20% of books by first-time authors; 50% of books from agented writers. "Harcourt Children's Books publishes hardcover picture books and fiction only."

- Harcourt Children's Books no longer accepts unsolicited manuscripts, queries or illustrations. Recent Harcourt titles *Tails*, by Matthew Van Fleet; *Leaf Man*, by Lois Ehlert; *The Great Fuzz Frenzy*, by Janet Stevens and Susan Steven Crummel; *How I Became a Pirate* and *Pirates* Don't *Change Diapers*, by Melinda Long, illustrated by David Shannon; and *Frankenstein Makes a Sandwich*, by Adam Rex, are all New York Times bestsellers. Harcourt title *Jazz Baby*, by Lisa Wheeler, illustrated by R. Gregory Christie, won a Theodor Seuss Geisel Award in 2008. See Lisa Wheelers article Great Opening Lines in Picture Books on page 37.

How to Contact Only interested in agented material.

Terms Pays authors and illustrators royalty based on retail price. Pays photographers by the project. Sends galleys to authors; dummies to illustrators. Original artwork returned at job's completion.

HARPERCOLLINS CHILDREN'S BOOKS

10 East 53rd St.New York NY 10022. (212)261-6500. Website: www.harpercollinschildrens.com. Book publisher. President and Publisher: Susan Katz. Associate Publisher/Editor-in-Chief: Kate Morgan Jackson. Associate Publisher, Fiction: Elise Howard. Editorial Directors: Margaret Anastas, Barbara Lalicki, Maria Modugno, Phoebe Yeh. **Art Acquisitions:** Martha Rago or Barbara Fitzsimmons, director. Imprints: HarperTrophy, HarperTeen, EOS, HarperFestival, Greenwillow Books, Joanna

Cotler Books, Laura Geringer Books, Katherine Tegen Books, Balzer and Bray.

- HarperCollins Children's Books is not accepting unsolicited and/or unagented manuscripts or queries. "Unfortunately, the volume of these submissions is so large that we cannot give them the attention they deserve. Such submissions will not be reviewed or returned." Agent submissions may be sent to Kate Morgan Jackson. Responses only if interested. Materials returned with SASE. HarperCollins Children's Books title *The Graveyard Book*, by Neil Gaiman won 2009 Newbury Medal, HarperTeen title *Jellicoe Road*, by Melina Marchetta won the 2009 Micael L. Printz Award, HarperCollins Children's Books title *Nation*, by Terry pratchett won the 2009 Michael L. Printz Honor.

Fiction Publishes picture, chapter, novelty, board and TV/movie books.

HARPERTEEN

10 East 53rd St.New York NY 10022. (212)261-6500. Fax: (212)261-6668. Web sites: www.harpercollins.com, www.harperteen.com. Book publisher. Imprint of HarperCollins Children's Books. Publishes 65-70 teen titles/year.

- HarperTeen is a teen imprint. HarperTeen also publishes hardcovers, paperback reprints and paperback originals.

How to Contact HarperCollins Children's Books is not accepting unsolicited and/or un-agented manuscripts or queries. "Unfortunately the volume of these submissions is so large that we cannot give them the attention they deserve. Such submissions will not be reviewed or returned."Manuscripts and queries: Agent submissions may be sent to Elise Howard. Responses only if interested. Materials returned with SASE.

HAYES SCHOOL PUBLISHING CO. INC.

321 Pennwood Ave.Wilkinsburg PA 15221-3398. (412)371-2373. Fax: (800)543-8771. E-mail: chayes@hayespub.com. Website: www.hayespub.com. Estab. 1940. **Acquisitions:** Mr. Clair N. Hayes. Produces folders, workbooks, stickers, certificates. Wants to see supplementary teaching aids for grades K-12. Interested in all subject areas. Will consider simultaneous and electronic submissions.

How to Contact Query with description or complete ms. Responds in 6 weeks. SASE for return of submissions.

Terms Work purchased outright. Purchases all rights.

HEALTH PRESS NA INC

P.O. Box 37470, Albuquerque NM 87176-7479. (505)888-1394 or (877)411-0707. Fax: (505)888-1521. E-mail: goodbooks@healthpress.com. Website: www.healthpress.com. **Acquisitions:** Editor. Publishes 4 young readers/year. 100% of books by first-time authors.

Fiction Picture books, young readers: health, special needs. Average word length: young readers—1,000-1,500; middle readers—1,000-1,500. Recently published *The Girl With No Hair*, by Elizabeth Murphy-Melas, illustrated by Alex Hernandez (ages 8-12, picture book); *The Peanut Butter Jam*, by Elizabeth Sussman-Nassau, illustrated by Margot Ott (ages 6-12, picture book).

Nonfiction Picture books, young readers: health, special needs, social issues, self help.

How to Contact Submit complete ms. Responds in 3 month. Publishes a book 9 months after acceptance. Will consider simultaneous submissions.

Terms Pays authors royalty. Sends galleys to authors. Book catalog available.

HENDRICK-LONG PUBLISHING COMPANY

10635 Tower Oaks, Suite D, Houston TX 77070. (832)912-READ. Fax: (832)912-7353. E-mail: hendrick-long@worldnet.att.net. **Acquisitions:** Vilma Long, vice president. Publishes 4 young readers/year; 4 middle readers/year. 20% of books by first-time authors. Publishes fiction/

nonfiction about Texas of interest to young readers through young adults/teens.

Fiction Young readers, middle readers: history books on Texas and the Southwest. No fantasy or poetry.

Nonfiction Young readers, middle readers: history books on Texas and the Southwest, biography, multicultural. "Would like to see more workbook-type manuscripts."

How to Contact Fiction/nonfiction: Query with outline/synopsis and sample chapter. Responds to queries in 5 months. Publishes a book 18 months after acceptance. No simultaneous submissions. Include SASE.

HOLIDAY HOUSE INC.

425 Madison Ave.New York NY 10017. (212)688-0085. Fax: (212)421-6134. Website: www. holidayhouse.com. Estab. 1935. Book publisher. **Vice President/Editor-in-Chief:** Mary Cash. **Acquisitions:** Acquisitions Editor. **Art Director:** Claire Counihan. Publishes 35 picture books/ year; 3 young readers/year; 15 middle readers/year; 8 young adult titles/year. 20% of books by first-time authors; 10% from agented writers. Mission Statement: "To publish high-quality books for children."

Fiction All levels: adventure, contemporary, folktales, ghost, historical, humor, literary, multicultural, school, suspense/mystery, sports. Recently published *Anansi's Party Time*, by Eric Kimmel, illustrated by Janet Stevens; *The Blossom Family series*, by Betsy Byars; *Washington at Valley Forge*, by Russell Freedman.

Nonfiction All levels, but more picture books and fewer middle-grade nonfiction titles: animal, biography, concept, contemporary, geography, historical, math, multicultural, music/dance, nature/environment, religion, science, social issues.

How to Contact Send queries only to editor. Responds to queries in 3 months; mss in 4 months. "If we find your book idea suits our present needs, we will notify you by mail." Once a ms has been requested, the writers should send in the exclusive submission, with a SASE, otherwise the ms will not be returned.

Terms Pays authors and illustrators an advance against royalties. Originals returned at job's completion. Book catalog, ms/artist's guidelines available for a SASE.

Tips "We need books with strong stories, writing and art. We do not publish board books or novelties. No easy readers."

HENRY HOLT & COMPANY

175 Fifth Ave, New York NY 10010. Unsolicited Manuscript Hotline: (646)307-5087. Website: www.HenryHoltKids.com. Submissions Website: www.HenryHoltKids.com/submissions.htm. **Manuscript Acquisitions:** Addressed to submissions/Henry Holt books for young readers. **Art Acquisitions:** Patrick Collins, creative director. Publishes 30-35 picture books/year; 6-8 chapter books/year; 10-15 middle readers/year; 8-10 young adult titles/year. 15% of books by first-time authors; 40% of books from agented writers. "Henry Holt and Company Books for Young Readers is known for publishing quality books that feature imaginative authors and illustrators. We tend to publish many new authors and illustrators each year in our effort to develop and foster new talent."

Fiction Picture books: animal, anthology, concept, folktales, history, humor, multicultural, nature/environment, poetry, special needs, sports. Middle readers and young adults: adventure, contemporary, fantasy, history, humor, multicultural, special needs, sports, suspense/mystery.

Nonfiction Picture books: animal, arts/crafts, biography, concept, geography, history, hobbies, multicultural, the arts, nature/environment, sports. Middle readers and young readers, young adult: biography, history, multicultural, sports.

How to Contact Writers Fiction/nonfiction: submit complete ms, attn: submissions; "no SASE please." Responds in 4-6 months only if interested, otherwise mss are not returned or responded to. Will not consider simultaneous or multiple submissions.

Illustration Works with 50-60 illustrators/year. Reviews ms/illustration packages from artists. Random samples ok. Illustrations only: submit tearsheets, slides. Do not send originals. Responds to art samples only if interested. Samples filed but not returned. If accepted, original artwork returned at job's completion. Portfolios are reviewed every Monday.

Terms Pays authors/illustrators royalty based on retail price. Sends galleys to authors; proofs to illustrators.

⚡ HOUGHTON MIFFLIN HARCOURT

Children's Trade Books, 222 Berkeley St.Boston MA 02116-3764. (617)351-5000. Fax: (617)351-1111. E-mail: Children'sBooks@hmhpub.com. Website: www.houghtonmifflinbooks.com. **Manuscript Acquisitions:** Submissions Coordinator; Betsy Groban, publisher; Margaret Raymo, editorial director; Ann Rider, executive editor; Mary Wilcox, franchise director, Julia Richardson, paperback director; Kate O'Sullivan, senior editor, Monica Perez, franchise senior editor; Erica Zappy, associate editor. **Art Acquisitions:** Sheila Smallwood, creative director. Imprints include Houghton Mifflin, Harcourt, Clarion, Sandpiper and Graphia. Averages 60 titles/year. Publishes hardcover originals and trade paperback reprints and originals. "Houghton Mifflin gives shape to ideas that educate, inform, and above all, delight."

- Houghton title *The House in the Night*, by Susan Marie Swanson, illustrated by Beth Krommes won the 2008 Caldecott award.

Fiction All levels: all categories except religion. "We do not rule out any theme, though we do not publish specifically religious material." Recently published *Red Sings from Treetops: a year in colors*, by Joyce Sidman, illustrated by Pamela Zagarenski (ages 5-8, picture book/poetry); *The Entomological Tales of Augustus T. Percival: Petronella Saves Nearly Everyone* (ages 5 and up, middle-grade); *Cashay* (ages 12 and up, YA novel).

Nonfiction All levels: all categories except religion. Recently published *Down, Down, Down; A Journey to the Bottom of the Sea,* by Steven Jenkins (ages 5-8, picture); *The Frog Scientist*, by Pamela S. Turner photographs by Andy Comins (ages 10 and up); How to Contact/Writers Fiction: Submit entire ms typed (letter quality), double-spaced manuscript on unfolded plain white paper in a 9x12 envelope. We do not accept manuscripts that are handwritten or submitted on computer disk. You do not have to furnish illustrations, but if you wish, copies of a few comprehensive sketches or duplicate copies of original art will suffice. Nonfiction: Submit outline/synopsis and sample chapters. Responds within 4 months ONLY if interested —DO NOT SEND SELF-ADDRESSED STAMPED ENVELOPE. All declined material will be recycled.

Illustration Works with 60 illustrators/year. Reviews ms/illustration packages or illustrations only from artists: Query with samples (colored photocopies are fine); provide tearsheets. Responds in 4 months if interested. Samples returned with SASE; samples filed if interested. Address art submissions to: Art Department, Children's Trade Books.

HUNTER HOUSE PUBLISHERS

P.O. Box 2914, Alameda CA 94501-0914. (510)865-5282. Fax: (510)865-4295. E-mail: acquisitions@ hunterhouse.com. Website: www.hunterhouse.com. **Manuscript Acquisitions:** Acquisitions editor. Publishes 0-1 nonfiction titles for teenage women/year. 50% of books by first-time authors; 5% of books from agented writers.

Nonfiction Young adults: self help, health, multicultural, violence prevention. "We emphasize that all our books try to take multicultural experiences and concerns into account. We would be interested in a self-help book on multicultural issues." Books are therapy/personal growth-oriented. Does *not* want to see books for young children, fiction, illustrated picture books, autobiography. Published *Turning Yourself Around: Self-Help Strategies for Troubled Teens*, by Kendall Johnson, Ph..; *Safe Dieting for Teens*, by Linda Ojeda, Ph..

How to Contact Query; submit overview and chapter-by-chapter synopsis, sample chapters and statistics on your subject area, support organizations or networks and marketing ideas. "Testimonials from professionals or well-known authors are crucial." Responds to queries in 3 months; mss in 6 months. Publishes a book 18 months after acceptance. Will consider simultaneous submissions.

Terms Payment varies. Sends galleys to authors. Book catalog available for 9 × 12 SAE and $1.25 postage; ms guidelines for standard SAE and 1 first-class stamp.

Tips Wants teen books with solid, informative material. "We do few children's books. The ones we do are for a select, therapeutic audience. No fiction! Please, no fiction."

IDEALS CHILDREN'S BOOKS AND CANDYCANE PRESS

Imprints of Ideals Publications, 2636 Elm Hill Pike, Suite 120, Nashville TN 37214. Website: www.idealsbooks.com. **Manuscript Acquisitions:** Submissions. **Art Acquisitions:** Art Director. Publishes 4-6 new picture books/year; 4-6 new board books/year. 50% of books by first-time authors.

Fiction Picture books: animal, concept, history, religion. Board books: animal, history, nature/environment, religion. Average word length: picture books—1,500; board books—200.

ILLUMINATION ARTS

P.O. Box 1865, Bellevue WA 98009. (425)644-7185. Fax: (425)644-9274. E-mail: liteinfo@illumin.com. Website: www.illumin.com. **Acquisitions:** Ruth Thompson, editorial director.

Fiction Word length: Prefers under 1,000, but will consider up to 1,500 words. Recently published *God's Promise*, by Maureen Moss, illustrated by Gerald Purnell; *Roonie B. Moonie: Lost and Alone*, by Emma Perry Roberts, illustrated by Robert Rogalski.

How to Contact Fiction: Submit complete ms. Responds to queries in 3 months with SASE only. No electronic or CD submissions for text or art. Publishes a book 1-2 years after acceptance. Will consider simultaneous submissions.

Terms Pays authors and illustrators royalty based on wholesale price. Book fliers available for SASE.

Tips "Read our books and follow our guidelines. Be patient. The market is competitive. We receive 2,000 submissions annually and publish 2-3 books a year. Sorry, we are unable to track unsolicited submissions."

IMPACT PUBLISHERS, INC.

P.O. Box 6016, Atascadero CA 93423-6016. (805)466-5917. Fax: (805)466-5919. E-mail: info@impactpublishers.com. Website: www.impactpublishers.com. **Manuscript Acquisitions:** Freeman Porter, submissions editor. **Art Acquisitions:** J. Trumbull, production. Imprints: Little Imp Books, Rebuilding Books, The Practical Therapist Series. Publishes 1 young reader/year; 1 middle reader/year; 1 young adult title/year. 20% of books by first-time authors. "Our purpose is to make the best human services expertise available to the widest possible audience. We publish only popular psychology and self-help materials written in everyday language by professionals with advanced degrees and significant experience in the human services."

Nonfiction Young readers, middle readers, young adults: self-help. Recently published *Jigsaw Puzzle Family: The Stepkids' Guide to Fitting It Together*, by Cynthia MacGregor (ages 8-12, children's/divorce/emotions).

How to Contact Nonfiction: Query or submit complete ms, cover letter, résumé. Responds to queries in 12 weeks; mss in 3 months. Will consider simultaneous submissions or previously published work.

Terms Pays authors royalty of 10-12%. Offers advances. Pays illustrators by the project. Book catalog available for #10 SAE with 2 first-class stamps; ms guidelines available for SASE. All imprints included in a single catalog.

Tips "Please do not submit fiction, poetry or narratives."

JEWISH LIGHTS PUBLISHING

P.O. Box 237, Rt. 4, Sunset Farm Offices, Woodstock VT 05091. (802)457-4000. Fax: (802)457-4004. E-mail: editorial@jewishlights.com. Website: www.jewishlights.com. **Manuscript Acquisitions:** Submissions Editor. **Art Acquisitions:** Tim Holtz. Publishes 2 picture books/year; 1 young reader/year. 50% of books by first-time authors; 25% of books from agented authors. All books have spiritual/religious themes. "Jewish Lights publishes books for people of all faiths and all backgrounds who yearn for books that attract, engage, educate and spiritually inspire. Our authors are at the forefront of spiritual thought and deal with the quest for the self and for meaning in life by drawing on the Jewish wisdom tradition. Our books cover topics including history, spirituality, life cycle, children, self-help, recovery, theology and philosophy. We do not publish autobiography, biography, fiction, haggadot, poetry or cookbooks. At this point we plan to do only two books for children annually, and one will be for younger children (ages 4-10)."

Fiction Picture books, young readers, middle readers: spirituality. "We are not interested in anything other than spirituality." Recently published *God's Paintbrush*, by Sandy Eisenberg Sasso, illustrated by Annette Compton (ages 4-9).

Nonfiction Picture book, young readers, middle readers: activity books, spirituality. Recently published *When a Grandparent Dies: A Kid's Own Remembering Workbook for Dealing with Shiva and the Year Beyond*, by Nechama Liss-Levinson, Ph.. (ages 7-11); *Tough Questions Jews Ask: A Young Adult's Guide to Building a Jewish Life*, by Rabbi Edward Feinstein (ages 12 and up).

How to Contact Fiction/nonfiction: Query with outline/synopsis and 2 sample chapters; submit complete ms for picture books. Include SASE. Responds to queries/mss in 4 months. Publishes a book 1 year after acceptance. Will consider simultaneous submissions and previously published work.

Terms Pays authors royalty of 10% of revenue received; 15% royalty for subsequent printings. Offers advances. Pays illustrators by the project or royalty. Pays photographers by the project or royalty. Sends galleys to authors; dummies to illustrators. Book catalog available for 6½ × 9½ SAE and 59¢ postage; ms guidelines available on Web site.

Tips "Explain in your cover letter why you're submitting your project to *us* in particular. Make sure you know what we publish."

JOURNEYFORTH BOB JONES UNIVERSITY PRESS

Imprint of Bob Jones University Press, 1700 Wade Hampton Blvd.Greenville SC 29614. (864)242-5100, ext. 4350. Fax: (864)298-0268. E-mail: jb@bjupress.com. Website: www.bjupress.com. Estab. 1974. Specializes in trade books, Christian material, and educational material. **Acquisitions Editor:** Nancy Lohr. Publishes 2 picture book/year; 4 young readers/year; 6 middle readers/year; 6 young adult titles/year. 10% of books by first-time authors. "We aim to produce well-written books for readers of varying abilities and interests and fully consistent with biblical truth."

Fiction Young readers, middle readers, young adults: adventure, animal, contemporary, fantasy, folktales, history, humor, multicultural, nature/environment, problem novels, suspense/mystery. Average word length: young readers—10,000-12,000; middle readers—10,000-40,000; young adult/teens—40,000-60,000. Recently published *Tommy's Race*, by Sharon Hambrick, illustrated by Maurie Manning (ages 6-7, contemporary fiction); *Regina Silsby's Secret War*, by Thomas J. Brodeur (young adult historical fiction); *Two Sides to Everything*, by Deb Brammer (ages 9-12, contemporary fiction).

Nonfiction Young readers, middle readers, young adult: biography. Average word length: young readers—10,000-12,000; middle readers—10,000-40,000; young adult/teens—40,000-60,000. Recently published *Children of the Storm*, by Natasha Vius (young adult autobiography); *Fanny Crosby*, by Rebecca Davis (Christian biography).

How to Contact Fiction: Query or submit outline/synopsis and 5 sample chapters. "Do not send stories with magical elements. We are not currently accepting picture books. We do not publish: romance, science fiction, poetry and drama." Nonfiction: Query or submit outline/synopsis and 5 sample chapters. Responds to queries in 4 weeks; mss in 3 months. Publishes book 12-15 months after acceptance. Will consider previously published work.

Terms Pays authors royalty based on wholesale price. Pays illustrators by the project. Originals returned to artist at job's completion. Book catalog and writers guidelines are at www.bjupress. com/books/freelance.html.

Tips "Review our backlist to be sure your work is a good fit."

JOURNEY STONE CREATIONS

3533 Danbury Rd, Fairfield OH 45014. Eestab 2004. (513)860-5616. Fax (513)860-0176. E-mail: pat@ jscbookscomsubmissions. E-mail: danelle@jscbookscom_art_dept. Website: wwwjscbookscom.

Fiction Picture books: adventure, animal, contemporary, history, humor, multicultural, nature/ environment, poetry, religion, sports. Early readers: adventure, animal, contemporary, health, history, humor, multicultural, nature/environment, poetry, religion, sports, suspense. "We are not accepting middle readers at this time."Word length: picture books—1200 or less; Early readers—5,000 or less. Recently published *Stranger Danger*, by Patricia Stirnkorb, illustrated by Claudia Wolf (ages 7-12, childhood saftey); *Caterpillars Dream*, by Sally Harris.

How to Contact Query only after reviewing needs on Web Site. Reports on queires in 4-6 weeks. Publishes a book up to 2 years after acceptance. Accepts simultaneous and electrionic submissions. "At this time we are only accepting picture books and early reader books with less than 5,000 words. We are reviewing books for publication 12-18 months away."However, we are seeking only specific topics and themes. **Do not submit without first checking our Web site."**

Terms Pays authors negotiable based on project price or preferes to purchase work outright. Pays illustrators by the project. Book catalog available on Web stie. Writer's/artist's guidelines available on Web site.

Tips "Make sure you submit only your best work. For writers, if it is not letter perfect, we don't want to see it. Review our guidelines." We cannot stress the importance of submitting only after you have read our needs. Don't waste your time and money submitting things we do not need. We are only publishing children's fiction/non-ficton, no adult or teen fiction at this time."

☐ KAEDEN BOOKS

P.O. Box 16190, Rocky River, OH 44116-6190. E-mail: lstenger@kaeden.com. Website: www.kaeden. com. **Contact:** Lisa Stenger, Editor. Kaeden Books produces high-quality children's books for the educational market.

Fiction Stories with humor, surprise endings and interesting characters suitable for the education market. "Must have well-developed plots with clear beginnings, middles and endings. No adult or religious themes." Word count range: 25-2,000.

Nonfiction Unique, interesting topics, supported with details and accurate facts. Word count range: 25-2000.

How to Contact Submit complete ms; include SASE. Do not send originals. Respond within 1 year. For complete guidelines see www.kaeden.com. No phone calls please.

Terms Work purchased outright from authors. Pays royalties to previous authors. Illustrators paid by project (range: $50-150/page).

Tips "We are particularly interested in humorous stories with surprise endings and beginning chapter books."

☐ KAMEHAMEHA PUBLISHING

567 South King St.Suite 118, Honolulu, HI 96813. 808-523-6200, Fax: 808-541-5305. E-mail: kspress@ ksbe.edu. Website: www.KamehamehaPublishing.org. **Manuscript Acquisitions:** Acquisitions Editor. "Kamehameha Schools Press publishes in the areas of Hawaiian history, Hawaiian culture, Hawaiian language and Hawaiian studies."

Fiction Young reader, middle readers, young adults: biography, history, multicultural, Hawaiian folklore.

Nonfiction Young reader, middle readers, young adults: biography, history, multicultural, Hawaiian folklore. How to Contact/Writers Query. Responds to queries in 3 months; mss in 3 months. Publishes a book up to 2 years after acceptance.

Terms Work purchased outright from authors or by royalty agreement. Pays illustrators by the project. Sends galleys to authors. Book catalog available (call or write for copy). All imprints included in a single catalog. Catalog available on Web site.

Tips "Writers and illustrators must be knowledgeable in Hawaiian history/culture and be able to show credentials to validate their proficiency. Greatly prefer to work with writers/illustrators available in the Honolulu area."

N KANE/MILLER BOOK PUBLISHERS, INC.

P.O. Box 8515, La Jolla CA 92038.Estab. 1985. (858)456-0540. Fax: (858)456-9641. E-mail: info@kanemiller.com. Website: www.kanemiller.com. Specializes in trade books, fiction, multicultural material. **Manuscript Acquisitions/Art Acquisitions:** Kira Lynn Editorial Dept. Publishes 20 picture books/year; 4 young readers/year; 8 middle readers/year. 50% of books by first-time authors.

Fiction Picture Books: concept, contemporary, health, humor, multicultural. Young Readers: contemporary, multicultural, suspense. Middle Readers: contemporary, humor, multicultural, suspense.

How to Contact Only interested in agented material. Fiction/nonfiction: submit outline/synopsis and 2 sample chapters. Responds to queries in 3 weeks; mss in 6 weeks. Publishes a book 1 year of acceptance. Will consider simultaneous submissions.

Terms Book catalog available online; All imprints included in a single catalog; Writer's and artist's guidelines are available. www.kanemiller.com.

KAR-BEN PUBLISHING, INC.

A division of Lerner Publishing Group, Inc. 241 First Ave. No.Minneapolis, MN 55401. (612)332-3344. Fax: (612)-332-7615. E-mail: editorial@karben.com. Website: www.karben.com. **Manuscript Acquisitions:** Joni Sussman, publisher. Publishes 10-15 books/year (mostly picture books); 20% of books by first-time authors. All of Kar-Ben's books are on Jewish themes for young children and families.

Fiction Picture books: adventure, concept, folktales, history, humor, multicultural, religion, special needs; must be on a Jewish theme. Average word length: picture books-1,000. Recently published *Engineer Ari and the Rosh Hashanah Ride,* by Deborah Bodin Cohen, illustrated by Shahar Kober; and *The Wedding That Saved a Town,* by Yale Strom, illustrated by Jenya Prosmitsky.

Nonfiction Picture books, young readers: activity books, arts/crafts, biography, careers, concept, cooking, history, how-to, multicultural, religion, social issues, special needs; must be of Jewish interest.

How to Contact Submit complete ms. Responds to queries/mss in 6 weeks. Publishes a book 24-36 months after acceptance. Will consider simultaneous submissions.

Terms Pays authors royalties of 3-5% of net against advance of $500-1,000; or purchased outright. Original artwork returned at job's completion. Book catalog free on request. Manuscript guidelines on Web site.

Tips Looks for books for young children with Jewish interest and content, modern, nonsexist, not didactic. Fiction or nonfiction with a Jewish theme can be serious or humorous, life cycle, Bible story, or holiday-related. L ooking in particular for stories that reflect the ethnic and cultural diversity of today's Jewish family."

KRBY CREATIONS, LLC

PO Box 327, Bay Head NJ 08742. Fax (815)846-0636. E-mail: info@krbycreationscom. Website: wwwkrbycreationscom.

Fiction Recently published *The Snowman in the Moon*, by Stephen Heigh (picture book); *Mulch the Lawnmower*, by Scott Nelson (picture book); *My Imagination*, by Katrina Estes-Hill (picture book).

How to Contact Fiction/nonfiction: Writers *must* request guidelines by e-mail prior to submitting mss. See Web site. Submissions without annotation found in guidelines will not be considered. Responds to e-mail queries in 1 week; mss in 1-3 months. Publishes book 1 year after acceptance. Considers simultaneous submissions.

Tips "Submit as professionally as possible; make your vision clear to us about what you are trying to capture. Know your market/audience and identify it in your proposal. Tell us what is new/unique with your idea. All writers submitting must first request guidelines by e-mail."

WENDY LAMB BOOKS

Imprint of Random House, 1745 Broadway, New York, NY 10019. Website: www.randomhouse.com. **Manuscript Acquisitions:** Wendy Lamb. Receives 1,500-2,000 submissions/year. Publishes 12-15 novels/year for middle grade and young adult readers. WLB does not publish picture books at present. 15% of books by first-time authors and 10% unagented writers.

Fiction Recently published *Eyes of the Emperor*, by Graham Salisbury; *A Brief Chapter in My Impossible Life*, by Dana Reinhardt; *What They Found: Love on 145th Street*, by Walter Dean Myers; *Eleven*, by Patricia Reilly Giff. Other WLB authors include Christopher Paul Curtis, Gary Paulsen, Donna Jo Napoli, Peter Dickinson, Marthe Jocelyn, Graham McNamee and Marcus Sedgwick.

How to Contact Query letter with SASE for reply. A query letter should briefly describe the book you have written, the intended age group, and your brief biography and publishing credits, if any. Please send the first 10 pages (or to the end of the chapter) of your manuscript. Our turn-around time is approximately 4 - 8 weeks.

LEE & LOW BOOKS INC.

95 Madison Ave.New York NY 10016-7801. (212)779-4400. Fax: (212) 683-1894. E-mail: info@leeandlow.com. Website: www.leeandlow.com. **Acquisitions:** Louise May, editor-in-chief; Jennifer Fox, senior editor. Publishes 12-14 children's books/year. 25% of books by first-time authors. Lee & Low Books publishes books with diverse themes. "One of our goals is to discover new talent and produce books that reflect the diverse society in which we live."

- Lee & Low Books is dedicated to publishing culturally authentic literature. The company makes a special effort to work with writers and artists of color and encourages new voices.

Fiction Picture books, young readers: anthology, contemporary, history, multicultural, poetry. "Are not considering folktales or animal stories." Picture book, middle reader: contemporary, history, multicultural, nature/environment, poetry, sports. Average word length: picture books—1,000-1,500 words. Recently published *Horse Song*, by Ted and Betsy Lewin; *Yum! ¡Mmmm! Quérico*, by Pat Mora; *Bird*, by Zetta Elliot.

Nonfiction Picture books: concept. Picture books, middle readers: biography, history, multicultural, science and sports. Average word length: picture books—1,500-3,000. Recently published *Honda: The Boy Who Dreamed of Cars*, by Mark Weston; *The Last Black King of the Kentucky Derby*, by Crystal Hubbard.

How to Contact Fiction/nonfiction: Submit complete ms. No e-mail submissions. Responds within 6 months, only if interested. Publishes a book 2-3 years after acceptance. Will consider simultaneous submissions. Guidelines on Web site.

Terms Pays authors advances against royalty. Pays illustrators advance against royalty. Photographers paid advance against royalty. Book catalog available for 9 × 12 SAE and $1.68 postage; catalog and ms and art guidelines available via Web site or with SASE.

Tips "We strongly urge writers to visit our Web site and familiarize themselves with our list before submitting. Materials will only be returned with SASE."

LEGACY PRESS

Legacy Press P.O. Box 261129 San Diego CA 92196. (858) 277-1167. Website: www.legacyxpress. com. Manuscript/Art Acquisitions: Editorial Department Publishes 3 young readers/year; 3 middle readers/year; 3 young adult titles/year. Publishes nonfiction, Bible-teaching books. "We publish books that build a legacy in kids' faith. Our books are non-denominational and are marketed primarily through bookstores." Nonfiction, devotional, journals, guide books, young readers, middle readers, young adults. Recently published The God And Me Bible for Girls." Nonfiction Young readers, middle readers, young adults: reference, religion. Recently published Bill the Warthog-Full Metal Trench Coat, by Dean Anderson, illustrated by Dave Carleson.;

How to Contact Nonfiction: Submit outline/synopsis and 3-5 sample chapters. Will consider simultaneous submissions and previously published work. Illustration Works with 5 illustrators/ year. Reviews ms/illustration packages from artists. Submit ms with 5-10 pieces of final art. Illustrations only: Query with samples to be kept on file. Terms Pays authors royalty or work purchased outright. Offers advances.

Tips "Become familiar with our products and get to know the Christian bookstore market. We are looking for innovative ways to teach and encourage children about the Christian life."

LERNER PUBLISHING GROUP

241 First Ave. N.Minneapolis MN 55401. (612)332-3344. Fax: (612)332-7615. E-mail: info@ lernerbooks.com. Website: www.lernerbooks.com. **Manuscript Acquisitions:** Jennifer Zimian, nonfiction submissions editor; Zelda Wagner, fiction submissions editor. Primarily publishes books for children ages 7-18. List includes titles in geography, natural and physical science, current events, ancient and modern history, high interest, sports, world cultures, and numerous biography series.

- Starting in 2007, Lerner Publishing Group no longer accepts submission in any of their imprints except for Kar-Ben Publishing.

How to Contact "We will continue to seek targeted solicitations at specific reading levels and in specific subject areas. The company will list these targeted solicitations on our Web site and in national newsletters, such as the SCBWI *Bulletin*."

ARTHUR A. LEVINE BOOKS

Imprint of Scholastic, Inc.557 Broadway, New York NY 10012. (212)343-4436. Fax: (212)343-4890. Website: www.arthuralevinebooks.com. **Acquisitions:** Arthur A. Levine, editorial director; Cheryl Klein, senior editor. Publishes approximately 8 picture books/year; 8 full-length works for middle grade and young adult readers/year. Approximately 25% of books by first-time authors.

Fiction Recently published *The Arrival*, by Shaun Tan (graphic novel); *Her Mother's Face*, by Roddy Doyle, illustrated by Freya Blackwood (picture book); *Moribito: Guardian of the Spirit*, by Nahoko Uehashi, trans. by Cathy Hirano (novel); *Deep Down Popular*, by Phoebe Stone (novel); and *Crossing to Paradise*, by Kevin Crossley-Holland (novel).

Nonfiction Recently published *The Secret World of Hildegard*, by Jonah Winter and Jeanette Winter (picture book); *Dizzy*, by Jonah Winter and Sean Qualls (picture book); and *The Adventures of Marco Polo*, by Russell Freedman and Bagram Ibatoulline (picture book).

How to Contact Fiction/nonfiction: Accepts queries only. Responds to queries in 1 month; mss in 5 months. Publishes a book 112 years after acceptance.

LILY RUTH PUBLISHING

P.O. Box 6622, Paris TX 75461.Estab. 2008. (903)715-0740. Fax: (903)737-9748. E-mail: lilyruthpublishing@yahoo.com. Website: www.lilyruthpublishing.com. Estab. 2008. Specializes in fiction. **Manuscript Acquisitions/Art Acquisitions:** Jennifer L. Stone. Publishes 2 middle readers/year. 50% of books by first-time authors. "Here at Lily Ruth Publishing we believe that literature for children should be above all, fun. Strong stories from authors with unique voices are what make reading entertaining and exciting, inspiring a love of reading that will last a life time."

Fiction Middle Readers: adventure, fantasy, history, humor. Young Adults/Teens: adventure, fantasy, humor. Average word length: middle readers—25,000; young adults— 50,000. Recently published *My Weird Family Series: My Vampire Cousin*, by J.k. Hawkins (middle reader, adventure, humor); *My Weird Family Series: My Werewolf Brothers*, by J.K. Hawkins (middle reader, adventures, humor).

How to Contact Fiction: query or submit outline/synopsis and 3 sample chapters. Responds 3 weeks; mss in 6 weeks. Publishes a book 6 mons - 1 year. Will consider simultaneous submissions.

Terms Pays authors 10%-15% based on retail price. Sends galleys to authors. Originals returned to artist at job's completion. Catalog available on web site.

▲ LITTLE, BROWN AND COMPANY BOOKS FOR YOUNG READERS

Hachette Book Group USA, 237 Park Ave, New York NY 10017. (212)364-1100. Fax: (212)364-0925. Web sites: www.lb-kids.com; www.lb-teens.com. **Senior Vice President, Publisher:** Megan Tingley. Editorial Director, Little, Brown Books for Young Readers (core hardcover and paperback list): Editor-in-Chief: Liza Baker. Senior Executive Editor: Andrea Spooner. Executive Editorial Director, Poppy (young women's commercial fiction imprint): Cynthia Eagan; Editorial Director: Jennifer Hunt. **Creative Director:** Gail Doobinin. Publishes picture books, board books, chapter books, novelty books, and general nonfiction and novels for middle and young adult readers.

• Little, Brown does not accept unsolicited mss or unagented material.

Fiction Picture books: humor, adventure, animal, contemporary, history, multicultural, folktales. Young adults: contemporary, humor, multicultural, suspense/mystery, chick lit. Multicultural needs include "any material by, for and about minorities." Average word length: picture books—1,000; young readers—6,000; middle readers—15,000- 50,000; young adults—50,000 and up. Recently published *South*, by Patrick McDonnell; *The I Love You Book*, by Todd Parr; *Wabi Sabi*, by Mark Reibstein, illustrated by Ed Young; *The Absolutely True Diary of a Part-time Indian*,by Sherman Alexie; *The Mysterious Benedict Society*, by Trenton Lee Stewart; *The Name Of This Book Is Secret*, by Pseudonymous Bosch; *Ghostgirl*, by Tonya Hurley; *North of Beautiful*, by Justina Chen Headley; *Sweethearts*, by Sara Zarr; *Maximum Ride*, by James Patterson; *The Gossip Girl* series, by Cecily Von Ziegesar; *The Clique* series, by Lisi Harrison; *The Twilight Saga*, by Stephanie Meyer.

Nonfiction Middle readers, young adults: arts/crafts, history, multicultural, nature, self help, social issues, sports, science. Average word length: middle readers—15,000-25,000; young adults—20,000-40,000. Recently published *American Dreaming*, by Laban Carrick Hill; *Exploratopia*, by the Exploratorium; *Yeah! Yeah! Yeah!: The Beatles, Beatlemania, and the Music that Changed the World*, by Bob Spitz.

How to Contact Only interested in solicited agented material. Fiction: Submit complete ms. Nonfiction: Submit cover letter, previous publications, a proposal, outline and 3 sample chapters. Do not send originals. Responds to queries in 2 weeks. Responds to mss in 2 months.

Terms Pays authors royalties based on retail price. Pays illustrators and photographers by the project or royalty based on retail price. Sends galleys to authors; dummies to illustrators.

Tips "In order to break into the field, authors and illustrators should research their competition and try to come up with something outstandingly different."

☐ LOLLIPOP POWER BOOKS

Imprint of Carolina Wren Press, 120 Morris Street, Durham NC 27701. (919)560-2738. Fax: (919)560-2759. E-mail: carolinawrenpress@earthlink.net. Website: www.carolinawrenpress.org. **Manuscript Acquisitions:** Children's Book Editor. **Art Acquisitions:** Art Director. "In the past, Carolina Wren Press and Lollipop Power specialize in children's books that counter stereotypes or debunk myths about race, gender, sexual orientation, etc. We are also interested in books that deal with health or mental health issues—our two biggest sellers are Puzzles (about a young girl coping with Sickle Cell Disease) and I like it when you joke with me, I don't like it when you touch me (about inappropriate touching) and we are currently promoting Peace Comes to Ajani, about anger management. Many of our children's titles are bilingual (English/Spanish)."Please note, however, that as of 2009, we are no longer holding open submission periods for children's literature.

Fiction Average word length: picture books—500.

How to Contact No open submissions at this time. Please check our Web site to see if we have re-opened submissions.

Terms Pays authors royalty of 10% minimum based on retail price or work purchased outright from authors (range: $500-$2,000). Pays illustrators by the project (range: $500-$2,000). Sends galleys to authors; dummies to illustrators. Originals returned to artist at job's completion. Catalog available on Web site.

LUCENT BOOKS

Imprint of Gale, 27550 Drake Road, Farmington Hills, MI 49331. E-mail: Kristine.burns@cengage.com. Website: www.gale.com/lucent. **Acquisitions:** Kristine Burns. Series publisher of educational nonfiction for junior high school and library markets.

• See also listing for Greenhaven Press.

Nonfiction Young adult circulating reference: current issues, diseases, drugs, biographies, geopolitics, history. Recently launched Crime Scene Investigations, and Hot Topics (both series). Recently published *Energy Alternatives*; *Hate Crimes*; *Human Papillomavirus*; *Malnutrition*; *Criminal Profiling*; *DNA Evidence*; *Tupac Shakur*; and *Zac Efron*.

How to Contact E-mail query with résumé or list of publications.

Terms Work purchased outright from authors; write-for-hire, flat fee.

Tips No unsolicited manuscripts.

Ⓝ MAGICAL CHILD

Shades of White. 301 Tenth St.Crystal City MO 63019.Estab. 2007. (314)740-0361. E-mail: acquisition@paganchildrensbookpublishing.com. Website: www.magicalchildbooks.com. Estab. 2007. Specializes in trade books, fiction. **Manuscript Acquisitions:** Acquisition Editor. **Art Acquisitions:** Art Director. Publishes 1-3 picture books/year; 1-3 young readers/year; 1-3 middle readers/year. 80% of books by first-time authors. "The Neo-Pagan Community is the fastest growing demographic in the spiritual landscape, and Pagan parents are crying out for books appropriate for the Pagan kids. It is our plan to fill this small, but growing a need."

Fiction Picture Books: adventure, contemporary, nature/environment, earth religions NOT native American. Young Readers: adventure, contemporary, nature/environment. Middle Readers: adventure, contemporary, nature/environment, earth religions NOT native American. Average word length; picture books— 500-8001; young readers—500-4,500; middle readers—11,200-28,000. Recently published *Aiden's First Full Moon Circle*, by W. Lyon Martin (ages 5-8, picture book); *An Ordinary Girl, A magical Child*, by W. Lyon Martin (ages 5-8, chapter book); *Rabbit's Song*, by S.J. Tucker (ages 4-8, picture book).

Nonfiction Middle Readers: biography, history (Earth Religion's only for both). Average word length: middle readers—11,200-28,000.

How to Contact Fiction: Query or submit outline/synopsis for Picture books only or submit outline/synopsis and 3 sample chapters. Nonfiction: Query or submit outline/synopsis and 3 sample chapters. Responds to queries 3 weeks; mss in 3-6 months. Publishes a book 18+ months after acceptance. Will consider simultaneous submissions.

Terms Pays authors royalty based on retail price. Offers advances. Pays illustrators royalty based on wholesale price. Sends galleys to authors; dummies to illustrators. Originals returned to artist at job's completion. Book catalog available for SASE (envelope size #10 and 1 first-class stamps) All imprints included in single catalog.

Tips "Visit our submissions guidelines on the web site. Follow the information provided there. We expect our authors to take an active role in promoting their books. If you can't do that, please don't submit your manuscript. NO CALLS, Please. Our list is VERY specific please do not send us manuscripts outside of our requested needs.

MAGINATION PRESS

750 First Street, NE, Washington DC 20002-2984. (202)336-5618. Fax: (202)336-5624. Website: www.maginationpress.com. **Acquisitions:** Kristine Enderle, managing editor. Publishes 12 books/year (picture books/year, middle readers/year, teen nonficition). 75% of books by first-time authors. "We publish books dealing with the psycho/therapeutic resolution of children's problems and psychological issues with a strong self-help component.";

• Magination Press is an imprint of the American Psychological Association.

Fiction All levels: psychological and social issues, self-help, health, parenting concerns and, special needs. Picture books, middle school readers. Recently published *Nobody's Perfect: A Story for Children about Perfection,* by Ellen Flanagan Burns, illustrated by, Erica Peltron Villnave (ages 8-12); *Murphey's Three Homes; A Story for Children in Foster Care,* by Jan Levinson Gilman, illustrated by Kathy O'Malley (ages 4-8).

Nonfiction All levels: psychological and social issues, self-help, health, multicultural, special needs. Recently published Putting on the Brakes: Understanding ad controlling your ADD or ADHD (ages 8-13), by Patricia Quinn and Judith M. Stern, illustrated by Joe Lee.

How to Contact Fiction/nonfiction: Submit complete ms. Responds to queries in 1-2 months; mss in 2-6 months. Will consider simultaneous submissions. Materials returned only with a SASE. Publishes a book 18-24 months after acceptance.

☐ MASTER BOOKS

Imprint of New Leaf Publishing Group, Inc, P.O. Box 726, Green Forest, AR 72638. (870)438-5288. Fax: (870)438-5120. E-mail: nlp@newleafpress.net. Website: www.nlpg.com. **Manuscript Acquisitions:** Craig Froman, acquisitions editor. **Art Acquisitions:** Diana Bogardus, art director. Publishes 2 picture books/year; 3 young readers/year; 3 middle readers/year; 2 young adult titles/year. 10% of books by first-time authors.

Nonfiction Picture books: activity books, animal, nature/environment, creation. Young readers, middle readers, young adults: activity books, animal, biography Christian, nature/environment, science, creation. Recently published *Whale of a Story*, by Buddy Davis (middle readers, Bible story); *Dinky Dinosaur*, by Darrell Wiskur (picture book, creation); *For Those Who Dare*, by John Hudson Tiner (young adult, biography).

How to Contact Nonfiction: Submit outline/synopsis and 3 sample chapters. Responds to queries/mss in 3 months. Publishes book 1 year after acceptance. Will consider simultaneous submissions. Must download submissions form from Web site.

Terms Pays authors royalty of 3-15% based on wholesale price. Sends galleys to authors. Book catalog available for 9 × 12 SAE and $1.85 postage; ms guidelines available for SASE. Catalog available on Web site.

Tips "All of our children's books are creation-based, including topics from the Book of Genesis. We look also for home school educational material that would be supplementary to a home school curriculum."

☑ MARGARET K. MCELDERRY BOOKS

Imprint of Simon & Schuster Children's Publishing Division, 1230 Avenue of the Americas, New York NY 10020. (212)698-7000. Website: www.simonsayskids.com. **Publisher**: Vice President, Publisher Emma D. Dryden. **Acquisitions:** Karen Wojtyla, editorial director; Lisa Cheng, associate editor; Emily Fabre, Editorial Assistant. **Art Acquisitions:** Ann Bobco, Executive Art Director. Imprint of Simon & Schuster Children's Publishing Division. Publishes 12 picture books/year; 5-8 middle readers/year; 8-10 young adult titles/year. "Margaret K. McElderry Books publishes hardcover and paperback trade books for children from pre-school age through young adult. This list includes picture books, middle grade and teen fiction, poetry, and fantasy. The style and subject matter of the books we publish is almost unlimited. We do not publish textbooks, coloring and activity books, greeting cards, magazines, pamphlets, or religious publications."

Fiction All levels. "Always interested in publishing young read-aloud picture books, humorous middle grade fiction, and original teen fiction or fantasy." Average word length: picture books-500; young readers-2,000; middle readers-10,000-20,000; young adults-45,000-50,000. Recently Published: *Monster Mess,* by Margery Cuyler; illustrated by S. D. Schindler (picture book); *The Joy of Spooking: Fiendish Deeds* by P. J. Bracegirdle (MGF); *Identical,* by Ellen Hopkins (teen); *Where is Home, Little Pip?,* by Karma Wilson; illustrated by Jane Chapman (picture book); *Dr. Ted,* by Andrea Beaty; illustrated by Pascal LeMaitre (picture book); *To Be Mona* by Kelly Easton (teen).

How to Contact Simon & Schuster children's publishing division does not accept unsolicited queries, manuscripts, or art samples unless submitted by an agent.

Terms Pays authors royalty based on retail price. Pays illustrator royalty of by the project. Pays photographers by the project. Original artwork returned at job's completion.

Tips "We're looking for strong, original fiction, especially mysteries and middle grade humor. We are always interested in picture books for the youngest age reader. Study our titles."

MEADOWBROOK PRESS

5451 Smetana Dr.Minnetonka MN 55343-9012. (952)930-1100. Fax: (952)930-1940. Website: www. meadowbrookpress.com. **Manuscript Acquisitions:** Submissions Editor. **Art Acquisitions:** Art Director. 20% of books by first-time authors; 10% of books from agented writers. Publishes children's poetry books, activity books, arts-and-crafts books and how-to books.

- Meadowbrook does not accept unsolicited children's picture books, short stories or novels. They are primarily a nonfiction press. The publisher offers specific guidelines for children's poetry. Be sure to specify the type of project you have in mind when requesting guideline, or visit their Web site.

Nonfiction Publishes activity books, arts/crafts, how-to, poetry. Average word length: varies. Recently published *The Siblings' Busy Book,* by Heather Kempskie & Lisa Hanson (activity book); *I Hope I Don't Strike Out,* by Bruce Lansky (poetry).

How to Contact Nonfiction: See guidelines on Web site before submitting. Responds only if interested. Publishes a book 1-2 years after acceptance. Will consider simultaneous submissions.

Terms Pays authors royalt y of 5-7% based on retail price. Offers average advance payment of $1,000-3,000. Pays illustrators per project. Pays photographers by the project. Book catalog available for 5 × 11 SASE and 2 first-class stamps; ms guidelines and artists guidelines available for SASE.

Tips "Writers should visit our Web site before submitting their work to us. Illustrators should take a look at the books we publish to determine whether their style is consistent with ours. Writers should also note the style and content patterns of our books. No phone calls, please—e-mail us. We work with the printed word and will respond more effectively to your questions if we have something in front of us."

MERIWETHER PUBLISHING LTD.

885 Elkton Dr.Colorado Springs CO 80907-3557. (719)594-9916. Fax: (719)594-9916. E-mail: editor@meriwether.com. Website: www.meriwetherpublishing.com. **Manuscript Acquisitions:** Ted Zapel, comedy plays and educational drama; Rhonda Wray, religious drama. "We do most of our artwork in-house; we do not publish for the children's elementary market." 75% of books by first-time authors; 5% of books from agented writers. "Our niche is drama. Our books cover a wide variety of theatre subjects from play anthologies to theatrecraft. We publish books of monologs, duologs, short one-act plays, scenes for students, acting textbooks, how-to speech and theatre textbooks, improvisation and theatre games. Our Christian books cover worship on such topics as clown ministry, storytelling, banner-making, drama ministry, children's worship and more. We also publish anthologies of Christian sketches. We do not publish works of fiction or devotionals."

Fiction Middle readers, young adults: anthology, contemporary, humor, religion. "We publish plays, not prose-fiction." Our emphasis is comedy plays instead of educational themes.

Nonfiction Middle readers: activity books, how-to, religion, textbooks. Young adults: activity books, drama/theater arts, how-to church activities, religion. Average length: 250 pages. Recently published *Acting for Life*, by Jack Frakes; *Scenes Keep Happening*, by Mary Krell-Oishi; *Service with a Smile*, by Daniel Wray.

How to Contact Nonfiction: Query or submit outline/synopsis and sample chapters. Responds to queries in 3 weeks; mss in 2 months or less. Publishes a book 6-12 months after acceptance. Will consider simultaneous submissions.

Terms Pays authors royalty of 10% based on retail or wholesale price. Book catalog for SAE and $2 postage; ms guidelines for SAE and 1 first-class stamp.

Tips "We are currently interested in finding unique treatments for theater arts subjects: scene books, how-to books, musical comedy scripts, monologs and short comedy plays for teens."

MILKWEED EDITIONS

1011 Washington Ave. S.Suite 300, Minneapolis MN 55415-1246. (612)332-3192. Fax: (612)215-2550. E-mail: editor@milkweed.org. Website: www.milkweed.org. **Manuscript Acquisitions:** Daniel Slager, publisher. Publishes 3-4 middle readers/year. 25% of books by first-time authors. "Milkweed Editions publishes with the intention of making a humane impact on society, in the belief that literature is a transformative art uniquely able to convey the essential experiences of the human heart and spirit. To that end, Milkweed Editions publishes distinctive voices of literary merit in handsomely designed, visually dynamic books, exploring the ethical, cultural, and esthetic issues that free societies need continually to address."

Fiction Middle readers: adventure, contemporary, fantasy, multicultural, nature/environment, suspense/mystery. Does not want to see folktales, health, hi-lo, picture books, poetry, religion, romance, sports. Average length: middle readers—90-200 pages. Recently published *Perfect*, by Natasha Friend (contemporary); *The Linden Tree*, by Ellie Mathews(contemporary); *The Cat*, by Jutta Richter (contemporary/translation).

How to Contact Fiction: Submit complete ms. Responds to mss in 6 months. Publishes a book 1 year after acceptance. Will consider simultaneous submissions.

Terms Pays authors variable royalty based on retail price. Offers advance against royalties. Sends galleys to authors. Book catalog available for $1.50 to cover postage; ms guidelines available for SASE or at Web site. Must include SASE with ms submission for its return.

☐ THE MILLBROOK PRESS

A division of Lerner Publishing Group, Inc.241 First Avenue North Minneapolis, MN 5540. (800)328-4929. Fax: (800)332-1132. Website: www.lernerbooks.com.

- Starting in 2007, Lerner Publishing Group no longer accepts submission in any of their imprints except for Kar-Ben Publishing.

How to Contact "We will continue to seek targeted solicitations at specific reading levels and in specific subject areas. The company will list these targeted solicitations on our Web site and in national newsletters, such as the SCBWI Bulletin."

MIRRORSTONE

Imprint of Wizards of the Coast, P.O. Box 707, Renton WA 98057. (425)254-2287. Website: www. mirrorstonebooks.com. **Manuscript and Art Acquisitions:** Nina Hess. Publishes **6** middle readers/ year; 4 young adult titles/year. 5% of books by first-time authors. "We publish fantasy novels for young readers based on the lore of the Dungeons & Dragons role-playing game."

Fiction Young readers, middle readers, young adults: fantasy only. Average word length: middle readers-30,000-40,000; young adults-60,000-75,000. Recently published *A Practical Guide to Dragon-Riding*, by Lisa Trumbauer (ages 6 and up); *The Stowaway, by R.A. Salvatore and Geno*

Salvatore (10 and up), *Red Dragon Codex*, by R. Henham (ages 8-12).

How to Contact Fiction: Query with samples, writing credits. "No manuscripts, please." Responds to queries if interested. Publishes book 9-24 months after acceptance.

Terms Pays authors royalty of 4-6% based on retail price. Offers advances (average amount: $4,000). Pays illustrators by the project. Ms guidelines available on our Web site. All imprints included in a single catalog. Catalog available on Web site.

Tips Editorial staff attended or plans to attend ALA conference.

MITCHELL LANE PUBLISHERS, INC.

P.O. Box 196, Hockessin DE 19707. (302)234-9426. Fax: (302)234-4742. E-mail: mitchelllane@mitchelllane.com. Website: www.mitchelllane.com. **Acquisitons:** Barbara Mitchell, president. Publishes 80 young adult titles/year. "We publish nonfiction for children and young adults."

Nonfiction Young readers, middle readers, young adults: biography, multicultural. Average word length: 4,000-50,000 words. Recently published *Rihanna, Taylor Swift* (both Blue Banner Biographies); *The Jonas Brothers* (A Robbie Reader).

How to Contact Most assignments are work-for-hire.

Terms Work purchased outright from authors (range: $350-2,000). Pays illustrators by the project (range: $40-400). Sends galleys to authors.

Tips "Most of our assignments are work-for-hire. Submit résumé and samples of work to be considered for future assignments."

NEW CANAAN PUBLISHING COMPANY LLC.

2384 N. Hwy 341, Rossville, GA 30741. (423)228-2409. Fax: (203)548-9072. E-mail: djm@newcanaanpublishing.com. Website: www.newcanaanpublishing.com. Book publisher. Publishes 1 picture book/year; 1 young reader/year; 1 middle reader/year; 1 young adult title/year. 50% of books by first-time authors. "We seek books with strong educational or traditional moral content and books with Christian themes."

- To curb the number of unsolicited submissions, New Canaan Publishing only accepts: 1—books for children of military families; and 2—middle readers and young adult books addressing Christian themes (e.g.devotionals, books addressing teen or pre-teen issues with a Christian focus, whether in a fictional context or otherwise).

Fiction All levels: adventure, history, religion (Christianity), suspense/mystery. Picture books: Christian themes. Average word length: picture books—1,000-3,000; young readers—8,000-30,000; middle readers—8,000-40,000; young adult s—15,000-50,000.

Nonfiction All levels: religion (Christian only), textbooks. Average word length: picture books—1,000-3,000; young readers—8,000-30,000; middle readers—8,000-40,000; young adults—15,000-50,000.

How to Contact Submit outline/synopsis with biographical information and writing credentials. Does not guarantee a response unless offer to publish is forthcoming. Responds where appropriate in 4-6 months. Publishes a book 12-18 months after acceptance.

Terms Pays authors royalty of 7-12% based on wholesale price. Royalty may be shared with illustrator where relevant. Pays illustrators royalty of 4-6% as share of total royalties. Submission guidelines available on Web site.

Tips "We are small, so please be patient."

Ⓝ NEW DAY PUBLISHING, INC

New Day Publishing, Inc. 26 Bluff Ridge Court, Greensboro NC 27455.Estab. 2006. (336)545-1545. Fax: (336)545-1640. E-mail: ateich@newdaypublishing. Website: www.newdaypublishing.com.

Fiction Picture Books: religion. Recently published *Who Made the Morning?*, by Jan Godfrey and Honor Ayers (ages 4-7 hardback), *Come to the Party with Jesus*, by Leena Lane and Chris Sanderson (paper back), *Stand up and Walk with Jesus,* by Leena Lane and Chris Sanderson (paper back).

Nonfiction Picture Books: Christian teaching activities-early children. Recently published *Make a Joyful Voice: Music, Movement and Creative Play to teach Bible Stories. Old Testaments Readers Theater-Read Aloud Scripts for Young Christians. New Testaments Readers Theater-Read Aloud Scripts for Young Christians.*

How to Contact Fiction/nonfiction: submit outline/synopsis. Responds to queries in 2-3 weeks/mss. Publishes 9-12 months after acceptance. Will consider simultaneous submissions.

Terms Pays royalty of 5-10% based on net sales. Pays illustrators by the project based on net sales. Originals returned to artist at job's completion with SASE. Catalog available on Web site will post writers guidelines soon.

Tips "Have background in early childhood. Must be appropriate for children ages 4-7."

NOMAD PRESS

2456 Christain St.White River Junction VT 05001. (802)649-1995. Fax: (802)649-2667. E-mail: rachel@nomadpress.net. Website: www.nomadpress.net. Estab. 2001. Specializes in nonfiction, educational material. **Contact:** Alex Kahan, publisher. Produces 8-12 young readers/year. 10% of books by first-time authors. "We produce nonfiction children's activity books that bring a particular science or cultural topic into sharp focus."

• Nomad Press does not accept picture books or fiction.

Nonfiction Middle readers: activity books, history, science. Average word length: middle readers—30,000. Recently published *The Human Body: 25 Fantastic Projects Illuminate How the Body Works,* by Kathleen M. Reilly (ages 9-12); *Great Medieval Projects You Can Build Yourself*, by Kris Bordessa (ages 9-12); *Great China Projects You Can Build Yourself*, by Lance Kramer (ages 9-12); *Planet Earth: 25 Environment Projects You Can Build Yourself*, by Kathleen M.Reilly (ages 9-12).

How to Contact Accepts international submissions. Nonfiction: "Nomad Press does not accept unsolicited manuscripts. If authors are interested in contributing to our children's series, please send a writing resume that includes relevant experience/expertise and publishing credits." Responds to queries in 1-2 months. Publishes book 1 year after acceptance.

Terms Pays authors royalty based on retail price or work purchased outright. Offers advance against royalties. Catalog on Web site. All imprints included in single catalog. See Web site for writer's guidelines.

Tips "We publish a very specific kind of nonfiction children's activity book. Please keep this in mind when querying or submitting."

☐ ONSTAGE PUBLISHING

190 Lime Quarry Road, Suite 106J, Madison AL 35601 35758-8962. (256)461-0661. E-mail: onstage123@knology.net. Website: www.onstagepublishing.com. **Manuscript Acquisitions:** Dianne Hamilton. Publishes 1-2 middle readers/year; 1-2 young adult titles/year. 80% of books by first-time authors.

Fiction Middle readers: adventure, contemporary, fantasy, history, nature/environment, science fiction, suspense/mystery. Young adults: adventure, contemporary, fantasy, history, humor, science fiction, suspense/mystery. Average word length: chapter books—4,000-6,000 words; middle readers—5,000 words and up; young adults—25,000 and up. Recently published *Flying Boats & Pies*, by Jamie Dodso (an adventure for boys ages 12+); *Finders Magic*, by C.M. Fleming (an historical novel for grades 4-8). "We do not produce picture books."

Nonfiction Query first; currently not producing nonfiction.

How to Contact Fiction: Send complete ms if under 20,000 words, otherwise send synopsis and first 3 chapters. Responds to queries/mss in 6-8 months. Publishes a book 1-2 years after acceptance. Will consider simultaneous submissions.

Terms Pays authors/illustrators/photographers advance plus royalties. Sends galleys to authors; dummies to illustrators. Catalog available on Web site.

Tips "Study our titles and get a sense of the kind of books we publish, so that you know whether your project is likely to be right for us."

OOLIGAN PRESS

P.O. Box 751, Portland OR 97213. (503)725-9410. E-mail: ooliganacquisitions@pdx.edu. Website: www.ooliganpress.pdx.edu. Estab. 2001. **Contact:** Acquisitions Committee. "Ooligan Press is a general trade press at Portland State University. As a teaching press, Ooligan makes as little distinction as possible between the press and the classroom. Under the direction of professional faculty and staff, the work of the press is done by students enrolled in the Book Publishing graduate program at PSU. We are especially interested in works with social, literary, or educational value. Though we place special value on local authors, we are open to all submissions, including translated works and writings by children and young adults. We do not currently publish picture books, board books, easy readers, or pop-up books or middle grade readers. 90% of books by first-time authors.

Fiction Young adult with an emphasis on historical fiction or works related to the Pacific Northwest Region. At this time we cannot accept science fiction or fantasy submissions. Recently published *Ricochet River*, by Robin Cody (YA novel); *A Heart for Any Fate* (YA novel).

Nonfiction Young adult: open to all categories.

How to Contact Query with SASE or submit proposal package including 4 sample chapters, projected page count, intended audience, and marketing ideas. Prefers traditional mail, but will read unattached queries. Do not send proposal package by e-mail. Response to queries in 4-6 weeks. Publishes a book 18 months after acceptance. Will consider simultaneous submissions and previously published work.

Terms Pays negotiable royalty based on retail price. Authors see galleys for review. Book catalog and writer's guidelines available on Web site.

ORCHARD BOOKS

Imprint of Scholastic, Inc.557 Broadway, New York NY 10012. (212)343-6782. Fax: (212)343-4890. Website: www.scholastic.com. Book publisher. Editorial Director: Ken Geist. **Manuscript Acquisitions:** Ken Geist, V.P.editorial director. **Art Acquisitions:** Elizabeth B. Parisi, executive art director. "Orchard publishes 30 books yearly including board books, early chapter books, fiction, poetry, picture books, novelty and young adult novels" 10% of books by first-time authors.

• Orchard is not accepting unsolicited manuscripts; query letters only.

Fiction All levels: animal, contemporary, history, humor, multicultural, poetry. Recently published *Maybe a Bear Ate It!*, by Robie Harris, illustrations by Michael Emberley; *Funny Farm*, by Mark Teague; *One Brown Bunny*, by Marion Dane Bauer, illustrations by Ivan Bates; *Charlie Bone and the Shadow*, by Jenny Nimmo; *Lyonesse: The Well Between the Worlds*, by Sam Llewellyn; *Ten Things I Hate About Me*, by Randa Abdel-Fattah. Upcoming publications:*Cat Dreams*, by Ursula Le Guin, illustrations by S.. Schindler; *Max Spaniel series*, by David Catrow; *There Was An Old Monster*, by Rebecca and Ed Emberley; *Dog's Don't Brush Their Teeth*, by Diane de Groat, *and Shelley Rotner and the Dragons of Wayward Crescent series*, by Chris d'Lacey.

Nonfiction "We publish nonfiction very selectively."

How to Contact Query only with SASE. Responds in 3-6 months.

Terms Most commonly offers an advance against list royalties. Sends galleys to authors; dummies to illustrators. Original artwork returned at job's completion.

Tips "Read some of our books to determine first whether your manuscript is suited to our list."

OUR CHILD PRESS

P.O. Box 4379, Philadelphia PA 19118. Phone/fax: (610)308-8088. E-mail: ourchildpress@aol.com. Website: www.ourchildpress.com. **Acquisitions:** Carol Perrott, president. 90% of books by first-time authors.

Fiction All levels: adoption, multicultural, special needs. Published *Like Me*, written by Dawn Martelli, illustrated by Jennifer Hedy Wharton; *Is That Your Sister?*, by Catherine and Sherry Burin; *Oliver: A Story About Adoption*, by Lois Wichstrom.

How to Contact : Query or submit complete ms. Responds to queries/mss in 6 months. Publishes a book 6-12 months after acceptance.

Terms Pays authors royalty of 5-10% based on wholesale price. Pays illustrators royalty of 5-10% based on wholesale price. Original artwork returned at job's completion. Book catalog for business-size SAE and 67¢ postage.

☐ OUR SUNDAY VISITOR, INC.

200 Noll Plaza, Huntington IN 46750. (260)356-8400. Fax: (260)359-9117. Website: www.osv. com. For guidelines: booksed@osv.com **Acquisitions:** Jacquelyn Lindsey, David Dziena and Bert Ghezzi. **Art Director:** Tyler Ottinger. Publishes religious, educational, parenting, reference and biographies. OSV is dedicated to providing books, periodicals and other products that serve the Catholic Church.

- Our Sunday Visitor, Inc.is publishing only those children's books that tie in to sacramental preparation and Catholic identity. Contact the acquisitions editor for manuscript guidelines.

Nonfiction Picture books, middle readers, young readers, young adults. Recently published *Living the Ten Commandments for Children*, by Rosemarie Gortler and Donna Piscitelli, illustrated by Mimi Sternhagen.

How to Contact Query, submit complete ms, or submit outline/synopsis and 2-3 sample chapters. Responds to queries/mss in 2 months. Publishes a book 18-24 months after acceptance. Will consider simultaneous submissions, electronic submissions via disk or modem, previously published work.

Terms Pays authors royalty of 10-12% net. Pays illustrators by the project (range: $200-1,500). Sends galleys to authors; dummies to illustrators. Book catalog available for SASE; ms guidelines available for SASE.

Tips "Stay in accordance with our guidelines."

RICHARD C. OWEN PUBLISHERS, INC.

P.O. Box 585, Katonah NY 10536. (800)336-5588. Fax: (914)232-3977. Website: www.rcowen. com. **Acquisitions:** Janice Boland, children's books editor/art director. 90% of books by first-time authors. We publish "child-focused books, with inherent instructional value, about characters and situations with which five-, six-, and seven-year-old children can identify—books that can be read for meaning, entertainment, enjoyment and information. We include multicultural stories that present minorities in a positive and natural way. Our stories show the diversity in America." Is not interested in lesson plans, or books of activities for literature studies or other content areas.

- Due to a high volume of submissions, Richard C. Owen Publishers are currently only accepting nonfiction pieces.

Nonfiction Picture books, young readers: animals, careers, hi-lo, history, how-to, music/dance, geography, multicultural, nature/environment, science, sports. Multicultural needs include: "Good stories respectful of all heritages, races, cultural—African-American, Hispanic, American Indian." Wants lively stories. No "encyclopedic" type of information stories. Average word length: under 500 words. Recently published *The Coral Reef*.

How to Contact Fiction/nonfiction: Submit complete ms and cover letter. Responds to mss in 1 year. Publishes a book 2-3 years after acceptance. See Web site for guidelines.

Terms Pays authors royalty of 5% based on net price or outright purchase (range: $25-500). Offers no advances. Pays illustrators by the project (range: $100-2,500). Pays photographers by the project (range: $100-2,000) or per photo ($100-150). Original artwork returned 12-18 months after job's completion. Book brochure, ms/artists guidelines available for SASE.

Tips Seeking "authentic nonfiction that has charm, magic, impact and appeal; that children living in today's society will want to read and reread; books with strong storylines, child-appealing characters, events, language, action. Write for the ears and eyes and hearts of your readers—use an economy of words. Visit the children's room at the public library and immerse yourself in the best children's literature."

PACIFIC PRESS

P.O. Box 5353, Nampa ID 83653-5353. (208)465-2500. Fax: (208)465-2531. E-mail: booksubmissions@ pacificpress.com. Website: www.pacificpress.com/writers/books.htm. **Manuscript Acquisitions:** Scott Cady. **Art Acquisitions:** Gerald Monks, creative director. Publishes 1 picture book/year; 2 young readers/year; 2 middle readers/year. 5% of books by first-time authors. Pacific Press brings the Bible and Christian lifestyle to children.

Fiction Picture books, young readers, middle readers, young adults: religious subjects only. No fantasy. Average word length: picture books—100; young readers—1,000; middle readers—15,000; young adults—40,000. Recently published *A Child's Steps to Jesus* (3 vols), by Linda Carlyle; *Octopus Encounter*, by Sally Streib; *Sheperd Warrior*, by Bradley Booth.

Nonfiction Picture books, young readers, middle readers, young adults: religion. Average word length: picture books—100; young readers—1,000; middle readers—15,000; young adults—40,000. Recently published *Escape*, by Sandy Zaugg; *What We Believe*, by Seth Pierce.

How to Contact Fiction/nonfiction: Query or submit outline/synopsis and 3 sample chapters. Responds to queries in 3 months; mss in 1 year. Publishes a book 6-12 months after acceptance. Will consider e-mail submissions.

Terms Pays author royalty of 6-15% based on wholesale price. Offers advances (average amount: $1,500). Pays illustrators royalty of 6-15% based on wholesale price. Pays photographers royalty of 6-15% based on wholesale price. Sends galleys to authors. Originals returned to artist at job's completion. Manuscript guidelines for SASE. Catalog available on Web site (www. adventistbookcenter.com).

Tips Pacific Press is owned by the Seventh-day Adventist Church. The Press rejects all material that is not Bible-based.

PACIFIC VIEW PRESS

P.O. Box 2897, Berkeley CA 94702. (510)849-4213. Fax: (510)843-5835. E-mail: pvpress@sprynet. com. Website: www.pacificviewpress.com. **Acquisitions:** Pam Zumwalt, president. Publishes 1-2 picture books/year. 50% of books by first-time authors. "We publish unique, high-quality introductions to Asian cultures and history for children 8-12, for schools, libraries and families. Our children's books focus on hardcover illustrated nonfiction. We look for titles on aspects of the history and culture of the countries and peoples of the Pacific Rim, especially China, presented in an engaging, informative and respectful manner. We are interested in books that all children will enjoy reading and using, and that parents and teachers will want to buy."

Nonfiction Young readers, middle readers: Asia-related multicultural only. Recently published *Cloud Weavers: Ancient Chinese Legends*, by Rena Krasno and Yeng-Fong Chiang (all ages); *Exploring Chinatown: A Children's Guide to Chinese Culture*, by Carol Stepanchuk (ages 8-12).

How to Contact Query with outline and sample chapter. Responds in 3 months.

Terms Pays authors royalty of 8-12% based on wholesale price. Pays illustrators by the project (range: $2,000-5,000).

Tips "We welcome proposals from persons with expertise, either academic or personal, in their area of interest. While we do accept proposals from previously unpublished authors, we would expect submitters to have considerable experience presenting their interests to children in classroom or other public settings and to have skill in writing for children."

PAULINE BOOKS & MEDIA

50 Saint. Pauls Ave.Boston MA 02130-3491. (617)522-8911. E-mail: editorial@paulinemedia.com.

Website: www.pauline.org. **Children's Editor:** Christina M. Wegendt, FSP; Diane Lynch. **Art Acquisitions:** Mary Joseph Peterson, FSP. Publishes 8 picture books/year; 2 board books/year; 5 young readers/year; 5 middle readers/year. One to two books per year by first-time authors. Through our children's literature we aim to provide wholesome and entertaining reading that can help children develop strong Christian values.

Nonfiction Picture books, young readers, middle readers: religion. Average word length: picture books—500-1,000; young readers—8,000-10,000; middle readers—15,000-25,000. Recently published *God Made Wonderful Me!*, by Genny Monchamp; *An Arkful of Animal Stories*, by John Goodwin; *Mother to the Poor*, by Jung-Wook Ko; *Adventrues of Saint Paul*, by Oldrich Selucky; *Saint John Vianney; A Priest for All People*, by Elizabeth Marie DeDominico.

How to Contact For board books and picture books, the entire manuscript should be submitted. For easy -to-read, young readers, and middle-reader books, please send a cover letter accompanied by a synopsis and two sample chapters. Electronic submissions are encouraged. We make every effort to respond to unsolicited submissions within two months.

Terms Varies by project, but generally are royalties with advance. flat fees sometimes considered for smaller works. Manuscript and art guidelines available by SASE or on Web site. Catalog available on Web site.

Tips "Manuscripts may or may not be explicitly catechetical, but we seek those that reflect a positive worldview, good moral values, awareness and appreciation of diversity, and respect for all people. All material must be relevant to the lives of young readers and must conform to Catholic teaching and practice."

PAULIST PRESS

97 Macarthur Blvd.Mahwah NJ 07430. Website: www.paulistpress.com. Acquisitions: Children's Editor. Publishes 6-8 titles/year. 10% of books by first-time authors. We usually use our current authors and illustrators. Our goal is to spread the good news about God's love, usually from a Catholic perspective.

Fiction and Poetry We are currently *not publishing fiction or poetry*. Please do not submit or query.

Nonfiction The very few books we consider are on explicitly Catholic doctrine, prayers, sacraments, or customs, all meant to be used in a catechetical setting. Activity book submissions must be writer/illustrator only. For examples see *My Catholic School Holiday Activity Book* and *Jesus Loves Me Activity Book*, both written and illustrated by Jennifer Galvin. Examples of other kinds of books are *Child's Guide to the Stations of the Cross*, by Sue Stanton, illustrated by Anne Catharine Blake; and *The Imitation of Christ for Children*, by Elizabeth Ficocelli with illustrations my Chris Sabatino.

How to Contact Send complete mss for short nonfiction; query, outline, and sample for longer books. No e-mail submissions. No pitching ideas over the phone. Include SASE. Responds in 4-6 months. Simultaneous submissions are OK.

Illustration Send non-returnable samples of your children's art, both color and b/w, or a link to your Web page showing the same. Receipt of art samples cannot be acknowledged. For activity books, send an outline and a few sample pages. Activity books must give permission for the pages to be reproducible in a classroom setting. This actually increases rather than decreases sales.

Terms Pays authors royalty of 4-8% based on net sales, depending on whether or not they are split between author and illustrator. Advance payment is $500, payable on publication. Illustrators sometimes receive a flat fee when all we need are spot illustrations.

PEACHTREE PUBLISHERS, LTD.

1700 Chattahoochee Ave.Atlanta GA 30318-2112. (404)876-8761. Fax: (404)875-2578. E-mail: hello@ peachtree-online.com. Website: www.peachtree-online.com. **Acquisitions:** Helen Harriss. **Art Director:** Loraine Joyner. Production Manager: Melanie McMahon Ives. Publishes 30-35 titles/year.

Fiction Picture books, young readers: adventure, animal, concept, history, nature/environment. Middle readers: adventure, animal, history, nature/environment, sports. Young adults: fiction, mystery, adventure. Does not want to see science fiction, romance.

Nonfiction Picture books: animal, history, nature/environment. Young readers, middle readers, young adults: animal, biography, nature/environment. Does not want to see religion.

How to Contact Fiction/nonfiction: Submit complete ms (picture books) or 3 sample chapters (chapter books) by postal mail only. Responds to queries/mss in 6-7 months. Publishes a book 1-2 years after acceptance. Will consider simultaneous submissions.

Terms "Manuscript guidelines for SASE, visit Web site or call for a recorded message. No fax or e-mail submittals or queries please."

PELICAN PUBLISHING CO. INC.

1000 Burmaster St.Gretna LA 70053-2246. (504)368-1175. Website: www.pelicanpub.com. **Manuscript Acquisitions:** Nina Kooij, editor-in-chief. **Art Acquisitions:** Terry Callaway, production manager. Publishes 20 young readers/year; 4 middle readers/year. **4% of books from agented writers**. "Pelican publishes hardcover and trade paperback originals and reprints. Our children's books (illustrated and otherwise) include history, biography, holiday, and regional. Pelican's mission is "To publish books of quality and permanence that enrich the lives of those who read them."

Fiction Young readers: history, holiday, science, multicultural and regional. Middle readers: Louisiana history. Multicultural needs include stories about African-Americans, Irish-Americans, Jews, Asian-Americans, and Hispanics. Does not want animal stories, general Christmas stories, "day at school" or"accept yourself" stories. Maximum word length: young readers-1,100; middle readers-40,000. Recently published *The Oklahoma Land Run*, by Una Belle Townsend (ages 5-8, historical/regional).

Nonfiction Young readers: biography, history, holiday, multicultural. Middle readers: Louisiana history, holiday, regional. Recently published *Batty about Texas*, by J. Jaye Smith (ages 5-8, science/regional).

How to Contact Fiction/nonfiction: Query. Responds to queries in 1 month; mss in 3 months. Publishes a book 9-18 months after acceptance.

Terms Pays authors in royalties; buys ms outright "rarely." Sends galleys to authors. Illustrators paid by "various arrangements." Book catalog and ms guidelines available on Web site or for SASE.

Tips "No anthropomorphic stories, pet stories (fiction or nonfiction), fantasy, poetry, science fiction or romance. Writers: be as original as possible. Develop characters that lend themselves to series and always be thinking of new and interesting situations for those series. Give your story a strong hook-something that will appeal to a well-defined audience. There is a lot of competition out there for general themes. We look for stories with specific 'hooks' and audiences, and writers who actively promote their work."

PHILOMEL BOOKS

Penguin Young Readers Group (USA), 345 Hudson St.New York NY 10014. (212)414-3610. Website: www.penguin.com. **Manuscript Acquisitions:** submissions editor. **Art Acquisitions:** Ryan Thomann, junior designer. Publishes 18 picture books/year; 2 middle-grades/year; 2 young readers/year; 4 young adult titles/year. 5% of books by first-time authors; 80% of books from agented writers. "We look for beautifully written, engaging manuscripts for children and young adults."

Fiction All levels: adventure, animal, contemporary, fantasy, folktales, hi-lo, history, humor, sports, multicultural. Middle readers, young adults: problem novels, science fiction, suspense/mystery. No concept picture books, mass-market "character" books, or series. Average word length: picture books—1,000; young readers—1,500; middle readers—14,000; young adult—20,000.

Nonfiction Picture books, young readers, middle readers: hi-lo. "Creative nonfiction on any subject." Average word length: picture books—2,000; young readers—3,000; middle readers—10,000.

How to Contact "As of January 1, 2007, Philomel will no longer respond to your unsolicited submission unless interested in publishing it. Rejected submissions postmarked January 1, 2007, or later will be recycled. Please *do not* include a self-addressed stamped envelope with your submission. You will not hear from Philomel regarding the status of your submission unless we are interested in publishing it, in which case you can expect a reply from us within approximately four months. We regret that we cannot respond personally to each submission, but rest assured that we do make every effort to consider each and every one we receive."

Terms Pays authors in royalties. Average advance payment "varies." Illustrators paid by advance and in royalties. Sends galleys to authors; dummies to illustrators. Book catalog, ms guidelines free on request with SASE (9 × 12 envelope for catalog).

Tips Wants "unique fiction or nonfiction with a strong voice and lasting quality. Discover your own voice and own story and persevere." Looks for "something unusual, original, well-written. Fine art. The genre (fantasy, contemporary, or historical fiction) is not so important as the story itself and the spirited life the story allows its main character. We are also interested in receiving adolescent novels, current, contemporary fiction with voice."

◻ PIANO PRESS

P.O. Box 85, Del Mar CA 92014-0085. (619)884-1401. Fax: (858)755-1104. E-mail: pianopress@pianopress.com. Website: www.pianopress.com. **Manuscript Acquisitions:** Elizabeth C. Axford, M.A, editor. "We publish music-related books, either fiction or nonfiction, coloring books, songbooks and poetry."

Fiction Picture books, young readers, middle readers, young adults: folktales, multicultural, poetry, music. Average word length: picture books—1,500-2,000. Recently published *Strum a Song of Angels*, by Linda Oatman High and Elizabeth C. Axford; *Music and Me*, by Kimberly White and Elizabeth C. Axford.

Nonfiction Picture books, young readers, middle readers, young adults: multicultural, music/dance. Average word length: picture books—1,500-2,000. Recently published *The Musical ABC*, by Dr. Phyllis J. Perry and Elizabeth C. Axford; *Merry Christmas Happy Hanukkah—A Multilingual Songbook & CD*, by Elizabeth C. Axford.

How to Contact Fiction/ nonfiction: Query. Responds to queries in 3 months; mss in 6 months. Publishes a book 1 year after acceptance. Will consider simultaneous submissions, electronic submissions via disk or modem.

Terms Pays authors, illustrators, and photographers royalty of 5-10% based on retail price. Sends galleys to authors; dummies to illustrators. Originals returned to artist at job's completion. Book catalog available for #10 SASE and 2 first-class stamps. All imprints included in a single catalog. Catalog available on Web site.

Tips "We are looking for music-related material only for any juvenile market. Please do not send nonmusic-related materials. Query first before submitting anything."

PIÑATA BOOKS

Imprint of Arte Publico Press, University of Houston, 452 Cullen Performance Hall, Houston TX 77204-2004. (713)743-2843. Fax: (713)743-3080. Website: www.artepublicopress.com. **Manuscript Acquisitions:** Dr. Nicholas Kanellos; Gabriela Baeza Ventura, executive editor. **Art Acquisitions:** Adelaida Mendoza, production manager. Publishes 6 picture books/year; 2 young readers/year; 5 middle readers/year; 5 young adult titles/year. 80% of books are by first-time authors. "Arte Publico's mission is the publication, promotion and dissemination of Latino literature for a variety of national and regional audiences, from early childhood to adult, through the complete gamut of delivery systems, including personal performance as well as print and electronic media."

Fiction Recently published *We Are Cousins/ Somos primos* by Diane Gonzales Betrand; *Butterflies* *on Carmen Street/ Mariposas en la calle Carmen* by Monica Brown*; and Windows into My World: Latino Youth Write Their Lives.*

Nonfiction Recently published *Cesar Chavez: The Struggle for Justice/Cesar Chavez: La Lucha Por La Justicia*, by Richard Griswold del Castillo, illustrated by Anthony Accardo (ages 3-7).

How to Contact Accepts material from U.S./Hispanic authors only (living abroad OK). Manuscripts, queries, synopses, etc. are accepted in either English or Spanish. Fiction: Submit complete ms. Nonfiction: Query. Responds to queries in 2-4 months; mss in 3-6 months. Publishes a book 2 years after acceptance. Will sometimes consider previously published work.

Terms Pays authors royalty of 10% minimum based on wholesale price. Offers advances (average amount $2,000). Pays illustrators advance and royalties of 10% based on wholesale price. Sends galleys to authors. Catalog available on Web site; ms guidelines available for SASE.

PINEAPPLE PRESS, INC.

P.O. Box 3889, Sarasota FL 34239. (941)739-2219. Fax: (941)739-2296. E-mail: info@pineapplepress. com. Website: www.pineapplepress.com. **Manuscript Acquisitions:** June Cussen. Publishes 1 picture book/year; 1 young reader/year; 1 middle reader/year; 1 young adult title/year. 50% of books by first-time authors. "Our mission is to publish good books about Florida."

Fiction Picture books, young readers, middle readers, young adults: animal, folktales, history, nature/environment. Recently published *The Treasure of Amelia Island* by M.C. Finotti (ages 8-12).

Nonfiction Picture books: animal, history, nature/environmental, science. Young readers, middle readers, young adults: animal, biography, geography, history, nature/environment, science. Recently published *Those Magical Manatees* by Jan Lee Wicker and *Those Beautiful Butterflies* by Sarah Cussen.

How to Contact/Writers Fiction: Query or submit outline/synopsis and 3 sample chapters. Nonfiction: Query or submit outline/synopsis and intro and 3 sample chapters. Responds to queries/samples/mss in 2 months. Will consider simultaneous submissions.

Terms Pays authors royalty of 10-15%. Pays illustrators royalties. Sends galleys to authors; dummies to illustrators. Originals returned to artist at job's completion. Book catalog available for 9 × 12 SAE with $1.06 postage; all imprints included in a single catalog. Catalog available on Web site at www. pineapplepress.com.

Tips "Learn about publishing and book marketing in general. Be familiar with the kinds of books published by the publishers to whom you are submitting."

PITSPOPANY PRESS

Simcha Media, P.O. Box 5329, Englewood NJ 07631. (212)444-1657. Fax: (866)205-3966. E-mail: pitspop@netvision.net.il. Website: www.pitspopany.com. Estab. 1992. Specializes in trade books, Judaica, nonfiction, fiction, multicultural material. **Manuscript Acquisitions:** Yaacov Peterseil, publisher. **Art Acquisitions:** Yaacov Peterseil, publisher. Produces 6 picture books/year; 4 young readers/year; 4 middle readers/year; 4 young adult books/year. 10% of books by first-time authors. "Pitspopany Press is dedicated to bringing quality children's books of Jewish interest into the marketplace. Our goal is to create titles that will appeal to the esthetic senses of our readers and, at the same time, offer quality Jewish content to the discerning parent, teacher, and librarian. While the people working for Pitspopany Press embody a wide spectrum of Jewish belief and opinion, we insist that our titles be respectful of the mainstream Jewish viewpoints and beliefs. We are especially interested in chapter books for kids. Most of all, we are committed to creating books that all Jewish children can read, learn from, and enjoy."

Fiction Picture books: animal, anthology, fantasy, folktales, history, humor, multicultural, nature/ environment, poetry. Young readers: adventure, animal, anthology, concept, contemporary, fantasy, folktales, health, history, humor, multicultural, nature/environment, poetry, religion, science fiction, special needs, sports, suspense. Middle readers: animal, anthology, fantasy, folktales, health, hi-lo, history, humor, multicultural, nature/environment, poetry, religion, science fiction, special needs, sports, suspense. Young adults/teens: animal, anthology, contemporary, fantasy, folktales, health, hi-lo, history, humor, multicultural, nature/environment, poetry, religion, science fiction, special needs, sports, suspense. Recently published *Hayyim's Ghost*, by Eric Kimmel, illustrated by Ari Binus (ages 6-9); *The Littlest Pair*, by Syliva Rouss, illustrated by Hally Hannan (ages 3-6); *The Converso Legacy*, by Sheldon Gardner (ages 10-14, historial fiction).

Nonfiction All levels: activity books, animal, arts/crafts, biography, careers, concept, cooking, geography, health, history, hobbies, how-to, multicultural, music/dance, nature/environment, reference, religion, science, self help, social issues, special needs, sports.

How to Contact Accepts international submissions. Fiction/nonfiction: Submit outline/synopsis. Responds to queries/mss in 6 weeks. Publishes book 9 months after acceptance. Considers simultaneous submissions, electronic submissions.

Terms Pays authors royalty or work purchased outright. Offers advance against royalties. Author sees galleys for review. Originals returned to artist at job's completion. Catalog on Web site. All imprints included in single catalog. Offers writer's guidelines for SASE.

PLAYERS PRESS, INC.

P.O. Box 1132, Studio City CA 91614-0132. (818)789-4980. **Manuscript Acquisitions:** Robert W. Gordon, vice president/editorial director. **Art Acquisitions:** Attention: Art Director. Publishes 7-25 young readers, dramatic plays and musicals/year; 2-10 middle readers, dramatic plays and musicals/year; 4-20 young adults, dramatic plays and musicals/year. 35% of books by first-time authors; 1% of books from agented writers. Players Press philosophy: "To create is to live life's purpose."

Fiction All levels: plays. Recently published *Play From African Folktales*, by Carol Korty (collection of short plays); *Punch and Judy*, a play by William-Alan Landes; *Silly Soup!*, by Carol Korty (a collection of short plays with music and dance).

Nonfiction Picture books, middle readers, young readers, young adults. "Any children's nonfiction pertaining to the entertainment industry, performing arts and how-to for the theatrical arts only." Needs include activity books related to theatre: arts/crafts, careers, history, how-to, music/dance, reference and textbook. Recently published *Scenery*, by J. Stell (How to Build Stage Scenery); *Monologues for Teens*, by Vernon Howard (ideal for teen performers); *Humorous Monologues*, by Vernon Howard (ideal for young performers); *Actor's Resumes*, by Richard Devin (how to prepare an acting résumé).

How to Contact Fiction/nonfiction: Submit plays or outline/synopsis and sample chapters of entertainment books. Responds to queries in 2 weeks; mss in 6 months-1 year. Publishes a book 10 months after acceptance. No simultaneous submissions.

Terms Pays authors royalty based on wholesale price. Pays illustrators by the project (range: $5-1,000). Pays photographers by the project (up to $100); royalty varies. Sends galleys to authors; dummies to illustrators. Book catalog and ms guidelines available for 9 × 12 SASE.

Tips Looks for "plays/musicals and books pertaining to the performing arts only. Illustrators: send samples that can be kept for our files."

PLUM BLOSSOM BOOKS

Parallax Press, P.O. Box 7355, Berkeley CA 94707. (510)525-0101. Fax: (510)525-7129. E-mail: rachel@parallax.org. Website: www.parallax.org. Estab. 1985. Specializes in nonfiction, fiction. **Writers contact:** Rachel Neuman, senior editor. Produces 2 picture books/year. 30% of books by first-time authors. "Plum Blossom Books publishes stories for children of all ages that focus on mindfulness in daily life, Buddhism, and social justice."

Fiction Picture books: adventure, contemporary, folktales, multicultural, nature/environment, religion. Young readers: adventure, contemporary, folktales, multicultural, nature/environment, religion. Middle readers: multicultural, nature/environment, religion. Young adults/teens: nature/

environment, religion. Recently published *The Hermit and the Well*, by Thich Nhat Hanh, illustrated by Dinh Mai (ages 4-8, hardcover); *Each Breath a Smile*, by Sister Thuc Nghiem and Thich Nhat Hanh, illustrated by T. Hop (ages 2-5, paperback picture book); *Meow Said the Mouse*, by Beatrice Barbey, illustrated by Philippe Ames (ages 5-8, picture and activity book).

Nonfiction All levels: nature/environment, religion (Buddhist), Buddhist counting books.

How to Contact Accepts international submissions. Fiction/nonfiction: Query or submit complete ms. Responds to queries in 1-2 weeks. Responds to mss in 4 weeks. Publishes book 9-12 months after acceptance. Considers electronic submissions.

Terms Pays authors royalty of 20% based on wholesale price. Pays illustrators by the project. Author sees galleys for review. Illustrators see dummies for review. Originals returned to artist at job's completion. Catalog available for SASE. Offers writer's, artist's guidelines for SASE. See Web site for writer's, artist's, photographer's guidelines.

Tips "Read our books before approaching us. We are very specifically looking for mindfulness and Buddhist messages in high-quality stories where the Buddhist message is implied rather than stated outright."

PRICE STERN SLOAN, INC.

Penguin Group (USA), 345 Hudson St.New York NY 10014. (212)414-3590. Fax: (212)414-3396. Estab. 1963. Website: http://us.penguingroup.com/youngreaders. **Acquisitions:** Debra Dorfman, president/publisher. "Price Stern Sloan publishes quirky mass market novelty series for children's as well as licensed movie tie-in books.

• Price Stern Sloan does not accept e-mail submissions.

Fiction Publishes picture books and novelty/board books including Mad Libs Movie and Television Tie-ins, and unauthorized biographies. "We publish unique novelty formats and fun, colorful paperbacks and activity books. We also publish the Book with Audio Series Wee Sing and Baby Loves Jazz." Recently published: Baby Loves Jazz Board Book with CD Series; New Formats in the Classic Mr. Men/Little Miss Series; Movie/TV tie-in titles: Speed Racers, Journey 3D. Unauthorized biographies: Mad for Miley and Jammin' with Jonas Brother.

How to Contact Query. Responds to queries in 6-8 weeks.

Terms Work purchased outright. Offers advance. Book catalog available for 9 × 12 SASE and 5 first-class stamps; address to Book Catalog. Manuscript guidelines available for SASE; address to Manuscript Guidelines.

Tips "Price Stern Sloan publishes unique, fun titles."

PUFFIN BOOKS

Penguin Group (USA), Inc.345 Hudson St.New York NY 10014-3657. (212)414-3600. Website: www. penguin.com/youngreaders. **Acquisitions:** Sharyn November, senior editor and editorial director of Firebird. Imprints: Speak, Firebird, Sleuth. Publishes trade paperback originals and reprints. Publishes 175-200 titles/year. Receives 600 queries and mss/year. 1% of books by first-time authors; 5% from unagented writers. "Puffin Books publishes high-end trade paperbacks and paperback originals and reprints for preschool children, beginning and middle readers, and young adults."

Fiction Picture books, young adult novels, middle grade and easy-to-read grades 1-3: fantasy and science fiction, graphic novels, classics. Recently Published *Three Cups of Tea Young Readers Edition*, by Greg Mortenson and David Oliver Relin; adapted for young readers by Sarah Thomson; *The Big Field*, by Mike Lupica; *Geek Charming*, by Robin Palmer**.**

Nonfiction Biography, illustrated books, young children's concept books (counting, shapes, colors). Subjects include education (for teaching concepts and colors, not academic), women in history. "Women in history books interest us."

How to Contact Fiction: Submit 3 sample chapters with SASE. Nonfiction: Submit 5 pages of ms with SASE. "It could take up to 5 months to get response." Publishes book 1 year after acceptance. Will consider simultaneous submissions, if so noted. Does not accept unsolicited picture book mss.

Terms Pays royalty. Offers advance (varies). Book catalog for 9 × 12 SASE with 7 first-class stamps; send request to Marketing Department.

Ⓐ PUSH

Scholastic, 557 Broadway, New York NY 10012-3999. Website: www.thisispush.com. Estab. 2002. Specializes in fiction. Produces 6-9 young adult books/year. 50% of books by first-time authors. PUSH publishes new voices in teen literature.

- PUSH does not accept unsolicited manuscripts or queries, only agented or referred fiction/ memoir.

Fiction Young adults: contemporary, multicultural, poetry. Recently published *Splintering*, by Eireann Corrigan; *Never Mind the Goldbergs*, by Matthue Roth; *Perfect World*, by Brian James.

Nonfiction Young adults: memoir. Recently published *Talking in the Dark*, by Billy Merrell; *You Remind Me of You*, by Eireann Corrigan.

How to Contact Only interested in agented material. Accepts international submissions. Fiction/nonfiction: Submit complete ms. Responds to queries in 2 months; mss in 4 months. No simultaneous, electronic, or previously published submissions.

Tips "We only publish first-time writers (and then their subsequent books), so authors who have published previously should not consider PUSH. Also, for young writers in grades 7-12, we run the PUSH novel Contest with the Scholastic Art & Writing Awards. Every year it begins in October and ends in March. Rules can be found on our Web site."

G.P. PUTNAM'S SONS

Penguin Putnam Books For Young Readers, 345 Hudson St.New York NY 10014. (212)414-3610. Website: www.penguinputnam.com. **Manuscript Acquisitions:** Susan Kochan, associate editorial director; John Rudolph, executive editor; Timothy Travaglini, senior editor; Stacey Barney, editor. **Art Acquisitions:** Cecilia Yung, art director, Putnam and Philomel. Publishes 25 picture books/ year; 15 middle readers/year; 5 young adult titles/year. 5% of books by first-time authors; 50% of books from agented authors.

- G.P. Putnam's Sons title *Feathers*, by Jacqueline Woodson, won a Newbery Honor Medal in 2008. See First Books on page 133 for an interview with Sarah S. Brannen, author and illustrator of Putnam title *Uncle Bobby's Wedding*.

Fiction Picture books: animal, concept, contemporary, humor, multicultural. Young readers: adventure, contemporary, history, humor, multicultural, special needs, suspense/mystery. Middle readers: adventure, contemporary, history, humor, fantasy, multicultural, problem novels, sports, suspense/mystery. Young adults: contemporary, history, fantasy, problem novels, special needs. Does not want to see series. Average word length: picture books—200-1,000; middle readers—10,000-30,000; young adults—40,000-50,000. Recently published *Good Night, Goon: A Parody,* by Michael Rex (ages 4-8); *Geek Magnet*, by Kieran Scott (ages 1 2 and up).

Nonfiction Picture books: animal, biography, concept, history, nature/environment, science. Subjects must have broad appeal but inventive approach. Average word length: picture books—200-1,500. Recently published *Art from Her Heart*, by Kathy Whitehead, illustrated by Shane W. Evans (ages 5 and up, 32 pages).

How to Contact Accepts unsolicited mss. No SASE required, as will only respond if interested. Picture books: send full mss. Fiction: Query with outline/synopsis and 10 manuscript pages. Nonfiction: Query with outline/synopsis, 10 manuscript pages, and a table of contents. Do not send art unless requested. Responds to mss within 4 months if interested. Will consider simultaneous submissions.

Terms Pays authors royalty based on retail price. Pays illustrators by the project or royalty based on retail price. Sends galleys to authors. Original artwork returned at job's completion.

Tips "Study our catalogs and get a sense of the kind of books we publish, so that you know whether your project is likely to be right for us."

RAINBOW PUBLISHERS

P.O. Box 261129, San Diego CA 92196. (858)277-1167. Website: www.rainbowpublishers.com. **Acquisitions:** Editorial Department. Publishes 5 young readers/year; 5 middle readers/year; 5 young adult titles/year. 50% of books by first-time authors. "Our mission is to publish Bible-based, teacher resource materials that contribute to and inspire spiritual growth and development in kids ages 2-12."

Nonfiction Young readers, middle readers, young adult/teens: activity books, arts/crafts, how-to, reference, religion. Does not want to see traditional puzzles. Recently published More Bible Puzzles (series of 4 books for ages 8 and up).

How to Contact Nonfiction: Submit outline/synopsis and 3-5 sample chapters. Responds to queries in 6 weeks; mss in 3 months. Publishes a book 36 months after acceptance. Will consider simultaneous submissions, submissions via disk and previously published work.

Terms For authors work purchased outright (range: $500 and up). Pays illustrators by the project (range: $300 and up). Sends galleys to authors. Book catalog available for 10 × 13 SAE and 2 first-class stamps; ms guidelines available for SASE.

Tips "Our Rainbow imprint carries reproducible books for teachers of children in Christian ministries, including crafts, activities, games and puzzles. Our Legacy imprint published titles for children such as devotionals, fiction and Christian living. Please write for guidelines and study the market before submitting material."

☐ ▣ RANDOM HOUSE-GOLDEN BOOKS FOR YOUNG READERS GROUP

Random House, Inc.1745 Broadway, New York NY 10019. (212)782-9000. Estab. 1925. Book publisher. "Random House Books aims to create books that nurture the hearts and minds of children, providing and promoting quality books and a rich variety of media that entertain and educate readers from 6 months to 12 years." Publisher/Vice President: Kate Klimo. VP & Associate Publisher/Art Director: Cathy Goldsmith. **Acquisitions:** Easy-to-Read Books (step-into-reading and picture books), board and novelty books, fiction and nonfiction for young and mid-grade readers: Heidi Kilgras, Editorial Director. Stepping Stones: Jennifer Arena, Executive Editor. Middle grade and young adult fiction: Jim Thomas, Editorial Director. 100% of books published through agents; 2% of books by first-time authors.

- Random House-Golden Books does not accept unsolicited manuscripts, only agented material. They reserve the right not to return unsolicited material.

How to Contact Only interested in agented material. Reviews ms/illustration packages from artists through agent only. Does not open or respond to unsolicited submissions.

Terms Pays authors in royalties; sometimes buys mss outright. Sends galleys to authors. Book catalog free on request.

☐ RAVEN TREE PRESS

1400 Miller Parkway McHenry, IL 60050. Phone: (800) 323-8270 / (815) 363-3582. Fax: (800) 909-9901. E-mail: raven@raventreepress.com. Website: www.raventreepress.com. Publishes 8-10 picture books/year. 50% of books by first-time authors. "We publish entertaining and educational picture books in a variety of formats..Bilingual (English/Spanish), English - Only, Spanish - Only and Wordless editions."

Fiction Picture books: K-3 focus. No word play or rhyme. Work will be translated into Spanish by publisher. Check Web site prior to any submissions for current needs. Average word length: 500.

How to Contact Check Web site for current needs, submission guidelines and deadlines.

Terms Pays authors and illustrators royalty. Offers advances against royalties. Pays illustrators by the project or royalty. Originals returned to artist at job's completion. Catalog available on Web site.

Tips "Submit only based on guidelines. No e-mail OR snail mail queries please. Word count is a definite issue, since we are bilingual." Staff attended or plans to attend the following conferences: BEA, NABE, IRA, ALA and SCBWI.

RAZORBILL

Penguin Group, 345 Hudson Street, New York NY 10014. Imprint estab. 2003. (212)414-3448. Fax: (212)414-3343. E-mail: razorbill@us.penguingroup.com. Website: www.razorbillbooks.com. Specializes in fiction. **Acquisitions:** Julianne Lowell; Editorial Assistant: Lexa Hillyer, Jessica Rothenberg, editors. Publishes about 30 middle grade and YA titles/year. "This division of Penguin Young Readers is looking for the best and the most original of commercial contemporary fiction titles for middle grade and YA readers. A select quantity of nonfiction titles will also be considered."

Fiction Middle Readers: adventure, contemporary, graphic novels, fantasy, humor, problem novels. Young adults/teens: adventure, contemporary, fantasy, graphic novels, humor, multicultural, suspense. Average word length: middle readers—40,000; young adult—60,000. Recently published *Influence*, by Mary-Kate Olsen and Ashley Olsen (ages 12 and up, full color, coffee table book of interviews and photographs); *Thirteen Reason Why*, by Jay Asher (ages 14 and up, a NY Times Bestseller); the NY Times bestselling *Vampire Academy series,* by Richelle Mead (ages 12 and up).

Nonfiction Middle readers and Young adults/teens: concept.

How to Contact Submit outline/synopsis and 3 sample chapters along with query and SASE. Responds to queries/mss in approx. 8 weeks. Publishes a book 1-2 years after acceptance. Will consider e-mail submissions and simultaneous submissions.

Terms Offers advance against royalties. Authors see galleys for review. Catalog available online at www.razorbillbooks.com.

Tips "New writers will have the best chance of acceptance and publication with original, contemporary material that boasts a distinctive voice and well-articulated world. Check out www.razorbillbooks.com to get a better idea of what we're looking for."

⊡ RED DEER PRESS

195 Allstate Parkway, Markham ON L9P 1R4 Canada. (800)-387-9776/(905)477-9700. Fax: (800)260-9777/(905)477-2834. E-mail: rdp@reddeerpress.com. Website: www.reddeerpress.com. **Manuscript/Art Acquisitions:** Peter Carver, children's editor. Publishes 3 to 5 picture books/year; 4 young adult titles/year per season. Red Deer Press is known for their "high-quality international children's program that tackles risky and/or serious issues for kids."

• Red Deer only publishes books written and illustrated by Canadians.

Fiction Picture books, young readers: adventure, contemporary, fantasy, folktales, history, humor, multicultural, nature/environment, poetry. Middle readers, young adult/teens: adventure, contemporary, fantasy, folktales, hi-lo, history, humor, multicultural, nature/environment, problem novels, suspense/mystery. Recently published *Egghead*, by Caroline Pignat; *Dooley Takes the Fall*, by Norah McClintock; *The End of The World As We Know It,* by Lesley Choyce.

How to Contact Fiction/nonfiction: Query or submit outline/synopsis. Responds to queries in 2 months; mss in 8 months. Publishes a book 18 months after acceptance.

Terms Pays authors royalty (negotiated). Advances (negotiated). Pays illustrators and photographers by the project or royalty (depends on the project). Sends galleys to authors. Originals returned to artist at job's completion. Guidelines not available on Web site.

Tips "Writers, illustrators, and photographers should familiarize themselves with Red Deer Press's children's publishing program, including the kinds of books we do and do not publish."

▢ ▢ RENAISSANCE HOUSE

Imprint of Laredo Publishing, Englewood, NJ 07631. (800)547-5113. Fax: (201)408-5011. E-mail: laredo@renaissancehouse.net. Website: www.renaissancehouse.net. **Manuscript Acquisitions:** Raquel Benatar. **Art Acquisitions:** Sam Laredo. Publishes 5 picture books/year; 10 young readers/year; 10 middle readers/year; 5 young adult titles/year. 10% of books by first-time authors.

Fiction Picture books: animal, folktales, multicultural. Young readers: animal, anthology, folktales, multicultural. Middle readers, young adult/teens: anthology, folktales, multicultural, nature/

environment. Recently published *Go Milka, Go* (English-Spanish, age 8-10, biography); *Stories of the Americas*, a series of legends by several authors (ages 9-12, legend).

How to Contact Submit outline/synopsis. Responds to queries/mss in 3 weeks. Publishes a book 1 year after acceptance. Will consider simultaneous submissions, e-mail submissions.

Terms Pays authors royalty of 5-10% based on retail price. Pays illustrators by the project. Sends galleys to authors; dummies to illustrators. Originals returned to artist at job's completion. Book catalog available for 9 × 12 SASE and $3 postage. All imprints included in a single catalog. Catalog available on website.

⊠ ROARING BROOK PRESS

175 Fifth Ave.New York NY 10010. (646)438-6157. **Manuscript/Art Acquisitions**: Simon Boughton, publisher. **Editorial Director, Neal Porter Books:** Neal Porter. **Executive Editor:** Nancy Mercado. **Senior Editor:** Dierdre Langeland. Publishes approximately 70 titles/year. 1% of books by first-time authors. This publisher's goal is "to publish distinctive high-quality children's literature for all ages. To be a great place for authors to be published. To provide personal attention and a focused and thoughtful publishing effort for every book and every author on the list."

- Roaring Brook Press is an imprint of MacMillan, a group of companies that includes Henry Holt and Farrar, Straus & Giroux. Roaring Brook is not accepting unsolicited manuscripts. Roaring Brook title *First the Egg*, by Laura Vaacaro Seeger, won a Caldecott Honor Medal and a Theodor Seuss Geisel Honor in 2008. Their title *Dog and Bear: Two Friends, Three Stories*, also by Laura Vaccaro Seeger, won the Boston Globe-Horn Book Picture Book Award in 2007.

Fiction Picture books, young readers, middle readers, young adults: adventure, animal, contemporary, fantasy, history, humor, multicultural, nature/environment, poetry, religion, science fiction, sports, suspense/mystery. Recently published *Dog and Bear*, by Laura Vaccaro Seeger; *Candyfloss*, by Jacqueline Wilson.

Nonfiction Picture books, young readers, middle readers, young adults: adventure, animal, contemporary, fantasy, history, humor, multicultural, nature/environment, poetry, religion, science fiction, sports, suspense/mystery.

How to Contact Primarily interested in agented material. Not accepting unsolicited mss or queries. Will consider simultaneous agented submissions.

Terms Pays authors royalty based on retail price. Pays illustrators royalty or flat fee depending on project. Sends galleys to authors; dummies to illustrators, if requested.

Tips "You should find a reputable agent and have him/her submit your work."

⊡ RUNNING PRESS KIDS

Imprint of Running Press Book Publishers, 125 S. 22nd St.Philadelphia PA 19103-4399. (215)567-5080. Fax: (800)453-2884. Website: www.runningpress.com. **Manuscript Acquisitions:** Submissions Editor. **Art Acquisitions:** Design Director. Publishes 5 picture books/year. 20% of books by first-time authors. "We want to publish the books and Running Press Kids products that parents, teachers, and librarians want their kids to experience, and that kids can't wait to get their hands on."

Fiction Picture books and YA novels: adventure, animal, anthology, concept, contemporary, fantasy, folktales, health, history, humor, multicultural, nature/environment, poetry, suspense/mystery. Recently published *Free to Be... You and me,* by Marlo Thomas and Freinds; *Cathy's Book, Cathy's Key and Cathy'sRing (Spring 2009),* by Sean Stewart and Jordan Weisman; *Creepers and The Plague (Spring 2009),* by Joanne Dahme; *Say a Little Prayer,* by Dionne Warwick..

Nonfiction Picture books: activity books, animal, biography, concept, history. Young readers, middle readers: activity books, animal, biography, concept, cooking, geography, history. Recently published *Wings, Horns, and Claws,* by Christopher Wormell; *The New Big Book of US Presidents,* by Todd Davis and Mark Frey; The Doodle Series, including Do you Doodle?, Beautiful Doodles, Ooodles of Doodles (Spring 2009) and others.

How to Contact Fiction: Submit complete ms. Nonfiction: Query. Responds to queries in 2 month; mss in 3 months. Publishes book 2 years after acceptance. Will consider simultaneous submissions and previously published work.

Terms Pays authors royalty or work purchased outright from authors. Offers advances. Pays illustrators by the project or royalties. Sends galleys to authors; dummies to illustrators. Originals returned to artist at job's completion. Book; ms guidelines available for SASE. All imprints included in a single catalog. Catalog available on Web site.

☑ SCHOLASTIC INC.

557 Broadway, New York NY 10012. (212)343-6100. Website: www.scholastic.com. Arthur A. Levine Books, Cartwheel Books®, Chicken House®, Graphix™, Little Scholastic™, Little Shepherd™, Michael di Capua Books, Orchard Books®, PUSH, Scholastic en español, Scholastic Licensed Publishing, Scholastic Nonfiction, Scholastic Paperbacks, Shcolastic Press, Scholastic Reference™, Tangerine Press®, and The Blue Sky Press® are imprints of Scholastic Trade Books Division. In addition, Scholastic Trade Books included Klutz®, a highly innovative publisher and creator of "books plus" for children.

- Scholastic Press title *The Invention of Hugo Cabret*, by Brian Selznick won the Caldecott Medal in 2008.

SCHOLASTIC PRESS

557 Broadway, New York NY 10012. (212)343-6100. Website: www.scholastic.com. **Manuscript Acquisitions:** David Saylor, editorial director, Scholastic Press, Creative director and Associate Publisher for all Scholastic hardcover imprints. David Levithan, Executive editorial director, Scholastic Press fiction, multimedia publishing, and Push Lisa Sandell, acquiring editor; Dianne Hess, executive editor (picture book fiction/nonfiction, 2nd-3rd grade chapter books, some middle grade fantasy that is based on reality); Tracy Mack, executive editor (picture book, middle grade, YA); Rachel Griffiths, editor: Jennifer Rees, associate editor (picture book fiction/nonfiction, middle grade, YA). **Art Acquisitions:** Elizabeth Parisi, art director, Scholastic Press; Marijka Kostiw, art director; David Saylor, creative director and associate publisher for all Scholastic hardcover imprints. Publishes 60 titles/year. 1% of books by first-time authors.

- Scholastic Press title *What I Saw and How I Lied* won the 2009 National Book Award; *Best-selling Hunger Games*, by Suzanne Collins; Best-selling 39 Clues Series; *Zen Ties*, by Jon J. Muth was 42 weeks on the New York Times Best seller list; *Elijah of Buxton*, by Christopher Paul Curtis won a Newbery Honor Medal and the Coretta Scott King Author Award in 2008. Their title *Henry's Freedom Box: A True Story from the Underground Railroad*, by Ellen Levine, illustrated by Kadir Nelson, won a Caldecott Honor Medal in 2008; Hugo Cabaret won the 2008 Caldecott Medal.

Fiction Looking for strong picture books, young chapter books, appealing middle grade novels (ages 8-11) and interesting and well written young adult novels.

Nonfiction Interested in "unusual, interesting, and very appealing approaches to biography, math, history and science."

How to Contact Fiction/nonfiction: "Send query with 1 sample chapter and synopsis. Don't call! Don't e-mail!" Picture books: submission accepted from agents or previously published authors only.

Terms Pays advance against royalty.

Tips "Read *currently* published children's books. Revise, rewrite, rework and find your own voice, style and subject. We are looking for authors with a strong and unique voice who can tell a great story and have the ability to evoke genuine emotion. Children's publishers are becoming more selective, looking for irresistible talent and fairly broad appeal, yet still very willing to take risks, just to keep the game interesting."

SEEDLING CONTINENTAL PRESS

520 E. Bainbridge St.Elizabethtown PA 17022. Website: www.continentalpress.com. **Acquisitions:** Megan Bergonzi. 20% of books by first-time authors. Publishes books for classroom use only for the beginning reader in English. "Natural language and predictable text are requisite. Patterned text is acceptable, but must have a unique story line. Poetry, books in rhyme and full-length picture books are not being accepted. Illustrations are not necessary."

Fiction Young readers: adventure, animal, folktales, humor, multicultural, nature/environment. Does not accept texts longer than 12 pages or over 300 words. Average word length: young readers—100.

Nonfiction Young readers: animal, arts/crafts, biography, careers, concept, multicultural, nature/environment, science. Does not accept texts longer than 12 pages or over 300 words. Average word length: young readers—100.

How to Contact Fiction/nonfiction: Submit complete ms with SASE. Responds in 6 months. Publishes a book 1-2 years after acceptance. Will consider simultaneous submissions. Prefers e-mail submissions from authors or illustrators outside the U.S.

Terms Work purchased outright from authors. Pays illustrators and photographers by the project. Original artwork is not returned at job's completion. Catalog available on Web site.

Tips "See our Web site. Follow writers' guidelines carefully and test your story with children and educators."

SHEN'S BOOKS

1547 Palos Verdes Mall, #291, Walnut Creek CA 94597. (925)262-8108. Fax: (888)269-9092. E-mail: info@shens.com. Website: www.shens.com. Estab. 1986. Specializes in multicultural material. **Acquisitions:** Renee Ting, president. Produces 2 picture books/year. 50% of books by first-time authors.

Fiction Picture books, young readers: folktales, multicultural with Asian Focus. Middle readers: multicultural. Recently published *Grandfather's Story Cloth*, by Linda Gerdner, illustrated by Stuart Loughridge (ages4-8); *The Wakame Gatherers*, by Holly Thompson, illustrated by Kazumi (ages 4-8); *Romina's Rangoli*, Malathi Michelle Iyengar, illustrated by Jennifer Wanardi (ages 4-8); *The Day the Dragon Danced*, by Kay Haugaard, illustrated by Carolyn Reed Barritt (ages 4-8).

Nonfiction Picture books, young readers: multicultural. Recently published *Selvakumar Knew Better*, by Virginia Kroll, illustrated by Xiaojun Li (ages 4-8).

How to Contact Accepts international submissions. Fiction/nonfiction: Submit complete ms. Responds to queries in 1-2 weeks; mss in 6-12 months. Publishes book 1-2 years after acceptance. Considers simultaneous submissions.

Terms Authors pay negotiated by the project. Pays illustrators by the project. Pays photographers by the project. Illustrators see dummies for review. Catalog on Web site.

Tips "Be familiar with our catalog before submitting."

☐ SILVER MOON PRESS

381 Park Avenue South, Suite 1121,New York NY 10016. (212)802-2890. Fax: (212)802-2893. E-mail: mail@silvermoonpress.com. Website: www.silvermoonpress.com. **Publisher:** David Katz. **Marketing Coordinator:** Karin Lillebo. Book publisher. Publishes 1-2 books for grades 4-6/year. 25% of books by first-time authors; 10% books from agented authors. Publishes mainly American historical fiction and books of educational value. Develops books which fit neatly into curriculum for grades 4-6. "History comes alive when children can read about other children who lived when history was being made!"

Fiction Middle readers: historical, multicultural and mystery. Average word length: 14,000. Recently published *Liberty on 23rd Street*, by Jacqueline Glasthal; *A Silent Witness in Harlem*, by Eve Creary; *In the Hands of the Enemy*, by Robert Sheely; *Ambush in the Wilderness*, by Kris Hemphill; *Race to Kitty Hawk*, by Edwina Raffa and Annelle Rigsby; *Brothers of the Falls*, by Joanna Emery.

How to Contact We are not accepting manuscript submissions at this time.

Terms Pays authors royalty or work purchased outright. Pays illustrators by the project, no royalty. Pays photographers by the project, per photo, no royalty. Sends galleys to authors; dummies to illustrators. Book catalog available for 8½ × 11 SASE and $1.11 postage.

Tips "We do not accept biographies, poetry, or romance. We do not accept fantasy, science fiction, or historical fiction with elements of either. No picture books. Submissions that fit into New York State curriculum topics such as the Revolutionary War, Colonial times, and New York State history in general stand a greater chance of acceptance than those that do not."

SIMON & SCHUSTER BOOKS FOR YOUNG READERS

1230 Avenue of the Americas, New York NY 10020. (212)698-7000. Fax: (212)698-2796. Website: www.simonsayskids.com. **Manuscript Acquisitions:** Justin Chanda, associate publisher; David Gale, vice president, editorial director; Kevin Lewis, executive director; Emily Meehan, executive editor, Paula Wiseman, VP, publisher, books. **Art Acquisitions:** Dan Potash, vice president, creative director. Publishes 95 books/year. "We publish high-quality fiction and nonfiction for a variety of age groups and a variety of markets. Above all we strive to publish books that will offer kids a fresh perspective on their world." **Simon & Schuster Books for Young Readers does not accept unsolicited manuscripts.** Queries are accepted via mail. Their title Wolves, by Emily Gravett, won a Boston Globe-Horn Book Picture Book Honor Award in 2007.

Fiction Picture books: animal, minimal text/very young readers. Middle readers, young adult: fantasy, adventure, suspense/mystery. All levels: contemporary, history, humor. Recently published *Orange Pear Apple Bear*, written and illustrated by Emily Gravett (picture book, ages 1-4); *Huge*, by Sasha Paley (young adult fiction, ages 13 and up).

Nonfiction Picture books: concept. All levels: narrative, current events, biography, history. "We're looking for picture book or middle grade nonfiction that have a retail potential. No photo essays." Recently published Insiders Series (picture book nonfiction, all ages).

How to Contact Do not accept unsolicited or unagented manuscripts.

Terms Pays authors royalty (varies) based on retail price. Pays illustrators or photographers by the project or royalty (varies) based on retail price. Original artwork returned at job's completion. Manuscript/artist's guidelines available via Web site or free on request. Call (212)698-2707.

Tips "We're looking for picture books centered on a strong, fully-developed protagonist who grows or changes during the course of the story; YA novels that are challenging and psychologically complex; also imaginative and humorous middle-grade fiction. And we want nonfiction that is as engaging as fiction. Our imprint's slogan is 'Reading You'll Remember.' We aim to publish books that are fresh, accessible and family-oriented; we want them to have an impact on the reader."

SKINNER HOUSE BOOKS

Unitarian Universalist Association. 25 Beacon St.Boston MA 02108. Estab. 1976. (617)742-2100. Fax: (617)742-7025. E-mail: skinnerhouse@uua.org. Website: www.uua.org/publications/skinnerhouse/. Estab. 1976. Specializes in nonfiction, educational material, multicultural material. **Manuscript Acquisitions:** Betsy Martin, Editorial Assistant. **Art Acquisitions:** Suzanne Morgan, Design Director. Publishes 1 picture books/ year; 1 young readers/year; 1 middle readers/year. 50% of books by first-time authors. "We publish books for Unitarian Universalists. Most of our children's' titles are intended for religious education or worship use. They reflect Unitarian Universalist values."

Fiction All levels: anthology, multicultural, nature/environment, religion. Recently published *A Child's Book of Blessings and Prayers*, by Eliza Blanchard (ages 4-8, picture book); *Meet Jesus: The Life and Lessons of a Beloved Teacher*, by Lynn Gunney (age's 5-8, picture book); *Magic Wanda's Travel Emporium*, by Joshua Searle-White (ages 9 and up, stories).

Nonfiction All levels: activity books, multicultural, music/dance, nature/environment, religion. *Unitarian Universalism Is a Really long Name*, by Jennifer Dant (picture book, resource that answers children's' questions about Unit. Univ. ages 5-9)

How to Contact Fiction/nonfiction: query or submit outline/synopsis and 2 sample chapters. Responds to queries in 3 weeks; Publishes a book 1 year after acceptance. Will consider but prefer e-mail submissions, simultaneous submissions, and sometimes previously published work.

Terms Pays authors royalty 8% based on retail price. Pays illustrators/photographers by the project. Sends galleys to authors; dummies to illustrators. Book catalog available for SASE.

Tips "Consult our Web site."

⬛ SLEEPING BEAR PRESS

Imprint of Gale Group, 310 N. Main St.Suite 300, Chelsea MI 48118. (734)475-4411. Fax: (734)475-0787. Website: www.sleepingbearpress.com. **Manuscript Acquisitions:** Heather Hughes. **Art Acquisitions:** Jennifer Bacheller, creative director. Publishes 30 picture books/year. 10% of books by first-time authors.

Fiction Picture books: adventure, animal, concept, folktales, history, multicultural, nature/environment, religion, sports. Young readers: adventure, animal, concept, folktales, history, humor, multicultural, nature/environment, religion, sports. Average word length: picture books—1,800. Recently published *Brewster the Rooster*, by Devin Scillian; *The Orange Shoes*, by Trinka Hakes Noble; *Yatandou*, by Gloria Whelan.

Nonfiction Average word length: picture books—1,800. Recently published *D is for Drinking Gourd: An African American Alphabet*, by E.B. Lewis.

How to Contact Fiction/nonfiction: Submit complete ms or proposal. "We do not return materials, so please only submit copies. SBP will contact you if interested." Publishes book 2 years after acceptance. Will consider e-mail submissions, simultaneous submissions.

Terms Pays authors royalty. Offers advances. Pays illustrators royalty. Sends galleys to authors. Originals returned to artist at job's completion. Book catalog available. All imprints included in a single catalog. Catalog available on Web site.

Tips "Please review our book on line before sending material or calling." Editorial staff attended or plans to attend the following conferences: BEA, IRA, Regional shows, UMBE, NEBA, AASL, ALA, and numerous local conferences.

SMALLFELLOW PRESS

Imprint of Tallfellow Press, 9454 Wilshire BLVD.Suite 550, Beverly Hills, CA 90212. E-mail: tallfellow@pacbell.net. Website: www.smallfellow.com. **Manuscript/Art Acquisitions:** Claudia Sloan.

• Smallfellow no longer accepts manuscript/art submissions.

⬛ SOUNDPRINTS/STUDIO MOUSE

Soundprints and Studio Mouse are imprints of Trudy Corporation, 353 Main St.Norwalk CT 06851. Estab. 1947. (800)228-7839. Fax: (203)864-1776. E-mail: info@soundprints.com. Website: www. soundprints.com. Publishes mass market books, educational material, multicultural material. **Manuscript Acquisitions:** Jamie McCune, editorial assistant. **Art Acquisitions:** Meredith Campbell Britton, senior designer. 10% of books by first-time authors.

Fiction Picture books, young readers: adventure, animal, fantasy, history, multicultural, nature/environment, sports. Recently published Smithsonian Alphabet of Earth, by Barbie Heit Schwaeber, and illustrated by Sally Vitsky (ages preschool-2, hardcover and paperback available with audio CD); Little Black Ant on Park Street, by Janet Halfmann and illustrated by Kathleen Rietz (ages preschool-grade 3, hardcover, paperback, micro book available with plush toy and cd); Oh Where, Oh Where Has My Little Dog Gone?, edited by Laura Gates Galvin and illustrated by Erica Pelton Villnave (ages 3 and up, die-cut handle paperback book with cd).

How to Contact/Writers Query of submit complete manuscript. Responds to queries/mss in 6 months. Publishes a book 1-2 years after acceptance. Illustration Works with 3-7 illustrators/year.

Uses color artwork only. Send tearsheets with contact information, "especially Web address if applicable." Samples not returned; samples filed.

Photography Buys stock and assign work. Model/property release and captions required. Send color promo sheet.

Terms Original artwork returned at jobs completion. Catalog available on Web site. Offers writer's/ artist's/photographer's guidelines with SASE.

N SPINNER BOOKS

Imprint of University Games, 2030 Harrison St.San Francisco CA 94107. Estab. 1985. (415)503-1600. Fax: (415)503-0085. E-mail: info@ugames.com. Website: www.ugames.com. Specializes in nonfiction. **Contact:** Editorial Department. Publishes 6 young readers/ year; 6 middle readers/year. "Spinners Books publishes books of puzzles, games and trivia."

Nonfiction Picture books: Games & Puzzles. Recently published *20 Questions*, by Bob Moog (adult); *20 Questions for Kids*, by Bob Moog (young adult).

How to Contact Only interested in agented material. Nonfiction: Query. Responds to queries in 3 months; mss in 2 months. Publishes a book 6 months after acceptance. Will consider e-mail submissions.

Terms Sends galleys to authors; dummies to illustrators. Originals returned to artist at job's completion. Book catalog available on Web site: www.ugames.com

STANDARD PUBLISHING

8805 Governor's Hill Drive, Suite 400, Cincinnati OH 45249. Website: www.standardpub.com. Publishes resources that meet church and family needs in the area of children's ministry. Visit the publisher's Web site for writer's guidelines and current publishing objectives.

STARSEED PRESS

Imprint of HJ Kramer in joint venture with New World Library, P.O. Box 1082, Tiburon CA 94920. (415)435-5367. Fax: (415)435-5364. Website: www.newworldlibrary.com. **Manuscript Acquisitions:** Jan Phillips. **Art Acquisitions:** Linda Kramer, vice president. Publishes 2 picture books/year. 50% of books by first-time authors. "We publish 4-color, 32-page children's picture books dealing with self-esteem and positive values, with a non-denominational, spiritual emphasis."

Fiction Picture books: self-esteem, multicultural, nature/environment. Average word length: picture books—500-1,500. Recently published *Lucky Goose Goes to Texas*, by Holly Bea, illustrated by Joe Boddy (ages 3-10, picture book).

Nonfiction Picture books: multicultural, nature/environment.

How to Contact Fiction/nonfiction: Submit outline/synopsis. Responds to queries/mss in 10 weeks. Publishes a book 18 months after acceptance. Will consider simultaneous submissions, previously published work.

Terms Negotiates based on publisher's net receipts. Split between author and artist. Originals returned to artist at job's completion. Book catalog available for 9 × 11 SAE with $1.98 postage; ms and art guidelines available for SASE. All imprints included in a single catalog.

STONE ARCH BOOKS

7825 Telegraph Rd.Minneapolis MN 55438. (952)224-0514. Fax: (952)933-2410. Website: www.stonearchbooks.com. **Acquisitions Editor:** Michael Dahl. **Art Director:** Heather Kindseth. Specializes in "safe graphic novels and high-interest fiction for striving readers, especially boys."

Fiction Young Readers, middle readers, young adults: adventure, contemporary, fantasy, humor, light humor, mystery, science fiction, sports, suspense. Average word length: young readers-1,000-3,000; middle readers and early young adults: 5,000-10,000.

How to Contact Submit outline/synopsis and 3 sample chapters. Electronic submissions are preferred and should be sent to www.author.sub@stonearchbooks.com. Accepts simulteous submissions. Only submissions with an e-mail addresses will receive a reply.

Terms Work purchased outright from authors. Illustrators paid by the project. Title list and catalog available on web site.

Tips "A high-interest topic or activity is one that a young person would spend their free time on without adult direction or suggestion."

SYLVAN DELL PUBLISHING

976 Houston Northcutt Blvd.Suite 3, Mount Pleasant SC 29464.Estab. 2004. E-mail: donnagerman@ sylvandellpublishing.com. Website: www.sylvandellpublishing.com. **Contact**: Donna German."The books that we publish are usually, but not always, fictional stories that relate to animals, nature, the environment, and science. All books should subtly convey an educational theme through a warm story that is fun to read and that will grab a children's attention. Each book has a 3-5 page "For Creative Minds" section in the back to reinforce the educational component of the book itself. This section will have a craft and/or game as well as "fun facts" to be shared by the parent, teacher, or other adult. Authors do not need to supply this information but may be actively involved in its development if they would like. Please read about our submission guidelines on our Web site."

• Sylvan Dell only accepts electronic submissions.

Fiction Picture Books: animal, folktales, nature/environment, math-related. Word length—picture books: no more than 1500. Recently published *Whistling Wings,* by first-time author Laura Goering, illustrated by Laura Jacques; *Sort it Out!,* by Barbara Mariconda, illustrated by Sherry Rogers; *River Beds: Sleeping in the World's Rivers,* by Gail Langer Karwoski, illustrated by Connie McLennan; *Saturn for my Birthday,* by first-time author John McGranaghan, illustrated by Wendy Edelson.

How to Contact Submit complete ms. Prefers to work with authors from the US and Canada because of marketing. Responds to mss in 3-4 months. Publishes a book about 2 years after acceptance. Accepts simultaneous submissions. Accepts electronic submissions only. Snail mail submissions are discarded without being opened.

Terms Pays authors and illustrators step-up, advance royalty. "Authors and illustrators see PDFs of book as it goes to the printer. Any concerns or changes are dealt with then. We keep cover art and return all other art to illustrators." Catalog available on Web site. Writer's and artist's guidelines available on Web site.

Tips "Please make sure that you have looked at our Web site to read our complete submission guidelines and to see if we are looking for a particular subject. Manuscripts must meet all four of our stated criteria. We look for fairly realistic, bright and colorful art—no cartoons."

TANGLEWOOD BOOKS

P.O. Box 3009, Terre Haute IN 47803. E-mail: ptierney@tanglewoodbooks.com. Website: www. tanglewoodbooks.com. Estab. 2003. Specializes in trade books. **Acquisitions Editor:** Erica Bennet. **Illustrators contact:** Peggy Tierney, publisher. Produces 2-3 picture books/year, 1-2 middle readers/year, 1-2 young adult titles/year. 20% of books by first-time authors. "Tanglewood Press strives to publishh entertaining, kid-centric books."

Fiction Picture books: adventure, animal, concept, contemporary, fantasy, humor. Average word length: picture books—800. Recently published *68 Knots*, by Micheal Robert Evans (young adult); *The Mice of Bistrot des Sept Freres*, written and illustrated by Marie Letourneau; *You Can't Milk a Dancing Cow,* by Tom Dunsmuir, illustrated by Brain Jones (ages 4-8, humorous).

How to Contact Accepts international submissions. Fiction: Query with 3-5 sample chapters. Responds to mss in up to 18 months. Publishes book 2 years after acceptance. Considers simultaneous submissions.

Terms Illustrators paid by the project for covers and small illustrations; royalty of 3-5% for picture books. Author sees galleys for review. Illustrators see dummies for review. Originals returned to artist at job's completion.

Tips "Please see lengthy 'Submissions' page on our Web site."

TILBURY HOUSE, PUBLISHERS

103 Brunswick Av.Gardiner ME 04345. (207)582-1899. Fax: (207)582-8227. E-mail: karen@ tilburyhouse.com. Website: www.tilburyhouse.com. **Publisher:** Jennifer Bunting. **Children's Book Editor:** Audrey Maynard. **Associate Children's Book Editor:** Karen Fisk. Publishes 2-4 picture book/year; 1-3 young readers/year.

Fiction Picture books, young readers, middle readers: multicultural, nature/environment. Special needs include books that teach children about tolerance and honoring diversity. Recently published *GIVE a GOAT*, by Jan West Schrock; *Amadi's Snowman*, by Katia Novet Saint-Lot; *Under the Night Sky*, by Amy Lundebrek.

Nonfiction Picture books, young readers, middle readers: multicultural, nature/environment. Recently published *Just for Elephants*, by Carol Buckley; *Life Under Ice*, by Mary Cerullo, with photography by Bill Curtsinger.

How to Contact Fiction/nonfiction: Submit complete ms or outline/synopsis. Responds to queries/mss in 1 month. Publishes a book 1-2 years after acceptance. Will consider simultaneous submissions "with notification."

Terms Pays authors royalty based on wholesale price. Pays illustrators/photographers by the project; royalty based on wholesale price. Sends galleys to authors. Book catalog available for SAE and postage.

Tips "We are always interested in stories that will encourage children to understand the natural world and the environment, as well as stories with social justice themes. We really like stories that engage children to become problem solvers as well as those that promote respect, tolerance and compassion." We do not publish books with personified animal characters; historical fiction; chapter books; fantasy. d

TOR BOOKS

175 Fifth Ave.New York NY 10010-7703. Fax: (212)388-0191. E-mail: Juliet.Pederson@Tor.com. Website: www.tor-forge.com. **Contact:** Juliet Pederson, assistant to publisher, children's/YA division. Publisher: Kathleen Doherty; Senior Editor: Susan Chang. Imprints: Forge, Orb, Starscape, Tor Teen. Publishes 5-10 middle readers/year; 5-10 young adult titles/year.

- Tor Books is the "world's largest publisher of science fiction and fantasy, with strong category publishing in historical fiction, mystery, western/Americana, thriller, YA."

Fiction Middle readers, young adult titles: adventure, animal, anthology, concept, contemporary, fantasy, history, humor, multicultural, nature/environment, problem novel, science fiction, suspense/mystery. Average word length: middle readers—30,000; young adults—60,000-100,000. Published *Hidden Talents, Flip*, by David Lubar (ages 10 and up, fantasy); *Briar Rose*, by Jane Yolen (ages 12 and up).

Nonfiction Middle readers and young adult: geography, history, how-to, multicultural, nature/ environment, science, social issues. Does not want to see religion, cooking. Average word length: middle readers—25,000-35,000; young adults—70,000. Published *Strange Unsolved Mysteries*, by Phyllis Rabin Emert; *Stargazer's Guide (to the Galaxy)*, by Q.L. Pearce (ages 8-12, guide to constellations, illustrated).

How to Contact Fiction/nonfiction: Submit outline/synopsis and complete ms. Responds to queries in 1 month; mss in 6 months for unsolicited work; 1 month or less for agented submissions. Note: We do not accept electronic submissions, synopsis or querys of any kind. Do not email your inquiries.

Illustration Query with samples. Contact: Irene Gallo, art director. Responds only if interested. Samples kept on file.

Terms Pays authors royalty. Offers advances. Pays illustrators by the project. Book catalog available for 9 × 12 SAE and 3 first-class stamps. See website, www.tor-forge.com for latest submission guidelines.

Tips "Know the house you are submitting to, familiarize yourself with the types of books they are publishing. Get an agent. Allow him/her to direct you to publishers who are most appropriate. It saves time and effort."

TRICYCLE PRESS

Imprint of Ten Speed Press, P.O. Box 7123, Berkeley CA 94707. (510)559-1600. Website: www.tricyclepress.com. **Acquisitions:** Nicole Geiger, publisher. Publishes 14-18 picture books/year; 2-4 middle readers/year; 3 board books/year. 25% of books by first-time authors. Press looks for something outside the mainstream; books that encourage children to look at the world from a different angle. We publish high-quality trade books."

Fiction Board books, picture books, young readers: concept. Middle grade: literary fiction, high-quality contemporary, fantasy, history, multicultural, nature, poetry, suspense/mystery; no mass market fiction. Average word length: picture books 500-1,000. Published *Rough, Tough Charley,* by Verla Kay, illustrated by Adam Gustavson (ages 5-7, picture book); *Hey, Little Ant,* by Phillip and Hannah Hoose, illustrated by Debbie Tiley (ages 4-8, picture book); *Shifty,* by Lynn E. Hazen (12 and up, novel); *Brand New Emily,* by Ginger Rue (ages 11-14, novel).

Nonfiction Picture books, middle readers: animal, arts/crafts, biography, careers, concept, cooking, history, how-to, multicultural, music/dance, nature/environment, science. Recently published *Wild Fibonacci,* by Joy N. Hulme, illustrated by Carol Schwartz (ages 7 and up, picture book); *Salad People and More Real Recipes: A New Cookbook for Preschoolers and Up,* by Mollie Katzen; *What the World Eats,* by Peter Menzel, (all ages, nonfiction, photographic picture book).

How to Contact Submit complete ms for picture books. Submit outline/synopsis and 2-3 sample chapters for middle grade, young adult and longer nonfiction. Responds to mss in 4-6 months. Publishes a book 1-2 years after acceptance. Welcomes simultaneous submissions and previously published work. Do not send original artwork; copies only, please. No electronic or faxed submissions.

Terms Pays authors royalty of 7.5% based on net receipts. Offers advances. Pays illustrators and photographers royalty of 7.5% based on net receipts. Sends galleys of novels to authors. Book catalog for 9 × 12 SASE (3 first-class stamps). Manuscript guidelines for SASE (1 first-class stamp). Guidelines available at Web site.

Tips "We are looking for something a bit outside the mainstream and with lasting appeal (no one-shot-wonders)."

TURTLE BOOKS

866 United Nations Plaza, Suite 525, New York NY 10017. (212)644-2020. Website: www.turtlebooks.com. **Acquisitions:** John Whitman. "Turtle Books publishes only picture books for young readers. Our goal is to publish a small, select list of quality children's books each spring and fall season. As often as possible, we will publish our books in both English and Spanish editions."

- Turtle Books does a small number of books and may be slow in responding to unsolicited manuscripts.

Fiction Picture books: adventure, animal, concept, contemporary, fantasy, folktales, hi-lo, history, humor, multicultural, nature/environment, religion, sports, suspense/mystery. Recently published *The Legend of Mexicatl,* by Jo Harper, illustrated by Robert Casilla (the story of Mexicatl and the origin of the Mexican people); *Vroom, Chugga, Vroom-Vroom,* by Anne Miranda, illustrated by David Murphy (a number identification book in the form of a race car story); *The Crab Man,* by Patricia VanWest, illustrated by Cedric Lucas (the story of a young Jamaican boy who must make the difficult decision between making an income and the ethical treatment of animals); *Prairie Dog Pioneers,* by Jo and Josephine Harper, illustrated by Craig Spearing (the story of a young girl who doesn't want to move, set in 1870s Texas); *Keeper of the Swamp,* by Ann Garrett, illustrated by

Karen Chandler (a dramatic coming-of-age story wherein a boy confronts his fears and learns from his ailing grandfather the secrets of the swamp); *The Lady in the Box*, by Ann McGovern, illustrated by Marni Backer (a modern story about a homeless woman named Dorrie told from the point of view of two children); *Alphabet Fiesta*, by Anne Miranda, illustrated by young schoolchildren in Madrid, Spain (an English/Spanish alphabet story).

How to Contact Send complete ms. "Queries are a waste of time." Response time varies.

Terms Pays royalty. Offers advances.

TWO LIVES PUBLISHING

191 Water St.Ambler PA 19002. (609)502-8147. Fax: (610)717-1460. E-mail: bcombs@twolives.com. Website: www.twolives.com. **Manuscript Acquisitions:** Bobbie Combs. Publishes 1 picture book/year; 1 middle reader/year. 100% of books by first-time authors. "We create books for children whose parents are lesbian, gay, bisexual or transgender. WE ONLY want stories featuring children and their gay or lesbian parents".

Fiction Picture books, young readers, middle readers: contemporary.

How to Contact Fiction: Query. Responds to queries/mss in 3 months. Publishes book 2-3 years after acceptance. Will consider e-mail submissions, simultaneous submissions, previously published work.

Terms Pays authors royalty of 5-10% based on retail price. Offers advances (average amount: $250). Pays illustrators royalty of 5-10% based on retail price. Sends galleys to authors. Originals returned to artist at job's completion. Catalog available on Web site.

ⒶTYNDALE HOUSE PUBLISHERS, INC.

351 Executive Dr.P.O. Box 80, Wheaton IL 60189. (630)668-8300. Website: www.tyndale.com. **Manuscript Acquisitions:** Katara Washington Patton. **Art Acquisitions:** Talinda Iverson. Publishes approximately 15 Christian children's titles/year.

• Tyndale House no longer reviews unsolicited mss, only agented material.

Fiction Juvenile.

Nonfiction Bible, devotionals, Bible storybooks.

Terms Pay rates for authors and illustrators vary.

Tips "All accepted manuscripts will appeal to Evangelical Christian children and parents."

VIKING CHILDREN'S BOOKS

Penguin Group Inc.345 Hudson St.New York NY 10014-3657. (212)414-3600. Fax: (212)414-3399. Website: www.penguin.com. **Acquisitions:** Catherine Frank, executive editor (picture books, middle grade and young adult fiction, and nonfiction); Tracy Gates, associate editorial director (picture books, middle grade, and young adult fiction); Joy Peskin, executive editor (middle grade and young adult fiction); Kendra Levin, associate editor (picture books, middle grade and young adult fiction); Leila Sales, editorial assistant. **Art Acquisitions:** Denise Cronin, Viking Children's Books. Publishes hardcover originals. Publishes 60 books/year. Receives 7,500 queries/year. 25% of books from first-time authors; 33% from unagented writers. "Viking Children's Books is known for humorous, quirky picture books, in addition to more traditional fiction. We publish the highest quality fiction, nonfiction, and trade books for pre-schoolers through young adults." Publishes book 1-2 years after acceptance of artwork. Hesitantly accepts simultaneous submissions.

• Viking Children's Books is not accepting unsolicited submissions at this time.

Fiction All levels: adventure, animal, contemporary, fantasy, hi-lo, history, humor, multicultural, nature/environment, poetry, problem novels, romance, science fiction, sports, suspense/mystery. Recently published *Llama Llama Misses Mama*, by Anna Dewdney (ages 2 up, picture book); *Wintergirls*, by Laurie Halse Anderson (ages 12 and up); *Good Luck Bear*, by Greg Foley (ages 2 up); Along for the Ride, by Sarah Dessen (ages 12 up).

Nonfiction All levels: animal, biography, concept, geography, hi-lo, history multicultural, music/

dance, nature/environment, science, and sports. Recently published *The Up Close Biography series* (ages 11 up, nonfiction*); Knucklehead,* by Jon Scieszka (ages 7up, nonfiction); John Lennon: All I Want is the Truth, by Elizabeth partridge (ages 11up, nonfiction).

Illustration Works with 30 illustrators/year. Responds to artist's queries/submissions only if interested. Samples returned with SASE only or samples filed. Originals returned at job's completion.

Terms Pays 2-10% royalty on retail price or flat fee. Advance negotiable.

⚡ WALKER & COMPANY

Books for Young Readers, 175 Fifth Ave.New York NY 10010. Website: www.walkeryoungreaders. com. **Manuscript Acquisitions:** Emily Easton, publisher; Stacy Cantor, associate editor Mary Kate Castellani, asistant editor. Publishes 20 picture books/year; 5-10 nonfiction books/year; 5-10 middle readers/year; 5-10 young adult titles/year. 5% of books by first-time authors; 75% of books from agented writers.

Fiction Picture books: adventure, history, humor. Middle readers: coming-of-age, adventure, contemporary, history, humor, multicultural. Young adults: adventure, contemporary, romance, humor, historical fiction, suspense/mystery. Recently published *Gimme Cracked Corn and I Will Share*, written and illustrated by Kevin O'Malley (ages 6-10, picture book); *Revenge of the Cheerleaders*, by Janette Rallison (12 and up, teen/young adult novel). *Skinny*, by Ibi Kaslik (ages 14 and up).

Nonfiction Picture book, middle readers: biography, history. Recently published *Blue Flame*, by K.M. Grant (ages 10-14); *I, Matthew Henson*, by Carole Boston Weahterford, illustrated by Eric Velasquez (ages 7-12, picture book history); *101 Things to Do Before You're Old and Boring*, by Richard Horne (ages 12 and up). Multicultural needs include "contemporary, literary fiction and historical fiction written in an authentic voice. Also high interest nonfiction with trade appeal."

How to Contact Fiction/nonfiction: Submit outline/synopsis and sample chapters; complete ms for picture books. Send SASE for writer's guidelines.

Terms Pays authors royalty of 5-10%; pays illustrators royalty or flat fee. Offers advance payment against royalties. Original artwork returned at job's completion. Sends galleys to authors. ms guidelines for SASE.

Tips Writers: "Make sure you study our catalog before submitting. We are a small house with a tightly focused list. Illustrators: Have a well-rounded portfolio with different styles." Does not want to see folktales, ABC books, paperback series. "Walker and Company is committed to introducing talented new authors and illustrators to the children's book field."

⬜ WEIGL PUBLISHERS INC.

350 5th Ave. Suite 3304, New York NY 10118-0069. (866)649-3445. Fax: (866)449-3445. E-mail: linda@weigl.com. Website: www.weigl.com. **Manuscript/Art Acquisitions:** Heather Hudak. Publishes 25 young readers/year; 40 middle readers/year; 20 young adult titles/year. 15% of books by first-time authors. "Our mission is to provide innovative high-quality learning resources for schools and libraries worldwide at a competitive price."

Nonfiction Young readers: animal, biography, geography, history, multicultural, nature/environment, science. Middle readers: animal, biography, geography, history, multicultural, nature/environment, science, social issues, sports. Young adults: biography, careers, geography, history, multicultural, nature/environment, social issues. Average word length: young readers—100 words/page; middle readers—200 words/page; young adults—300 words/page. Recently published *Amazing Animals* (ages 9 and up, science series); *U.S. Sites and Symbols* (ages 8 and up, social studies series); *Science Q&A* (ages 9 and up, social studies series).

How to Contact Nonfiction: Query, by e-mail only. Publishes book 6-9 months after acceptance. Will consider e-mail submissions, simultaneous submissions.

Terms Work purchased outright from authors. Pays illustrators by the project. Pays photographers per photo. Originals returned to artist at job's completion. Book catalog available for 9½ × 11 SASE. Catalog available on website.

☐ WESTWINDS PRESS/ALASKA NORTHWEST BOOKS

Graphic Arts Center Publishing Company, P.O. Box 10306, Portland OR 97296-0306. (503)226-2402. Fax: (503)223-1410. E-mail: editorial@gacpc.com. Website: www.gacpc.com. Independent book packager/producer. **Writers contact:** Tim Frew, executive editor. **Illustrators contact:** same. Produces 4 picture books/year, 1-2 young readers/year. 10% of books by first-time authors. "Graphic Arts Center Publishing Company publishes and distributes regional titles through its three imprints: Graphic Arts Books, Alaska Northwest Books and WestWinds Press. GAB is known for its excellence in publishing high-end photo-essay books. Alaska Northwest, established in 1959, is the premier publisher of nonfiction Alaska books on subjects ranging from cooking, Alaska Native culture, memoir, history, natural history, reference, biography, humor and children's books. WestWinds Press, established in 1999, echoes those themes with content that focuses on the Western States."

Fiction Picture books: animal, folktales, nature/environment. Young readers: adventure, animal, folktales, nature/environment. Average word length: picture books—1,100; young readers—9,000. Recently published *Kumak's Fish*, by Michael Bania (folktale, ages 6 and up); *Sweet Dreams, Polar Bear*, by Mindy Dwyer (3 and up); *Seldovia Sam and the Sea Otter Rescue*, by Susan Springer, illustrated by Amy Meissner (adventure, beginning chapter book).

Nonfiction Picture books: animal, nature/environment. Young readers: animal, nature/environment. Middle readers: nature/environment. Average word length: picture books—1,100; young readers—9,000. Recently published *Sharkabet*, by Ray Troll (ages 5 and up); *Winter Is*, by Anne Dixon, illustrated by Mindy Dwyer (environment/nature, ages 3-6).

How to Contact Accepts international submissions. Fiction/nonfiction: Submit complete ms. Responds to queries in 3 months; mss in 6 months. Publishes book 1-2 years after acceptance. Considers simultaneous submissions, electronic submissions, previously published work. "Please include SASE for response and return of materials."

Terms Offers advance against royalties. Originals returned to artist at job's completion. All imprints included in single catalog.

WHITE MANE KIDS

Imprint of White Mane Publishing, P.O. Box 708, Shippensburg PA 17257. (717)532-2237. Fax: (717)532-6110. Website: www.whitemane.com. **Manuscript Acquisitions:** Send attention acquisitions dept.

Fiction Middle readers, young adults/teens: history. Recently published *Drumbeat: The Story of a Civil War Drummer Boy*, by Rober J. Trout; *The Witness Tree and the Shadow of the Noose: Mystery, Lies, and Spies in Manassas*, by K.E.M. Johnston

Nonfiction Middle readers, young adults: history. Recently published *Hey, History Isn't Boring Anymore! A Creative Approach to Teaching the Civil War*, by Kelly Ann Butterbaugh.

How to Contact Fiction/nonfiction: Query. Responds to queries in 1 month; mss in 3-4 months. Publishes book 12-18 months after acceptance. Will consider simultaneous submissions.

Terms Pays authors royalties. Pays illustrators by the project. Sends galleys to authors. Originals returned to artist at job's completion. Book catalog available; ms guidelines available for SASE. All imprints included in a single catalog.

Tips "We are interested in historically accurate fiction for middle and young adult readers. We do *not* publish picture books." Our primary focus is the American Civil War and some America Revolution topics.

ALBERT WHITMAN & COMPANY

6340 Oakton St, Morton Grove, IL 60053-2723. (847)581-0033. Fax: (847)581-0039. Website: www.albertwhitman.com. **Manuscript Acquisitions:** Kathleen Tucker, editor-in-chief. Art Acquisitions: Carol Gildar. Publishes 30 books/year. 20% of books by first-time authors; 15% off books from agented authors.

Fiction Picture books, young readers, middle readers: adventure, concept (to help children deal with problems), fantasy, history, humor, multicultural, suspense. Middle readers: problem novels, suspense/mystery. "We are interested in contemporary multicultural stories-stories with holiday themes and exciting distinctive novels. We publish a wide variety of topics and are interested in stories that help children deal with their problems and concerns. Does not want to see, "religion-oriented, ABCs, pop-up, romance, counting."Recently published fiction: *Three Little Gators*, by Hellen Ketteman, illustrated by Will Terry; *Peace Week in Miss Fox's Class,* by Eileen Spinelli, Ane Kennedy (Illustrator); *The Bully-Blockers Club*, by Teresa Bateman, illustrated by Jackie Urbanovic; *The Truth about Truman School*, by Dori Hillestad Butler.

Nonfiction Picture books, young readers, middle readers: animal, arts/crafts, health, history, hobbles, multicultural, music/dance, nature/environment, science, sports, special needs. Does not want to see, "religion, any books that have to be written in, or fictionalized biographies."Recently published *Abe lincoln Loved Animals*, by Ellen Jackson, illustrated by Doris Etllinger; *An Apple for Harriet Tubman* by Glennette Tilly Turner.

How to Contact Fiction/nonfiction: Submit query, outline, and sample chapter. For picture books send entire ms. Include cover letter. Responds to submissions in 4 months. Publishes a book 18 months after acceptance. Will consider simultaneous submissions "if notified."

Terms Pays author's, illustrator's, and photographer's royalties. Book catalog for 8 × 10 SAE and 3 first-class stamps.

Tips "In both picture books and nonfiction, we are seeking stories showing life in other cultures and the variety of multicultural life in the U.S. We also want fiction and nonfiction about mentally or physically challenged children-some recent topics have been autism, stuttering, and diabetes. Look up some of our books first to be sure your submission is appropriate for Albert Whitman & Co."

WILLIAMSON BOOKS

An imprint of Ideals Publications, 2636 Elm Hill Pike, Ste. 120, Nashville TN 37214. Website: www.idealsbooks.com. **Manuscript and Art Acquisitions:** Williamson Books Submission. Publishes 2-4 titles/year. 50% of books by first-time authors; 10% of books from agented authors. Publishes "very successful nonfiction series (Kids Can!® Series) on subjects such as history, science, arts/crafts, geography, diversity, multiculturalism. Little Hands® series for ages 2-6, Kaleidoscope Kids® series (age 7 and up) and Quick Starts for Kids!® series (ages 8 and up). "Our goal is to help every child fulfill his/her potential and experience personal growth."

Nonfiction Hands-on active learning books, animals, African-American, arts/crafts, Asian, biography, diversity, careers, geography, health, history, hobbies, how-to, math, multicultural, music/dance, nature/environment, Native American, science, writing and journaling. Does not want to see textbooks, picture books, fiction. "Looking for all things African American, Asian American, Hispanic, Latino, and Native American including crafts and traditions, as well as their history, biographies, and personal retrospectives of growing up in U.S. for grades pre-K-8th. We are looking for books in which learning and doing are inseparable." Recently published *Keeping Our Earth Green; Leap Into Space; China! and Big Fun Craft Book.*

How to Contact Query with annotated TOC/synopsis and 1 sample chapter. Responds to queries/mss in 4 months. Publishes book "about 1 year" after acceptance. Writers may send a SASE for guidelines or e-mail.

Terms Pays authors advance against future royalties based on wholesale price or purchases outright. Pays illustrators by the project. Pays photographers per photo. Sends galleys to authors.

Tips "Please do not send any fiction or picture books of any kind—those should go to Ideals Children's Books. Look at our books to see what we do. We're interested in interactive learning books with a creative approach packed with interesting information, written for young readers ages 3-7 and 8-14. In nonfiction children's publishing, we are looking for authors with a depth of knowledge shared with children through a warm, embracing style. Our publishing philosophy is based on the idea that all children can succeed and have positive learning experiences. Children's lasting learning experiences involve their participation."

WINDWARD PUBLISHING

An imprint of the Finney Company, 8075 215th Street West, Lakeville MN 55044. (952)469-6699. Fax: (952)469-1968. E-mail: feedback@finneyco.com. Website: www.finneyco.com. **Manuscript/Art Acquisitions:** Alan E. Krysan. Publishes 2 picture books/year; 4-6 young readers, middle readers, young adult titles/year. 50% of books by first-time authors.

Fiction Young readers, middle readers, young adults: adventure, animal, nature/environment. Recently published *Storm Codes*, by Tracy Nelson Maurer (ages 6-12, picture book); *Wild Beach*, by Marion Coste (ages 4-8, picture book).

Nonfiction Young readers, middle readers, young adults: activity books, animal, careers, nature/environment, science. Young adults: textbooks. Recently published *My Little Book of Manatees*, by Hope Irvin Marston (ages 4-8, introductions to the wonders of nature); *Space Station Science*, by Marianne Dyson (ages 8-13, science).

How to Contact Fiction: Query. Nonfiction: Submit outline/synopsis and 3 sample chapters. Responds to queries in 1 month; mss in 2 months. Publishes book 6-12 months after acceptance. Will consider simultaneous submissions and previously published work.

Terms Author's payment negotiable by project. Offers advances (average amount: $500). Illustrators and photographers payment negotiable by project. Sends galleys to authors; dummies to illustrators. Originals returned to artist at job's completion. Book catalog available for 6 × 9 SAE and 3 first-class stamps; ms guidelines available for SASE on web site, www.finneyco.com/authoring.html. Catalog mostly available on Web site.

PAULA WISEMAN BOOKS

Imprint of Simon & Schuster, 1230 Sixth Ave.New York NY 10020. (212)698-7000. Website: http://kids.simonandschuster.com/. Publishes 15 picture books/year; 4 middle readers/year; 2 young adult titles/year. 10% of books by first-time authors.

Fiction Considers all categories. Average word length: picture books—500; others standard length. Recently published *Which Puppy?*, by Kate Feiffer, illustrated by Jules Feiffer.

Nonfiction Picture books: animal, biography, concept, history, nature/environment. Young readers: animal, biography, history, multicultural, nature/environment, sports. Average word length: picture books—500; others standard length.

How to Contact Do not submit original artwork. DO NOT ACCEPT UNSOLICTED OR UNAGENTED MANUSCRIPT SUBMISSIONS.

WM KIDS

Imprint of White Mane Publishing Co.Inc.P.O. Box 708, 73 W. Burd St.Shippensburg PA 17257. (717)532-2237. Fax: (717)532-6110. E-mail: marketing@whitemane.com. Website: www.whitemane.com. Acquisitions: Harold Collier, acquisitions editor. Imprints: White Mane Books, Burd Street Press, White Mane Kids, Ragged Edge Press. Publishes 7 middle readers/year. 50% of books are by first-time authors.

Fiction Middle readers, young adults: history (primarily American Civil War). Average word length: middle readers—30,000. Does not publish picture books. Recently published *The Witness Tree and the Shadow of the Noose: Mystery, Lies, and Spies in Manassas,* by K.E.M. Johnston and *Drumbeat:*

The Story of a Civil War Drummer Boy, by Robert J. Trout (grades 5 and up).
Nonfiction Middle readers, young adults: history. Average word length: middle readers—30,000. Does not publish picture books. Recently published *Hey, History Isn't Boring Anymore! A Creative Approach to Teaching the Civil War,* by Kelly Ann Butterbaugh (young adult).
How to Contact Fiction: Query. Nonfiction: Submit outline/synopsis and 2-3 sample chapters. Responds to queries in 1 month; mss in 3 months. Publishes a book 18 months after acceptance. Will consider simultaneous submissions.
Terms Pays authors royalty of 7-10%. Pays illustrators and photographers by the project. Sends galleys for review. Originals returned to artist at job's completion. Book catalog and writer's guidelines available for SASE. All imprints included in a single catalog.

WORDSONG

815 Church St.Honesdale PA 18431. Website: www. wordsongpoetry.com. Estab. 1990. An imprint of Boyds Mills Press, Inc. 5% of books from agented writers. "We publish fresh voices in contemporary poetry."
Fiction/Nonfiction All levels: All types of quality children's poetry.
How to Contact Fiction/ nonfiction: Submit complete ms or submit through agent. Label package "Manucript Submission" and include SASE. "Please send a book-length collection of your ow n poems. Do not send an initial query." Responds in 3 months.
Terms Authors paid royalty or work purchased outright. Offers advances. Illustrators paid by the project or royalties; varies. Photographers paid by the project, per photo, or royalties; varies. Manuscripts/artist's guidelines available on Web site.
Tips "Collections of original poetry, not anthologies, are our biggest need at this time. Keep in mind that the strongest collections demonstrate a facility with multiple poetic forms. Check to see what's already on the market and on our Web site before submitting. "

WORLD BOOK, INC.

233 N. Michigan Ave.Suite 2000, Chicago IL 60601. (312)729-5800. Fax: (312)729-5600. Website: www.worldbook.com. **Manuscript Acquisitions:** Paul A. Kobasa, Editor-in-Chief. **Art Acquisitions:** Sandra Dyrlund, art/design manager. World Book, Inc. (publisher of The World Book Encyclopedia), publishes reference sources and nonfiction series for children and young adults in the areas of science, mathematics, English-language skills, basic academic and social skills, social studies, history, and health and fitness. We publish print and non-print material appropriate for children ages 3-14. WB does not publish fiction, poetry, or wordless picture books."
Nonfiction Young readers: animal, arts/crafts, careers, concept, geography, health, reference. Middle readers: animal, arts/crafts, careers, geography, health, history, hobbies, how-to, nature/ environment, reference, science. Young adult: arts/crafts, careers, geography, health, history, hobbies, how-to, nature/environment, reference, science.
How to Contact Nonfiction: Submit outline/synopsis only; no mss. Responds to queries/mss in 2 months. Unsolicited mss will not be returned. Publishes a book 18 months after acceptance. Will consider simultaneous submissions.
Terms Payment negotiated on project-by-project basis. Sends galleys to authors. Book catalog available for 9 × 12 SASE. Manuscript and art guidelines for SASE.

Canadian & International Book Publishers

While the United States is considered the largest market in children's publishing, the children's publishing world is by no means strictly dominated by the U.S. After all, the most prestigious children's book extravaganza in the world occurs each year in Bologna, Italy, at the Bologna Children's Book Fair and some of the world's most beloved characters were born in the United Kingdom (i.e., Winnie-the-Pooh and Mr. Potter).

In this section you'll find book publishers from English-speaking countries around the world from Canada, Australia, New Zealand and the United Kingdom. The listings in this section look just like the U.S. Book Publishers section; and the publishers listed are dedicated to the same goal—publishing great books for children.

Like always, be sure to study each listing and research each publisher carefully before submitting material. Determine whether a publisher is open to U.S. or international submissions, as many publishers accept submissions only from residents of their own country. Some publishers accept illustration samples from foreign artists, but do not accept manuscripts from foreign writers. Illustrators do have a slight edge in this category as many illustrators generate commissions from all around the globe. Visit publishers' Web sites to be certain they publish the sort of work you do. Visit online bookstores to see if publishers' books are available there. Write or e-mail to request catalogs and submission guidelines.

When mailing requests or submissions out of the United States, remember that U.S. postal stamps are useless on your SASE. Always include International Reply Coupons (IRCs) with your SAE. Each IRC is good for postage for one letter. So if you want the publisher to return your manuscript or send a catalog, be sure to enclose enough IRCs to pay the postage. For more help visit the United State Postal Service Web site at www.usps.com/global. Visit www.timeanddate. com/worldclock and American Computer Resources, Inc.'s International Calling Code Directory at www.the-acr.com/codes/cntrycd.htm before calling or faxing internationally to make sure you're calling at a reasonable time and using the correct numbers.

As in the rest of *Children's Writer's & Illustrator's Market*, the maple leaf ◪ symbol identifies Canadian markets. Look for International ⊛ symbol throughout *Children's Writer's & Illustrator's Market* as well. Several of the Society of Children's Book Writers and Illustrator's (SCBWI) international conferences are listed in the Conferences & Workshops section along with other events in locations around the globe. Look for more information about SCBWI's international chapters on the organization's Web site, www.scbwi.org. You'll also find international listings in Magazines and Young Writer's & Illustrator's Markets. See Useful Online Resources on page 370 for sites that offer additional international information.

◪ ANNICK PRESS LTD.

15 Patricia Ave.Toronto ON M2M 1H9 Canada. (416)221-4802. Fax: (416)221-8400. E-mail: annickpress@annickpress.com. Website: www.annickpress.com. **Creative Director:** Sheryl Shapiro. Publishes 5 picture books/year; 6 young readers/year; 8 middle readers/year; 9 young adult titles/year. 25% of books by first-time authors. "Annick Press maintains a commitment to high-quality books that entertain and challenge. Our publications share fantasy and stimulate judgment and abilities."

• Annick Press does not accept unsolicited manuscripts.

Fiction Recently published *The Apprentice's Masterpiece: A Story of Medieval Spain*, by Melanie Little, ages 12 and up; *Monks in Space,* by David Jones, ages 10-14; *Mattland,* by Hazel Hutchins and Gail Herbert, illustrated by Dusan Petricic, ages 4-7;*Baboon: A Novel*, by David Jones, (ages 10-14); *The Night Wanderer: A Native Gothic Novel*, by Drew Hayden Taylor, (ages 12 and up); *Shoe Shakes,* by Loris Lesynski, illustrated by Michael Martchenko,(picture book, ages 3-5).

Nonfiction Recently published *The Bite of the Mango*, written by Mariatu Kamara with Susan McClelland, ages 14 and up; *A Native American Thought of It: Amazing Inventions and Innovations*, by Rocky Landon with David MacDonald, Ages 9-11; *Super Crocs & Monster Wings: Modern Animals' Ancient Past*, by Claire Eamer, ages 9-12.

Terms Pays authors royalty of 5-12% based on retail price. Offers advances (average amount: $3,000). Pays illustrators royalty of 5% minimum. Originals returned to artist at job's completion. Book catalog available on Web site.

▦ BUSTER BOOKS

Imprint of Michael O'Mara Books, 16 Lion Yard, Tremadoc Rd.London SW4 7NQ United Kingdom. (44)(207)772-8643. Fax: (44)(207)819-5934 E-mail: enquiries@mombooks.com. Website: www.mombooks.com/busterbooks. "We are dedicated to providing irresistible and fun books for children of all ages. We typically publish black-and-white nonfiction for children aged 8-12 novelty titles-including doodle books."

Nonfiction Middle readers.

How to Contact Prefers synopsis and sample text over complete mss. Responds to queries/mss in 6 weeks. Will consider e-mail submissions.

Tips "We do not accept fiction submissions. Please do no send original artwork as we cannot guarantee its safety." Visit website before submitting.

▦ CHILD'S PLAY (INTERNATIONAL) LTD.

Child's Play International, Ashworth Rd.Bridgemead, Swindon, Wiltshire SN5 7YD United Kingdom. (44)(179)361-6286. Fax: (44)(179)351-2795. E-mail:office@childs-play.co. Website: www.childs-play.com. Estab. 1972. Specializes in nonfiction, fiction, educational material, multicultural material. **Manuscript Acquisitions:** Sue Baker, Neil Burden. **Art Acquisitions:** Annie Kubler, art director. Produces 30 picture books/year; 10 young readers/year; 2 middle readers/year. 20% of books by first-time authors. "A child's early years are more important than any other. This is when children learn most about the world around them and the language they need to survive and grow. Child's Play aims to create exactly the right material for this all-important time."

Fiction Picture books: adventure, animal, concept, contemporary, folktales, multicultural, nature/environment. Young readers: adventure, animal, anthology, concept, contemporary, folktales, humor, multicultural, nature/environment, poetry. Average word length: picture books—0-1,500; young readers—2,000. Recently published *The Wim Wom from the Mustard Mill*, by Polly Peters (ages 3-8, traditional tale); *Ten Little Ducks,* illustrated Airlie Anderson (ages 3-6 years, novelty); *Pick and Choose,* illustrated Anthony Lewis (ages 0-2 years, novelty board).

Nonfiction Picture books: activity books, animal, concept, multicultural, music/dance, nature/environment, science. Young readers: activity books, animal, concept, multicultural, music/dance, nature/environment, science. Average word length: picture books—2,000; young readers—3,000. Recently published *Roly Poly Discovery,* by Kees Moerbeek (ages 3 + years, novelty).

How to Contact/Writers Accepts international submissions. Fiction/nonfiction: Query or submit complete ms. Responds to queries in 10 weeks; mss in 15 weeks. Publishes book 2 years after acceptance. Considers simultaneous submissions, electronic submissions.

Terms Work purchased outright from authors (range: $500-15,000). Pays illustrators by the project (range: $500-15,000). Author sees galleys for review. Originals not returned. Catalog on Web site. Offers writer's, artist's guidelines for SASE.

Tips "Look at our Web site to see the kind of work we do before sending. Do not send cartoons. We do not publish novels. We do publish lots of books with pictures of babies/toddlers."

▣ CHRISTIAN FOCUS PUBLICATIONS

Geanies House, Tain Ross-shire IV20 1TW, Scotland, UK. Estab. 1975. 44 (0) 1862 871 011. Fax: 44 (0) 1862 871 699. E-mail: info@christianfocus.com. Website: www.christianfocus.com. Specializes in Christian material, nonfiction, fiction, educational material. **Manuscript Acquisitions:** Catherine Mackenzie. Publishes 4-6 picture books/year; 4-6 young readers/year; 10-15 middle readers/year; 4-6 for young adult books/year. 2% of books by first-time authors.

Fiction Picture books, young readers, adventure, history, religion. Middle readers: adventure, problem novels, religion. Young adult/teens: adventure, history, problem novels religion. Average word length: young readers—5,000; middle readers—max 10,000; young adult/teen—max 20,000. Recently published *Back Leg of a Goat,* by Penny Reeve, illustrated by Fred Apps (middle reader Christian/world issues); *Trees in the Pavement, by* Jennifer Grosser (teen fiction/Christian/Islamic and multicultural issues); *The Duke's Daughter*, by Lachlan Mackenzie; illustrated by Jeff Anderson (young reader folk tale/Christian).

Nonfiction All levels: activity books, biography, history, religion, science. Average word length: picture books—2-5,000; young readers—5,000; middle readers—5,000-10,000; young adult/ teens-10,000-20,000. Recently published *Moses the Child—Kept by God*, by Carine Mackenzie, illustrated by Graham Kennedy (young reader, bible story); *Hearts and Hands—History Lives vol. 4,* by Mindy Withrow, cover illustration by Jonathan Williams (teen, church history); *Little Hands Life of Jesus,* by Carine Mackenzie, illustrated by Rafaella Cosco (picture book, bible stories about Jesus).

How to Contact Fiction/nonfiction: Query or submit outline/synopsis submit outline/synopsis and 3 sample chapters. Responds to queries in 2 weeks/mss in 3 months. Publishes 1 year after acceptance. Will consider electronic submissions and previously published work.

Terms Authors: "We do not discuss financial details of this type in public. Contracts can vary depending on the needs of author/publisher. Illustrators/Photographers: "Each project varies—we determine our budget by determining possible sales—but each illustrator is paid a fee. Originals generally are not returned. We keep them on file so that we can rescan if necessary in the future but they may be sent back to the artist on the proviso that we will be able to obtain them again for the future reprints if necessary. For catalog visit our Web site at www.christianfocus.com."Writers and artists are available for SASE.

Tips "Be aware of the international market as regards writing style/topics as well as illustration styles. Our company sells rights to European as well as Asian countries. Fiction sales are not as good as they were. Christian fiction for youngsters is not a product that is performing well in comparison to non-fiction such as Christian Biography/bible stories/church history etc."

▣ COTEAU BOOKS LTD.

2517 Victoria Ave.Regina SK S4P 0T2 Canada. (306)777-0170. E-mail: coteau@coteaubooks.com. Website: www.coteaubooks.com. **Acquisitions:** Acquistion editor. Publishes 6 juvenile and/or young adult books/year; 14-16 books/year; 25% of books by first-time authors. "Coteau Books publishes the finest Canadian fiction, poetry, drama and children's literature, with an emphasis on western writers."

• Coteau Books publishes Canadian writers and illustrators only; mss from the U.S. are returned unopened.

Fiction Young readers, middle readers, young adults: adventure, contemporary, fantasy, history, humor, multicultural, nature/environment, science fiction, suspense/mystery. "No didactic, message pieces, nothing religious, no horror. No picture books. Recently published *New: Run Like Jaäger*, by Karen Bass (ages 15 and up); *Longhorns & Outlaws*, by Linda Aksomitis (ages 9 and up); *Graveyard of the Sea*, by Penny Draper (ages 9 and up).

Nonfiction Young readers, middle readers, young adult/teen: biography, history, multicultural, nature/environment, social issues.

How to Contact Fiction: Submit complete ms or sample chapters to acquisitions editor. No e-mail submissions or queries. Include SASE. Responds to queries/mss in 4 months. Publishes a book 1-2 years after acceptance.

Terms Pays authors royalty based on retail price. Pays illustrators and photographers by the project. Sends galleys to authors; dummies to illustrators. Original artwork returned at job's completion. Book catalog free on request with 9 × 12 SASE.

Tips "Truthfully, the work speaks for itself! Be bold. Be creative. Be persistent! There is room, at least in the Canadian market, for quality novels for children, and at Coteau, this is a direction we will continue to take."

⊞ Ⓐ EMMA TREEHOUSE

Treehouse Children's Books, The Studio, Church Street, Nunney, Somerset BA11 4LW, United Kingdom. (44)(373)836-233. Fax: (44)(373)836-299. E-mail: sales@emmatreehouse.com. Website: www.emmatreehouse.com. Estab. 1992. Publishes mass market books, trade books. We are an independent book packager/producer. **Manuscript Acquisitions:** David Bailey, director. **Art Acqusitions:** Richard Powell, creative director. Imprints: Treehouse Children's Books. Produces 100 young readers/year.

Fiction Picture books: adventure, animal, concept, folktales, humor.

Nonfiction Picture books: activity books, animal, concept.

How to Contact Only interested in agented material. Accepts international submissions. Fiction: Submit outline/synopsis. Nonfiction: Submit complete ms. Responds to queries in 3 weeks. No simultaneous, electronic, or previously published submissions.

Terms Work purchased outright. Pays illustrators by the project. Illustrators see dummies for review. Catalog available for SASE. All imprints included in single catalog.

⊞ DAVID FICKLING BOOKS

31 Beaumont St.Oxford OX1 2NP United Kingdom. (018)65-339000. Fax: (018)65-339009. E-mail: tburgess@randomhouse.co.uk. Website: www.avidficklingbooks.co.uk/. Publishes 12 fiction titles/year.

Fiction Considers all categories. Recently published *Once Upon a Time in the North*, by Phillip Pullman; *The Curious Incident of the Dog in the Night-time*, by Mark Haddon; *The Boy in the Striped Pyjamas*, by John Boyne.

How to Contact Submit 3 sample chapters to David Fickling. Please send submission rather than query letter. Responds to mss in approx. Three months.

▣ FITZHENRY & WHITESIDE LTD.

195 Allstate Pkwy.Markham ON L3R 4T8 Canada. (905)477-9700. Fax: (905)477-9179. E-mail: gailwinskill@fitzhenry.ca. Website: www.fitzhenry.ca. Book publisher. **President:** Sharon Fitzhenry; Children's Publisher: Gail Winskill. Publishes 3 picture books/year; 4 middle novels/year; 3 young adult titles/year; 3 juvenile nonfiction titles/year. 10% of books by first-time authors. Publishes fiction and nonfiction—social studies, visual arts, biography, environment. Emphasis on Canadian authors and illustrators, subject or perspective.

How to Contact Fiction/nonfiction. Publishes a book 12-24 months after acceptance. See full submission guidelines on Web site www.fitzhenry.com.

Terms Pays authors 8-10% royalty with escalations. Offers "respectable" advances for picture books, 50/50 splite between author and illustrator. Pays illustrators by the project and royalty. Pays photographers per photo. Sends galleys to authors; dummies to illustrators.

Tips "We respond to quality."

N ⊞ FRANCES LINCOLN CHILDREN'S BOOKS

Frances Lincoln. 4 Torriano Mew, Torriano Ave.London NW5 2RZ. +00442072844009. E-mail: flcb@franceslincoln.com. Website: www.franceslincoln.com. Estab. 1977. Specializes in trade books, nonfiction, fiction, multicultural material. **Manuscript Acquisitions:** Emily Sharatt, editor assistant. **Art Acquisitions:** Jane Donald, designer. Publishes 84 picture books/year; 2 young readers/year; 11 middle readers/year; 2 young adult titles/readers; 6% of books by first-time authors. "Our company was founded by Frances Lincoln in 1977. We published our first books two years later, and we have been creating illustrated books of the highest quality ever since, with special emphasis on gardening, walking and the outdoors, art, architecture, design and landscape. In 1983 we started to publish illustrated books for children. Since then we have won many awards and prizes with both fiction and non-fiction children's books.

Fiction Picture books, young readers, middle readers, young adults: adventure, animal, anthology, fantasy, folktales, health, history, humor, multicultural, nature/environment, special needs, sports. Average word length: picture books—1,000; young readers— 9,788; middle readers— 20,653; young adults— 35,407. Recently published *The Sniper*, by James Riordan (young adult/teen novel); *Amazons! Women Warriors of the World*, by Sally Pomme Clayton, illustrated by Sophie Herxheimer (picture book);*Young Inferno*, by John Agard, illustrated by Satoshi Kitamura (graphic novel/picture book).

Nonfiction Picture books, young readers, middle readers, young adult: activity books, animal, biography, careers, cooking, graphic novels, history, multicultural, nature/environment, religion, social issues, special needs. Average word length: picture books—1,000; middle readers—29,768. Recently published *Tail-End Charlie*, by Mick Manning and Brita Granstroöm. (picture book); *Our World of Water*, by Beatrice Hollyer, with photographers by Oxfam (picture book); *Look! Drawing the Line in Art*, by Gillian Wolfe (picture book).

How to Contact Fiction/nonfiction: Submit query (by e-mail- letter queries are rarely responded to). Responds as soon as possible; mss in minimum 6 weeks. Publishes a book 18 months after acceptance. Will consider e-mail submissions, simultaneous submissions, and previously published work.

Terms Pays authors royalty. Offers advances. Originals returned to artist at job's completion. Catalog available on Web site.

◪ GROUNDWOOD BOOKS

110 Spadina.Suite 801, Toronto ON M5V 2K4 Canada. (416)363-4343. Fax: (416)363-1017. Website: www.groundwoodbooks.com. **Manuscript Acquisitions:** Acquisitions Editor. **Art Acquisitions:** Art Director. Publishes 10 picture books/year; 3 young readers/year; 5 middle readers/year; 5 young adult titles/year, approximately 2 nonfiction titles/year. 10% of books by first-time authors. Non-fiction: Recently published *Off to War*, by Deborah Ellis (9+); *Children of War*, by Deborah Ellis (12+); *Groundwork Guides Cities*, by John Lorinc; *Slavery Today*, by Kevin Bales and Becky Cornell. Picture Books: Recently published *The Sleeping Porch*, by Ian Wallace (ages 4-7), *Abuelos*, by Pat Mora, illustrated by Amelia Lau Carling and *Oloyou*, by Teresa Cardenas, illustrated by Margaria Sada, translated by Elisa Amado.

Fiction Recently published *The Shepherd's Granddaughter*, by Anne Laurel Carter (y/a);*The Saver*, by Edeet Ravel (y/a).

How to Contact Fiction: Submit synopsis and sample chapters. Responds to mss in 6-8 months. Will consider simultaneous submissions.

Terms Offers advances. Pays illustrators by the project for cover art; otherwise royalty. Sends galleys to authors; dummies to illustrators. Originals returned to artist at job's completion. Backlist available on Web site.

Tips "Try to familiarize yourself with our list before submitting to judge whether or not your work is appropriate for Groundwood. Visit our Web site for guidelines."

🌐 🗋 🎞 HINKLER BOOKS

45-55 Fairchild St.Heatherton, Victoria Australia 3202. (61)(3)9552-1333. Fax: (61)(3)9552-2566. E-mail: tracey.ahern@hinkler.com.au. Website: www.hinklerbooks.com. **Acquisitions:** Tracey Ahern, publisher. "Hinkler Books publishes quality books affordable to the average family."

🌀 🅰 KEY PORTER BOOKS

6 Adelaide St. E, Toronto ON M5C 1H6 Canada. (416)862-7777. Fax: (416)862-2304. E-mail: info@ keyporter.com. Website: www.keyporter.com. Book publisher. Key Porter Books is the largest independent, 100% Canadian-owned trade publisher.

Fiction Picture books: biographies, memoirs. Middle readers, young adult: adventure, anthology, sports. Recently published *Shooting Water*, by Devyani Saltzman; *Duty: The Life of a Cop*; by Julian Fantino with Jerry Amernic; *Consequences,* by Penelope Lively; *Last Sam's Cage*, by David A. Poulsen; *The Alchemist's Dream* and *Where Soldiers Lie*, by John Wilson; *The Feathered Cloak*, by Sean Dixon; *Rink of Dreams* and *So Long, Jackie Robinson*, by Nancy L.M. Russell; *Past Crimes*, by Carol Matas; *Carew*, by J. C. Mills; *Sundancer*, by Shelley Peterson; *Alligator Tales: Alligator Pie*, by Dennis Lee, illustrated by Nora Hilb (board book).

Nonfiction Picture books: animal, arts/crafts, cooking, geography, nature/environment, reference, science. Middle readers: animal, nature/environment, reference, science. Recently published *Taken by Storm*, by Christopher Essex and Ross McKitrick; *Sharkwater*. by Rob Stewart; *Dancing Elephants & Floating Continents*, by John Wilson; *Being a Girl*, by Kim Cattrall.

How to Contact Only interested in agented material; no unsolicited mss. "Although Key Porter Books does not review unsolicited manuscript submissions, we do try and review queries and proposals." Responds to queries/proposals in 6 months.

Tips "Please note that all proposals and accompanying materials will be discarded unless sufficient postage has been provided for their return. Please do not send any original artwork or other irreplaceable materials. We do not accept responsibility for any materials you submit."

🌀 KIDS CAN PRESS

29 Birch Ave.Toronto ON M4V 1E2 Canada. E-mail: info@kidscan.com. Website: www.kidscanpress. com. **Manuscript Acquisitions**: Acquisitions Editor. Art Acquisitions: **Art Director**. Publishes 6-10 picture books/year; 10-15 young readers/year; 2-3 middle readers/year; 2-3 young adults/year. 10-15% of books by first-time authors.

- Kids Can Press is currently accepting unsolicited manuscripts from Canadian adult authors only.

Fiction Picture books, young readers: concepts. We do not accept young adult fiction or fantasy novels for any age. adventure, animal, contemporary, folktales, history, humor, multicultural, nature/environment, special needs, sports, suspense/mystery. Average word length: picture books 1,000-2,000; young readers 750-1,500; middle readers 10,000-15,000; young adults over 15,000. Recently published *Rosie & Buttercup*, by Chieri Ugaki, illustrated by Shephane Jorisch (picture book); *The Landing*, by John Ibbitson (novel); *Scaredy Squirrel*, by Melanie Watt, illustrated by Melanie Watt, (picture book).

Nonfiction Picture books: activity books, animal, arts/crafts, biography, careers, concept, health, history, hobbies, how-to, multicultural, nature/environment, science, social issues, special needs, sports. Young readers: activity books, animal, arts/crafts, biography, careers, concept, history, hobbies, how-to, multicultural. Middle readers: cooking, music/dance. Average word length: picture books 500-1,250; young readers 750-2,000; middle readers 5,000-15,000. Recently published *The Kids Book of Canadian Geography*, by Jane Drake and Ann Love, illustrated by Heather Collins, written and illustrated by Briony Penn (informational activity); *Science, Nature, Environment*; *Moving Day*, by Pamela Hickman, illustrated by Geraldo Valerio (animal/nature); *Everywear*, by Ellen Warwick, illustrated by Bernice Lum (craft book).

How to Contact Fiction/nonfiction: Submit outline/synopsis and 2-3 sample chapters. For picture books submit complete ms. Responds in 6 months only if interested. Publishes a book 18-24 months after acceptance.

🌐 KOALA BOOKS

P.O. Box 626, Mascot NSW 1460 Australia. (61)02 9667-2997. Fax: (61)02 9667-2881. E-mail: admin@koalabooks.com.au. Website: www.koalabooks.com.au. **Manuscript Acquisitions:** Children's Editor. Art Acquisitions: Children's Designer, deb@koalabooks.com.au. **KOALA** Books is an independent wholly Australian-owned children's book publishing house. Our strength is providing quality books for children at competitive prices.

How to Contact Accepts material from residents of Australia only. Hard copy only. Picture books only: Submit complete ms, blurb, brief author biography, list of author's published works. Also SASE large enough for ms return. Responds to mss in 3 months.

Terms Pays authors royalty of 10% based on retail price or work purchased outright occasionally (may be split with illustrator).

Tips a look at our Web site to get an idea of the kinds of books we publish. A few hours research in a quality children's bookshop would be helpful when choosing a publisher."

🌐 LITTLE TIGER PRESS

Imprint of Magi Publications, 1 The Coda Centre, 189 Munster Rd.London SW6 6AW, United Kingdom. (44)20-7385 6333. Fax: (44)20 7385 7333. Website: www.littletigerpress.com. "Our aim is to create beautiful books that our readers will love as much as we do, helping them develop a passion for books that offer laughter, comfort, learning or exhilarating flights of the imagination!";

Fiction Picture books: animal, concept, contemporary, humor. Average word length: picture books - 750 words or less. Recently published Sylvia and Bird, By Catherine Rayner (ages 4-7, picture book); Little Bear's Big Jumper, by David Bedford and Caroline Pedler (ages 4-7, touch-and-feel, picture book).

Tips "Every reasonable care is taken of the manuscripts and samples we receive, but we cannot accept responsibility for any loss or damage. Try to read or look at as many books on the Little Tiger Press list before sending in your material. Refer to our website www.littletigerpress.com for further details."

▣ LOBSTER PRESS

1620 Sherbrooke St. W.Suites C&D, Montreal QC H3H 1C9 Canada. (514)904-1100. Fax: (514)904-1101. E-mail: editoria@lobsterpress.com. Website: www.lobsterpress.com. **Editorial Director**: Meghan Nolan. Publishes picture books, young readers and YA fiction and nonfiction. "Driven by a desire to produce quality books that bring families together." **Lobster Press is currently accepting manuscripts and queries for everything except picture books.**

Fiction Young readers, middle readers, young adults: adventure, animal, contemporary, health, history, literary, multicultural, nature/environment, special needs, sports, suspense/mystery, science fiction, historical fiction, teen issues. Average word length: picture books—200-1,000. Average word length: middle, YA readers—40,000-70,000. Recently published When I Visited the Farm, written and illustrated by Crystal Beshara (picture book, 3-5); Grim Hill; The Forgotten Secret (ages 9 +); If You Live Like Me, by Lori Weber (novel, 13 +).

Nonfiction Young readers, middle readers and adults/teens: animal, biography, Canadian history/ culture, careers, geography, hobbies, how-to, multicultural, nature/environment, references, science, self-help, social issues, sports, travel. Recently published Our *Powerful Planet: The Curious Kid's guide to Tornadoes, Earthquakes, and other Phenomena*, by Tim O'Shei (ages 8 +); *Pier 21: Stories from Near & Far*, by Anne Renaud (ages 8 +).

How to Contact "Please address all submissions to Editorial, Lobster Press and specify the genre of your work on the envelope; e-mailed or faxed submissions will not be considered. No editorial comment will be forthcoming unless Lobster Press feels that a manuscript is publishable."

Terms Pays authors 5-10% royalty based on retail price. Original artwork returned to artist at job's completion. Writer's and artist's guidelines available on Web site.

🌐 MANTRA LINGUA

Global House, 303 Ballards Lane, London N12 8NP United Kingdom. (44)(208)445-5123. Website: www.mantralingua.com. **Manuscript Acquisitions:** Series Editor. Mantra Lingua "multicultural resources and innovative technologies to support teachers and children."

- Mantra Lingua publishes dual-language books in English and more that 42 languages. They also publish talking books and resources with their Talking Pen technology, which brings sound and interactivity to thier products. They will consider good contemporary stories, myths and folklore for picture books only.

Fiction Picture books, young readers, middle readers: folktales, multicultural stories, myths. Average word length: picture books—1,000-1,500; young readers—1,000-1,500. Recently published *Keeping Up With Cheetah*, by Lindsay Camp, illustrated by Jill Newton (ages 3-7); *Lion Fables*, by Heriette Barkow, illustrated by Jago Ormerod (ages 6-10).

How to Contact Fiction: Submit outline/synopsis (250 words); mail submissions. Include SASE if you'd like ms returned.

⬆ MOOSE ENTERPRISE BOOK & THEATRE PLAY PUBLISHING

Imprint of Moose Hide Books, 684 Walls Rd.Sault Ste. Marie ON P6A 5K6 Canada. E-mail: mooseenterprises@on.aibn.com. Website: www.moosehidebooks.com. **Manuscript Acquisitions:** Edmond Alcid. Publishes 2 middle readers/year; 2 young adult titles/year. 75% of books by first-time authors. Editorial philosophy: "To assist the new writers of moral standards."

- This publisher does not offer payment for stories published in its anthologies and/or book collections. Be sure to send a SASE for guidelines.

Fiction Middle readers, young adults: adventure, fantasy, humor, suspense/mystery, story poetry. Recently published *Realm of the Golden Feather*, by C.R. Ginter (ages 12 and up, fantasy); *Tell Me a Story*, short story collection by various authors (ages 9-11, humor/adventure); *Spirits of Lost Lake*, by James Walters (ages 12 and up, adventure); *Rusty Butt—Treasure of the Ocean Mist*, by R.E. Forester.

Nonfiction Middle readers, young adults: biography, history, multicultural.

How to Contact Fiction/nonfiction: Query. Responds to queries in 1 month; mss in 3 months. Publishes book 1 year after acceptance. Will consider simultaneous submissions.

Terms Pays royalties.Originals returned to artist at job's completion. Manuscript and art guidelines available for SASE.

Tips "Do not copy trends, be yourself, give me something new, something different."

⬆ ORCA BOOK PUBLISHERS

1016 Balmoral St.Victoria BC V8T 1A8 Canada. (250)380-1229. Fax: (250)380-1892. Website: www. orcabook.com. **Acquisitions:** Christi Howes, children's book editor (young readers); Andrew Wooldridge, editor (Orca Soundings); Bob Tyrrell, editor (teen fiction); Sarah Harvey, editor (juvenile fiction); Melanie Jeffs, editor (Orca Currents). Publishes 7 picture books/year; 16 middle readers/year; 10 young adult titles/year. 25% of books by first-time authors.

- Orca only considers authors who are Canadian or who live in Canada.

Fiction Picture books: animals, contemporary, history, nature/environment. Middle readers: contemporary, history, fantasy, nature/environment, problem novels, graphic novels. Young adults: adventure, contemporary, hi-lo (Orca Soundings), history, multicultural, nature/environment, problem novels, suspense/mystery, graphic novels. Average word length: picture books—500-1,500; middle readers—20,000-35,000; young adult—25,000-45,000; Orca Soundings—13,000-15,000; Orca Currents—13,000-15,000. Published *Tall in the Saddle*, by Anne Carter, illustrated by David McPhail (ages 4-8, picture book); *Me and Mr. Mah*, by Andrea Spalding, illustrated by Janet Wilson (ages 5 and up, picture book); *Alone at Ninety Foot*, by Katherine Holubitsky (young adult).

How to Contact Fiction: Submit complete ms if picture book; submit outline/synopsis and 3 sample chapters. "All queries or unsolicited submissions should be accompanied by a SASE." Responds to queries in 2 months; mss in 3 months. Publishes a book 18-36 months after acceptance. Submission guidelines available online.

Terms Pays authors royalty of 5% for picture books, 10% for novels, based on retail price. Offers advances (average amount: $2,000). Pays illustrators royalty of 5% minimum based on retail price and advance on royalty. Sends galleys to authors. Original artwork returned at job's completion if picture books. Book catalog available for SASE with $2 first-class postage. Manuscript guidelines available for SASE. Art guidelines not available.

Tips "We are not seeking seasonal stories, board books, or 'I Can Read' Books. Orca Sounding/ Currents lines offer high interest teen novels aimed at reluctant readers. The story should reflect the universal struggles young people face, but need not be limited to 'gritty' urban tales. Can include adventure, mystery/suspense, fantasy, etc. There's a definite need for humorous stories that appeal to boys and girls. Protagonists are between 14 and 17 years old."

⊞ PICCADILLY PRESS

5 Castle Rd.London NW1 8PR United Kingdom. (44)(207)267-4492. Fax: (44)(207)267-4493. E-mail: books@piccadillypress.co.uk Website: www.piccadillypress.co.uk.

Fiction Picture books: animal, contemporary, fantasy, nature/environment.Young adults: contemporary, humor, problem novels. Average word length: picture books-500-1,000; young adults-25,000-35,000. Recently published *Saxby Smart: Private Detective- The Hangman's Lair and other case files,* by Simon Cheshire (young adult); *Mates, Dates the Secret Story,* by Cathy Hopkins (young adult); *Hattori Hachi: The Revenge of Praying Mantis*, by Jane Prowse (young adult); Where's the Bus?, by Eileen Browne and James Croft (picture book).

Nonfiction Young adults: self help (humorous). Average word length: young adults-25,000-35,000. Recently published *Mates, Dates & Saving the Planet a girl's guide to going green*, by Cathy Hopkins; *Totally Pants A brilliant guide to boys'bits*, by Tricia Kreitman, Dr. Neil Simpson, Dr. Rosemary Jones.

How to Contact Fiction: Submit complete ms for picture books or submit outline/synopsis and 2 sample chapters for YA. Enclose a brief cover letter and SASE for reply. Nonfiction: Submit outline/ synopsis and 2 sample chapters. Responds to mss in approximately 6 weeks.

Tips "Keep a copy of your manuscript on file."d

⊞ PIPERS' ASH LTD.

Church Rd.Christian Malford, Chippenham Wiltshire SN15 4BW United Kingdom. (44) (124) 972-0563. E-mail: pipersash@supamasu.com. Website: www.supamasu.com. **Manuscript Acquisitions:** Manuscript Evaluation Desk. Publishes 1 middle reader/year; 2 young adult titles/ year. 90% of books by first-time authors. Editorial philosophy is "to discover new authors with talent and potential."

Fiction Young readers, middle readers: adventure. Young adults: problem novels. Average word length: young readers—10,000; middle readers—20,000; young adults—30,000. Visit Web site.

Nonfiction Young readers: history, multicultural, nature/environment. Middle readers: biography, history, multicultural, nature/environment, sports. Young adults: self help, social issues, special needs. Average word length: young readers—10,000; middle readers—20,000; young adults—30,000.

How to Contact Fiction/nonfiction: Query. Responds to queries in 1 week; mss in 3 months. Publishes book 2 months after acceptance. Will consider e-mail submissions, previously published work.

Terms Pays authors royalty of 10% based on wholesale price. Sends galleys to authors. Offers ms guidelines for SASE. "Include adequate postage for return of manuscript plus publisher's guidelines."

Tips "Visit our Web site—note categories open to writers and word link to pages of submission guidelines."

🌐 MATHEW PRICE LTD.

E-mail: mathewp@mathewprice.com. Website: www.mathewprice.com. **Manuscript Acquisitions:** Mathew Price, chairman. Publishes 2 picture books/year; 2 young readers/year; 3 novelties/year; 1 gift book/year. Looking especially for stories for 2- to 4-year-olds. "Mathew Price Ltd. works to bring to market talented authors and artists profitably by publishing books for children that lift the hearts of people young and old all over the world."

Fiction Will consider any category.

Terms Originals returned to artist at job's completion. Book catalog available. All imprints included in a single catalog. Catalog available on Web site.

Tips "Study the market, keep a copy of all your work, and include a SAE if you want materials returned."

🌐 QED PUBLISHING

Quarto Publishing plc, 226 City Road, London EC1V 2TT United Kingdom. (44)(207)812-8600. Fax: (44)(207)253-4370. E-mail: zetad@quarto.com and AmandaA@quarto.com. Website: www.qed-publishing.co.uk. Estab. 2003. Specializes in trade books, educational material, multicultural material. **Manuscripts Acquisitions:** Amanda Askew, managing editor. **Art Acquisitions:** Zeta Davies, creative director. Produces 8 picture books/year; 20 nonfiction readers/year, 40 general reference book/year. Strives for "editorial excellence with ground-breaking design."

Fiction Average word length: picture books—500; young readers—3,000; middle readers—3,500. Recently published *The Tickety Tale Teller*, by Maureen Haselhurst, illustrated by Barbara Vagnozzi (ages 4+); *The Thief of Bracken Farm*, by Emma Barnes, illustrated by Hannah Wood (ages 4+); *The Big Fuzzy*, by Caroline Castle, illustrated by Daniel Howarth (ages 4+).

Nonfiction Picture books: animal, arts/crafts, biography, geography, reference, science. Young readers: activity books, animal, arts/crafts, biography, geography, reference, science. Middle readers: activity books, animal, arts/crafts, biography, geography, science. Average word length: picture books—500; young readers—3,000; middle readers—3,500. Recently published *Exploring the Earth*, by Peter Grego (ages 7 and up); *The Ancient Egyptians*, by Fiona Macdonald (ages 7+, science); *The Great Big Book of Pirated,* by John Malam (ages 7+, history).

How to Contact Fiction/nonfiction: Query.

Tips "Be persistent."

🌐 RANDOM HOUSE CHILDREN'S BOOKS

61-63 Uxbridge Rd. London W5 5SA England. (44)(208)579-2652. Fax: (44)(208)579-5479. E-mail: enquiries@randomhouse.co.uk. Website: www.kidsatrandomhouse.co.uk. Book publisher. **Manuscript Acquisitions:** Philippa Dickinson, managing director. Imprints: Doubleday, Corgi, Johnathan Cape, Hutchinson, Bodley Head, Red Fox, David Fickling Books, Tamarind Books. Publishes 120 picture books/year; 120 fiction titles/year.

Fiction Picture books: adventure, animal, anthology, contemporary, fantasy, folktales, humor, multicultural, nature/environment, poetry, suspense/mystery. Young readers: adventure, animal, anthology, contemporary, fantasy, folktales, humor, multicultural, nature/environment, poetry, sports, suspense/mystery. Middle readers: adventure, animal, anthology, contemporary, fantasy, folktales, humor, multicultural, nature/environment, problem novels, romance, sports, suspense/mystery. Young adults: adventure, contemporary, fantasy, humor, multicultural, nature/environment, problem novels, romance, science fiction, suspense/mystery. Average word length: picture books—800; young readers—1,500-6,000; middle readers—10,000-15,000; young adults—20,000-45,000.

How to Contact Only interested in agented material. No unsolicited mss or picture books.

Terms Pays authors royalty. Offers advances. Pays illustrators by the project or royalty. Pays photographers by the project or per photo.

Tips "Although Random House is a big publisher, each imprint only publishes a small number of books each year. Our lists for the next few years are already full. Any book we take on from a previously unpublished author has to be truly exceptional. Manuscripts should be sent to us via literary agents."

⚅ RED DEER PRESS

195 Allstate Parkway, Markham ON L9P 1R4 Canada. (800)-387-9776/(905)477-9700. Fax: (800)260-9777/(905)477-2834. E-mail: rdp@reddeerpress.com. Website: www.reddeerpress.com. **Manuscript/Art Acquisitions:** Peter Carver, children's editor. Publishes 3 to 5 picture books/year; 4 young adult titles/year per season. Red Deer Press is known for their "high-quality international children's program that tackles risky and/or serious issues for kids."

• Red Deer only publishes books written and illustrated by Canadians.

Fiction Picture books, young readers: adventure, contemporary, fantasy, folktales, history, humor, multicultural, nature/environment, poetry. Middle readers, young adult/teens: adventure, contemporary, fantasy, folktales, hi-lo, history, humor, multicultural, nature/environment, problem novels, suspense/mystery. Recently published *Egghead*, by Caroline Pignat; *Dooley Takes the Fall*, by Norah McClintock; *The End of The World As We Know It*, by Lesley Choyce.

How to Contact Fiction/nonfiction: Query or submit outline/synopsis. Responds to queries in 2 months; mss in 8 months. Publishes a book 18 months after acceptance.

Terms Pays authors royalty (negotiated). Advances (negotiated). Pays illustrators and photographers by the project or royalty (depends on the project). Sends galleys to authors. Originals returned to artist at job's completion. Guidelines not available on Web site.

Tips "Writers, illustrators, and photographers should familiarize themselves with Red Deer Press's children's publishing program, including the kinds of books we do and do not publish."

⚅ RONSDALE PRESS

3350 W. 21st Ave.Vancouver BC V6S 1G7 Canada. (604)738-4688. Fax: (604)731-4548. E-mail: ronsdale@shaw.ca. Website: ronsdalepress.com. Estab. 1988. Book publisher. **Manuscript/Art Acquisitions:** Veronica Hatch, children's editor. Publishes 3 children's books/year. 40% of titles by first-time authors. "Ronsdale Press is a Canadian literary publishing house that publishes 12 books each year, three of which are children's titles. Of particular interest are books involving children exploring and discovering new aspects of Canadian history."

Fiction Young adults: Canadian historical novels. Average word length: middle readers and young adults—50,000. Recently published *Red Goodwin*, by John Wilson (ages 10-14); *Tragic Links*, by Cathy Beveridge (ages 10-14); *Dark Times*, edited by Ann Walsh (anthology of short stories, ages 10 and up); *Rosie's Dream Cape*, by Zelda Freedman (ages 8-14); *The Way Lies North*, by Jean Rae Baxter (ages 10-14).

Nonfiction Middle readers, young adults: animal, biography, history, multicultural, social issues. Average word length: young readers—90; middle readers—90.

How to Contact Accepts material from residents of Canada only. Fiction/nonfiction: Submit complete ms. Responds to queries in 2 weeks; mss in 2 months. Publishes a book 1 year after acceptance. Will consider simultaneous submissions.

Terms Pays authors royalty of 10% based on retail price. Pays illustrators by the project $400-800. Sends galleys to authors. Book catalog available for 8½ × 11 stet and $1 postage; ms and art guidelines available for SASE.

Tips "Ronsdale Press publishes well-written books that have a new slant on things and that can take an age-old story and give it a new spin. We are particularly interested in novels for young adults with a historical component that offers new insights into a part of Canada's history. We publish only Canadian authors."

▣ SCHOLASTIC CANADA LTD.

604 King St. West, ON M5V 1E1 Canada. (416)915-3500. Fax: (416)849-7912. Website: www.scholastic.ca; for ms/artist guidelines: www.scholastic.ca/aboutscholastic/manuscripts.htm. **Acquisitions:** Editor, children's books. Publishes hardcover and trade paperback originals. Imprints: Scholastic Canada; North Winds Press; Les Editions Scholastic. Publishes 70 titles/year; imprint publishes 4 titles/year. 3% of books from first-time authors; 50% from unagented writers. Canadian authors, theme or setting required.

- At presstime Scholastic Canada was not accepting unsolicited manuscripts. For up-to-date information on their current submission policy, call their publishing status line at (905)887-7323, ext. 4308 or view their submission guidelines on their Web site.

Fiction Picture books, young readers, young adult. Average word length: picture books—under 1,000; young readers—7,000-10,000; middle readers—15,000-30,000; young adult—25,000-40,000.

Nonfiction Animals, biography, history, hobbies, nature, recreation, science, sports. Reviews artwork/photos as part of ms package. Send photocopies.

How to Contact Query with synopsis, 3 sample chapters and SASE. Nonfiction: Query with outline, 1-2 sample chapters and SASE (IRC or Canadian stamps only). Responds in 3 months. Publishes book 1 year after acceptance.

Terms Pays authors royalty of 5-10% based on retail price. Offers advances. Book catalog for 8½ × 11 SAE with $2.55 postage stamps (IRC or Canadian stamps only).

▣ SECOND STORY PRESS

20 Maud St.Suite 401, Toronto ON M5V 2M5 Canada. (416)537-7850. Fax: (416)537-0588. E-mail: info@secondstorypress.ca. Website: www.secondstorypress.ca.

Fiction Considers nonsexist, nonracist, and nonviolent stories, as well as historical fiction, chapter books, picture books. Recently published *Lilly and the Paper Man*, by Rebecca Upjohn; *Mom and Mum Are Getting Married!*, by Ken Setterington.

Nonfiction Picture books: biography. Recently published *Hiding Edith: A True Story*, by Kathy Kacer (a new addition to our Holocaust remembrance series for young readers).

How to Contact Accepts appropriate material from residents of Canada only. Fiction and nonfiction: Submit complete ms or submit outline and sample chapters by postal mail only. No electronic submissions or queries.

▣ THISTLEDOWN PRESS LTD.

633 Main St.Saskatoon SK S7H 0J8 Canada. (306)244-1722. Fax: (306)244-1762. E-mail: tdpress@thistledown.sk.com. Website: www.thistledown.com. **Acquisitions:** Allan Forrie, publisher. Publishes numerous middle reader and young adult titles/year. "Thistledown originates books by Canadian authors only, although we have co-published titles by authors outside Canada. We do not publish children's picture books."

- Thistledown publishes books by Canadian authors only.

Fiction Middle readers, young adults: adventure, anthology, contemporary, fantasy, humor, poetry, romance, science fiction, suspense/mystery, short stories. Average word length: young adults—40,000. Recently published *Up All Night*, edited by R.P. MacIntyre (young adult, anthology); *Offside*, by Cathy Beveridge (young adult, novel); *Cheeseburger Subversive*, by Richard Scarsbrook; *The Alchemist's Daughter*, by Eileen Kernaghan.

How to Contact Submit outline/synopsis and sample chapters. "We do not accept unsolicted full-length manuscripts. These will be returned." Responds to queries in 4 months. Publishes a book about 1 year after acceptance. No simultaneous submissions. No e-mailed submissions.

Terms Pays authors royalty of 10-12% based on net dollar sales. Pays illustrators and photographers by the project (range: $250-750). Sends galleys to authors. Original artwork returned at job's completion. Book catalog free on request. Manuscript guidelines for #10 envelope and IRC.

Tips "Send cover letter including publishing history and SASE."

⚡ TRADEWIND BOOKS

202-1807 Maritime Mews, Vancouver BC V6H 3W7 Canada.(604)662-4405. Fax: (604)730-0454. E-mail: tradewindbooks@yahoo.com. Web site:www.tradewindbooks.com. **Manuscript Acquisitions**: Michael Katz, publisher. **Art Acquisitions:** Carol Frank, art director. Senior Editor: R. David Stephens. Publishes 2-3 picture books; 3 young adult titles/year; 1 book of poetry; 1 chapter book.15% of books by first-time authors.

Fiction Picture books: adventure, multicultural, folktales. Average word length: 900 words. Recently published *Broken*, by Alyxandra Harvey-Fitzhenry;The Graveyard Hounds, by Vi Hughes and illustrated by Christina Leist; Viva Zapata!, by Emilie Smith and illustrated by Stefan Czernecki.

How to Contact Picture books: submit complete ms. YA novels by Canadian authors only. Chapter books by US authors considered. Will consider simultaneous submissions. Do not send query letter. Responds to mss in 12 weeks. Unsolicited submissions accepted only if authors have read a selection of books published by Tradewind Books. Submissions must include a reference to these books.

Terms Royalties negotiable. Offers advances against royalties. Originals returned to artist at job's completion. Catalog available on Web site.

⊞ USBORNE PUBLISHING

83-85 Saffron Hill, London EC1N 8RT United Kingdom. Fax: (44)(20)743-1562. Website: www.usborne.com. **Manuscript Acquisitions:** Fiction Editorial Assistant. **Art Acquisitions:** Usborne Art Department. "Usborne Publishing is a multiple-award winning, world-wide children's publishing company specializing in superbly researched and produced information books with a unique appeal to young readers."

Fiction Young readers, middle readers: adventure, contemporary, fantasy, history, humor, multicultural, nature/environment, science fiction, suspense/mystery, strong concept-based or character-led series Average word length: young readers—5,000-10,000; middle readers—25,000-50,000. Recently publshed Secret Mermaid series, by Sue Mongredien (ages 7 and up); SCholl Friends, by Ann Bryant (ages 9 and up).

How to Contact Refer to guidelines on Web site or request from above address. Fiction: Submit 3 sample chapters and a full synopsis with SASE. Does not accept submissions for nonfiction or picture books. Responds to queries in 1 month; mss in 4 months.

Terms Pays authors royalty.

Tips "Do not send any original work and, sorry, but we cannot guarantee a reply."

⚡ WHITECAP BOOKS

351 Lynn Ave.North Vancouver BC V7J 2C4 Canada. (604)980-9852. Fax: (604)980-8197. E-mail: whitecap@whitecap.ca. Website: www.whitecap.ca. **Manuscript Acquisitions:** Rights and Acquisitions. **Illustration Acquisitions:** Michelle Mayne, art director. Publishes 0-1 young readers/year; 0-1 middle readers/year; 3-4 young adult/year.

Fiction Whitecap Books is currently de-emphasizing the children's and YA adventure in series only. Recently published *Wild Horse Cree #2; Coyote Canyon*, by Sharon Siamon.

Nonfiction Young Children's and middle reader's non-fiction focusing mainly on nature, wildlife and animals. Recently published *Canadian Girls Who Rocked The World; Revised and Expanded Edition*, by Tanya Lloyd Kyi.

How to Contact Query to Rights and Acquisitions. Accepts unagented work and multiple submissions. Responds to queries/ms in 6 months. Publishes a book approximately 1 year after acceptance. Include SASE with sufficient return postage. Mark envelopes "submissions." Please send international postal vouchers with SASE if submission is form U.S.A. No e-mail submissions.

Terms Pays authors a negotiated royalty or purchases work outright. Offers advances. Pays illustrators and photographers negotiated amount. Originals returned to artist at job's completion. Manuscript guidelines available on website.

Tips "Check submission guidelines on our web site before submitting. Don't send U.S. postage SASE to Canada. It can't be used in Canada and no reply will be sent."

Magazines

Children's magazines are a great place for unpublished writers and illustrators to break into the market. Writers, illustrators and photographers alike may find it easier to get book assignments if they have tearsheets from magazines. Having magazine work under your belt shows you're professional and have experience working with editors and art directors and meeting deadlines.

But magazines aren't merely a breaking-in point. Writing, illustration and photo assignments for magazines let you see your work in print quickly, and the magazine market can offer steady work and regular paychecks (a number of them pay on acceptance). Book authors and illustrators may have to wait a year or two before receiving royalties from a project. The magazine market is also a good place to use research material that didn't make it into a book project you're working on. You may even work on a magazine idea that blossoms into a book project.

TARGETING YOUR SUBMISSIONS

It's important to know the topics typically covered by different children's magazines. To help you match your work with the right publications, we've included several indexes in the back of this book. The **Subject Index** lists both book and magazine publishers by the fiction and nonfiction subjects they're seeking.

If you're a writer, use the Subject Index in conjunction with the **Age-Level Index** to narrow your list of markets. Targeting the correct age group with your submission is an important consideration. Many rejection slips are sent because a writer has not targeted a manuscript to the correct age. Few magazines are aimed at children of all ages, so you must be certain your manuscript is written for the audience level of the particular magazine you're submitting to. Magazines for children (just as magazines for adults) may also target a specific gender.

If you're a poet, refer to the **Poetry Index** to find which magazines publish poems.

Each magazine has a different editorial philosophy. Language usage also varies between periodicals, as does the length of feature articles and the use of artwork and photographs. Reading magazines *before* submitting is the best way to determine if your material is appropriate. Also, because magazines targeted to specific age groups have a natural turnover in readership every few years, old topics (with a new slant) can be recycled.

If you're a photographer, the **Photography Index** lists children's magazines that use photos from freelancers. Using it in combination with the subject index can narrow your search. For instance, if you photograph sports, compare the Magazine list in the Photography Index with the list under Sports in the Subject Index. Highlight the markets that appear on both lists, then read those listings to decide which magazines might be best for your work.

Since many kids' magazines sell subscriptions through direct mail or schools, you may not be able to find a particular publication at bookstores or newsstands. Check your local library, or send for copies of the magazines you're interested in. Most magazines in this section have sample copies available and will send them for a SASE or small fee.

Also, many magazines have submission guidelines and theme lists available for a SASE. Check magazines' websites, too. Many offer excerpts of articles, submission guidelines, and theme lists and will give you a feel for the editorial focus of the publication.

Watch for the Canadian 🍁 and International 🌐 symbols. These publications' needs and requirements may differ from their U.S. counterparts.

ADVENTURES

WordAction Publications,, 6401 The Paseo, Kansas City MO 64131.(816)333-7000. Fax: (816)333-4439. E-mail: dfillmore@nazarene.org. **Articles Editor:** Donna Filmore. Weekly magazine. "Adventures is a full-color story paper for first and second graders. It is designed to connect Sunday School learning with the daily living experiences of the early elementary child. The reading level should be beginning. The intent of Adventures is to provide a life-related paper enabling Christian values, encouraging good choices and providing reinforcement for biblical concepts taught in WordAction Sunday School curriculum." Entire publication aimed at juvenile market.

Fiction Picture-Oriented Material: contemporary, inspirational, religious. Young Readers: contemporary, inspirational, religious.. Byline given.

How to Contact Fiction: Send complete ms. Responds to queries in 6 weeks; to mss in 6 weeks.

Terms Pays on acceptance. Buys all rights. Writer's guidelines free for SASE.

Tips "Send SASE for themes and guidelines or e-mail acallison@nazarene.org. Stories should realistically portray the life experiences of first- and second-grade children from a variety of ethnic and social backgrounds. We also need simple puzzles, easy recipes and easy-to-do craft ideas."

ADVOCATE, PKA'S PUBLICATION

PKA Publication, 1881 Little Westkill Rd.Prattsville NY 12468. (518)299-3103. **Publisher:** Patricia Keller. Bimonthly tabloid. Estab. 1987. Circ. 12,000. "Advocate advocates good writers and quality writings. We publish art, fiction, photos and poetry. Advocate 's submitters are talented people of all ages who do not earn their livings as writers. We wish to promote the arts and to give those we publish the opportunity to be published."

- Gaited Horse Association newsletter is included in this publication. Horse-oriented stories, poetry, art and photos are currently needed.

Fiction Middle readers, young adults/teens; adults: adventure, animal, contemporary, fantasy, folktales, health, humorous, nature/environment, problem-solving, romance, science fiction, sports, suspense/mystery. Looks for "well written, entertaining work, whether fiction or nonfiction." Buys approximately 42 mss/year. Prose pieces should not exceed 1,500 words. Byline given. Wants to see more humorous material, nature/environment and romantic comedy.

Nonfiction Middle readers, young adults/teens: animal, arts/crafts, biography, careers, concept, cooking, fashion, games/puzzles, geography, history, hobbies, how-to, humorous, interview/profile, nature/environment, problem-solving, science, social issues, sports, travel. Buys 10 mss/year. Prose pieces should not exceed 1,500 words. Byline given.

Poetry Reviews poetry any length.

How to Contact Fiction/nonfiction: send complete ms. Responds to queries in 6 weeks; mss in 2 months. Publishes ms 2-18 months after acceptance.

Illustration Uses b&w artwork only. Uses cartoons. Reviews ms/illustration packages from artists. Submit a photo print (b&w or color), an excellent copy of work (no larger than 8 × 10) or original. Prints in black and white but accepts color work that converts well to gray scale. Illustrations only: "Send previous unpublished art with SASE, please." Responds in 2 months. Samples returned with SASE; samples not filed. Credit line given.

Photos Buys photos from freelancers. Model/property releases required. Uses color and b&w prints (no slides). Send unsolicited photos by mail with SASE. Responds in 2 months. Wants nature, artistic and humorous photos.

Terms Pays on publication with contributor's copies. Acquires first rights for mss, artwork and photographs. Pays in copies. Sample copies for $ 5. For a yearly subscription, published 6 times per year $16.50. Writer's/illustrator/photo guidelines with sample copy.

Tips "Please, no simultaneous submissions, work that has appeared on the Internet, po rnography, overt religiousity, anti-environmentalism or gratuitous violence. Artists and photographers should keep in mind that we are a b&w paper. Please do not send postcards. Use envelope with SASE."

AIM MAGAZINE, America's Intercultural Magazine

P.O. Box 390, Milton WA 98354-0390. Website: www.aimmagazine.org. **Contact:** Ruth Apilado, associate editor. Quarterly magazine. Circ. 8,000. "Readers are high school and college students, teachers, adults interested in helping to purge racism from the human blood stream by the way of the written word—that is our goal!" 15% of material aimed at juvenile audience.

Fiction Young adults/teens: adventure, folktales, humorous, history, multicultural, "stories with social significance." Wants stories that teach children that people are more alike than they are different. Does not want to see religious fiction. Buys 20 mss/year. Average word length: 1,000-4,000. Byline given.

Nonfiction Young adults/teens: biography, interview/profile, multicultural, "stuff with social significance." Does not want to see religious nonfiction. Buys 20 mss/year. Average word length: 500-2,000. Byline given.

How to Contact Fiction: Send complete ms. Nonfiction: Query with published clips. Responds to queries/mss in 1 month. Will consider simultaneous submissions.

Illustration Buys 6 illustrations/issue. Preferred theme: Overcoming social injustices through nonviolent means. Reviews ms/illustration packages from artists. Query first. Illustrations only: Query with tearsheets. Responds to art samples in 1 month. Samples filed. Original artwork returned at job's completion "if desired." Credit line given.

Photos Wants "photos of activists who are trying to contribute to social improvement."

Terms Pays on acceptance. Buys first North American serial rights. Pays $15-25 for stories/articles. Pays in contributor copies if copies are requested. Pays $25 for b&w cover illustration. Photographers paid by the project. Sample copies for $5.

Tips "Write about what you know."

AMERICAN CAREERS

Career Communications, Inc.6701 W. 64th St.Overland Park KS 66202. (913)362-7788. Fax: (913)362-4864. Website: www.carcom.com. **Articles Editor:** Mary Pitchford. **Art Director:** Jerry Kanabel. Published 1 time/year. Estab. 1990. Circ. 400,000. Publishes career and education information for students in grades 6-12.

Nonfiction Buys 5 mss/year. Average word length: 300-800. Byline given.

How to Contact Nonfiction: Query with résumé and published clips. Acknowledges queries within 30 days. Keeps queries on file up to 2 years. Accepts simultaneous submissions with notification.

Terms Pays on acceptance. Pays writers variable amount.

Tips Send a query in writing with résumé and clips.

AMERICAN GIRL

8400 Fairway Place, Middleton WI 53562-0984. (608)836-4848. Website: www.americangirl.com. **Contact**: Editorial Dept. Assistant. Bimonthly magazine. Estab. 1992. Circ. 600,000. girls ages 8-12.

Fiction Not currently accepting fiction.

Nonfiction How-to, interview/profile, history. Any articles aimed at girls ages 8-12. Buys 3-10 mss/year. Average word length: 600. Byline sometimes given. No historical profiles about obvious female heroines: Annie Oakley, Amelia Earhart; no romance or dating.

How to Contact Fiction: Query with published clips. Nonfiction: Query. Responds to queries/mss in 3 months. Will consider simultaneous submissions.

Illustration Works on assignment only.

Terms Pays on acceptance. Buys first North American serial rights. Pays $500 minimum for stories; $300 minimum for articles. Sample copies for $4.50 and 9 1/2x12 SASE with $1.98 in postage (send to Magazine Department Assistant). Writer's guidelines free for SASE.

Tips Keep (stories and articles) simple but interesting. Kids are discriminating readers, too. They won't read a boring or pretentious story. We're looking for short (maximum 175 words) how-to stories and short profiles of girls for 'Girls Express' section.

APPLESEEDS

30 Grove Street, Peterborough, NH 03458. E-mail (for writers queries): susanbuckleynyc@gmail. com. Website: www.cobblestonepub.com. **Editor:** Susan Buckley. Magazine published 9 times annually. AppleSeeds is a 36-page, multidisciplinary, nonfiction social studies magazine from Cobblestone Publishing for ages 8-10. Each issue focuses on one theme.

- Requests for sample issues should be mailed to Cobblestone directly. See Web site for current theme list.

How to Contact Nonfiction: Query only. Send all queries to Susan Buckley. See Web site for submission guidelines and theme list. E-mail queries only. See Web site for editorial guidelines.

Illustration Contact Ann Dillon at Cobblestone. See Web site for illustration guidelines.

Tips "Submit queries specifically focused on the theme of an upcoming issue. We generally work 6 months ahead on themes. We look for unusual perspectives, original ideas, and excellent scholarship. We accept **no unsolicited manuscripts**. Writers should check our Web site at cobblestonepub. com/pages/writersAPPguides/html for current guidelines, topics, and query deadlines. We use very little fiction. Illustrators should not submit unsolicited art."

ℕ 🌐 AQUILA

New Leaf Publishing, P.O. Box 2518, Eastbourne BN22 8AP United Kingdom. (44)(132)343-1313. Fax: (44)(132)373-1136. E-mail: info@aquila.co.uk. Website: www.aquila.co.uk. **Submissions Editor:** Jackie Berry and Anji Ansty-Holroyd. Monthly magazine. Estab. 1993. "Aquila is an educational magazine for readers ages 8-13 including factual articles (no pop/celebrity material), arts/crafts and puzzles." Entire publication aimed at juvenile market.

Fiction Young Readers: animal, contemporary, fantasy, folktales, health, history, humorous, multicultural, nature/environment, problem solving, religious, science fiction, sports, suspense/ mystery. Middle Readers: animal, contemporary, fantasy, folktales, health, history, humorous, multicultural, nature/environment, problem solving, religious, romance, science fiction, sports, suspense/mystery. Buys 6-8 mss/year. Byline given.

Nonfiction Considers Young Readers: animal, arts/crafts, concept, cooking, games/puzzles, health, history, how-to, interview/profile, math, nature/environment, science, sports. Middle Readers: animal, arts/crafts, concept, cooking, games/puzzles, health, history, interview/profile, math, nature/environment, science, sports. Buys 48 mss/year. Average word length: 350-750.

How to Contact Fiction: Query with published clips. Nonfiction: Query with published clips. Responds to queries in 6-8 weeks.Publishes ms 1 year after acceptance. Considers electronic submissions via disk or e-mail, previously published work.

Illustration Color artwork only.Works on assignment only. For first contact, query with samples. Submit samples to Jackie Berry, Editor. Responds only if interested. Samples not returned. Samples filed.

Terms Buys exclusive magazine rights. Buys exclusive magazine rights rights for artwork. Pays 150-200 for stories; 50-100 for articles. Additional payment for ms/illustration packages. Additional payment for ms/photo packages. Pays illustrators $130-150 for color cover. Sample copies (€5 sterling) this must be bankers cheque in sterling, not US dollars. Writer's guidelines free for SASE. Publishes work by children.

Tips "We only accept a high level of educational material for children ages 8-13 with a good standard of literacy and ability."

ASK

Arts and Sciences for Kids, 70 E. Lake Street, Suite 300, Chicago IL 60601. (312)701-1720. E-mail: ask@caruspub.com. Website: www.askmagkids.com. **Editor:** Liz Huyck. **Art Director:** Karen Kohn. Magazine published 9 times/year. Estab. 2002. "ASK invites curious kids between the ages of 7 and 10 into the world of science."

Nonfiction Young readers, middle readers: science, machines, archaeology, animal, nature/environment, history of science. Average word length: 150-1,500. Byline given.

How to Contact *Ask* does not accept unsolicited mss or queries. All articles are commissioned. To be considered for assignments, experienced science writers may send a résumé and 3 published clips.

Illustration Buys 10 illustrations/issue; 60 illustrations/year. Works on assignment only. Illustrations only: Query with samples.

BABAGANEWZ

Jewish Family & Life, P.O. Box 9129, Newton, MA 02464. (888) 458-8535. Fax: (617) 965-7772. Website: www.babaganewz.com. **Articles Editor:** Mark Levine. **Managing Editor:**Jean Max. Monthly magazine. Estab. 2001. Circ. 40,000. "BabagaNewz helps middle school students explore Jewish values that are at the core of Jewish beliefs and practices."

Fiction Middle readers: religious, Jewish themes. Buys 1 ms/year. Average word length: 1,000-1,500. Byline given.

Nonfiction Middle readers: arts/crafts, concept, games/puzzles, geography, history, humorous, interview/profile, nature/environment, religion, science, social issues. Most articles are written by assignment. Average word length: 350-1,000. Byline given.

How to Contact Queries only for fiction; queries preferred for nonfiction. No unsolicited manuscripts.

Illustration Uses color artwork only. Works on assignment only. Illustrations only: Send postcard sample with promo sheet, resume, URL. Responds only if interested. Credit line given.

Photos Photos by assignment.

Terms Pays on acceptance. Usually buys all rights for mss. Original artwork returned at job's completion only if requested. Sample copies free for SAE 9 × 12 and 4 first-class stamps.

Tips "Most work is done on assignment. We are looking for freelance writers with experience writing non-fiction for 9- to 13-year-olds, especially on Jewish-related themes. No unsolicited manuscripts."

BABYBUG

Carus Publishing Company, 70 E. Lake St.Suite 300, Chicago IL 60601. Website: www.babybugmagkids.com. **Editor:** Alice Letvin. **Art Director:** Suzanne Beck. Published 10 times/year (monthly except for combined May/June and July/August issues). Estab. 1994. "A listening and looking magazine for infants and toddlers ages 6 to 24 months, Babybug is 6 × 7, 24 pages long, printed in large type on high-quality cardboard stock with rounded corners and no staples."

Fiction Looking for very simple and concrete stories, 4-6 short sentences maximum.

Nonfiction Must use very basic words and concepts, 10 words maximum.

Poetry Maximum length 8 lines. Looking for rhythmic, rhyming poems.

How to Contact "Please do not query first." Send complete ms with SASE. "Submissions without SASE will be discarded." Responds in 6 months.

Illustration Uses color artwork only. Works on assignment only. Reviews ms/illustration packages from artists. "The manuscripts will be evaluated for quality of concept and text before the art is considered." Contact: Suzanne Beck. Illustrations only: Send tearsheets or photo prints/photocopies with SASE. "Submissions without SASE will be discarded." Responds in 3 months. Samples filed.

Terms Pays on publication for mss; after delivery of completed assignment for illustrators. Rights purchased vary. Original artwork returned at job's completion. Rates vary ($25 minimum for mss; $250 minimum for art). Sample copy for $5. Guidelines free for SASE or available on Web site, FAQ at www.cricketmag.com.

Tips "*Babybug* would like to reach as many children's authors and artists as possible for original contributions, but our standards are very high, and we will accept only top-quality material. Before attempting to write for *Babybug*, be sure to familiarize yourself with this age child."

BOYS' LIFE

Boy Scouts of America, 1325 W. Walnut Hill Lane, Irving TX 75015-2079. (972)580-2366. Fax: (972)580-2079. Website: www.boyslife.org. **Managing Editor:** Michael Goldman. **Senior Writer:** Aaron Derr. **Fiction Editor:** Paula Murphey. **Director of Design:** Scott Feaster. Monthly magazine. Estab. 1911. Circ. 11,000,000. Boys' Life is "a 4-color general interest magazine for boys 8 to 18 who are members of the Cub Scouts, Boy Scouts or Venturers."

Fiction Young readers, middle readers, young adults: adventure, animal, contemporary, history, humor, multicultural, nature/environment, problem-solving, sports, science fiction, spy/mystery. Does not want to see animals and adult reminiscence." Buys only 12-16 mss/year. Average word length: 1,000-1,500. Byline given.

Nonfiction Young readers, middle readers, young adult: animal, arts/crafts, biography, careers (middle readers and young adults only), cooking, health, history, hobbies, how-to, interview/profile, multicultural, nature/environment, problem-solving, science, sports. Matter is broad. We cover everything from professional sports to American history to how to pack a canoe. A look at a current list of the BSA's more than 100 merit badge pamphlets gives an idea of the wide range of subjects possible. Even better, look at a year's worth of recent issues. Column subjects are science, nature, earth, health, sports, space and aviation, cars, computers, entertainment, pets, history, music and others." Average word length: 500-1,500. Columns 300-750 words. Byline given.

How to Contact Fiction: Send complete ms with cover letter and SASE to fiction editor. Nonfiction: Major articles query senior editor. Columns query associate editor with SASE for response. Responds to queries/mss in 2 months.

Illustration Buys 10-12 illustrations/issue; 100-125 illustrations/year. Works on assignment only. Reviews ms/illustration packages from artists. "Query first." Illustrations only: Send tearsheets. Responds to art samples only if interested. Samples returned with SASE. Original artwork returned at job's completion. Credit line given.

Terms Pays on acceptance. Buys first rights. Pays $750 and up for fiction; $400-1,500 for major articles; $150-400 for columns; $250-300 for how-to features. Pays illustrators $1,500-3,000 for color cover; $100-1,500 color inside. Pays photographers by the project. Sample copies for $3.95 plus 9 × 12 SASE. Writer's/illustrator's/photo guidelines available for SASE.

Tips "We strongly urge you to study at least a year's issues to better understand the type of material published. Articles for *Boys' Life* must interest and entertain boys ages 8 to 18. Write for a boy you know who is 12. Our readers demand crisp, punchy writing in relatively short, straightforward sentences. The editors demand well-reported articles that demonstrate high standards of journalism. We follow *The New York Times* manual of style and usage. All submissions must be accompanied by SASE with adequate postage."

BOYS' QUEST

P.O. Box 227, Bluffton OH 45817-0227. (419)358-4610. Fax: (419)358-5027. Website: www.boysquest.com. **Articles Editor:** Marilyn Edwards. Bimonthly magazine. Estab. 1995. "Boys' Quest is a magazine created for boys from 5 to 14 years, with youngsters 8, 9 and 10 the specific target age. Our point of view is that every young boy deserves the right to be a young boy for a number of years before he becomes a young adult. As a result, Boys' Quest looks for articles, fiction, nonfiction, and poetry that deal with timeless topics, such as pets, nature, hobbies, science, games, sports, careers, simple cooking, and anything else likely to interest a young boy."

Fiction Picture-oriented material, young readers, middle readers: adventure, animal, history, humorous, multicultural, nature/environment, problem-solving, sports. Does not want to see violence, teenage themes. Buys 30 mss/year. Average word length: 200-500. Byline given.

Nonfiction Picture-oriented material, young readers, middle readers: animal, arts/crafts, cooking, games/puzzles, history, hobbies, how-to, humorous, math, problem-solving, sports. Prefer photo support with nonfiction. Buys 30 mss/year. Average word length: 200-500. Byline given.

Poetry Reviews poetry. Maximum length: 21 lines. Limit submissions to 6 poems.

How to Contact All writers should consult the theme list before sending in articles. To receive current theme list, send a SASE. Fiction/nonfiction: Query or send complete ms (preferred). Send SASE with correct postage. No faxed or e-mailed material. Responds to queries in 2 weeks; mss in 2 weeks (if rejected); 5 weeks (if scheduled). Publishes ms 3 months-3 years after acceptance. Will consider simultaneous submissions and previously published work.

Illustration Buys 10 illustrations/issue; 60-70 illustrations/year. Uses b&w artwork only. Works on assignment only. Reviews ms/illustration packages from artists. Illustrations only: Query with samples, tearsheets. Responds in 1 month only if interested and a SASE. Samples returned with SASE; samples filed. Credit line given.

Photos Photos used for support of nonfiction. "Excellent photographs included with a nonfiction story is considered very seriously." Model/property releases required. Uses b&w, 5 × 7 or 3 × 5 prints. Query with samples; send unsolicited photos by mail. Responds in 3 weeks.

Terms Pays on publication. Buys first North American serial rights for mss. Buys first rights for artwork. Pays 5/word for stories and articles. Additional payment for ms/illustration packages and for photos accompanying articles. Pays $150-200 for color cover; $25-35 for b&w inside. Pays photographers per photo (range: $5-10). Originals returned to artist at job's completion. Sample copies for $6 (there is a direct charge by the post office of $4.50 per issue for airmail to other countries); $8 for Canada, and $10.50 for all other countries. Writer's/illustrator's/photographer's guidelines and theme list are free for SASE.

Tips "First be familiar with our magazines. We are looking for lively writing, most of it from a young boy's point of view—with the boy or boys directly involved in an activity that is both wholesome and unusual. We need nonfiction with photos and fiction stories—around 500 words—puzzles, poems, cooking, carpentry projects, jokes and riddles. Nonfiction pieces that are accompanied by black and white photos are far more likely to be accepted than those that need illustrations. We will entertain simultaneous submissions as long as that fact is noted on the manuscript."

BREAD FOR GOD'S CHILDREN

Bread Ministries, Inc.P.O. Box 1017, Arcadia FL 34265-1017. (863)494-6214. Fax: (863)993-0154. E-mail: bread@breadministries.org. Website: www.breadministries.org. **Editor:** Judith M. Gibbs. Bimonthly magazine. Estab. 1972. Circ. 10,000 (U.S. and Canada). "Bread is designed as a teaching tool for Christian families." 85% of publication aimed at juvenile market.

Fiction Young readers, middle readers, young adult/teen: adventure, religious, problem-solving, sports. Looks for "teaching stories that portray Christian lifestyles without preaching." Buys approximately 20 mss/year. Average word length: 900-1,500 (for teens); 600-900 (for young children). Byline given.

Nonfiction All levels: how-to. "We do not want anything detrimental to solid family values. Most topics will fit if they are slanted to our basic needs." Buys 3-4 mss/year. Average word length: 500-800. Byline given.

How to Contact Fiction/nonfiction: Send complete ms. Responds to mss in 6 months "if considered for use." Will consider simultaneous submissions and previously published work.

Illustration "The only illustrations we purchase are those occasional good ones accompanying an accepted story."

Terms Pays on publication. Pays $30-50 for stories; $30 for articles. Sample copies free for 9 × 12 SAE and 5 first-class stamps (for 2 copies).

Tips "We want stories or articles that illustrate overcoming obstacles by faith and living solid, Christian lives. Know our publication and what we have used in the past. Know the readership and publisher's guidelines. Stories should teach the value of morality and honesty without preaching. Edit carefully for content and grammar."

BRILLIANT STAR

National Spiritual Assembly of the Báha'ís of the U.S.1233 Central St.Evanston IL 60201. (847)853-2354. Fax: (847)425-7951. E-mail: brilliant@usbnc.org. Website: www.brilliantstarmagazine.org. **Associate Editor:** Susan Engle. **Art Director:** Amethel Parel-Sewell. Publishes 6 issues/year. Estab. 1969. Magazine is designed for children ages 8-12. Brilliant Star # presents Báha'í history and principles through fiction, nonfiction, activities, interviews, puzzles, cartoons, games, music, and art. Universal values of good character, such as kindness, courage, creativity, and helpfulness are incorporated into the magazine.

Fiction Middle readers: contemporary, fantasy, folktale, multicultural, nature/environment, problem-solving, religious. Average word length: 700-1,400. Byline given.

Nonfiction Middle readers: arts/crafts, games/puzzles, geography, how-to, humorous, multicultural, nature/environment, religion, social issues. Buys 6 mss/year. Average word length: 300-700. Byline given.

Poetry Only publish poetry written by children at the moment."

How to Contact Fiction: Send complete ms. Nonfiction: Query. Responds to queries/mss in 6 weeks. Publishes ms 6 months-1 year after acceptance. Will consider e-mail submissions.

Illustration Works on assignment only. Reviews ms/illustration packages from artists. Illustrations only: Query with samples. Contact: Aaron Kreader, graphic designer. Responds only if interested. Samples kept on file. Credit line given.

Photos Buys photos with accompanying ms only. Model/property release required; captions required. Responds only if interested.

Terms Pays 2 copies of issue. Buys first rights and reprint rights for mss. Buys first rights and reprint rights for artwork; first rights and reprint rights for photos. Sample copies for $3. Writer's/illustrator's/photo guidelines for SASE.

Tips "*Brilliant Star's* content is developed with a focus on children in their 'tween' years, ages 8-12. This is a period of intense emotional, physical, and psychological development. Familiarize yourself with the interests and challenges of children in this age range. Protagonists in our fiction are usually in the upper part of our age-range: 10-12 years old. They solve their problems without adult intervention. We appreciate seeing a sense of humor but not related to bodily functions or put-downs. Keep your language and concepts age-appropriate. Use short words, sentences, and paragraphs. Activities and games may be submitted in rough or final form. Send us a description of your activity along with short, simple instructions. We avoid long, complicated activities that require adult supervision. If you think they will be helpful, please try to provide step-by-step rough sketches of the instructions. You may also submit photographs to illustrate the activity."

CADET QUEST

Calvinist Cadet Corps, P.O. Box 7259, Grand Rapids MI 49510. (616)241-5616. E-mail: submissions@calvinistcadets.org. Website: www.calvinistcadets.org. **Editor:** G. Richard Broene. Magazine published 7 times/year. Circ. 9,000."Our magazine is for members of the Calvinist Cadet Corps—boys aged 9-14. Our purpose is to show how God is at work in their lives and in the world around them. Our magazine offers nonfiction articles and fast-moving fiction—everything to appeal to the interests and concerns of boys and teach Christian values."

Fiction Middle readers, boys/early teens: adventure, humorous, multicultural, problem-solving, religious, sports. Buys 12 mss/year. Average word length: 900-1,500.

Nonfiction Middle readers, boys/early teens: arts/crafts, games/puzzles, hobbies, how-to, humorous, interview/profile, problem-solving, science, sports. Buys 6 mss/year. Average word length: 400-900.

How to Contact Fiction/nonfiction: Send complete ms by mail with SASE or by e-mail. Please note: e-mail submissions must have material in the body of the e-mail. Will not open attachments." Responds to mss in 2 months. Will consider simultaneous submissions.

Illustration Buys 2 illustration/issue; buys 12 illustrations/year. Works on assignment only. Reviews ms/illustration packages from artists. Responds in 5 weeks. Samples returned with SASE. Originals returned to artist at job's completion. Credit line given.

Photos Buys photos from freelancers. Wants nature photos and photos of boys.

Terms Pays on acceptance. Buys first North American serial rights; reprint rights. Pays 4-5 cent a word for stories/articles. Pays illustrators $200-300 for full page illustrations— inside or cover and $100 - $200 for smaller illustrations—inside. Sample copy free with 9 × 12 SAE and 3 first-class stamps.

Tips "Our publication is mostly open to fiction; look for new themes at our Web site. We use mostly fast-moving fiction from a Christian perspective and based on our themes for each issue. Articles on sports, outdoor activities, science, crafts, etc. should emphasize a Christian perspective. Best time to submit material is February-April. Themes available on our Web site February 1."

CALLIOPE, Exploring World History

30 Grove St.Peterborough NH 03458. (603)924-7209. Fax: (603)924-7380. Website: www. cobblestonepub.com. **Editorial Director:** Lou Waryncia. **Co-editors:** Rosalie Baker and Charles Baker. **Art Director:** Ann Dillon. Magazine published 9 times/year. "Calliope covers world history (East/West), and lively, original approaches to the subject are the primary concerns of the editors in choosing material."

- For themes and queries deadlines, visit the Calliope web site at: www.cobblestonepub.com/ magazine/CAL.

Fiction Middle readers and young adults: adventure, folktales, plays, history, biographical fiction. Material must relate to forthcoming themes. Word length: up to 1,000.

Nonfiction Middle readers and young adults: arts/crafts, biography, cooking, games/puzzles, history. Material must relate to upcoming themes. Word length: 300-1,000.

How to Contact "A query must consist of the following to be considered (please use nonerasable paper): a brief cover letter stating subject and word length of the proposed article; a detailed one-page outline explaining the information to be presented in the article; an bibliography of materials the author intends to use in preparing the article; a self-addressed stamped envelope. Writers new to *Calliope* should send a writing sample with query. In all correspondence, please include your complete address as well as a telephone number where you can be reached. A writer may send as many queries for one issue as he or she wishes, but each query must have a separate cover letter, outline and bibliography as well as a SASE. Telephone and e-mail queries are not accepted. Handwritten queries will not be considered. Queries may be submitted at any time, but queries sent well in advance of deadline *may not be answered for several months*. Go-aheads requesting material proposed in queries are usually sent 10 months prior to publication date. Unused queries will be returned approximately three to four months prior to publication date."

Illustration Illustrations only: Send tearsheets, photocopies. Original work returned upon job's completion (upon written request).

Photos Buys photos from freelancers. Wants photos pertaining to any upcoming themes. Uses b&w/color prints, 35mm transparencies and 300 DPI digital images. Send unsolicited photos by mail (on speculation).

Terms Buys all rights for mss and artwork. Pays 20-25¢/word for stories/articles. Pays on an individual basis for poetry, activities, games/puzzles. "Covers are assigned and paid on an individual basis." Pays photographers per photo ($15-100 for b $25-100 for color). Sample copy for $5.95 and SAE with $2 postage. Writer's/illustrator's/photo guidelines for SASE.

CAMPUS LIFE'S IGNITE YOUR FAITH

Christianity Today, International, 465 Gundersen Dr.Carol Stream IL 60188. (630)260-6200. Fax: (630)260-2004. E-mail: iyf@igniteyourfaith.com. Website: www.igniteyourfaith.com. **Articles and Fiction Editor:** Chris Lutes. Magazine published 4 times yearly. Estab. 1944. Circ. 100,000. "Our purpose is to creatively engage and empower Christian teens to become fully devoted followers of Jesus Christ."

Fiction Young adults: humorous, problem-solving with a Christian worldview. Buys 1-3 mss/year. Byline given.

Poetry Reviews poetry.

How to Contact Fiction/nonfiction: Query only.

Terms Pays on acceptance. Writer's guidelines available on Web site.

CAREERS AND COLLEGES

A division of Alloy Education, an Alloy Media + Marketing Company, 10 Abeel Road, Cranbury NJ 08512. (609) 619- 8739. Website: www.careersandcolleges.com. **SVP/Managing Director:** Jayne Pennington. Editor: Don Rauf. Magazine published 3 times a year (2 issues direct-to-home in July and 1 to 10,000 high schools in December). Circulation: 760,000. Distributed to 760,000 homes of 15- to 17-year-olds and college-bound high school graduates, and 10,000 high schools. Careers and Colleges magazine provides juniors and seniors in high school with editorial, tips, trends, and Web sites to assist them in the transition to college, career, young adulthood, and independence.

Nonfiction Young adults/teens: careers, college, health, how-to, humorous, interview/profile, personal development, problem-solving, social issues, sports, travel. Buys 10-20 mss/year. Average word length: 1,000-1,500. Byline given.

How to Contact Nonfiction: Query. Responds to queries in 6 weeks. Will consider electronic submissions.

Illustration Buys 2 illustrations/issue; buys 8 illustrations/year. Works on assignment only. Reviews samples online. Query first. Credit line given.

Terms Pays on acceptance plus 45 days. Buys all rights. Pays $100-600 for assigned/unsolicited articles. Additional payment for ms/illustration packages "must be negotiated." Pays $300-1,000 for color illustration; $200-700 for b&w/color inside illustration. Pays photographers by the project. Sample copy $5. Contributor' s Guidelines are available electronically.

Tips "Articles with great quotes, good reporting, good writing. Rich with examples and anecdotes. Must tie in with the objective to help teenaged readers plan for their futures. Current trends, policy changes and information regarding college admissions, financial aid, and career opportunities."

CARUS PUBLISHING COMPANY

P.O. Box 300, Peru IL 61354.

- See listings for *Babybug*, *Cicada*, *Click*, *Cricket*, *Ladybug*, *Muse*, *Spider* and *ASK*. Carus Publishing owns Cobblestone Publishing, publisher of *AppleSeeds*, *Calliope*, *Cobblestone*, *Dig*, *Faces* and *Odyssey*.

CATHOLIC FORESTER

Catholic Order of Foresters, P.O. Box 3012, 355 Shuman Blvd.Naperville IL 60566-7012. (630)983-4900. E-mail: magazine@CatholicForester.com. Website: www.catholicforester.com. **Articles Editor:** Patricia Baron. **Assistant V.P. Communication:** Mary Ann File. **Art Director:** Keith Halla. Quarterly magazine. Estab. 1883. Circ. 85,000. Targets members of the Catholic Order of Foresters. In addition to the organization's news, it offers general interest pieces on health, finance, family life. Also use inspirational and humorous fiction.

Fiction Buys 6-10 mss/year. Average word length: 500-1,500.

How to Contact Fiction: Submit complete ms. Responds in 4 months. Will consider previously published work.

Illustration Buys 2-4 illustrations/issue. Uses color artwork only. Works on assignment only.

Photos Buys photos with accompanying ms only.

Terms Pays on acceptance. Buys first North American serial rights, reprint rights, one-time rights. Sample copies for 9 × 12 SASE with 3 first-class stamps. Writer's guidelines free for SASE.

CELEBRATE

Word Action Publishing Co.Church of the Nazarene, 2923 Troost Ave, Kansas City MO 64109. (816)931-1900, ext. 8228. Fax: (816)412-8306. E-mail: dxb@nph.com. Website: www.wordaction. com. **Editor:** Abigail L. Takala. **Assistant Editor:** Danielle J. Broadbooks. Weekly publication. Estab. 2001. Circ. 30,000. "This weekly take-home paper connects Sunday School learning to life for preschoolers (age 3 and 4), kindergartners (age 5 and 6) and their families." 75% of publication aimed at juvenile market; 25% parents.

Nonfiction Picture-oriented material: arts/crafts, cooking, poems, action rhymes, piggyback songs (theme based). 50% of mss nonfiction. Byline given.

Poetry Reviews poetry. Maximum length: 4-8 lines. Unlimited submissions.

How to Contact Nonfiction: query. Responds to queries in 1 month. Responds to mss in 6 weeks. Publishes ms 1 year after acceptance. Will accept electronic submission via e-mail.

Terms Pays on acceptance. Buys all rights, multi-use rights. Pays $15 for activities, crafts, recipes, songs, rhymes, and poems. Compensation includes 2 contributor copies. Sample copy for SASE.

Tips "We are accepting submissions at this time."

▣ CHALLENGE

Pearson Education Australia, 20 Thackray Rd.Port Melbourne VIC 3205 Australia. (61)03 9245 7111. Fax: (61)03 9245 7333. E-mail: magazines@pearson.com.au. Website: www.pearson.com.au/schools. **Articles Editor:** Petra Poupa. **Fiction Editor:** Meredith Costain. Quarterly Magazine. Circ. 20,000. "Magazines are educational and fun. We publish mainly nonfiction articles in a variety of genres and text types. They must be appropriate, factually correct, and of high interest. We publish interviews, recounts, informational and argumentative articles."

- *Challenge* is a theme-based publication geared to ages 11-14. Check the Web site to see upcoming themes and deadlines.

Fiction Middle readers, young adults: adventure, animal, contemporary, fantasy, folktale, humorous, multicultural, problem-solving, science fiction, sports, suspense/mystery. Buys 12 mss/year. Average word length: 400-1,000. Byline given.

Nonfiction Middle readers, young adults: animal, arts/crafts, biography, careers, cooking, fashion, geography, health, history, hobbies, how-to, humorous, interview/profile, math, multicultural, nature/environment, problem-solving, science, social issues, sports, travel (depends on theme of issue). Buys 100 ms/year. Average word length: 200-600. Byline given.

Poetry Reviews poetry.

How to Contact Fiction/nonfiction: Send complete ms. Responds to queries in 4-5 months; mss in 3 months. Publishes ms 3 months after acceptance. Will consider simultaneous submissions and electronic submissions via disk or e-mail.

Photos Looking for photos to suit various themes; photos needed depend on stories. Model/property release required; captions required. Uses color, standard sized, prints, high resolution digital images and 35mm transparencies. Provide résumé, business card, promotional literature and tearsheets to be kept on file.

Terms Pays on publication. Buys first Australian serial rights. Pays $80-200 (Australian) for stories; $100-220 (Australian) for articles.

Tips "Check out our Web site for information about our publications." Also see listings for *Comet* and *Explore*.

☐ CHEMMATTERS

American Chemical Society, 1155 16th Street, NW, Washington DC 20036. (202)872-6164. Fax: (202)833-7732. E-mail: chemmatters@acs.org. Website: http://www.acs.org/chemmatters. **Editor:** Pat Pages. **Art Director:** Cornithia Harris. Quarterly magazine. Estab. 1983. Circ. 35,000. "ChemMatters accepts both e-mail and mail submissions."

• *ChemMatters* only accepts e-mail submissions.

How to Contact Query with published clips. E-mail or mail submissions will be considered. Responds to queries/mss in 2 weeks. Publishes ms 6 months after acceptance. Will consider simultaneous submissions, e-mail submissions.

Illustration Buys 3 illustrations/issue; 12 illustrations/year. Uses color artwork only. Works on assignment only. Reviews manuscript/illustration packages from artists. Query. Contact: Cornithia Harris, art director *ChemMatters*. Illustrations only: Query with promo sheet, resume. Responds in 2 weeks. Samples returned with self-addressed stamped envelope; samples not filed. Credit line given.

Photos Looking for photos of high school students engaged in science-related activities. Model/property release required; captions required. Uses color prints, but prefers high-resolution PDFs. Query with samples. Responds in 2 weeks.

Terms Pays on acceptance. Minimally buys first North American serial rights, but prefers to buy all rights, reprint rights, electronic rights for manuscripts. Buys all rights for artwork; non-exclusive first rights for photos. Pays $500-$1,000 for article. Additional payment for manuscript/illustration packages and for photos accompanying articles. **Sample copies** free for self-addressed stamped envelope 10 inches × 13 inches and 3 first-class stamps. **Writer's guidelines** free for self-addressed stamped envelope (available as e-mail attachment upon request).

Tips Be aware of the content covered in a standard high school chemistry textbook. Choose themes and topics that are timely, interesting, fun, *and* that relate to the content and concepts of the first-year chemistry course. Articles should describe real people involved with real science. Best articles feature young people making a difference or solving a problem.

CHILDREN'S BETTER HEALTH INSTITUTE

1100 Waterway Blvd.P.O. Box 567, Indianapolis IN 46206. See listings for Children's Digest, Children's Playmate, Humpty Dumpty's Magazine, Jack and Jill, Turtle and U*S* Kids.

CHILDREN'S DIGEST

Children's Better Health Institute, 1100 Waterway Blvd.P.O. Box 567, Indianapolis IN 46206. (317)634-1100. Fax: (317)684-8094. Website: www.childrensdigestmag.org. For children ages 10-12.

• See Web site for submission guidelines.

CHILDREN'S PLAYMATE

Children's Better Health Institute, 1100 Waterway Blvd.Box 567, Indianapolis IN 46206. (317)634-1100. Fax: (317)684-8094. Website: www.childrensplaymatemag.org. **Editor:** Terry Harshman. **Art Director:** Rob Falco. Magazine published 6 times/year. Estab. 1929. Circ. 135,000. For children ages 6-8 years; approximately 50% of content is health-related.

Fiction Average word length: 100-300. Byline given. Sample copies $2.95.

Nonfiction Young readers: easy recipes, games/puzzles, health, medicine, safety, science. Buys 16-20 mss/year. Average word length: 300-500. Byline given.

Poetry Maximum length: 20-25 lines.

How to Contact Fiction/nonfiction: Send complete ms. Responds to mss in 3 months. Do not send queries.

Illustration Works on assignment only. Reviews ms/illustration packages from artists. Query first.

Terms Pays on publication for illustrators and writers. Buys all rights for mss and artwork. Pays 17¢/word for stories. Pays minimum $25 for poems. Pays $275 for color cover illustration; $90 for b&w inside; $70-155 for color inside. Sample copy $3.95. Writer's/illustrator's guidelines for SASE.

CICADA

Carus Publishing Company, 70 East Lake Street, Suite 300, Chicago IL 60601. E-mail: mail@cicadamag.com. Website: www.cricketmag.com. **Editor-in-Chief:** Marianne Carus. **Executive Editor:** Deborah Vetter. **Art Director**: John Sandford. Bimonthly magazine. Estab. 1998. Cicada publishes fiction and poetry with a genuine teen sensibility, aimed at the high school and college-age market. The editors are looking for stories and poems that are thought-provoking but entertaining.

Fiction Young adults: adventure, contemporary, fantasy, historical, humor/satire, multicultural, nature/environment, romance, science fiction, sports, suspense/mystery. Buys up to 42 mss/year. Average word length: about 5,000 words for short stories; up to 10,000 for novellas (one novella per issue).

Nonfiction Young adults: first-person, coming-of-age experiences that are relevant to teens and young adults (example: life in the Peace Corps). Buys up to 6 mss/year. Average word length: about 5,000 words. Byline given.

Poetry : Reviews serious, humorous, free verse, rhyming (if done well) poetry. Maximum length: up to 25 lines. Limit submissions to 5 poems.

How to Contact Fiction/nonfiction: send complete ms. Responds to mss in 3 months. Publishes ms 1-2 years after acceptance. Will consider simultaneous submissions if author lets us know. Important: See www.cricketmag.com. For updated submissions guidelines as editorial needs fluctuate.

Illustration Buys 20 illustrations/issue; 120 illustrations/year. Uses color artwork for cover; b&w for interior. Works on assignment only. Reviews ms/illustration packages from artists. To submit samples, e-mail a link to your online portfolio to: mail@cicadamag.com. You may also e-mail a sample up to a maximum attachment size of 50 KB. We will keep your samples on file and contact you if we find an assignment that suits your style. Credit line given.

Photos Wants documentary photos (clear shots that illustrate specific artifacts, persons, locations, phenomena, etc.cited in the text) and "art" shots of teens in photo montage/lighting effects etc.

Terms Pays on publication. Rates and contract rights vary.

Tips "Cicada is currently open to submissions from adult contributors who have previously published in the magazine. We are also open to general submissions from young people ages 14-23. See YA guidelines at www.cicadamag.com. In addition, The Slam, our online micro fiction and poetry forum, is open to young people ages 14-23. Check www.cricketmag.com for updates on our submissions policy."

⚅ THE CLAREMONT REVIEW

4980 Wesley Road, Victoria BC V8Y 1Y9 Canada. (250)685-5221. Fax: (250)658-5387. E-mail: bashford@islandnet.com. Website: www.theClaremontReview.ca. Magazine 2 times/year. Estab. 1992. Circ. 500. "Publish quality fiction and poetry of emerging writers aged 13 to 19."

Fiction Young adults: multicultural, problem-solving, social issues, relationships. Average word length: 1,500-3,000.

Poetry Maximum length: 60 lines. No limit on submissions.

How to Contact Fiction: Send complete ms. Responds to queries in 2 weeks; mss in 2 months. Publishes ms 6 months after acceptance.

Illustration Illustrations only: Send postcard sample with samples, SASE. Contact: Janice McCachen, editor. Responds in 2 months. Samples returned with SASE. Credit line given.

Terms Buys first North American rights for mss. Pays contributor's copies when published. Sample copies for $10. Writer's guidelines for SASE.

Tips "Looking for good, concrete narratives with credible dialogue and solid use of original detail. It must be unique, honest and have a glimpse of some truth. Send an error-free final draft with a short covering letter and bio. Read our magazine first to familiarize yourself with what we publish."

CLICK

30 Grove Street, Suite C, Peterborough, NH 03458. E-mail: click@caruspub.com. Website: www. cricketmag.com. **Editor:** Amy Tao. **Art Director:** Deb Porter. 9 issues/year. Estab. 1998. "Click is a science and exploration magazine for children ages 3 to 7. Designed and written with the idea that it's never too early to encourage achild's natural curiosity about the world, Click 's 40 full-color pages are filled with amazing photographs, beautiful illustrations, and stories and articles that are both entertaining and thought-provoking."

Nonfiction Young readers: animals, nature/environment, science. Average word length:100-900. Byline given.

How to Contact *Click* does not accept unsolicited manuscripts or queries. All articles are commissioned. To be considered for assignments, experienced science writers may send a resume and three published clips.

Illustration Buys 10 illustrations/issue; 100 illustrations/year. Works on assignment only. Query with samples. Responds only if interested. Credit line given.

COBBLESTONE

Discover American History30 Grove St.Suite C, Peterborough NH 03458. (603)924-7209. Fax: (603)924-7380. Website: www.cobblestonepub.com. **Editor:** Meg Chorlian. **Art Director:** Ann Dillon. **Editorial Director:** Lou Waryncia. Magazine published 9 times/year. Circ. 27,000. "Cobblestone is theme-related. Writers should request editorial guidelines which explain procedure and list upcoming themes. Queries must relate to an upcoming theme. It is recommended that writers become familiar with the magazine (sample copies available).": Discover American History30 Grove St.Suite C, Peterborough NH 03458. (603)924-7209. Fax: (603)924-7380. Website: www. cobblestonepub.com. **Editor:** Meg Chorlian. **Art Director:** Ann Dillon. **Editorial Director:** Lou Waryncia. Magazine published 9 times/year. Circ. 27,000. "Cobblestone is theme-related. Writers should request editorial guidelines which explain procedure and list upcoming themes. Queries must relate to an upcoming theme. It is recommended that writers become familiar with the magazine (sample copies available)."

• *Cobblestone* themes and deadline are available on Web site or with SASE.

Fiction Middle readers, young adults: folktales, history, multicultural.

Nonfiction Middle readers (school ages 9-14): arts/crafts, biography, geography, history (world and American), multicultural, social issues. All articles must relate to the issue's theme. Buys 120 mss/year. Average word length: 600-800. Byline given.

Poetry Up to 100 lines. "Clear, objective imagery. Serious and light verse considered." Pays on an individual basis. Must relate to theme.

How to Contact Fiction/nonfiction: Query. "A query must consist of all of the following to be considered: a brief cover letter stating the subject and word length of the proposed article, a detailed one-page outline explaining the information to be presented in the article, an extensive bibliography of materials the author intends to use in preparing the article, a SASE. Writers new to *Cobblestone* should send a writing sample with query. If you would like to know if your query has been received, please also include a stamped postcard that requests acknowledgment of receipt. In all correspondence, please include your complete address as well as a telephone number where you can be reached. A writer may send as many queries for one issue as he or she wishes, but each query must have a separate cover letter, outline, bibliography and SASE. Telephone queries are not accepted. Handwritten queries will not be considered. Queries may be submitted at any time, but queries sent well in advance of deadline *may not be answered for several months.* Go-aheads requesting material proposed in queries are usually sent five months prior to publication date. Unused queries will not be returned."

Illustration Buys 5 color illustrations/issue; 45 illustrations/year. Preferred theme or style: Material that is fun, clear and accurate but not too juvenile. Historically accurate sources are a must. Works on assignment only. Reviews ms/illustration packages from artists. Query. Illustrations only: Send photocopies, tearsheets, or other nonreturnable samples. "Illustrators should consult issues of *Cobblestone* to familiarize themselves with our needs." Responds to art samples in 1 month. Samples are not returned; samples filed. Original artwork returned at job's completion (upon written request). Credit line given.

Photos Photos must relate to upcoming themes. Send transparencies and/or color prints. Submit on speculation.

Terms Pays after publication. Buys all rights to articles and artwork. Pays 20-25¢/word for articles/ stories. Pays on an individual basis for poetry, activities, games/puzzles. Pays photographers per photo ($50-100 for color). Sample copy $5.95 with 9 × 12 SAE and 4 first-class stamps; writer's/ illustrator's/photo guidelines free with SAE and 1 first-class stamp.

Tips Writers: "Submit detailed queries which show attention to historical accuracy and which offer interesting and entertaining information. Study past issues to know what we look for. All feature articles, recipes, activities, fiction and supplemental nonfiction are freelance contributions." Illustrators: "Submit color samples, not too juvenile. Study past issues to know what we look for. The illustration we use is generally for stories, recipes and activities."

CRICKET

Carus Publishing Company, 70 East Lake, Suite 300, Chicago, IL 60601. (312)701-1270. Website: www.cricketmag.com. **Editor-in-Chief:** Marianne Carus. **Executive Editor:** Lonnie Plecha. **Senior Art Director:** Karen Kohn. Publishes 9 issues/year. Estab. 1973. Circ. 55,000. Children's literary magazine for ages 9-14.

Fiction Middle readers, young adults/teens: contemporary, fantasy, folk and fairy tales, history, humorous, science fiction, suspense/mystery. Buys 70 mss/year. Maximum word length: 2,000. Byline given.

Nonfiction Middle readers, young adults/teens: adventure, architecture, archaeology, biography, foreign culture, games/puzzles, geography, natural history, science and technology, social science, sports, travel. Multicultural needs include articles on customs and cultures. Requests bibliography with submissions. Buys 30 mss/year. Average word length: 200-1,500. Byline given.

Poetry Reviews poems, 1-page maximum length. Limit submission to 5 poems or less.

How to Contact Send complete ms. Do not query first. Responds to mss in 4-6 months. Does not like but will consider simultaneous submissions. SASE required for response, IRC's for international submissions.

Illustration Buys 22 illustrations (7 separate commissions)/issue; 198 illustrations/year. Preferred theme for style: "stylized realism; strong people, especially kids; good action illustration; whimsical and humorous. All media, generally full color." Reviews ms/illustration packages from artists, "but reserves option to re-illustrate." Send complete ms with sample and query. Illustrations only: Provide link to web site or tearsheets and good quality photocopies to be kept on file. SASE required for response/return of samples.

Photos Purchases photos with accompanying ms only. Model/property releases required. Uses 300 DPI digital files, color glossy prints.

Terms Pays 30 days after publication. Rights purchased vary. Do not send original artwork. Pays up to 25¢/word for unsolicited articles; up to $3/line for poetry. Pays $750 for color cover; $150-250 for color inside. Writer's/illustrator's guidelines for SASE. Sample issue for $5, check made out to Cricket Magazine Group.

Tips Writers: "Read copies of back issues and current issues. Adhere to specified word limits. *Please* do not query." Would currently like to see more fantasy and science fiction." Illustrators:

"Send only your best work and be able to reproduce that quality in assignments. Put name and address on *all* samples. Know a publication before you submit your style appropriate?"

DAVEY AND GOLIATH'S DEVOTIONS

Augsburg Fortress Publishers, P.O. Box 1209, Minneapolis MN 55440-1209. E-mail: cllsub@augsburgfortress.org. Website: www.augsburgfortress.org. **Editor:** Becky Carlson. Quarterly magazine. Circ. approximately 40,000. This is a booklet of interactive conversations and activities related to weekly devotional material. Used primarily by Lutheran families with elementary school-aged children."Davey and Goliath's devotions is a magazine with concrete ideas that families can use to build biblical literacy and share faith and serve others. It includes bible stories, family activities, crafts, games, and a section of puzzles, and mazes."

How to Contact Visit www.augsburgfortress.org/media/company/downloads/FamilyDevotional SampleBriefing.oc to view sample briefing. Follow instructions in briefing if interested in submitting a sample for the devotional. Published material is 100% assigned.

Terms Pays on acceptance of final ms assignment. Buys all rights. Pays $40/printed page on assignment. Free sample and information for prospective writers. Include 6 × 9 SAE and postage.

Tips "Pay attention to details in the sample devotional. Follow the process laid out in the information for prospective writers. Ability to interpret Bible texts appropriately for children is required. Content must be doable and fun for families on the go."

DIG

Cobblestone Publishing, 30 Grove St.Suite C, Peterborough NH 03450. (603)924-7209. Fax: (603)924-7380. E-mail: cfbakeriii@meganet.net. Website: www.igonsite.com. **Editor:** Rosalie Baker. **Editorial Director:** Lou Waryncia. **Art Director:** Ann Dillon. Magazine published 9 times/year. Estab. 1999. Circ. 18,000. An archaeology magazine for kids ages 8-14. Publishes entertaining and educational stories about discoveries, artifacts, archaeologists.

• *Dig* was purchased by Cobblestone Publishing, a division of Carus Publishing.

Nonfiction Middle readers, young adults: biography, games/puzzles, history, science, archaeology. Buys 50 mss/year. Average word length: 400-800. Byline given.

How to Contact Fiction/nonfiction: Query. "A query must consist of all of the following to be considered: a brief cover letter stating the subject and word length of the proposed article, a detailed one-page outline explaining the information to be presented in the article, a bibliography of materials the author intends to use in preparing the article, and a SASE. Writers new to *Dig* should send a writing sample with query." Multiple queries accepted, may not be answered for many months. Go-aheads requesting material proposed in queries are usually sent 10 months prior to publication date. Unused queries will be returned approximately 3-4 months prior to publication date.

Illustration Buys 10-15 illustrations/issue; 60-75 illustrations/year. Prefers color artwork. Works on assignment only. Reviews ms/illustration packages from artists. Query. Illustrations only: Query with samples. Arrange portfolio review. Send tearsheets. Responds in 2 months only if interested. Samples not returned; samples filed. Credit line given.

Photos Uses anything related to archaeology, history, artifacts, and current archaeological events that relate to kids. Uses color prints and 35mm transparencies and 300 DPI digital images. Provide resume, promotional literature or tearsheets to be kept on file. Responds only if interested.

Terms Pays on publication. Buys all rights for mss. Buys first North American rights for photos. Original artwork returned at job's completion. Pays 20-25¢/word. Additional payment for ms/illustration packages and for photos accompanying articles. Pays per photo.

Tips "We are looking for writers who can communicate archaeological concepts in a conversational, interesting, informative and *accurate* style for kids. Writers should have some idea where photography can be located to support their articles."

DRAMATICS MAGAZINE

Educational Theatre Association, 2343 Auburn Ave.Cincinnati OH 45219. (513)421-3900. E-mail: dcorathers@edta.org. Website: www.edta.org. **Articles Editor:** Don Corathers. **Graphic Design:** Kay Walters. Published monthly September-May. Estab. 1929. Circ. 35,000. "Dramatics is for students (mainly high school age) and teachers of theater. Mix includes how-to (tech theater, acting, directing, etc.), informational, interview, photo feature, humorous, profile, technical. We want our student readers to grow as theater artists and become a more discerning and appreciative audience. Material is directed to both theater students and their teachers, with strong student slant."

Fiction Young adults: drama (one-act and full-length plays). Does not want to see plays that show no understanding of the conventions of the theater. No plays for children, no Christmas or didactic "message" plays. "We prefer unpublished scripts that have been produced at least once." Buys 5-9 plays/year. Emerging playwrights have better chances with résumé of credits.

Nonfiction Young adults: arts/crafts, careers, how-to, interview/profile, multicultural (all theater-related). "We try to portray the theater community in all its diversity." Does not want to see academic treatises. Buys 50 mss/year. Average word length: 750-3,000. Byline given.

How to Contact Send complete ms. Responds in 3 months (longer for plays). Published ms 3 months after acceptance. Will consider simultaneous submissions and previously published work occasionally.

Illustration Buys 0-2 illustrations/year. Works on assignment only. Arrange portfolio review; send résumé, promo sheets and tearsheets. Responds only if interested. Samples returned with SASE; sample not filed. Credit line given.

Photos Buys photos with accompanying ms only. Looking for "good-quality production or candid photography to accompany article. We very occasionally publish photo essays." Model/property release and captions required. Prefers hi-res jpg files. Will consider prints or transparencies. Query with résumé of credits. Responds only if interested.

Terms Pays on acceptance. Buys one-time print and short term Web rights. Buys one-time rights for artwork and photos. Original artwork returned at job's completion. Pays $100-500 for plays; $50-500 for articles; up to $100 for illustrations. Pays photographers by the project or per photo. Sometimes offers additional payment for ms/illustration packages and photos accompanying a ms. Sample copy available for 9 × 12 SAE with 4 ounces first-class postage. Writer's and photo guidelines available for SASE or via Web site.

Tips "Obtain our writer's guidelines and look at recent back issues. The best way to break in is to know our audience—drama students, teachers and others interested in theater—and write for them. Writers who have some practical experience in theater, especially in technical areas, have an advantage, but we'll work with anybody who has a good idea. Some freelancers have become regular contributors."

⊕ EXPLORE

Pearson Education Australia, 20 Thackray Rd.Port Melbourne VIC 3207 Australia. (61)03 3245 7111. Fax: (61)03 9245 7333. E-mail: magazines@pearson.com.au. Website: www.pearson.com.au/schools. Quarterly Magazine. Circ. 20,000. Pearson Education publishes "educational magazines that include a variety of nonfiction articles in a variety of genres and text types (interviews, diary, informational, recount, argumentative, etc.). They must be appropriate, factually correct and of high interest.

- *Explore* is a theme based publication. Check the Web site to see upcoming themes and deadlines.

Fiction Young readers, middle readers: adventure, animal, contemporary, fantasy, folktale, humorous, multicultural, nature/environment, problem-solving, suspense/mystery. Middle readers: science fiction, sports. Average word length: 400-1,000. Byline given.

Nonfiction Young readers, middle readers: animal, arts/crafts, biography, careers, cooking, health, history, hobbies, how-to, interview/profile, math, multicultural, nature/environment, problem-solving, science, social issues, sports, travel. Young readers: games/puzzles. Middle readers: concept, fashion, geography. Average word length: 200-600. Byline given.

Poetry Reviews poetry.

How to Contact Fiction/nonfiction: Send complete ms. Responds to queries in 1 month; mss in 3 months. Publishes ms 3 months after acceptance. Will consider simultaneous submissions and electronic submissions via disk or e-mail.

Photos Looking for photos to suit various themes; photos needed depend on stories. Model/property release required; captions required. Uses color, standard sized, prints, high resolution digital images and 35mm transparencies. Provide résumé, business card, promotional literature and tearsheets to be kept on file.

Terms Pays on publication. Buys first Australian rights. Pays $80-200 (Australian) for stories; $100-220 (Australian) for articles.

Tips "Check out our Web site for information about our publications." Also see listings for *Challenge* and *Comet*.

FACES, People, Places & Cultures

30 Grove St.Peterborough NH 03458. (603)924-7209. Fax: (603)924-7380. E-mail: facesmag@yahoo.com. Website: www.cobblestonepub.com. **Editor:** Elizabeth Crooker Carpentiere. **Editorial Director:** Lou Warnycia. **Art Director:** Ann Dillon. Magazine published 9 times/year (September-May) with combined issues in May/June, July/August, and November/December. Circ. 15,000. Faces is a theme-related magazine; writers should send for theme list before submitting ideas/queries. Each month a different world culture is featured through the use of feature articles, activities and photographs and illustrations.

• See Web site for 2009-2010 theme list for *Faces*.

Fiction Middle readers, young adults/teens: adventure, folktales, history, multicultural, plays, religious, travel. Does not want to see material that does not relate to a specific upcoming theme. Buys 9 mss/year. Maximum word length: 800. Byline given.

Nonfiction Middle readers and young adults/teens: animal, anthropology, arts/crafts, biography, cooking, fashion, games/puzzles, geography, history, how-to, humorous, interview/profile, nature/environment, religious, social issues, sports, travel. Does not want to see material not related to a specific upcoming theme. Buys 63 mss/year. Average word length: 300-600. Byline given.

How to Contact Fiction/nonfiction: Query with published clips and 2-3 line biographical sketch. "Ideas should be submitted six to nine months prior to the publication date. Responses to ideas are usually sent approximately four months before the publication date." Guidelines on Web site.

Illustration Buys 3 illustrations/issue; buys 27 illustrations/year. Preferred theme or style: Material that is meticulously researched (most articles are written by professional anthropologists); simple, direct style preferred, but not too juvenile. Works on assignment only. Roughs required. Reviews ms/illustration packages from artists. Illustrations only: Send samples of b&w work. "Illustrators should consult issues of *Faces* to familiarize themselves with our needs." Responds to art samples only if interested. Samples returned with SASE. Original artwork returned at job's completion (upon written request). Credit line given.

Photos Wants photos relating to forthcoming themes.

Terms Pays on publication. Buys all rights for mss and artwork. Pays 20-25¢/word for articles/stories. Pays on an individual basis for poetry. Covers are assigned and paid on an individual basis. Pays illustrators $50-300 for color inside. Pays photographers per photo ($25-100 for color). Sample copy $6.95 with 7½ × 10½ SAE and 5 first-class stamps. Writer's/illustrator's/photo guidelines via Web site or free with SAE and 1 first-class stamp.

Tips "Writers are encouraged to study past issues of the magazine to become familiar with our style and content. Writers with anthropological and/or travel experience are particularly encouraged; *Faces* is about world cultures. All feature articles, recipes and activities are freelance contributions."

Illustrators: "Submit b&w samples, not too juvenile. Study past issues to know what we look for. The illustration we use is generally for retold legends, recipes and activities."

THE FRIEND MAGAZINE

The Church of Jesus Christ of Latter-day Saints, 50 E. North Temple St.Salt Lake City UT 84150-3226. (801)240-2210. E-mail: friend@ldschurch.org. Website: www.lds.org. **Editor:** Vivian Paulsen. **Art Director:** Mark Robison. Monthly magazine for 3-12 year olds. Estab. 1971. Circ. 275,000.

Nonfiction Publishes children's/true stories—adventure, ethnic, some historical, humor, mainstream, religious/inspirational, nature. Length: 1,000 words maximum. Also publishes family- and gospel-oriented puzzles, games and cartoons. Simple recipes and handicraft projects welcome.

Poetry Reviews poetry. Maximum length: 20 lines. "We are looking for easy-to-illustrate peoms with catchy cadences. Poems should convey a sense of joy adn reflect gospel teachings. Also brief poems that will appeal to preschoolers."

How to Contact Send complete ms. Responds to mss in 2 months.

Illustration Illustrations only: Query with samples; arrange personal interview to show portfolio; provide résumé and tearsheets for files.

Terms Pays on acceptance. Buys all rights for mss. Pays $100-150 (400 words and up) for stories; $30 for poems; $20 minimum for activities and games. Contributors are encouraged to send for sample copy for $1.50, 9 × 12 envelope and four 41-cent stamps. Free writer's guidelines.

Tips "*The Friend* is published by The Church of Jesus Christ of Latter-day Saints for boys and girls up to eleven years of age. All submissions are carefully read by the *Friend* staff, and those not accepted are returned within two months for SASE. Submit seasonal material at least one year in advance. Query letters and simultaneous submissions are not encouraged. Authors may request rights to have their work reprinted after their manuscript is published."

FUN FOR KIDZ

P.O. Box 227, Bluffton OH 45817-0227. (419)358-4610. Fax: (419)358-5027. Website: www.funforkidz.com. **Articles Editor:** Marilyn Edwards. Bimonthly magazine. Estab. 2002. "Fun for Kidz is a magazine created for boys and girls ages 5-14, with youngsters 8, 9, and 10 the specific target age. The magazine is designed as an activity publication to be enjoyed by both boys and girls on the alternative months of Hopscotch and Boys' Quest magazines."

• *Fun for Kidz* is theme-oriented. Send SASE for theme list and writer's guidelines.

Fiction Picture-oriented material, young readers, middle readers: adventure, animal, history, humorous, problem-solving, multicultural, nature/environment, sports. Average word length: 300-700.

Nonfiction Picture-oriented material, young readers, middle readers: animal, arts/crafts, cooking, games/puzzles, history, hobbies, how-to, humorous, problem-solving, sports, carpentry projects. Average word length: 300-700. Byline given.

Poetry Reviews poetry.

How to Contact Fiction/nonfiction: Send complete ms. Responds to queries in 2 weeks; mss in 5 weeks. Will consider simultaneous submissions. "Will not respond to faxed/e-mailed queries, mss, etc."

Illustration Works on assignment mostly. "We are anxious to find artists capable of illustrating stories and features. Our inside art is pen & ink." Query with samples. Samples kept on file.

Photos "We use a number of back & white photos inside the magazine; most support the articles used."

Terms Pays on publication. Buys first American serial rights. Buys first American serial rights and photos for artwork. Pays 5/word; $10/poem or puzzle; $35 for art (full page); $25 for art (partial page). Pays illustrators $5-10 for b&w photos. Sample copies available for $6 (there is a direct charge by the post office of $4.50 per issue for airmail to other countries); $8 for Canada, and $10.50 for all other countries.

Tips "Our point of view is that every child deserves the right to be a child for a number of years before he or she becomes a young adult. As a result, *Fun for Kidz* looks for activities that deal with timeless topics, such as pets, nature, hobbies, science, games, sports, careers, simple cooking, and anything else likely to interest a child."

GIRLS' LIFE

Monarch, 4529 Harford Rd.Baltimore MD 21214. (410)426-9600. Fax: (410)254-0991. E-mail: katiea@girlslife.com. Website: www.girlslife.com. **Contact:** Katie Abbondanza, associate editor. Bimonthly magazine for girls, ages 9-15. Estab.1994. Circ. 400,000.

Fiction "We accept short fiction. They should be stand-alone stories and are generally 2,500-3,500 words."

Nonfiction "Features and articles should speak to young women ages 10-15 looking for new ideas about relationships, family, friends, school, etc. with fresh, savvy advice. Front-of-the -book columns and quizzes are a good place to start."Buys 40mss/year. Length: 700-2,000 words. Pays $350/regular column; $500/feature.

How to Contact Accepts queries by mail or e-mail. Query by with published clips. Submit complete mss on spec only. Responds in 3 month to queries.

Photos State availability with submission if applicable. Reviews contact sheets, negatives, transparencies. Negotiates payment individually. Captions, identification of subjects, model releases required.

Terms Pays on publication. Publishes ms an average of 3 months after acceptance Byline given. Buys all rights. Editorial lead time 4 months. Submit seasonal material 5 months in advance. Sample copy for $5 or online. Writer's guidelines online.

Tips "Send thought-out queries with published writing samples and detailed résumé. Have fresh ideas and a voice that speaks to our audience-not down to them. And check out a copy of the magazine or visit girlslife.com before submitting."

Ⓝ ⬛ GREEN TEACHER

Green Teacher, 95 Robert Street, Toronto ON M2S 2K5.(416)960-1244. Fax: (416)925-3474. E-mail: info@greenteacher.com. Website: www.greenteacher.com. **Article Editor/Photo Editor:** Gail Littlejohn and Tim Grant. Estab. 1991. Circ. 15,000. "Green Teacher is a magazine that helps youth educators enhance environmental and global education inside and outside of schools."

Nonfiction Considers all levels: multicultural, nature/environment. Buys 0 — volunteer mss/year. Average word length: 750-2,500.

How to Contact Nonfiction: Query. Responds to queries in 1 weeks; Publishes ms 8 months after acceptance. Considers electronic submissions via disk or e-mail.

Illustration Buys 3 illustrations/issue from freelancers; 10 illustrations/year from freelancers. Black & white artwork only. Works on assignment only. Reviews ms/illustration packages from artists. Query. **Contact:** Gail Littlejohn, Editor. Illustrations only: Query with samples; tearsheets. Contact: Gail Littlejohn, Editor. Responds only if interested. Samples not returned. Samples filed. Credit line given.

Photos Purchases photos both separately and with accompanying mss. "Activity photos, environmental photos." Uses b&w prints. Query with samples. Responds only of interested.

Terms Pays on acceptance.

GUIDE MAGAZINE

Review and Herald Publishing Association, 55 W. Oak Ridge Dr.Hagerstown MD 21740. (301)393-4037. Fax: (301)393-4055. E-mail: guide@rhpa.org. Website: www.guidemagazine.org. **Editor:** Randy Fishell. **Designer:** Brandon Reese. Weekly magazine. Estab. 1953. Circ. 27,000. "Ours is a weekly Christian journal written for middle readers and young teens (ages 10-14), presenting true stories relevant to the needs of today's young person, emphasizing positive aspects of Christian living."

Nonfiction Middle readers, young adults/teens: adventure, animal, character-building, contemporary, games/puzzles, humorous, multicultural, problem-solving, religious. "We need true, happenings, not merely true-to-life. Our stories and puzzles must have a spiritual emphasis." No violence. No articles. "We always need humor and adventure stories." Buys 150 mss/year. Average word length: 500-600 minimum, 1,200-1,300 maximum. Byline given.

How to Contact Nonfiction: Send complete ms. Responds in 6 weeks. Will consider simultaneous submissions. "We can pay half of the regular amount for reprints." Responds to queries/mss in 6 weeks. Credit line given. "We encourage e-mail submissions."

Terms Pays on acceptance. Buys first world serial rights; first rights; one-time rights; second serial (reprint rights); simultaneous rights. Pays 6-12¢/word for stories and articles. "Writer receives three complimentary copies of issue in which work appears." Sample copy free with 6 × 9 SAE and 2 first-class stamps. Writer's guidelines for SASE.

Tips "Children's magazines want mystery, action, discovery, suspense and humor—no matter what the topic. For us, truth is stronger than fiction."

HIGHLIGHTS FOR CHILDREN

803 Church St.Honesdale PA 18431. (570)253-1080. E-mail: eds@highlights-corp.com. Website: www.highlights.com. **Contact:** Manuscript Coordinator. **Editor in Chief:** Christine French Clark. **Art Director:** Cindy Smith. Monthly magazine. Estab. 1946. Circ. 2 million. "Our motto is 'Fun With a Purpose.' We are looking for quality fiction and nonfiction that appeals to children, encourages them to read, and reinforces positive values. All art is done on assignment."

Fiction Picture-oriented material, young readers, middle readers: adventure, animal, contemporary, fantasy, folktales, history, humorous, multicultural, problem-solving, sports. Multicultural needs include first-person accounts of children from other cultures and first-person accounts of children from other countries. Does not want to see war, crime, violence. "We see too many stories with overt morals." Would like to see more contemporary, multicultural and world culture fiction, mystery stories, action/adventure stories, humorous stories, and fiction for younger readers. Buys 150 mss/year. Average word length: 500-800. Byline given.

Nonfiction Picture-oriented material, young readers, middle readers: animal, arts/crafts, biography, careers, games/puzzles, geography, health, history, hobbies, how-to, interview/profile, multicultural, nature/environment, problem-solving, science, sports. Multicultural needs include articles set in a country *about* the people of the country. Does not want to see trendy topics, fads, personalities who would not be good role models for children, guns, war, crime, violence. "We'd like to see more nonfiction for younger readers—maximum of 500 words. We still need older-reader material, too—500-800 words." Buys 200 mss/year. Maximum word length: 800. Byline given.

How to Contact Send complete ms. Responds to queries in 1 month; mss in 6 weeks.

Illustration Buys 25-30 illustrations/issue. Preferred theme or style: Realistic, some stylization. Works on assignment only. Reviews ms/illustration packages from artists. Illustrations only: photocopies, promo sheet, tearsheets, or slides. Résumé optional. Portfolio only if requested. Contact: Art Director. Responds to art samples in 2 months. Samples returned with SASE; samples filed. Credit line given.

Terms Pays on acceptance. Buys all rights for mss. Pays $50 and up for unsolicited articles. Pays illustrators $1,000 for color cover; $25-200 for b&w inside, $100-500 for color inside. Sample copies $3.95 and send SASE with 4 first-class stamps. Writer's/illustrator's guidelines free with SASE and on Web site.

Tips "Know the magazine's style before submitting. Send for guidelines and sample issue if necessary." Writers: "At *Highlights* we're paying closer attention to acquiring more nonfiction for young readers than we have in the past. Illustrators: "Fresh, imaginative work encouraged. Flexibility in working relationships a plus. Illustrators presenting their work need not confine themselves to just children's illustrations as long as work can translate to our needs. We also use animal illustrations, real and imaginary. We need crafts, puzzles and any activity that will stimulate children mentally and creatively. We are always looking for imaginative cover subjects. Know our publication's standards and content by reading sample issues, not just the guidelines. Avoid tired themes, or put a fresh twist on an old theme so that its style is fun and lively. We'd like to see stories with subtle messages, but the fun of the story should come first. Write what inspires you, not what you think the market needs."

HOPSCOTCH, The Magazine for Girls

P.O. Box 164, Bluffton OH 45817-0164. (419)358-4610. Fax: (419)358-5027. Website: hopscotchmagazine.com. **Editor:** Marilyn Edwards. Bimonthly magazine. Estab. 1989. Circ. 14,000. For girls from ages 5- 14, featuring traditional subjects—pets, games, hobbies, nature, science, sports, etc.—with an emphasis on articles that show girls actively involved in unusual and/or worthwhile activities."

Fiction Picture-oriented material, young readers, middle readers: adventure, animal, history, humorous, nature/environment, sports, suspense/mystery. Does not want to see stories dealing with dating, sex, fashion, hard rock music. Buys 30 mss/year. Average word length: 300-700. Byline given.

Nonfiction Picture-oriented material, young readers, middle readers: animal, arts/crafts, biography, cooking, games/puzzles, geography, hobbies, how-to, humorous, math, nature/environment, science. Does not want to see pieces dealing with dating, sex, fashion, hard rock music. "Need more nonfiction with quality photos about a *Hopscotch*-age girl involved in a worthwhile activity." Buys 46 mss/year. Average word length: 400-700. Byline given.

Poetry Reviews traditional, wholesome, humorous poems. Maximum word length: 300; maximum line length: 20. Will accept 6 submissions/author.

How to Contact All writers should consult the theme list before sending in articles. To receive a current theme list, send a SASE. Fiction: Send complete ms. Nonfiction: Query or send complete ms. Responds to queries in 2 weeks; mss in 5 weeks. Will consider simultaneous submissions.

Illustration Buys approximately 10 illustrations/issue; buys 60-70 articles/year. "Generally, the illustrations are assigned after we have purchased a piece (usually fiction). Occasionally, we will use a painting—in any given medium—for the cover, and these are usually seasonal." Uses b&w artwork only for inside; color for cover. Reviews ms/illustration packages from artists. Query first or send complete ms with final art. Illustrations only: Send résumé, portfolio, client list and tearsheets. Responds to art samples only if interested and SASE in 1 month. Samples returned with SASE. Credit line given.

Photos Purchases photos separately (cover only) and with accompanying ms only. Looking for photos to accompany article. Model/property releases required. Uses 5 × 7, b&w prints; 35mm transparencies. Black & white photos should go with ms. Should show girl or girls ages 6-12.

Terms For mss: pays on publication. For mss, artwork and photos, buys first North American serial rights; second serial (reprint rights). Original artwork returned at job's completion. Pays 5¢/word and $5-10/photo. "We always send a copy of the issue to the writer or illustrator." Text and art are treated separately. Pays $200 maximum for color cover; $25-35 for b&w inside. Sample copy for $6 (there is a direct charge by the post office of $4.50 per issue for airmail to other countries) and 8 × 12 SASE; $8 for Canada, and $10.50 for all other countries. Writer's/illustrator's/photo guidelines, theme list free for #10 SASE.

Tips "Remember we publish only six issues a year, which means our editorial needs are extremely limited. Please look at our guidelines and our magazine... and remember, we use far more nonfiction than fiction. Guidelines and current theme list can be downloaded from our Web site. If decent photos accompany the piece, it stands an even better chance of being accepted. We believe it is the responsibility of the contributor to come up with photos. Please remember, our readers are 6-12 years—most are 8-10—and your text should reflect that. Many magazines try to entertain first and educate second. We try to do the reverse. Our magazine is more simplistic, like a book to be read from cover to cover. We are looking for wholesome, non-dated material."

HORSEPOWER, Magazine for Young Horse Lovers

Magazine for Young Horse Lovers, P.O. Box 670, Aurora ON L4G 4J9 Canada. (800)505-7428. Fax: (905)841-1530. E-mail: info@horse-canada.com. Website: www.horse-canada.com. **Editor:** Susan Stafford. Bimonthly 16-page magazine, bound into Horse Canada, a bimonthly family horse magazine. Estab. 1988. Circ. 17,000. "Horsepower offers how-to articles and stories relating to horse care for kids ages 6-16, with a focus on safety."

• *Horsepower* no longer accepts fiction.

Nonfiction Middle readers, young adults: arts/crafts, biography, careers, fashion, games/puzzles, health, history, hobbies, how-to, humorous, interview/profile, problem-solving, travel. Buys 6-10 mss/year. Average word length: 500-1,200. Byline given.

How to Contact Fiction: query. Nonfiction: send complete ms. Responds to queries in 6 months; mss in 3 months. Publishes ms 6 months after acceptance. Will consider simultaneous submissions, electronic submission via disk or e-mail, previously published work.

Illustration Buys 3 illustrations/year. Reviews ms/illustration packages from artists. Contact: Editor. Query with samples. Responds only if interested. Samples returned with SASE; samples kept on file. Credit line given.

Photos Look for photos of kids and horses, instructional/educational, relating to riding or horse care. Uses color matte or glossy prints. Query with samples. Responds only if interested. Accepts TIFF or JPEG 300 dpi, disk or e-mail. Children on horseback must be wearing riding helmets or photos cannot be published.

Terms Pays on publication. Buys one-time rights for mss. Original artwork returned at job's completion if SASE provided. Pays $50-75 for stories. Additional payment for ms/illustration packages and for photos accompanying articles. Pays illustrators $25-50 for color inside. Pays photographers per photo (range: $15). Sample copies for $4.50. Writer's/illustrator's/photo guidelines for SASE.

Tips "Articles must be easy to understand, yet detailed and accurate. How-to or other educational features must be written by, or in conjunction with, a riding/teaching professional. Fiction is not encouraged, unless it is outstanding and teaches a moral or practical lesson. Note: preference will be given to Canadian writers and photographers due to Canadian content laws. Non-Canadian contributors accepted on a very limited basis."

HUMPTY DUMPTY'S MAGAZINE

Children's Better Health Institute, 1100 Waterway Blvd.Indianapolis IN 46206. (317)636-8881. Fax: (317)684-8094. Website: www.humptydumptymag.org. **Editor/Art Director:** Phyllis Lybarger. Magazine published 6 times/year. HDM is edited for children ages 4-6. It includes fiction (easy-to-reads; read alouds; rhyming stories; rebus stories), nonfiction articles (some with photo illustrations), poems, crafts, recipes, and puzzles. Content encourages development of better health habits.

• *Humpty Dumpty's* publishes material promoting health and fitness with emphasis on simple activities, poems and fiction.

Fiction Picture-oriented stories: adventure, animal, contemporary, fantasy, folktales, health, humorous, multicultural, nature/environment, problem-solving, science fiction, sports. Also, talking inanimate objects are very difficult to do well. Beginners (and maybe everyone) should avoid these." Buys 8-10 mss/year. Maximum word length: 300. Byline given.

Nonfiction Picture-oriented articles: animal, arts/crafts, concept, games/puzzles, health, how-to, humorous, nature/environment, no-cook recipes, science, social issues, sports. Buys 6-10 mss/year. Prefers very short nonfiction pieces—200 words maximum. Byline given. Send ms with SASE if you want ms returned.

How to Contact Send complete ms. Nonfiction: Send complete ms with bibliography if applicable. "No queries, please!" Responds to mss in 3 months. Send seasonal material at least 8 months in advance.

Illustration Buys 5-8 illustrations/issue; 30-48 illustrations/year. Preferred theme or style: Realistic or cartoon. Works on assignment only. Illustrations only. Query with slides, printed pieces or photocopies. Samples are not returned; samples filed. Responds to art samples only if interested. Credit line given.

Terms Writers: Pays on publication. Artists: Pays within 2 months. Buys all rights. "One-time book rights may be returned if author can provide name of interested book publisher and tentative date of publication." Pays up to 22¢/word for stories/articles; payment varies for poems and activities. 10 complimentary issues are provided to author with check. Pays $275 for color cover illustration; $35-90 per page b&w inside; $70-155 for color inside. Sample copies for $3.95. Writer's/illustrator's guidelines free with SASE.

⃞ IMAGINATION CAFÉ

Imagination Cafe, P.O. Box 1536, Valparaiso IN 46384.(219)510-4467. E-mail: editor@imagination-cafe.com. Website: www.imagionation-cafe.com. **Articles Editor:** Rosanne Tolin. **Art Director:** Photo Editor. Estab. 2006. "Imagination Café is dedicated to empowering kids and tweens by encouraging curiosity in the world around them, as well as exploration of their talents and aspirations. Imagination Café's mission is to offer children tools to discover their passions by providing them with reliable information, resources and safe opportunities for self-expression. Imagination Café publishes general interest articles with an emphasis on career exploration for kids. There is also material on school, science, history, and sports. Plus, celebrity briefs, recipes, animals, and other general interest pieces." Publication is aimed at juvenile market.

Nonfiction Buys 72 mss/year. Average word length: 150-500. Byline given.

How to Contact Agented submissions only. Nonfiction: Query or query with published clips. Send complete ms. Responds to queries in 1 day to 2 weeks. Publishes ms 1 month after acceptance. Considers simultaneous submissions.

Terms Pays on acceptance. Buys electronic and non-exclusive print rights. Originals not returned. Pays 15-75 for stories. Additional payment for ms/illustration packages.

Tips "Imagination Café is not a beginner's market. Most of our contributors are published writers. Please study the web site before submitting, and make sure your writing is clearly directed to a kid audience, no adults. That means informative, interesting text written in a clear, concise, even clever manner that suitable for the online reader. Have fun with it and be sure include web-friendly, relevant links and sidebars."

JACK AND JILL

Children's Better Health Institute, 1100 Waterway Blvd.P.O. Box 567, Indianapolis IN 46202. (317)634-1100. Fax: (317)684-8094. Website: www.cbhi.org/magazines/jackandjill/index.shtml. **Editor:** Daniel Lee. **Art Director:** Jennifer Webber. Magazine for children ages 7-10, published 6 times/year. Estab. 1938. Circ. 360,000. "Write entertaining and imaginative stories for kids, not just about them. Writers should understand what is funny to kids, what's important to them, what excites them. Don't write from an adult 'kids are so cute' perspective. We're also looking for health and healthful lifestyle stories and articles, but don't be preachy."

Fiction Young readers and middle readers: adventure, contemporary, folktales, health, history, humorous, nature, sports. Buys 30-35 mss/year. Average word length: 700. Byline given.

Nonfiction Young readers, middle readers: animal, arts/crafts, cooking, games/puzzles, history, hobbies, how-to, humorous, interview/profile, nature, science, sports. Buys 8-10 mss/year. Average word length: 500. Byline given.

Poetry Reviews poetry.

How to Contact Fiction/nonfiction: Send complete ms. Queries not accepted. Responds to mss in 3 months. Guidelines by request with a #10 SASE.

Illustration Buys 15 illustrations/issue; 90 illustrations/year. Responds only if interested. Samples not returned; samples filed. Credit line given.

Terms Pays on publication; up to 17¢/word. Pays illustrators $275 for color cover; $35-90 for b&w, $70-155 for color inside. Pays photographers negotiated rate. Sample copies $1.25. Buys all rights to mss and one-time rights to photos.

Tips Publishes writing/art/photos by children.

KEYS FOR KIDS

CBH Ministries, Box 1001, Grand Rapids MI 49501-1001. (616)647-4971. Fax: (616)647-4950. E-mail: hazel@cbhministries.org. Website: www.cbhministries.org. **Fiction Editor:** Hazel Marett. Bimonthly devotional booklet. Estab. 1982. "This is a devotional booklet for children and is also widely used for family devotions."

Fiction Young readers, middle readers: religious. Buys 60 mss/year. Average word length: 400.

How to Contact Fiction: Send complete ms. Will consider simultaneous submissions,

Terms Pays on acceptance. Buys reprint rights or first rights for mss. Pays $25 for stories. Sample copies free for SAE 6 × 9 and 3 first-class stamps. Writer's guidelines for SASE.

Tips "Be sure to *follow*guidelines after studying sample copy of the publication."

THE KIDS HALL OF FAME NEWS

The Kids Hall of Fame, 3 Ibsen Court, Dix Hills NY 11746. (631)242-9105. Fax: (631)242-8101. E-mail: VictoriaNesnick@TheKidsHallofFame.com. Website: www.TheKidsHallofFame.com. **Publisher:** Dr. Victoria Nesnick. **Art/Photo Editor:** Amy Gilvary. Online publication. Estab. 1998. "We spotlight and archive extraordinary positive achievements of contemporary and historical kids internationally under age 20. These inspirational stories are intended to provide positive peer role models and empower others to say, 'If that kid can do it, so can I,' or 'I can do better.' Our magazine is the prelude to The Kids Hall of Fame set of books (one volume per age) and museum."

How to Contact Query with published clips or send complete mss with SASE for response. Go to Web site for sample stories and for The Kids Hall of Fame nomination form.

Tips "Nomination stories must be positive and inspirational, and whenever possible, address the 7 items listed in the 'Your Story and Photo' page of our Web site. Request writers' guidelines and list of suggested nominees. Day and evening telephone queries acceptable."

KIDZ CHAT®

Standard Publishing. Website: www.standardpub.com. **Editor:** Marjorie Redford. Weekly magazine. Circ. 55,000.

- *Kidz Chat*® has decided to reuse much of the material that was a part of the first publication cycle. They will not be sending out theme lists, sample copies or writers guidelines or accepting any unsolicited material because of this policy.

KID ZONE

WordAction Publishing Co.2923 Troost Ave.Kansas City MO 64109. (816)931-1900. Fax: (816)412-8306. E-mail: lslohberger@wordaction.com. **Editor:** Virginia L. Folsom. **Senior Editor:** Donna L. Fillmore. **Assistant Editor:** Laura Lohberger. Take-home paper. "Kid Zone is a leisure-reading piece for third- and fourth-graders. It is published weekly by WordAction Publishing. The major purpose of the magazine is to provide a leisure-reading piece which will build Christian behavior and values and provide reinforcement for Biblical concepts taught in the Sunday School curriculum. The focus of the reinforcement will be life-related, with some historical appreciation. Kid Zone'target audience is children age's eight to ten in grades three and four. The readability goal is third to fourth grade." Request guidelines and theme list by e-mail or send SASE.

LADYBUG, The Magazine for Young Children

70 E. Lake St.Suite 300, Chicago IL 60601. (312)701-1720. **Editor:** Alice Letvin. **Art Director:** Suzanne Beck. Monthly magazine. Estab. 1990. Circ. 130,000. Literary magazine for children 3-6, with stories, poems, activities, songs and picture stories.

Fiction Picture-oriented material: adventure, animal, fantasy, folktales, humorous, multicultural, nature/environment, problem-solving, science fiction, sports, suspense/mystery. "Open to any easy fiction stories." Buys 50 mss/year. Story length: limit 800 words. Byline given.

Nonfiction Picture-oriented material: activities, animal, arts/crafts, concept, cooking, humorous, math, nature/environment, problem-solving, science. Buys 35 mss/year. Story length: limit 800 words.

Poetry Reviews poems, 20-line maximum length; limit submissions to 5 poems. Uses lyrical, humorous, simple language, action rhymes.

How to Contact Fiction/nonfiction: Send complete ms. Queries not accepted. Responds to mss in 6 months. Publishes ms up to 3 years after acceptance. Will consider simultaneous submissions if informed. Submissions without SASE will be discarded.

Illustration Buys 12 illustrations/issue; 145 illustrations/year. Prefers "bright colors; all media, but use watercolor and acrylics most often; same size as magazine is preferred but not required." To be considered for future assignments: Submit promo sheet, slides, tearsheets, color and b&w photocopies. Responds to art samples in 3 months. Submissions without SASE will be discarded.

Terms Pays on publication for mss; after delivery of completed assignment for illustrators. Rights purchased vary. Original artwork returned at job's completion. Pays 25¢/word for prose; $3/line for poetry. Pays $750 for color (cover) illustration, $50-100 for b&w (inside) illustration, $250/page for color (inside). Sample copy for $5. Writer's/illustrator's guidelines free for SASE or available on Web site, FAQ at www.cricketmag.com.

Tips Writers: "Get to know several young children on an individual basis. Respect your audience. We want less cute, condescending or 'preachy-teachy' material. Less gratuitous anthropomorphism. More rich, evocative language, sense of joy or wonder. Keep in mind that people come in all colors, sizes, physical conditions. Be inclusive in creating characters. Set your manuscript aside for at least a month, then reread critically." Illustrators: "Include examples, where possible, of children, animals, and—most important—action and narrative (i.e.several scenes from a story, showing continuity and an ability to maintain interest)." (See listings for *Babybug, Cicada, Cricket, Muse* and *Spider*.)

LEADING EDGE

4087 JKB, Provo UT 84602. (801)378-3553. E-mail: fiction@leadingedgemagazine.com. Website: www.leadingedgemagazine.com. Twice yearly magazine. Estab. 1981."We strive to encourage developing and established talent and provide high quality speculative fiction to our readers." Does not accept mss with sex, excessive violence, or profanity.

Fiction Young adults: fantasy, science fiction. Buys 16 mss/year. Average word length: up to 15,000. Byline given.

How to Contact Fiction: Send complete ms c/o Fiction Director. Responds to queries/mss in 4 months. Publishes ms 2-6 months after acceptance.

Illustration Buys 24 illustrations/issue; 48 illustrations/year. Uses b&w artwork only. Works on assignment only. Contact: Art Director. Illustrations only: Send postcard sample with portfolio, samples, URL. Responds only if interested.Samples filed. Credit line given.

Terms Pays on publication. Buys first North American serial rights for mss. Buys first North American serial rights for artwork. Original artwork returned at job's completion. Pays $0.01/word for stories. Pays illustrators $50 for color cover, $30 for b&w inside. Sample copies for $5.95. Writer's/illustrator's guidelines for SASE or visit the web site.

LISTEN, Drug-Free Possibilities for Teens

55 West Oak Ridge Dr.Hagerstown MD 21740. (301)393-4019. Fax: (301)393-3294. E-mail: listen@ healthconnection.org. **Editor:** Céleste Perrino-Walker. Monthly magazine, 9 issues. Estab. 1948. Circ. 12,000. "Listen offers positive alternatives to drug use for its teenage readers. Helps them have a happy and productive life by making the right choices."

Nonfiction How-to, health, humorous, life skills, problem-solving, social issues, drug facts, drug-free living. Wants to see more factual articles on drug abuse. Buys 50 mss/year. Average word length: 500. Byline given.

How to Contact Fiction/nonfiction: Query. Considers manuscripts once a year, in October. Will consider simultaneous submissions, e-mail and previously published work.

Illustration Buys 3-6 illustrations/issue; 50 illustrators/year. Reviews ms/illustration packages from artists. Manuscript/illustration packages and illustration only: Query. Contact: Bill Kirstein bkirstein@rhpa.org, designer. Responds only if interested. Originals returned at job's completion. Samples returned with SASE. Credit line given.

Photos Purchases photos from freelancers. Photos purchased with accompanying ms only. Uses color and b&w photos; digital, 35mm, transparencies or prints. Query with samples. Looks for "youth oriented—action (sports, outdoors), personality photos."

Terms Pays on acceptance. Buys exclusive magazine rights for mss. Buys one-time rights for artwork and photographs. Pays $80-200 for articles. Pays illustrators $500 for color cover; $75-225 for b&w inside; $135-450 for color inside. Pays photographers by the project (range: $125-500); pays per photo (range: $125-500). Additional payment for ms/illustration packages and photos accompanying articles. Sample copy for $2 and 9 × 12 SASE and 2 first class stamps. Writer's guidelines free with SASE.

Tips "*Listen* is a magazine for teenagers. It encourages development of good habits and high ideals of physical, social and mental health. It bases its editorial philosophy of primary drug prevention on total abstinence from tobacco, alcohol, and other drugs. Because it is used extensively in public high school classes, it does not accept articles and stories with overt religious emphasis. Four specific purposes guide the editors in selecting materials for *Listen*: (1) To portray a positive lifestyle and to foster skills and values that will help teenagers deal with contemporary problems, including smoking, drinking, and using drugs. This is *Listen*'s primary purpose. (2) To offer positive alternatives to a lifestyle of drug use of any kind. (3) To present scientifically accurate information about the nature and effects of tobacco, alcohol, and other drugs. (4) To report medical research, community programs, and educational efforts which are solving problems connected with smoking, alcohol, and other drugs. Articles should offer their readers activities that increase one's sense of self-worth through achievement and/or involvement in helping others. They are often categorized by three kinds of focus: (1) Hobbies. (2) Recreation. (3) Community Service."

LIVE WIRE®

Standard Publishing. E-mail: Website: www.standardpub.com. **Editor:** Marjorie Redford. Published quarterly in weekly parts. Circ. 40,000.

- *Live Wire*® has decided to reuse much of the material that was a part of the first publication cycle. They will not be sending out theme lists, sample copies, or writers guidelines or accepting any unsolicited material because of this policy.

MUSE

Carus Publishing, 70 E Lake St.Suite 300, Chicago IL 60601. (312)701-1720. Fax: (312)701-1728. E-mail: muse@caruspub.com. Website: www.cricketmag.com. **Editor:** Elizabeth Preston. **Art Director:** John Sandford. **Photo Editor:** Carol Parden. Estab. 1996. Circ. 40,000. "The goal of Muse is to give as many children as possible access to the most important ideas and concepts underlying the principal areas of human knowledge. Articles should meet the highest possible standards of clarity and transparency aided, wherever possible, by a tone of skepticism, humor, and irreverence."

Nonfiction Middle readers, young adult: animal, arts, history, math, nature/environment, problem-solving, science, social issues.

How to Contact *Muse* is not accepting unsolicited mss or queries. All articles are commissioned. To be considered for assignments, experienced science writers may send a résumé and 3 published clips.

Illustration Works on assignment only. Credit line given. Send prints or tearsheets, but please, no portfolios or original art, and above all, DO NOT SEND SAMPLES THAT NEED TO BE RETURNED.

Photos Needs vary. Query with samples to photo editor.

NATIONAL GEOGRAPHIC KIDS

National Geographic Society, 1145 17th St. NW, Washington DC 20036-4688. (202)857-7000. Fax: (202)775-6112. Website: www.nationalgeographic.com/ngkids. **Editor:** Melina Gerosa Bellows. **Art Director:** Jonathan Halling. **Photo Director:** Jay Sumner. Monthly magazine. Estab. 1975. Circ. 1.3 million.

NATURE FRIEND MAGAZINE

4253 Woodcock Lane, Dayton, VA 22821 (540)867-0764. Fax: (540)867-9516. Website: www.naturefriendmagazine.com. **Articles Editor:** Kevin Shank. Monthly magazine. Estab. 1983. Circ. 10,000.

Fiction Picture-oriented material, conversational, no talking animal stories.

Nonfiction Picture-oriented material: animal, how-to, nature, photo-essays. No talking animal stories. No evolutionary material. Buys 50 mss/year. Average word length: 500. Byline given.

Photos Submit on CD with a color printout. Photo guidelines free with SASE.

Terms Pays on publication. Buy one-time rights. Pays $75 for front cover photo; $50 for back cover photo, $25 inside photo. Offers sample copy is and writer's/photographer's guidelines for $10.

Tips Needs stories about unique animals or nature phenomena. "Please examine samples and writer's guide before submitting." The best way to learn what we use is to be a subscriber.

NEW MOON

The Magazine for Girls & Their Dreams New Moon Girl Media, LLC.2 W. First St.#101, Duluth MN 55802. (218)728-5507. Fax: (218)728-0314. E-mail: girl@newmoongirlmedia.com. Website: www.newmoongirls.com. **Managing Editor:** Heather Parfitt. Bimonthly magazine. Estab. 1992. Circ. 30,000. "New Moon Girls is for every girl who wants her voice heard and her dreams taken seriously. New Moon Girls portrays strong female role models of all ages, backgrounds and cultures now and in the past.": The Magazine for Girls & Their Dreams New Moon Girl Media, LLC.2 W. First St.#101, Duluth MN 55802. (218)728-5507. Fax: (218)728-0314. E-mail: girl@newmoongirlmedia.com. Website: www.newmoongirls.com. **Managing Editor:** Heather Parfitt. Bimonthly magazine. Estab. 1992. Circ. 30,000. "New Moon Girls is for every girl who wants her voice heard and her dreams taken seriously. New Moon Girls portrays strong female role models of all ages, backgrounds and cultures now and in the past."

Fiction Middle readers, young adults: adventure, contemporary, fantasy, folktales, history, humorous, multicultural, nature/environment, problem-solving, religious, science fiction, sports, suspense/mystery, travel. Buys 6 mss/year. Average word length: 1,200-1,600. Byline given.

Nonfiction Middle readers, young adults: animal, arts/crafts, biography, careers, cooking, games/puzzles, health, history, hobbies, humorous, interview/profile, math, multicultural, nature/environment, problem-solving, science, social issues, sports, travel, stories about real girls. Does not want to see how-to stories. Wants more stories about real girls doing real things written *by girls*. Buys 6-12 adult-written mss/year; 30 girl-written mss/year. Average word length: 600. Byline given.

How to Contact Fiction/Nonfiction: Does not return or acknowledge unsolicited mss. Send copies only. Responds only if interested. Will consider simultaneous and e-mail submissions.

Illustration Buys 6-12 illustrations/year from freelancers. *New Moon Girls* seeks 4-color cover illustrations. Reviews ms/illustrations packages from artists. Query. Submit ms with rough sketches. Illustration only: Query; send portfolio and tearsheets. Samples not returned; samples filed. Responds in 6 months only if interested. Credit line given.

Terms Pays on publication. Buys all rights for mss. Buys one-time rights, reprint rights, for artwork. Original artwork returned at job's completion. Pays 6-12 ¢/word for stories and articles. Pays in contributor's copies. Pays illustrators $400 for color cover; $50-300 for color inside. Sample copies for $7. Writer's/cover art guidelines for SASE or available on Web site.

Tips "Please refer to a copy of *New Moon Girls* to understand the style and philosophy of the magazine, or visit us online at www.NewMoonGirls.com. Writers and artists who understand our goals have the best chance of publication. We're looking for stories about real girls, women's careers, and historical profiles. We publish girl's and women's writing only." Publishes writing/art/photos by girls.

NICK JR. FAMILY MAGAZINE

Nickelodeon Magazine Group, 1515 Broadway, 37th Floor, New York NY 10036. (212)846-4985. Fax: (212)846-1690. Website: www.nickjr.com/magazine. **Deputy Editor:** Wendy Smolen. **Creative Director:** Don Morris. Published 9 times/year. Estab. 1999. Circ. 1,100,000. A magazine where kids play to learn and parents learn to play. 30% of publication aimed at juvenile market.

Fiction Picture-oriented material: adventure, animal, contemporary, humorous, multicultural, nature/environment, problem-solving, sports. Byline sometimes given.

Nonfiction Picture-oriented material: animal, arts/crafts, concept, cooking, games/puzzles, hobbies, how-to, humorous, math, multicultural, nature/environment, problem-solving, science, social issues, sports. Byline sometimes given.

How to Contact Fiction/nonfiction: Query or submit complete ms. Responds to queries/mss in 3-12 weeks.

Illustration Only interested in agented material. Works on assignment only. Reviews ms/illustration packages from artists. Query or send ms with dummy. Contact: Don Morris, creative director. Illustrations only: arrange portfolio review; send résumé, promo sheet and portfolio. Responds only if interested. Samples not returned; samples kept on file. Credit line sometimes given.

Tips "Writers should study the magazine before submitting stories. Read-Together Stories must include an interactive element that invited children to participate in telling the story: a repeating line, a fill-in-the-blank rhyme, or rebus pictures."

ODYSSEY, Adventures in Science

30 Grove St. Suite C, Peterborough NH 03458. (603)924-7209. Fax: (603)924-7380. E-mail: odyssey@caruspub.com. Website: www.odysseymagazine.com. **Editor:** Elizabeth E. Lindstrom. **Executive Director:** Lou Waryncia. **Art Director:** Ann Dillon. Magazine published 9 times/year. Estab. 1979. Circ. 22,000. Magazine covers general science and technology for children ages 10-16. All material must relate to the theme of a specific upcoming issue in order to be considered.

• *Odyssey* themes can be found on www.odysseymagazine.com.

Fiction Middle readers and young adults/teens: science fiction, science, astronomy. Does not want to see anything not theme-related. Average word length: 900-1,200 words.

Nonfiction Middle readers and young adults/teens: interiors, activities. Don't send anything not theme-related. Average word length: 750-1,200, depending on section article is used in.

How to Contact Query by mail. "A query must consist of all of the following to be considered (please use nonerasable paper): a brief cover letter stating the subject and word length of the proposed article; a detailed one-page outline explaining the information to be presented in the article; an extensive bibliography of materials/interviews the author intends to use in preparing the article; a SASE. Writers new to *Odyssey* should send a writing sample with query. If you would like to know if your query has been received, please also include a stamped postcard that requests acknowledgment of receipt. In all correspondence, please include your complete address as well as a telephone number and e-mail address where you can be reached. A writer may send as many queries for one issue as he or she wishes, but each query must have a separate cover letter, outline, bibliography, and SASE. Telephone queries are not accepted. Handwritten queries will not be considered. Queries may be submitted at any time."

Illustration Buys 4 illustrations/issue; 36 illustrations/year. Works on assignment only. Reviews ms/illustration packages from artists. Query. Contact: Beth Lindstrom, editor. Illustration only: Query with samples. Send tearsheets, photocopies. Responds in 2 weeks. Samples returned with SASE; samples not filed. Original artwork returned upon job's completion (upon written request).

Photos Wants photos pertaining to any of our forthcoming themes. Uses color prints; 35mm transparencies, digital images. Photographers should send unsolicited photos by mail on speculation.

Terms Pays on publication. Buys all rights for mss and artwork. Pays 20-25¢/word for stories/articles. Covers are assigned and paid on an individual basis. Pays photographers per photo ($15-100 for b $25-100 for color). Sample copy for $4.95 and SASE with $2 postage. Writer's/illustrator's/photo guidelines for SASE. (See listings for *AppleSeeds*, *Calliope*, *Cobblestone*, *Dig*, and *Faces*.)

ON COURSE, A Magazine for Teens

1445 Boonville Ave.Springfield MO 65802-1894. (417)862-2781. Fax: (417)862-1693. E-mail: oncourse@ag.org. Website: www.oncourse.ag.org. **Editor:** Amber Weigand-Buckley. **Art Director:** Ryan Strong. Bi- annual magazine. Estab. 1991. Circ. 160,000. On Course is a magazine to empower students to grow in a real-life relationship with Christ.

• *On Course* no longer uses illustrations, only photos.

Fiction Young adults: Christian discipleship, contemporary, humorous, multicultural, problem-solving, sports. Average word length: 800. Byline given.

Nonfiction Young adults: careers, interview/profile, multicultural, religion, social issues, college life, Christian discipleship.

How to Contact Works on assignment basis only. Resumes and writing samples will be considered for inclusion in Writer's File to receive story assignments.

Photos Buys photos from freelancers. "Teen life, church life, college life; unposed; often used for illustrative purposes." Model/property releases required. Uses color glossy prints and 35mm or 2¼ × 2¼ transparencies. Query with samples; send business card, promotional literature, tearsheets or catalog. Responds only if interested.

Terms Pays on acceptance. Buys first or reprint rights for mss. Buys one-time rights for photographs. Pays $30 per assigned stories/articles. Pays illustrators and photographers "as negotiated." Sample copies free for 9 × 11 SA SE. Writer's guidelines for SASE.

PASSPORT

Sunday School Curriculum, 2923 Troost Ave.Kansas City MO 64109. (816)931-1900. Fax: (816)412-8343. E-mail: lsl@nph.com. Website: www.nph.com. **Editor:** Ryan R. Pettit. Weekly take-home paper. "Passport looks for a casual, witty approach to Christian themes. We want hot topics relevant to preteens. We are not accepting stories."

POCKETS, Devotional Magazine for Children

1908 Grand Ave.P.O. Box 340004, Nashville TN 37203-0004. (615)340-7333. Fax: (615)340-7267. E-mail: pockets@upperroom.org. Website: www.pockets.org. **Articles/Fiction Editor:** Lynn W. Gilliam. **Art Director:** Chris Schechner, 408 Inglewood Dr.Richardson TX 75080. Magazine published 11 times/year. Estab. 1981. "Pockets is a Christian devotional magazine for children ages 6-11. Stories should help children experience a Christian lifestyle that is not always a neatly wrapped moral package but is open to the continuing revelation of God's will."

Fiction Picture-oriented, young readers, middle readers: adventure, contemporary, occasional folktales, multicultural, nature/environment, problem-solving, religious. Does not accept violence or talking animal stories. Buys 25-30 mss/year. Average word length: 600-1,400. Byline given. *Pockets* also accepts short-short stories (no more than 600 words) for children 5-7. Buys 11 mss/year.

Nonfiction Picture-oriented, young readers, middle readers: cooking, games/puzzles. "*Pockets* seeks biographical sketches of persons, famous or unknown, whose lives reflect their Christian commitment, written in a way that appeals to children." Does not accept how-to articles. "Nonfiction reads like a story." Multicultural needs include: stories that feature children of various racial/ethnic groups and do so in a way that is true to those depicted. Buys 10 mss/year. Average word length: 400-1,000. Byline given.

How to Contact Fiction/nonfiction: Send complete ms. "We do not accept queries." Responds to mss in 6 weeks. Will consider simultaneous submissions.

Illustration Buys 25-35 illustrations/issue. Preferred theme or style: varied; both 4-color. Works on assignment only. Illustrations only: Send promo sheet, tearsheets.

RAINBOW RUMPUS, The Magazine for Kids with LGBT Parents

P.O. Box 6881, Minneapolis MN 55406.(612)721-6442. E-mail: fictionandpoetry@rainbowrumpus. org. Website: www.rainbowrumpus.org. **Article Editors:** Danaca Booth, Al Onkka and Alison Walkley. **Fiction Editor:** Beth Wallace. **Art/photo Acquisitions:** Beth Wallace. Monthly online magazine. Estab. 2005. Circ. 250 visits/day. "Rainbow Rumpus is an online magazine for 4- to 24-year-olds who have lesbian, gay, bisexual or transgender (LGBT) parents. The magazine has three sections: one for children, one for young adults, and one for parents, teachers and friends. We are looking for children's fiction, young adult fiction, and poetry. Rainbow Rumpus publishes and reviews work that is written from the point of view of youth who have LGBT parents or connections with the LGBT community, celebrates the diversity of LGBT-headed families, and is of high quality." 75% of publication aimed at young readers.

Fiction All levels: adventure, animal, contemporary, fantasy, folktales, history, humorous, multicultural, nature/environment, problem solving, science fiction, sports, suspense/mystery. Buys 24 mss/year. Average word length: 800-5,000. Byline given.

Nonfiction All levels: interview/profile, social issues. Average word length: 800-5,000. Byline given.

Poetry Maximum of 5 poems per submission.

How to Contact Send complete ms via email to fictionandpoetry@rainbowrumpus.org with the word "Submission"in the subject line. Responds to mss in 6 weeks. Considers electronic submission and previously published work.

Illustration Buys 1 illustration/issue. Uses both b&w and color artwork. Reviews ms/illustration packages from artists: Query. Illustrations only: query with samples. Contact: Beth Wallace, Editor in Chief. Samples not returned; samples filed depending on the level of interest. Credit line given.

Terms Pays on publication. Buys first rights for mss; may request print anthology and audio or recording rights. Buys first rights rights for artwork. Pays $75 per story. Pays illustrators $100 for b $300 for color. Writer's guidelines available on Web site.

Tips If you wish to submit nonfiction, please query by e-mail to editorinchief@rainbowrumpus.org. Emerging writers encouraged to submit. You do not need to be a member of the LGBT community to participate.

RANGER RICK

National Wildlife Federation, 11100 Wildlife Center Dr.Reston VA 20190. (703)438-6000. Website:

www.nwf.org/rangerrick. **Editor:** Mary Dalheim. **Design Director:** Donna Miller. Monthly magazine. Circ. 550,000. "NWF's mission is to inspire Americans to protect wildlife for our children's future."

• Ranger Rick does not accept submissions or queries.

Fiction Middle readers: animal (wildlife), fables, fantasy, humorous, multicultural, plays, science fiction. Average word length: 900. Byline given.

Nonfiction Middle readers: animal (wildlife), conservation, humorous, nature/environment, outdoor adventure, travel. Buys 15-20 mss/year. Average word length: 900. Byline given.

How to Contact No longer accepting unsolicited queries/mss.

Illustration Buys 5-7 illustrations/issue. Preferred theme: nature, wildlife. Works on assignment only. Illustrations only: Send résumé, tearsheets. Responds to art samples in 2 months.

Terms Pays on acceptance. Buys exclusive first-time worldwide rights and non-exclusive worldwide rights thereafter to reprint, transmit, and distribute the work in any form or medium. Original artwork returned at job's completion. Pays up to $700 for full-length of best quality. For illustrations, buys one-time rights. Pays $150-250 for b $250-1,200 for color (inside, per page) illustration. Sample copies for $2.15 plus a 9 × 12 SASE.

READ

Weekly Reader Publishing Group, 1 Reader's Digest Rd.Pleasantville, N.Y. 10570. Website: www. weeklyreader.com. **READ no longer accepts unsolicited manuscripts. Those that are sent will not be read, responded to, or returned.**

REUNIONS MAGAZINE

Reunions magazine, Inc.P.O. Box 11727, Milwaukee WI 53211.(414)263-4567. Fax: (414)263-6331. E-mail: editor@reunionsmag.com. Website: reunionsmag.com. Articles Editor: Edith Wagner. Art Director: Jennifer Rueth. Quarterly Monthly magazine. Estab. 1990. Circ. 20,000. "Reunions magazine is a reader driven how-to book for persons planning family, class, military and other reunions. Includes articles about the detao's pf reunion planning.

Nonfiction For parents of all ages of kids: cooking, games, genealogy/history. Must be about Reunions. Buys 85% mss/year. Average word length: 300-1,500. Byline given.

How to Contact Prefer e-mailed Microsoft Word attachments or responds to queries quickly instead if they're e-mailed; mss up to 1 year. Publishes ms can be up to a year for seasonal material after acceptance. Considers simultaneous submissions, electronic submissions via disk or e-mail, previously published work.

Illustration Uses material that illustrates copy. Samples returned with SASE. Credit line given.

Photos Buys photos including payments: no extra pay. Uses digital: 300 dpi or higher.

Terms Pays on publication. Buys first rights for mss. We don't buy any rights for artwork. Included in whatever we pay rights for photos. Pays $40 for stories; Pays with contributor copies. "Almost all: we pay very few contributors" No additional payment for ms/illustration packages. Free for SASE. Sample copies for $3. Writer's guidelines free for SASE and available on our web site.

Tips "Do not waste your time sending anything other that material about reunions and reunion planning.

SCIENCE WEEKLY

P.O. Box 70638, Chevy Chase MD 20813. (301)680-8804. Fax: (301)680-9240. E-mail: scienceweekly@ erols.com. Website: www.scienceweekly.com. **Publisher:** Dr. Claude Mayberry, CAM Publishing Group, Inc. Magazine published 14 times/year. Estab. 1984. Circ. 200,000.*Science Weekly* uses freelance writers to develop and write an entire issue on a single science topic. Send résumé only, not submissions. Authors preferred within the greater D.C.Virginia, Maryland area. Science Weekly works on assignment only.

Nonfiction Young readers, middle readers, (K-6th grade): science/math education, education, problem-solving.

Terms Pays on publication. Prefers people with education, science and children's writing background. *Send resume only.* Samples copies free with SAE and 3 first-class stamps. Free samples on Web site www.scienceweekly.com

SHARING THE VICTORY, Fellowship of Christian Athletes

8701 Leeds, Kansas City MO 64129. (816)921-0909. Fax: (816)921-8755. Website: www.sharingthevictory.com. **Articles/Photo Editor:** Jill Ewert. **Art Director:** Mat Casner. Magazine published 9 times a year. Estab. 1982. Circ. 80,000. Purpose is to serve as a ministry tool of the Fellowship of Christian Athletes (FCA) by aligning with its mission to present to athletes and coaches and all whom they influence, the challenge and adventure of receiving Jesus Christ as Savior and Lord.

Nonfiction Young adults/teens: religion, sports. Average word length: 700-1,200. Byline given. How to Contact/Writers Nonfiction: Query with published clips. Publishes ms 3 months after acceptance. Will consider electronic submissions via e-mail.

Photos Purchases photos separately. Looking for photos of sports action. Uses color prints and high resolution electronic files of 300 dpi or higher.

Terms Pays on publication. Buys first rights and second serial (reprint) rights. Pays $150-400 for assigned and unsolicited articles. Photographers paid per photo. Sample copies for 9 × 12 SASE and $1. Writer's/photo guidelines for SASE.

Tips "All stories must be tied to FCA ministry."

SHINE BRIGHTLY

GEMS Girls' Clubs, P.O. Box 7259, Grand Rapids MI 49510. (616)241-5616. Fax: (616)241-5558. E-mail: sara@gemsgc.org. Website: www.gemsgc.org. **Editor:** Jan Boone. **Senior Editor:** Sara Lynne Hilton. Monthly (with combined June/July/August summer issue) magazine. Circ.17000. "SHINE brightly is designed to help girls ages 9-14 see how God is at work in their lives and in the world around them."

Fiction Middle readers: adventure, animal, contemporary, health, history, humorous, multicultural, nature/environment, problem-solving, religious, sports. Does not want to see unrealistic stories and those with trite, easy endings. We are interested in manuscripts that show how girls can change the world. Buys 30 mss/year. Average word length: 400-900. Byline given.

Nonfiction Middle readers: animal, arts/crafts, careers, cooking, fashion, games/puzzles, health, hobbies, how-to, humorous, nature/environment, multicultural, problem-solving, religious, service projects, social issues, sports, travel, also movies, music and musicians, famous people, interacting with family and friends. We are currently looking for inspirational biographies, stories from Zambia, Africa, and articles about living a green lifestyle. Buys 9 mss/year. Average word length: 100- 800. Byline given.

How to Contact Annual theme update available online. Fiction/nonfiction: Send complete ms. Responds to mss in 3 months. Will consider simultaneous submissions. Guidelines on Web site.

Illustration Buys 3 illustrations/year. Prefers ms/illustration packages. Works on assignment only. Responds to submissions in 3 months. Samples returned with SASE. Credit line given.

Terms Pays on publication. Buys first North American serial rights, first rights, second serial (reprint rights) or simultaneous rights. Original artwork not returned at job's completion. Pays $35 for stories, assigned articles and unsolicited articles. Poetry is $5-15. Games and Puzzles are $5-10. "We send complimentary copies in addition to pay." Pays $25-50 for color inside illustration. Writer's guidelines online at www.gemsgc.org

Tips Writers: "Please check our website before submitting. We have a specific style and theme that deals with how girls can impact the world. The stories should be current, deal with pre-adolescent problems and joys, and help girls see God at work in their lives through humor as well as problem-solving."

☑ SKIPPING STONES

A Multicultural Children's Magazine, P.O. Box 3939, Eugene OR 97403. (541)342-4956. E-mail: editor@skippingstones.org. Website: www.skippingstones.org. **Articles/Photo/Fiction Editor:** Arun N. Toke. Bimonthly magazine. Estab. 1988. Circ. 2,500. "Skipping Stones is an award-winning multicultural, nonprofit magazine designed to encourage cooperation, creativity and celebration of cultural and ecological richness. We encourage submissions by children of color, minorities and under-represented populations."

• Send SASE for *Skipping Stones* guidelines and theme list for detailed descriptions of the topics they want. *Skipping Stones*, now in it's 21st year, has won EDPRESS, National Association for Multicultural Education (N.A.M.E.), Writer Magazine, Newsstand Resources and Parent's Choice Awards.

Fiction Middle readers, young adult/teens: contemporary, meaningful, humorous. All levels: folktales, multicultural, nature/environment. Multicultural needs include: bilingual or multilingual pieces; use of words from other languages; settings in other countries, cultures or multi-ethnic communities.

Nonfiction All levels: animal, biography, cooking, games/puzzles, history, humorous, interview/profile, multicultural, nature/environment, creative problem-solving, religion and cultural celebrations, sports, travel, social and international awareness. Does not want to see preaching, violence or abusive language; no poems by authors over 18 years old; no suspense or romance stories. Average word length: 1,000, max. Byline given.

How to Contact Fiction: Query. Nonfiction: Send complete ms. Responds to queries in 1 month; mss in 4 months. Will consider simultaneous submissions; reviews artwork for future assignments. Please include your name and address on each page.

Illustration Prefers illustrations by teenagers and young adults. Will consider all illustration packages. Manuscript/illustration packages: Query; submit complete ms with final art; submit tearsheets. Responds in 4 months. Credit line given.

Photos Black & white photos preferred, but color photos with good contrast are welcome. Needs: youth 7-17, international, nature, celebrations.

Terms Acquires first and reprint rights for mss and photographs. Pays in copies for authors, photographers and illustrators. Sample copy for $5 with SAE and 4 first-class stamps. Writer's/illustrator's guidelines for 4 × 9 SASE.

Tips "We want material meant for children and young adults/teenagers with multicultural or ecological awareness themes. Think, live and write as if you were a child, tween or teen." Wants "material that gives insight to cultural celebrations, lifestyle, customs and traditions, glimpse of daily life in other countries and cultures. Photos, songs, artwork are most welcome if they illustrate/highlight the points. Translations are invited if your submission is in a language other than English. Upcoming themes will include cultural celebrations, living abroad, challenging, hospitality customs of various cultures, cross-cultural understanding, African, Asian and Latin American cultures, humor, international understanding, turning points and magical moments in life, caring for the earth, spirituality, and Multicutural Awareness."

SPARKLE

GEMS Girls' Clubs, 1333 Alger SE, P,P. Box 7295, Grand Rapids MI 49510. (616)241-5616. Fax: (616)241-5558. E-mail: sara@gemsgc.org. Website: www.gemsgc.org. **Senior Editor:** Sara Lynn Hilton **Art Director/Photo Editor:** Sara DeRidder. Magazine published 6 times/year. Estab. 2002. Circ. 5,119. "Our mission is to prepare young girls to live out their faith and become world-changers-. We strive to help girls make a difference in the world. We look at the application of scripture to everyday life. We strive to delight the reader and cause the reader to evelute her own life in light of the truth presented. Finally, we strive to teach practical life skills.

Fiction Young readers: adventure, animal, contemporary, fantasy, folktale, health, history, humorous, multicultural, music and musicians, nature/environment, problem-solving, religious, recipes, service projects, sports, suspense/mystery, interacting with family and friends. We currently Looking for sinspirational biographies, stories form Zambia, Africa, and ideas on how to live a green lifestyle. Buys 10 mss/year. Average word length: 100-400. Byline given.

Nonfiction Young readers: animal, arts/crafts, biography, careers, cooking, concept, games/puzzles, geography, health, history, hobbies, how-to, interview/profile, math, multicultural, nature/environment, problem-solving, quizzes, science, social issues, sports, travel, personal experience, inspirational, music/drama/art. Buys 15 mss/year. Average word length: 100-400. Byline given.

Poetry Looks for simple poems about God's creation or traditional Bible truths. Maximum lenth: 15 lines.

How to Contact Fiction/nonfiction: Send complete ms. Responds to ms in 6 weeks. Publishes ms 6 months after acceptance. Will consider simultaneous submissions, and previously published work.

Illustration Buys 1-2 illustrations/issue; 8-10 illustrations/year. Uses color artwork only. Works on assignment only. Reviews ms/illustration packages from artists. Send ms with dummy. Contact: Sara DeRidder, graphic and web designer. Illustrations only: send promo sheet. Contact: Sara DeRidder. Responds in 3 weeks only if interested. Samples returned with SASE; samples filed. Credit line given.

Terms Pays on publication. Buys first North American serial rights, second serial (reprint rights) or simultaneous rights for mss, artwork and photos. Pays $20 minimum for stories and articles. Pays illustrators $50 for color cover; $25 for color inside. Original artwork not returned at job's completion. Sample copies for $1. Writer's/illustrator/photo guidelines free for SASE or available on Web site.Tips "Keep it simple. We are writing to 1st-3rd graders. It must be simple yet interesting. Manuscripts should build girls up in Christian character but not be preachy. They are just learning about God and how He wants them to live. Manuscripts should be delightful as well as educational and inspirational."

SPIDER, The Magazine for Children

70 E. Lake St.Suite 300, Chicago IL 60601. (312) 701-1720. Website: www.cricketmag.com and www.spidermagkids.com. **Editor-in-Chief:** Alice Letvin. **Editor:** May-May Sugihara. **Art Director:** Suzanne Beck. Monthly magazine. Estab. 1994. Circ. 70,000. Spider publishes high-quality literature for beginning readers, primarily ages 6-9.

Fiction Young readers: adventure, contemporary, fantasy, folktales, humor, science fiction. "Authentic stories from all cultures are welcome. No didactic, religious, or violent stories, or anything that talks down to children." Average word length: 300-1,000. Byline given.

Nonfiction Young readers: animal, arts/crafts, cooking, games/puzzles, geography, history, human interest, math, multicultural, nature/environment, problem-solving, science. "Well-researched articles on topics are welcome. Would like to see more games, puzzles and activities, especially ones adaptable to *Spider*'s takeout pages. No encyclopedic or overtly educational articles." Average word length: 300-800. Byline given.

Poetry Serious, humorous. Maximum length: 20 lines.

How to Contact Fiction/nonfiction: Send complete ms with SASE. Do not query. Responds to mss in 6 months. Publishes ms 2-3 years after acceptance. Will consider simultaneous submissions and previously published work.

Illustration Buys 20 illustrations/issue; 240 illustrations/year. Uses color artwork only. "We prefer that you work on flexible or strippable stock, no larger than 20 × 22 (image area 19 × 21). This will allow us to put the art directly on the drum of our separator's laser scanner. Art on disck CMYK, 300 dpi. We use more realism than cartoon-style art." Works on assignment only. Reviews ms/illustration packages from artists. Illustrations only: Send promo sheet and tearsheets. Responds in 3 months. Samples returned with SASE; samples filed. Credit line given.

Photos Buys photos from freelancers. Buys photos with accompanying ms only. Model/property releases and captions required. Uses 35mm, 2¼ × 2¼ transparencies or digital files. Send unsolicited photos by mail; provide résumé and tearsheets. Responds in 3 months.

Terms Pays on publication. Rights purchased vary. Buys first and promotional rights for artwork; one-time rights for photographs. Original artwork returned at job's completion. Pays up to 25¢/word for previously unpublished stories/articles. Authors also receive 6 complimentary copies of the issue in which work appears. Additional payment for ms/illustration packages and for photos accompanying articles. Pays illustrators $750 for color cover; $200-300 for color inside. Pays photographers per photo (range: $25-75). Sample copies for $5. Writer's/illustrator's guidelines online at www.cricketmag.com or for SASE.

Tips Writers: "Read back issues before submitting."

TURTLE MAGAZINE

, For Preschool Kids, 1100 Waterway Blvd.Indianapolis IN 46206-0567. (317)636-8881. Fax: (317)684-8094. Website: www.turtlemag.org. **Editor:** Terry Harshman. **Art Director:** Bart Rivers. Bimonthly magazine published 6 times/year. Circ. 300,000. Turtle uses read-aloud stories, especially suitable for bedtime or naptime reading, for children ages 2-5. Also uses poems, simple science experiments, easy recipes and health-related articles.

Fiction Picture-oriented material: health-related, medical, history, humorous, multicultural, nature/environment, problem-solving, sports, recipes, simple science experiments. Avoid stories in which the characters indulge in unhealthy activities. Buys 20 mss/year. Average word length: 150-300. Byline given. Currently accepting submissions for Rebus stories only.

Nonfiction Picture-oriented material: cooking, health, sports, simple science. "We use very simple experiments illustrating basic science concepts. These should be pretested. We also publish simple, healthful recipes." Buys 24 mss/year. Average word length: 100-300. Byline given.

Poetry "We're especially looking for short poems (4-8 lines) and slightly longer action rhymes to foster creative movement in preschoolers. We also use short verse on our inside front cover and back cover."

How to Contact Fiction/nonfiction: Send complete mss. Queries are not accepted. Responds to mss in 3 months.

Terms Pays on publication. Buys all rights for mss. Pays up to 22¢/word for stories and articles (depending upon length and quality) and 10 complimentary copies. Pays $25 minimum for poems. Sample copy $ 3.95. Writer's guidelines free with SASE and on Web site.

Tips "Our need for health-related material, especially features that encourage fitness, is ongoing. Health subjects must be age-appropriate. When writing about them, think creatively and lighten up! Always keep in mind that in order for a story or article to educate preschoolers, it first must be entertaining—warm and engaging, exciting, or genuinely funny. Here the trend is toward leaner, lighter writing. There will be a growing need for interactive activities. Writers might want to consider developing an activity to accompany their concise manuscripts." (

U.S. KIDS

Children's Better Health Institute, 1100 Waterway Blvd.P.O. Box 567, Indianapolis IN 46202. (317)636-8881. Website: www.uskidsmag.org. **Editor:** Daniel Lee. **Art Director:** Greg Vanzo. Magazine for children ages 6-11, published 6 times a year. Estab. 1987. Circ. 230,000.

Fiction Young readers: adventure, animal, contemporary, health, history, humorous, multicultural, nature/environment, problem-solving, sports, suspense/mystery. Buys limited number of stories/year. Query first. Average word length: 500-800. Byline given.

Nonfiction Young readers: animal, arts/crafts, cooking, games/puzzles, health, history, hobbies, how-to, humorous, interview/profile, multicultural, nature/environment, science, social issues, sports, travel. Wants to see interviews with kids ages 5-10, who have done something unusual or different. Buys 30-40 mss/year. Average word length: 400. Byline given.

Poetry Maximum length: 8-24 lines.

How to Contact Fiction: Send complete ms. Responds to queries and mss in 3 months.

Illustration Buys 8 illustrations/issue; 70 illustrations/year. Color artwork only. Works on assignment only. Reviews ms/illustration packages from artists. Query. Illustrations only: Send resume and tearsheets. Responds only if interested. Samples returned with SASE; samples kept on file. Does not return originals. Credit line given.

Photos Purchases photography from freelancers. Looking for photos that pertain to children ages 5-10. Model/property release required. Uses color and b&w prints; 35mm, 2¼ × 2¼, 4 × 5 and 8 × 10 transparencies. Photographers should provide resume, business card, promotional literature or tearsheets to be kept on file. Responds only if interested.

Terms Pays on publication. Buys all rights for mss. Purchases all rights for artwork. Purchases one-time rights for photographs. Pays 17¢/word minimum. Additional payment for ms/illustration packages. Pays illustrators $155/page for color inside. Photographers paid by the project or per photo (negotiable). Sample copies for $3.95. Writer's/illustrator/photo guidelines for #10 SASE.

Tips "Write clearly and concisely without preaching or being obvious."

⚄ WHAT IF?, Canada's Fiction Magazine for Teens

19 Lynwood Place, Guelph ON N1G 2V9 Canada. (519)823-2941. Fax: (519)823-8081. E-mail: editor@whatifmagazine.com. Website: www.whatifmagazine.com. **Articles/Fiction Editor:** Mike Leslie. **Art Director:** Jean Leslie. Quarterly magazine. Estab. 2003. Circ. 5,000. "The goal of What If? is to help Canadian young adults get published for the first time in a quality literary setting."

Fiction Young adults: adventure, contemporary, fantasy, folktale, health, humorous, multicultural, nature/environment, problem-solving, science fiction, sports, suspense/mystery. Buys 48 mss/year. Average word length: 500-3,000. Byline given.

Nonfiction Young adults: Personal essays and opinion pieces to a maximum of 1,500 words. Byline given.

Poetry Reviews poetry: all styles. Maximum length: 20 lines. Limit submissions to 4 poems.

How to Contact Fiction/Nonfiction: Send complete ms. Responds to mss in 3 months. Publishes ms 4 months after acceptance. Will consider e-mail submissions, previously published work if the author owns all rights.

Illustration Uses approximately 150 illustrations/year. Reviews ms/illustration packages from young adult artists. Send ms with dummy. Query with samples. Contact: Jean Leslie, production manager. Responds in 2 months. Samples returned with SASE. Credit line given.

Terms Pays on publication. Acquires first rights for mss and artwork. Original artwork returned at job's completion. Pays 2 copies for stories; 2 copy for articles; 2 copies for illustration and 2 copies for poems. Sample copies for $8.50 Writer's/illustrator's guidelines for SASE or available by e-mail.

Tips "Read our magazine. The majority of the material we publish (90%) is by Canadian young adults. Another 10% is staff written. We are currently accepting material from Canadian teens only."

WINNER

The Health Connection, 55 W. Oak Ridge Dr. Hagerstown MD 21740. (301)393-4017. Fax: (301)393-4055. E-mail: jschleifer@rhpa.org. Website: www.winnermagazine.org. **Editor:** Jan Schleifer. **Art Director:** Madelyn Gatz. Monthly magazine (September-May). Estab. 1958. Publishes articles that will promote children in grades 4-6 choosing a positive lifestyle and choosing to be drug-free.

Fiction Young readers, middle readers: contemporary, health, nature/environment, problem-solving, anti tobacco, alcohol, and drugs. Byline given.

Nonfiction Young readers, middle readers: positive role model personality features, health. Buys 10-15 mss/year. Average word length: 600-650 (in addition, needs 3 related thought questions and one puzzle/activity). Byline given.

How to Contact Fiction/nonfiction: Send complete ms; prefers e-mail submissions. Responds in 2 months. Publishes ms 6-12 months after acceptance. Will consider simultaneous.

Illustration Buys up to 3 illustrations/issue; up to 30 illustrations/year. Uses color artwork only. Works on assignment only. Reviews ms/illustration packages from artists; send ms with dummy. Responds only if interested. Samples returned with SASE.

Terms Pays on acceptance. Buys first rights for mss. Original artwork returned at job's completion. Additional payment for ms/illustration packages. Sometimes additional payment when photos accompany articles. Writer's guidelines for SASE. Sample magazine $2; include 9 × 12 envelope with 3 first-class stamps.

Tips "Keep material upbeat and positive for elementary age children."

YES MAG, Canada's Science Magazine for Kids

501-3960 Quadra St.Victoria, BC, V8X 4A3 Canada. Fax: (250)477-5390. E-mail. Web site:www. yesmag.ca. **Publisher:** David Garrison. **Editor:** Shannon Hunt. **Art/Photo Director:** Sam Logan. Managing Editor: Jude Isabella. Bimonthly magazine. Estab. 1996. Circ. 22,000. "YES Mag is designed to make science accessible, interesting, exciting, and fun. Written for children ages 10 to 15, YES Mag covers a range of topics including science and technology news, environmental updates, do-at-home projects and articles about Canadian science and scientists."

Nonfiction Middle readers: all the sciences-math, engineering, biology, physics, chemistry, etc. Buys 30 mss/year. Average word length: 250- 800. Byline given.

How to Contact Nonfiction: Query with published clips. "We prefer e-mail queries." Responds to queries/mss in 6 weeks. Generally publishes ms 3 months after acceptance. **Emphasis on Canadian writers.**

Illustration Buys 2 illustrations/issue; 10 illustrations/year. Uses color artwork only. Works on assignment only. Reviews ms/illustration packages from artists. Query. Illustration only: Query with samples. Responds in 6 weeks. Samples filed. Credit line given.

Photos "Looking for science, technology, nature/environment photos based on current editorial needs." Photo captions required. Uses color prints. Provide resume, business card, promotional literature, tearsheets if possible. Will buy if photo is appropriate. Usually uses stock agencies.

Terms Pays on publication. Buys one-time rights for mss. Buys one-time rights for artwork/photos. Original artwork returned at job's completion. Pays $ 70-200 for stories and articles. Sample copies for $5. Writer's guidelines available on the Web site under "Contact" information.

Tips We do not publish fiction or science fiction or poetry. Visit our Web site for more information and sample articles. Articles relating to the physical sciences and mathematics are encouraged."

YOUNG RIDER, THE MAGAZINE FOR HORSE AND PONY LOVERS

P.O. Box 8237, Lexington KY 40533. (859)260-9800. Fax: (859)260-9814. Website: www.youngrider. com. **Editor:** Lesley Ward. Bimonthly magazine. Estab. 1994. "Young Rider magazine teaches young people, in an easy-to-read and entertaining way, how to look after their horses properly, and how to improve their riding skills safely."

Fiction Young adults: adventure, animal, horses, horse celebrities, famous equestrians. Buys 10 mss/year. Average word length: 1,500 maximum. Byline given.

Nonfiction Young adults: animal, careers, health (horse), sports, riding. Buys 20-30 mss/year. Average word length: 1,000 maximum. Byline given.

How to Contact Fiction/nonfiction: Query with published clips. Responds to queries in 2 weeks. Publishes ms 6-12 months after acceptance. Will consider simultaneous submissions, electronic submissions via disk or modem, previously published work.

Illustration Buys 2 illustrations/issue; 10 illustrations/year. Works on assignment only. Reviews ms/illustration packages from artists. Query. Contact: Lesley Ward, editor. Illustrations only: Query with samples. Contact: Lesley Ward, editor. Responds in 2 weeks. Samples returned with SASE. Credit line given.

Photos Buys photos with accompanying ms only. **Uses high-res digital images only-in focus,**

good light. Model/property release required; captions required. Query with samples. Responds in 2 weeks.

Terms Pays on publication. Buys first North American serial rights for mss, artwork, photos. Original artwork returned at job's completion. Pays $150 maximum for stories; $250 maximum for articles. Additional payment for ms/illustration packages and for photos accompanying articles. Pays $70-140 for color inside. Pays photographers per photo (range: $65-155). Sample copies for $3.50. Writer's/illustrator's/photo guidelines for SASE.

Tips "Fiction must be in third person. Read magazine before sending in a query. No 'true story from when I was a youngster.' No moralistic stories. Fiction must be up-to-date and humorous, teen-oriented. Need horsy interest or celebrity rider features. No practical or how-to articles-all done in-house."

Agents & Art Reps

This section features listings of literary agents and art reps who either specialize in, or represent a good percentage of, children's writers and/or illustrators. While there are a number of children's publishers who are open to non-agented material, using the services of an agent or rep can be beneficial to a writer or artist. Agents and reps can get your work seen by editors and art directors more quickly. They are familiar with the market and have insights into which editors and art directors would be most interested in your work. Also, they negotiate contracts and will likely be able to get you a better deal than you could get on your own.

Agents and reps make their income by taking a percentage of what writers and illustrators receive from publishers. The standard percentage for agents is 10 to 15 percent; art reps generally take 25 to 30 percent. We have not included any agencies in this section that charge reading fees.

WHAT TO SEND

When putting together a package for an agent or rep, follow the guidelines given in their listings. Most agents open to submissions prefer initially to receive a query letter describing your work. For novels and longer works, some agents ask for an outline and a number of sample chapters, but you should send these only if you're asked to do so. Never fax or e-mail query letters or sample chapters to agents without their permission. Just as with publishers, agents receive a large volume of submissions. It may take them a long time to reply, so you may want to query several agents at one time. It's best, however, to have a complete manuscript considered by only one agent at a time. Always include a self-addressed, stamped envelope (SASE).

For initial contact with art reps, send a brief query letter and self-promo pieces, following the guidelines given in the listings. If you don't have a flier or brochure, send photocopies. Always include a SASE.

For those who both write and illustrate, some agents listed will consider the work of author/illustrators. Read through the listings for details.

As you consider approaching agents and reps with your work, keep in mind that they are very choosy about who they take on to represent. Your work must be high quality and presented professionally to make an impression on them. For more information on approaching agents and additional listings, see *Guide to Literary Agents* (Writer's Digest Books). For additional listings of art reps see *Artist's & Graphic Designer's Market* (Writer's Digest Books).

An Organization for Agents

In some listings of agents you'll see references to AAR (The Association of Authors' Representatives). This organization requires its members to meet an established list of professional standards and code of ethics.

The objectives of AAR include keeping agents informed about conditions in publishing and related fields; encouraging cooperation among literary organizations; and assisting agents in representing their author-clients' interests. Officially, members are prohibited from directly or indirectly charging reading fees. They offer writers a list of member agents on their website. They also offer a list of recommended questions an author should ask an agent and other FAQs, all found on their website. They can be contacted at AAR, 676A 9th Ave. #312, New York NY 10036. (212)840-5777. E-mail: aarinc@mindspring.com. Website: www.aar-online.org.

AGENTS

ADAMS LITERARY

7845 Colony Rd.#215, Charlotte NC 28226. (704)542-1440. Fax: (704)542-1450. E-mail: info@adamsliterary.com. Website: www.adamsliterary.com. **Contact:** Tracey Adams, Josh Adams. Estab. 2004. Member of AAR and SCBWI. 20% of clients are new/previously unpublished writers. 100% of material handled is books for young readers.

- Prior to becoming an agent, Tracey Adams worked in the editorial and marketing departments at several children's publishing houses. Also Josh Adams, a former executive editor, has an MBA from Columbia Business School.

Terms Agent receives 15% commission on domestic sales; 20% on foreign sales. Offers written contract.

How to Contact See Web site for updates on submission policy.

Tips "We represent authors, not books, so we enjoy forming long-term relationships with our clients. We work hard to be sure we are submitting work which is ready to be considered, but we respect the role of editors and don't over-edit manuscripts ourselves. Our style is assertive yet collaborative."

BOOKS & SUCH

52 Mission Circle, Suite 122, PMB 170.Santa Rosa CA 95409-5370. (707)538-4184. E-mail: etta@booksandsuch.biz. Website: www.booksandsuch.biz. **Contact:** Etta Willson. Estab. 1996. Member of SCWBI, WNBA, and associate member of CBA. Represents 35 clients. 4% of clients are new/unpublished writers. Places projects in the general market.Represents 70% juvenile books. Considers: nonfiction, fiction for middle grades, and picture books.

- Before becoming an agent with Books & Such, Etta Wilson was a book passenger and agent with March Media and an editor at Abingdon Press.

Recent Sales *Precious Girls Club Series* (Precious Moments); *Rumble, Zap, Pow* (Tyndale); *Police Officers on Patrol* (Viking).

Terms Agent receives 15% commission on domestic and foreign sales. Offers written contract.

Tips "The heart of my motivation is to help authors develop their writing talent for children and to be successful in having it published."

BOOKSTOP LITERARY AGENCY

67 Meadow View Rd.Orinda CA 94563. Website: www.bookstopliterary.com. Seeking both new and established writers and illustrators. Estab. 1983. 100% of material handled is books for children and young adults.

Terms Agent receives 15% commission on domestic sales. Offers written contract, binding for 1 year.

How to Contact Please send: cover letter, entire ms for picture books; and first 50 pages of novels, proposal and sample chapters ok for nonfiction. Send sample illustrations only if you are an illustrator.

CURTIS BROWN, LTD.

Ten Astor Place.New York NY 10003. (212)473-5400. Fax: (212)598-0917. Website: www. curtisbrown.com. Seeking both new and established writers. Estab. 1914. Members of AAR and SCBWI. Signatory of WGA. **Staff includes:** Nathan Bransford, Ginger Clark, Elizabeth Harding, Ginger Knowlton, Mitchell Waters, and Anna J. Webman.

Terms Agent receives 15% commission on domestic sales; 20% on foreign sales. Offers written contract. 75 days notice must be given to terminate contract.

How to Contact Query with SASE. If a picture book, send only one picture book ms. Considers simultaneous queries, "but please tell us." Returns material only with SASE. Obtains clients through recommendations from others, queries/solicitations, conferences.

BROWNE & MILLER LITERARY ASSOCIATES, LLC

410 S. Michigan Ave.Suite 460, Chicago IL 60605. (312)922-3063. Fax: (312)922-1905. E-mail: mail@browneandmiller.com. Website: www.browneandmiller.com. **Contact:** Danielle Egan-Miller, president. Prefers to work with established writers. Handles only certain types of work. Estab. 1971. Member of AAR, RWA, MWA. Represents 85+ clients. 5% of clients are new/previously unpublished writers. 15% of material handled is books for young readers.

• Prior to opening the agency, Danielle Egan-Miller worked as an editor.

Recent Sales Sold 10 books for young readers in the last year.

Terms Agent receives 15% commission on domestic sales; 20% on foreign sales. Offers written contract. Offers written contract, binding for 2 years. 30 days notice must be given to terminate contract.

How to Contact Query with SASE. Accepts queries by e-mail. Considers simultaneous queries. Responds in 2-4 weeks to queries; 4-6 months to mss. Returns material only with SASE. Obtains clients through recommendations from others.

Tips "We are very hands-on and do much editorial work with our clients. We are passionate about the books we represent and work hard to help clients reach their publishing goals."

PEMA BROWNE LTD.

11 Tena Place, Valley Cottage NY 10989. (845)268-0029. **Contact:** Pema Browne. Estab. 1966. Represents 2 illustrators. 10% of artwork handled is children's book illustration. Specializes in general commercial. Markets include: all publishing areas; children's picture books. Clients include HarperCollins, Holiday House, Bantam Doubleday Dell, Nelson/Word, Hyperion, Putnam. Client list available upon request.

Represents Fiction, nonfiction, picture books, middle grade, young adult, manuscript/illustration packages. Looking for "professional and unique" talent.

Recent Sales *The Daring Ms. Quimby*, by Suzanne Whitaker (Holiday House).

Terms Rep receives 30% illustration commission; 20% author commission. Exclusive area representation is required. For promotional purposes, talent must provide color mailers to distribute. Representative pays mailing costs on promotion mailings.

How to Contact For first contact, send query letter, direct mail flier/brochure and SASE. If interested will ask to mail appropriate materials for review. Portfolios should include tearsheets and transparencies or good color photocopies, plus SASE. Accepts queries by mail only. Obtains new talent through recommendations and interviews (portfolio review).

Tips "We are doing more publishing-all types-less advertising." Looks for "continuity of illustration and dedication to work."d

ANDREA BROWN LITERARY AGENCY, INC.

1076 Eagle Dr.Salinas CA 93905. (831)422-5925. Website: www.andreabrownlit.com. **President:** Andrea Brown. Estab. 1981. Member of SCBWI and WNBA. 20% of clients are new/previously unpublished writers. Specializes in "all kinds of children's books—illustrators and authors."

- Prior to opening her agency, Andrea Brown served as an editorial assistant at Random House and Dell Publishing and as an editor with Alfred A. Knopf.

Recent Sales *Thirteen Reasons Why,* by Jay Asher (Penguin); three book series, by Ellen Hopkins (S&S); *Downside Up,* by Neal Shusterman (Simon & Schuster).

Terms Agent receives 15% commission on domestic sales; 20% on foreign sales. Written contract.

How to Contact Query. Responds in 3 months to queries and mss. E-mail queries only.

Tips Query first. "Taking on very few picture books. Must be unique—no rhyme, no anthropomorphism. Do not call or fax queries or manuscripts. E-mail queries first. Check Web site for details."

LIZA DAWSON ASSOCIATES

350 7th Ave, Suite 2003, New York, NY 10001. E-mail: anna@olswanger.com. Website: www. olswanger.com. **Contact**: Anna Olswanger. Member of SCBWI, WNBA, Authors Guild. Represents 10 clients. 30% of clients are new/unpublished writers. 75% of material handled is books for young readers.

- Anna Olswanger coordinates the Jewish Childrens's Book Writers' Conference each fall at the 92nd Street Y in New York City and is a children's book author.

Terms Agent receives 15% commission on domestic sales; 20% commission on foreign sales. Offers written contract. Charges client for color photocopying and overseas postage.

How to Contact Query with first 5 pages. Must include e-mail address for response. Considers simultaneous queries. Responds in 4 weeks to queries; 8 weeks to mss. Obtains most new clients through recommendations and queries.

DUNHAM LITERARY, INC.

156 Fifth Ave.Suite 625, New York NY 10010-7002. Website: www.unhamlit.com. **Contact:** Jennie Dunham. Seeking both new and established writers but prefers to work with established writers. Estab. 2000. Member of AAR, signatory of SCBWI. Represents 50 clients. 15% of clients are new/ previously unpublished writers. 50% of material handled is books of young readers.

Recent Sales Sold 30 books for young readers in the last year. *Peter Pan,* by Robert Sabuda (Little Simon); *Flamingos On the Roof,* by Calef Brown (Houghton); *Adele and Simon In America,* by Barbara McClintock (Farrar, Straus & Giroux); *Caught Between the Pages,* by Marlene Carvell (Dutton); *Waiting For Normal,* by Leslie Connor (HarperCollins), *The Gollywhopper Games,* by Jody Feldman (Greenwillow).

Terms Agent receives 15% commission on domestic sales; 20-25% on foreign sales. Offers written contract. 60 days notice must be given to terminate contract.

How to Contact Query with SASE. Consider simultaneous queries and submissions. Responds in 2 week s to queries; 2 months to mss. Returns material only with SASE. Obtains clients through recommendations from others.

EDUCATIONAL DESIGN SERVICES LLC

5750 Bou Ave, Ste. 1508, N. Bethesda, MD 20852. E-mail: blinder@educationaldesignservices.com. Website: www.educationaldesignservices.com. **Contact:** B. Linder. Handles only certain types of work. Estab. 1981. 80% of clients are new/previously unpublished writers.

Recent Sales *How to Solve Word Problems in Mathematics*, by Wayne (McGraw-Hill*); Preparing for the 8th Grade Test in Social Studies*, by Farran-Paci (Amsco); *Minority Report*, by Gunn-Singh (Scarecrow Education); *No Parent Left Behind*, by Petrosino & Spiegel (Rowman & Littlefield); *Teaching Test-taking Skills* (R&L Education); *10 Languages You'll Need Most in the Classroom*, by Sundem, Krieger, Pickiewicz (Corwin Press); *Kids, Classrooms & Capital Hill*, by Flynn (R&L Education).

Terms Agent receives 15% commission on domestic sales; 25% on foreign sales. Offers written contract, binding until any party opts out. Terminate contract through certified letter.

How to Contact Query by e-mail or with SASE or send outline and 1 sample chapter. Considers simultaneous queries and submissions if so indicated. Responds in 6-8 weeks to queries/mss. Returns material only with SASE. Obtains clients through recommendations from others, queries/ solicitations, or through conferences.

ETHAN ELLENBERG LITERARY AGENCY

548 Broadway, #5-E, New York NY 10012. (212)431-4554. Fax: (212)941-4652. E-mail: agent@ ethanellenberg.com. Website: EthanEllenberg.com. **Contact:** Ethan Ellenberg. Estab. 1983. Represents 80 clients. 10% of clients are new/previously unpublished writers. "Children's books are an important area for us."

- Prior to opening his agency, Ethan Ellenberg was contracts manager of Berkley/Jove and associate contracts manager for Bantam. Represents 2002 Cladecott Medal winner Eric Rohmann, for *My Friend Rabbit*, adapted by Nelvana and running in an animated series fall 2007 on NBC.

Terms Agent receives 15% on domestic sales; 20% on foreign sales. Offers written contract, "flexible." Charges for "direct expenses only: photocopying for manuscript submissions, postage for submission and foreign rights sales."

How to Contact Picture books—send full ms with SASE. Illustrators: Send a representative portfolio with color copies and SASE. No original artwork. Young adults—send outline plus 3 sample chapters with SASE. Accepts queries by e-mail; does not accept attachments to e-mail queries or fax queries. Considers simultaneous queries and submissions. Responds in six weeks to snail mail queries; only responds to e-mail queries if interested. Returns materials only with SASE. "See Web site for detailed instructions, please follow them carefully." No phone calls.

Tips "We are actively taking new clients, both published and unpublished, in all areas of children's books. We're most interested in natural storytellers, people who let their imaginations soar. This includes all age groups and genres. If we love your work, we'll also give you sound editorial feedback and help you develop it so it can be successfully sold." For illustrators we must love you artwork and prefer author/illustrators. This continues to be a prime area of our interest and we look forward to your submission.

BARRY GOLDBLATT LITERARY LLC

320 Seventh Ave.#266, Brooklyn NY 11215. (718)832-8787. Fax: (718)832-5558. Website: www. bgliterary.com. Estab. 2000. Member of AAR, SCBWI. **Staff includes:**Barry Goldblatt, Beth Fleisher and Joe Monti. Represents 95% juvenile and young adult books. Considers picture books, graphic novels, fiction, nonfiction, middle grade, and young adult.

Recent Sales The Infernal Devices trilogy, by Cassandra Clare; *Clappy as a Ham*, by Michael Ian Black; *Pearl*, by Jo Knowles

Terms Agent receives 15% commission on domestic sales; 20% on foreign and dramatic sales. Offers written contract. 60 days notice must be given to terminate contract.

How to Contact "Please see our Web site for specific submission guidelines and information on agents' particular tastes." Obtains clients through referrals, queries, and conferences.

Tips "We're a group of hands-on agents, with wide ranging interests. Get us hooked with a great query letter, then convince us with an unforgettable manuscript."

THE GREENHOUSE LITERARY AGENCY

11308 Lapham Drive, Oakton VA 22124. E-mail: submissions@greenhouseliterary.com. Website: www.greenhouseliterary.com. **Contact:** Sarah Davies. Young agency actively seeking clients. Seeking both new and established writers. Estab. 2008. Member of SCBWI. Represents 7 debut authors. 100% new writers. 100% books for young readers. Staff includes Sarah Davies.

- Sarah Davies has had an editorial and management career in children's publishing spanning 25 years; for 5 years prior to launching the Greenhouse she was Publishing Director of Macmillan Children's Books in London, working with and publishing leading authors from both sides of the Atlantic.

Recent Sales The Devil's Kiss, by Sarwat Chadda (Hyperion); The Others Side of Blue, by Valerie Patterson (Clarion), Of All the Stupid Things, by Alexandra Diaz (Egmont USA).

Terms Receives 15% commission on sales to both US and UK; 25% on foreign sales. Offers written contract.Sarah Davies attends Bologna Children's Bookfair in Bologna, Italy; SCBWI conferences; BookExpo America; and other conference—see Web site for information.

How to Contact See website for full submission criteria. Email queries only; one page containing a short outline, biography and any writing 'credentials'. Up to the first five pages of text may be pasted into the email. Only submissions of interest can be replied to; allow 2 weeks (sometimes a little longer). If a full manuscript is requested allow 6-8 weeks for response. Obtains new authors through recommendations from other, queries/solicitations, conferences.

Tips "It's very important to me to have a strong, long-term relationship with clients. Having been 25 years in the publishing industry, I know the business from the inside and have excellent contacts in both the US and UK. I work hard to find every client the very best publisher and deal for their writing. My editorial background means I can work creatively with authors where necessary; I aim to submit high-quality manuscripts to publishers while respecting the role of the editor who will have their own publishing vision. Before submitting, prospective authors should look at the Greenhouse's 'Top 10 tips for authors of children's fiction', which can be found on our **www. greenhouseliterary.com.**

BARBARA S. KOUTS, LITERARY AGENT

P.O. Box 560, Bellport NY 11713. (631)286-1278. **Contact:** Barbara Kouts. Currently accepting new clients. Estab. 1980. Member of AAR. Represent 50 clients. 10% of clients are new/previously unpublished writers. Specializes in children's books.

Recent Sales Code Talker, by Joseph Bruchac (Dial); The Penderwicks, by Jeanne Birdsall (Knopf); Frogg y's Baby Sister, by Jonathan London (Viking).

Terms Agent receives 10% commission on domestic sales; 20% on foreign sales. Charges for photocopying.

How to Contact Accepts queries by mail only. Responds in 1 week to queries; 6 weeks to mss.

Tips "Write, do not call. Be professional in your writing."

McINTOSH & OTIS, INC.

353 Lexington Ave.New York NY 10016. (212)687-7400. Fax: (212)687-6894. **Contact:** Edward Necarsulmer IV. Seeking both new and established writers. Estab. 1927. Member of AAR and SCBWI. 30% of clients are new/previously unpublished writers. 90% of material handled is books for young readers.

Terms Agent receives 15% commission on domestic sales; 20% on foreign sales.

How to Contact Query with SASE. Exclusive submission only. Responds in 6 -8 weeks. Returns material only with SASE. Obtains clients through recommendations from others, editors, conferences and queries.

Tips "No e-mail or phone calls!"

THE McVEIGH AGENCY

345 West 21st St.New York NY 10011. (917)913-6388. Fax: (646)619-4944. E-mail: mark@themcveighagency.com. Website: www.themcveighagency.com. Contact: Mark McVeigh.

Recent Sales Sold 1 book last year. Also represents: Steve Bjoörkman (Illustrator of over 80 children's books, including NY TIMES best seller *Dirt On My Shirt*); Jim Colucci and Bonnie Datt (Authors); Stacia Deutsch and Rhody Cohon, (Co-authors of over 20 books); Chris Eboch (Author of over ten books, including the Haunted series for Simon and Schuster.); April Young Fritz; Verge Entertainment, Inc: Joseph Phillip Illidge, Shawn Martinbrough, Milo Stone Wilfred Santiago (Graphic novelist, author of 21: The Romberto Clemente story (Fantagraphics, 2010). Rebecca Van Slyke (Picture book author); BD Wong (actor, author); Linda Zinnen Author of *The Truth About Rats, Rules and The Seventh Grade*; *The Dragons Of Spratt, Ohio* (both HarperCollins), and Third (Dutton).

Terms Agent receives 15% on domestic sales, 15% on foreign sales. Offers written contract. 30 days notice must be given for termination of contract.

How to Contact E-mail query. Considers simultaneous queries, submissions. Responds 2 weeks after query; 4 weeks after ms. Returns mss only with SASE. Obtains new clients through recommendations from others, queries/solicitations, conferences.

Tips "I am a very hands-on, old-school agent who likes to edit manuscripts as much as I like to negotiate deals. My favorite agents were always what I called "honest sharks,'out to get the best deal for their client, always looking ahead, but always conduced business in such a way that everyone came away as happy as possible. In short-they had integrity and determination to represent their clients to the best of their abilities, and that's what I aspire to."

MEWS BOOKS

20 Bluewater Hill, Westport CT 06880. (203)227-1836. Fax: (203)227-1144. E-mail: mewsbooks@aol.com. **Contact:** Sidney B. Kramer. Seeking both new and established writers. Estab. 1974. 50% of material handled is books for young readers. Staff includes Sidney B. Kramer and Fran Pollak.

- Previously Sidney Kramer was Senior Vice President and founder of Bantam Books, President of New American Library, Director and Manager of Corgi Books in London; He is an attorney specializing in literary matters.

Recent Sales Sold 10 books for young readers in the last year.

Terms Agent receives 15% commission on domestic sales; 20% on foreign sales. Offers written contract, binding for 1-2 years. "We never retain an unhappy author, but we cannot terminate in the middle of activity. If submission is accepted, we ask for $100 against all expenses. We occasionally make referrals to editing services."

How to Contact Query with SASE, send outline and 2 sample chapters by regular mail only. Accepts short e-mail specific queries but not submissions or attachments. Prefers to read material exclusively. Responds in a few weeks to queries. Returns material only with SASE. Obtains clients through recommendations from others.

ERIN MURPHY LITERARY AGENCY

2700 Woodlands Village, #300-458, Flagstaff AZ 86001-7127. (928)525-2056. **Web site:** www.publishersmarketplace.com/members/ErinMurphy/. **Contact**: Erin Murphy. Closed to unsolicited queries and submissions. Considers both new and established writers, by referral from industry professionals she knows or personal contact (such as conferences) only. Estab. 1999. Member of SCBWI. Represents 50 active clients. 25% of clients are new/previously unpublished writers. 100% of material handled is books of young readers.

- Prior to opening her agency, Erin Murphy was editor-in-chief at Northland Publishing/Rising Moon. (Agency is not currently accepting unsolicited queries or submissions.)

Recent Sales Sold 20 books for young readers in the last year. Recent releases: *Dogs on the Bed*, by Elizabeth Bluemle (Candlewick); *A Curse Dark As Gold*, by Elizabeth C. Bunce (Levine/ Scholastic); *10 Lucky Things That Have Happened to me since I Nearly Got Hit by Lightning*, by Mary Hershey (Lamb/Random House); *Theodosia and the Staff of Osiris*, by R.L. Lafevers (Houghton); *Maybelle Goes to Tea*, by Katie Speck (Holt).

Terms Agent receives 15% commission on domestic sales; 20% on foreign sales. Offers written contract. 30 days notice must be given to terminate contract.

MUSE LITERARY MANAGEMENT

189 Waverly Place #4, New York NY 10014-3135.(212)925-3721. E-mail: MuseLiteraryMgmt@aol. com. Website: www.museliterary.com. Seeking both new and established writers. Estab. 1998. Agency is member of Children's Literature Network. Represents 10 clients. 90% new writers. 60% books for young readers. **Contact:** Deborah Carter.

Recent Sales Sold 1 book for young readers in 2008. *The Adventures of Molly Whuppie and Other Appalachian Folktales*, by Anne Shelby (University of North Carolina Press). Winner of 2008 AESOP Accolade from American Folklore Society.

Terms Agent receives 15% commission on domestic sales; 20% on foreign sales. Offers written contract. Contract binding for 1 year. One day's notice must be given for termination of contract.

How to Contact Accepts queries by e-mail, mail. Considers simultaneous queries, submissions. Responds in 1-2 weeks to queries; 2-3 weeks to ms.

Tips "I give editorial feedback and work on revisions on spec. Agency agreement is offered when the writer and I feel the manuscript is ready for submission to publishers. Writers should also be open to doing revisions with editors who express serious interest in their work, prior to any offer of a publishing contract. All aspects of career strategy are discussed with writers, and all decisions are ultimately theirs. I make multiple and simultaneous submissions when looking for rights opportunities, and share all correspondence. All agreements are signed by the writers. Reimbursement for expenses is subject to client's approval, limited to photocopying (usually press clips) and postage. I always submit fresh manuscripts to publishers printed in my office with no charge to the writer."

JEAN V. NAGGAR LITERARY AGENCY, INC.

216 E. 75th Street, Suite 1E, New York NY 10021.(212)794-1082. Fax: (212)794-3605. E-mail: jregel@jvnla.com (all first initial last name@jvnla.com). Website: www.jvnla.com. Seeking both new and established writers. Estab. 1978. Member of AAR, SCBWI. Represents 150 clients. Large percentage of clients are new/previously unpublished writers. 25% material handled is books for young readers.

Recent Sales See Web site for information.

How to Contact Accepts queries by e-mail. Prefers to read materials exclusively. Responds in 2 weeks to queries; response time for ms depends on the agent. Obtains new clients through recommendations from others, queries/solicitations, conferences.

ALISON PICARD, LITERARY AGENT

P.O. Box 2000, Cotuit MA 02635. Phone/fax: (508)477-7192. E-mail: ajpicard@aol.com. **Contact:** Alison Picard. Seeking both new and established writers. Estab. 1985. Represents 50 clients. 40% of clients are new/previously unpublished writers. 20% of material handled is books for young readers.

- Prior to opening her agency, Alison Picard was an assistant at a large New York agency before co-founding Kidde, Hoyt & Picard in 1982. She became an independent agent in 1985.

Recent Sales *Funerals and Fly Fishing*, by Mary Bartek (Henry Holt & Co.); *Playing Dad's Song*, by Dina Friedman (Farrar Straus & Giroux); *Escaping into the Night*, by Dina Friedman (Simon & Schuster); *Celebritrees* and *The Peace Bell*, by Margi Preus (Henry Holt & Co.)

Terms Receives 15% commission on domestic sales; 20-25% on foreign sales. Offers written contract, binding for 1 year. 1-week notice must be given to terminate contract.

How to Contact Query with SASE. Accepts queries by e-mail with no attachments. Considers simultaneous queries and submissions. Responds in 2 weeks to queries; 4 months to mss. Returns material only with SASE. Obtains clients through queries/solicitations.

Tips "We currently have a backlog of submissions."

PROSPECT AGENCY

285 5th Ave.PMB 445, Brooklyn NY 11215. (718)788-3217. Fax: (718)360-9582. E-mail: esk@ prospectagency.com. Website: www.prospectagency.com. **Contact:** Emily Sylvan Kim, Becca Stumpf, Rachel Orr, Vivian Chum. Seeking both new and established writers. Estab. 2005. Agent is member of AAR. Represents 55 clients aand growing. 70% of clients are new/previously unpublished writers. 60% of material handled is books for young readers. taff includes Emily Sylvan, Becca Stumpf, and Rachel Orr are agents. Emily handles Young Adult, tween and middle grade literary and commercial ficion, with a special interest in edgy books and books for boys. Becca Stumpf handels Young adult and middle grade literary and commercial fiction, with a special interest in fantasy and science fiction with cross-genre appeal. Rachel Orr handles picture books, beginning readers, chapter books, middle-grade/YA novels, children's non-fiction, and children's illustrators. Vivian Chum, a junior agent is seeking YA and middle-grade fiction and non-fiction. She also seeks children's picture book illustrators and graphic novels.

- For some of us, it's all we've ever known. Others have worked in various facets of publishing and law.

Recent Sales Sold 2 books for young readers in the last year. (Also represents adult fiction.) Recent sales include: *Waterloo Plot*, by Marissa Doyle (Holt); *Rocky Road*, by Rose Kent (Knopf); *Struts and Frets*, by Jon Skovron (Abrams); *I Think My Teacher is Superhero*, by Jake Bell (Scholastic).

Terms Agent receives 15% on domestic sales, 20% on foreign sales. Offers written contract.

How to Contact Send outline and 3 sample chapters. Accepts queries through Web site ONLY. Considers sumultaneous queries submissions. However, we do not accept submissions to multiple Prospect agents (please submit to only one agent at Prospect Agency). Responds in 1 week to 3 months following an initial quiery. 1 week to two months after a mss has been requested. All submissions are elcetronc; manuscripts and queries that are not a good fit for our agency are rejected via e-mail. We obtain new clients through conferences, recommendations, queries, and some scouting.

SUSAN SCHULMAN LITERARY AGENCY

454 W. 44th, New York NY 10036. (212)713-1633. Fax: (212)581-8830. E-mail: schulman@aol.com. Website: www.Schulmanagency.com. **Contact**: Susan Schulman. Seeking both new and established writers. Estab. 1980. Member of AAR, WGA, SCBWI, Dramatists Guild, New York Women in Film, League of New York Theater Professional Women; 15% of material handled is books for young readers. Staff includes Emily Uhry, YA; Linda Kiss, picture books.

Recent Sales Of total agency sales, approximately 20% is children's literature. Recent sales include: *Pirates of Crocodile Swamp*, by Jim Arnosky; *Spotting for Nelliel*, by Pamela Lowell (Marshall Cavendish); *I Get All Better*, by Vickie Cobb (4-book series with Lerner); film rights to *100 Girls to MTV*; film rights to *Social Climbers Guide to High School*, by Robyn Schneider to ABC Family.

Terms Agent receives 15% on domestic sales, 20% on foreign sales.

How to Contact Query with SASE. Accepts queries by e-mail but responds only to e-mail queries which interest agency. Considers simultaneous queries and submissions. Returns mss only with SASE. Obtains new clients through recommendations from others, queries/solicitations, conferences.

Tips Schulman describes her agency as "professional boutique, long-standing, eclectic."

SERENDIPITY LITERARY AGENCY

305 Gates Ave.Brooklyn NY 11216.(718)230-7689. Fax: (718)230-7829. E-mail: rbrooks@ serendipitylit.com. Website: www.serendipitylit.com. Contact: Regina Brooks. Estab. 2000. Represents 50 clients. 65% of clients are new/unpublished writers. 50% of material handled is books for young readers.

- Prior to becoming an agent, Regina Brooks was an acquisitions editor for John Wiley & Sons and McGraw-Hill Companies.

Recent Sales *A Wreath for Emmitt Till*, by Marilyn Nelson (Houghton Mifflin); *A Song for Present Existence*, by Marilyn Nelson and Tonya Hegamin (Scholastic); *Ruby and the Booker Boys*, by Derrick Barnes (Scholastic); *Brenda Buckley's Universe and Everything In It*, by Sundee Frazier (Delacorte Books for Young Readers); *Wait Until the Black Girl Sings*, by Bil Wright Simon and Schuster (Scholastic); *First Semester*, by Cecil R. Cross II (KimaniTru/ Harlequin).

Terms Agent receives 15% commission on domestic sales; 20% on foreign sales. Offers written contract. Terminations notice—2 months.

How to Contact Prefers to read material exclusively. For nonfiction, submit outline, 1 sample chapter and SASE. Accepts e-mail queries. Responds to queries in 4 weeks; mss in 1 month. Obtains new clients through writer's conferences and referrals.

Tips "I adore working with first-time authors whose books challenge the readers emotionally; tears and laughter. I also represent award-winning illustrators."

STIMOLA LITERARY STUDIO, LLC

306 Chase Court, Edgewater NJ 07020. Phone/fax: (201)945-9353. E-mail: info@stimolaliterarystudio. com. Website: www.stimolalitrarystudio.com. **Contact:** Rosemary B. Stimola. Seeking both new and established writers. Estab. 1997. Member of AAR, SCBWI, ALA, NCTE. Represents 45+ clients. 25% of clients are new/previously unpublished writers. 85% of material handled is books for young readers. Represents Preschool through young adult, fiction and nonfiction. Agency is owned and operated by a former educator and children's bookseller with a Ph.. in Linguistics. Actively seeking remarkable young adult fiction and debut picture book author/illustrators. No institutional books.

How to Contact Query via e-mail here listed. No attachments, please! Considers simultaneous queries. Responds in 3 weeks to queries of interest; 6-8 weeks to requested mss. Returns snail mail material with SASE. While unsolicited queries are welcome, most clients come through editor, agent, client referrals.

- Prior to opening her agency Rosemary Stimola was an independent children's bookseller.

Recent Sales Sold 35 books for young readers in the last year. Among these, *Soul Enchilada*, by David Gill (Greenwillow books); *Panda Bear and Polar Bear*, by Matthew Baek (Dial Books/ Penguin); *The Flying Beaver Brothers*, by Maxwell Eaton III (Knopf/RH; *Neil Armstrong is my Uncle and other Lies Muscle Man McFinty Told me*, by Nan Marino (Roaring Brook Press); *Past Perfect*, by Siobhan Vivian (Push/Scholastic).

Terms Agent receives 15% commission on domestic sales; 20% on foreign sales (if subagents used). Offers written contract, binding for all children's projects. 60 days notice must be given to terminate contract. Charges $85 one-time fee per project to cover expenses. Client provides all hard copy and e-files required for submission."

S©OTT TREIMEL NY

434 Lafayette St., New York ny 10003. (212)505-8353. E-mail: stny@verizonnet. Website: scotttreimelnycom

Recent Sales Sold 36 titles in the last year. *The Hunchback Assignments* by Arthur Slade (Random House U.S. and HarperCollins Canada); *One Little Flower Girl*, illustrations by Janie Bynum

(Scholastic); *ROAWR!* by Barbara Joosse (Philomel); *My Life From Airbras to Zits* by Barbara Haworth-Attard (Flux); *Play, Louis, Play* by Muriel Weinstein (Bloomsbury); *Cakes and Miracles* by Barbara Golden (Marshall Cavendish); *Dog Parade* by Barbara Joosse (Harcourt); Cyndy Szekeres Golden Books Backlist (Sterling); *Laundry Day* by Maurie Manning (Clarion); *One Hockey Night* by David Ward (Scholastic Canada); many titles to Audible.

Terms Agent receives 15-20% commission on domestic sales; 20-25% on foreign sales. Offers verbal or written contract, binding on a "contract-by-contract basis." Charges for photocopying, overnight/express postage, messengers. Offers editorial guidance, if extensive charges higher commission.

How to Contact Please check Web sites for submission policies.

Tips "I look for dedicated authors and illustrators willing to work hard in our increasingly competitive field. I want fresh story conceits, not derivative stories we have read and read. I am always mindful of an authentic (to the age) point-of-view. We spend a lot of time hunting for the best work, and do launch new talent each year."

WRITERS HOUSE

21 W. 26th St.New York NY 10010. (212)685-2400. Fax: (212)685-1781. Website: www.writershouse. com. Estab. 1974. Member of AAR. Represents 280 clients. Specializes in all types of popular fiction and nonfiction especially children's and young adult literature. No scholarly, professional, poetry or screenplays.

How to Contact Query. Please check our Web site for more specific submission guidelines and info about our agents.

Needs Obtains new clients through referrals and unsolicited submissions. **Terms** Agent receives 15% commission on domestic sales; 20% on foreign sales. Offers written contract, binding for 1 year.

Tips "Do not send manuscripts. Write a compelling letter. If you do, we'll ask to see your work."

ART REPS

ART FACTORY

925 Elm Grove Rd.Elm Grove WI 53122. (262)785-1940. Fax: (262)785-1611. E-mail: tstocki@ artfactoryltd.com. Website: www.artfactoryltd.com. **Contact:** Tom Stocki. Commercial illustration representative. Estab. 1978. Represents 9 illustrators including: Tom Buchs, Tom Nachreiner, Todd Dakins, Linda Godfrey, Larry Mikec, Bill Scott, Gary Shea, Terry Herman, Troy Allen. 10% of artwork handled is children's book illustration. Currently open to illustrators seeking representation. Open to both new and established illustrators.

Represents Illustration.

Terms Receives 25-30% commission. Offers written contract. Advertising costs are split: 75% paid by illustrators; 25% paid by rep. "We try to mail samples of all our illustrators at one time and we try to update our Web site; so we ask the illustrators to keep up with new samples." Advertises in *Picturebook*, *Workbook*.

How to Contact For first contact, send query letter, tearsheets. Responds only if interested. Call to schedule an appointment. Portfolio should include tearsheets. Finds illustrators through queries/ solicitations.

Tips "Have a unique style."

ASCIUTTO ART REPS.INC.

1712 E. Butler Circle, Chandler AZ 85225. (480)899-0600. Fax: (480)899-3636.Website: www. Aartreps.com E-mail: Aartreps@cox.net. **Contact:** Mary Anne Asciutto, art agent, Children's book illustration representative since 1980. Specializing in childrens illustrations for childrens educational

text books, grades K thru 8, childrens trade books, childrens magazines, posters, packaging, etc.
Recent Sales *Bats, Sharks, Whales, Snakes, Penguins, Alligators and Crocodiles*, illustrated by Meryl Henderson for Boyds Mills Press.
Terms Agency receives 25% commission. Advertising and promotion costs are split: 75% paid by talent; 25% paid by representative. US citizens only.
How to Contact Send samples via email with a cover letter résumé. Submit sample portfolio for review with an SASE for it's return. Responds in 2 to 4 weeks. Portfolio should include at least 12 samples of original art, printed tearsheets, photocopies or color prints of most recent work.
Tips In obtaining representation, "be sure to connect with an agent who handles the kind of work, you (the artist) *want."*

CAROL BANCROFT & FRIENDS

P.O. Box 2030, Danbury, CT 06813 (203)730-8270 or (800)720-7020. Fax: (203)730-8275. E-mail: artists@carolbancroft.com. Website: www.carolbancroft.com. **Owner:** Joy Elton Tricarico. **Founder:** Carol Bancroft. Estab. 1972. Illustration representative for all aspects of children's publishing and design. Text and trade; any children's related material. Member of, Society of Illustrators, Graphic Artists Guild, National Art Education Association, SCBWI. Represents 30+ illustrators. Specializes in illustration for children's publishing-text and trade; any children's-related material. Clients include, but not limited to, Scholastic, Houghton Mifflin, HarperCollins, Dutton, Harcourt, Marshall Cavendish, Mcgraw Hill, Hay House.
Represents Illustration for children of all ages including young adult.
Terms Rep receives 25% commission. Advertising costs are split: 75% paid by talent; 25% paid by representative. For promotional purposes, artists must provide "laser copies (not slides), tearsheets, promo pieces, good color photocopies, etc.; 6 pieces or more is best; narrative scenes and children interacting." Advertises in Picture Book, Directory of Illustration.
How to Contact Send either 2-3 samples with your **address** to the e-mail address above or mail 6-10 samples, along with a self Addressed, stamped envelope (SASE) to the above p.o. box."

SHERYL BERANBAUM

(401)737-8591. E-mail: SBeranbaum@aol.com. Website: www.beranbaum.com. **Contact:**Sheryl Beranbaum. Commercial illustration representative. Estab. 1985. Member of Graphic Artists Guild. Represents 17 illustrators. 75% of artwork handled is children's book illustration. Currently open to illustrators seeking representation. Open to new and established illustrators only. Submission guidelines available by phone.
• Sheryl Beranbaum is currently not taking on new artists.
Represents Illustration. "My illustrators are diversified and their work comes from a variety of the industry's audiences."
Terms Receives 30% commission. Charges marketing-plan fee or Web-only fee. Offers written contract. Advertising costs are split: 75% paid by illustrators; 25% paid by rep. Requires Itoya portfolio; postcards only for promotion.
How to Contact For first contact, send direct mail flier/brochure, tearsheets, photocopies. Responds only if interested. Portfolio should include photocopies.

PEMA BROWNE LTD.

11 Tena Place, Valley Cottage NY 10989. (845)268-0029. **Contact:** Pema Browne. Estab. 1966. Represents 2 illustrators. 10% of artwork handled is children's book illustration. Specializes in general commercial. Markets include: all publishing areas; children's picture books. Clients include HarperCollins, Holiday House, Bantam Doubleday Dell, Nelson/Word, Hyperion, Putnam. Client list available upon request.
Represents Fiction, nonfiction, picture books, middle grade, young adult, manuscript/illustration packages. Looking for "professional and unique" talent.
Recent Sales *The Daring Ms. Quimby*, by Suzanne Whitaker (Holiday House).

Terms Rep receives 30% illustration commission; 20% author commission. Exclusive area representation is required. For promotional purposes, talent must provide color mailers to distribute. Representative pays mailing costs on promotion mailings.

How to Contact For first contact, send query letter, direct mail flier/brochure and SASE. If interested will ask to mail appropriate materials for review. Portfolios should include tearsheets and transparencies or good color photocopies, plus SASE. Accepts queries by mail only. Obtains new talent through recommendations and interviews (portfolio review).

Tips "We are doing more publishing—all types—less advertising." Looks for "continuity of illustration and dedication to work."

CATUGEAU: ARTIST AGENT, LLC

3009 Margaret Jones Lane, Williamsburg VA 23185. (757)221-0666. Fax: (757)221-6669. E-mail: chris@catugeau.com. Website: www.CATugeau.com. **Owner/Agent:** Chris Tugeau. Children's publishing trade book, mass market, educational. Estab. 1994. Member of SPAR, SCBWI, Graphic Artists Guild. Represents 35 illustrators. 95% of artwork handled is children's book illustration.

• Accepting limited new artists from North America only.

Represents Illustration ONLY.

Terms Receives 25% commission. "Artists responsible for providing samples for portfolios, promotional books and mailings." Exclusive representation required in educational. Trade "house accounts" acceptable. Offers written contract. Advertises in *Picturebook*.

How to Contact For first contact, e-mail samples with note. No CDs. Responds ASAP. Finds illustrators through recommendations from others, conferences, personal search.

Tips "Do research, read articles on CAT Web site, study picture books at bookstores, promote yourself a bit to learn the industry. Be professional... know what you do best, and be prepared to give rep what they need to present you! Do have e-mail and scanning capabilities, too."

CORNELL & McCARTHY, LLC

2-D Cross Hwy. Westport CT 06880. (203)454-4210. Fax: (203)454-4258. E-mail: contact@cmartreps. com. Website: www.cmartreps.com. **Contact:** Merial Cornell. Children's book illustration representatives. Estab. 1989. Member of SCBWI and Graphic Artists Guild. Represents 30 illustrators. Specializes in children's books: trade, mass market, educational.

Represents Illustration.

Terms Agent receives 25% commission. Advertising costs are split: 75% paid by talent; 25% paid by representative. For promotional purposes, talent must provide 10-12 strong portfolio pieces relating to children's publishing.

How to Contact For first contact, send query letter, direct mail flier/brochure, tearsheets, photocopies and SASE or e-mail. Responds in 1 month. Obtains new talent through recommendations, solicitation, conferences.

Tips "Work hard on your portfolio."

CREATIVE FREELANCERS, INC.

4 Greenwich Hills Drive, Greenwich CT 06831 (800)398-9544. Website: www.illustratorsonline. com. **Contact:** Marilyn Howard. Commercial illustration representative. Estab. 1988. Represents over 30 illustrators. "Our staff members have art direction, art buying or illustration backgrounds." Specializes in children's books, advertising, architectural, conceptual. Markets include: advertising agencies; corporations/client direct; design firms; editorial/magazines; paper products/greeting cards; publishing/books; sales/promotion firms.

Represents Illustration. Artists must have published work.

Terms Rep receives 30% commission. Exclusive area representation is preferred. Advertising costs are split: 75% paid by talent; 25% paid by representative. For promotional purposes, talent must provide scans of artwork. Advertises in *American Showcase, Workbook*.

How to Contact For first contact, send tearsheets, low res jpegs or "whatever best shows work." Responds back only if interested.

Tips Looks for experience, professionalism and consistency of style. Obtains new talent through "word of mouth and Web site."

DIMENSION

13420 Morgan Ave. S.Burnsville MN 55337. (952)201-3981. Fax: (952)895-9315. E-mail: jkoltes@ dimensioncreative.com. Website: www.imensioncreative.com. **Contact:** Joanne Koltes. Commercial illustration representative. Estab. 1982. Member of MN Book Builder. Represents 12 illustrators. 65% of artwork handled is children's book illustration. Staff includes Joanne Koltes.

Terms Advertises in *Picturebook* and *Minnesota Creative*.

How to Contact Contact with samples via e-mail. Responds only if interested.

PAT HACKETT/ARTIST REP

7014 N. Mercer Way, Mercer Island WA 98040-2130. (206)447-1600. Fax: (206)447-0739. Website: www.pathackett.com. **Contact:** Pat Hackett. Commercial illustration representative. Estab. 1979. Member of Graphic Artists Guild. Represents 12 illustrators. 10% of artwork handled is children's book illustration. Currently open to illustrators seeking representation. Open to both new and established illustrators.

Represents Illustration. Looking for illustrators with unique, strong, salable style.

Terms Receives 25-33% commission. Advertising costs are split: 75% paid by illustrators; 25% paid by rep. Illustrator must provide portfolios (2-3) and promotional pieces. Advertises in *Picturebook*, *Workbook*.

How to Contact For first contact, send query letter, tearsheets, SASE, direct mail flier/brochure. Responds only if interested. Wait for response. Portfolio should include tearsheets. Lasers OK. Finds illustrators through recommendations from others, queries/solicitations.

Tips "Send query plus 1-2 samples, either by regular mail or e-mail."

HANNAH REPRESENTS

14431 Ventura Blvd.#108, Sherman Oaks CA 91423. (818)378-1644. E-mail: hannahrepresents@ yahoo.com. **Contact:** Hannah Robinson. Literary representative for illustrators. Estab. 1997. 100% of artwork handled is children's book illustration. Looking for established illustrators only.

Represents Manuscript/illustration packages.

HERMAN AGENCY

350 Central Park West, New York NY 10025. (212)749-4907. E-mail: ronnie@hermanagencyinc. com. Website: www.hermanagencyinc.com. **Contact:** Ronnie Ann Herman. Literary and artistic agency. Estab. 1999. Member of SCBWI and Graphic Artists Guild. Illustrators include: Joy Allen, Tom Arma, Durga Bernhard, Marion Billet, Mary Bono, Elizabeth Buttler, Chris Case, Jason Chapman, Seymour Chwast, Pascale Constantin, Kathy Couri, Troy Cummings, Doreen Gay-Kassel, Jan Spivey Gilchrist, Barry Gott, Liora Grossman, Steve Haskamp, Jago, Gideon Kendall, Ana Martin Larranaga, Mike Lester, Viqui Maggio, Lisa McCue, Bob McMahon, Margie Moore, Alexi Natchev, Jill Newton, John Nez, Tamara Petrosino, Michael Rex, David Sheldon, Richard Torrey, Mark Weber, Pete Whitehead, Candace Whitman, Deborah Zemke. Authors include: Eloise Greenfield, John Herman, R.A. Herman, Deloris Jordan, Nataniel Lachenmeyer, The Lorigs. 90% of artwork handled is children's book illustration and related markets. Currently not accepting new clients unless they have been successfully published by major trade publishing houses.

Terms Receives 25% commission for illustration assignments; 15% for ms assignments. Artists pay 75% of costs for promotional material, about $200 a year. Exclusive representation usually required. Offers written contract. Advertising costs are split: 75% paid by illustrator; 25% paid by rep.

How to Contact Not looking for new artists or authors unless previously published by major houses. For first contact, e-mail link to Web site. Authors should e-mail with a query. Responds in 1 month or less. I will contact you only if I like your samples or if I am interested in your writing. Finds illustrators and authors through recommendations from others, conferences, queries/solicitations.

LEVY CREATIVE MANAGEMENT

300 E. 46th St.Suite 8E, New York NY 10017. (212)687-6465. Fax: (212)661-4839. E-mail: info@ levycreative.com. Website: www.levycreative.com. **Contact:** Sari Levy. Estab. 1998. Member of Society of Illustrators, Graphic Artists Guild, Art Directors Club. Represents 13 illustrators including: Mike Byers, Alan Dingman, Marcos Chin, Robin Eley, Chrisopher Nielsen, Laura Osorno, Kyung Soon Park, Trip Park, Jason Seiler, Koren Shadmi, Jason Tharp, and Andrea Wicklund. 30% of artwork handled is children's book illustration. Currently open to illustrators seeking representation. Open to both new and established illustrators. Submission guidelines available on Web site.
Represents Illustration, manuscript/illustration packages.
Terms Exclusive representation required. Offers written contract. Advertising costs are split: 75% paid by illustrators; 25% paid by rep. Advertises in *Picturebook, American Showcase, Workbook, Alternative Pick and others.***How to Contact** For first contact, send tearsheets, photocopies, SASE. "See Web site for submission guidelines." Responds only if interested. Portfolio should include professionally presented materials. Finds illustrators through recommendations from others, word of mouth, competitions.

MARLENA AGENCY, INC.

322 Ewing St.Princeton NJ 08540. (609)252-9405. Fax: (609)252-1949. E-mail: marlena@ marlenaagency.com. Website: www.marlenaagency.com. Commercial illustration representative. Estab. 1990. Member of Society of Illustrators. Represents 30 international illustrators including: Gerard Dubois, Linda Helton, Paul Zwolak, Martin Jarrie, Serge Bloch, Hadley Hooper, Jean-François Martin Perre Mornet, Pep Montserrat, Tomasz Walenta, Istvan Orosz and Carmen Segovia. Staff includes Marlena Torzecka, Simone Stark, Ella Lupo, Marie Joanne Wimmr, Anna Pluskota. Currently open to illustrators seeking representation. Open to both new and established illustrators. Submission guidelines available for #10 SASE.
Represents Illustration.
Recent Sales *Sees Behind Trees*, by Linda Helton (Harcourt); *Ms. Rubinstein's Beauty, by Pep Montserrat* (Sterling);*ABC USA*, by Martin Jarrie (Sterling); *My Cat*, by Linda Helton (Scholastic); *The McElderry Book of Greek Myths*, by Pep Monserrat (McElderly Books)
Terms Exclusive representation required. Offers written contract. Requires printed portfolios, transparencies, direct mail piece (such as postcards) printed samples. Advertises in *Workbook*.
How to Contact For first contact, send tearsheets, photocopies, or e-mail low resolution samples only. Responds only if interested. Drop off or mail portfolio, photocopies. Portfolio should include tearsheets, photocopies. Finds illustrators through queries/solicitations, magazines and graphic design.
Tips "Be creative and persistent."

MB ARTISTS

(formerly HK Portfolio), 10 E. 29th St.40G, New York NY 10016. (212)689-7830. E-mail: mela@ mbartists.com. Website: www.mbartists.com. **Contact:** Mela Bolinao. Illustration representative. Estab. 1986. Member of SPAR, Society of Illustrators and Graphic Artists Guild. Represents 45 illustrators. Specializes in illustration for juvenile markets. Markets include: advertising agencies; editorial/magazines; publishing/books, Tos, games boards, stationary, etc.
Represents Illustration.
Recent Sales *Sweet Tooth*, illustrated by Jack E. Davis (Simon & Schuster); *The Perfect Nest*, illustrated by John Manders (Candlewick); *The Goodnight Train*, illustrated by by Laura Huliska

Beith (Harcourt); *Ducks Dunk*, illustrated by Hiroe Nakata (Henry Holt); *Here Comes T. Rex Cottontail*, illustrated by Jack E. Davis (HarperCollins).

Terms Rep receives 25% commission. No geographic restrictions. Advertising costs are split: 75% paid by talent; 25% paid by representative. Advertises in *Picturebook*, *Directory of Illustration*, *Play* and *Workbook*.

How to Contact No geographic restrictions. For first contact, send query letter, direct mail flier/brochure, Web site address, tearsheets, slides, photographs or color copies and SASE or send Web site link to mela@mbartists.com. Responds in 1 week. Portfolio should include at least 12 images appropriate for the juvenile market.

THE NEIS GROUP

14600 Sawyer Ranch Rd. Dripping Springs TX 78620. (616)450-1533 Fax: (512)-829-4508. E-mail: jneis@neisgroup.com. Website: www.neisgroup.com. **Contact:** Judy Neis. Commercial illustration representative. Estab. 1982. Represents 45 illustrators including: Lyn Boyer, Pam Thomson, Dan Sharp, Terry Workman, Liz Conrad, Garry Colby, Clint Hansen, Julie Borden, Diana Magnuson, Jacqueline Rogers, Johnna Bandle, Jack Pennington, Gary Ferster, Erika LeBarre, Mark and Lee Fullerton, James Palmer, Brandon Reese, Joel Spector, John White, Neverne Covington, Ruth Pettis. 60% of artwork handled is children's book illustration. Currently open to illustrators seeking representation. Looking for established illustrators only.

Represents Illustration, photography and calligraphy/manuscript packages.

Terms Receives 25% commission. "I prefer portfolios on disc, color printouts and e-mail capabilities whenever possible." Advertises in *Picturebook*, & *Creative Black Book*.

How to Contact For first contact, send bio, tearsheets, direct mail flier/brochure. Responds only if interested. After initial contact, drop off portfolio of nonreturnables. Portfolio should include tearsheets, photocopies. Obtains new talent through recommendations from others and queries/solicitations.

REMEN-WILLIS DESIGN GROUP—ANN REMEN-WILLIS

2964 Colton Rd.Pebble Beach CA 93953. (831)655-1407. Fax: (831)655-1408. E-mail: remenwillis@comcast.net. Web sites: www.annremenwillis.com or www.picture-book.com. **Contact:**Ann Remen-Willis. Specializes in childrens' book illustration trade/education. Estab. 1984. Member of SCBWI. Represents 18 illustrators including: Dominic Catalano, Siri Weber Feeney, Doug Roy, Susan Jaekel, Dennis Hockerman, Rosiland Solomon, Meredith Johnson, Renate Lohmann, Robin Kerr, Len Ebert, Gary Undercuffler, Sheila Bailey, Jon Goodell, Frank Hill, Carol Heyer is children's book illustration.

Terms Offers written contract. Advertising costs are split: 50% paid by illustrators; 50% paid by rep. Illustrator must provide small precise portfolio for promotion. Advertises in *Picturebook*, *Workbook*.

How to Contact For first contact, send tearsheets, photocopies or e-mail. Responds in 1 week.

Tips "Send samples of only the type of work you are interested in receiving as an assignment. Check out rep's Web sites first."

LIZ SANDERS AGENCY

2415 E. Hangman Creek Lane, Spokane WA USA 99224-8514. E-mail: liz@lizsanders.com. Website: ww.lizsanders.com. **Contact:** Liz Sanders. Commercial illustration representative. Estab. 1985. Represents Kyle Poling, Jared Beckstand, Craig Orback, Amy Ning, Tom Pansini, Chris Lensch, Lynn Gesue, Poozie, Susan Synarski, Sudi McCollum, Suzanne Beaky and more. Currently open to illustrators seeking representation. Open to both new and established illustrators. Handles Illustration. Markets include publishing, licensed properties, entertainment and advertising.

Terms Receives 30% commission against pro bono mailing program. Offers written contract. Advertises in Picturebook and picture-book.com, Directory of Illustration, childrensillustrators.com, theispot.com, folioplanet.com. No geographic restrictions.

How to Contact For first contact, send tearsheets, direct mail flier/brochure, color copies, non-returnable or e-mail to submissions@lizsanders.com. Responds only if interested. Obtains new talent through recommendations from industry contacts, conferences and queries/solicitations, Literary Market Place.

S.I. INTERNATIONAL

43 E. 19th St.New York NY 10003. (212)254-4996. Fax: (212)995-0911. E-mail: information@si-i.com. Website: www.si-i.com. Commercial illustration representative. Estab. 1983. Member of SPAR, Graphic Artists Guild. Represents 50 illustrators. Specializes in license characters, educational publishing and children's illustration, digital art and design, mass market paperbacks. Markets include design firms; publishing/books; sales/promotion firms; licensing firms; digital art and design firms.

Represents Illustration. Looking for artists "who have the ability to do children's illustration and to do license characters either digitally or reflectively."

Terms Rep receives 25-30% commission. Advertising costs are split: 70% paid by talent; 30% paid by representative. "Contact agency for details. Must have mailer." Advertises in *Picturebook*.

How to Contact For first contact, send query letter, tearsheets. Responds in 3 weeks. After initial contact, write for appointment to show portfolio of tearsheets, slides.

WENDYLYNN & CO.

504 Wilson Rd.Annapolis MD 21401. (401)224-2729. Fax: (410)224-2183. E-mail: wendy@wendylynn.com. Website: www.wendylynn.com. **Contact:** Wendy Mays. Children's illustration representative. Estab. 2002. Member of SCBWI. Represents 30 illustrators. 100% of artwork handled is children's illustration. Staff includes Wendy Mays, Janice Onken. Currently open to considering illustrators seeking representation. Open to both new and established illustrators. Not interested in cartoon style illustration. Submission guidelines available on Web site.

Represents Illustration.

Terms Receives 25% commission. Exclusive representation required. Offers written contract. Requires 20 images submitted on disk in high and low resolution versions. Requires participation in a children's illustrators Web site that cost the artist $200 annually. Pays 100% of all other promotion.

How to Contact For first contact, e-mail 4-5 jpg samples and link to Web site. Responds if interested. Portfolio should include a minimum of 20 strong images. Finds illustrators through recommendations from others and from portfolio reviews.

Tips "Incest in the best quality scanner you can afford and be able to scan your own artwork and send files digitally to publishers. Also, having your own Web site is important, and knowing how to use Photoshop is a plus." Portfolio should show a consistency of style.

DEBORAH WOLFE LTD.

731 N. 24th St.Philadelphia PA 19130. (215)232-6666. Fax: (215)232-6585. E-mail: inquiry@illustrationonline.com. Website: www.illustrationOnline.com. **Contact:** Deborah Wolfe. Commercial illustration representative. Estab. 1978. Member of Graphic Artist Guild. Represents 30 illustrators. Currently open to illustrators seeking representation.

Represents Illustration.

Terms Receives 25% commission. Exclusive representation required. Offers written contract. Advertising costs are split: 75% paid by illustrators; 25% paid by rep. Advertises in *Picturebook*, *Directory of Illustration*, *The Workbook*.

How to Contact Responds in 2 weeks. Portfolio should be sent as jpgs or you should direct us to your Web site." Finds illustrators through queries/solicitations.

Clubs & Organizations

Contacts made through organizations such as the ones listed in this section can be quite beneficial for children's writers and illustrators. Professional organizations provide numerous educational, business, and legal services in the form of newsletters, workshops, or seminars. Organizations can provide tips about how to be a more successful writer or artist, as well as what types of business cards to keep, health and life insurance coverage to carry, and competitions to consider.

An added benefit of belonging to an organization is the opportunity to network with those who have similar interests, creating a support system. As in any business, knowing the right people can often help your career, and important contacts can be made through your peers. Membership in a writer's or artist's organization also shows publishers you're serious about your craft. This provides no guarantee your work will be published, but it gives you an added dimension of credibility and professionalism.

Some of the organizations listed here welcome anyone with an interest, while others are only open to published writers and professional artists. Organizations such as the Society of Children's Book Writers and Illustrators (SCBWI, www.scbwi.org) have varying levels of membership. SCBWI offers associate membership to those with no publishing credits, and full membership to those who have had work for children published. International organizations such as SCBWI also have regional chapters throughout the U.S. and the world. Write or call for more information regarding any group that interests you, or check the websites of the many organizations that list them. Be sure to get information about local chapters, membership qualifications, and services offered.

AMERICAN ALLIANCE FOR THEATRE & EDUCATION

4811 Saint Elmo Ave, Unit B, Bethesda, MD 20814. (301)951-7977. E-mail: info@aate.com. Website: www.aate.com. Purpose of organization: to promote standards of excellence in theatre and drama education. "We achieve this by assimilating quality practices in theatre and theatre education, connecting artists, educators, researchers and scholars with each other, and by providing opportunities for our members to learn, exchange and diversify their work, their audiences and their perspectives." Membership cost: $115 annually for individual in U.S. and Canada, $220 annually for organization, $60 annually for students, and $70 annually for retired people, $310 annually for University Departmental memberships; add $30 outside Canada and U.S. Holds annual conference (July or August). Contests held for unpublished play reading project and annual awards in various categories. Awards plaque and stickers for published playbooks. Publishes list of unpublished plays deemed worthy of performance and stages readings at conference. Contact national office at number above or see Web site for contact information for Playwriting Network Chairpersons.

ARIZONA AUTHORS ASSOCIATION

6145 West Echo Lane, Glendale AZ 85302. E-mail: info@azauthors.com. Website: www.azauthors.com. **President:** Toby Heathcotte. Purpose of organization: to offer professional, educational and social opportunities to writers and authors, and serve as a network. Members must be authors, writers working toward publication, agents, publishers, publicists, printers, illustrators, etc. Membership cost: $45/year writers; $30/year students; $60/year other professionals in publishing industry. Holds regular workshops and meetings. Publishes bimonthly newsletter and Arizona Literary Magazine. Sponsors Annual Literary Contest in poetry, essays, short stories, novels, and published books with cash prizes and awards bestowed at a public banquet in Phoenix. Winning entries are also published or advertised in the Arizona Literary Magazine. First and second place winners in poetry, essay and short story categories are entered in the Pushcart Prize. Winner is published categories receive free listings by www.fivestarpublications.com. Send SASE or view Web site for guidelines.

THE AUTHORS GUILD

31 East 32nd Street 7th floor; New York, NY 10016. (212)563-5904. Fax: (212)564-5363. E-mail: staff@authorsguild.org. Website: www.authorsguild.org. **Executive Director:** Paul Aiken. Purpose of organization: to offer services and materials intended to help authors with the business and legal aspects of their work, including contract problems, copyright matters, freedom of expression and taxation. Guild has 8,000 members. Qualifications for membership: Must be book author published by an established American publisher within 7 years or any author who has had 3 works (fiction or nonfiction) published by a magazine or magazines of general circulation in the last 18 months. Associate membership also available. Annual dues: $90. Different levels of membership include: associate membership with all rights except voting available to an author who has a firm contract offer or is currently negotiating a royalty contract from an established American publisher. "The Guild offers free contract reviews to its members. The Guild conducts several symposia each year at which experts provide information, offer advice and answer questions on subjects of interest and concern to authors. Typical subjects have been the rights of privacy and publicity, libel, wills and estates, taxation, copyright, editors and editing, the art of interviewing, standards of criticism and book reviewing. Transcripts of these symposia are published and circulated to members. The Authors Guild Bulletin, a quarterly journal, contains articles on matters of interest to writers, reports of Guild activities, contract surveys, advice on problem clauses in contracts, transcripts of Guild and League symposia and information on a variety of professional topics. Subscription included in the cost of the annual dues."

☙ CANADIAN SOCIETY OF CHILDREN'S AUTHORS, ILLUSTRATORS AND PERFORMERS, (CANSCAIP)

104-40 Orchard View Blvd.Toronto ON M4R 1B9 Canada. (416)515-1559. E-mail: office@canscaip.org. Website: www.cansaip.org. **Office Manager:** Lena Coakley. Purpose of organization: development of Canadian children's culture and support for authors, illustrators and performers working in this field. Qualifications for membership: Members—professionals who have been published (not self-published) or have paid public performances/records/tapes to their credit. Friends—share interest in field of children's culture. Membership cost: $75 (Members dues), $35 (Friends dues), $45 (Institution dues). Sponsors workshops/conferences. Publishes newsletter: includes profiles of members; news round-up of members' activities countrywide; market news; news on awards, grants, etc; columns related to professional concerns.

LEWIS CARROLL SOCIETY OF NORTH AMERICA

11935 Beltsville Dr.Beltsville MD 20705. E-mail: imholtz99@atlantech.net. Website: www.lewiscarroll.org/lcsna.html. **Secretary:** Clare Imholtz. "We are an organization of Carroll admirers of all ages and interests and a center for Carroll studies." Qualifications for membership: "An interest in Lewis Carroll and a simple love for Alice (or the Snark for that matter)." Membership cost: $35 (regular membership), $50 (foreign membership), $100 (sustaining membership). The Society meets twice a year—in spring and in fall; locations vary. Publishes a semi-annual journal, Knight Letter, and maintains an active publishing program.

THE CHILDREN'S BOOK COUNCIL, INC.

12 W. 37th St.2nd Floor, New York NY 10018. (212)966-1990. Fax: (212)966-2073. E-mail: info@ cbcbooks.org. Website: www.cbcbooks.org. **Executive Director:** Robin Adelson. Purpose of organization: A nonprofit trade association of children's and young adult publishers and packagers, CBC promotes the enjoyment of books for children and young adults and works with national and international organizations to that end. The CBC has sponsored Children's Book Week since 1945 and Young People's Poetry Week since 1999. Qualifications for membership: trade publishers and packagers of children's and young adult books and related literary materials are eligible for membership. Publishers wishing to join should contact the CBC for dues information. Sponsors workshops and seminars for publishing company personnel. Children's Book Week poster and downloadable bookmark available, information at www.bookweekonline.com.

FLORIDA FREELANCE WRITERS ASSOCIATION

Writers-Editors Network, P.O. Box A, North Stratford NH 03590. (603)922-8338. E-mail: FFWA@ Writers-Editors.com. Web sites: www.ffwamembers.com and www.writers-editors.com **Executive Director:** Dana K. Cassell. Purpose of organization: To provide a link between Florida writers and buyers of the written word; to help writers run more effective editorial businesses. Qualifications for membership: "None. We provide a variety of services and information, some for beginners and some for established pros." Membership cost: $90/year. Publishes a newsletter focusing on market news, business news, how-to tips for the serious writer. Annual Directory of Florida Markets included in FFWA newsletter section and electronic download. Publishes annual Guide to CNW/Florida Writers, which is distributed to editors around the country. Sponsors contest: annual deadline March 15. Guidelines on Web site. Categories: juvenile, adult nonfiction, adult fiction and poetry. Awards include cash for top prizes, certificate for others. Contest open to nonmembers.

GRAPHIC ARTISTS GUILD

32 Broadway, Suite 1114, New York NY 10004. (212)791-3400. Fax: (212) 791-0333. E-mail: admin@ gag.org. Website: www.gag.org. **Executive Director:** Patricia Mckiernan. Purpose of organization: "To promote and protect the economic interests of member artists. It is committed to improving conditions for all creators of graphic arts and raising standards for the entire industry." Qualification for full membership: 50% of income derived from the creation of artwork. Associate members include those in allied fields, students and retirees. Initiation fee: $30. Full memberships: $200; student membership: $75/year. Associate membership: $170/year. Publishes Graphic Artists Guild Handbook, Pricing and Ethical Guidelines (members receive a copy as part of their membership).

HORROR WRITERS ASSOCIATION

244 5th Avenue, Suite 2767, New York, NY 10001. E-mail: hwa@horror.org. Website: www.horror. org. **Office Manager:** Lisa Morton. Purpose of organization: To encourage public interest in horror and dark fantasy and to provide networking and career tools for members. Qualifications for membership: Complete membership rules online at www.horror.org/memrule.htm. At least one low-level sale is required to join as an affiliate. Non-writing professionals who can show income from a horror-related field may join as an associate (booksellers, editors, agents, librarians, etc.). To qualify for full active membership, you must be a published, professional writer of horror. Membership cost: $65 annually. Holds annual Stoker Awards Weekend and HWA Business Meeting. Publishes monthly newsletter focusing on market news, industry news, HWA business for members. Sponsors awards. We give the Bram Stoker Awards for superior achievement in horror

annually. Awards include a handmade Stoker trophy designed by sculptor Stephen Kirk. Awards open to nonmembers.

INTERNATIONAL READING ASSOCIATION

800 Barksdale Rd.P.O. Box 8139, Newark DE 19714-8139. (302)731-1600, ext. 293. Fax: (302)731-1057. E-mail: pubinfo@reading.org. Website: www.reading.org. Purpose of organization: "Formed in 1956, the International Reading Association seeks to promote high levels of literacy for all by improving the quality of reading instruction through studying the reading process and teaching techniques; serving as a clearinghouse for the dissemination of reading research through conferences, journals, and other publications; and actively encouraging the lifetime reading habit. Its goals include professional development, advocacy, partnerships, research, and global literacy development." **Open to students.** Sponsors annual convention. Publishes a newsletter called "Reading Today." Sponsors a number of awards and fellowships. Visit the IRA Web site for more information on membership, conventions and awards.

THE INTERNATIONAL WOMEN'S WRITING GUILD

P.O. Box 810, Gracie Station, New York NY 10028. (212)737-7536. Fax: (212) 737-9469. E-mail: dirhahn@iwwg.org. Website: www.iwwg.org. **Executive Director and Founder:** Hannelore Hahn. IWWG is "a network for the personal and professional empowerment of women through writing." Qualifications: open to any woman connected to the written word regardless of professional portfolio. Membership cost: $45 annually. "IWWG sponsors several annual conferences a year in all areas of the U.S. The major conference is held in June of each year at Skidmore College in Saratoga Springs, NY. It is a week-long conference attracting over 500 women internationally." Also publishes a 32-page newsletter, Network, 4 times/year; offers dental and vision insurance at group rates, referrals to literary agents.

■ LEAGUE OF CANADIAN POETS

920 Yonge St.Suite 608, Toronto ON M4W 3C7 Canada. (416)504-1657. Fax: (416)504-0096. Website: www.poets.ca. **Acting Executive Director:** Joanna Poblocka. President: Mary Ellen Csamer. Inquiries to Program Manager: Joanna Poblocka. The L.C.P. is a national organization of published Canadian poets. Our constitutional objectives are to advance poetry in Canada and to promote the professional interests of the members. Qualifications for membership: full—publication of at least 1 book of poetry by a professional publisher; associate membership—an active interest in poetry, demonstrated by several magazine/periodical publication credits; student—an active interest in poetry, 12 sample poems required; supporting—any friend of poetry. Membership fees: full—$175/year, associate—$60, student—$20, supporting—$100. Holds an Annual General Meeting every spring; some events open to nonmembers. "We also organize reading programs in schools and public venues. We publish a newsletter which includes information on poetry/poetics in Canada and beyond. Also publish the books Poetry Markets for Canadians; Who's Who in the League of Canadian Poets; Poets in the Classroom (teaching guide), and online publications. The Gerald Lampert Memorial Award for the best first book of poetry published in Canada in the preceding year and The Pat Lowther Memorial Award for the best book of poetry by a Canadian woman published in the preceding year. Deadline for awards: November 1. Visit www.poets.ca for more details. Sponsors youth poetry competition. Visit www.youngpoets.ca for details.

LITERARY MANAGERS AND DRAMATURGS OF THE AMERICAS

P.O. Box 36. 20985, P.A.C.C.New York NY 10129. E-mail: lmda@lmda.org or lmdanyc@hotmail.com. Website: www.lmda.org. LMDA is a not-for-profit service organization for the professions of literary management and dramaturgy. Student Membership: $25/year. Open to students in dramaturgy, performing arts and literature programs, or related disciplines. Proof of student status required. Includes national conference, New Dramaturg activities, local symposia, job phone and select membership meetings. Active Membership: $60/year. Open to full-time and part-time professionals working in the fields of literary management and dramaturgy. All privileges and services including voting rights and eligibility for office. Institutional Membership: $200/year. Open to theaters, universities, and other organizations. Includes all privileges and services except voting rights and eligibility for office. Publishes a newsletter featuring articles on literary management, dramaturgy, LMDA program updates and other articles of interest.

THE NATIONAL LEAGUE OF AMERICAN PEN WOMEN

1300 17th St. N.W.Washington DC 20036-1973. (202)785-1997. E-mail: nlapw1@verizon.net. Website: www.americanpenwomen.org. **President:** N. Taylor Collins. Purpose of organization: to promote professional work in art, letters, and music since 1897. Qualifications for membership: An applicant must show "proof of sale" in each chosen category—art, letters, and music. Levels of membership include: Active, Associate, International Affiliate, Members-at-Large, Honorary Members (in one or more of the following classifications: Art, Letters, and Music). Holds workshops/conferences. Publishes magazine 4 times/year titled The Pen Woman. Sponsors various contests in areas of Art, Letters, and Music. Awards made at Biennial Convention. Biannual scholarships awarded to non-Pen Women for mature women. Awards include cash prizes—up to $1,000. Specialized contests open to nonmembers.

NATIONAL WRITERS ASSOCIATION

10940 S. Parker Rd.#508, Parker CO 80138. (303)841-0246. Fax: (303)841-2607. E-mail: natlwritersassn@hotmail.com. Website: www.nationalwriters.com. **Executive Director:** Sandy Whelchel. Purpose of organization: association for freelance writers. Qualifications for membership: associate membership—must be serious about writing; professional membership—must be published and paid writer (cite credentials). Membership cost: $65 associate; $85 professional; $35 student. Sponsors workshops/conferences: TV/screenwriting workshops, NWAF Annual Conferences, Literary Clearinghouse, editing and critiquing services, local chapters, National Writer's School. Open to non-members. Publishes industry news of interest to freelance writers; how-to articles; market information; member news and networking opportunities. Nonmember subscription: $20. Sponsors poetry contest; short story contest; article contest; novel contest. Awards cash for top 3 winners; books and/or certificates for other winners; honorable mention certificate places 5-10. Contests open to nonmembers.

NATIONAL WRITERS UNION

E-mail: nwu@nwu.org. Website: www.nwu.org. Students welcome. Purpose of organization: Advocacy for freelance writers. Qualifications for membership: "Membership in the NWU is open to all qualified writers, and no one shall be barred or in any manner prejudiced within the Union on account of race, age, sex, sexual orientation, disability, national origin, religion or ideology. You are eligible for membership if you have published a book, a play, three articles, five poems, one short story or an equivalent amount of newsletter, publicity, technical, commercial, government or institutional copy. You are also eligible for membership if you have written an equal amount of unpublished material and you are actively writing and attempting to publish your work" Membership cost: annual writing income less than $5000-$120/year; $5001-15,000-$195; $15,001-30,000-$265/year; $30,001-$45,000-$315 a year; $45,001- and up -$340/year. Monthly deductions to charge cards. Holds workshops throughout the country. Members only section on web site offers rich resources for freelance writers. Skilled contract advice and grievance help for members.

PEN AMERICAN CENTER

588 Broadway, Suite 303, New York NY 10012. (212)334-1660. Fax: (212)334-2181. E-mail: pen@pen.org. Website: www.pen.org. Purpose of organization: "An associate of writers working to

advance literature, to defend free expression, and to foster international literary fellowship." Qualifications for membership: "The standard qualification for a writer to become a member of PEN is publication of two or more books of a literary character, or one book generally acclaimed to be of exceptional distinction. Also eligible for membership: editors who have demonstrated commitment to excellence in their profession (usually construed as five years' service in book editing); translators who have published at least two book-length literary translations; playwrights whose works have been produced professionally; and literary essayists whose publications are extensive even if they have not yet been issued as a book. Candidates for membership may be nominated by a PEN member or they may nominate themselves with the support of two references from the literary community or from a current PEN member. Membership dues are $75 per year and many PEN members contribute their time by serving on committees, conducting campaigns and writing letters in connection with freedom-of-expression cases, contributing to the PEN journal, participating in PEN public events, helping to bring literature into underserved communities, and judging PEN literary awards. PEN members receive a subscription to the PEN journal, the PEN Annual Report, and have access to medical insurance at group rates. Members living in the New York metropolitan and tri-state area, or near the Branches, are invited to PEN events throughout the year. Membership in PEN American Center includes reciprocal privileges in PEN American Center branches and in foreign PEN Centers for those traveling abroad. Application forms are available on the Web at www.pen.org. Associate Membership is open to everyone who supports PEN's mission, and your annual dues ($40; $20 for students) provides crucial support to PEN's programs. When you join as an Associate Member, not only will you receive a subscription to the PEN Journal http://pen.org/page.php/prmID/150 and notices of all PEN events but you are also invited to participate in the work of PEN. PEN American Center is the largest of the 141 centers of International PEN, the world's oldest human rights organization and the oldest international literary organization. International PEN was founded in 1921 to dispel national, ethnic, and racial hatreds and to promote understanding among all countries. PEN American Center, founded a year later, works to advance literature, to defend free expression, and to foster international literary fellowship. The Center has a membership of 2,900 distinguished writers, editors, and translators. In addition to defending writers in prison or in danger of imprisonment for their work, PEN American Center sponsors public literary programs and forums on current issues, sends prominent authors to inner-city schools to encourage reading and writing, administers literary prizes, promotes international literature that might otherwise go unread in the United States, and offers grants and loans to writers facing financial or medical emergencies. In carrying out this work, PEN American Center builds upon the achievements of such dedicated past members as W.H. Auden, James Baldwin, Willa Cather, Robert Frost, Langston Hughes, Thomas Mann, Arthur Miller, Marianne Moore, Susan Sontag, and John Steinbeck. The Children's Book Authors' Committee sponsors annual public events focusing on the art of writing for children and young adults and on the diversity of literature for juvenile readers. The PEN/Phyllis Naylor Working Writer Fellowship was established in 2001 to assist a North American author of fiction for children or young adults (E-mail: awards@pen.org). Visit www.pen.org for complete information. Sponsors several competitions per year. Monetary awards range from $2,000-35,000.

⊕ PLAYMARKET

P.O. Box 9767, Te Aro Wellington New Zealand. (64)4 3828462. Fax: (64)4 3828461. E-mail: info@ playmarket.org.nz. Website: www.playmarket.org.nz. **Director:** Mark Amery. **Script Development**: Jean Betts & Janie Walker. **Administrator:** Pania Stevenson. **Agency Coordinator:** Katrina Chandra. Purpose of organization: funded by Creative New Zealand, Playmarket serves as New Zealand's script advisory service and playwrights' agency. Playmarket offers script assessment, development and agency services to help New Zealand playwrights secure professional production for their plays. Playmarket runs the NZ Young Playwrights Competition, The Aotearoa Playwrights Conference and the Adam Playreading Series and administers the annual Bruce Mason Playwrighting Award.

The organization's magazine, Playmarket News, is published biannually. Inquiries e-mail info@ playmarket.org.nz.

PUPPETEERS OF AMERICA, INC.

Membership Office: 26 Howard Ave, New Haven, CT 06519-2809. (888)568-6235. E-mail: membership@puppeteers.org. Website: www.puppeteers.org. **Membership Officer:** Fred Thompson. Purpose of organization: to promote the art and appreciation of puppetry as a means of communications and as a performing art. The Puppeteers of America boasts an international membership. Qualifications for membership: interest in the art form. Membership cost: single adult, $55; seniors (65 +) and youth members, (6-17 years of age), $35; full-time college student, $35; family, $75; couple, $65; senior couple, $55, Company, $90. Membership includes a bimonthly newsletter (Playboard). Discounts for workshops/conferences, access to the Audio Visual Library & Consultants in many areas of Puppetry. The Puppetry Journal, a quarterly periodical, providing a color photo gallery, news about puppeteers, puppet theaters, exhibitions, touring companies, technical tips, new products, new books, films, television, and events sponsored by the Chartered Guilds in each of the 8 P of A regions. Playboard, a bimonthly newsletter; access to the AV Library, the Puppetry Store and Consultants. Subscription to the Puppetry Journal only, $40 (libraries/ institutions only).

SCIENCE-FICTION AND FANTASY WRITERS OF AMERICA, INC.

P.O. Box 877, Chestertown MD 21620. E-mail: execdir@sfwa.org. Website: www.sfwa.org. **Executive Director:** Jane Jewell. Purpose of organization: to encourage public interest in science fiction literature and provide organization format for writers/editors/artists within the genre. Qualifications for membership: at least 1 professional sale or other professional involvement within the field. Membership cost: annual active dues—$70; affiliate—$55; one-time installation fee of $10; dues year begins July 1. Different levels of membership include: active—requires 3 professional short stories or 1 novel published; associate—requires 1 professional sale; or affiliate— which requires some other professional involvement such as artist, editor, librarian, bookseller, teacher, etc. Workshops/conferences: annual awards banquet, usually in April or May. Open to nonmembers. Publishes quarterly journal, the SFWA Bulletin. Nonmember subscription: $18/year in U.S. Sponsors Nebula Awards for best published science fiction or fantasy in the categories of novel, novella, novelette and short story. Awards trophy. Also presents the Damon Knight Memorial Grand Master Award for Lifetime Achievement, and, beginning in 2006, the Andre Norton Award for Outstanding Young Adult Science Fiction or Fantasy Book of the Year.

SOCIETY OF CHILDREN'S BOOK WRITERS AND ILLUSTRATORS

8271 Beverly Blvd.Los Angeles CA 90048. (323)782-1010. Fax:(323)782-1892 E-mail: scbwi@ scbwi.org. Website: www.scbwi.org. **President:** Stephen Mooser. **Executive Director:** Lin Oliver. Chairperson, Board of Advisors: Frank Sloan. Purpose of organization: to assist writers and illustrators working or interested in the field.Qualifications for membership: an interest in children's literature and illustration. Membership cost: $70/year. Plus one time $85 initiation fee.ifferent levels of membership include: P.A.L. membership—published by publisher listed in SCBWI Market Surveys; full membership—published authors/illustrators (includes self-published); associate membership—unpublished writers/illustrators. Holds 100 events (workshops/conferences) worldwide each year. National Conference open to nonmembers. Publishes bi-monthly magazine on writing and illustrating children's books. Sponsors annual awards and grants for writers and illustrators who are members.

SOCIETY OF ILLUSTRATORS

128 E. 63rd St.New York NY 10065. (212)838-2560. Fax: (212)838-2561. E-mail: info@ societyillustrators.org. Website: www.societyillustrators.org. **Contact:** Anelle Miller, director. "Our

mission is to promote the art and appreciation of illustration, its history and evolving nature through exhibitions, lectures and education." Cost of membership. Annual dues for nonresident Illustrator members (those living more than 125 air miles from SI's headquarters): $300. Dues for Resident Illustrator Members: $500 per year; Resident Associate Members: $500." Artist Members shall include those who make illustration their profession and earn at least 60% of their income from their illustration. Associate Members are those who earn their living in the arts or who have made a substantial contribution to the art of illustration. This includes art directors, art buyers, creative supervisors, instructors, publishers and like categories. The candidate must complete and sign the application form which requires a brief biography, a listing of schools attended, other training and a résumé of his or her professional career. Candidates for Illustrators membership, in addition to the above requirements, must submit examples of their work."

SOCIETY OF SOUTHWESTERN AUTHORS

P.O. Box 30355, Tucson AZ 85751-0355. Fax: (520)751-7877. E-mail: Information: Penny Porter wporter202@aol.com. Website: www.ssa-az.org. Purpose of organization: to promote fellowship among professional and associate members of the writing profession, to recognize members' achievements, to stimulate further achievement, and to assist persons seeking to become professional writers. Qualifications for membership: Professional Membership: proof of publication of a book, articles, TV screenplay, etc. Associate Membership: proof of desire to write, and/or become a professional. Self-published authors may receive status of Professional Membership at the discretion of the board of directors. Membership cost: $25 initiation plus $25/year dues. The Society of Southwestern Authors sponsors an annual 2-day Writers' Conference (all genres) held September 26-27, 2009(check Web site for updated information). SSA publishes a bimonthly newsletter, The Write Word, promoting members' published works, advice to fellow writers, and up-to-the-minute trends in publishing and marketing. Yearly writing contest open to all writers; short story, memoir, poetry, children's stories. Applications available in February—write Mary Ann Hutchinson douglashutchinson@comcast.net; Subject Line: SSA Writer's Contest.

SOUTHWEST WRITERS

3721 Morris NE, Suite A, Albuquerque NM 87111. (505)265-9485. Fax: (505)265-9483. E-mail: swwriters@juno.com. Website: www.southwestwriters.org. Non-profit organization dedicated to helping members of all levels in their writing. Members enjoy perks such as networking with professional and aspiring writers; substantial discounts on mini-conferences, workshops, writing classes, and annual and quarterly SWW writing contest; monthly newsletter; two writing programs per month; critique groups, critique service (also for nonmembers); discounts at bookstores and other businesses; and website linking. Cost of membership: Individual, $60/year, $100/2 years; Two People, $50 each/year; Student, $40/year; Student under 18, $25/year; Outside U.S.$65/year; Lifetime, $750. See Web site for information.

TEXT AND ACADEMIC AUTHORS ASSOCIATION

P.O. Box 76477, St. Petersburg FL 33734-6477. (727)563-0020. Fax: (727)563-0500. E-mail: TextandAcademicAuthors@taaonline.net. Website: www.taaonline.net. **President:** Paul Siegel. Purpose of organization: the only nonprofit membership association dedicated solely to assisting textbook and academic authors. TAA's overall mission is to enhance the quality of textbooks and other academic materials, such as journal articles, monographs and scholarly books, in all fields and disciplines, by networking opportunities. Qualifications for membership: all authors and prospective authors are welcome. Membership cost: $30 first year; graduated levels for following years. Workshops/conferences: June each year. Newsletter focuses on all areas of interest to text book and academic authors.

THEATRE FOR YOUNG AUDIENCES/USA

2936 N. Southport Ave 3rd floor Chicago, IL 60657. E-mail: info@tyausa.org. Website: www.tyausa. org. Purpose of organization: to promote theater for children and young people by linking professional theaters and artists together; sponsoring national, international and regional conferences and providing publications and information. Also serves as U.S. Center for International Association of the Theatre for Children and Young People. Different levels of memberships include: organizations, individuals, students, retirees, libraries. TYA Today includes original articles, reviews and works of criticism and theory, all of interest to theater practitioners (included with membership). Publishes Marquee, a directory that focuses on information on members in U.S.

VOLUNTEER LAWYERS FOR THE ARTS

1 E. 53rd St.6th Floor, New York NY 10022-4201. (212)319-ARTS, ext. 1 (the Art Law Line). Fax: (212)752-6575. E-mail: askvla@vlany.org. Website: www.vlany.org. **Executive Director:** Elena M. Paul. Purpose of organization: Volunteer Lawyers for the Arts is dedicated to providing free arts-related legal assistance to low-income artists and not-for-profit arts organizations in all creative fields. Over 1,000 attorneys in the New York area donate their time through VLA to artists and arts organizations unable to afford legal counsel. Everyone is welcome to use VLA's Art Law Line, a legal hotline for any artist or arts organization needing quick answers to arts-related questions. VLA also provides clinics, seminars and publications designed to educate artists on legal issues which affect their careers. Members receive discounts on publications and seminars as well as other benefits. Some of the many publications we carry are All You Need to Know About the Music Business; Business and Legal Forms for Fine Artists, Photographers & Authors & Self-Publishers; Contracts for the Film & TV Industry, plus many more.

WESTERN WRITERS OF AMERICA, INC.

1012 Mesa Vista Hall, MSCO6 3770, 1 University of New Mexico, Albuquerque NM 87131-0001. (505)277-5234. E-mail: wwa@unm.edu; rod@holmesco.com. Website: www.westernwriters.org. **Executive Director:** Paul Andrew Hutton. Open to students. Purpose of organization: to further all types of literature that pertains to the American West. Membership requirements: must be a published author of Western material. Membership cost: $75/year ($90 foreign). Different levels of membership include: Active and Associate-the two vary upon number of books or articles published. Holds annual conference. The 2008 conference held in Scottsdale, AZ; 2009 held in Midwest City, Oklahoma. Publishes bimonthly magazine focusing on western literature, market trends, bookreviews, news of members, etc. Nonmembers may subscribe for $30 ($50 foreign). Sponsors youth writing contests. Spur awards given annually for a variety of types of writing. Awards include plaque, certificate, publicity. Contest and Spur Awards open to nonmembers.

WOMEN WRITING THE WEST

8547 E. Arapahoe Rd.#J-541, Greenwood Village CO 80112. (303)773-8349. E-mail: WWW1@lohseworks.com. Website: www.womenwritingthewest.org. **Contact:** Joyce Lohse, administrator. Purpose of organization: Women writing the West is a nonprofit association of writers, editors, publishers, agents, booksellers, and other professionals writing and promoting the Women's West. As such, Women writing their stories in the American West in a way that illuminates them authentically. In addition, the organization provides support, encouragement, and inspiration to all women writing about any facet of the American West. Membership is open to all interested persons worldwide. **Open to students.** Cost of membership: Annual membership dues $60. Publisher dues are $60. International dues are $70. In addition to the annual dues, there is an option to become a sustaining member for $100. Sustaining members receive a WWW enamel logo pin, prominent listing in WWW publications, and the knowledge that they are assisting the organization. Members actively exchange ideas on a list e-bulletin board. WWW membership also allows the choice of participation in our marketing marvel, the annual WWW Catalog of Author's Books. An annual conference is held every fall. Our WWW newsletter is current WWW activities; features market research, and experience articles of interest pertaining to American West literature and member news. Sponsors annual WILLA Literary Award, which is given in several categories for outstanding literature featuring women's stories, set in the West. The winner of a WILLA literary Award receives a cash award and a trophy at the annual conference. Contest open to non-members.

⚡ WRITERS' FEDERATION OF NEW BRUNSWICK

Box 37, Station A, Fredericton E3B 4Y2 Canada. (506)459-7228. E-mail: wfnb@nb.aibn.com. Website: www.umce.ca/wfnb. **Executive Director:** Lee Thompson. Purpose of organization: "to promote New Brunswick writing and to help writers at all stages of their development." Qualifications for membership: interest in writing. Membership cost: $40, basic annual membership; $20, high school students; $45, family membership; $50, institutional membership; $100, sustaining member; $250, patron; and $1,000, lifetime member. Holds workshops/conferences. Publishes a newsletter with articles concerning the craft of writing, member news, contests, markets, workshops and conference listings. Sponsors annual literary competition, $15 entry fee for members, $20 for nonmembers. Categories: fiction, nonfiction, poetry, children's literature—3 prizes per category of $150, $75, $50; Alfred Bailey Prize of $400 for poetry ms; The Richards Prize of $400 for short novel, collection of short stories or section of long novel; The Sheree Fitch Prize for writing by young people (14-18 years of age). Contest open to nonmembers (residents of Canada only).

⚡ WRITERS GUILD OF ALBERTA

11759 Groat Rd.Edmonton AB T5M 3K6 Canada. (780)422-8174. Fax: (780)422-2663. E-mail: mail@writersguild.ab.ca. Website: www.writersguild.ab.ca. Purpose of organization: to provide meeting ground and collective voice for the writers in Alberta. Membership cost: $60/year; $30 for seniors/students. Holds workshops/conferences. Publishes a newsletter focusing on markets, competitions, contemporary issues related to the literary arts (writing, publishing, censorship, royalties etc.). Sponsors annual Literary Awards in six categories (novel, nonfiction, short fiction, children's literature, poetry, drama). Awards include $1,000, leather-bound book, promotion and publicity. Open to nonmembers.

WRITERS OF KERN

P.O. Box 22335, Bakersfield CA 93390. (661)399-0423. E-mail: mispegg@aol.com. Website: www. writersofkern.com. **Membership:** Beth Davisson. Open to published writers and any person interested in writing. Dues: $45/year, $20 for students; $20 initiation fee. Types of memberships: Active Writers with published work; Associate Writers working toward publication, affiliate— beginners and students. Monthly meetings held on the third Saturday of every month. Annual writers' workshops, with speakers who are authors, agents, etc.on topics pertaining to writing; critique groups for several fiction genres, poetry, children's, nonfiction, journalism and screenwriting which meet bimonthly. Members receive a monthly newsletter from WOK and CWC with marketing tips, conferences and contests.

Conferences & Workshops

Writers and illustrators eager to expand their knowledge of the children's publishing industry should consider attending one of the many conferences and workshops held each year. Whether you're a novice or seasoned professional, conferences and workshops are great places to pick up information on a variety of topics and network with experts in the publishing industry, as well as with your peers.

Listings in this section provide details about what conference and workshop courses are offered, where and when they are held, and the costs. Some of the national writing and art organizations also offer regional workshops throughout the year. Write, call or visit websites for information.

Writers can find listings of more than 1,000 conferences (searchable by type, location, and date) at The Writer's Digest/Shaw Guides Directory to Writers' Conferences, Seminars, and Workshop—www.writersdigest.com/conferences.

Members of the Society of Children's Book Writers and Illustrators can find information on conferences in national and local SCBWI newsletters. Nonmembers may attend SCBWI events as well. SCBWI conferences are listed in the beginning of this section under a separate subheading. For information on SCBWI's annual national conferences, contact them at (323)782-1010 or check their website for a complete calendar of national and regional events (www.scbwi.org).

CONFERENCES & WORKSHOPS CALENDAR

To help you plan your conference travel, here is a month-by-month calendar of all the conferences, workshops and retreats included in this section. The calendar lists conferences alphabetically by the month in which they occur.

January
Indianapolis Youth Lit Conference (Indianapolis IN)
Kindling Words East (Burlington VT)
San Diego State University Writers' Conference (San Diego CA)
SCBWI—Florida Regional Conference (Miami FL)
South Coast Writers Conference (Gold Beach OR)
Winter Poetry & Prose Getaway in Cape May (Cape May NJ)

February
San Francisco Writers Conference (San Francisco CA)
SCBWI; Annual Conference on Writing and Illustrating for Children (New York NY)
SCBWI—Norca (San Francisco/South); × Retreat at Asilomar (Pacific Grove CA)
SCBWI—Southern Breeze; Spring Mingle (Atlanta GA)

South Coast Writers Conference (Gold Beach OR)

March

Florida Christian Writers Conference (Bradenton FL)
Kentucky Writer's Workshop (Pineville KY)
SCBWI—Bologna Biennial Conference & SCBWI Showcase Booth at the Bologna Children's Book Fair (Bologna, Italy)
Virginia Festival of the Book (Charlottesville VA)
Whidbey Island Writers' Conference (Langley WA)
Tennessee Williams/New Orleans Literary Festival (New Orleans LA)

April

AEC Conference on Southern Literature (Chattanooga TN)
Festival of Faith and Writing (Grand Rapids MI)
Missouri Writers' Guild Annual State Conference (St. Charles MO)
SCBWI New Mexico Handsprings: A Conference for Children's Writers and Illustrators (Albuquerque NM)

May

Annual Spring Poetry Festival (New York NY)
BookExpo America/Writer's Digest Books Writers Conference (New York NY)
Kindling Words West (Abiquiu NM)
Oklahoma Writers' Federation, Inc. Annual Conference (Oklahoma City OK)
Pima Writers' Workshop (Tucson AZ)

June

East Texas Christian Writers Conference (Marshall TX)
The Environmental Writers' Conference and Workshop in Honor of Rachel Carson (Boothbay Harbor ME)
Great Lakes Writers Conference (Milwaukee WI)
Highland Summer Conference (Radford VA)
International Creative Writing Camp (Minot ND)
Iowa Summer Writing Festival (Iowa City IA)
Manhattanville Summer Writers' Week (Purchase NY)
Outdoor Writers Association of America Annual Conference (Lake Charles LA)
SCBWI—Florida Mid-Year Writing Workshop (Orlando FL)
SCBWI—New Jersey; Annual Spring Conference (Princeton NJ)
Southeastern Writer's Association—Annual Writer's Workshop (Athens GA)
Wesleyan Writers Conference (Middleton CT)
Write! Canada (Guelph ON Canada)
Write-by-the-Lake Writer's Workshop & Retreat (Madison WI)
Write-to-Publish Conference (Wheaton IL)
Writers Retreat Workshop (Erlanger KY)

July

Conference for Writers & Illustrators of Children's Books (Corte Madera CA)
Highlights Foundation Writers Workshop at Chautauqua (Chautauqua NY)
Maritime Writers' Workshop (Fredericton NB Canada)
Midwest Writers Workshop (Muncie IN)

Montrose Christian Writer's Conference (Montrose PA)
Pacific Northwest Children's Book Conference (Portland OR)
Pacific Northwest Writer Assn. Summer Writer's Conference (Seattle WA)
Robert Quackenbush's Children's Book Writing and Illustrating Workshop (New York NY)
Sage Hill Writing Experience (Saskatoon SK Canada)
Saskatchewan Festival of Words and Workshops (Moose Jaw SK Canada)
Steamboat Springs Writers Conference (Steamboat Springs CO)

August

Cape Cod Writer's Conference (Cape Cod MA)
The Columbus Writers Conference (Columbus OH)
Green Lake Writers Conference (Green Lake WI)
The Manuscript Workshop in Vermont (Londonderry VT)
Moondance International Film Festival (Hollywood CA)
The Pacific Coast Children's Writer's Workshop (Aptos CA)
SCBWI; Annual Conference on Writing and Illustrating for Children (Los Angeles CA)
Willamette Writers Annual Writers Conference (Portland OR)

September

League of Utah Writers' Roundup (Ogden UT)
Maui Writers Conference (Kihei HI)
SCBWI—Carolinas; Annual Fall Conference (Durham NC)
SCBWI—Eastern Pennsylvania; Fall Philly Conference (Exton PA)
SCBWI—Idaho; Editor Day (Boise ID)
SCBWI—Midsouth Fall Conference (Nashville TN)
SCBWI—Northern Ohio; Annual Conference (Cleveland OH)
Society of Southwestern Authors' Wrangling with Writing (Tucson AZ)

October

Flathead River Writers Conference (Whitefish MT)
Ozark Creative Writers, Inc. Conference (Eureka Springs AR)
SCBWI—Midatlantic; Annual Fall Conference (Arlington VA)
SCBWI—Oregon Conferences (Portland OR)
SCBWI—Southern Breeze; Writing and Illustrating for Kids (Birmingham AL)
SCBWI—Ventura/Santa Barbara; Fall Conference (Thousand Oaks CA)
SCBWI—Wisconsin; Fall Retreat for Working Writers (Milton WI)
Surrey International Writer's Conference (Surrey BC Canada)
Vancouver Internatinoal Writers Festival (Vancouver BC Canada)
Write on the Sound Writers Conference (Edmonds WA)

November

Jewish Children's Book Writers' Conference (New York NY)
LaJolla Writers Conference (LaJolla CA)
North Carolina Writers' Network Fall Conference (Durham NC)
SCBWI—Illinois; Prairie Writers Day
SCBWI—Missouri; Children's Writer's Conference (St. Peters MO)

December

Big Sur Writing Workshop (Big Sur CA)

Multiple or Seasonal Events

The conference listings below include information on multiple or year-round events or events that are seasonal (held in fall or spring, for example). Please read the listings for more information on the dates and locations of these events and check the conferences' websites.

American Christian Writers Conference

Booming Ground Online Writers Studio

Cat Writers' Association Annual Writers Conference

Children's Authors' Bootcamp

The DIY Book Festival

Duke University Youth Programs: Creative Writers' Workshop

Duke University Youth Programs: Young Writers' Camp

Gotham Writers' Workshop (New York NY)

Highlights Foundation Founders Workshops (Honesdale PA)

Mount Herman Christian Writer's Conference (Mount Herman CA)

Publishinggame.com Workshop

SCBWI—Arizona; Events

SCBWI—Eastern Canada; Annual Events

SCBWI—Dakotas

SCBWI—Idaho; Editor Day

SCBWI—Iowa Conferences

SCBWI—Los Angeles; Events

SCBWI—Metro New York; Professional Series (New York NY)

SCBWI—Michigan; Conferences

SCBWI—New Jersey; Mentoring Workshops (Princeton NJ)

SCBWI—Oregon Conferences

SCBWI—Pocono Mountains Retreat (Sterling PA)

SCBWI—Taiwan; Events

SCBWI—Ventura/Santa Barbara; Retreat for Children's Authors and Illustrators (Santa Barbara CA)

SCBWI—Western Washington State; Retreats & Conference

Southwest Writers Conferences

Split Rock Arts Program (St. Paul MN)

Sydney Children's Writers and Illustrators Network (Woollahra NSW Australia)

UMKC/Writers Place Writers Workshops (Kansas City MO)

Writers' League of Texas Workshop Series (Austin TX)

The Writers' Retreat Writing Workshop at Castle Hill

SCBWI CONFERENCES

SCBWI; ANNUAL CONFERENCES ON WRITING AND ILLUSTRATING FOR CHILDREN

8271 Beverly Blvd. Los Angeles CA 90048. (323)782-1010. Fax: (323)782-1892. E-mail: scbwi@scbwi.org. Website: www.scbwi.org. **Conference Director:** Lin Oliver. Writer and illustrator workshops geared toward all levels. **Open to students.** Covers all aspects of children's book and magazine publishing—the novel, illustration techniques, marketing, etc. Annual conferences held in August in Los Angeles and in New York in February. Cost of conference (LA): approximately $390; includes all 4 days and one banquet meal. Write for more information or visit web site.

SCBWI—ARIZONA; EVENTS

P.O. Box 26384, Scottsdale AZ 85255-0123. E-mail: RegionalAdvisor@scbwi-az.org. Website: www.scbwi-az.org. **Regional Advisor:** Michelle Parker-Rock. SCBWI Arizona will offer a variety of workshops, retreats, intensives, conferences, meetings and other craft and industry-related events throughout 2010-2011. Open to members and nonmembers, published and nonpublished. Registration to major events is usually limited. Pre-registration always required. Visit Web site, write or e-mail for more information.

▦ SCBWI BOLOGNA BIENNIAL CONFERENCE

& SCBWI SHOWCASE BOOTH AT THE BOLOGNA CHILDREN'S BOOK FAIR SCBWI @ Bologna - a writer and illustrator conference for children's book held in the spring every two years in association with the largest annual international children's book rights fair in the world, the Bologna Children's Book Fair (www.bookfair.bolognafiere.it) Next conference date: 21 March 2010. A professional workshops with a chance to pitch and present to editors, art directors, agents and children's book creators. Registration limited to 100 attendees to enhance networking opportunities. Manuscript and illustration critiques available by reservation for an additional fee. Featuring award winning and bestselling YA author Ellen Hopkins, author of 20 nonfiction children's books and 5 NY Times bestselling young adult novels in verse. Featured Agent Scott Treimel of S©ott Treimel (US) will hone pitches for authors and illustrators. Editor Tessa Strickland of Barefoot Books (UK), Editor Sarah Grant of Working Partners (UK). Agent Sarah Davies of Greenhouse Literary (US and UK), Editor Sarah Foster of Walker Books (Australia), Marcia Wernick of Sheldon Fogelman Agency (US), Agent Frances Plumpton of Richards Literary Agency (New Zealand). And many more publishers, editors, art directors and a gents from around the world. Attendance at the conference includes an access to all activities at the SCBWI showcase and a four-day general admission to the Bologna Rights fair (a 60 Euro value). SCBWI showcase at the Bologna Children's Book Fair: SCBWI PAL members may send proposals for 2-hour stand-time at the SCBWI Showcase booth at the Book Fair. Send proposals to bologna@scbwi.org only between September 1 and October 31 of 2009. Please request to join http://groups.yahoo.com/group/BolognaSCBWI/ for more details.

SCBWI—CAROLINAS; ANNUAL FALL CONFERENCE

E-mail: write_something@earthlink.net; jhackl1@charter.net. **Regional Advisor:** Teresa Fannin. Sept 25-27, 2009 at the Sheraton Imperial Airport Hotel, Durham, NC. **Speakers include**: Namrata Tripathi, Executive Editor, Atheneum Books for Young Readers, Simon & Schuster Children's Publishing and Bonnie Bader, Editor-in-Chief of Grosset and Dunlap and Price Stern Sloan, two imprints of the Penguin Young Readers Group. Friday afternoon manuscript and portfolio critiques, workshops in mystery, fantasy, non-fiction, craft, and more. Visit www.scbwicarolinas.org for more information.

SCBWI—DAKOTAS; SPRING CONFERENCE

100 N. Sanborn Blvd. #210, Mitchell SD 57301. E-mail: jean@santel.net. Website: www.scbwidakotas.

org. **Regional Advisor:** Jean Patrick. Conference for writers of all levels. "In addition to providing the basics about picture books and novels, we strive to offer unique information about other avenues for publication, including magazine writing, craft writing, work-for-hire writing and more. Recent conferences included keynote speakers Marilyn Kratz and Rose Ross Zebiker." Annual event held every spring. Check Web site for details.

SCBWI—DAKOTAS
Grand Forks ND 58202-7209. (701)777-3321. E-mail: jean@jeanpatrick.com. Website: www.und.edu/dept/english/ChildrensLit.html or www.scbwidakotas.org. **Regional Advisor:** Jean Patrick. Conference sessions geared toward all levels. "Although the conference attendees are mostly writers, we encourage & welcome illustrators of every level." Open to students. "Our conference offers 3-4 children's authors, editors, publishers, illustrators, or agents. Past conferences have included Kent Brown (publisher, Boyds Mills Press); Alexandra Penfold (Editor, Simon & Schuster); Jane Kurtz (author); Anastasia Suen (author); and Karen Ritz (illustrator). Conference held each fall. "Please call or e-mail to confirm dates. Writers and illustrators come from throughout the northern plains, including North Dakota, South Dakota, Montana, Minnesota, Iowa, and Canada." Writing facilities available: campus of University of North Dakota. Local art exhibits and/or concerts may coincide with conference. Cost of conference includes Friday evening reception and sessions, Saturday's sessions, and lunch. A manuscript may be submitted 1 month in advance for critique (extra charge). E-mail for more information.

SCBWI—DAKOTAS/UND WRITERS CONFERENCE IN CHILDREN'S LITERATURE
Department. of English, Merrifield Hall, Room 110, 276 Centennial Drive, Stop 7209, Univeristy of North Dakota, Grand Forks ND 58202. (701)777-3321 or (701)777-3984. E-mail: jean@jeanpatrick.com. Website: www.und.edu or www.scbwidakotas.com. **Regional Advisor:** Jean Patrick. Conference for all levels. "Our conference offers 3-4 chlidren's authors, editors, publishers, illustrators or agents. Past conferences have included Elaine Marie Alphin (author), Jane Kurtz (author), Alexandra Penfold (editor), Kent Brown (publisher), and Karen Ritz (illustrator)." Annual conference held every fall. "Please call or e-mail to confirm dates." Cost of conference to be determined. Cost included Friday evening sessions, Saturday sessions, and Saturday lunch. "We welcome writers, illustrators, and others who are interested in children's literature."

SCBWI—EASTERN CANADA; ANNUAL EVENTS
E-mail: araEast@scbwicanada.org; raEast@scbwicanada.org. Website: www.scbwicanada.org/east. **Regional Advisor:** Lizann Flatt. Writer and illustrator events geared toward all levels. Usually offers one event in spring and another in the fall. Check Web site Events pages for updated information.

SCBWI—EASTERN PENNSYLVANIA; FALL PHILLY CONFERENCE
Whitford Country Club, Exton PA. Website: www.scbwiepa.org. Conference focuses on writing skills, the publishing market, and finding inspiration. Manuscript and Portfolio critiques with editors available for an additional fee. Conference held in October 10. Registration is limited to 150. Information will be posted on the Web site in July. Cost: $100. Registration includes buffet lunch.

SCBWI—FLORIDA; MID-YEAR WRITING WORKSHOP
(305)382-2677. E-mail: lindabernfeld@hotmail.com. Website: www.scbwiflorida.com. **Regional Advisor:** Linda Rodriguez Bernfeld. Annual workshop held in June in Orlando. Workshop is geared toward helping everyone hone their writing skills. Attendees choose one track and spend the day with industry leaders who share valuable information about that area of children's book writing. There are a minimum of 3 tracks, picture book, middle grade and young adult. The 4th and 5th

tracks are variable, covering subjects such as poetry, non-fiction, humor or writing for magazines. Speakers in 2008 included Ellen Hopkins, Bruce Hale, Debra Garfinkle, Lisa McCourt, Linda Shulte, Nancy Springer, Nina Hess (senior editor at Mirrorstone), Nancy Siscoe, associate publishing director and executive editor at Knopf and Crown), Krista Marino, (editor at Delacorte), Andrea Tompa, (associate editor at Candlewick) and Nicole Kasprzak (assistant editor at G.P. Putnam). E-mail for more information.

SCBWI—FLORIDA; REGIONAL CONFERENCE

(305)382-2677. E-mail: lindabernfeld@gmail.com. Website: www.scbwiflorida.com. **Regional Advisor:** Linda Rodriguez Bernfeld. Annual conference held in January in Miami. 2009 conference will be held January 16-18, 2009. Speakers included Linda Sue Park (A Single Shard), Lisa Yee (Millicent Min), Ginger Knowlton (Curtis Brown LTD), and Alexandra Cooper, editor, Simon and Schuster. Cost of conference: approximately $225. The 3-day conference will have workshops Friday afternoon and a field trip to Books and Books Friday evening. There will be a general session all day Saturday covering all aspects of writing for children. There will be hands on workshops Sunday morning led by industry leaders. There is a Saturday only option. Past speakers have included Judy Blume, Paula Danziger, Bruce Coville, Arthur Levine, Libba Bray and Kate DiCamillo. For more information, contact e-mail Linda Rodriguez Bernfeld at lindabernfeld@gmail.com.

SCBWI—IDAHO; EDITOR DAY

Email: neysajensen@msn.com. **Regional Advisor:** Sydney Husseman; **Assistant Regional Advisor:** Neysa Jensen. One day workshop focuses on the craft of writing, as well as getting to know an editor. One-on-one critiques available for an additional fee. Event held in Boise, Idaho every fall.

SCBWI—ILLINOIS; PRAIRIE WRITERS DAY

Chicago, IL Email: biermanlisa@hotmail.com. Website: www.scbwi-illinois.org/events. Regional Advisors: Lisa Bierman and Alice McGinty. All-day conference November 14, 2009, at the Wojcik Conference Center, Harper College, 1200 W. Algonquin Rd.Palatine, IL 60067. Theme: Telling Our Good Stories Well Across All Formats. Speakers include Walker Books for Young Readers Associate Editor Stacy Cantor, Random House Associate Editor Nick Eliopulous, Little, Brown Assistant Editor T.S. Ferguson, Charlesbridge Editorial Director Yolanda LeRoy, author Cynthia Leitich Smith, who writes and publishes across all formats, and Firebrand Literary Agent Michael Stearns. Ms. critiques available as well as break-out sessions on career and craft. Visit website for more information on this and other SCBWI-Illinois events or contact Lisa Bierman at biermanlisa@hotmail.com.

SCBWI—IOWA CONFERENCES

E-mail: hecklit@aol.com. Website: www.scbwi-iowa.org. **Regional Advisor:** Connie Heckert. Writer and illustrator workshopsin all genres of children writing. The Iowa Region offers conferences of high quality events usually over a three-day period with registration options. Recent speakers included Jane Yolen, Adam Stemple, Bruce Coville and well-known edtiors from the finest publisheing houses, Holds spring and fall events on a regional level, and network events across that state. Individual critiques and portfolio review offerings vary with the program and presenters. For more information e-mail or visit Web site.

SCBWI—LOS ANGELES; EVENTS

P.O. Box 1728, Pacific Palisades CA 90272. (310)573-7318. Website: www.scbwisocal.org. **Co-regional Advisors:** Claudia Harrington (claudiascbwi@verizon.net) and Edie Pagliasotti (ediescbwi@sbcgloablnet). SCBWI—Los Angeles hosts 6 major events each year: **Writer's Workshop** (winter)—half-day workshop featuring speaker demonstrating nuts and bolts techniques on the craft of writing for childrens; **Writer's Day** (spring)—a one-day conference featuring speakers, a professional forum, writing contests and awards; **Critiquenic** (summer)—a free informal critiquing session for writers and illustrators facilitated by published authors/illustrators, held after a picnic lunch; **Writers & Illustrator's Sunday Field Trip** (fall)—hands-on creative field trip for writers and illustrators; **Illustrator's Day** (winter)—a one-day conference featuring speakers, juried art competition, contests, and portfolio review//display;. **Working Writer's Retreat** (fall)—a 3-day, 2-night retreat featuring an editor, speakers, and intensive critiquing. See calendar of events on Web site for more details and dates.

SCBWI—METRO NEW YORK; PROFESSIONAL SERIES

P.O. Box 1475, Cooper Station, New York NY 10276-1475. (212)545-3719. E-mail: scbwi_metrony@ yahoo.com. Website: http://metro.nyscbwi.org. **Regional Advisors:** Nancy Lewis and Seta Toroyan. Writer and illustrator workshops geared toward all levels. The Metro New York Professional Series generally meets the second Tuesday of each month, from October to June, 7-9 p.m. Check Web site to confirm location, dates, times and speakers. Cost of workshop: $15 for SCBWI members; $20 for nonmembers. "We feature an informal, evening with coffee, cookies, and top editors, art directors, agents, publicity and marketing people, librarians, reviewers and more."

SCBWI—MICHIGAN; CONFERENCES

Website: www.Kidsbooklink.org. **Co-Regional Advisors:** Monica Harris and Leslie Helakoski. One-day conference held in April/May and 3-day fall conference held in October. Workshops periodically. Speakers TBA. See Web site for details on all upcoming events.

SCBWI—MIDATLANTIC; ANNUAL FALL CONFERENCE

Mid-Atlantic SCBWI, P.O. Box 3215, Reston, VA 20195-1215. E-mail: sydney.unlap@adelphia.net or midatlanticscbwi@tidalwave.net. Website: www.scbwi-midatlantic.org. **Conference Co-Chairs:** Sydney Dunlap and Erin Teagan. Regional Advisor: Ellen Braaf. Conference takes place Saturday, November 13, 2010 in Arlington, VA from 8 to 5. Keynote speaker TBA. For updates and details visit Web site. Registration limited to 200. Conference fills quickly. Cost: $95 for SCBWI members; $120 for nonmembers. Includes continental breakfast. Lunch is on your own. (The food court at the Ballston Common Mall is two blocks away.)

SCBWI—MIDSOUTH FALL CONFERENCE

P.O. Box 120061, Nashville TN 37212.E-mail: expressdog@bellsouth.net or cameron_s_e@yahoo. com. Website: www.scbwi-midsouth.org. **Conference Coordinators:** Genetta Adair and Sharon Cameron. Conference for writers and illustrators of all experience. In the past, workshops were offered on Plotting You Novel, Understanding the Language of Editors, Landing an Agent, How to Prepare a Portfolio, Negotiating a Contract, The Basics for Beginners, and many others. Attendees are invited to bring a manuscript and/or art portfolio to share in the optional, no-charge critique group session. Illustrators are invited to bring color copies of their art (not originals) to be displayed in the illustrators' showcase. For an additional fee, attendees may schedule a 15-minute manuscript critique or portfolio critique by the editor, art director or other expert consultant. Annual conference held in September. Registration limited to 120 attendees. Cost to be determined. The 2009 Midsouth Fall Conference included Arthur A. Levine Books, Senior Editor Cheryl Klein; Agent Michael Stearns of Firebrand Literary Agency; Award-winning Author Carolina Cooney; and more.

SCBWI—MISSOURI; CHILDREN'S WRITER'S CONFERENCE

St. Charles County Community College, P.O. Box 76975, 103 CEAC, St. Peters MO 63376-0975. (314)213-8000, ext. 4108. Website: www.scbwi-mo.org. **Regional Advisor:** Lynnea Annette. Writer and illustrator conference geared toward all levels. **Open to students.** Speakers include editors, writers, agents, and other professionals. Topics vary from year to year, but each conference offers sessions for both writers and illustrators as well as for newcomers and published writers. Previous topics included: "What Happens When Your Manuscript is Accepted" by Dawn Weinstock, editor; "Writing—Hobby or Vocation?" by Chris Kelleher; "Mother Time Gives Advice: Perspectives from a 25 Year Veteran" by Judith Mathews, editor; "Don't Be a Starving Writer" by Vicki Berger Erwin, author; and "Words & Pictures: History in the Making," by author-illustrator Cheryl Harness. Annual conference held in early November. For exact date, see SCBWI Website: www.scbwi.org or the events page of the Missouri SCBWI Web site. Registration limited to 75-90. Cost of conference includes one-day workshop (8 a.m. to 5 p.m.) plus lunch. Write for more information.

SCBWI—NEW JERSEY; ANNUAL SPRING CONFERENCE

E-mail: njscbwi@newjerseyscbwi.com. Website: www.newjerseyscbwi.com. **Regional Advisor:** Kathy Temean. This two day conference is always held the first weekend in June at the Princeton Theological Seminary in Princeton, NJ. "How to" workshops, first page sessions, pitch sessions and interaction with the faculty of editors, agents, art director and authors are some of the highlights of the weekend. Writers and illustrators will find workshops to fit their level of expertise. Illustrators can attend a special session with an art director to discuss promotional mmaterials. Published authors attending the conference are invited to do a book signing and sell their books on Saturday afternoon, also Illustrators have the opportunity to sell their artwork during this time. Attendees have the option to participate in group critiques, one-on-one critiques and portfolio reviews. Continental breakfast and lunch is included with the cost of admission.

SCBWI—NEW JERSEY; FIRST PAGE SESSIONS

E-mail: njscbwi@newjerseyscbwi.com. Website: www.newjerseyscbwi.com. Held 4 times a year at the Princeton Theological Seminary in Princeton, NJ. Two editors/agents give their first impression of a first page and let participants know if they would read more. These sessions are held late afternoon during the week and are limited to 30 people. Attendees can choose to have dinner with the editors after the session. Please visit www.newjerseyscbwi.com for more information.

SCBWI—NEW JERSEY; MENTORING WORKSHOPS

E-mail: njscbwi@newjerseyscbwi.com. Website: www.newjerseyscbwi.com. **Regional Advisor:** Kathy Temean. These workshops have become very popular and fill quickly. Workshops provide an inspiring environment for writers to work on their manuscript and have personal contact with their mentor/editor. Each workshop consists of 14 writers and two editors or 28 people and 4 editors. Weekend workshops allow writers to spend 45 minutes, one-on-one, with their mentor to discuss their manuscript and career direction, first page critiques, pitch sessions and other fun writing activities. One day workshops consist of 20 minute one-on-one critiques, plus first page critiques. These workshops are held in the Spring and Fall each year at The Princeton Theological Seminary in Princeton, New Jersey. Please visit www.newjerseyscbwi.com for more information

SCBWI—NEW MEXICO; HANDSPRINGS: A CONFERENCE FOR CHILDREN'S WRITERS AND ILLUSTRATORS

P.O. Box 1084, Socorro NM. E-mail: handsprings@scbwi-nm.org. Website: www.scbwi-nm.org. **Registrar:** Lucy Hampson. **Regional Advisor:** Chris Eboch. Conference for beginner and intermediate writers and illustrators. "Each conference features three keynote speakers—editors, agents, [ART DIRECTORS] and/or illustrators and authors. 2009 speakers include Ruta Rimas, editorial assistant, Balzer & Bray, Harpercollins Childrens Books; Chris Richman, Literary Agent, Firebrand Literary; and [Margaret Chodos-Irvine, illustrator/author. Writers and illustrators lead breakout sessions. Workshop topics included: Creating unforgettable characters, creating unforgettable settings, illustrator portfolio critique." Annual conference held in April or May. Registration limited to 100.

"Offers classroom-style workshops and large-group presentations." Cost: $95-110 for basic Saturday registration; $15-20 for Friday evening party with editor panel; $40-50 for private critiques (lowest prices are for SCBWI members). "The Friday evening party included social time, a First Page critique panel with our visiting editors, mini book launches and an illustrators' portfolio display. Saturday features a full day of keynote speeches by visiting editors, agents and/or art directors; breakout workshops on the craft and business of writing; and optional one-on-one critiques with the editors or portfolio review by the art director."

SCBWI—NORCA (SAN FRANCISCO/SOUTH); GOLDEN GATE CONFERENCE AT ASILOMAR

Website: www.scbwisf.org. **Co-Regional Advisors:** Amy Laughlin and Amanda Materne. We welcome published and "not-yet-published" writers and illustrators. Lectures and workshops are geared toward professionals and those striving to become professional. Program topics cover aspects of writing or illustrating, from picture books to young adult novels. Past speakers include editors, art directors, Newbery Award-winning authors, and Caldecott Award-winning illustrators. Annual conference, generally held last weekend in February; Friday evening through Sunday lunch. Registration limited to approximately 100. Most rooms shared with one other person. Additional charge for single when available. Desks available in most rooms. All rooms have private baths. Conference center is set in wooded campus on Asilomar Beach in Pacific Grove, California. Approximate cost: $460 for SCBWI members, $600 for nonmembers; includes shared room, 6 meals, ice breaker party and all conference activities. Vegetarian meals available. Coming together for shared meals and activities builds a strong feeling of community amount the speakers and conferees. Scholarships available to SCBWI members. Registration opens end of September/ early October and the conference sells out within one or two days. A waiting list is then formed. Coming together for shared meals and activities builds a strong feeling of community among the speakers and conferees. For more information, including exact costs and dates, visit our Web site in September.

SCBWI—NORTHERN OHIO; ANNUAL CONFERENCE

c/o Northern Ohio SCBWI, P.O. Box 195, Medina, Ohio 44258. E-mail: rwranch55@aol.com. Website: www.nohscbwi.org. **Regional Advisor:** Laurie Knowlton. Northern Ohio's conference is crafted for all levels of writers and illustrators of children's literature. We are incorporating hands-on activities to our September 11th and 12th, 2009 Conference. Not only will we cover the ins and outs of the whole process from idea through publication and promotion, we are also going to give participants the opportunity to dissect their own work with seasoned professionals such as Harold Underdown. Our annual event will be held at the Sheraton Cleveland Airport Hotel. Conference costs will be posted on our Web site with registration information. SCBWI members receive a discount. Additional fees apply for late registration, critiques, or portfolio reviews. Cost includes an optional Friday evening Opening Banquet form 6-10 p.m. with a keynote speaker; Saturday event from 8:30 a.m. to 5 p.m. which includes breakfast snack, full-day conference with headliner presentations, general sessions, breakout workshops, lunch, panel discussion, bookstore, and autograph session. We are also offering a social track for illustrators. Illustrator Showcase is open to all attendees at no additional cost. Grand door prize drawn at the end of the day Saturday, is free admission to the following year's conference.

SCBWI—OREGON CONFERENCES

E-mail: robink@scbwior.com. Website: www.scbwior.com. **Regional Advisor:** Robin Koontz. Writer and illustrator workshops and presentations geared toward all levels. "We invite editors, teachers, agents, attorneys, authors, illustrators and others in the business of writing and illustrating for children. They present lectures, workshops, and on-site critiques on a first-registered basis." Critique group network for local group meetings and regional retreats; see Web site for details.

Two main events per year: Writers and Illustrators Retreat: Retreat held near Portland Thursday-Sunday the 2nd weekend in October. Cost of retreat: $345 plus $35.00 critique fee includes double occupancy and all meals; Spring Conference: Held in the Portland area (2 day event the third Fri-Sat in May); cost for presentations and workshops: about $130 includes continental breakfast and lunch on Saturday, critique fee $35.00-attendees only; Friday intensive cost about $30 per a-la-carte-session with writer and illustrator tracks includes snacks and coffee. Registration limited to 300 for the conference and 55 for the retreat. SCBWI Oregon is a regional chapter of the SCBWI. SCBWI Members receive a discount for all events. Oregon and S. Washington members get preference.

SCBWI—POCONO MOUNTAINS RETREAT
Website: www.scbwiepa.org. Held in the spring at Shawnee Inn, Shawnee on the Delaware, PA. Faculty addresses craft, web design, school visits, writing, illustration and publishing. Registration limited to 150. Cost of retreat: tuition $140, meals, room and board averages $250 for the weekend. For information, online registration and brochure, visit Web site.

SCBWI—ROCKY MOUNTAIN; EVENTS
E-mail: denise@rmcscbwi.org. or ttuell@yahoo.com. Website: www.rmcscbwi.org. Co-Regional Advisors: Denise Vega and Todd Tuell. SCBWI Rocky Mountain chapter offers various special events, schmoozes, meetings and conferences throughout the year. 2009 major events: Summer Retreat with freelance editor Nora Cohen, July 10-12, Colorado Springs, CO, Fall Conference September 19-20, Sheraton Denver West Hotel, Lakewood, CO. More info on Web site.

SCBWI—SAN DIEGO; CHAPTER MEETINGS & WORKSHOPS
San Diego—SCBWI, San Diego CA. E-mail: ra-sd@sandiego-scbwi.org. Website: www.sandiego-scbwi.org. **Regional Advisor:** Janice M. Yuwiler. Writer and illustrator meetings and workshops geared toward all levels. Topics vary but emphasize writing and illustrating for children. Check Web site, e-mail or write for more information. "The San Diego chapter holds meetings the second Saturday of each month from September-May at the University of San Diego's from 2-4 p.m.; cost $7 (members), $9 (nonmembers). Check web site for room, speaker and directions." 2010 meeting schedule: January 9, February 13, March 13, April 10, May 8, September 11, October 9, November 13, and December 11. December 2009 meeting: Published members share lessons learned and holiday book sale. 2010 conference/retreat to be held the second Saturday or weekend of January, February or March—Check Web site for date and faculty. Season tickets include all regular chapter meetings during the season and newsletter issues for one calendar year as well as discounts on workshops/conferences. If interested in taking a class, Inside Children's books through University of San Diego Continuing Education for 2 units college credit. Class in 2010 begins in September 11, 2010 and ends May 14, 2011. See the Web site for conference/workshop dates, times and prices. Chapter also helps members find critique groups for on-going enhancements of skills.

SCBWI—SOUTHERN BREEZE; SPRINGMINGLE
P.O. Box 26282, Birmingham AL 35260. E-mail: JSKittinger@bellsouth.net. Website: www.southern-breeze.org. **Regional Advisors:** Jo Kittinger and Donna Bowman. Writer and illustrator workshops geared toward intermediate, advanced and professional levels. Speakers typically include agents, editors, authors, art directors, illustrators. **Open to SCBWI members, non-members and college students.** Annual conference held in Atlanta, Georgia. Usually held in late February. Registration limited. Cost of conference: approximately $225; includes Friday dinner, Saturday lunch and Saturday banquet. Manuscript critiques and portfolio reviews available for addtional fee. Pre-registration is necessary. Send a SASE to Southern Breeze, P.O. Box 26282, Birmingham AL 35260 for more information or visit Website: www.southern-breeze.org.

SCBWI—SOUTHERN BREEZE; WRITING AND ILLUSTRATING FOR KIDS

P.O. Box 26282, Birmingham AL 35260. E-mail: jskittinger@bellsouth.net. Website: www.southern-breeze.org. **Regional Advisors:** Jo Kittinger and Donna Bowman. Writer and illustrator workshops geared toward all levels. Open to SCBWI members, non-members and college students. All sessions pertain specifically to the production and support of quality children's literature. This one-day conference offers about 30 workshops on craft and the business of writing. Picture books, chapter books, novels covered. Entry and professional level topics addressed by published writers and illustrators, editors and agents. Annual conference. Fall conference is held the third weekend in October in the Birmingham, AL metropolitan area. (Museums, shopping, zoo, gardens, universities and colleges are within a short driving distance.) All workshops are limited to 30 or fewer people. Pre-registration is necessary. Some workshops fill quickly. Cost of conference: approximately $110 for members, $135 for nonmembers, $120 for students; program includes keynote speaker, 4 workshops (selected from 30), lunch, and Friday night dessert party. Mss critiques and portfolio reviews are available for an additional fee; mss must be sent early. Registration is by mail ahead of time. Manuscript and portfolio reviews must be pre-paid and scheduled. Send a SASE to: Southern Breeze, P.O. Box 26282, Birmingham AL 35260 or visit Web site. Fall conference is always held in Birmingham, Alabama. Room block at a hotel near conference site (usually a school) is by individual reservation and offers a conference rate. Keynote for WIK08 is Paul Fleischman. Additional speakers include editor Harold Underdown; Laurent Linn, Associate Art Director at Hernry Holt; and Author Sarah Campbell. WIK09 speakers to be announced.

SCBWI—TAIWAN; EVENTS

Fax: (886)2363-5358. E-mail: scbwi_taiwan@yahoo.com. Website: www.scbwi.tw. Mailing list: http://groups.yahoo.com/group/scbwi_taiwan. **Regional Advisor:**Kathleen Ahrens. Writer and illustrator workshops geared toward intermediate level. Open to students. Topics emphasized: "We regularly hold critiques for writers and for illustrators, and invite authors and illustrators visiting Taipei to give talks. See our Web site for more information."

SCBWI—VENTURA/SANTA BARBARA; FALL CONFERENCE

Simi Valley CA 93094-1389. (805)581-1906. E-mail: alexisinca@aol.com. Website: www.scbwisocal.org/calendar. Writers'conference geared toward all levels. Speakers include editors, authors, illustrators and agents. Fiction and nonfiction picture books, middle grade and YA novels, and magazine submissions addressed. Annual writing contest in all genres plus illustration display. Conference held October 24, 2009 at California Lutheran University in Thousand Oaks, California in cooperation with the CLU School of Education. For fees and other information e-mail or go to Web site.

SCBWI—VENTURA/SANTA BARBARA; RETREAT FOR CHILDREN'S AUTHORS AND ILLUSTRATORS

E-mail: alexisinca@aol.com. Website: www.scbwisocal.org. The Winter Retreat, usually held in Santa Barbara in January, focuses on craft or business issues. Go to Web site or e-mail for current theme and fee.

SCBWI—WESTERN WASHINGTON STATE; RETREATS & CONFERENCE

P.O. Box 156, Enumclaw WA 98022. Email: info@scbwi-washington.org. Website: www.scbwi-washington.org. **Co-Regional Advisors:** Joni Sensel and Laurie Thompson. "The Western Washington region of SCBWI hosts an annual conference in May, as well as a weekend retreat in November. Please visit the Web site for complete details."

SCBWI—WISCONSIN; FALL RETREAT FOR WORKING WRITERS

3446 Hazelnut Lane, Milton WI 53563. E-mail: pjberes@centurytel.net. Website: www.scbwi-wi-com. **Regional Advisor:** Pam Beres. Writer and illustrator conference geared toward all levels. All our sessions pertain to children's writing/illustration. Faculty addresses writing/illustrating/publishing. Annual conference held October. Registration limited to 90. Conference center has retreat-style bedrooms with desks that can be used to draw/write. Cost of conference: $375 for SBCWI member; $450 for non-members; includes program, meals, lodging, ms critique. Write or go to our Web site for more information: www.scbwi-wi.com.

OTHER CONFERENCES

AEC CONFERENCE ON SOUTHERN LITERATURE

3069 South Broad Street, Suite 2, Chattanooga TN 37408-3056. (423)267-1218. Fax: (423)267-1018. E-mail: info@artsedcouncil.org. Website: www.artsedcouncil.org. **Executive Director:** Susan Robinson. **Open to students.** Conference is geared toward readers. Biennial conference held April 2-4, 2009. Cost of conference: $125 for 3 days. Visit Web site for more information. Features panel discussions, readings and commentaries for adults and students by today's foremost Southern writers.

AMERICAN CHRISTIAN WRITERS CONFERENCE

P.O. Box 110390, Nashville TN 37222-0390. 1(800)21-WRITE or (615)834-0450. Fax: (615)834-7736. Website: www.ACWriters.com. **Director:** Reg Forder. Writer and illustrator workshops geared toward beginner, intermediate and advanced levels. Classes offered include: fiction, nonfiction, poetry, photography, music, etc. Workshops held in 3 dozen U.S. cities. Call or write for a complete schedule of conferences. 75 minutes. Maximum class size: 30 (approximate). Cost of conference: $119, 1-day session; $209, 2-day session (discount given if paid 30 days in advance) includes tuition only.

ANNUAL SPRING POETRY FESTIVAL

City College, New York NY 10031. (212)650-6356. E-mail: plaskin@ccny.cuny.edu. **Director, Poetry Outreach Center:** Pam Laskin. Writer workshops geared to all levels. **Open to students.** Annual poetry festival. Festival held May 16, 2008. Registration limited to 325. Cost of workshops and festival: free. Write for more information.

BIG SUR WRITING WORKSHOP

Henry Miller Library, Highway One, Big Sur CA 93920. Phone/fax: (831)667-2574. E-mail: magnus@henrymiller.org. Website: www.henrymiller.org/CWW.html. **Contact:** Magnus Toren, executive director. Annual workshops are held in December and March focusing on children's and young adult writing. Workshop held in Big Sur Lodge in Pfeiffer State Park. Cost of workshop: $720; included meals, lodging, workshop, Saturday evening reception; $600 if lodging not needed. www.henerymiller.org.

BOOKEXPO AMERICA/WRITER'S DIGEST BOOKS WRITERS CONFERENCE

4700 East Galbraith Rd.Cincinnati OH 45236. (513) 531-2690. Fax: (513) 891-7185. E-mail: writersdigestconference@writersdigest.com. Website: www.writersdigest.com/bea. Contact: Greg Hatfield, Events Manager. Estab. 2003. Annual. Conference duration: one day, usually in May. Average attendance: 600. "The purpose of the conference is to prepare writers hoping to get their work published. We offer instruction on the craft of writing, as well as advice for submitting their work to publications, publishing houses and agents. We provide breakout sessions on these topics, including expert advice from industry professionals, and offer workshops on fiction and nonfiction, in the various genres (literary, children's, mystery, romance, etc.). We also provide attendees the opportunity to actually pitch their work to agents." Site: New York. Past speakers included Jodi Picoult, Jacquelyn Mitchard, Jerry B. Jenkins, Steve Almond, Loren Estelman and Donald Maass. The price in 2009 was $199. For brochure, visit Web site. Agents and editors participate in conference..

⬛ BOOMING GROUND ONLINE WRITERS STUDIO

Buch E-462, 1866 Main Mall, UBC, Vancouver BC V6T 1Z1 Canada. (604)822-0257. Fax: (604)648-8848. E-mail: apply@boomingground.com. Website: www.boomingground.com. **Director:** Brianna Brash-Nyberg. Writer mentorships geared toward beginner, intermediate, and advanced levels. **Open to students.** Online mentorship program—students work for 4-8 months with a mentor by e-mail. Program cost: $780 Canadian. Individual manuscript evaluation also available. Apply online; send manuscript sample with application. No art classes offered. Visit Web site for more information.

CAPE COD WRITER'S CONFERENCE

Cape Cod Writer's Center, P.O. Box 408, Osterville MA 02655. (508)420-0200. Fax: (508)420-0212. E-mail: writers@capecodwriterscenter.org; www.capecodwriterscenter.org. Annual conference held third week in August in a rustic retreat center on Nantucket Sound, Cape Cod; 47th annual conference: August 15-22, 2009. This year a double conference, each three days of classes with 14 full length (seven-and-a-half-hour) workshops, four short courses, and two Master Classes. Workshops geared toward beginner/intermediate, and advanced levels include writing for children and for young adults (Master Class on this subject as well), fiction, nonfiction (including memoir), poetry, and screenwriting. Evening programs include speakers, Master Classes, panels, poetry, and prose readings. Manuscript evaluations and mentoring with faculty, literary agents, publishers, and editors. No registration fee for Cape Cod Writers Center members. The Young Writers' Workshop for 12- to 16-year-olds on prose and poetry held concurrent with the conference. Pricing available on the web page by May 1.

CAT WRITERS' ASSOCIATION ANNUAL WRITERS CONFERENCE

President Amy D. Shojai, P.O. Box 1904, Sherman TX 75091. (903) 868-1022. E-mail:shojai@verizon.ne. Website: www.catwriters.org. The Cat Writers' Association holds an annual conference at varying locations around the US. The agenda for the conference is filled with seminars, editor appointments, an autograph party, networking breakfast, reception and annual awards banquet, as well as the annual meeting of the association. See Web site for details.

CHILDREN'S AND YOUNG ADULT LITERATURE & ILLUSTRATION FESTIVAL

The Loft Literary Center, Suite 200, Open Book, 1011 Washington Avenue South, Minneapolis MN 55415. (612)379-8999. E-mail: loft@loft.org. Website: www.loft.org. Craft and publication sessions for writers and illustrators plus an opportunity for portfolio critique for illustrators at 2009 Festival, April 18 & 19. Registration limited to 175 people. Cost of conference: approximately $250; includes admission to full and break-out sessions. Find more information at www.loft.org or call (612)379-8999. The Loft also offers creative writing classes for beginning to advanced writers in nearly every form and genre, offers Minnesota writers readings, fellowships, mentorships and awards and has writing studios available for rental.

CHILDREN'S AUTHORS' BOOTCAMP

P.O. Box 231, Allenspark CO 80510. (303)747-1014. E-mail: CABootcamp@msn.com. Website: www.WeMakeWriters.com. **Contact:** Linda Arms White. Writer workshops geared toward beginner and intermediate levels. "Children's Authors' Bootcamp provides two full, information-packed days on the fundamentals of writing fiction for children. The workshop covers developing strong, unique characters; well-constructed plots; believable dialogue; seamless description and pacing; point of view; editing your own work; marketing your manuscripts to publishers, and more. Each day also includes in-class writing exercises and small group activities." Workshop held several times per year at various locations throughout the United States. Please check our Web site for upcoming dates and locations. Maximum size is 55; average workshop has 40-50 participants. Cost of workshop varies; see Web site for details. Cost includes tuition for both Saturday and Sunday (9:00 a.m. to 4:30 p.m.); morning and afternoon snacks; lunch; handout packet. "Check website for details."

THE COLUMBUS WRITERS CONFERENCE

P.O. Box 20548, Columbus OH 43220-0176. (614)451-3075. Fax: (614)451-0174. E-mail: angelaPL28@aol.com. Website: www.creativevista.com. **Director:** Angela Palazzolo. "In addition to consultations with agents and editor, this two-day conference offers a wide variety of topics and has included writing in the following markets: children's, young adult, novel, short story, science fiction, fantasy, humor, mystery, finding and working with a literary agent, book proposals, working with an editor, query writing, screenwriting, magazine writing, travel, humor, and freelance writing. Specific sessions that have pertained to children: fiction, nonfiction, children's writing, children's markets, young adult, pitching children's books to agents and editors, and publishing children's poetry and stories. Annual conference. Conference held in August. Cost of conference is TBA. E-mail or call to request brochure or visit the Web site creativevista.com.

CONFERENCE FOR WRITERS & ILLUSTRATORS OF CHILDREN'S BOOKS

Book Passage, 51 Tamal Vista Blvd.Corte Madera CA 94925. (415)927-0960, ext. 234. Fax: (415)927-3069. E-mail: kathryn@bookpassage.com. Website: www.bookpassage.com. **Conference Coordinator:** Kathryn Petrocelli. Writer and illustrator conference geared toward beginner and intermediate levels. Sessions cover such topics as the nuts and bolts of writing and illustrating, publisher's spotlight, market trends, developing characters/finding voice in your writing, and the author/agent relationship. Four-day conference held each summer. Includes opening night dinner, 3 lunches and a closing reception.

THE DIY BOOK FESTIVAL

7095 Hollywood Blvd.Suite 864, Los Angeles CA 90028-0893. (323)665-8080. Fax: (323)372-3883. E-mail: diyconvention@aol.com. Website: www.iyconvention.com. **Managing Director:** Bruce Haring. Writer and illustrator workshops geared toward beginner and intermediate levels. **Open to students.** Festival focus on getting your book into print, book marketing and promotion. Annual workshop. Workshop held February-October, various cities. Cost of workshop: $50; includes admission to event, entry to prize competition, lunch for some events. Check out our Web site for current dates and locations: www.iyconvention.com.

DUKE UNIVERSITY YOUTH PROGRAMS: CREATIVE WRITERS' WORKSHOP

P.O. Box 90702, Durham NC 27708. (919)684-6259. Fax: (919)681-8235. E-mail: youth@duke.edu. Website: www.learnmore.uke.edu/youth. **Contact:** Duke Youth Programs. Writer workshops geared toward intermediate to advanced levels. **Open to students.** The Creative Writers' Workshop provides an intensive creative writing experience for advanced high school age writers who want to improve their skills in a community of writers. "The interactive format gives participants the opportunity to share their work in small groups, one-on-one with instructors, and receive feedback in a supportive environment. The review and critique process helps writers sharpen critical thinking skills and learn how to revise their work." Annual workshop. Every summer there is one 2-week residential session. Costs for 2008—$1,655 for residential campers; $1,065 for extended day campers; $825 for day campers. Visit Web site for more information.

DUKE UNIVERSITY YOUTH PROGRAMS: YOUNG WRITERS' CAMP

P.O. Box 90702, Durham NC 27708. (919)684-2827. Fax: (919)681-8235. E-mail: youth@duke.edu. Website: www.learnmore.uke.edu/youth. **Contact:** Duke Youth Programs (919)684-6259. Beginner and intermediate levels writing workshops for middle and high school students. **Open to students** (grades 6-11). Summer Camp. The Young Writers' Camp offers courses to enhance participants skills in creative and expository writing. "Through a core curriculum of short fiction, poetry, journalism and playwriting students choose two courses for study to develop creative and analytical processes of writing. Students work on assignments and projects in and out of class, such as newspaper features, short stories, character studies, and journals." Annual workshop. Every summer there are three 2-week sessions with residential and day options. Costs for 2008—$1,655 for residential campers; $1,065 for extended day campers; $825 for day campers. Visit Web site or call for more information.

EAST TEXAS CHRISTIAN WRITERS CONFERENCE

East Texas Baptist University, 1209 North Grove Street, Marshall TX 75670. (903)923-2083. Fax: (903)923-2077. E-mail: jcornish@etbu.edu or jhopkins@etbu.edu. Website: www.etbu.edu/News/CWC/default.htm. **Humanities Secretary:** Joy Cornish. Writer workshops geared toward beginner, intermediate and advanced levels. **Open to students.** Children's literature, books, stories, plays, art, and general literature. Annual conference. Workshop held first Friday and Saturday in June each year. Cost of workshop: $70/individual; $50/student; includes 5 writing workshops, materials, Friday evening dinner and luncheon; pre-conference workshops extra. Write, e-mail or call for more information.

THE ENVIROMENTAL WRITERS' CONFERENCE AND WORKSHOP IN HONOR OF RACHEL CARSON

The Spruce Point Inn, Boothbay Harbor ME. (845)398-4247. Fax: (845)398-4224. E-mail: info@new-cue.org. Website: www.new-cue.org. **President:** Barbara Ward Klein. Writer and illustrator workshops geared toward beginner, intermediate, advanced and professional levels. Our conference emphasizes environmental and nature writing for juvenile fiction and non-fiction. Workshop held in June every 2 years on the even numbered year. Registration limited to 100 participants. Writing/art facilities available: Large meeting rooms for featured authors/speakers. Smaller break-out rooms for concurrent sessions. Cost of workshop: $395/returning participants; $445/new-before 5/1/10. Includes all featured and keynote addresses, concurrent sessions, workshops, guided outdoor activities and almost all meals. Submit writing sample, no longer than 3 pages. Write for more information. Additional information about featured speakers, The Spruce Point Inn, and the Boothbay Harbor Area is available on-line at www.new-cue.org.

FESTIVAL OF FAITH AND WRITING

Department of English, Calvin College 1795 Knollcrest Circle SE, Grand Rapids MI 49546. (616)526-6770. E-mail: ffw@calvin.edu. Website: www.calvin.edu/festival. E-mail all inquiries about attendance (for registration brochures, program information, etc.). Geared toward all levels of readers and writers. Open to students. The Festival of Faith and Writing has talks, panel discussions, and workshops by nearly 100 individuals, many of whom compose, write, illustrate, and publish children's books and books for young adults. Each break-out will have a session on children's books/young adult books. Conference held in April of the even years. Registration limited to approximately 1,900 people. This conference is geared towards a variety of writers and readers. The Festival brings together writers and readers who wonder about the intersections of faith with words on a page, lyrics in a melody, or images on a screen. Novelists, publishers, musicians, academics, poets, playwrights, editors, screenwriters, agents, journalists, preachers, students, and readers of every sort sit down together for three days of conversation and celebration.

FISHTRAP, INC.

400 Grant Street, P.O. Box 38, Enterprise OR 97828-0038. (541)426-3623. E-mail: director@fishtrap. org. Website: www.fishtrap.org. **Director:** Rick Bombaci. Writer workshops geared toward beginner, intermediate, advanced and professional levels. Open to students, scholarships available. A series of eight writing workshops and a writers' gathering is held each July; a winter gathering concerning writing and issues of public concern is held each February. During the school year Fishtrap brings writers into local schools and offers workshops for teachers and writers of children's and young adult books. A **Children's Lit Writing Workshop is held each fall.** Other programs include writing and K-12 teaching residencies, writers' retreats, and lectures. College credit available for many workshops. See Web site for full program descriptions and to get on the e-mail and mail lists.

FLATHEAD RIVER WRITERS CONFERENCE

P.O. Box 7711, Kalispell MT 59904. E-mail: conference@authorsoftheflathead.org. **Director:** Conference Coordinator. Two, 12 person, intense workshops geared toward beginner, intermediate, advanced and professional levels. **Open to students of any age.** Along with our presenters, we periodically feature a children's writer workshop/speaker. Annual conference held early-October at the Flathead Valley Community College. Registration limited to 100. Cost of the weekend conference: $150; includes all lectures and a choice of weekend workshops plus breakfast and lunch. Lodging not included.Write for more information.

FLORIDA CHRISTIAN WRITERS CONFERENCE

Lake Yale Conference center, Leesburg FL. E-mail: billiewilson@cfl.rr.com. Website: www. flwriters.org. **Conference Director:** Billie Wilson. Writer workshops geared toward all levels. **Open to students.** "We offer 80 one-hour workshops and 11 six-hour classes. Approximately 15 of these are for the children's genre." Annual workshop held in March. "We have 30 publishers and publications represented by editors teaching workshops and reading manuscripts from the conferees. The conference is limited to 200 people. Advanced or professional workshops are by invitation only via submitted application. Cost of conference: $440; includes tuition and ms critiques and editor review of your ms plus personal appointments with editors. Write or e-mail for more information.

GOTHAM WRITERS' WORKSHOP

New York NY 10018. (877)974-8377. (212)307-6325. E-mail: dana@write.org. Website: www. WritingClasses.com. **Director, Student Affairs:** Dana Miller. Creative writing workshops taught by professional writers are geared toward beginner, intermediate and advanced levels. **Open to students.** "Workshops cover the fundamentals of plot, structure, voice, description, characterization, and dialogue appropriate to all forms of fiction and nonfiction for pre-schoolers through young adults. Students can work on picture books or begin middle-readers or young adult novels." Annual workshops held 4 times/year (10-week and 1-day workshops). Workshops held January, April, July, September/October. Registration limited to 14 students/in-person (NYC) class; 18 students/ online class; 40 students for in-person (NYC) one-day workshops are held 4 times per year. Cost of workshop: $420 for 10-week workshops; $150 for 1-day workshops; 10-week NYC classes meet once a week for 3 hours; 10-week online classes include 10 week-long, asynchronous "meetings"; 1-day workshops are 7 hours and are held 8 times/year. E-mail for more information.

GREAT LAKES WRITER'S WORKSHOP

Real Writing for Real People, Alverno College Milwaukee WI 53234-3922. (414)382-6176. Fax: (414)382-6332. E-mail: nancy.krase@alverno.edu. Website: www.alverno.edu. **Coordinator:** Nancy Krase. Annual writing workshops geared toward beginner and intermediate levels; subjects include publishing, short story writing, novel writing, poetry, writing techniques/focus in character development, techniques for overcoming writers block and children's writing. Workshop held saturday, June 27, 2009. Cost of workshop: $115/entire workshop; $99 if you register before June 5, 2009 conference includes continental breakfast, and lunch along with author's keynote followed by choice of 2 workshops. See online brochure. Featured at lunch will be a panel on publishing. Online brochure will be available for viewing March 16 at alverno.edu.

GREEN LAKE WRITERS CONFERENCE

Real Writing for Real People, Alverno College Milwaukee WI 53234-3922. (414)382-6176. Fax: (414)382-6332. E-mail: nancy.krase@alverno.edu. Website: www.alverno.edu. **Coordinator:** Nancy Krase. Annual writing workshops geared toward beginner and intermediate levels; subjects include publishing, short story writing, novel writing, poetry, writing techniques/focus in character development, techniques for overcoming writers block and children's writing. Workshop held saturday, June 27, 2009. Cost of workshop: $115/entire workshop; $99 if you register before June 5, 2009 conference includes continental breakfast, and lunch along with author's keynote followed by choice of 2 workshops. See online brochure. Featured at lunch will be a panel on publishing. Online brochure will be available for viewing March 16 at alverno.edu.

HIGHLAND SUMMER CONFERENCE

P.O. Box 7014, Radford University, Radford VA 24142-7014. (540)831-5366. Fax: (540)831-5951. E-mail: rbderrick@radford.edu. Website: www.radford.edu/~arsc. **Director:** Grace Toney Edwards. **Assistant to the Director:** Ruth Derrick. **Open to students.** Writer workshops geared toward beginner, intermediate and advanced levels. Emphasizes Appalachian literature, culture and heritage. Annual workshop. Workshop held first 2 weeks in June annually each year. Registration limited to 20. Writing facilities available: computer center. Cost of workshop: Regular tuition (housing/meals extra). Must be registered student or special status student. E-mail, fax or call for more information. Past visiting authors include: Ron Rash, Sharon McCrumb, George Ella Lyon, and Frank X Walker.

HIGHLIGHTS FOUNDATION FOUNDERS WORKSHOPS

814 Court St.Honesdale PA 18431. (570)253-1192. Fax: (570)253-0179. E-mail: contact@highlightsfoundation.org. Website: www.highlightsfoundation.org. **Contact:** Kent Brown, director. Workshops geared toward those interested in writing and illustrating for children, intermediate and advanced levels. Classes offered include: Writing Novels for Young Adults, Biography, Nonfiction Writing, Writing Historical Fiction, Wordplay: Writing Poetry for Children, Heart of the Novel, Nature Writing for Kids, Visual Art of the Picture Book, The Whole Novel Workshop, and more (see Web site for updated list). Workshops held near Honesdale, PA. Workshops limited to between 8 and 14 people. Cost of workshops range from $695 and up. Cost of workshop includes tuition, meals, conference supplies and private housing. Call for application and more information.

HIGHLIGHTS FOUNDATION WRITERS WORKSHOP AT CHAUTAUQUA

814 Court St.Honesdale PA 18431. (570) 253-1192. Fax: (570) 253-0179. E-mail: contact@highlightsfoundation.org. To view faculty and other details please got to Website: www.highlightsfoundation.org. **Contact:** Kent Brown, Director. Writer Workshops geared toward those interested in writing for children; beginner, intermediate and advanced levels. Classes include: Writing Poetry, Book Promotion, Characterization, Developing a Plot, How to Promote Your Book, and many many more. Annual workshop held: July 10-17, 2010, at Chautauqua Institution, Chautauqua, NY. Registration limited to 100. Tuition, meals, conference supplies. Cost does not include housing. Call for availability and pricing. Scholarships are available for first-time attendees. Call for more information or visit the Web site.

INDIANAPOLIS YOUTH LITERATURE CONFERENCE

2060 E. 54th Street, Indianapolis IN 46220. (317)254-0830. E-mail: kidsink@indy.net. Website: www.butler.edu/childlit/about.htm. **Chaired:** Dr. Marilyn Irwin **Contact:** Rebecca Mullin. Writer and illustrator conference geared toward all levels. **Open to college students.** Annual conference held the last Saturday of the month of January each year featuring top writers in the field of children's literature. Includes sessions such as Nuts and Bolts for Beginning Writers. Registration limited to 350. Cost of conference: $85; includes SCBWI Networking Luncheon, registration, 3 plenary addresses, 2 workshops, book signing, reception and conference bookstore. Cisit the web site for more information. "The conference is geared toward three groups: teachers, librarians and writers/illustrators."

INTERNATIONAL CREATIVE WRITING CAMP

111-11th Ave Sw.Suit 3, Minot, ND 58701. (701)838-8472. Fax: (701)838-1351. E-mail: info@internationalmusiccamp.com. Website: www.internationalmusiccamp.com. **Camp Director:** Dr. Timothy Wollenzien. Writer and illustrator workshops geared toward beginner, intermediate and advanced levels. **Open to students.** Sessions offered include those covering poems, plays, mystery stories, essays. Workshop held June 21-27, 2008. Registration limited to 40. The summer camp location at the International Peace Garden on the Border between Manitoba and North Dakota is an ideal site for creative thinking. Excellent food, housing and recreation facilities are available. Cost of workshop: Before May 1st -$315.00; after May 1st - $340.00. Write for more information.

IOWA SUMMER WRITING FESTIVAL

C215 Seashore Hall, Iowa City IA 52242. (319)335-4160. Fax: (319)335-4743. E-mail: iswfestival@uiowa.edu. Website: www.uiowa.edu/~iswfest. **Director:** Amy Margolis. Writer workshops geared toward beginner, intermediate and advanced levels. Open to writers age 21 and over. "We offer writing workshops across the genres, including workshops for children's writers in picture books, structuring writing for children, the young adult novel, and nonfiction." Annual workshop held June and July. Registration limited to 12/workshop. Workshops meet in university classrooms. Cost of workshop: $500-525/week-long session; $250/weekend. Housing is separate and varies by facility. Write or call for more information.

KENTUCKY WRITER'S WORKSHOP

1050 State Park Road, Pineville KY 40977. (606)337-3066. Fax: (606)337-7250. Email: Dean.Henson@ky.gov. Website: http://parks.ky.gov. **Event Coordinator:** Dean Henson. Writer workshops featuring published authors and geared toward beginner and intermediate levels. **Open to students.** Annual workshop. Workshop will next be held March 27-28, 2009. Writing facilities available: classroom setup. An all-inclusive, on-site package is available and includes two nights accommodations, two evening buffet meals, and admission to all sessions. Write or call for more information.

KINDLING WORDS EAST

Web site (for registration and information): www.kindlingwords.org. Annual retreat held in late January near Burlington, Vermont. A retreat with three strands: writer, illustrator and editor; professional level. Intensive workshops for each strand, and an open schedule for conversations and networking. Registration limited to approximately 70. Tuition: $205. Hosted by the 4-star Inn at Essex (room and board extra). Participants must be published by a CCBC listed publisher, or if in publishing, occupy a professional position. Registration opens August 1 or as posted on the Web site, and fills quickly. Check Web site to see if spaces are available, to sign up to be notified when registration opens each year, or for more information.

KINDLING WORDS WEST

Web site (for registration and information): www.kindlingwords.org. Annual retreat held in late May at a stunning and sacred location: Mable Dodge Luhan House, in Taos New Mexico. KWW is an artist's colony- style week with workshops by gifted teachers followed by a working retreat. Participants gather just before dinner to have white-space discussions; evenings include fireside readings, star gazing and songs. $400 tuition; room/board extra. Participants must be published by CBC-recognized publisher. Go to www.kindlingwords.org to view speakers and register.

LAJOLLA WRITERS CONFERENCE

FROM PEN TO PAPER TO PUBLICATION P.O. Box 2068, Cedar Rapids IA 52406. (319)398-1057. Fax: (319)398-5432. E-mail: heather.willard@kirkwood.edu. Website: www.kirkwood.edu/ writersworkshop. **Program Director:** Heather Willard. Writer workshop geared toward all levels. "We do not have any illustrator workshops, but would be interested in making contact with illustration professionals for future workshops." **Open to students.** "We cover all facets of writing from childrens to adult, fiction to nonfiction. Some of our presenters include Katie Brogan (Writer's Digest Books), Don Harstad, Stephanie Gordon & Judy Enderle and many more. Stephanie and Judy focus primarily on children's writing. Two of their workshops are "First Pages: How to Grab an Editor" and "The Nitty Gritty of Editing." Annual event. Held in October. Writing facilities available: computer labs and atrium. Cost of workshop: $249; includes keynote and 3 days of workshops (3-4 each day, with 4-5 choices in each). Also available for extra charge: Brown Bag Lunch Panel, 1-on-1 critiques. Some workshops require a writing sample prior to the workshop. Write or e-mail for more information.P.O. Box 178122, San Diego CA 92177. (858)467-1978. Website: www.lajollawritersconference.com. **Contact:** Jared Kuritz, Director. Established 2001. Annual. 2009 Conference held November 6-8. Conference duration: 3 days. Maximum attendance limited to 200. The La Jolla Writers Conference welcomes writers of all levels of experience. This three-day event, now in its 9th year, always boasts exciting, interactive workshops, lectures, and presentations by an outstanding and freely accessible faculty comprised of best-selling authors, editors from major publishing houses, and literary agents, all of whom value meeting and working with a diverse group of creative people passionate about writing. The LJWC uniquely covers the art, craft, and business of writing for both fiction and non-fiction. **Costs** $285 before April 1; $385 April 1 through August 1; $425 after August 1. Conference registration includes access to more than 85 classes, three keynote addresses, two meals, appetizer reception, and faculty author singing. **Additional Information:** Private Read & Critiques for an additional fee.

LEAGUE OF UTAH WRITERS' ANNUAL ROUNDUP

P.O. Box 18430, Kearns UT 84118. (435) 313-4459. E-mail: natpace@yahoo.com. Website: www. luwrite.com. **President:** Natalie Pace. **President Elect**: Mike Eldredge. **Membership Chairman:** Dorothy Crofts. Writer workshops geared toward beginner, intermediate or advanced. Annual conference. Roundup will be held at the HOmestead in Midway Utah, September 18-19, 2009. Registration limited to 300. Cost is $99 for members/$129 for nonmembers registering before August 15; $120 for members; $150 non-members after August 19. Cost includes 3 meals, all workshops, general sessions, a syllabus, handouts and conference packet. Contact Natalie Pace - natpace@yahoo.com with questions or (435)674-9792 or above e-mail address. Send registration to Dorothy Crofts, Membership Chairman, P.O. Box 18430, Kearns, UT 84118. Check Web site for updates, price changes and specifics.

MANHATTANVILLE SUMMER WRITERS' WEEK

2900 Purchase Street, Purchase NY 10577-2103. (914)323-5239. Fax: (914)694-3488. E-mail: sirabian@mville.edu. Website: www.manhattanville.edu. **Program Director:** Karen Sirabian. Writer workshops geared toward writers and aspiring writers. **Open to students.** Writers' week offers a special workshop for writers interested in children's/young adult writing. We have featured such workshop leaders as: Patricia Gauch, Richard Peck, Elizabeth Winthrop and Janet Lisle. In 2009, James Howe will conduct a workshop entitled "Writing for Children & Young Adults." Annual workshop held in June 22-26. Length of each session: one week. Cost of workshop: $725 (non-credit); includes a full week of writing activities, 5-day workshop on children's literature; lectures; readings; sessions with editors and agents; major speaker, Rick Moody; etc. Workshop may be taken for 2 graduate credits. Write or e-mail for more information.

THE MANUSCRIPT WORKSHOP IN VERMONT

P.O. Box 529, Londonderry VT 05148. (802)824-3968 or (212)877-4457. E-mail: aplbrk2@earthlink. net. Website: www.barbaraseuling.com. **Director:** Barbara Seuling. Writer workshop for all levels. Annual workshop estab. 1992. Generally held mid to late July and August and sometimes early September. Intensive workshop spans 5 days, from dinner on Monday evening to lunch on Friday. The time is divided among instructive hands-on sessions in the mornings, writing time in the afternoons, and critiquing in the evenings. A guest speaker from the world of children's books appears at each workshop. Registration is limited to 8; smaller workshops are considered for specialized workshops. Cost of workshop: $895 per person; includes a shared room and all meals. Private room available for additional cost. Inquire about smaller, specialized workshops in novel writing and picture books.

◪ MARITIME WRITERS' WORKSHOP

UNB College of Extended Learning, P.O. Box 4400, Fredericton NB E3B 5A3 Canada. E-mail: ahowells @unb.ca. Website: www.cel.unb.ca/pce. **Coordinator:** Alison Howells. Day-long workshops during the week of July 6-10, 2009. Workshops run from 9 a.m.- 4 p.m. daily, on topics such as life writing, ficiton, and how to get published. Group workshop plus individual conferences, public readings, etc. Registration limited to 20/class. Daily workshop cost is $115. Discount of 5 workshops for the price of 4.

MAUI WRITERS CONFERENCE

4224 Wailae Avenue, Suite 586, Honula, HI 96816. (808)739-5500. E-mail: writers@mauiwriters. com. Website: www.mauiwriters.com. **Director:** Shannon Tullius. Writers workshops geared toward beginner, intermediate, advanced. **Open to students.** "We offer a small children's writing section covering picture books, middle grade and young adult. We invite one New York Times Bestselling Author plus agents and editors, who give consultations to attendees for a fee." Workshop held annually over the Labor Day weekend. Cost includes admittance to all conference sessions and classes only—. No airfare, food or consultations.

MIDWEST WRITERS WORKSHOP

Department of Journalism, Ball State University, Muncie IN 47306. (765)282-1055. Fax: (765)285-7997. Website: www.midwestwriters.org. **Director:** Jama Kehoe Bigger. Writer workshops geared toward intermediate level. Topics include most genres. Our faculty/speakers have included Joyce Carol Oates, George Plimpton, Clive Cussler, Haven Kimmel, James Alexander Thom, Wiliam Zinsser, Phillip Gulley, and children's writers Rebecca Kai Dotlich, April Pulley Sayre, Peter Welling, Claire Ewert and Michelle Medlock Adams. Workshop also includes agent pitch sessions ms evaluation and a writing contest. Annual workshop held in late July. Registration tentatively limited to 125. Most meals included. Offers scholarships. Write for more information.

MISSOURI WRITERS' GUILD ANNUAL STATE CONFERENCE

(816)361-1281. E-mail: conferenceinfo@missouriwritersguild.org. Website: www.missouriwritersguild. org. **Contact:** Karen Heywood, vice president and conference chairman. Writer and illustrator workshops geared to all levels. **Open to students.** Annual conference held early April or early May each year. Cost of conference: $139-159.

MONTROSE CHRISTIAN WRITER'S CONFERENCE

5 Locust St.Montrose PA 18801-1112. (570)278-1001. Fax: (570)278-3061. E-mail: mbc@montrosebible.org. Website: www.montrosebible.org. **Executive Director:** Jim Fahringer. **Secretary-Registrar:** Donna Kosik. **Open to adults and students.** Writer workshops geared toward beginner, intermediate and advanced levels. Annual workshop held in July. Cost of workshop: $150 tuition, 2008 rate. Brochure available in April.

MOONDANCE INTERNATIONAL FILM FESTIVAL

970 Ninth St.Boulder CO 80302. (303)545-0202. E-mail: info@moondancefilmfestival.com (with MIFF or MOONDANCE in the subject line). Website: www.moondancefilmfestival.com. **Executive Director:** Elizabeth English. Moondance Film Festival Workshop Sessions include screenwriting, playwriting, short stories, filmmaking (feature, documentary, short, animation), TV and video filmmaking, writing for TV (MOW, sitcoms, drama), writing for animation, adaptation to screenplays (novels and short stories), how to get an agent, what agents want to see, and pitch panels. 2009 workshops and film festival held August, 2009 (exact date and location TBA). Cost of workshops, seminars, panels, pitch session: $50 each. Check website for more information and registration forms. The 2008 competition deadline for entries in the first or second week of April. "The Moondance competition includes special categories for writers and filmmakers who create work for the children's market!" Entry forms and guidelines are on the Web site.

MOUNT HERMON CHRISTIAN WRITERS CONFERENCE

Mount Hermon Christian Conference Center, Mount Hermon CA 95041-0413. (831)335-4466. Fax: (831)335-9413. E-mail: rachelw@mhcamps.org. Website: www.mounthermon.org/writers. **Writers Conferences Director:** Rachel A. Williams; **Conference Host:** David Talbott. Writer workshops geared toward all levels. **Open to students over 16 years** with special teen track. All genre of writing. 12 Major Morning Sessions, 70 optional afternoon workshops offered include every genre of writing. Held annually over Palm Sunday weekend: April 3-7, 2009 and March 26-30, 2010. Length of each session: 5-day residential conferences held annually. Registration limited 45/class, but most are 20-30. Conference center with hotel-style accommodations. Cost of workshop: $600-1100 variable; includes tuition, resource notebook, refreshment breaks, full room and board for 13 meals and 4 nights. Conference information posted annually on Web site by December 1. Write or e-mail for more information or call toll-free to 1-888-MH-CAMPS.

NORTH CAROLINA WRITERS' NETWORK FALL CONFERENCE

P.O. Box 954, Carrboro NC 27510-0954. (919)967.9540. Fax: (919)929.0535. E-mail: mail@ncwriters.org. Website: www.ncwriters.org. Writing workshops and services geared toward beginning, intermediate and advanced or published levels. **Open to students.** We offer workshops, keynote, presentations and critique sessions in a variety of genres: fiction, poetry, creative nonfiction, children, youth, etc. Past youth and children writing faculty include Louise Hawes, Jackie Ogburn, Clay Carmichael, Carole Boston Weatherford, Susie Wilde, Stephanie Greene, Joy Neaves, and Frances O'Roark Dowell. Annual Conference to be held next at the Marriott Winston-Salem Twin City Quarter. Date: Usually the second weekend of November. Cost of conference usually $250/members, $350/nonmembers, including all workshops, panels, roundtables, social activities and four meals. Extra costs for accommodations, master classes and critique sessions.

OKLAHOMA WRITERS' FEDERATION, INC. ANNUAL CONFERENCE

3925 S. Boulevard St.Edmond, OK 73013. (405)348-3325. Marcia@marciapreston.com. **Contact: 2009 President: Marcia Preston** (please see Web site for most current info): www.owfi.org. Writer workshops geared toward all levels. **Open to students.** "Forty seminars, with 30 speakers consisting of editors, literary agents and many best-selling authors. Topics include writing for children, publishing law, and digital forensics for writers, book publicity, romantic suspense, developing characters and setting, and much more." Annual conference. Held first weekend in May each year. Writing facilities available: book room, autograph party, two lunch workshops. Cost of conference: $150 before March 15; $175 after March 15; $70 for single days; $25 for lunch workshops. Full tuition includes 2-day conference (all events except lunch workshops) and 2 dinners plus one 10-minute appointment with an attending editor or agent of your choice (must be reserved in advance). "If writers would like to participate in the annual writing contest, they must become members of OWFI. You don't have to be a member to attend the conference." Write or e-mail for more information.

OUTDOOR WRITERS ASSOCIATION OF AMERICA ANNUAL CONFERENCE

121 Hickory St.Missoula, MT 59801. (406)728-7434. Fax: (406)728-7445. E-mail: rginer@owaa. org. **Meeting Planner:** Robin Giner. Writer workshops geared toward all levels. Annual four-day conference. Craft Improvement seminars; newsmaker sessions. Workshop held in June. 2009 conference to be held in Grand Rapids, Michigan. Cost of workshop: $380; includes attendance at all workshops and most meals. Attendees must have prior approval from Executive Director before attendance is permitted. Write for more information.

OZARK CREATIVE WRITERS, INC. CONFERENCE

Open to professional and amateur writers, workshops are geared to all levels and all forms of the creative process and literary arts. Sessions sometimes include songwriting, with presentations by best-selling authors, editors, and agents. The OCW Conference promotes writing by offering competition in all genres. The annual event is held on the second full weekend in October (October 8-10, 2009) at the Best Western Inn of the Ozarks, in the resort town of Eureka Springs, Arkansas. Approximately 200 attend each year; many also enter the creative writing competitions. The cost of registration is approximately $80-100, and includes attendance at al session presentations, continental breakfast, and contest entry fees; banquet meals and lodging not included. For more information' Website: ozarkcreativwriters.org Program Chair: Chrissy Willis. E-mail: ozarkcreativewriters@ clarissawillis.com. Mail: 223 Sycamore Dr.Bluff City, TN 37618

THE PACIFIC COAST CHILDREN'S WRITERS WORKSHOP

for Novelists, P.O. Box 244, Aptos CA 95001. Website: www.childrenswritersworkshop.com. **Founding Director:** Nancy Sondel. This eighth annual workshop "Vision and Voice," is geared toward intermediate through professional levels; beginners may attend with some limits in participation. Intensive focus on craft with an eye to publication. **Open to students.** "As with all enrollees, students must demonstrate competence in story-crafting and/or come prepared to learn from highly skilled writers. (Discount for students age 16-24.) Our keynotes, master-class open clinics, and hands-on focus sessions whole-novel vision and ongoing re-vision. Presenters include an established NY editor and agent, plus literary masters Marion Dane Bauer (2009) and Darcy Pattison (2010). Some of our enrollees have landed contracts as a direct result of our event." Annual seminar; held August 21-23, 2008 and August 20-22 2010. Registration limited to 30. Pajaro Dunes' gated beachfront facility offers free use of business center; enrollees' condos have DSL Internet access. "Our private conference building is available 24 hours per day." **Cost of workshop**: $299-599, which includes basic program, most meals, up to 3 faculty critiques per enrollee (written and/or in person). Additional fee for add-on workshop wit faculty author, and/or for academic credit conferred by the University of California. Discounts available. "Our e-application includes essay questions about each writer's manuscript; sample chapters and synopsis must be submitted with the application, by mid -April for the most critique options. **Content:** We focus on literary, character-driven, realistic novels with protagonists ages 11 and older. Our seminar-style, master-class format is 90 percent hands-on—highly interactive, with continuous dialogues between seasoned faculty and savvy, congenial peers. Manuscript clinics are team-taught by our nationally-known agent, editor, and author. Critiques may address enrollees' opening and later chapters and brief synopses. Our pre-workshop prep (personalized manuscript worksheets, peer critiques) maximizes learning and networking with the pros. For more information, please reach us via our Web site's contact form."

PACIFIC NORTHWEST CHILDREN'S BOOK CONFERENCE

Portland State University, Continuing Education, Graduate School of Education, P.O. Box 751, Portland OR 97207. (503)725-9786 or (800)547-8887, ext. 9786. Fax: (503)725-5595. E-mail:katagiri@pdx.ed. Website: www.ceed.pdx.edu/children/. Focus on the craft of writing and illustrating for children while working with an outstanding faculty of acclaimed editors, authors, and illustrators. Daily afternoon faculty-led writing and illustration workshops. Acquire specific information on how to become a professional in the field of children's literature. Annual workshop for all levels. Conference held July 13-17 2009 on the campus of Reed College, Portland, Oregon. Cost depends on options selected, including: noncredit or 3 graduate credits or graduate credits; individual ms/portfolio reviews and room and board at Reed campus. E-mail katagiri@pdx.edu for more information. Linda Zuckerman, editor, coordinates conference and brings together knowledgeable and engaging presenters every year.

PACIFIC NORTHWEST WRITER ASSN. SUMMER WRITER'S CONFERENCE

PMB 2717, 1420 NW Gilman Blvd, Suite 2, Issaquah, WA 98027. (425) 673-BOOK (2665). E-mail: staff@pnwa.org. Website: www.pnwa.org. Writer conference geared toward beginner, intermediate, advanced and professional levels. Meet agents and editors. Learn craft from renowned authors. Uncover new marketing secrets. PNWA's 54th Anniversary Conference was held July 30-August 2, 2009 at the Seattle Airport Hilton, Seattle, WA 98188. Annual conference held every July.

PIMA WRITERS' WORKSHOP

Pima College, 2202 W. Anklam Rd.Tucson AZ 85709-0170. (520)206-6084. Fax: (520)206-6020. E-mail: mfiles@pima.edu. **Director:** Meg Files. Writer conference geared toward beginner, intermediate and advanced levels. **Open to students.** The conference features presentations and writing exercises on writing and publishing stories for children and young adults, among other genres. Annual conference. Workshop held in May. Cost of workshop: $80; includes tuition, manuscript consultation. Write for more information.

ROBERT QUACKENBUSH'S CHILDREN'S BOOK WRITING AND ILLUSTRATING WORKSHOP

Studio address: 223 East 79th St.New York, NY 10075. Mailing address: 460 East 79th St.New York, NY 10075. (212)744-3822. Fax: (212)861-2761. E-mail: Rqstudios@aol.com. Website: www.rquackenbush.com. **Contact:** Robert Quackenbush. A four-day extensive workshop on writing and illustrating books for young readers held annually the second week in July at author/artist Robert Quackenbush's Manhattan studio for beginning and advance writers and illustrators. The focus of this workshop is on creating manuscripts and/or illustrated book dummies from start to finish for picture books and beginning reader chapter books ready to submit to publishers. Also covered is writing fiction and nonfiction for middle grades and young adults, if that is the attendee's interest. In addition, attention is given to review of illustrator's portfolios and new trends in illustration, including animation for films, are explored. During the four days, the workshop meets from 9 a.m-4 p.m. including one hour for lunch. Registration is limited to 10. Some writing and/or art supplies are available at the studio and there is an art store nearby, if needed. There are also electrical outlets for attendee's laptop computers. Cost of workshop is $750. A $100 non-refundable deposit is required tro enroll; balace is due three weeks prior the workshop. Attendees are responsible for arranging for their own hotel and meals. On request, suggestions are given for economical places to stay and eat. Recommended by Foder's Great American Learning Vacations, which says,

"This unique workshop, held annually since 1982, provides the opportunity to work with Robert Quackenbush, a prolific author and illustrator of children's books with more than 200 fiction and nonfiction books for young readers to his credit, including mysteries, biographies and songbooks. The workshop attracts both professional and beginning writers and artists of different ages from all over the world." Brochure available. Also inquire about fall, winter and spring workshops that meet once a week for ten weeks each that are offered to artists and writers in the New York area.

◘ SAGE HILL WRITING EXPERIENCE, Writing Children's & Young Adult Fiction Workshop

Box 1731, Saskatoon SK S7K 3S1 Canada. Phone: (306) 652-7395. Fax: (306)244-0255. E-mail: sage. hill@sasktel.net. Website: www.sagehillwriting.ca. **Executive Director:** Paula Jane Remlinger. Writer conference geared toward intermediate level. This program occurs every 3 years. Most recently in summer 2009. The Sage Hill Conference is annual. Conference held in July. Registration limited to 6 participants for this program, and to 37 for full program. Cost of conference approximately $ 1195; includes instruction, meals, accommodation. Require ms samples prior to registration. Write or visit the Web site for more information and workshop dates. Summer 2009 facilitator: Arthur Slade. Program dates: July 20-31, 2009.

SAN DIEGO STATE UNIVERSITY WRITERS' CONFERENCE

The College of Extended Studies, San Diego CA 92182-1920. (619)594-2517. Fax: (619)594-8566. E-mail: extended.std@sdsu.edu. Website: www.ces.sdsu.edu/writers **Conference Facilitator:**Rose Brown. Writer workshops geared toward beginner, intermediate and advanced levels. Emphasizes nonfiction, fiction, screenwriting, advanced novel writing; includes sessions specific to writing and illustrating for children. Workshops offered by children's editors, agents and writers. Annual workshops. Workshops held February 6-8 2009. Registration limited. Cost of workshops: approximately $350. Call for more information or visit Web site.

SAN FRANCISCO WRITERS CONFERENCE

1029 Jones St, San Francisco CA 94l09. (415)673-0939. Website: wwwsfwritersorg.

◘ SASKATCHEWAN FESTIVAL OF WORDS AND WORKSHOPS

217 Main Street, Moose Jaw SK S6H 0W1 Canada. (306)691-0557. Fax: (306)693-2994. E-mail: word.festival@sasktel.net. Website: www.festivalofwords.com. **Artistic Coordinator:** Donna Lee Howes. Writer workshops geared toward beginner and intermediate levels. **Open to students.** Readings that include a wide spectrum of genres—fiction, creative non-fiction, poetry, songwriting, screenwriting, playwriting, children's writing, panels, interviews and performances. Annual festival. Workshop held third weekend in July. Cost of workshop: $8/session—$125 for full festival pass. Write, e-mail, or visit Web site for more information.

SOCIETY OF SOUTHWESTERN AUTHORS' WRANGLING WITH WRITING

P.O. Box 30355, Tucson AZ 85751-0355. (520)296-5299. Fax: (520)296-0409. E-mail: wporter202@ aol.com. Website: www.ssa-az.org. **Wrangling With Writing Conference Director:** Penny Porter. 36 Writer workshops geared to all genres. "Limited scholarships available." Sessions include Writing and Publishing the Young Adult Novel, What Agents Want to See in a Children's Book, Writing Books for Young Children, Writing the Children's Story. One-on-one interviews with agents prescheduled prior to conference at an additional cost of $20 for a 15-minute meeting. "Three children's books agents interested in meeting with children's writers." Annual conferences held September 26-27, 2009. Registration limited to 400. Hotel rooms have data ports for internet access. Tentative cost: $350 nonmembers, $275 for SSA members; includes selections from all workshop sessions-and individual appointments with keynoters, authors, agents and teachers. Hotel accommodations are not included. "Write for more information. SSA has put on this conference for over 36 years now. "It's hands-on, it's friendly, and every year writers sell their manuscripts."

SOUTH COAST WRITERS CONFERENCE

P.O. Box 590, 29392 Ellensburg Ave.Gold Beach OR 97444. (541)247-2741. E-mail: scwc@socc.edu. **Coordinator:** Janet Pretti. Writer workshops geared toward beginner, intermediate levels. **Open to students.** Include fiction, nonfiction, nuts and bolts, poetry, feature writing, children's writing, publishing. Annual workshop. Workshop held Friday and Saturday of President's Day weekend in February. Registration limited to 25-30 students/workshop. Cost of workshop: $55 before January 31, $65 after; includes Friday night author's reading and book signing, Saturday conference, choice of 4 workshop sessions, Saturday evening writers' circle (networking and critique). Write or email for more information. "We also have four six-hour workshops Friday for more intensive writing exercises. The cost is an additional $40."

SOUTHEASTERN WRITERS ASSOCIATION—29TH ANNUAL WRITERS WORKSHOP

161 Woodstone, Athens GA 30605. E-mail: purple@southeasternwriters.com. Website: www. southeasternwriters.com. President: Lee Clevinger. **Open to all writers**. Contests with cash prizes. Instruction offered for novel and short fiction, nonfiction, children's books, humor, inspirational writing, and poetry. Manuscript deadline April 1st, includes evaluation conference with instructor(s). Agent and editors in residence. Annual 4-day workshop held in June. Cost of workshop: $395 for four days or $150-350 daily tuition. Accommodations: Offers overnight accommodations on workshop site. Visit Web site for more information and cost of overnight accommodations. E-mail or send SASE for brochure.

SOUTHWEST WRITERS CONFERENCES

3721 Morris NE, Suite A, Albuquerque NM 87111. (505)265-9485. Fax: (505)265-9483. E-mail: swwriters@juno.com. Website: www.southwestwriters.org. **Open to adults and students.** Writer workshops geared toward all genres at all levels of writing. Various aspects of writing covered, including children's. Mini-conference, periodic workshops, and writing classes. Examples from mini-conferences: Suzy Capozzi and Delacorte Press Editor Claudia Gable; Pitch, Publish and Promote conference with Literary Agent Katherine Sands, Mundania Press Publisher Bob Sanders and Literary Agent Jerry D. Simmons. Cracking the Code: Secrets of Writing and Selling Compelling Nonfiction conference featured literary agents Michael Larsen, Elizabeth Pomoda and Jeff Herman; Lee Gutkind, publisher; David Fryxell, editor; Lucinda Schroeder, criminologist/writer; and a panel of New Mexico publishers. Making a Good Script Great: All-day seminar with Dr. Linda Seger and other speakers. Dimension in Fiction and Non-fiction: All-day screenwriting conference. Prices vary, but usually $79-$179. Also offers annual and other contests, two monthly programs, writing classes, periodic workshops, monthly newsletter, critique service, e-lerts, Web site linking and various discount perks. See Web site for information.

SPLIT ROCK ARTS PROGRAM

Twin Cities Campus University of Minnesota, Twin Cities Campus, 360 Coffey Hall, 1420 Eckles Ave.St. Paul MN 55108-6084. (612)625-8100. Fax: (612)624-6210. E-mail: splitrockarts@umn.edu. Website: www.cce.umn.edu/splitrockarts. Workshops, including poetry, fiction, nonfiction, young-adult literature, and picture books, among others, are taught by renowned writers and illustrators. Past and current faculty includes Marcia Brown, Marion Dane Bauer, Candace Fleming, Jan Spivey Gilchrist, David Haynes, Jaqueline Kolosov, Gerald McDermott, Daniel Powers, Ilse Plume, Eric Rohmann, Lauren Stringer, Jane Resh Thomas, and others. Weeklong workshops run June through July. Registration limited to 16/workshop. Graduate/undergraduate credit, scholarships and on-campus accommodations available. Cost of workshop: $375-550 and up. Print and online catalogs are available in late February.

STEAMBOAT SPRINGS WRITERS CONFERENCE

P.O. Box 774284, Steamboat Springs CO 80477. (970)879-8138. E-mail: info@steamboats.com. Website: www.steamboatwriters.com. **Conference Director:** Susan de Wardt. Writers' workshops geared toward intermediate levels. **Open to students.** Some years offer topics specific to children's writing. Annual conference since 1982. Workshops will be held in July. Registration limited to 35. Cost of workshop: $50; includes 4 seminars and luncheon. Write, e-mail or see website for more information.

☑ SURREY INTERNATIONAL WRITER'S CONFERENCE

Guildford Continuing Education, 10707 146th St.Surrey BC U3R IT5 Canada. (604)589-2221. Fax: (604)588-9286. E-mail: contest@siwc.ca. Website: www.siwc.ca. **Coordinator:** kc dyer. Writer and illustrator workshops geared toward beginners, intermediate and advanced levels. Topics include marketing, children's agents and editors. Annual Conference. Conference held in October. Cost of conference includes all events for 3 days and most meals. Check our website for more information.

▦ SYDNEY CHILDREN'S WRITERS AND ILLUSTRATORS NETWORK

The Hughenden Boutique Hotel, Woollahra NSW 2025 Australia. (61)(2)9363-4863. Fax: (61) (2) 93620398. E-mail: admin@hughendenhotel.com.au. Website: www.hughendenhotel.com. au. **Contact:** Susanne Gervay. Writer and illustrator network geared toward professionals. Topics emphasized include networking, information and expertise about Australian children's publishing industry. Network held the first Wednesday of every month, except for January, commencing at 10:30 a.m. Registration limited to 30. Writing facilities available: internet and conference facilities. No Cost. As a prerequisite must be published in a commercial or have a book contract. E-mail for more information. "This is a professional meeting which aims at an interchange of ideas and information between professional children's authors and illustrators. Editors and other invited guests speak from time to time."

UMKC/WRITERS PLACE WRITERS WORKSHOPS

5300 Rockhill Rd.Kansas City MO 64110-2450. (816)235-2736. Fax: (816)235-5279. E-mail: seatons@ umkc.edu. Website: www.newletters.org/writingConferences.asp. **Contact:** Kathi Wittfeld. Mark Twain Workshop will be Monday, June 8 -26, 2009 in 104 Cockefair Hall and New Letters Weekend Writing Conference will be held on Friday, June 26-28, 2009 at Diastole. New Letters Writer's Conference and Mark Twain Writer's Workshop is geared toward intermediate, advanced and professional levels. Workshops open to students and community. Annual workshops. Workshops held in Summer. Cost of workshop varies. Write for more information.

☑ VANCOUVER INTERNATIONAL WRITERS & READERS FESTIVAL

1398 Cartwright St.Vancouver BC V6H 3R8 Canada. (604)681-6330. Fax: (604)681-8400. E-mail: viwf@writersfest.bc.ca. Website: www.writersfest.bc.ca. **Artistic Director:** Hal Wake. Annual literary festival. The Vancouver International Writers Festival strives to encourage an appreciation of literature and to promote literacy by providing a forum where writers and readers can interact. The VIWF produces special events and an annual Festival that feature writers from around the world. The Festival attracts over 12,000 readers of all ages to 70 events including Spreading the World events for grades K-12. Held in late October on Granville Island, located in the heart of Vancouver. All writers who participate are invited by the A.. The events are open to anyone who wishes to purchase tickets. Cost of events ranges from $10-30.

VIRGINIA FESTIVAL OF THE BOOK

145 Ednam Dr.Charlottesville VA 22903. (434)924-6890. Fax: (434)296-4714. E-mail: vabook@

virginia.edu. Website: www.vabook.org. **Program Director:** Nancy Damon. **Open to Students.** Readings, panel discussions, presentations and workshops by author, and book-related professionals for children and adults. Most programs are free and open to the public. Held March 18-22, 2009. See Web site for more information. Applications for 2010 Festival will be accepted beginning in May 2009.

WESLEYAN WRITERS CONFERENCE

Wesleyan University, Middletown CT 06459. (860)685-3604. Fax: (860)685-2441. E-mail: agreene@ wesleyan.edu. Website: www.wesleyan.edu/writers. **Director:** Anne Greene. Seminars, workshops, readings, ms advice; geared toward all levels. This conference is useful for writers interested in how to structure a story, novel, poem, nonfiction or mixed genre piece. Although we don't always offer classes in writing for children, the advice about plot, character, and story is useful for writers of any sort, no matter who their audience is." One of the nation's best-selling children's authors was a student here. Classes in the novel, short story, fiction techniques, poetry, journalism, literary nonfiction and mixed media work. Guest speakers, readings, lectures, workshops, and panels offer discussion of fiction, poetry, nonfiction, memoir, reviewing, editing and publishing. Individual ms consultations available. Conference held annually the third week in June. Length of each session: 5 days. Approximately 100 participants attend. Classrooms, meals, lodging, library, computer, and athletic facilities available on campus. Cost of conference 2008: tuition—$850, room—$175, meals-$275. Open to new writers, experienced writers and everyone interested in the writer's craft. To register, see the web site. Scholarships available.

WHIDBEY ISLAND WRITERS' CONFERENCE (10TH ANNUAL)

P.O. Box 1289, Langley WA 98260. (360)331-6714. E-mail: writers@whidbey.com. Website: www. writeonwhidbey.org. **Writers Contact:** Pam Owen, conference director. Three days focused on the tools you need to become a great writer. Learn from a variety of award-winning children's book authors and very experienced literary agents. Variety of preconference workshops and conference topics. Conference held February 27-March 1, 2009. Registration limited to 290. Cost: $395; early bird and member discounts available. Registration includes workshops, fireside chats, book-signing reception, various activities, and daily luncheons. The conference offers consultation appointments with editors and agents. Preconference workshops available on February 28. Registrants may reduce the cost of their conference by volunteering. See the Web site for more information. "The uniquely personal and friendly weekend is designed to be highly interactive."

WILLAMETTE WRITERS ANNUAL WRITERS CONFERENCE

9045 SW Barbur Blvd.Suite 5A, Portland OR 97219. (503)452-1592. Fax: (503)452-0372. E-mail: wilwrite@willamettewriters.com. Website: www.willamettewriters.com. **Office Manager:** Bill Johnson. Writer workshops geared toward all levels. Emphasizes all areas of writing, including children's and young adult. Opportunities to meet one-on-one with leading literary agents and editors. Workshops held in August. Cost of conference: $230-$430; includes membership.

TENNESSEE WILLIAMS/NEW ORLEANS LITERARY FESTIVAL

938 Lafayette St.Suite 514, New Orleans LA 70113. (504)581-1144. Fax: (504)523-3680. E-mail: info@tennesseewilliams.net. Website: www.tennesseewilliams.net. **Executive Director:** Paul J. Willis. Writer workshops geared toward beginner, intermediate, advanced, and professional levels. **Open to students.** Annual workshop. Workshop held around the third week in March (March 25-29, 2009). Master classes are limited in size to 100—all other panels offered have no cap. Cost of workshop: prices range from $15-35. Visit Web site for more information. "We are a literary festival and may occasionally offer panels/classes on children's writing and/or illustration, but this is not done every year."

WINTER POETRY & PROSE GETAWAY IN CAPE MAY

18 N. Richards Ave.Ventnor NJ 08406. (609)823-5076. E-mail: info@wintergetaway.com. Website: www.wintergetaway.com. **Director:** Peter E. Murphy. Estab. 1994. **Locations**: The Grand Hotel on the Oceanfront in Historic Cape May, NJ. Average attendance: 200 (10 or fewer participants in each workshop). **Features**: January 15-18, 2010. Thousands of people have enjoyed the Winter Poetry & Prose Getaway over the past 16 years, developing their craft as writers and making lifelong friends. The focus isn't on the award-winning faculty, it's on helping you improve and advance your skills. Our Writing for the Children's Market workshop explores different genres of juvenile literature and focuses on creating character, plot, setting, and dialogue. Writing exercises and prompts provide springboards for discussion and feedback. Previous faculty has included Pamela Curtis Swallow, Carol Plum-Ucci, and Joyce McDonald. This intensive weekend conference offers plenty to do beyond your workshop. Late afternoons allow you to choose from tutorials, panels, talks, walking on the beach, or you may continue working. Evenings include special activities, receptions, open mics, socializing, a bookstore on Sunday night and more.

WRITE-BY-THE-LAKE WRITER'S WORKSHOP & RETREAT

610 Langdon St.Room 621, Madison WI 53703. (608)262-3447. E-mail: cdesmet@dcs.wisc.edu. Website: www.cs.wisc.edu/lsa/writing. **Coordinator:** Christine DeSmet. Writer workshops geared toward beginner, intermediate, and advanced levels. **Open to students** (1-3 graduate credits available in English). "One week-long session is devoted to writing for children." Annual workshop. Workshop held the third week of June. Registration limited to 15. Writing facilities available: computer labs. Cost of workshop: $325 before May 18; $355 after May 18. Cost includes instruction, reception, and continental breakfast each day. E-mail for more information. "Brochure goes online every January for the following June."

▌▌WRITE! CANADA

698A Highpoint Ave, Waterloo, ON N2V 1G9 Canada. (519)886-4196. Fax: (905)471-6912. E-mail: info@thewordguild.com. Website: www.thewordguild.com. Estab. 1984. Annual conference for writers who are Christian. Hosted by The Word Guild, an association of Canadian writers and editors who are Christian. The Word Guild seeks to connect, develop, and promote its members. Keynote speaker, continuing classes, workshops, panels, editor appointments, reading times, critiques, and more. For all levels of writers from beginner to professional. Held in mid-June. This year: June 18-20, 2009 at Guelph Bible Conference Centre. Check web site for details.

WRITE ON THE SOUND WRITERS CONFERENCE

700 Main St.Edmonds WA 98020-3032. (425)771-0228. Fax: (425)771-0253. E-mail: wots@ci.edmonds.wa.us. Website: www.ci.edmonds.wa.us/ArtsCommission/wots.stm. **Conference Organizer:** Kris Gillespie. Writer workshops geared toward beginner, intermediate, advanced and professional levels with some sessions on writing for children. Annual conference held in Edmonds, on Puget Sound, on the first weekend in October with 2.5 days of workshops. Registration limited to 200. Cost of conference: approximately $112 for early registration, $137 for late registration; includes two days of workshops plus one ticket to keynote lecture. Brochures are mailed in August. Attendees must pre-register. Write, e-mail or call for brochure. Writing contest and manuscript critique appointments for conference participants.

WRITERS' LEAGUE OF TEXAS SUMMER WRITING ACADEMY AND WORKSHOPS

611 S. Congress Ave.Suite 130, Austin TX 78704. (512)499-8914. Fax: (512)499-0441. E-mail: wlt@writersleague.org. Website: www.writersleague.org. **Contact:** Kristy Bordine, Program and Membership Coordinator. "Classes and workshops provide practical advice and guidance on the craft of writing for writers at all stages of their career." Retreat: Annual Summer Writing Academy

in Alpine, TX, is a weeklong writing intensive with four tracks. Special presentations: "The Secrets of the Agents" series of workshops with visiting literary agents. Classes and Workshops: Topics: E-publishing; creative nonfiction; screenwriting; novel writing; short fiction; journaling; manuscript revision; memoir writing; poetry; essays; freelance writing; publicity; author/book web sites; and blogging. Instructors include Suzy Spencer, Karleen Koen, Scott Wiggerman, Diane Fanning, Marion Winik, Carol Dawson, Marsha Moyer, Susan Wade, Lila Guzman, Laurie Lynn Drummond, Jesse Sublett, David Wilkinson, John Pipkin, Ann McCutchan, and Dao Strom.

THE WRITERS' RETREAT

E-mail: info@writersretreat.com. Website: www.writersretreat.com. Contact: Micheline Cote. This is the only organization featuring a network of worldwide residential retreats opened year-round with on-site mentoring. The retreats cater to writers of all genres and offer on-site support such as mentoring, workshops, editing, and lodging. Residency rates vary between $475 and $1,000 per week depending on the location. There's no application process to stay at the writers retreat, first reserved basis. To start and operate a retreat in your area, contact The Writers' Retreat.

WRITERS RETREAT WORKSHOP

E-mail: wrw04@netscape.net (brochure and other information). Website: www.writersretreat workshop.com. **Director:** Jason Sitzes. Intensive workshops geared toward beginner, intermediate and advanced levels. Workshops are appropriate for writers of full length novels for children/YA. Also, for writers of all novels or narrative nonfiction. Annual workshop, held in Marydale Retreat Center, Erlanger KY in late May early June. Registration limited to 32: beginners and advanced. Writing facilities available: private rooms with desks. Cost includes tuition, food and lodging for nine nights, daily classes, writing space, time and assignments, consultation and instruction. One annual scholarship available: February deadline. Requirements: short synopsis required to determine appropriateness of novel for our nuts and bolts approach to getting the work in shape for publication. Write for more information. For complete updated details, visit www. writersretreatworkshop.com.

WRITE-TO-PUBLISH CONFERENCE

9118 W. Elmwood Dr.#1G, Niles IL 60714-5820. (847)296-3964. Fax: (847)296-0754. E-mail: lin@ writetopublish.com. Website: www.writetopublish.com. **Director:** Lin Johnson. Writer workshops geared toward all levels. **Open to students.** Conference is focused for the Christian market and includes classes on writing for children. Annual conference held in June. Cost of conference approximately: $450; includes conference and banquet. For information e-mail brochure@ writetopublish.com. Conference takes place at Wheaton College in the Chicago area.

WRITING WORKSHOP AT CASTLE HILL

1 Depot Road, P.O. Box 756, Truro MA 02666-0756. (508)349-7511. Fax: (508)349-7513. E-mail: castlehill@gis.net. Website: www.castlehill.org **Director:** Cherie Mittenthal. Poetry, Fiction, Memoir workshops geared toward intermediate and advanced levels. **Open to students.** Workshops by Espada, Doty, Hoagland, Feldman, Unger, Lerman, Laux, Seligson, Loomis, Campion, Millar, Lisicky, Bernays, Kaplan and more! Workshop are week-long and begin June 23 through August 28th. Registration limited to 10-12. Writing/art facilities available: classroom space. Cost of workshop: $325; includes week long workshop and one-on-one conference with teacher. Write for more information.

Contests, Awards & Grants

Publication is not the only way to get your work recognized. Contests and awards can also be great ways to gain recognition in the industry. Grants, offered by organizations like SCBWI, offer monetary recognition to writers, giving them more financial freedom as they work on projects.

When considering contests or applying for grants, be sure to study guidelines and requirements. Regard entry deadlines as gospel and follow the rules to the letter.

Note that some contests require nominations. For published authors and illustrators, competitions provide an excellent way to promote your work. Your publisher may not be aware of local competitions such as state-sponsored awards—if your book is eligible, have the appropriate person at your publishing company nominate or enter your work for consideration.

To select potential contests and grants, read through the listings that interest you, then send for more information about the types of written or illustrated material considered and other important details. A number of contests offer information through Web sites given in their listings.

If you are interested in knowing who has received certain awards in the past, check your local library or bookstores or consult *Children's Books: Awards & Honors*, compiled and edited by the Children's Book Council (www.cbcbooks.org). Many bookstores have special sections for books that are Caldecott and Newbery Medal winners. Visit the American Library Association website, www.ala.org, for information on the Caldecott, Newbery, Coretta Scott King and Printz Awards. Visit www.hbook.com for information on The Boston Globe-Horn Book Award. Visit www.scbwi.org/awards.htm for information on The Golden Kite Award.

ACADEMY OF CHILDREN'S WRITERS' WRITING FOR CHILDREN COMPETITION

Academy of Children's Writers, P.O. Box 95, Huntington Cambridgeshire PE28 5RL England. 01487 832752. Fax: 01487 832752. E-mail: enquiries@childrens-writers.co.uk **Contact:** Roger Dewar, contest director. Annual contest for the best unpublished short story writer for children. **Deadline:** March 31.Visit Web site for guidelines: www.chidrens-writers.co.uk. **Charges $10 (US) Bill;** Prize: 1st Prize: $4,000; 2nd Prize: $600; 3rd Prize: $400. Judged by a panel appointed by the Academy of Children's Writers. Open to any writer.

AIM MAGAZINE SHORT STORY CONTEST

P. O. Box 390, Milton, WA 98354-0390. (773)874-6184. **Contest Director:** Ruth Apilado, associate editor. Annual contest. **Open to students.** Estab. 1983. Purpose of contest: "We solicit stories with lasting social significance proving that people from different racial/ethnic backgrounds are more alike than they are different." Unpublished submissions only. Deadline for entries: August 15. SASE for contest rules and entry forms. SASE for return of work. No entry fee. Awards $100. Judging by editors. Contest open to everyone. Winning entry published in fall issue of AIM. Subscription rate: $20/year. Single copy: $5.

⚡ ALCUIN CITATION AWARD

The Alcuin Society, P.O. Box 3216, Vancouver BC V6B 3X8 Canada. (604)732-5403. E-mail: awards@alcuinsociety.com. Website: www.alcuinsociety.com /awards. Annual award. Estab. 1981. Purpose of contest: Alcuin Citations are awarded annually for excellence in Canadian book design. Previously published submissions from the year prior to the Award's Call for Entries (i.e.2005 awards went to books published in 2004). Submissions made by the publisher, author or designer. Deadline for entries: mid-March. Entry fee is $25/book for Society members; $30/book for non-members; include cheque and entry form with book; downloadable entry form available at web site. Awards certificate. Winning books are exhibited nationally, and internationally at the Frankfurt and Leipzig Book Fairs, and are Canada's entries in the international competition in Leipzig, "Book Design from all over the World" in the following Spring. Judging by professionals and those experienced in the field of book design. Requirements for entrants: Winners are selected from books designed and published in Canada. Awards are presented annually at an appropriate ceremonies held in early June each year.

AMERICA & ME ESSAY CONTEST

Farm Bureau Insurance, P.O. Box 30400, 7373 W. Saginaw, Lansing MI 48909-7900. (517)323-7000. Fax: (517)323-6615. E-mail: lfedewa@fbinsmi.com. Website: www.farmbureauinsurance-mi.com. **Contest Coordinator:** Lisa Fedewa. Annual contest. **Open to students only.** Estab. 1968. Purpose of the contest: to give Michigan 8th graders the opportunity to express their thoughts/feelings on America and their roles in America. Unpublished submissions only. Deadline for entries: mid-November. SASE for contest rules and entry forms. "We have a school mailing list. Any school located in Michigan is eligible to participate." Entries not returned. No entry fee. Cash awards savings bonds and plaques for state top ten ($1,000), certificates and plaques for top 3 winners from each school. Each school may submit up to 10 essays for judging. Judging by home office employee volunteers. Requirements for entrants: participants must work through their schools or our agents' sponsoring schools. No individual submissions will be accepted. Top ten essays and excerpts from other essays are published in booklet form following the contest. State capitol/ schools receive copies."

AMERICAN ASSOCIATION OF UNIVERSITY WOMEN, NORTH CAROLINA DIVISION, AWARD IN JUVENILE LITERATURE

North Carolina Literary and Historical Association, 4610 Mail Service Center, Raleigh NC 27699-4610. (919)807-7290. Fax: (919)733-8807. E-mail: michael.hill@ncmail.net. **Award Coordinator:** Mr. Michael Hill. Annual award. Purpose of award: to recognize the year's best work of juvenile literature by a North Carolina resident. Book must be published during the year ending June 30. Submissions made by author, author's agent or publisher. Deadline for entries: July 15. SASE for contest rules. Awards a cup to the winner and winner's name inscribed on a plaque displayed within the North Carolina Office of Archives and History. Judging by Board of Award selected by sponsoring organization. Requirements for entrants: Author must have maintained either legal residence or actual physical residence, or a combination of both, in the state of North Carolina for three years immediately preceding the close of the contest period. Only published work (books) eligible.

AMERICAS AWARD

CLASP Committee on Teaching and Outreach, c/o Center for Latin American and Caribbean Studies, P.O. Box 413, Milwaukee WI 53201. (414)229-5986. Fax: (414)229-2879. E-mail: jkline@uwm.edu. Web site:http://www4.uwm.edu/clacs/aa/index.cfm. **Coordinator:** Julie Kline. Annual award. Estab. 1993. Purpose of contest: Up to two awards are given each spring in recognition of U.S. published works (from the previous year) of fiction, poetry, folklore or selected nonfiction (from picture books to works for young adults) in English or Spanish which authentically and engagingly relate to Latin America, the Caribbean, or to Latinos in the United States. By combining both and linking the "Americas," the intent is to reach beyond geographic borders, as well as multicultural-international boundaries, focusing instead upon cultural heritages within the hemisphere. Previously published submissions only. Submissions open to anyone with an interest in the theme of the award. Deadline for entries: January 15. Visit Web site or send SASE for contest rules and any committee changes. Awards $500 cash prize, plaque and a formal presentation at the Library of Congress, Washington DC. Judging by a review committee consisting of individuals in teaching, library work, outreach and children's literature specialists.

HANS CHRISTIAN ANDERSEN AWARD

IBBY International Board on Books for Young People, Nonnenweg 12, Postfach CH-4003 Basel Switzerland. (004161)272 29 17. Fax: (004161)272 27 57. E-mail: ibby@ibby.org. Website: www. ibby.org. **Director:** Liz Page. Award offered every two years. Purpose of award: A Hans Christian Andersen Medal shall be awarded every two years by the International Board on Books for Young People (IBBY) to an author and to an illustrator, living at the time of the nomination, who by the outstanding value of their work are judged to have made a lasting contribution to literature for children and young people. The complete works of the author and of the illustrator will be taken into consideration in awarding the medal, which will be accompanied by a diploma. Published work only. Candidates are nominated by National Sections of IBBY in good standing.The Hans Christian Andersen Award, is the highest international recognition given to an author and an illustrator of children's books. The Author's Award has been given since 1956, the Illustrator's Award since 1966. Her Majesty Queen Margrethe of Denmark is the Patron of the Hans Christian Andersen Awards. The Hans Christian Andersen Jury judges the books submitted for medals according to literary and artistic criteria. The awards are presented at the biennial congresses of IBBY.

ATLANTIC WRITING COMPETITION

Writer's Federation of Nova Scotia, 1113 Marginal Rd.Halifax NS B3H 4P7 Canada. (902)423-8116. Fax: (902)422-0881. E-mail: talk@writers.ns.ca. Website: www.writers.ns.ca/awc.html. Annual contest. Purpose is to encourage emerging writers in Atlantic Canada to explore their talents by sending unpublished work to any of five categories: novel, short story, poetry, writing for younger children, writing for juvenile/young adult. Unpublished submissions only. Only open to residents of Atlantic Canada who are unpublished in category they enter. Visit Web site for more information.

BAKER'S PLAYS HIGH SCHOOL PLAYWRITING CONTEST

Baker's Plays, 45 W. 25th St.New York NY 10010. E-mail: publications@bakersplays.com Website: www.bakersplays.com. **Contest Director:** Roxanne Heinze-Bradshaw. **Open to any high school students.** Annual contest. Estab. 1990. Purpose of the contest: to encourage playwrights at the high school level and to ensure the future of American theater. Unpublished submissions only. Postmark deadline: January 30. Notification: May. SASE for contest rules and entry forms. No entry fee. Awards $500 to the first place playwright with publication by Baker's Plays; $250 to the second place playwright with an honorable mention; and $100 to the third place playwright with an honorable mention in the series. Judged anonymously. Plays must be accompanied by the signature of a sponsoring high school drama or English teacher, and it is recommended that the play receive a production or a public reading prior to the submission. To ensure return of manuscripts, please include SASE. Teachers must not submit student's work. The winning work will be listed in the Baker's Plays Catalogue, which is distributed to 50,000 prospective producing organizations.

• Baker's Plays is now encouraging submission via e-mail at publications@bakersplay.com.

JOHN AND PATRICIA BEATTY AWARD

California Library Association, 717 20th Street, Suite 200, Sacramento CA 95811. (916)447-8541. Fax: (916)447-8394. E-mail: info@cla-net.org. Website: www.cla-net.org. **Executive Director:** Susan Negreen. Annual award. Estab. 1987. Purpose of award: "The purpose of the John and Patricia Beatty Award is to encourage the writing of quality children's books highlighting California, its culture, heritage and/or future." Previously published submissions only. Submissions made by the author, author's agent or review copies sent by publisher. The award is given to the author of a children's book published the preceding year. Deadline for entries: Submissions may be made January-December. Contact CLA Executive Director who will liaison with Beatty Award Committee. Awards cash prize of $500 and an engraved plaque. Judging by a 5-member selection committee appointed by the president of the California Library Association. Requirements for entrants: "Any children's or young adult book set in California and published in the U.S. during the calendar year preceding the presentation of the award is eligible for consideration. This includes works of fiction as well as nonfiction for children and young people of all ages. Reprints and compilations are not eligible. The California setting must be depicted authentically and must serve as an integral focus for the book." Winning selection is announced through press release during National Library Week in April. Author is presented with award at annual California Library Association Conference in November.

[N] [C] THE GEOFFREY BILSON AWARD FOR HISTORICAL FICTION FOR YOUNG PEOPLE

The Canadian Children's Book Centre, 40 Orchard View Blvd.Suite 101, Toronto ON M4R 1B9 Canada. (416)975-0010. Fax: (416)975-8970. E-mail: naseem@bookcentre.ca. Website: www.bookcentre.ca. **Contact:** Naseem Hrab, librarian. Created in Geoffrey Bilson's memory in 1988. Offered annually for a previously published "outstanding work of historical fiction for young people by a Canadian author." Open to Canadian citizens and residents of Canada for at least 2 years. Deadline: December 15. Prize: $5,000. Judged by a jury selected by the Canadian Children's Book Centre.

THE IRMA S. AND JAMES H. BLACK BOOK AWARD

Bank Street College of Education, New York NY 10025-1898. (212)875-4458. Fax: (212)875-4558. E-mail: kfreda@bankstreet.edu. Website: http://streetcat.bnkst.edu/html/isb.html. **Contact:** Kristin Freda. Annual award. Estab. 1972. Purpose of award: "The award is given each spring for a book for young children, published in the previous year, for excellence of both text and illustrations." Entries must have been published during the previous calendar year (between January '08 and December '08 for 2009 award). Deadline for entries: mid-December. "Publishers submit books to us by sending them here to me at the Bank Street Library. Authors may ask their publishers to submit their books. Out of these, three to five books are chosen by a committee of older children and children's literature professionals. These books are then presented to children in selected first, second, and third grade classes here and at a number of other cooperating schools. These children are the final judges who pick the actual award winner. A scroll (one each for the author and illustrator, if they're different) with the recipient's name and a gold seal designed by Maurice Sendak are awarded in May."

WALDO M. AND GRACE C. BONDERMAN BIENNIAL NATIONAL YOUTH THEATRE PLAYWRITING COMPETITION AND DEVELOPMENT WORKSHOP AND SYMPOSIUM

Bonderman Youth Theatre Playwriting Workshop, Indiana Repertory Theatre, 140 West Washington St.Indianapolis, IN 46204. E-mail: bonderma@iupui.edu. Website: www.Irtlive.com. **Artistic Director:** Dorothy Webb. Open to professional and non-professional American playwrights. Next deadline, (Tentative) August 15, 2010. Established 1985. Entries not returned. No entry fee. Judging by professional theatre directors, teachers, and artists. Requirements for entrants: Contest opens only to American playwrights with plays not previously produced professionally and not currently in development with a theatre.

N ⊕ BOOKTRUST EARLY YEARS AWARDS

Booktrust, Book House, 45 E. Hill, Wandsworth, London SW18 2QZ United Kingdom. Fax: (00 44)20 8516 2978. E-mail: tarryn@booktrust.org.uk. Website: www.booktrust.org.uk. **Contact:** Tarryn McKay, and Megan Farr. The Booktrust Early Years Awards were initially established in 1999 and are awarded annually. The awards are given to the best books, published between September 1 and the following August 31, in the opinion of the judges in each category. The categories are: Baby Book Award, Pre-School Award, and Best Emerging New Illustrator Award. Authors and illustrators must be of British nationality, or other nationals who have been residents in the British Isles for at least 10 years. Books can be any format. Deadline: June. Prize: £2,000 and a crystal award to each winner (to be split between author/illustrator if necessary). In addition, the publisher receives a crystal award naming them as "The Booktrust Early Years Awards Publisher of the Year."

THE BOSTON GLOBE-HORN BOOK AWARDS

The Boston Globe & The Horn Book, Inc.The Horn Book, 56 Roland St.Suite 200, Boston MA 02129. (617)628-0225. Fax: (617)628-0882. E-mail: info@hbook.com. Website: www.hbook.com/awards/bghb/submissions_bghb.asp. Annual award. Estab. 1967. Purpose of award: To reward literary excellence in children's and young adult books. Awards are for picture books, nonfiction, fiction and poetry. Up to two honor books may be chosen for each category. Books must be published between June 1, 2008 and May 31, 2009. Deadline for entries: May 31, 2009. Textboks, e-books, and audiobooks will not be considered, nor will manuscripts. Books should be submitted by publishers, although the judges reserve the right to honor any eligible book. Award winners receive $500 and silver engraved bowl, honor book winners receive a silver engraved plate. Judging by 3 judges involved in children's book field. The Horn Book Magazine publishes speeches given at awards ceremonies. The book must have been published in the U.S.

ANN ARLYS BOWLER POETRY CONTEST

Bowler Poetry Contest, Read Magazine, Weekly Reader Corporation, 1 Reader's Digest Rd.Pleasantville, NY 10570. Contest infromation and entry forms at: www.weeklyreader.com/read. **Open to students.** Annual contest. Estab. 1988. Purpose of the contest: to reward young-adult poets (grades 6-12). Unpublished submissions only. Submissions. Entry form must include signature of teacher, parent or guardian, and student verifying originality. Maximum number of submissions per student: 3 poems. Deadline for entries: December 31. No entry fee. Awards 6 winners $100 each, medal of honor and publication in Read. Judging by Read and Weekly Reader editors and the Bowler family.

⊠ ANN CONNOR BRIMER AWARD

Nova Scotia Library Association, P.O. Box 36036, Halifax NS B3J 3S9 Canada. (902)490-5875. Fax: (902)490-5893. Website: http://nsla.ns.ca/aboutnsla/brimeraward.html. **Award Director:** Heather MacKenzie. Annual award. Estab. 1991. Purpose of the contest: to recognize excellence in writing. Given to an author of a children's book who resides in Atlantic Canada. Previously published submissions only. Submissions made by the author's agent or nominated by a person or group of people. Must be published in previous year. Deadline for entries: October 15. SASE for contest rules and entry forms. No entry fee. Awards $1,000 and framed certificate. Judging by a selection committee. Requirements for entrants: Book must be intended for use up to age 15; in print and readily available; fiction or nonfiction except textbooks.

BUCKEYE CHILDREN'S BOOK AWARD

Website: www.bcbookaward.info. **President:** Christine Watters. Correspondence should be sent to Christine Watters via the Web site. **Open to Ohio students.** Award offered every year. Estab. 1981. Purpose of the award: The Buckeye Childerens Book Award Program was designed to encourage children to read literatrue critically, to promote teacher and librarian involvement in children's literature programs, and to commend authors of such literature, as well as to promote the use of libraries. Nominees are submitted by students between January 1 and March 15. Votes are cast between September 1 and November 10.

BYLINE MAGAZINE CONTESTS

P.O. Box 111, Albion, NY 14411. E-mail: robbi@bylinemag.com. Website: www.bylinemag.com. **Contest Director:** Robbi Hess. Purpose of contest: ByLine runs 4 contests a month on many topics to encourage and motivate writers. Past topics include first chapter of a novel, new talent short story, juvenile fiction, nonfiction, personal essay, general short stories, various poetry contests, etc. Send SASE for contest flier with topic list and rules, or see Web site. Unpublished submissions only. Submissions made by the author. "On occasion we will print winning submissions." Entry fee is $3-5. Awards cash prizes for first, second and third place. Amounts vary. Judging by qualified writers or editors. List of winners will appear in magazine.

RANDOLPH CALDECOTT MEDAL

Association for Library Service to Children, Division of the American Library Association, 50 E. Huron, Chicago IL 60611. (312)280-2163. E-mail: alsc@ala.org. Website: http://www.ala.org/ala/mgrps/divs/alsc/awardsgrants/bookmedia/caldecottmedal/caldecottapp/caldecottapplication.cfm. **Executive Director:** Diane Foote. Annual award. Estab. 1938. Purpose of the award: to honor the artist of the most outstanding picture book for children published in the U.S. (Illustrator must be U.S. citizen or resident.) Must be published year preceding award. Deadline for entries: December 31. SASE for award rules. Entries not returned. No entry fee. "Medal given at ALA Annual Conference during the Newbery/Caldecott Banquet."

CALIFORNIA YOUNG PLAYWRIGHTS CONTEST

Playwrights Project, 2356 Moore Street, #204, San Diego CA 92110. (619)239-8222. Fax: (619)239-8225. E-mail: write@playwrightsproject.org. Website: www.playwrightsproject.org. **Managing Director:** Cecelia Kouma. **Open to Californians under age 19.** Annual contest. Estab. 1985. "Our organization and the contest is designed to nurture promising young writers. We hope to develop playwrights and audiences for live theater. We also teach playwriting." Submissions required to be unpublished and not produced professionally. Submissions made by the author. Deadline for entries: June 1. SASE for contest rules and entry form. No entry fee. Award is professional productions of 8-10 short plays each year, participation of the writers in the entire production process, with a royalty awarded. Judging by professionals in the theater community, a committee of 5-7; changes somewhat each year. Works performed in San Diego at a professional theatre. Writers submitting scripts of 10 or more pages receive a detailed script evaluation letter upon request.

CALLIOPE FICTION CONTEST

Writers' Specialized Interest Group (SIG) of American Mensa, Ltd.2506 SE Bitterbrush Dr.Madras, OR 97741. E-mail: cynthia@theriver.com. Website: www.calliopewriters.org. **Fiction Editor:** Sandy Raschke. **Open to students.** Annual contest. Estab. 1991. Purpose of contest: "To promote good writing and opportunities for getting published. To give our member/subscribers and others an entertaining and fun exercise in writing." Unpublished submissions only (all genres, no violence, profanity or extreme horror). Submissions made by author. Deadline for entries: changes annually but usually around September 15. Entry fee is $5 for nonsubscribers; subscribers get first entry fee. Awards small amount of cash (up to $75 for 1st place, to $10 for 3rd), certificates, full or mini-subscriptions to Calliope and various premiums and books, depending on donations. All winners are published in subsequent issues of Calliope. Judging by fiction editor, with concurrence of other editors, if needed. Requirements for entrants: winners must retain sufficient rights to have their stories published in the January/February issue, or their entries will be disqualified; one-time rights. Open to all writers. No special considerations—other than following the guidelines. Contest theme, due dates and sometimes entry fees change annually. Always send SASE for complete rules; available after March 15 each year. Sample copies with prior winners are available for $3.

⊞ CANADA COUNCIL GOVERNOR GENERAL'S LITERARY AWARDS

350 Albert St.Ottawa ON K1P 5V8 Canada. (613)566-4410, ext. 5573. Fax: (613)566-4410. E-mail: diane.miljours@canadacouncil.ca. **Program Officer, Writing and Publishing Section:** Diane Miljours. Annual award. Estab. 1937. Purpose of award: given to the best English-language and the best French-language work in each of the seven categories of Fiction, Literary Non-fiction, Poetry, Drama, Children's Literature (text), Children's Literature (illustration) and Translation. Books must be first-edition trade books that have been written, translated or illustrated by Canadian citizens or permanent residents of Canada. In the case of Translation, the original work written in English or French, must also be a Canadian-authored title. English titles must be published between September 1, 2008 and September 30, 2009. Books must be submitted by publishers. Books must reach the Canada Council for the Arts no later than August 7, 2009. The deadlines are final; no bound proofs or books that miss the applicable deadlines will be given to the peer assessment committees. The awards ceremony is scheduled mid-November. Amount of award: $25,000 to winning authors; $1,000 to non-winning finalists.

⊞ SANDRA CARON YOUNG ADULT POETRY PRIZE

National League of American Pen Women, Nob Hill, San Francisco Branch, 1544 Sweetwood Dr.Broadmoor Vlg.Colma CA 94015-2029. E-mail: pennobhill@aol.com. Website: www. soulmakingcontest.us. **Contact:** Eileen Malone. **Open to students.** Three poems/entry; one poem/ page; one-page poems only from poets in grades 9-12 or equivalent. Annually. Deadline: November 30. Guidelines for SASE. Charges $5/entry (make checks payable to NLAPW, Nob Hill Branch). Prize: 1st Place: $100; 2nd Place: $50; 3rd Place: $25. Open to any writer in grade 9-12.

⊞ CHILDREN'S AFRICANA BOOK AWARD

Outreach Council of the African Studies Association, c/o Rutgers University, 132 George St.New Brunswick NJ 08901. (732)932-8173. Fax: (732)932-3394. Website: www.africanstudies.org. Administered by Africa Access, P.O. Box 8028, Silver Spring MD 20910. (301)587-3040. Fax: (301)562-5244. E-mail: africaaccess@aol.com. Website: www.africaaccessreview.org. **Chairperson**: Brenda Randolph. Annually. Estab. 1991. Purpose of contest: "The Children's Africana Book Awards are presented annually to the authors and illustrators of the best books on Africa for children and young people published or republished in the U.S. The awards were created by the Outreach Council of the African Studies Association (ASA) to dispel stereotypes and encourage the publication and use of accurate, balanced children's materials about Africa. The awards are presented in 2 categories: Young Children and Older Readers. Since 1991, 51 books have been recognized." Entries must have been published in the calendar year previous to the award. No entry fee. Awards plaque, announcement each spring, reviews published at Africa Access Review website and in Sankofa: Journal of African Children's & Young Adult Literature. Judging by Outreach Council of ASA and children's literature scholars. "Work submitted for awards must be suitable for children ages 4-18; a significant portion of books' content must be about Africa; must by copyrighted in the calendar year prior to award year; must be published or republished in the US."

CHILDREN'S WRITER WRITING CONTESTS

93 Long Ridge Rd.West Redding CT 06896-1124. (203)792-8600. Fax: (203)792-8406. Website: www. childrenswriter.com. Contest offered twice per year by Children's Writer, the monthly newsletter of writing and publishing trends. Purpose of the award: To promote higher quality children's literature. "Each contest has its own theme. Any original unpublished piece, not accepted by any

publisher at the time of submission, is eligible." Submissions made by the author. Deadline for entries: Last weekday in February and October. "We charge a $10 entry fee for nonsubscribers only, which is applicable against a subscription to Children's Writer Awards: 1st place—$250 or $500, a certificate and publication in Children's Writer; 2nd place—$100 or $250, and certificate; 3rd-5th places—$50 or $100 and certificates. To obtain the rules and theme for the current contest go to the website and click on "Writing Contests," or send a SASE to Children's Writer at the above address. Put "Contest Request" in the lower left of your envelope. Judging by a panel of 4 selected from the staff of the Institute of Children's Literature. "We acquire First North American Serial Rights (to print the winner in Children's Writer), after which all rights revert to author." Open to any writer. Entries are judged on age targeting, originality, quality of writing and, for nonfiction, how well the information is conveyed and accuracy. "Submit clear photocopies only, not originals; submission will not be returned. Manuscripts should be typed double-spaced. No pieces containing violence or derogatory, racist or sexist language or situations will be accepted, at the sole discretion of the judges."

CHRISTIAN BOOK AWARDS

Evangelical Christian Publishers Assocation, 9633 South 48th Street, Suite 140, Phoenix, AZ 85044. (480)966-3998. Fax: (480)966-1944. E-mail: info@ecpa.org. Website: www.ecpa.org. **President:** Mark W. Kuyper. Annual award. Established 1978. Categories include Children & Youth. " All entries must be evangelical in nature and cannot be contrary to ECPA's Statement of Faith (stated in official rules)." Deadline for entry: January (see Web site for specific date). Guidelines available on Web site in October. " The work must be submitted by an ECPA member publisher." Awards a Christian Book Award plaque.

COLORADO BOOK AWARDS

1490 Lafayette Street, Suite 101, Denver CO 80218. (303)894-7951, ext. 21. Fax: (303) 864-9361, E-mail: bookawardinfo@coloradohumanities.org. Website: www.ceh.org. Annual award established 1993. Previously published submissions only. Submissions are made by the author, author's agent, nominated by a person or group of people. Requires Colorado residency by author, illustrator, photographer, editor, or other major contributor. Deadline for entries: January 31, 2009. Entry fee is $50. Awards $250 and plaque. Judging by a panel of literary agents, booksellers and librarians. See Web site for complete contest guidelines and entry form.

THE COMMONWEALTH CLUB'S BOOK AWARDS CONTEST

The Commonwealth Club of California, 595 Market St.San Francisco CA 94105. (415)597-6703. Fax: (415)597-6729. E-mail: bookawards@commonwealthclub.org. Website: www.commonwealthclub. org/features/cabookawards. **Contact:** Gina Baleria. Annual contest. Estab. 1932. Purpose of contest: the encouragement and production of literature in California. Juvenile and Young Adult categories included. Previously published submissions; must be published from January 1 to December 31, no self published or on-demand entries. Deadline for entries: December 18, 2009. SASE for contest rules and entry forms. No entry fee. Awards gold and silver medals. Judging by the Book Awards Jury. The contest is only open to California writers/illustrators (must have been resident of California when ms was accepted for publication). The award winners will be honored at the Annual Book Awards Program on June 3, 2010 at 6pm. Winning entries are displayed at awards program and advertised in newsletter.

CRICKET LEAGUE

Cricket magazine, P.O. Box 300, 315 Fifth St.Peru IL 61354. mail@cricketmagkids.com. Website: ww.cricketmagkids.com/league. Address entries to: Cricket League. Open to students. Nine contests per year. Estab. 1973. " The purpose of Cricket League contests is to encourage creativity and give young people an opportunity to express themselves in writing, drawing, painting or photography.

There is a contest in each issue. Possible categories include story, poetry, art, or photography. Each contest relates to a specific theme described on each Cricket issue's Cricket League page and on the Web site. Signature verifying originality, age and address of entrant and permission to publish required. Entries which do not relate to the current month's theme cannot be considered." Unpublished submissions only. Deadline for entries: the 25th of the month. Cricket League rules, contest theme, and submission deadline information can be found in the current issue of Cricket and via Web site. " We prefer that children who enter the contests subscribe to the magazine or that they read Cricket in their school or library." No entry fee. Awards certificate suitable for framing and children's books or art/writing supplies. Judging by Cricket editors. Obtains right to print prizewinning entries in magazine and/or on the Web site. Refer to contest rules in current Cricket issue. Winning entries are published on the Cricket League pages in a subsequent Cricket magazine. Current theme, rules, and prizewinning entries also posted on the Web site.\ltrpar

DELACORTE DELL YEARLING CONTEST FOR A FIRST MIDDLE-GRADE NOVEL

Delacorte Press, Random House, Inc.1745 Broadway, 9th Floor, New York NY 10019. Estab. 1992. (212)782-9000 Website: www.randomhouse.com. Annual award. Purpose of the award: to encourage the writing of fiction for children ages 9-12, either contemporary or historical; to encourage unpublished writers in the field of middle grade fiction. Unpublished submissions only. No simultaneous submissions. Length: between 96-160 pages. Submissions made by author only. Must not be out with an agent. Entries should be postmarked between April 1 and June 30. Letter sized SASE for notification. Because of new postal regulations no manuscripts can be returned. No entry fee. Awards a $1,500 cash prize plus a hardcover and paperback book contract with a $7,500 advance against a royalties. Judging by Delacorte Press Books for Young Readers editorial staff. Open to U.S. and Canadian writers who have not previously published a novel for middle-grade readers (ages 9-12).

DELACORTE PRESS CONTEST FOR A FIRST YOUNG ADULT NOVEL

Delacorte Press, Books for Young Readers Department, 1745 Broadway, 9th Floor, New York NY 10019. Website: www.randomhouse.com/kids/writingcontests. Annual award. Estab. 1982. Purpose of award: to encourage the writing of contemporary young adult fiction (for readers ages 12-18). Previously unpublished submissions only. Manuscripts sent to Delacorte Press may not be submitted to other publishers or literary agents while under consideration for the prize. Entries must be submitted between October 1 and December 31. Length: between 100-224 pages. No entry fee. Awards a $1,500 cash prize and a $7,500 advance against royalties for world rights on a hardcover and paperback book contract. Works published in an upcoming Delacorte Press, an imprint of Random House, Inc.Books for Young Readers list. Judged by the editors of the Books for Young Readers Department of Delacorte Press. Requirements for entrants: The writer must be American or Canadian and must not have previously published a young adult novel but may have published anything else. Foreign-language mss and translations and mss submitted to a previous Delacorte Press are not eligible. Send SASE for notification. Guidelines are also available on our Web site.

MARGARET A. EDWARDS AWARD

50 East Huron St.Chicago IL 60611-2795. (312)280-4390 or (800)545-2433. Fax: (312)280-5276. E-mail: yalsa@ala.org. Website: www.ala.org/yalsa/edwards. Annual award administered by the Young Adult Library Services Association (YALSA) of the American Library Association (ALA) and sponsored by School Library Journal magazine. Purpose of award: ALA's Young Adult Library Services Association (YALSA), recognizes an author and a specific work or works for significant and lasting contribution to young adult literature. Submissions must be previously published no less than five years prior to the first meeting of the current Margaret A. Edwards Award Committee at Midwinter Meeting. Nomination form is available on the YALSA Web site. No entry fee. Judging

by members of the Young Adult Library Services Association. Deadline for entry: December 1. "The award will be given annually to an author whose book or books, over a period of time, have been accepted by young adults as an authentic voice that continues to illuminate their experiences and emotions, giving insight into their lives. The book or books should enable them to understand themselves, the world in which they live, and their relationship with others and with society. The book or books must be in print at the time of the nomination."

DOROTHY CANFIELD FISHER CHILDREN'S BOOK AWARD

Vermont Department of Libraries, Northeast Regional Library, 109 State St.,Montpelier VT 05609. (802)828-6954. Fax: (802)828-2199. E-mail: ggreene@dol.state.vt.us. Website: www.cfaward.org. **Chair:** Steve Madden. Annual award. Estab. 1957. Purpose of the award: to encourage Vermont children to become enthusiastic and discriminating readers by providing them with books of good quality by living American or Canadian authors published in the current year. Deadline for entries: December of year book was published. SASE for award rules and entry forms or e-mail. No entry fee. Awards a scroll presented to the winning author at an award ceremony. Judging is by the children grades 4-8. They vote for their favorite book. Requirements for entrants: "Titles must be original work, published in the United States, and be appropriate to children in grades 4 through 8. The book must be copyrighted in the current year. It must be written by an American author living in the U.S. or Canda, or a Canadian author living in Canada or the U.S."

N ☑ THE NORMA FLECK AWARD FOR CANADIAN CHILDREN'S NONFICTION

The Canadian Children's Book Centre, 40 Orchard View Blvd.Suite 101, Toronto ON M4R 1B9 Canada. (416)975-0010. Fax: (416)975-8970. E-mail: info@bookcentre.ca. Website: www. bookcentre.ca. **Contact:** Naseem Hrab, librarian. The Norma Fleck Award was established by the Fleck Family Foundation in May 1999 to honor the life of Norma Marie Fleck, and to recognize exceptional Canadian non-fiction books for young people. Publishers are welcome to nominate books using the online form. Offered annually for books published between January 1, 2009, and December 31, 2009. Open to Canadian citizens or landed immigrants. The jury will always include at least 3 of the following: a teacher, a librarian, a bookseller, and a reviewer. A juror will have a deep understanding of, and some involvement with, Canadian children's books. The Canadian Children's Book Centre will select the jury members. **Deadline: December 15 (annually).** Prize: $10,000 goes to the author (unless 40% or more of the text area is composed of original illustrations, in which case the award will be divided equally between the author and the artist).

FLICKER TALE CHILDREN'S BOOK AWARD

Flicker Tale Award Committee, North Dakota Library Association, Morton Mandan Public Library, 609 West Main St.Mandan ND 58554. Website: www.ndla.info/ftaward.htm. **Contact:** Linda Austin. Estab. 1979. Purpose of award: to give children across the state of North Dakota a chance to vote for their book of choice from a nominated list of 20: 4 in the picture book category; 4 in the intermediate category; 4 in the juvenile category (for more advanced readers); 4 in the upper grage level non-fiction category. Also, to promote awareness of quality literature for children. Previously published submissions only. Submissions nominated by librarians and teachers across the state of North Dakota. Awards a plaque from North Dakota Library Association and banquet dinner. Judging by children in North Dakota. Entry deadline in April.

DON FREEMAN MEMORIAL GRANT-IN-AID

Society of Children's Book Writers and Illustrators, 8271 Beverly Blvd.Los Angeles CA 90048. (323)782-1010 Fax: (323) 782-1892 E-mail: scbwi@scbwi.org. Website: www.scbwi.org. Estab. 1974. Purpose of award: to "enable picture book artists to further their understanding, training and work in the picture book genre." Applications and prepared materials are available in October and must be postmarked between February 1 and March 1. Grant awarded and announced in August.

SASE for award rules and entry forms. SASE for return of entries. No entry fee. Annually awards one grant of $1,500 and one runner-up grant of $500. "The grant-in-aid is available to both full and associate members of the SCBWI who, as artists, seriously intend to make picture books their chief contribution to the field of children's literature."

🆕 FRIENDS OF THE AUSTIN PUBLIC LIBRARY AWARD FOR BEST CHILDREN'S AND BEST YOUNG ADULT'S BOOK

Website: www.smu.edu/english/creativewriting/The_Texas_Institute_of_Letters.htm. Offered annually for work published January 1-December 31 of previous year to recognize the best book for children and young people. Writer must have been born in Texas or have lived in the state for at least 2 consecutive years at one time, or the subject matter must be associated with the state. See Web site for information on eligibility, deadlines, and the judges names and addresses to whom the books should be sent. Prize: $500 for each award winner.

🆕 THEODOR SEUSS GEISEL AWARD

Association for Library Service to Children, Division of the American Library Association, 50 E. Huron, Chicago IL 60611.1(800)-545-2433. E-mail: alsc@ala.org. Website: www.ala.org/ala/mgrps/divs/alsc/awardsgrants/bookmedia/geiselaward/geiselawardapplicationprocess/index.cfm. The Theodor Seuss Geisel Award, established in 2004, is given annually beginning in 2006 to the author(s) and illustrator(s) of the most distinguished American Book for beginning readers published in English in the United States during the preceding year. The award is to recognize the author(s) and illustrator(s) who demonstrate great creativity and imagination in his/her/their literary and artistic achievements to engage children in reading. Deadline for entries: December 31. Entries not returned. Not entry fee. Medal given at awards ceremony during ALA Annual Conference.

🎨 AMELIA FRANCES HOWARD GIBBON AWARD FOR ILLUSTRATION

Canadian Library Association, 328 Frank St.Ottawa ON K2P 0X8 Canada. (613)232-9625; Fax: (613)563-9895. Website: www.cla.ca. **Contact:** Chairperson, Canadian Association of Children's Librarians. Annual award. Estab. 1971. Purpose of the award: "to honor excellence in the illustration of children's book(s) in Canada. To merit consideration the book must have been published in Canada and its illustrator must be a Canadian citizen or a permanent resident of Canada." Previously published submissions only; must be published between January 1 and December 31 of the previous year. Deadline for entries: December 31. SASE for award rules. Entries not returned. No entry fee. Judging by selection committee of members of Canadian Association of Children's Librarians. Requirements for entrants: illustrator must be Canadian or Canadian resident.

GOLDEN KITE AWARDS

Society of Children's Book Writers and Illustrators, 8271 Beverly Blvd.Los Angeles CA 90048. (323)782-1010. E-mail: scbwi@scbwi.org. Website: www.scbwi.org. **Contact:** SCBWI Golden Kite Coordinator. Annual award. Estab. 1973. "The works chosen will be those that the judges feel exhibit excellence in writing, and in the case of the picture-illustrated books—in illustration, and genuinely appeal to the interests and concerns of children. For the fiction and nonfiction awards, original works and single-author collections of stories or poems of which at least half are new and never before published in book form are eligible—anthologies and translations are not. For the picture-illustration awards, the art or photographs must be original works (the texts—which may be fiction or nonfiction—may be original, public domain or previously published). Deadline for entries: December 15. SASE for award rules. No entry fee. Awards, in addition to statuettes and plaques, the four winners receive $2,500 cash award plus trip to LA SCBWI Conference. Editors of four winning books receive $1,000 cash award. The panel of judges will consist of professional authors, illustrators, editors or agents." Requirements for entrants: "must be a member of SCBWI and books must be published in that year." Winning books will be displayed at national conference in August. Books to be entered, as well as further inquiries, should be submitted to: The Society of Children's Book Writers and Illustrators, above address.

N ⌷ GOVERNOR GENERAL'S LITERARY AWARDS

Canada Council for the Arts, 350 Albert St.P.O. Box 1047, Ottawa ON K1P 5V8 Canada. (613)566-4414, ext. 5573. Fax: (613)566-4410. Website: www.canadacouncil.ca/prizes/ggla. Submissions in English must be published between September 1, 2008 and September 30, 2009; submissions in French between July 1, 2008 and June 30, 2009. Publishers submit titles for consideration. Deadline: March 15, June 1 and August 7, depending on the book's publication date. Prize: Each laureate receives $25,000; nonwinning finalists receive $1,000.

N THE MARILYN HALL AWARDS FOR YOUTH THEATRE

Beverly Hills Theatre Guild, P.O. Box 148, Beverly CA 90213. Website: www.beverlyhillstheatreguild. org. **Contact:** Candace Coster. **Open to students.** Annual contest. Estab. 1998/99. Purpose of contest: "To encourage the creation and development of new plays for youth theatre." Unpublished submissions only. Authors must be U.S. citizens or legal residents and must sign entry form personally. Deadline for entries: between January 15 and last day of February each year (postmark accepted). Playwrights may submit up to two scripts. One nonprofessional production acceptable for eligibility. SASE for contest rules and entry forms. No entry fee. Awards: $700, 1st prize; $300, 2nd prize. Judging by theatre professionals cognizant of youth theatre and writing/producing.

HIGHLIGHTS FOR CHILDREN FICTION CONTEST

803 Church St.Honesdale PA 18431-1895. (570)253-1080. Fax: (570)251-7847. Website: www. highlights.com. **Fiction Contest Editor:** Christine French Clark. Annual contest. Estab. 1980. Purpose of the contest: to stimulate interest in writing for children and reward and recognize excellence. Unpublished submissions only. Deadline for entries: January 31; entries accepted after January 1 only. SASE for contest rules and return of entries. No entry fee. Awards 3 prizes of $1,000 each in cash and a pewter bowl (or, at the winner's election, attendance at the Highlights Foundation Writers Workshop at Chautauqua) and a pewter bowl. Judging by a panel of Highlights editors and outside judges. Winning pieces are purchased for the cash prize of $1,000 and published in Highlights; other entries are considered for purchase at regular rates. Requirements for entrants: open to any writer 16 years of age or older. Winners announced in May. Length up to 800 words. Stories for beginning readers should not exceed 500 words. Stories should be consistent with Highlights editorial requirements. No violence, crime or derogatory humor. Send SASE or visit Web site for guidelines and current theme.

THE MARILYN HOLINSHEAD VISITING SCHOLARS FELLOWSHIP

Kerlan Grant-in-Aid, University of Minnesota, 113 Anderson Library, 222 21st Ave. South, Minneapolis MN 55455.E-mail: circ@umn.edu. Website: http://special.lib.umn.edu/clrc/kerlan/index.php. This fellowship provides grants-in-aid for travel to the Kerlan Collection. These grants will be available for research study in 2007. The Kerlan Collection is one of the world's finest research collections in children's literature and contains over 100,000 books and original art and manuscript material for approximately 16,000 titles. For more information about our holdings, please visit the Kerlan Collection's Web site. Applicants may request up to $1,500. Send a letter with the proposed purpose, a plan to use specific research materials (manuscripts and art), dates, and budget (including airfare and per diem) to above address. The deadline for receipt of all materials is December 30, 2009. Travel and a written report on the project must be completed and submitted in 2010.

IMPRINT OF MIDLAND COMMUNITY THEATRE

Midland Community Theatre, 2000 W. Wadley, Midland TX 79705. (432)682-2544. Fax: (432)682-6136. E-mail: mclaren@mctmidland.org. Website: www.mctmidland.org. **Chair** : Andy Salcedo. Estab. 1989. Open to students. Annual contest. Purpose of conference: "The McLaren Memorial Comedy Play Writing Competition was established in 1989 to honor long-time MCT volunteer Mike McLaren who loved a good comedy, whether he was on stage or in the front row." Unpublished submissions only. Submissions made by author. Deadline for entries: February 28th (scripts are accepted January 1st through the end of February each year). SASE for contest rules and entry forms. Entry fee is $10 per script. Awards $400 for full-length winner and $200 for one-act winner as well as staged readings for 3 finalists in each category. Judging by the audience present at the McLaren festival when the staged readings are performed. Rights to winning material acquired or purchased. 1st right of production or refusal is acquired by MCT. Requirements for entrants: "Yes, the contest is open to any playwright, but the play submitted must be unpublished and never produced in a for-profit setting. One previous production in a nonprofit theatre is acceptable. 'Readings' do not count as productions."

INSIGHT WRITING CONTEST

Insight Magazine, 55 W. Oak Ridge Dr.Hagerstown MD 21740-7390. (301) 393-4038; Website: www.insightmagazine.org. **Open to students.** Annual contest. Unpublished submissions only. Submissions made by author. Deadline for entries: June. SASE for contest rules and entry forms. Awards first prizes, $ 100-250; second prizes, $75-200; third prizes, $50-150. Winning entries will be published in Insight. Contest includes three categories: Student Short Story, General Short Story and Student Poetry. You must be age 22 or under to enter the student categories. Entries must include cover sheet form available with SASE or on Web site.

IRA CHILDREN'S AND YOUNG ADULT'S BOOK AWARD

International Reading Association, 800 Barksdale Rd.P.O. Box 8139, Newark DE 19714-8139. (302)731-1600. Fax: (302)731-1057. E-mail: exec@reading.org. Website: www.reading.org. Annual award. Awards are given for an author's first or second published book for fiction and nonfiction in three categories: primary (ages preschool-8), intermediate (ages 9-13), and young adult (ages 14-17). This award is intended for newly published authors who show unusual promise in the children's book field. Deadline for entries: November 1. Awards $1000. For guidelines write or e-mail exec@reading.org.

JOSEPH HENRY JACKSON AND JAMES D. PHELAN LITERARY AWARDS

Sponsored by The San Francisco Foundation. Administered by Intersection for the Arts, 446 Valencia St.San Francisco CA 94103. (415)626-2787. Fax: (415)626-1636. Website: www.theintersection.org/resource_awards.php. Submit entries to Awards Coordinator. **Open to Students.** Annual award. Estab. 1937. Purpose of award: to encourage young writers for an unpublished manuscript-in-progress. Submissions must be unpublished. Submissions made by author. Deadline for entry: March 31. SASE for contest rules and entry forms. Judging by established peers. All applicants must be 20-35 years of age. Applicants for the Henry Jackson Award must be residents of northern California or Nevada for 3 consecutive years immediately prior to the March 31 deadline. Applicants for the James D. Phelan awards must have been born in California but need not be current residents.

EZRA JACK KEATS/KERLAN COLLECTION MEMORIAL FELLOWSHIP

Ezra Jack Keats/Kerlan Collection, Memorial Fellowship Committee, 113 Andersen Library, 222 21st Avenue South, University of Minnesota, Minneapolis, MN 55455. Website: http://special.lib.umn.edu/clrc/kerlan/awards.php. This fellowship from the Ezra Jack Keats Foundation will provide $1,500 to a "talented writer and/or illustrator of children's books who wishes to use the Kerlan Collection for the furtherance of his or her artistic development." Special consideration will be given to someone who would find it difficult to finance a visit to the Kerlan Collection. The Ezra Jack Keats Fellowship recipient will receive transportation costs and a per diem allotment. Applications for 2010 must be postmarked by December 30, 2009. For digital application materials, please visit Web site. For paper copies of the application send a large (6 × 9 or 9 × 12) self- addressed envelope with 97¢ postage envelope to above address.

THE EZRA JACK KEATS NEW WRITER AND NEW ILLUSTRATOR AWARDS

Ezra Jack Keats Foundation/Administered by The Office of Children's Services, The New York Public Library, 450 14th St.Brooklyn NY 11215. E-mail: mtice@nypl.org. Website: www.ezra-jack-keats.org. **Program Coordinator:** Margaret Tice. Annual awards. Purpose of the awards: "The awards will be given to a promising new writer of picture books for children and a promising new illustrator of picture books for children. Selection criteria include books for children (ages 9 and under) that reflect the tradition of Ezra Jack Keats. These books portray: the universal qualities of childhood, strong and supportive family and adult relationships, the multicultural nature of our world." Submissions made by the publisher. Must be published in the preceding year. Deadline for entries: mid-December. SASE for contest rules and entry forms or email Margaret Tice at mtice@nypl.org. No entry fee. Awards $1,000 coupled with Ezra Jack Keats Bronze Medal. Judging by a panel of experts. "The author or illustrator should have published no more than 3 children's books. Entries are judged on the outstanding features of the text, complemented by illustrations. Candidates need not be both author and illustrator. Entries should carry a 2006 copyright (for the 2007 award)." Winning books and authors to be presented at reception at The New York Public Library.

KENTUCKY BLUEGRASS AWARD

Kentucky Reading Association, c/o, Kay Renee Hensley, Lincoln County High School Media Center, 60 Education Way, Stanford, KY 404 84. (606) 365- 9111. Fax: (606) 365- 1750. E-mail: kay. hensley@ lincoln.kyschools.us. Website: www.kyreading.org. **Award Director:** Kay Renee Hensley. Submit entries to: Kay Renee Hensley. Annual award. Estab. 1983. Purpose of award: to promote readership among young children and young adolescents. Also to recognize exceptional creative efforts of authors and illustrators. Previously published submissions only. Submissions made by author, made by author's agent, nominated by teachers or librarians. Must be published no more than 3 years prior to the award year. Deadline for entries: March 15. Contest rules and entry forms are available from the Web site. No entry fee. Awards a framed certificate and invitation to be recognized at the annual luncheon of the Kentucky Bluegrass Award. Judging by children who participate through their schools or libraries. "Books are reviewed by a panel of teachers and librarians before they are placed on a Master List for the year. These books must have been published within a three year period prior to the review. Winners are chosen from this list of preselected books. Books are divided into four divisions, K-2, 3-5, 6-8, 9-12 grades. Winners are chosen by children who either read the books or have the books read to them. Children from the entire state of Kentucky are involved in the selection of the annual winners for each of the divisions."

CORETTA SCOTT KING BOOK AWARDS

Coretta Scott King Book Awards Committee, Ethnic and Multicultural Information Exchange Round Table, American Library Association, 50 E. Huron St.Chicago IL 60611. (800)545-2433 ext: 4297. Fax: (312)280-3256. E-mail: olos@ala.org. Website: www.ala.org/csk. "The Coretta Scott King Book Awards is an annual award celebrating African American experience. A new talent award may also be selected. An awards jury of Children's Librarians judge the books form the previous year, and select the winners in January at the ALA Midwinter meeting. A copy of an entry must be sent to each juror by December 1 of the juried year. A copy of the jury list and directions for submitting titles can be found on Web site. Call or e-mail ALA Office for Literacy and Outreach

Services for jury list. Awards breakfast held on Tuesday morning during ALA. Annual Conference in June. See schedule at Web site.

LOUISE LOUIS/EMILY F. BOURNE STUDENT POETRY AWARD

Poetry Society of America, 15 Gramercy Park South, New York NY 10003-1705. (212)254-9628. Fax: (212)673-2352. E-mail: eve@poetrysociety.org. Website: www.poetrysociety.org. **Contact:** Program Director. **Open to students.** Annual award. Purpose of the award: award is for the best unpublished poem by a high or preparatory school student (grades 9-12) from the U.S. and its territories. Unpublished submissions only. Deadline for entries: Oct. 1 to Dec. 22. SASE for award rules and entry forms. Entries not returned. "High schools can send an unlimited number of submissions with one entry per individual student for a flat fee of $20. (High school students may send a single entry for $5.)" Award: $250. Judging by a professional poet. Requirements for entrants: Award open to all high school and preparatory students from the U.S. and its territories. School attended, as well as name and address, should be noted. PSA submission guidelines must be followed. These are printed in our fall calendar on our Web site and are readily available if those interested send us a SASE. Line limit: none. "The award-winning poem will be included in a sheaf of poems that will be part of the program at the award ceremony and sent to all PSA members."

MCLAREN MEMORIAL COMEDY PLAY WRITING COMPETITION

Midland Community Theatre, Inc.2000 W. Wadley, Midland TX 79705.(432)682-2554. Website: www.mctmidland.org. **Contact:** Andy Salcedo. Annual competition. Accepts submissions in 2 division: one-act and full-length. Accepts submissions January 1, through the last day of February every year. Entries must be comedies for adults, teens or children; musical comedies not accepted. Work must never have been produced professionally or published. See Web site for competitions guidelines and required brochure with entry form. Entry fee: $20/script. Awards $400 for winning full-length play; $200 for winning one-act play; staged reading for full-length finalists.

▧ ▨ THE VICKY METCALF AWARD FOR CHILDREN'S LITERATURE

The Writers' Trust of Canada, 90 Richmond St. E.Suite 200, Toronto ON M5C 1P1 Canada. (416)504-8222. Fax: (416)504-9090. E-mail: info@writerstrust.com. Website: www.writerstrust. com. **Contact:** James Davies. The Vicky Metcalf Award is presented each spring to a Canadian writer for a body of work in children's literature at The Writers' Trust Awards event in Toronto. Prize: $20,000. Open to Canadian residents only.

MILKWEED PRIZE FOR CHILDREN'S LITERATURE

Milkweed Editions, 1011 Washington Ave. S.Suite 300, Minneapolis MN 55415-1246. (612)332-3192. Fax: (612)215-2550. E-mail: editor@milkweed.org. Website: www.milkweed.org. **Award Director:** Daniel Slager, Publisher. Annual award. Estab. 1993. Purpose of the award: to recognize an outstanding literary novel for readers ages 8-13 and encourage writers to turn their attention to readers in this age group. Unpublished submissions only "in book form." Please send SASE or visit Web site for award guidelines. The prize is awarded to the best work for children ages 8-13 that Milkweed agrees to publish in a calendar year. The Prize consists of a $10,000 advance against royalties agreed to at the time of acceptance. Submissions must follow our usual children's guidelines.

MINNESOTA BOOK AWARDS

The Friends of the Saint Paul Public Library, 325 Cedar Street, Suite 555, Saint Paul, MN 55101. (651)366-6497. Fax: (651)222-1988. E-mail: mnbookawards@thefriends.org. Website: www. thefriends.org. **Contact:** Ann Nelson. Annual award, established 1988. Purpose of contest: To recognize and honor achievement by members of Minnesota's book community.

NATIONAL CHILDREN'S THEATRE FESTIVAL

Actors' Playhouse at the Miracle Theatre, 280 Miracle Mile, Coral Gables FL 33134. (305)444-9293, ext. 615. Fax: (305)444-4181. E-mail: maulding@actorsplayhouse.org. Website: www.actorsplayhouse. org. **Director:** Earl Maulding. **Open to students.** Annual contest. Estab. 1994. Purpose of contest: to bring together the excitement of the theater arts and the magic of young audiences through the creation of new musical works and to create a venue for playwrights/composers to showcase their artistic products. Submissions must be unpublished. Submissions are made by author or author's agent. Deadline for entries: April 1 annually. Visit Web site or send SASE for contest rules and entry forms. Entry fee is $10. Awards: first prize of $500, full production, and transportation to Festival weekend based on availability. Final judges are of national reputation. Past judges include Joseph Robinette, Moses Goldberg and Luis Santeiro.

NATIONAL FOUNDATION FOR ADVANCEMENT IN THE ARTS

youngARTS, 444 Brickell Ave.P-14, Miami FL 33131. (305)377-1140. Fax: (305)377-1149. E-mail: info@nfaa.org. Website: www.youngARTS.org. **Contact:** Carla Hill. **Open to students/high school seniors or other 17- and 18-year-olds.** Created to recognize and reward outstanding accomplishment in cinematic arts, dance, jazz, music, photography, theater, voice, visual arts and/or writing. youngARTS is an innovative national program of the National Foundation for Advancement in the Arts (NFAA). Established in 1981, youngARTS touches the lives of gifted young people across the country, providing financial support, scholarships and goal-oriented artistic, educational and career opportunities. Each year, from a pool of more than 8,000 applicants, an average of 800 youngARTS winners are chosen for NFAA support by panels of distinguished artists and educators. Deadline for registration: June 1 (early) and October 1. Deadline for submission of work: Nov. 3. Entry fee is $35(online)/40(paper). Fee waivers available based on need. Awards $100-10,000—unrestricted cash grants. Judging by a panel of artists and educators recognized in the field. Rights to submitted/winning material: NFAA/youngARTS retains the right to duplicate work in an anthology or in Foundation literature unless otherwise specified by the artist. Requirements for entrants: Artists must be high school seniors or, if not enrolled in high school, must be 17 or 18 years old. Applicants must be U.S. citizens or residents, unless applying in jazz. Literary and Visual works will be published in an anthology distributed during youngARTS Week in Miami when the final adjudication takes place. NFAA invites up to 150 finalists to participate in youngARTS Week in January in Miami-Dade County, Florida. youngARTS Week is a once-in-a-lifetime experience consisting of performances, master classes, workshops, readings, exhibits, and enrichment activities with renowned artists and arts educators. All expenses are paid by NFAA, including airfare, hotel, meals and ground transportation.

NATIONAL PEACE ESSAY CONTEST

United States Institute of Peace, 1200 17th St. NW, Washington DC 20036. (202)457-1700. Fax: (202)429-6063. E-mail: education@usip.org. Website: www.usip.org. **Open to high school students.** Annual contest. Estab. 1987. "The contest gives students the opportunity to do valuable research, writing and thinking on a topic of importance to international peace and conflict resolution. Teaching guides are available for teachers who allow the contest to be used as a classroom assignment." Deadline for entries is February 1, 2007. "Interested students, teachers and others may write or call to receive free contest kits. Please do not include SASE." Guidelines and rules on Web site. No entry fee. State Level Awards are $1,000 college scholarships. National winners are selected from among the 1st place state winners. National winners receive scholarships in the following amounts: first place $10,000; second $5,000; third $2,500. National amount includes State Award. First place state winners invited to an expenses-paid awards program in Washington, DC in June. Judging is conducted by education professionals from across the country and by the Board of Directors of the United States Institute of Peace. "All submissions become property of the U.S. Institute of Peace to use at its discretion and without royalty or any limitation. Students grades

9-12 in the U.S.its territories and overseas schools may submit essays for review by completing the application process. U.S. citizenship required for students attending overseas schools. National winning essays will be published by the U.S. Institute of Peace."

THE NENE AWARD

Hawaii State Library, Honolulu HI 96813. (808)586-3510. Fax: (808)586-3584. E-mail: neneaward@ gmail.com. Estab. 1964. "The Nene Award goal is to help the children of Hawaii become acquainted with the best contemporary writers of fiction, become aware of the qualities that make a good book and choose the best for themselves. Works are nominated by students, teachers and librarians in Hawaii. Nominations by publishers or authors are not accepted. Ballots are usually due around the middle of March. Winning authors are invited to a awards ceremony in Honolulu and presented with a plaque. Judging is done by the children of Hawaii in grades 4-6. Requirements for entries: books must be fiction, written by a living author, published in the last six years and suitable for children in grades 4, 5 and 6. Nene winners and nominees are displayed in all participating school and public libraries. The award winner is announced in May.

JOHN NEWBERY MEDAL

Association for Library Service to Children, Division of the American Library Association, 50 E. Huron, Chicago IL 60611. (800)545-2433 ext.2162; Fax: (312)280-5271 E-mail: alsc@ala.org. Website: www.ala.org/ala/mgrps/divs/alsc/awardsgrants/bookmedia/newberymedal/newberyapp/ newberyapplication.cfm. **Executive Director, ALSC:** Diane Foote. Annual award. Estab. 1922. Purpose of award: to recognize the most distinguished contribution to American children's literature published in the U.S. Previously published submissions only; must be published prior to year award is given. Deadline for entries: December 31. SASE for award rules. Entries not returned. No entry fee. Medal awarded at Caldecott/Newbery banquet during ALA annual conference. Judging by Newbery Award Selection Committee.

NEW ENGLAND BOOK AWARDS

New England Independent Booksellers Association, 297 Broadway, #212, Arlington MA 02474. (781)316-8894. Fax: (781)316-2605. E-mail: nan@neba.org. Website: www.newenglandbooks.org/ Default.aspx?pageId=23404. **Assistant Executive Director:** Nan Sorensen. Annual award. Estab. 1990. Purpose of award: "to promote New England authors who have produced a body of work that stands as a significant contribution to New England's culture." Previously published submissions only. Submissions made by New England booksellers; publishers. "Award given to authors 'body of work' not a specific book." Entries must be still in print and available. No entry fee. Judging by NEIBA membership. Requirements for entrants: Author/illustrator must live in New England. Submit written nominations only; actual books should not be sent. Member bookstores receive materials to display winners' books. Submission deadline: March 1.

NEW VOICES AWARD

Lee & Low Books, 95 Madison Ave.New York NY 10016. (212)779-4400. Fax: (212)532-6035. E-mail: general@leeandlow.com. Website: www.leeandlow.com/editorial/voices.html. **Editor-in-chief:** Louise May. **Open to students.** Annual award. Estab. 2000. Purpose of contest: To encourage writers of color to enter the world of children's books. Lee & Low Books is one of the few minority-owned publishing companies in the country. We have published more than 85 first-time writers and illustrators. Winning titles include The Blue Roses, winner of a Patterson Prize for Books for Young People, Janna and the Kings, an IRA Children's Book Award Notable, and Sixteen Years in Sixteen Seconds, selected for the Texas Bluebonnet Award Masterlist. Submissions made by author. Deadline for entries: October 31. SASE for contest rules or visit Web site. No entry fee. Awards New Voices Award—$1,000 prize and standard publication contract (regardless of whether or not writer has an agent) along with an advance on royalties; New Voices Honor Award—$500 prize. Judging by Lee & Low editors. Restrictions of media for illustrators: The author must be a writer of color who is a resident of the U.S. and who has not previously published a children's picture book. For additional information, send SASE or visit Lee & Low's Web site, (www.leeandlow.com/editorial/voices8.html).

NORTH AMERICAN INTERNATIONAL AUTO SHOW HIGH SCHOOL POSTER CONTEST

Detroit Auto Dealers Association, 1900 W. Big Beaver Rd.Troy MI 48084-3531. (248)643-0250. Fax: (248)283-5148. E-mail: sherp@dada.org. Website: www.naias.com. **Contact:** Sandy Herp. **Open to students.** Annual contest. Submissions made by the author and illustrator. Contact D.A..A. for contest rules and entry forms or retrieve rules from Web site. No entry fee. Awards in the High School Poster Contest are as follows: Chairman's Award—$1,000; Designer's Best of Show (Digital and Traditional)—$500; Best Theme—$250; Best Use of Color—$250; Most Creative—$250. A winner will be chosen in each category from grades 10, 11 and 12. Prizes: 1st place in 10, 11, 12—$500; 2nd place—$250; 3rd place—$100. The winners of the Designer's Best of Show Digital and Traditional will each receive $500. The winner of the Chairman's Award will receive $1,000. Entries will be judged by an independent panel of recognized representatives of the art community. Entrants must be Michigan high school students enrolled in grades 10-12. Winning posters may be displayed at the NAIAS 2009 and reproduced in the official NAIAS program, which is available to the public, international media, corporate executives and automotive suppliers. Winning posters may also be displayed on the official NAIAS Web site at the sole discretion of the NAIAS.

OHIOANA BOOK AWARDS

Ohioana Library Association, 274 East First Ave.Suite 300, Columbus OH 43201. (614)466-3831. Fax: (614)728-6974. E-mail: ohioana@ohioana.org. Website: www. oplin.org. Director: Linda R. Hengst. Annual award. "The Ohioana Book Awards are given to books of outstanding literary quality. Purpose of contest: to provide recognition and encouragement to Ohio writers and to promote the work of Ohio writers. Up to six are given each year. Awards may be given in the following categories: fiction, nonfiction, children's/juvenile, poetry and books about Ohio or an Ohioan. Books must be received by the Ohioana Library during the calendar year prior to the year the award is given and must have a copyright date within the last two calendar years." Deadline for entries: December 31. SASE for award rules and entry forms (or downloaded from Ohioana's website at www.ohioana.org/awards/books.asp). No entry fee. Winners receive citation and glass sculpture. "Any book that has been written or edited by a person born in Ohio or who has lived in Ohio for at least five years is eligible."

OKLAHOMA BOOK AWARDS

Oklahoma Center for the Book, 200 NE 18th, Oklahoma City OK 73105. (405)521-2502. Fax: (405)525-7804. E-mail: gcarlile@oltn.odl.state.ok.us. Website: www.odl.state.ok.us/ocb. **Executive Director:** Glenda Carlile. Annual award. Estab. 1989. Purpose of award: "to honor Oklahoma writers and books about our state." Previously published submissions only. Submissions made by the author, author's agent, or entered by a person or group of people, including the publisher. Must be published during the calendar year preceding the award. Awards are presented to best books in fiction, nonfiction, children's, design and illustration, and poetry books about Oklahoma or books written by an author who was born, is living or has lived in Oklahoma. Deadline for entries: early January. SASE for award rules and entry forms. Entry fee $25. Awards a medal—no cash prize. Judging by a panel of 5 people for each category—a librarian, a working writer in the genre, booksellers, editors, etc. Requirements for entrants: author must be an Oklahoma native, resident, former resident or have written a book with Oklahoma theme. Winner will be announced at banquet in Oklahoma City. The Arrell Gibson Lifetime Achievement Award is also presented each year for a body of work.

ONCE UPON A WORLD CHILDREN'S BOOK AWARD

Simon Wiesenthal Center and Museum of Tolerance Library and Archives, 1399 S. Roxbury Dr.Los Angeles, CA 90035-4709. (310)772-7605. Fax: (310)772-7628. E-mail: bookaward@wiesenthal.net. Website: www.wiesenthal.com/library. Award Director: Adaire J. Klein. Submit 4 copies of each entry to: Adaire J. Klein, Director of Library and Archival Services. Annual award. Estab. 1996. Submissions made by publishers, author or author's agent. Suggestions from educators, libraries, and others accepted. Must be published January-December of previous year. Deadline for entries: March 30. SASE for contest rules and entry forms. Awards $1,000 each to two authors honoring a book for children age 6-10 and one for age 11 and up. Recognition of Honor Books if deemed appropriate. Judging is by 6 independent judges familiar with children's literature. Award open to any writer with work in English language on subjects of tolerance, diversity, human understanding, and social justice. Next award will be presented on Sunday November 1, 2009. Book Seals available from the Library.

ORBIS PICTUS AWARD FOR OUTSTANDING NONFICTION FOR CHILDREN

The National Council of Teachers of English, 1111 W. Kenyon Rd.Urbana IL 61801-1096. (217)328-3870. Fax: (217)328-0977. E-mail: dzagorski@ncte.org. Website: www.ncte.org/awards/orbispictus. **Chair, NCTE Committee on the Orbis Pictus Award for Outstanding Nonfiction for Children:** Kim Ford, Memphis TN. Annual award. Estab. 1989. Purpose of award: To promote and recognize excellence in the writing of nonfiction for children. Previously published submissions only. Submissions made by author, author's agent, by a person or group of people. Must be published January 1-December 31 of contest year. Deadline for entries: November 30. Call for award information. No entry fee. Awards a plaque given at the NCTE Elementary Section Luncheon at the NCTE Annual Convention in November. Judging by a committee. "The name Orbis Pictus commemorates the work of Johannes Amos Comenius, 'Orbis Pictus—The World in Pictures' (1657), considered to be the first book actually planned for children."

THE ORIGINAL ART

Museum of American Illustration at the Society of Illustrators, 128 E. 63rd St.New York NY 10021-7303. (212)838-2560. Fax: (212)838-2561. E-mail: kate@societyillustrators.org or info@societyillustrators.org. Website: www.societyillustrators.org. **Exhibition Director:** Kate Feirtag. Annual contest. Estab. 1981. Purpose of contest: to celebrate the fine art of children's book illustration. Previously published submissions only. Deadline for entries: August 21. Request "call for entries" to receive contest rules and entry forms. Entry fee is $20/book. Judging by seven professional artists and editors. Works will be displayed at the Society of Illustrators Museum of American Illustration in New York City October-November annually. Medals awarded; catalog published.

HELEN KEATING OTT AWARD FOR OUTSTANDING CONTRIBUTION TO CHILDREN'S LITERATURE

Church and Synagogue Library Association, 2920 SW Dolph Ct Ste 3A, Portland OR 97219. (503)244-6919. Fax: (503)977-3734. E-mail: csla@worldaccessnet.com. Website: www.cslainfo.org. **Chair of Committee:** Jeri Baker. Annual award. Estab. 1980. "This award is given to a person or organization that has made a significant contribution to promoting high moral and ethical values through children's literature." Deadline for entries: April 1. "Recipient is honored in July during the conference." Awards certificate of recognition and a conference package consisting of all meals, day of awards banquet, two nights' housing and a complimentary 1 year membership. "A nomination for an award may be made by anyone. It should include the name, address and telephone number of the nominee, plus the church or synagogue relationship where appropriate. Nominations of an organization should include the name of a contact person. A detailed description of the reasons for the nomination should be given, accompanied by documentary evidence of accomplishment. The person(s) making the nomination should give his/her name, address and telephone number and a brief explanation of his/her knowledge of the nominee's accomplishments. Elements of creativity and innovation will be given high priority by the judges."

PATERSON PRIZE FOR BOOKS FOR YOUNG PEOPLE

Poetry Center at Passaic County Community College, One College Blvd.Paterson NJ 07505-1179. (973)684-6555. Fax: (973)523-6085. E-mail: mgillan@pccc.edu. Website: www.pccc.edu/poetry. **Director:** Maria Mazziotti Gillan. Estab. 1996. Part of the Poetry Center's mission is "to recognize excellence in books for young people." Published submissions only. Submissions made by author, author's agent or publisher. Must be published between January 1-December 31 of year previous to award year. Deadline for entries: March 15. SASE for contest rules and entry forms or visit Web site. Awards $500 for the author in either of 3 categories: PreK-Grade 3; Grades 4-6, Grades 7-12. Judging by a professional writer selected by the Poetry Center. Contest is open to any writer/illustrator.

PENNSYLVANIA YOUNG READERS' CHOICE AWARDS PROGRAM

Pennsylvania School Librarians Association, 148 S. Bethlehem Pike, Ambler PA 19002-5822. (215)643-5048. Fax: (215)646-7250. E-mail: bellavance@verizon.net. Website: www.psla.org. **Coordinator:** Jean B. Bellavance. Annual award. Estab. 1991. Submissions nominated by a person or group. Must be published within 5 years of the award for example, books published in 2005 to present are eligible for the 2009-2010 award. Deadline for entries: September 1. SASE for contest rules and entry forms. No entry fee. Framed certificate to winning authors. Judging by children of Pennsylvania (they vote). Requirements for entrants: currently living in North America. Reader's Choice Award is to promote reading of quality books by young people in the Commonwealth of Pennsylvania, to promote teacher and librarian involvement in children's literature, and to honor authors whose work has been recognized by the children of Pennsylvania. Four awards are given, one for each of the following grade level divisions: K-3, 3-6, 6-8, YA. View information at the Pennsylvania School Librarians Web site.

PEN/PHYLLIS NAYLOR WORKING WRITER FELLOWSHIP

PEN, 588 Broadway, New York NY 10012. (212)334-1660, ext. 108. Fax: (212)334-2181. E-mail: awards@pen.org. Website: www.pen.org. Submit entries to: awards coordinator. Must have published 2 books for children or young adults to be eligible. Annual contest. Estab. 2001. To support writers with a financial need and recognize work of high literary caliber. Unpublished submissions only. Submissions nominated. Deadline for entries: January 15, 2010. Awards $5,000. Upon nomination by an editor or fellow writer, a panel of judges will select the winning book. Open to a writer of children's or young adult fiction in financial need, who has published at least two books. Please visit our Web site for full guidelines.

JAMES D. PHELAN AWARD

Intersection for the Arts, 446 Valencia Street, San Francisco CA 94103. (415)626-2787. Fax: (415)626-1636. E-mail: info@theintersection.org. Website: www.theintersection.org. **Contest Director:** Kevin B. Chen. Submit entries to: Awards Coordinator. Annual contest. Estab. 1935. Purpose of contest: "To support unpublished manuscripts in progress." Unpublished submissions only. Submissions made by author. Postmark deadline for entries: March 31. Visit www.theintersection. org for complete contests guidelines and application form. No entry fee. Awards: $2,000. Judging by 3 independent judges to be determined. "Must be born in California, but need not reside in California, and must be between ages 20-35."

PLEASE TOUCH MUSEUM BOOK AWARD

Please Touch Museum, Memorial Hall in Fairmont Park, 4231 Ave.of the Republic, Philadelphia

PA 19131. (215)578-5153. Fax: (215)578-5171. E-mail: brafter@pleasetouchmuseum.org. Website: www.pleasetouchmuseum.org. **Contact:** Brian Rafter. Annual award. Estab. 1985. Purpose of the award: "to recognize and encourage the publication of high-quality books for young children. The award is given to books that are imaginative, exceptionally illustrated, and help to foster a child's life-long love of reading. Each year, the museum selects one winner in two age categories— ages 3 and under and ages 4 to 7. These age categories reflect the age of the children Please Touch Museum serves. To be eligible for consideration, a book must: (1) Be distinguished in text, illustration, and ability to explore and clarify an idea for young children (ages 7 and under). (2) Be published within the last year by an American publisher. (3) Be by an American author and/or illustrator." SASE for award rules and entry forms. No entry fee. Publishing date deadlines apply. Judging by jury of select museum staff, children's literature experts, librarians, and early childhood educators. Please Touch Museum's Kid's Store purchases books for selling at Annual Book Award Ceremony and throughout the year. Winning author autographing sessions may be held at Please Touch Museum, and at the Delaware Valley Association for the Education of Young Children' Annual Conference in Philadelphia.

PNWA ANNUAL LITERARY CONTEST

Pacific Northwest Writers Association, PMB 2717-1420 NW Gilman Blvd, Ste 2, Issaquah, WA 98027. (425)673-2665. E-mail: staff@pnwa.org. Website: www.pnwa.org. **Open to students.** Annual contest. Purpose of contest: "Valuable tool for writers as contest submissions are critiqued (2 critiques)." Unpublished submissions only. Submissions made by author. Deadline for entries: February 20, 2009. Entry fee is $35/entry for members, $50/entry for nonmembers. Awards $600-1st; $300-2nd; $150-3rd. Awards in all 12 categories.

POCKETS MAGAZINE FICTION CONTEST

Pockets Magazine, The Upper Room, P.O. Box 340004, Nashville TN 37203-0004. (615)340-7333. Fax: (615)340-7267. E-mail: pockets@upperroom.org. Website: www.pockets.org. **Contact:** Lynn W. Gilliam, senior editor. The purpose of the contest is to find new freelance writers for the magazine therefore previous winners are not eligible. Annual competition for short stories. Award: $1,000 and publication in Pockets. Competition receives 400 submissions. Judged by Pockets editors and editors of other Upper Room publications. Guidelines available on website or upon request and SASE. No entry fee. No entry form. Note on envelope and first sheet: Fiction Contest. Submissions must be postmarked between March 1 and August 15 of the current year. **Unpublished submissions only.** Word length: 1,000-1,600 words. Winner notified November 1. Submissions returned after November 1 if accompanied by SASE.

EDGAR ALLAN POE AWARD

Mystery Writers of America, Inc.1140 Broadway, Suite 1507, New York NY 10001. (212)888-8171. Fax: (212)888-8107. E-mail: mwa@mysterywriters.org. Website: www.mysterywriters.org. **Administrative Manager:** Margery Flax. Annual award. Estab. 1945. Purpose of the award: to honor authors of distinguished works in the mystery field. Previously published submissions only. Submissions made by the author, author's agent; "normally by the publisher." Work must be published/produced the year of the contest. Deadline for entries: Must be received by November 30. Submission information can be found at: www.mysterywriters.org. No entry fee. Awards ceramic bust of "Edgar" for winner; scrolls for all nominees. Judging by professional members of Mystery Writers of America (writers). Nominee press release sent in mid January. Winner announced at the Edgar® Banquet, held in late April/early May.

MICHAEL L. PRINTZ AWARD

Young Adult Library Services Association, Division of the American Library Association, 50 E. Huron, Chicago IL 60611. Fax: (312)280-5276. E-mail: yalsa@ala.org. Website: www.ala.org/

yalsa. Annual award. The Michael L. Printz Award is an award for a book that exemplifies literary excellence in young adult literature. It is named for a Topeka, Kansas school librarian who was a long-time active member of the Young Adult Library Services Association. It will be selected annually by an award committee that can also name as many as 4 honor books. The award-winning book can be fiction, nonfiction, poetry or an anthology, and can be a work of joint authorship or editorship. The books must be published between January 1 and December 31 of the preceding year and be designated by its publisher as being either a young adult book or one published for the age range that YALSA defines as young adult, e.g. ages 12 through 18. The deadline for both committee and field nominations will be December 1.

QUILL AND SCROLL INTERNATIONAL WRITING/PHOTO CONTEST

Quill and Scroll, School of Journalism and Mass Communication, University of Iowa, Iowa City IA 52242-1528 -2004. (319)335-3457. Fax: (319)335-3989. E-mail: quill-scroll@uiowa.edu. Website: www.uiowa.edu/~quill-sc. **Contest Director:** Vanessa Shelton. **Open to students.** Annual contest. Previously published submissions only. Submissions made by the author or school newspaper adviser. Must be published within the last year. Deadline for entries: February 5. SASE for contest rules and entry forms or visit Web site for more information and forms. Entry fee is $2/entry. Awards engraved plaque to junior high and high school level sweepstakes winners. Judging by various judges. Quill and Scroll acquires the right to publish submitted material in the magazine if it is chosen as a winning entry. Requirements for entrants: must be students in grades 9-12 for high school division; grades 6-8 for junior high school division. Entry form available on Web site.

🌐 RED HOUSE CHILDREN'S BOOK AWARD

Federation of Children's Book Groups, 2 Bridge Wood View, Horsforth, Leeds LS18 5PE England. (44)(113)258-8910. E-mail: marianneadey@aol.com. Website: www.redhousechildrensbookawards. co.uk. **Coordinator:** Sinead Kromer. Purpose of the award: "The R.H.C.B.A. is an annual prize for the best children's book of the year judged by the children themselves." Categories: (I) books for younger children, (II) books for younger readers, (III) books for older readers. Estab. 1980. Works must be published in the United Kingdom. Deadline for entries: December 31. SASE or e-mail for rules. Entries not returned. Awards "a magnificent silver and oak trophy worth over €6,000." Silver dishes to each category winner. Portfolios of children's work to all Top Ten authors and illustrators. Judging by children. Requirements for entrants: Work must be fiction and published in the UK during the current year (poetry is ineligible). Top 50 Books of the year will be published in current "Pick of the Year" publication.

TOMAS RIVERA MEXICAN AMERICAN CHILDREN'S BOOK AWARD

Texas State University-San Marcos, EDU, 601 University Dr.San Marcos TX 78666-4613. (512)245-3839. Fax: (512)245-7911. E-mail: jb23@txstate.edu. Website: www.education.txstate.edu **Award Director:** Dr. Jennifer Battle. Competition open to adults. Annual contest. Estab. 1995. Purpose of award: "To encourage authors, illustrators and publishers to produce books that authentically reflect the lives of Mexican Americans appropriate for children and young adults in the United States." Unpublished mss not accepted. Submissions made by "any interested individual or publishing company." Must be published during the two years prior to the year of consideration for the appropriate category "Works for Younger Children" or " Works for Older Children". Deadline for entries: November 1 of publication year. Contact Dr. Jennifer Battle for nomination forms, or send copy of book. No entry fee. Awards $3,000 per book. Judging of nominations by a regional committee, national committee judges finalists. Annual ceremony honoring the book and author/illustrator is held during Hispanic Heritage Month at Texas State University-San Marcos and a selected city.

◩ ROCKY MOUNTAIN BOOK AWARD: ALBERTA CHILDREN'S CHOICE BOOK AWARD

Rocky Mountain Book Award Committee, Box 42, Lethbridge AB T1J 3Y3 Canada. (403)381-0855. E-mail: rockymountainbookaward@shaw.ca. Website: http://rmba.lethsd.ab.ca. **Contest Director:** Michelle Dimnik. Submit entries to: Richard Chase, board member. Open to students. Annual contest. Estab. 2001. Purpose of contest: "Reading motivation for students, promotion of Canadian authors, illustrators and publishers." Previously unpublished submissions only. Submissions made by author's agent or nominated by a person or group. Must be published between 2006-2009. Deadline for entries: January 17, 2009. SASE for contest rules and entry forms. No entry fee. Awards: Gold medal and author tour of selected Alberta schools. Judging by students. Requirements for entrants: Canadian authors and illustrators only.

◩ SASKATCHEWAN BOOK AWARDS: CHILDREN'S LITERATURE

Saskatchewan Book Awards, 205B-2314 11th Avenue, Regina SK S4P 0K1 Canada. (306)569-1585. Fax: (306)569-4187. E-mail: director@bookawards.sk.ca. Website: www.bookawards.sk.ca. **Award Director:** Glenda James. Open to Saskatchewan authors only. Annual award. Estab. 1995. Purpose of contest: to celebrate Saskatchewan books and authors and to promote their work. Previously published submissions only. Submissions made by author, author's agent or publisher by September 15. SASE for contest rules and entry forms. Entry fee is $20 (Canadian). Awards $2,000 (Canadian). Judging by two children's literature authors outside of Saskatchewan. Requirements for entrants: Must be Saskatchewan resident; book must have ISBN number; book must have been published within the last year. Award-winning book will appear on TV talk shows and be pictured on bookmarks distributed to libraries, schools and bookstores in Saskatchewan.

SCBWI MAGAZINE MERIT AWARDS

Society of Children's Book Writers and Illustrators, 8271 Beverly Blvd.Los Angeles CA 90048. Fax: (323)782-1010. E-mail: scbwi@scbwi.org. Website: www.scbwi.org. **Award Coordinator:** Dorothy Leon. Annual award. Estab. 1988. Purpose of the award: "to recognize outstanding original magazine work for young people published during that year and having been written or illustrated by members of SCBWI." Previously published submissions only. Entries must be submitted between January 1 and December 15 of the year of publication. For rules and procedures see Web site. No entry fee. Must be a SCBWI member. Awards plaques and honor certificates for each of 4 categories (fiction, nonfiction, illustration, poetry). Judging by a magazine editor and two "full" SCBWI members. "All magazine work for young people by an SCBWI member—writer, artist or photographer—is eligible during the year of original publication. In the case of co-authored work, both authors must be SCBWI members. Members must submit their own work." Requirements for entrants: 4 copies each of the published work and proof of publication (may be contents page) showing the name of the magazine and the date of issue. The SCBWI is a professional organization of writers and illustrators and others interested in children's literature. Membership is open to the general public at large.

SCBWI WORK-IN-PROGRESS GRANTS

Society of Children's Book Writers and Illustrators, 8271 Beverly Blvd.Los Angeles CA 90048. (323)782-1010. Fax: (323)782-1892. E-mail: scbwi@scbwi.org. Website: www.scbwi.org. Annual award. "The SCBWI Work-in-Progress Grants have been established to assist children's book writers in the completion of a specific project." Four categories: (1) General Work-in-Progress Grant. (2) Grant for a Contemporary Novel for Young People. (3) Nonfiction Research Grant. (4) Grant for a Work Whose Author Has Never Had a Book Published. Requests for applications may be made beginning October 1. Completed applications accepted February 1-April 1 of each year. SASE for applications for grants. In any year, an applicant may apply for any of the grants except the one awarded for a work whose author has never had a book published. (The recipient of this grant will be chosen from entries in all categories.) Five grants of $1,500 will be awarded annually. Runner-up grants of $500 (one in each category) will also be awarded. "The grants are available to both full and associate members of the SCBWI. They are not available for projects on which there are already contracts." Previous recipients not eligible to apply.

SHUBERT FENDRICH MEMORIAL PLAYWRITING CONTEST

Pioneer Drama Service, Inc.P.O. Box 4267, Englewood CO 80155-4267. Fax: (303)779-4315. E-mail: submissions@pioneerdrama.com. Website: www.pioneerdrama.com. **Director:** Lori Conary. Annual contest. Estab. 1990. Purpose of the contest: "To encourage the development of quality theatrical material for educational and family theater." Previously unpublished submissions only. Open to all writers not currently published by Pioneer Drama Service. Deadline for entries: December 31. SASE for contest rules and guidelines. No entry fee. Cover letter, SASE for return of ms, and proof of production or staged reading must accompany all submissions. Awards $1,000 royalty advance and publication. Upon receipt of signed contracts, plays will be published and made available in our next catalog. Judging by editors. All rights acquired with acceptance of contract for publication. Restrictions for entrants: Any writers currently published by Pioneer Drama Service are not eligible.

SKIPPING STONES BOOK AWARDS

Skipping Stones, P.O. Box 3939, Eugene OR 97403-0939. (541)342-4956. E-mail: info@skippingstones. org. Website: www.skippingstones.org. Open to published books, magazines, educational videos, and DVDs. Annual awards since 1994. Purpose of contest: To recognize contributions to children's literature, teaching resources and educational audio/video resources in the areas of multicultural awareness, nature and ecology, social issues, peace and nonviolence. Submissions made by the author or publishers and/or producers. Deadline for entries: February 1. Send request for contest rules and entry forms or visit Web site. Entry fee is $50; 50% discount for nonprofit publishers. Each year, an honor roll of about 20 books and A/V resources are selected by a multicultural selection committee of editors, students, parents, teachers and librarians. Winners receive gold honor award seals, certificates and publicity via multiple outlets. Many educational publications announce the winners of our book awards. The reviews of winning books and educational videos/ DVDs are published in the May-August issue of Skipping Stones, now in its 21st year.

SKIPPING STONES YOUTH HONOR AWARDS

Skipping Stones, P.O. Box 3939, Eugene OR 97403-0939. (541)342-4956. E-mail: editor@ SkippingStones.org. Website: www.SkippingStones.org. **Open to students.** Annual awards. Purpose of contest: "to recognize youth, 7 to 17, for their contributions to multicultural awareness, nature and ecology, social issues, peace and nonviolence. Also to promote creativity, self-esteem and writing skills and to recognize important work being done by youth organizations." Submissions made by the author. Deadline for entries: June 25. SASE for contest rules. Entries must include certificate of originality by a parent and/or teacher and a cover letter that included cultural background information on the author. Entry fee is $3. Everyone who enters the contest receives the September-October issue featuring Youth Awards. Judging by Skipping Stones ' staff. "Up to ten awards are given in three categories: (1) Compositions—(essays, poems, short stories, songs, travelogues, etc.) should be typed (double-spaced) or neatly handwritten. Fiction or nonfiction should be limited to 1,000 words; poems to 30 lines. Non-English writings are also welcome. (2) Artwork—(drawings, cartoons, paintings or photo essays with captions) should have the artist's name, age and address on the back of each page. Send the originals with SASE. Black & white photos are especially welcome. Limit: 8 pieces. (3) Youth Organizations—Tell us how your club or group works to: (a) preserve the nature and ecology in your area, (b) enhance the quality of life for low-income, minority or disabled or (c) improve racial or cultural harmony in your school or community. Use the same format as for compositions." The winners are published in the September-October issue of Skipping Stones. Now in its 2 1st year, Skipping Stones is a winner of N.A.M.E.EDPRESS, Newsstand Resources and Parent's Choice Awards.

KAY SNOW WRITERS' CONTEST

Williamette Writers, 9045 SW Barbur Blvd. #5A, Portland OR 97219-4027. (503)452-1592. Fax: (503)452-0372. E-mail: wilwrite@willamettewriters.com. Website: www.willamettewriters.com. **Contest Director:** Patricia MacAodha. Annual contest. **Open to students.** Purpose of contest: "to encourage beginning and established writers to continue the craft." Unpublished, original submissions only. Submissions made by the author. Deadline for entries: April 23rd. SASE for contest rules and entry forms. Entry fee is $10, Williamette Writers' members; $15, nonmembers; free for student writers grades 1-12. Awards cash prize of $300 per category (fiction, nonfiction, juvenile, poetry, script writing), $50 for students in three divisions: 1-5, 6-8, 9-12. Judges are anonymous.

SOUTHWEST WRITERS ANNUAL CONTEST

SouthWest Writers, 3721 Morris NE, Suite A, Albuquerque NM 87111. (505)265-9485. Fax: (505)265-9483. E-mail: swwriters@juno.com. Website: www.southwestwriters.org. Submit entries to: Contest Chair. **Open to adults and students.** Annual contest. Estab. 1982. Purpose of contest: to encourage writers of all genres. Also offers mini-conferences, critique service (for $60/year, offers 2 monthly programs, monthly newsletter, annual writing and quarterly writing contests, other workshops, various discount perks, Web site linking, e-mail addresses, classes and critique service (open to nonmembers). See Web site for more information or call or write.

SUGARMAN FAMILY AWARD FOR JEWISH CHILDREN'S LITERATURE

Washington District of Columbia Jewish Community Center, 1529 16th St. N.W.Washington DC 20036. (202)518-9400. Fax: (202)777-3254. E-mail: lilikg@washingtondcjcc.org. Website: www.washingtondcjcc.org/literary. **Award Director:** Lili Kalish Gersch. Biannual award. Estab. 1994. Purpose of contest: to enrich children's appreciation of Jewish culture and to inspire writers and illustrators for children. Submissions are made by the author, illustrator or agent. Must be published between October 2007 and October 2009, no self-published books. Deadline: June 1, 2009. See website for award rules and entry forms. Entry fee is $25. Award at least $750. Requirements for entrants: must live in the United States, be available to receive award on October 8, 2009, at the Washington DCJCC's Hyman S. & Freda Bernstein Jewish Literary Festival.

N SYDNEY TAYLOR BOOK AWARD

Association of Jewish Libraries, P.O. Box 1118, Teaneck, NJ 07666. (212)725-5359. E-mail: chair@sydneytaylorbookaward.org. Website: www.sydneytaylorbookaward.org. **Contact:** Kathe Pinchuck, chair. Offered annually for work published during the current year. "Given to distinguished contributions to Jewish literature for children. One award for younder readers, one for older readers, and one for teens." Publishers submit books. Deadline: December 31, but we cannot guarantee that books received after December 1 will be considered. Guidelines on Web site. Awards certificate, cash award, and gold or silver seals for cover of winning book.

SYDNEY TAYLOR MANUSCRIPT COMPETITION

Association of Jewish Libraries, 204 Park St.Montclair NJ 07042. E-mail: stmacajl@aol.com. Website: www.jewishlibraries.org. **Coordinator:** Aileen Grossberg. **Open to students** and to any unpublished writer of fiction.Annual contest. Estab. 1985. Purpose of the contest: "This competition is for unpublished writers of fiction. Material should be for readers ages 8-11, with universal appeal that will serve to deepen the understanding of Judaism for all children, revealing positive aspects of Jewish life." Unpublished submissions only. Deadline for entries: December 15. Download rules and forms from website or send SASE for contest rules and entry forms. No entry fee. Awards $1,000. Award winner will be notified in April, and the award will be presented at the convention in June. Judging by qualified judges from within the Association of Jewish Libraries. Requirements for entrants: must be an unpublished fiction writer; also, books must range from 64-200 pages in length. "AJL assumes no responsibility for publication, but hopes this cash incentive will serve to encourage new writers of children's stories with Jewish themes for all children."

THE TORONTO BOOK AWARDS

City of Toronto, 100 Queen St. W, 2nd Floor, West Tower, Toronto ON M5H 2N2 Canada. (416)392-7666. E-mail: bkurmey@toronto.ca. **Submit entries to:** Bev Kurmey, Protocol Officer. Annual award. Estab. 1974. Recognizes books of literary or artistic merit that are evocative of Toronto. Submissions made by author, author's agent or nominated by a person or group. Must be published the calendar year prior to the award year. Deadline for entries: last week day of March annually. Awards $15,000 in prize money. Judging by committee.

MUNICIPAL CHAPTER OF TORONTO IODE JEAN THROOP BOOK AWARD

Toronto Municipal IODE, 40 St. Clair Ave. E.Suite 205, Toronto ON M4T 1M9 Canada. (416)925-5078. Fax: (416)925-5127. E-mail: iodetoronto@bellnet.ca; http://www.bookcentre.ca/awards/iode_book_award_municipal_chapter_toronto. **Contest Director:** Jennifer Werry. Submit entries to: Theo Heras, Lillian Smith Library, 239 College St.Toronto. Annual contest. Estab. 1974. Previously published submissions only. Submissions made by author. Deadline for entries: November 1. No entry fee. Awards: $1,000. If the illustrator is different from the author, the prize money is divided. Judging by Book Award Committee comprised of members of Toronto Municipal Chapter IODE. Requirements for entrants: Authors and illustrators must be Canadian and live within the GTA.

VEGETARIAN ESSAY CONTEST

The Vegetarian Resource Group, P.O. Box 1463, Baltimore MD 21203. (410)366-VEGE. Fax: (410)366-8804. E-mail: vrg@vrg.org. Website: www.vrg.org. Annual contest. **Open to students.** Estab. 1985. Purpose of contest: to promote vegetarianism in young people. Unpublished submissions only. Deadline for entries: May 1 of each year. SASE for contest rules and entry forms. No entry fee. Awards $50 savings bond. Judging by awards committee. Acquires right for The Vegetarian Resource Group to reprint essays. Requirements for entrants: age 18 and under. Winning works may be published in Vegetarian Journal, instructional materials for students. Submit 2-3 page essay on any aspect of vegetarianism, which is the abstinence of meat, fish and fowl. Entrants can base paper on interviewing, research or personal opinion. Need not be vegetarian to enter.

VFW VOICE OF DEMOCRACY

Veterans of Foreign Wars of the U.S.406 W. 34th St.Kansas City MO 64111. (816)968-1117. Fax: (816)968-1149. Website: www.vfw.org. **Open to high school students.** Annual contest. Estab. 1960. Purpose of contest: to give high school students the opportunity to voice their opinions about their responsibility to our country and to convey those opinions via the broadcast media to all of America. Deadline for entries: November 1. No entry fee. Winners receive awards ranging from $1,000-16,000. Requirements for entrants: "Ninth-twelfth grade students in public, parochial, private and home schools are eligible to compete. Former first place state winners are not eligible to compete again. Contact your participating high school teacher, counselor, our Web site www.vfw.org or your local VFW Post to enter."

VIRGINIA LIBRARY ASSOCIATION/JEFFERSON CUP

Virginia Library Association, P.O. Box 8277, Norfolk, VA 23503-0277. (757)583-0041; Fax: (757)583-5041. E-Mail lhahne@coastalnet.com. Website: www.vla.org. **Executive Director:** Linda Hahne. Award director changes year to year. 2009 Jefferson Cup Director: Connie J. Moore, e-mail cjmoore@ms.spotsylvvania.k12.va.us. Annual award. Estab. 1983. Purpose of award "The Jefferson Cup honors a distinguished biography, historical fiction or American history book for young people.

Presented since 1983, the Jefferson Cup Committee's goal is to promote reading about America's past; to encourage the quality writing of United States history, biography and historical fiction for young people and to recognize authors in these disciplines." Entries must be published in the year prior to selection. Deadline for entries, January 31st. Additional information on the Jefferson Cup and criteria on making submissions is available on the VLA Web site at http://www.vla.org/demo/Youth-Serv/JC-How-To.html. Judging by committee. The book must be about US history or an American person, 1492 to present, or fiction that highlights the US past; author must reside in the US. The book must be published especially for young people.

WASHINGTON CHILDREN'S CHOICE PICTURE BOOK AWARD

Washington Library Media Association, 10924 Mukilteo Speedway PMB 142, Mukilteo WA 98275. E-mail: wlma@earthlink.net. Website: www.wlma.org/wccpba.htm. **Award Directors:** Dave Sonnen and Karen Heubschman. Submit nominations to: Barb Engvall, chairman; mail to Barb Engvall, WCCPBA Ballot, John Campbell Elementary School, 408 N. 1St St, Selah WA 98942. Annual award. Estab. 1982. Previously published submissions only. Submissions nominated by a person or group. Must be published within 2-3 years prior to year of award. Deadline for entries: April 1. SASE for contest rules and entry forms. Awards pewter plate, recognition. Judging by WCCPBA committee.

WASHINGTON POST/CHILDREN'S BOOK GUILD AWARD FOR NONFICTION

E-mail: theguild@childrensbookguild.org. Website: www.childrensbookguild.org. **President:** changes yearly. Annual award. Estab. 1977. Purpose of award: "to honor an author or illustrator whose total work has contributed significantly to the quality of nonfiction for children." Award includes a cash prize and an engraved crystal paperweight. Judging by a jury of Children's Book Guild specialists, authors, illustrators and a Washington Post book critic. "One doesn't enter. One is selected. Our jury annually selects one author for the award."

WE ARE WRITERS, TOO!

Creative With Words Publications, Carmel CA 93922. Fax: (831)655-8627. E-mail: geltrich@mbay.net. Website: members.tripod.com/CreativeWithWords. **Contest Director:** Brigitta Geltrich. **Open to all ages:** pre-school, school, and adult. Eight times a year. Estab. 1975. Purpose: to further creative writing in children and offer all ages an opportunity to be published. Unpublished submissions only. Can submit year round on any theme (theme list available upon request and SASE). Deadlines for entries: year round. SASE for guidelines and submittal forms. SASE for return of entries "if not accepted." No entry fee. All selected poems are published in an anthology. Judging by selected guest editors and educators. Anthologies open to all ages. Writer should request guidelines. Include SASE with all correspondence. Age of child and home address must be stated and ms must be verified of its authenticity. Each story or poem must have a title. Creative with Words Publications (CWW) publishes the top 50-100 mss submitted to any theme. CWW also publishes two anthologies for adult poets and writers only. Focus of all anthologies is on Nature, Seasons, Animals, School/Education, and on Folklore.

WESTERN HERITAGE AWARDS

National Cowboy & Western Heritage Museum, 1700 NE 63rd St.Oklahoma City OK 73111-7997. (405)478-2250. Fax: (405)478-4714. E-mail: ssimpson@nationalcowboymuseum.org. Website: www.nationalcowboymuseum.org. **Western Heritage Award:** Shayla Simpson. Annual award. Estab. 1961. Purpose of award: The WHA are presented annually to encourage the accurate and artistic telling of great stories of the West through 16 categories of western literature, television, film and music; including fiction, nonfiction, children's books and poetry. Previously published submissions only; must be published the calendar year before the awards are presented. Deadline for literary entries: November 30. Deadline for film, music and television entries: December 31.

Entries not returned. Entry fee is $50/entry. Awards a Wrangler bronze sculpture designed by famed western artist, John Free. Judging by a panel of judges selected each year with distinction in various fields of western art and heritage. Requirements for entrants: The material must pertain to the development or preservation of the West, either from a historical or contemporary viewpoint. Literary entries must have been published between December 1 and November 30 of calendar year. Film, music or television entries must have been released or aired between January 1 and December 31 of calendar year of entry. Works recognized during special awards ceremonies held annually at the museum. There is an autograph party preceding the awards. Awards ceremonies are sometimes broadcast.

JACKIE WHITE MEMORIAL NATIONAL CHILDREN'S PLAY WRITING CONTEST

Columbia Entertainment Company, 1800 Nelwood.Columbia MO 65202-1447. (573)874-5628. E-mail: bybetsy@yahoo.com. Website: www.cectheatre.org. **Contest Director:** Betsy Phillips. Annual contest. Estab. 1988. Purpose of contest: "To encourage writing of family-friendly scripts." Previously unpublished submissions only. Submissions made by author. Deadline for entries: June 1, 2009. SASE for contest rules and entry forms. Entry fee is $20. Awards $500 with production possible. Judging by current and past board members of CEC and at least one theater school parent. Play may be performed during the following season. We reserve the right to award 1st place and prize monies without a production. All submissions will be read by at least three readers. Author will receive a written evaluation of the script.

LAURA INGALLS WILDER METAL

Association for Library Service to Children, Division of the American Library Association, 50 E. Huron, Chicago IL 60611. (800)545-2433; Fax:(312)280-5271. E-mail: alsc@ala.org. Website: www. ala.org/ala/alsc/awardsscholarships/literaryawds/wildermedal/wildermedal.htm. **Executive Director:** Diane Foote. Award offered every 2 years. Purpose of the award: to recognize an author or illustrator whose books, published in the U.S.have over a period of years made a substantial and lasting contribution to children's literature. The candidates must be nominated by ALSC members. Medal presented at Newbery/Caldecott banquet during annual conference. Judging by Wilder Award Selection Committee.

▧ RITA WILLIAMS YOUNG ADULT PROSE PRIZE

National League of American Pen Women, Nob Hill, San Francisco Branch, 1544 Sweetwood Dr.Broadmoor Vlg.CA 94015-2029. E-mail: pennobhill@aol.com. Website: www.soulmakingcontest. us. **Contact:** Eileen Malone. **Open to students.** Up to 3,000 words in story, essay, journal entry, creative nonfiction, or memoir by writers in grades 9-12. Annual prize. Deadline: November 30. Guidelines for SASE or at www.soulmakingcontest.us. Charges $5/entry (make checks payable to NLAPW, Nob Hill Branch) International entrants please send Travelers Check drawn on a USA Bank. Prize: 1st Place: $100; 2nd Place: $50; 3rd Place: $25. Open to any writer in grade 9-12.or equivalent.

PAUL A. WITTY OUTSTANDING LITERATURE AWARD

International Reading Association, Special Interest Group, Reading for Gifted and Creative Learning, School of Education, P.O. Box 10034, Lamar University, Beaumont, TX 77710. (409)286-5941. Fax: (409)880-8384. Website: www.reading.org/association/awards/sig_witty.html. **Award Director:** Dr. Cathy Dorothy Sisk. **Open to students.** Annual award. Estab. 1979. Categories of entries: poetry/ prose at elementary, junior high and senior high levels. Unpublished submissions only. Deadline for entries: February 1. SASE for award rules and entry forms. SASE for return of entries. No entry fee. Awards $25 and plaque, also certificates of merit. Judging by 2 committees for screening and awarding. "The elementary students' entries must be legible and may not exceed 1,000 words. Secondary students' prose entries should be typed and may exceed 1,000 words if necessary. At both elementary and secondary levels, if poetry is entered, a set of five poems must be submitted. All entries and requests for applications must include a self-addressed, stamped envelope."

PAUL A. WITTY SHORT STORY AWARD

International Reading Association, P.O. Box 8139, 800 Barksdale Rd.Newark DE 19714-8139. (302)731-1600. E-mail: exec@reading.org. Website: www.reading.org. "The entry must be an original short story appearing in a young children's periodical for the first time. The short story should serve as a literary standard that encourages young readers to read periodicals." Deadline for entries: The entry must have been published for the first time in the eligibility year; the short story must be submitted during the calendar year of publication. Anyone wishing to nominate a short story should send it to the designated Paul A. Witty Short Award Subcommittee Chair by December 1. Award is $1,000 and recognition at the annual IRA Convention.

JOHN WOOD COMMUNITY COLLEGE CREATIVE WRITING CONTEST

Business Office—Writing Contest, John Wood Community College, 1301 S. 48th Street, Quincy IL 62305. (217)641-4940. Fax: (217)641-4900. E-mail: KLangston@jwcc.edu. Website: www.jwcc.edu. **Contact:** Kelli Langston, education specialist. The college sponsors a writing contest for poetry, fiction and nonfiction. Entries for the contest are accepted January-March of each year. Please see the JWCC Web site for more details or e-mail. KLangston@jwcc.edu for more information. In addition, the college sponsors a student art show in February. A recycled art contest in April. A photography show in May and an annual art competition for adults only in November.

N ALICE WOOD MEMORIAL OHIOANA AWARD FOR CHILDREN'S LITERATURE

Ohioana Library Association, 274 E. First Ave.Suite 300, Columbus OH 43201. (614)466-3831. Fax: (614)728-6974. E-mail: ohioana@sloma.state.oh.us or Ohioana@Ohioana.org. Website: www. ohioana.org. **Contact:** Linda R. Hengst. Offered to an author whose body of work has made, and continues to make, a significant contribution to literature for children or young adults and through their work as a writer, teacher, administrator, and community member, interest in children's literature has been encouraged and children have become involved with reading. Nomination forms for SASE. Recipient must have been born in Ohio or lived in Ohio at least 5 years. Deadline: December 31. Awards $1,000 cash prize.

WRITE IT NOW!

SmartWriters.com, 10823 Worthing Ave.San Diego CA 92126-2665. (858)689-2665. E-mail: e ditor@ smartwriters.com. Website: www.SmartWriters.com. **Editorial Director:** Roxyanne Young. Estab. 1994. Annual contest. "Our purpose is to encourage new writers and help get their manuscripts into the hands of people who can help further their careers." Unpublished submissions only. Submissions made by author. Deadline for entries: May 1. SASE for contest rules and entry forms; also see Web site. Entry fee is $15 for initial entry, $10 for additional entries. Awards a cash prize, books about writing, and an editorial review of the winning manuscripts. 2007's cash prize was $250, plus $100 cash prizes for category winners. Judging by published writers and editors. Requirement for entrants: "This contest is open to all writers age 18 and older. There are 5 categories: Young Adult, Mid-grade, Picture Book, Nonfiction, and Illustration." See Web site for more details, FAQ, and rules updates.

WRITERS-EDITORS NETWORK ANNUAL INTERNATIONAL WRITING COMPEITION

(formerly Florida State Writing Competition), CNW/FFWA, P.O. Box A, North Stratford NH 03590. (603)922-8338. Fax: (603)922-8339. E-mail: contest@writers-editors.com. Website: www. writers-editors.com. **Executive Director:** Dana K. Cassell. Annual contest. Estab. 1984. Categories include children's literature (length appropriate to age category). Entry fee is $5 (members), $10 (nonmembers) or $10-20 for entries longer than 3,000 words. Awards $100 first prize, $75 second prize, $50 third prize, certificates for honorable mentions. Judging by librarians, editors and published authors. Judging criteria: interest and readability within age group, writing style and mechanics, originality, salability. Deadline: March 15. For copy of official entry form, send #10 SASE or visit Web site. List of winners on Web site.

✍ WRITERS' LEAGE OF TEXAS BOOK AWARDS

Writers' League of Texas, 611 S. Congress Ave.Suite 130, Austin TX 78704. (512)499-8914. Fax: (512)499-0441. E-mail: wlt@writersleague.org. Website: www.writersleague.org. **Contact:** Kristy Bordine, membership administrator. Offered annually for books published in the previous year. Honors outstanding children's books in short-works categories. Awards at the Texas Book Festival in Austin, Texas. Deadline: May 31. Entry Fee: $25. Prize: Two prizes of $1,000.

WRITING CONFERENCE WRITING CONTESTS

The Writing Conference, Inc.P.O. Box 664, Ottawa KS 66067. Phone/fax: (785)242-1995. E-mail: jbushman@writingconference.com. Website: www.writingconference.com. **Contest Director:** John H. Bushman. **Open to students.** Annual contest. Estab. 1988. Purpose of contest: to further writing by students with awards for narration, exposition and poetry at the elementary, middle school and high school levels. Unpublished submissions only. Submissions made by the author or teacher. Deadline for entries: January 8. Consult Web site for guidelines and entry form. No entry fee. Awards plaque and publication of winning entry in The Writers' Slate online, April issue. Judging by a panel of teachers. Requirements for entrants: must be enrolled in school—K-12th grade- - or home schooled.

✍ WRITING FOR CHILDREN COMPETITION

90 Richmond St. E, Suite 200, Toronto ON M5C 1P1 Canada. (416)703-8982, ext. 226. Fax: (416)504-9090. E-mail: competitions@writersunion.ca. Website: www.writersunion.ca. **Open to students** and Canadian citizens or landed immigrants who have not had a book published. Annual contest. Estab. 1997. Purpose of contest: to discover, encourage and promote new writers of children's literature. Unpublished submissions only. Submissions made by author. Deadline for entries: April 24. Entry fee is $15. Awards $1,500 and submission of winner and finalists to 3 publishers of children's books. Word limit: 1,500. Judging by members of the Writers Union of Canada (published book authors). Requirements for entrants: Open only to unpublished writers. Please do not send illustrations.

YEARBOOK EXCELLENCE CONTEST

Quill and Scroll Society, School of Journalism and Mass Communication, 100 Adler Building, Room E346, Iowa City IA 52242- 2004. (319)335-3457. Fax: (319)335-3989. E-mail: quill-scroll@uiowa. edu. Website: www.uiowa.edu/~quill-sc. **Executive Director:** Vanessa Shelton. **Open to students whose schools have Quill and Scroll charters.** Annual contest. Estab. 1987. Purpose of contest: to recognize and reward student journalists for their work in yearbooks and to provide student winners an opportunity to apply for a scholarship to be used freshman year in college for students planning to major in journalism. Previously published submissions only. Submissions made by the author or school yearbook adviser. Must be published between in the 12-month span prior to contest deadline. Deadline for entries: November 1. Visit our web site for list of current and previous winners.

✍ YOUNG ADULT CANADIAN BOOK AWARD

Canadian Library Association/ Association canndienne des bibliothèques, 328 Frank St.Ottawa ON K2P 0X8 Canada. (613)232-9625. Fax: (613)563-9895. Website: www.cla.ca. **Contact:** Committee Chair. Annual award. Estab. 1981. This award recognizes an author of an outstanding English language Canadian book which appeals to young adults between the ages of 13 and 18. To be eligible for consideration, the following must apply; it must be a work of fiction (novel, collection of short stories, or graphic novel), the title must be a Canadian publication in either hardcover or paperback, and the author must be a Canadian citizen or landed immigrant. The award is given annually, when merited, at the Canadian Library Association's annual conference. The winner will receive a leather-bound book wit the title, author and award seal embossed on the cover in gold. Established in 1980 by the Young Adult Caucus of the Saskatchewan Library Association, the Young Adult Canadian Book Award is administered by the Young Adult Services Interest Group of the Canadian Library Association. Nominations should be sent by December 31, annually.

YOUNG READER'S CHOICE AWARD

3738 W. Central, Missoula MT 59804. (406)542-4055. Fax: (406)543-5358. E-mail: monlux@ montana.com. Website: www.PNLA.org. **Award Director:** Carole Monlux, chair YRCA. "This award is not for unsolicited books—the short list for this award is nominated by students, teachers and librarians and it is only for students in the Pacific Northwest to vote on the winner." YRCA is intended to be a Book Award chosen by students—not adults. It is the oldest children's choice award in U.S. and Canada. Previously published submissions only (the titles are 3 years old when voted upon). Submissions nominated by a person or group in the Pacific Northwest. Deadline for entries: February 1—Pacific Northwest nominations only. SASE for contest rules and entry forms. Awards medal made of Idaho silver, depicting eagle and salmon in northwest. Native American symbols. Judging by students in Pacific Northwest. "The Pacific Northwest Library Association's Young Reader's Choice Award is the oldest children's choice award in the U.S. and Canada. Only 4th- through 12th-graders in the Pacific Northwest are eligible to vote. PNLA strongly encourages people to nominate titles to be included in the ballot."

THE YOUTH HONOR AWARD PROGRAM

Skipping Stones, P.O. Box 3939, Eugene OR 97403. (514)342-4956. E-mail: info@skippingstones. org. Website: www.skippingstones.org. **Director of Public Relations:** Arun N. Toke. **Open to students.** Annual contest. Estab. 1994. Purpose of contest: "To recognize creative and artistic works by young people that promote multicultural awareness and nature appreciation." Unpublished submissions only. Submissions made by author. Deadline for entries: June 25. SASE for contest rules and entry forms. Entry fee is $3; low-income entrants, free. "Ten winners will be published in our fall issue. Winners will also receive an Honor Award Certificate, a subscription to Skipping Stones and five nature and/or multicultural books." Requirements for entrants: Original writing (essays, interviews, poems, plays, short stories, etc.) and art (photos, paintings, cartoons, etc.) are accepted from youth ages 7 to 17. Non-English and bilingual writings are welcome. Also, you must include a certificate of originality signed by a parent or teacher. "Include a cover letter telling about yourself and your submissions, your age, and contact information. Every student who enters will receive a copy of Skipping Stones featuring the ten winning entries."

THE ANNA ZORNIO MEMORIAL CHILDREN'S THEATRE PLAYWRITING AWARD

University of New Hampshire, Department of Theatre and Dance, Paul Creative Arts Center, 30 College Rd.Durham NH 03824-3538. (603)862-3038. Fax: (603)862-0298. E-mail: mike.wood@unh. edu. Website: www.unh.edu/theatre-dance/zornio.html. **Contact:** Michael Wood. Contest every 4 years; next contest is November 2012 for 2013-2014 season. Estab. 1979. Purpose of the award: "to honor the late Anna Zornio, an alumna of The University of New Hampshire, for dedication to and inspiration of playwriting for young people, K-12th grade. Open to playwrights who are residents of the U.S. and Canada. Plays or musicals should run about 45 minutes." Unpublished submissions only. Submissions made by the author. Deadline for entries: March 2, 2012. SASE for award rules and entry forms. No entry fee. Awards $500 plus guaranteed production. Judging by faculty committee. Acquires rights to campus production. For entry form and more information visit www.unh.edu/theatre-dance/zornio.

Helpful Books & Publications

The editors of *Children's Writer's & Illustrator's Market* suggest the following books and periodicals to keep you informed on writing and illustrating techniques, trends in the field, business issues, industry news and changes, and additional markets.

BOOKS

An Author's Guide to Children's Book Promotion, Ninth edition, by Susan Salzman Raab, 345 Millwood Rd., Chappaqua NY 10514. (914)241-2117. E-mail: info@raabassociates. com. Web site: www.raabassociates.com/authors.htm.

The Business of Writing for Children, by Aaron Shepard, Shepard Publications. Available on www.amazon.com.

Children's Writer Guide, (annual), The Institute of Children's Literature, 93 Long Ridge Rd., West Redding CT 06896-0811. (800)443-6078. Web site: www.writersbookstore.com.

The Children's Writer's Reference, by Berthe Amoss and Eric Suben, Writer's Digest Books, 4700 E. Galbraith Rd., Cincinnati OH 45236. (800)448-0915. Web site: www.writersdigest. com.

Children's Writer's Word Book, Second edition, by Alijandra Mogilner & Tayopa Mogilner, Writer's Digest Books, 4700 E. Galbraith Rd., Cincinnati OH 45236. (800)448-0915. Web site: www.writersdigest.com.

The Complete Idiot's Guide(r) to Publishing Children's Books, Second Edition, by Harold D. Underdown, Alpha Books, 201 W. 103rd St., Indianapolis IN 46290. Web site: www. un derdown.org/cig.htm.

Creating Characters Kids Will Love, by Elaine Marie Alphin, Writer's Digest Books, 4700 E. Galbraith Rd., Cincinnati OH 45236. (800)448-0915. Web site: www.writersdigest.com.

Formatting & Submitting Your Manuscript, Second Edition, by Cynthia Laufenberg and the editors of Writer's Market, Writer's Digest Books, 4700 E. Galbraith Rd., Cincinnati OH 45236. (800)448-0915. Web site: www.writersdigest.com.

Guide to Literary Agents, edited by Chuck Sambuchino, Writer's Digest Books, 4700 E. Galbraith Rd., Cincinnati OH 45236. (800)448-0915. Web site: www.writersdigest.com.

How to Write a Children's Book and Get It Published, Third Edition, by Barbara Seuling, John Wiley & Sons, 111 River St., Hoboken NJ 07030. (201)748-6000. Web site: www. wiley.com.

How to Write and Illustrate Children's Books and Get Them Published, edited by Treld Pelkey Bicknell and Felicity Trottman, Writer's Digest Books, 4700 E. Galbraith Rd., Cincinnati OH 45236. (800)448-0915. Web site: www.writersdigest.com.

How to Write Attention-Grabbing Query & Cover Letters, by John Wood, Writer's Digest Books, 4700 E. Galbraith Rd., Cincinnati OH 45236. (800)448-0915. Web site: www.writers digest.com.

Illustrating Children's Books: Creating Pictures for Publication, by Martin Salisbury, Barron's Educational Series, 250 Wireless Blvd., Hauppauge NY 11788. (800)645-3476. Web site: www.barronseduc.com.

It's a Bunny-Eat-Bunny World: A Writer's Guide to Surviving and Thriving in Today's Competitive Children's Book Market, by Olga Litowinsky, Walker & Company, 104 Fifth Ave., New York NY 10011. (212)727-8300. Web site: www.walkerbooks.com.

Page After Page: discover the confidence & passion you need to start writing & keep writing (no matter what), by Heather Sellers, Writer's Digest Books, 4700 E. Galbraith Rd., Cincinnati OH 45236. (800)448-0915. Web site: www.writersdigest.com.

Picture Writing: A New Approach to Writing for Kids and Teens, by Anastasia Suen, Writer's Digest Books, 4700 E. Galbraith Rd., Cincinnati OH 45236. (800)448-0915. Web site: www.writersdigest.com.

Story Sparkers: A Creativity Guide for Children's Writers, by Marcia Thornton Jones and Debbie Dadey, Writer's Digest Books, 4700 E. Galbraith Rd., Cincinnati OH 45236. (800)448-0915. Web site: www.writersdigest.com.

Take Joy: A Writer's Guide to Loving the Craft, by Jane Yolen, Writer's Digest Books, 4700 E. Galbraith Rd., Cincinnati OH 45236. (800)448-0915. Web site: www.writersdigest.com.

A Teen's Guide to Getting Published; Publishing for Profit, Recognition and Academic Success, Second edition, by Jessica Dunn & Danielle Dunn, Prufrock Press, P.O. Box 8813, Waco TX 76714-8813. (800)998-2208. Web site: www.prufrock.com.

The Writer's Guide to Crafting Stories for Children, by Nancy Lamb, Writer's Digest Books, 4700 E. Galbraith Rd., Cincinnati OH 45236. (800)448-0915. Web site: www.writersdigest.com.

Writing and Illustrating Children's Books for Publication: Two Perspectives, Revised Edition, by Berthe Amoss and Eric Suben, Writer's Digest Books, 4700 E. Galbraith Rd., Cincinnati OH 45236. (800)448-0915. Web site: www.writersdigest.com.

Writing & Selling the YA Novel, by K.L. Going, Writer's Digest Books, 4700 E. Galbraith Rd., Cincinnati OH 45236. (800)448-0915. Web site: www.writersdigest.com.

Writing for Young Adults, by Sherry Garland, Writer's Digest Books, 4700 E. Galbraith Rd., Cincinnati OH 45236. (800)448-0915. Web site: www.writersdigest.com.

Writing With Pictures: How to Write and Illustrate Children's Books, by Uri Shulevitz, Watson-Guptill Publications, 770 Broadway, New York NY 10003. (800)278-8477. Web site: www.watsonguptill.com/products.html.

You Can Write Children's Books, by Tracey E. Dils, Writer's Digest Books, 4700 E. Galbraith Rd., Cincinnati OH 45236. (800)448-0915. Web site: www.writersdigest.com.

You Can Write Children's Books Workbook, by Tracey E. Dils, Writer's Digest Books, 4700 E. Galbraith Rd., Cincinnati OH 45236. (800)448-0915. Web site: www.writersdigest.com.

PUBLICATIONS

Book Links: Connecting Books, Libraries and Classrooms, editor Laura Tillotson, American Library Association, 50 E. Huron St., Chicago IL 60611. (800)545-2433. Web site: www.ala.org/BookLinks. *Magazine published 6 times a year (September-July) for the purpose of connecting books, libraries and classrooms. Features articles on specific topics followed by bibliographies recommending books for further information. Subscription: $39.95/year.*

Children's Book Insider, editor Laura Backes, 901 Columbia Rd., Ft. Collins CO 80525-1838. (970)495-0056 or (800)807-1916. E-mail: mail@write4kids.com. Web site: www.write4ki ds.com. *Monthly newsletter covering markets, techniques and trends in children's publishing. Subscription: $29.95/year; electronic version $26.95/year.*

Children's Writer, editor Susan Tierney, The Institute of Children's Literature, 93 Long Ridge Rd., West Redding CT 06896-0811. (800)443-6078. Web site: www.childrenswriter.com. *Monthly newsletter of writing and publishing trends in the children's field. Subscription: $24/year; special introductory rate: $19.*

The Five Owls, editor Dr. Mark West, P.O. Box 235, Marathon TX 79842. (432)386-4257. Web site: www.fiveowls.com. *Quarterly online newsletter for readers personally and professionally involved in children's literature. Subscription: $35/year.*

The Horn Book Magazine, editor-in-chief Roger Sutton, The Horn Book Inc., 56 Roland St., Suite 200, Boston MA 02129. (800)325-1170. E-mail: info@hbook.com or cgross@hbook.com. Web site: www.hbook.com. *Bimonthly guide to the children's book world including views on the industry and reviews of the latest books. Subscription: $34.95/year for new subscriptions; $49/year for renewals.*

The Lion and the Unicorn: A Critical Journal of Children's Literature, editors George Bodmer, Lisa Paul and Sandra Beckett, The Johns Hopkins University Press, P.O. Box 19966, Baltimore MD 21211-0966. (800)548-1784 or (410)516-6987 (outside the U.S. and Canada). E-mail: jrlncirc@press.jhu.edu. Web site: www.press.jhu.edu/journals/lion and the unicorn/. *Magazine published 3 times a year serving as a forum for discussion of children's literature featuring interviews with authors, editors and experts in the field. Subscription: $33/year.*

Once Upon a Time, editor Audrey Baird, 553 Winston Court, St. Paul MN 55118. (651)457-6223. E-mail: audreyouat@comcast.net. Web site: www.onceuponatimemag.com. *Quarterly support magazine for children's writers and illustrators and those interested in children's literature. Subscription: $27/year.*

Publishers Weekly, editor-in-chief Sara Nelson, Reed Business Information, a division of Reed Elsevier Inc., 360 Park Ave. S., New York NY 10010. (800)278-2991. Web site: www.publishersweekly.com. *Weekly trade publication covering all aspects of the publishing industry; includes coverage of the children's field and spring and fall issues devoted solely to children's books. Subscription: $239.99/year. Available on newsstands for $8/issue. (Special issues are higher in price.)*

Society of Children's Book Writers and Illustrators Bulletin, editors Stephen Mooser and Lin Oliver, SCBWI, 8271 Beverly Blvd., Los Angeles CA 90048. (323)782-1010. E-mail: bulletin@scbwi.org. Web site: www.scbwi.org/pubs.htm. *Bimonthly newsletter of SCBWI covering news of interest to members. Subscription with $60/year membership.*

Useful Online Resources

The editors of *Children's Writer's & Illustrator's Market* suggest the following Web sites to keep you informed on writing and illustrating techniques, trends in the field, business issues, industry news and changes, and additional markets.

Amazon.com: www.amazon.com

Calling itself "A bookstore too big for the physical world," Amazon.com has more than 3 million books available on their Web site at discounted prices, plus a personal notification service of new releases, reader reviews, bestseller and suggested book information.

America Writes for Kids: http://usawrites4kids.drury.edu

Lists book authors by state along with interviews, profiles and writing tips.

Artlex Art Dictionary: www.artlex.com

Art dictionary with more than 3,200 terms

Association for Library Service to Children: www.ala.org

This site provides links to information about Newbery, Caldecott, Coretta Scott King, Michael L. Printz and Theodor Seuss Geisel Awards as well as a host of other awards for notable children's books.

Association of Authors' Representatives: www.aar-online.org

The Web site of the AAR offers a list of agent members, links, and frequently asked questions including useful advice for authors seeking representation.

Association of Illustrators: www.theaoi.com

This U.K.-based organization has been working since 1973 to promote illustration, illustrators' rights and standards. The Web site has discussion boards, artists' directories, events, links to agents and much more.

Authors and Illustrators for Children Webring: www.geocities.com/heartland/shores/2084/

Here you'll find a list of links of sites of interest to children's writers and illustrators or created by them.

The Authors Guild Online: www.authorsguild.org

The Web site of The Authors Guild offers articles and columns dealing with contract issues, copyright, electronic rights and other legal issues of concern to writers.

Barnes & Noble Online: www.barnesandnoble.com

The world's largest bookstore chain's Web site contains 600,000 in-stock titles at discount prices as well as personalized recommendations, online events with authors and book forum access for members.

The Book Report Network: includes www.bookreporter.com; www.readinggroupguides.com; www.authorsontheweb.com; www.teenreads.com and www.kidsreads.com.

All the sites feature giveaways, book reviews, author and editor interviews, and recommended reads. A great way to stay connected.

Bookwire: www.bookwire.com

A gateway to finding information about publishers, booksellers, libraries, authors, reviews and awards. Also offers frequently asked publishing questions and answers, a calendar of events, a mailing list and other helpful resources.

Canadian Children's Book Centre: www.bookcentre.ca

The site for the CCBC includes profiles of illustrators and authors, information on recent books, a calendar of upcoming events, information on CCBC publications, and tips from Canadian children's authors.

Canadian Society of Children's Authors, Illustrators and Performers: www.canscaip.org

This organization promotes all aspects of children's writing, illustration and performance.

The Children's Book Council: www.cbcbooks.org

This site includes a complete list of CBC members with addresses, names and descriptions of what each publishes, and links to publishers' Web sites. Also offers previews of upcoming titles from members; articles from *CBC Features*, the Council's newsletter; and their catalog.

Children's Literature: www.childrenslit.com

Offers book reviews, lists of conferences, searchable database, links to over 1,000 author/illustrator Web sites and much more.

Children's Literature Web Guide: www.ucalgary.ca/~dkbrown

This site includes stories, poetry, resource lists, lists of conferences, links to book reviews, lists of awards (international), and information on books from classic to contemporary.

Children's Writer's & Illustrator's Market Web Page: www.cwim.com

Visit the new web page for market updates and sign up for a free e-newsletter.

Children's Writing Supersite: www.write4kids.com

This site (formerly Children's Writers Resource Center) includes highlights from the newsletter *Children's Book Insider*; definitions of publishing terms; answers to frequently asked questions; information on trends; information on small presses; a research center for Web information; and a catalog of material available from *CBI*.

The Colossal Directory of Children's Publishers Online: www.signaleader.com/

This site features links to Web sites of children's publishers and magazines and includes information on which publishers offer submission guidelines online.

Cynthia Leitich Smith's Web site: www.cynthialeitichsmith.com

In addition to information about her books and appearances and a blog, Cynthia Leitich Smith has assembled a site chock full of great useful and inspiring information including interviews with writers and illustrators, favorite reads, awards, bibliographies, and tons of helpful links, many to help writers explore diversity.

Database of Award-Winning Children's Literature: www.dawcl.com

A compilation of over 4,000 records of award-winning books throughout the U.S., Canada, Australia, New Zealand and the U.K. You can search by age level, format, genre, setting, historical period, ethnicity or nationality of the protagonist, gender of protagonist, publication year, award name, or even by keyword. Begin here to compile your reading list of award-winners.

The Drawing Board: http://thedrawingboardforillustrators.blogspot.com

This site for illustrators features articles, interviews, links and resources for illustrators from all fields.

Editor & Publisher: www.editorandpublisher.com

The Internet source for *Editor & Publisher*, this site provides up-to-date industry news, with other opportunities such as a research area and bookstore, a calendar of events and classifieds.

International Board on Books for Young People: www.ibby.org

Founded in Switzerland in 1953, IBBY is a nonprofit that seeks to encourage the creation and distribution of quality children's literature. They cooperate with children's organizations and children's book institutions around the world.

International Reading Association: www.reading.org

This Web site includes articles; book lists; event, conference and convention information; and an online bookstore.

Kid Magazine Writers: www.kidmagwriters.com

Writer Jan Fields created this site to offer support and information to the often-neglected children's magazine writer. The Web site features editor interviews, articles on technique, special reports, an A to Z magazine market guide, and archives of monthly features.

National Association for the Education of Young Children: www.naeyc.org

This organization is comprised of over 100,000 early childhood educators and others interested in the development and education of young children. Their Web site makes a great introduction and research resource for authors and illustrators of picture books.

National Writers Union: www.nwu.org

The union for freelance writers in U.S. Markets. The NWU offers contract advice, grievance assistance, health and liability insurance and much more.

Once Upon a Time: www.onceuponatimemag.com

This companion site to *Once Upon A Time* magazine offers excerpts from recent articles, notes for prospective contributors, and information about *OUAT*'s 11 regular columnists.

Picturebook: www.picture-book.com

This site brought to you by *Picturebook* sourcebook offers tons of links for illustrators, portfolio searching, and news, and offers a listserv, bulletin board and chatroom.

Planet Esme: A Wonderful World of Children's Literature: www.planetesme.com

This site run by author Esme Raji Codell, offers extensive lists of children's book recommendations, including the latest titles of note for various age groups, a great list of links, and more. Be sure to click on "join the club" to receive Codell's delightful e-mail newsletter.

Publishers' Catalogues Home Page: www.lights.ca/publisher

A mammoth link collection of more than 6,000 publishers around the world arranged geographically. This site is one of the most comprehensive directories of publishers on the Internet.

The Purple Crayon: www.underdown.org

Editor Harold Underdown's site includes articles on trends, business, and cover letters and queries as well as interviews with editors and answers to frequently asked questions. He also includes links to a number of other sites helpful to writers and excerpts from his book *The Complete Idiot's Guide to Publishing Children's Books*.

Slantville: www.slantville.com

An online artists community, this site includes a yellow pages for artists, frequently asked questions and a library offering information on a number of issues of interest to illustrators. This is a great site to visit to view artists' portfolios.

Smartwriters.com: www.smartwriters.com

Writer, novelist, photographer, graphic designer, and co-founder of 2-Tier Software, Inc., Roxyanne Young, runs this online magazine, which is absolutely stuffed with resources for children's writers, teachers and young writers. It's also got contests, interviews, free books, advice and well—you just have to go there.

Society of Children's Book Writers and Illustrators: www.scbwi.org

This site includes information on awards and grants available to SCBWI members, a calendar of events listed by date and region, a list of publications available to members, and a site map for easy navigation. Follow the Regional Chapters link to find the SCBWI chapter in your area.

The Society of Illustrators: www.societyillustrators.org

Since 1901, this organization has been working to promote the interest of professional illustrators. Information on exhibitions, career advice, and many other links provided.

U.K. Children's Books: www.ukchildrensbooks.co.uk

Filled with links to author sites, illustrator sites, publishers, booksellers, and organizations—not to mention help with Web site design and other technicalities—visit this site no matter which side of the Atlantic you rest your head.

United States Board on Books for Young People: www.usbby.org

Serves as the U.S. national section of the International Board on Books for Young People.

United States Postal Service: www.usps.com

Offers domestic and International postage rate calculator, stamp ordering, zip code look up, express mail tracking and more.

Verla Kay's Web site: www.verlakay.com

Author Verla Kay's Web site features writer's tips, articles, a schedules of online workshops (with transcripts of past workshops), a good news board and helpful links.

Writersdigest.com: www.writersdigest.com

Brought to you by *Writer's Digest* magazine, this site features articles, resources, links, writing prompts, a bookstore, and more.

Writersmarket.com: www.writersmarket.com

This gateway to the *Writer's Market* online edition offers market news, FAQs, tips, featured markets and web resources, a free newsletter, and more.

Writing-world.com: www.writing-world.com/children/

Site features reams of advice, links and offers a free bi-weekly newsletter.

Glossary

AAR. Association of Authors' Representatives.

ABA. American Booksellers Association.

ABC. Association of Booksellers for Children.

Advance. A sum of money a publisher pays a writer or illustrator prior to the publication of a book. It is usually paid in installments, such as one half on signing the contract, one half on delivery of a complete and satisfactory manuscript. The advance is paid against the royalty money that will be earned by the book.

ALA. American Library Association.

All rights. The rights contracted to a publisher permitting the use of material anywhere and in any form, including movie and book club sales, without additional payment to the creator.

Anthology. A collection of selected writings by various authors or gatherings of works by one author.

Anthropomorphization. The act of attributing human form and personality to things not human (such as animals).

ASAP. As soon as possible.

Assignment. An editor or art director asks a writer, illustrator or photographer to produce a specific piece for an agreed-upon fee.

B&W. Black and white.

Backlist. A publisher's list of books not published during the current season but still in print.

BEA. BookExpo America.

Biennially. Occurring once every 2 years.

Bimonthly. Occurring once every 2 months.

Biweekly. Occurring once every 2 weeks.

Book packager. A company that draws all elements of a book together, from the initial concept to writing and marketing strategies, then sells the book package to a book publisher and/or movie producer. Also known as book producer or book developer.

Book proposal. Package submitted to a publisher for consideration usually consisting of a synopsis, outline and sample chapters. (See Before Your First Sale, page 8.)

Business-size envelope. Also known as a #10 envelope. The standard size used in sending business correspondence.

Camera-ready. Refers to art that is completely prepared for copy camera platemaking.

Caption. A description of the subject matter of an illustration or photograph; photo captions include persons' names where appropriate. Also called cutline.

CBC. Children's Book Council.

Clean-copy. A manuscript free of errors and needing no editing; it is ready for typesetting.

Clips. Samples, usually from newspapers or magazines, of a writer's published work.

Concept books. Books that deal with ideas, concepts and large-scale problems, promoting an understanding of what's happening in a child's world. Most prevalent are alphabet and counting books, but also includes books dealing with specific concerns facing young people (such as divorce, birth of a sibling, friendship or moving).

Contract. A written agreement stating the rights to be purchased by an editor, art director or producer and the amount of payment the writer, illustrator or photographer will receive for that sale. (See Running Your Business, page 13.)

Contributor's copies. The magazine issues sent to an author, illustrator or photographer in which her work appears.

Co-op publisher. A publisher that shares production costs with an author, but, unlike subsidy publishers, handles all marketing and distribution. An author receives a high percentage of royalties until her initial investment is recouped, then standard royalties. (*Children's Writer's & Illustrator's Market* does not include co-op publishers.)

Copy. The actual written material of a manuscript.

Copyediting. Editing a manuscript for grammar usage, spelling, punctuation and general style.

Copyright. A means to legally protect an author's/illustrator's/photographer's work. This can be shown by writing ©, the creator's name, and year of work's creation. (See Running Your Business, page 13.)

Cover letter. A brief letter, accompanying a complete manuscript, especially useful if responding to an editor's request for a manuscript. May also accompany a book proposal. (See Before Your First Sale, page 8.)

Cutline. See caption.

Division. An unincorporated branch of a company.

Dummy. A loose mock-up of a book showing placement of text and artwork.

Electronic submission. A submission of material by modem or on computer disk.

Final draft. The last version of a polished manuscript ready for submission to an editor.

First North American serial rights. The right to publish material in a periodical for the first time, in the United States or Canada. (See Running Your Business, page 13.)

F&Gs. Folded and gathered sheets. An early, not-yet-bound copy of a picture book.

Flat fee. A one-time payment.

Galleys. The first typeset version of a manuscript that has not yet been divided into pages.

Genre. A formulaic type of fiction, such as horror, mystery, romance, science fiction or western.

Glossy. A photograph with a shiny surface as opposed to one with a non-shiny matte finish.

Gouache. Opaque watercolor with an appreciable film thickness and an actual paint layer.

Halftone. Reproduction of a continuous tone illustration with the image formed by dots produced by a camera lens screen.

Hard copy. The printed copy of a computer's output.

Hardware. All the mechanically-integrated components of a computer that are not software—circuit boards, transistors and the machines that are the actual computer.

Hi-Lo. High interest, low reading level.

Home page. The first page of a Web site.

IBBY. International Board on Books for Young People.

Imprint. Name applied to a publisher's specific line of books.

Internet. A worldwide network of computers that offers access to a wide variety of electronic resources.

IRA. International Reading Association.

IRC. International Reply Coupon. Sold at the post office to enclose with text or artwork sent to a recipient outside your own country to cover postage costs when replying or returning work.

Keyline. Identification of the positions of illustrations and copy for the printer.

Layout. Arrangement of illustrations, photographs, text and headlines for printed material.

Line drawing. Illustration done with pencil or ink using no wash or other shading.

Mass market books. Paperback books directed toward an extremely large audience sold in supermarkets, drugstores, airports, newsstands, online retailers, and bookstores.

Mechanicals. Paste-up or preparation of work for printing.

Middle grade or mid-grade. See middle reader.

Middle reader. The general classification of books written for readers approximately ages 9-11. Often called middle grade or mid-grade.

Ms (mss). Manuscript(s).

Multiple submissions. See simultaneous submissions.

NCTE. National Council of Teachers of English.

One-time rights. Permission to publish a story in periodical or book form one time only. (See Running Your Business, page 13.)

Outline. A summary of a book's contents; often in the form of chapter headings with a descriptive sentence or two under each heading to show the scope of the book.

Package sale. The sale of a manuscript and illustrations/photos as a "package" paid for with one check.

Payment on acceptance. The writer, artist or photographer is paid for her work at the time the editor or art director decides to buy it.

Payment on publication. The writer, artist or photographer is paid for her work when it is published.

Picture book. A type of book aimed at preschoolers to 8-year-olds that tells a story using a combination of text and artwork, or artwork only.

Print. An impression pulled from an original plate, stone, block, screen or negative; also a positive made from a photographic negative.

Proofreading. Reading text to correct typographical errors.

Query. A letter to an editor or agent designed to capture interest in an article or book you have written or propose to write. (See Before Your First Sale, page 8.)

Reading fee. Money charged by some agents and publishers to read a submitted manuscript. (*Children's Writer's & Illustrator's Market* does not include agencies that charge reading fees.)

Reprint rights. Permission to print an already published work whose first rights have been sold to another magazine or book publisher. (See Running Your Business, page 13.)

Response time. The average length of time it takes an editor or art director to accept or reject a query or submission and inform the creator of the decision.

Rights. The bundle of permissions offered to an editor or art director in exchange for printing a manuscript, artwork or photographs. (See Running Your Business, page 13.)

Rough draft. A manuscript that has not been checked for errors in grammar, punctuation, spelling or content.

Roughs. Preliminary sketches or drawings.

Royalty. An agreed percentage paid by a publisher to a writer, illustrator or photographer for each copy of her work sold.

SAE. Self-addressed envelope.

SASE. Self-addressed, stamped envelope.

SCBWI. The Society of Children's Book Writers and Illustrators. (See listing in Clubs & Organizations section.)

Second serial rights. Permission for the reprinting of a work in another periodical after its first publication in book or magazine form. (See Running Your Business, page 13.)

Semiannual. Occurring every 6 months or twice a year.

Semimonthly. Occurring twice a month.

Semiweekly. Occurring twice a week.

Serial rights. The rights given by an author to a publisher to print a piece in one or more periodicals. (See Running Your Business, page 13.)

Simultaneous submissions. Queries or proposals sent to several publishers at the same time. Also called multiple submissions. (See Before Your First Sale, page 8.)

Slant. The approach to a story or piece of artwork that will appeal to readers of a particular publication.

Slush pile. Editors' term for their collections of unsolicited manuscripts.

Software. Programs and related documentation for use with a computer.

Solicited manuscript. Material that an editor has asked for or agreed to consider before being sent by a writer.

SPAR. Society of Photographers and Artists Representatives.

Speculation (spec). Creating a piece with no assurance from an editor or art director that it will be purchased or any reimbursements for material or labor paid.

Subsidiary rights. All rights other than book publishing rights included in a book contract, such as paperback, book club and movie rights. (See Running Your Business, page 13.)

Subsidy publisher. A book publisher that charges the author for the cost of typesetting, printing and promoting a book. Also called a vanity publisher. (*Children's Writer's & Illustrator's Market* does not include subsidy publishers.)

Synopsis. A brief summary of a story or novel. Usually a page to a page and a half, single-spaced, if part of a book proposal.

Tabloid. Publication printed on an ordinary newspaper page turned sideways and folded in half.

Tearsheet. Page from a magazine or newspaper containing your printed art, story, article, poem or photo.

Thumbnail. A rough layout in miniature.

Trade books. Books sold in bookstores and through online retailers, aimed at a smaller audience than mass market books, and printed in smaller quantities by publishers.

Transparencies. Positive color slides; not color prints.

Unsolicited manuscript. Material sent without an editor's, art director's or agent's request.

Vanity publisher. See subsidy publisher.

Work-for-hire. An arrangement between a writer, illustrator or photographer and a company under which the company retains complete control of the work's copyright. (See Running Your Business, page 13.)

YA. See young adult.

Young adult. The general classification of books written for readers approximately ages 12-18. Often referred to as YA.

Young reader. The general classification of books written for readers approximately ages 5-8.

Names Index

This index lists the editors, art directors, agents and art reps listed in *Children's Writer's & Illustrator's Market*, along with the publisher, publication or company for which they work. Names were culled from Book Publishers, Canadian & International Books Publishers, Magazines, and Agents & Art Reps.

M

Age-Level Index

This index lists book and magazine publishers by the age-groups for which they publish. Use it to locate appropriate markets for your work, then carefully read the listings and follow the guidelines of each publisher. Use this index in conjunction with the Subject Index to further narrow your list of markets. **Picture Books and Picture-Oriented Material** are for preschoolers to 8-year-olds; **Young Readers** are for 5- to 8-year-olds; **Middle Readers** are for 9- to 11-year-olds; and **Young Adults** are for ages 12 and up.

BOOK PUBLISHERS
Middle Readers

Picture Books

Young Readers

MAGAZINES
Middle Readers

Subject Index

This index lists book and magazine publishers by the fiction and nonfiction subject areas in which they publish. Use it to locate appropriate markets for your work, then carefully read the listings and follow the guidelines of each publisher. Use this index in conjunction with Age-Level Index to further narrow your list of markets.

BOOK PUBLISHERS - FICTION

Adventure

Animal

Folktales

Humor

Multicultural

Nature/Environment

BOOK PUBLISHERS - NONFICTION

Activity Books

Hobbies

How-to

Multicultural

Music/Dance

Nature/Environment

Subject Index

Reference

Religion

Special Needs

Sports

MAGAZINES - FICTION

Adventure

Animal

Humorous

Interview/Profile

Math

Photography Index

This index lists markets that buy photos from freelancers and is divided into Book Publishers and Magazines. Its important to carefully read the listings and follow the guidelines of each publisher to which you submit.

BOOK PUBLISHERS

MAGAZINES

General Index